9TH EDITION

NEW PERSPECTIVES ON

COMPUTER CONCEPTS

W9-APT-153

by June Jamrich Parsons and Dan Oja

INTRODUCTORY

Includes access to an integrated companion Web site and an interactive BookOnCD. The companion Web site offers audio clips, labs, games, relevant links, practice tests, and more. The BookOnCD contains the entire contents of the textbook with figures that come to life as videos, software tours, and animations. See the Preface for more information!

THOMSON
COURSE TECHNOLOGY

Australia · Canada · Denmark · Japan · Mexico · New Zealand · Philippines · Puerto Rico · Singapore · South Africa · Spain · United Kingdom · United States

EXECUTIVE EDITOR
Rachel Goldberg

SENIOR EDITOR
Amanda Shelton

SENIOR PRODUCT MANAGER
Kathy Finnegan

PRODUCT MANAGER
Brianna Hawes

ASSOCIATE PRODUCT MANAGER
Shana Rosenthal

EDITORIAL ASSISTANT
Janine Tangney

MARKETING MANAGER
Joy Stark

DEVELOPMENTAL EDITOR
Amanda Brodkin

**TECHNOLOGY PROJECT
MANAGER**
Nick Quintanilla

PRODUCTION EDITOR
Jennifer Goguen McGrail

COMPOSITION
GEX Publishing Services

TEXT DESIGNER
Joel Sadagursky

COVER DESIGNER
Deborah VanRooyen

New Perspectives on Computer Concepts 9th Edition—Introductory is published by Thomson Course Technology.

COPYRIGHT © 2007 Thomson Course Technology, a division of Thomson Learning, Inc. Thomson Learning™ is a trademark used herein under license.

Printed in the United States of America

1 2 3 4 5 6 7 8 9 BM 10 09 08 07 06

For more information, contact Course Technology, 25 Thomson Place, Boston, Massachusetts, 02210.

Or find us on the World Wide Web at: www.course.com

ALL RIGHTS RESERVED. No part of this work covered by the copyright hereon may be reproduced or used in any form or by any means—graphic, electronic, or mechanical, including photocopying, recording, taping, Web distribution, or information storage and retrieval systems—without the written permission of the publisher.

For permission to use material from this text or product, submit a request online at www.thomsonrights.com

Any additional questions about permissions can be submitted by e-mail to thomsonrights@thomson.com

Disclaimer
Thomson Course Technology reserves the right to revise this publication and make changes from time to time in its content without notice.

Disclaimer
Any fictional URLs used throughout this book are intended for instructional purposes only. At the time this book was printed, any such URLs were fictional and not belonging to any real persons or companies.

Some of the product names and company names used in this book have been used for identification purposes only and may be trademarks or registered trademarks of their respective manufacturers and sellers.

Microsoft and the Office logo are either registered trademarks or trademarks of Microsoft Corporation in the United States and/or other countries. Course Technology is an independent entity from the Microsoft Corporation, and not affiliated with Microsoft in any manner.

ISBN-13: 978-1-4188-3945-1
ISBN-10: 1-4188-3945-0

CONTENTS AT A GLANCE

TABLE OF CONTENTS

CHAPTER 1
COMPUTER, INTERNET, WEB, AND E-MAIL BASICS

ON THE WEB

ON THE BOOKONCD

CHAPTER 2
COMPUTER HARDWARE

ON THE WEB

ON THE BOOKONCD

CHAPTER 3
COMPUTER SOFTWARE

ON THE WEB

ON THE BOOKONCD

CHAPTER 4
FILE MANAGEMENT, VIRUS PROTECTION, AND BACKUP

ON THE WEB

ON THE BOOKONCD

CHAPTER 5
INTERNET AND LAN TECHNOLOGY

ON THE WEB

ON THE BOOKONCD

CHAPTER 6
WEB PAGES, WEB SITES, AND E-COMMERCE

ON THE WEB

ON THE BOOKONCD

CHAPTER 7
DIGITAL MEDIA

ON THE WEB

ON THE BookOnCD

Preface

Study Smarter: The NP9 Experience

You have purchased more than just a book.

New Perspectives on Computer Concepts 9th Edition includes a printed book, an integrated Web site, and an interactive BookOnCD designed to be used together to provide a cutting-edge learning experience.

Want to study smarter? The NP9 Web site offers tools to help you understand the material from all angles and to thoroughly prepare you for exams. Want to see the concepts in the book in action? The BookOnCD brings concepts to life by directly linking to videos, screentours, and animations.

The *New Perspectives on Computer Concepts* pedagogy is designed to help you focus your learning, study more efficiently, and retain the information you learn well after completing the course. Chapters in this book follow a logical progression of chapter opener activities, chapter activities, and end-of-chapter exercises to keep you engaged throughout. This organization is further enhanced by the robust labs, compelling videos, and dynamic games and exercises on the NP9 Web site and BookOnCD. This truly unique model ensures that you have the reinforcement you need to gain a complete understanding of computer concepts.

CREATE YOUR OWN LEARNING PLAN

Engaging **Chapter Opener** activities draw you into the chapter material and help you to assess your knowledge of the material before digging in.

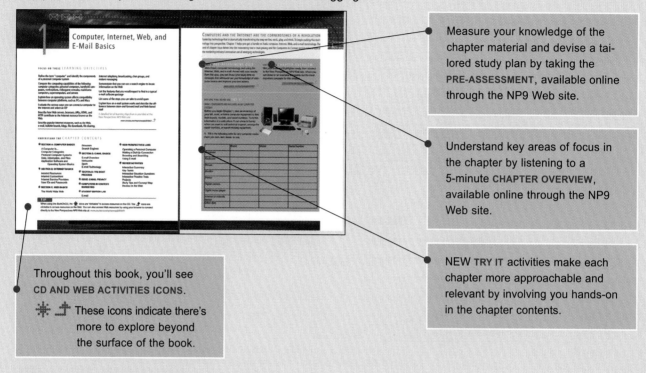

Measure your knowledge of the chapter material and devise a tailored study plan by taking the PRE-ASSESSMENT, available online through the NP9 Web site.

Understand key areas of focus in the chapter by listening to a 5-minute CHAPTER OVERVIEW, available online through the NP9 Web site.

Throughout this book, you'll see CD AND WEB ACTIVITIES ICONS.

These icons indicate there's more to explore beyond the surface of the book.

NEW TRY IT activities make each chapter more approachable and relevant by involving you hands-on in the chapter contents.

EXPLORE TIMELY TOPICS

Chapter features, such as **InfoWebLinks**, **Issues**, and **Computers in Context**, help you understand concepts, put information in context, and explore topics beyond those presented in the text.

TechTalk

Each chapter includes a TechTalk section that presents challenging technical information in an easy-to-understand way. **TechTalk** helps you delve deeper into the mechanics of how computers and computer technologies work.

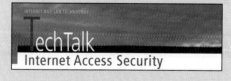

Issue

Each chapter also explores a contemporary **Issue** and gives you the opportunity to express your opinion through "What Do You Think" questions.

Computers in Context

In the **Computers in Context** section, you'll discover how technology plays a role in careers such as film-making, architecture, banking, and fashion.

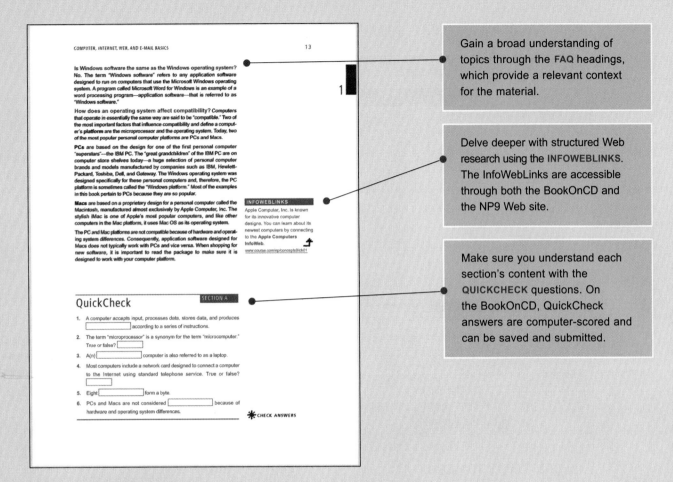

Gain a broad understanding of topics through the FAQ headings, which provide a relevant context for the material.

Delve deeper with structured Web research using the INFOWEBLINKS. The InfoWebLinks are accessible through both the BookOnCD and the NP9 Web site.

Make sure you understand each section's content with the QUICKCHECK questions. On the BookOnCD, QuickCheck answers are computer-scored and can be saved and submitted.

APPLY YOUR KNOWLEDGE

The end-of-chapter exercises and assignments offer a wealth of opportunities to test your comprehension of the material in the chapter, as well as to apply the concepts and skills that you learned.

Labs

You can master hundreds of computer concepts including file management, desktop applications, computer privacy, virus protection and more using the Labs that accompany this book. **Student Edition Labs**, available through the NP9 Web site, help you learn through dynamic observation, step-by-step practice and challenging review questions.

STUDENT EDITION LABS are available through the NP9 Web site and cover over thirty subject areas, including file management, virus protection, wireless networking, and computer ethics.

New Perspectives Labs are available on the BookOnCD and also give you hands-on experience applying concepts and using software.

Interactive Review Activities

Prove your mastery of the concepts in each chapter with the Interactive Summary, Interactive Situation Questions, and Interactive Practice Tests. These activities are printed in the book and also accessible in an interactive format on the BookOnCD and NP9 Web site.

NP9 Projects

Work with the NP9 **Projects** to apply the concepts you have learned from reading and lab activities. NEW to the 9th Edition, each chapter includes critical thinking, group, cyberclassroom, globalization, multimedia, and resume-buider projects.

Study Tips and Concept Maps

Study Tips help you organize and consolidate the information in a chapter by making lists, outlines, charts, and sketches. NEW to the 9th Edition, **Concept Maps** test your broader understanding of the material in the chapter by completing a hierarchy chart of key terms and concepts. Concept Maps are also accessible in an interactive format on the BookOnCD and NP9 Web site.

Review on the Web

Review on the Web provides you with even more activities and projects to help you apply the concepts you learned in the chapter.

The TECHTV VIDEO projects keep you up-to-date on the latest technology trends and technology-related issues through timely video clips and projects.

ONLINE GAMES give you a rewarding, interactive way to reinforce concepts learned in each chapter.

Use the ONLINE INTERACTIVE REVIEW ACTIVITIES to track your progress and save your results to share with your instructor.

NP9 WEB SITE

Follow the directions on the inside front cover of this book to create a CoursePort user profile to access all the resources and learning tools on the NP9 Web site. The CoursePort system allows you to save your results from the Web site activities and share them with your instructor using the Universal Gradebook. Trackable Web activities include:

- **Pre-Assessments**
- **Interactive Practice Tests**
- **Student Edition Labs**
- **Concept Maps**
- **Interactive Summaries**
- **Online Games**
- **Interactive Situation Questions**

NP9 BOOKONCD

The interactive BookOnCD includes the entire contents of the printed book and brings the concepts to life through videos, animations and software screentours that are included throughout each chapter.

The BookOnCD also allows you to track and save your results on the following activities:

- **QuickCheck Questions**
- **New Perspectives Labs**
- **Interactive Summaries**
- **Interactive Situation Questions**
- **Interactive Practice Tests**
- **Concept Maps**

INSTRUCTOR RESOURCES

New Perspectives instructional resources and technology provide instructors with a wide range of tools that enhance teaching and learning. These tools can be accessed from the Instructor Toolkit package or at www.course.com.

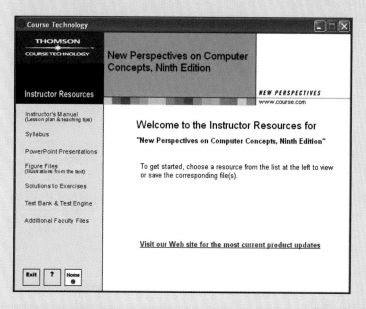

Instructor's Manual: Help is Only a Few Keystrokes Away
An enhanced Instructor's Manual offers an outline for each chapter, plus instructional suggestions and teaching tips, including how to effectively use and integrate the Web site content, CD content, and labs.

ExamView: Our Powerful Testing Software Package
With ExamView, instructors can generate printed tests, create LAN-based tests, or test over the Internet.

Course Presenter
Instructors can deliver engaging and visually impressive lectures for each chapter with the professionally-designed Course Presenter. The Course Presenter is a PowerPoint presentation that is multimedia-enhanced with screentours, animations, and videos.

Instructor Edition and Instructor Toolkit

The Instructor Edition content provides suggestions on how to use New Perspectives on Computer Concepts technology in the classroom. The Instructor Toolkit includes CDs for the Instructor Resources, Course Presenter, and the CourseCoach. The CourseCoach CD explains in depth the New Perspectives Computer Concepts pedagogy and technology resources.

BlackBoard and WebCT Content

We offer a full range of content for use with BlackBoard and WebCT to simplify the use of New Perspectives in distance education settings.

SAM

In addition to these Instructor Resources, Course Technology is also proud to offer SAM: Software to help you teach, test, and train. You can reinforce the lessons presented in this text and create realistic hands-on exams with SAM Computer Concepts. For a total solution to your introductory computer course, SAM for Computer Concepts is available with SAM for Office 2003. This integrated offering provides seamless training, testing, and reporting for everything you'd want to cover in your introduction to computers course.

For more information on how to make SAM Computer Concepts Training and Assessment work for you, please visit samcentral.course.com.

FROM THE AUTHORS

Thirty years ago on April Fool's day 1976, a fledgling computer company released the Apple I computer. Its 8-bit 6502 microprocessor ambled along at 1 megahertz shuttling data to a paltry 8 kilobytes of RAM. How technology has changed! Today's digital world is measured in gigahertz and gigabytes. We have the Internet and LANs, wireless hotspots and smartphones. Entertainment has gone digital, too, and computers play a role in photography, videos, and music. To help instructors and students stay in step with the march of technology, we produced this media-rich and Web-enhanced 9th Edition of *New Perspectives on Computer Concepts*.

Our philosophy is that interaction enhances learning. The NP9 Web site and BookOnCD offer a profusion of opportunities for interacting with concepts and structured, hands-on activities. The Orientation Chapter at the beginning of the book has been reorganized to create a separate section dedicated to using our popular BookOnCD technology and another on using the wide array of learning tools at the NP9 Web site. Expanding on the theme of interaction, we added a Try It activity to the beginning of each chapter to get students engaged right from the start. Each chapter now concludes with a Concept Map activity designed to help students internalize the metastructure underlying the concepts they've learned.

Based on feedback from students, instructors, and reviewers, we focused on making technology concepts even more understandable by streamlining explanations and honing figures for the clearest presentation possible. We logged countless hours of research to bring you the most up-to-date information about new products and trends in computers, software, and the Internet. Please make sure to check the InfoWebLinks for important updates on post-publication events.

Many of today's students have substantially more practical experience with computers than their counterparts of 10 years ago, and yet other students enter college with inadequate technology preparation. The goal of *New Perspectives on Computer Concepts* is to bring every student up to speed with computer basics, and then go beyond basic computer literacy to provide students with technical information that every college-educated person would be expected to know. Whether you are an instructor or a student, we hope that you enjoy the learning experience provided by our text-based and technology-based materials.

ACKNOWLEDGEMENTS

The book would not exist—and certainly wouldn't arrive on schedule—were it not for the efforts of our media, editorial, and production teams. We thank Amanda Young Shelton and Shana Rosenthal for tireless work on every detail of the project; Rachel Goldberg for her leadership for the entire New Perspectives series; Keefe Crowley for supervising alpha and beta testing of the BookOnCD plus maintaining our InfoWebLinks site; Nick Quintanilla for his project management of the NP9 Web site and QA testing of the BookOnCD; Karen McCutcheon for her QA testing of the BookOnCD; Brian Campbell for an innovative Web site design; Jennifer Goguen McGrail for managing production; Donna Mulder, Tensi Parsons, Keefe Crowley, and Joe Bush, for creating videos, screentours, interactive tests, photos, illustrations, and animations; Chris Robbert for his clear narrations; Sue Oja, Debora Elam, Marilou Potter, Deana Martinson, Karen Kangas, Jaclyn Kangas, and Kevin Lappi for checking and double-checking the alpha and beta versions of the BookOnCD; Amanda Brodkin for her insightful developmental edit and making sure that every comma is in the right place; artist Joel Sadagursky for a stunning interior design; artist Deborah VanRooyen for a striking cover design; and Christina Micek for photo research. We want to thank you all!

We also want to give special thanks to Officer David Zittlow of the City of Fond du Lac Police Department for providing photos of computer technology used in law enforcement; Bob Metcalf for giving us permission to use his original sketch of Ethernet; The University of Illinois for supplying photos of PLATO; and Rob Flickenger for providing the photo of his Pringles can antenna.

June Parsons and Dan Oja

NEW PERSPECTIVES ON COMPUTER CONCEPTS
ADVISORY COMMITTEE

Dori McPherson
Schoolcraft College

Bob Irvine
American River
College

Saeed Molki
South Texas College

Michael Wiemann
Blue River Community
College

Bobbye Haupt
Cecil Community
College

Heith Hennel
Valencia Community
College

Gerald Hensel
Valencia Community
College

Pat Frederick
Del Mar College

Barbara Burns
St. Johns River
Community College

Dottie Baumeister
Harford Community
College

Richard Linge
Arizona Western
College

Robert Moore
Laredo Community
College

Karl Smart Lyman
Central Michigan
University

Patti Impink
Macon State College

Linda Cooper
Macon State College

Kathy Winters
University of
Tennessee—
Chattanooga

Dr. Nazih Abdallah
University of Central
Florida

John Gammell
St. Cloud State
University

We would also like to thank reviewers and members of past Advisory Committees who helped provide valuable feedback that is still an influence on the 9th Edition:

Academic Reviewers

Dr. Nazih Abdallah,
University of Central
Florida

Paula Bell,
Lock Haven University
of Pennsylvania

Wendy Chisholm,
Barstow College

Dave Courtaway,
Devry University,
Ponoma

Sallie Dodson,
Radford University

Phil Funk,
Southern New
Hampshire University

Michael Gaffney,
Century College

Ernest Gines,   Tarrant
County College SE

Ione Good,
Southeastern
Community College

Tom Gorecki,
College of Southern
Maryland

Steve Gramlich,
Pasco-Hernando
Community College

Michael Hanna,
Colorado State
University

Stan Leja,
Del Mar College

Martha Lindberg,
Minnesota State
University

Terry Long,
Valencia Community
College

Dr. W. Benjamin Martz,
University of Colorado,
Colorado Springs

Deann McMullen,
Western Kentucky
Community and
Technical College

Robert Moore,
Laredo Community
College

Dr. Rodney Pearson,
Mississippi State
University

Lana Shryock,
Monroe County
Community College

Betty Sinowitz,
Rockland Community
College

Martin Skolnik,
Florida Atlantic
University

Jerome Spencer,
Rowan University

Beverly Amer, Northern
Arizona University

Ken Baldauf,
Florida State University

Mary Caldwell,
Rollins College

Becky Curtin,
William Rainey Harper
College

Eric Daley,
University of
New Brunswick

Robert Erickson,
University of Vermont

Mike Feiler,
Merritt College

Ed Mott,
Central Texas College

Catherine Perlich,
MediaTechnics

Gregory Stefanelli,
Carroll Community
College

Martha J. Tilmann,
College of San Mateo

Mary Zayac,
University of the Virgin
Islands

Chuck Calvin,
Computer Learning
Centers

David Primeaux,
Virginia
Commonwealth
University

Student Reviewers

Kitty Edwards

Heather House

Technical Reviewers

Jeff Harrow

Barbra D. Letts

John Lucas

Ramachandran Bharath

Karl Mulder

NEW PERSPECTIVES

9TH EDITION

COMPUTER CONCEPTS

June Jamrich Parsons, Dan Oja

Orientation

THE PURPOSE OF THIS ORIENTATION IS TO GET YOU UP AND RUNNING WITH

your computer and all the technology tools that accompany your textbook. If you have had little or no experience with computers, you'll find the basics in Sections A and B. Whether you're a beginner or a more experienced computer user, the activities in Section C offer some practical tips on online security. To learn how to use the BookOnCD and NP9 Web site that accompany your textbook, check out Sections D and E.

TAKE A PRE-ASSESSMENT QUIZ

Take the pre-assessment quiz to find out how much you know about basic computer operations, using software, communicating with your instructor via e-mail, online security, and using the BookOnCD and Web site for this textbook.

www.course.com/np/concepts9/ch00

LISTEN TO A CHAPTER OVERVIEW

Get your book and highlighter ready, then connect to the New Perspectives NP9 Web site, where you can listen to an overview that points out the most important concepts for this chapter.

www.course.com/np/concepts9/ch00

BEFORE YOU READ ON, TRY IT!

WHAT DO I NEED TO GET STARTED?

To complete the activities in the Orientation, you'll need access to a computer, the BookOnCD packaged with your textbook, Internet access, an e-mail address for yourself, and your instructor's e-mail address.

To make sure you have what you need, use the following checklist. Check off the boxes for each item that you have.

☐ Access to a computer. If you're using your own computer, you might need a user ID and password to log into Windows. Don't write your password down, but make sure you know what it is.

☐ Access to a school computer network. You might need a user ID and password if you'll be using a lab computer or accessing your school's network. Check with your instructor or lab manager to learn how your school handles network access.

☐ BookOnCD. The BookOnCD should be packaged with your textbook and requires a computer CD or DVD drive to run. If your computer does not have this type of drive, check with your instructor. Your school network might provide access to the BookOnCD from lab computers.

☐ E-mail address. Your instructor should explain how you can obtain an e-mail address if you don't already have one. Write your e-mail address here:

_____

☐ Instructor e-mail address. To mail in assignments, you'll need your instructor's e-mail address. Write it here:

_____

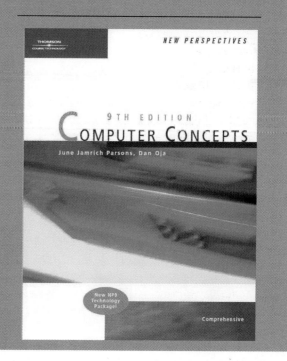

THOMSON
COURSE TECHNOLOGY

NEW PERSPECTIVES

9TH EDITION
COMPUTER CONCEPTS

June Jamrich Parsons, Dan Oja

New NP9
Technology
Package!

Comprehensive

TIP

⌨ Keyboard icons indicate hands-on activities. When using the BookOnCD, the ✳ icons are "clickable" to access resources on the CD. The ⚜ icons are clickable to access resources on the Web. You can also access Web resources by using your browser to connect directly to the New Perspectives NP9 Web site at: www.course.com/np/concepts9/ch00

Getting Started

When you use the *New Perspectives on Computer Concepts* textbook, you not only learn about computers, you also use computers as learning tools. Therefore, it is a good idea to have a basic understanding of how to use your computer. Section A is designed to get computer novices quickly up to speed with computing basics, such as turning on computer equipment, using Windows, using a computer mouse, using a computer keyboard, and accessing Help. It is a good idea to work through this section with your textbook next to a computer so that you can do the TRY IT! activities.

COMPUTER EQUIPMENT

What do I need to know about my computer? Your computer—the one you own, the one you use in a school lab, or the one provided to you at work—is technically classified as a microcomputer and sometimes referred to as a personal computer. A computer runs software (or "programs") that help you accomplish a variety of tasks. A typical computer system consists of several devices—you must be able to identify these devices to use them.

What are the important components of my computer system? The system unit contains your computer's circuitry, such as the microprocessor that is the "brain" of your computer and memory chips that temporarily store information. It also contains storage devices, such as a hard disk drive.

Your computer system includes basic hardware devices that allow you to enter information and commands, view work, and store information for later retrieval. Devices for entering information include a keyboard and mouse. A display device, such as a TV-like monitor, allows you to view your work, a printer produces "hard copy" on paper, and speakers produce beeps and chimes that help you pay attention to what happens on the screen.

Where are the important components of a desktop computer system? A desktop computer is designed for stationary use on a desk or table. Figure 1 shows the key components of a desktop computer system.

PC OR MAC?

Microcomputers can be divided into two camps: PCs and Macs. The CD that comes with this book is designed for use with PCs, and the TRY IT! instructions apply specifically to PCs.

To determine whether you have a PC or Mac check your computer's brand name. PC brands include Dell, IBM, Levono, Hewlett-Packard, Compaq, Sony, and Gateway. You can use the software that accompanies your textbook with these and other PC brands.

Macintosh computers are manufactured by Apple Computers, Inc. and sport a rainbow-colored logo of an apple. If you have a Mac, check with your instructor for the location of your school's PC lab.

FIGURE 1

A desktop computer system includes several components, usually connected by cables.

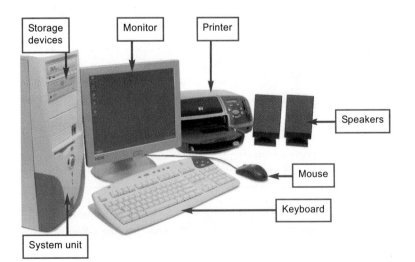

Storage devices

Monitor

Printer

Speakers

Mouse

Keyboard

System unit

Where are the important components of a notebook computer system? Notebook computers (sometimes called "laptops") are small, lightweight computers designed to be carried from place to place. The components of a notebook computer system, except the printer, are housed in a single unit, as shown in Figure 2.

FIGURE 2

A notebook computer includes a flat-panel LCD screen, keyboard, speakers, and touchpad in the same unit that contains the microprocessor, memory, and storage devices. An external mouse is sometimes used instead of the touchpad.

How do I identify my computer's storage devices? Your computer contains a hard disk, housed inside the system unit. It is also likely to have a floppy disk drive and some type of drive that works with CDs. Figure 3 can help you identify your computer's storage devices and their uses.

FIGURE 3

You should use the hard disk to store most of your data, but to transport or back up data, you can use floppy disks, CDs, DVDs, or USB flash drives.

Floppy disk drive

Low-capacity storage for only 1.44 million characters, but handy for transferring work between home and school labs.

CD drive

A CD-ROM drive reads CDs, but does not allow you to store your own data on them. CD-R or CD-RW drives allow you to store 640 million characters of data.

DVD drive

DVD-ROM drives read CDs and DVDs, but do not let you store your own data. Recordable and rewritable DVD drives allow you to store 4.7 billion characters of data.

USB flash drive

A USB flash drive is about the size of a highlighter and plugs directly into the computer system unit. Capacity ranges from 32 million to 4 billion characters.

HOW TO TURN YOUR COMPUTER ON AND OFF

How do I turn it on? A notebook computer typically has one switch that turns on the entire system. Look for the switch along the sides of the computer or above the keyboard. When using a desktop computer, turn on the monitor, printer, and speakers before you flip the switch on the system unit.

Most computers take a minute or two to power up, and you might be required to log in by entering a user ID and password. Your computer is ready to use when the Windows desktop (Figure 4 on the next page) appears on the computer screen and you can move the arrow-shaped pointer with your mouse.

How do I turn it off? Your computer is designed to turn itself off after you initiate a shutdown sequence by clicking the onscreen Start button, selecting "Shut Down" or "Turn Off Computer," and following the instructions on the screen. After the computer shuts itself off, you can turn off the monitor, speakers, and printer. When using computers in a school lab, ask about the shutdown procedure. Your lab manager might ask that you log out but do not turn the computer off.

TRY IT!

Turn your computer on

1. Locate the power switch for any devices connected to your computer and turn them on.

2. Locate the power switch for your computer and turn it on.

3. If a message asks for your user ID and/or password, type them in, and then press the **Enter** key on your computer's keyboard.

4. Wait for the Windows desktop to appear.

WINDOWS BASICS

What is Windows? Microsoft Windows is an example of a type of software called an operating system. The operating system controls all the basic tasks your computer performs, such as running application software, manipulating files on storage devices, and transferring data to and from printers, digital cameras, and other devices. The operating system also controls the user interface—the way software appears on the screen and the way you control what it does.

What is the Windows desktop? The Windows desktop is your base of operations for using your computer. It displays small pictures called "icons" that help you access software, documents, and the components of your computer system. The desktop is divided into several areas, as shown in Figure 4.

FIGURE 4

The Windows Desktop

[A] The main part of the desktop displays icons that represent software, files, and folders containing documents, graphics, and other data.

[B] The taskbar contains the Start button, Quick Start bar, and Notification area.

[C] The Start button is used to display the Start menu, which lists all the programs installed on your computer.

[D] The Quick Start bar is always visible, making it a good place for icons that represent the programs you frequently use.

[E] The Notification area displays the current time and the status of programs, devices, and Internet connections.

When working with your computer, you'll frequently use the Start button in the lower-left corner of the screen to display the Start menu that provides options for accessing software, finding data, configuring hardware, and finding answers to your questions about using Windows (Figure 5).

How do I manipulate icons and other Windows controls? To use the Start button and other desktop controls, you'll need to become familiar with how to use a mouse to control an on-screen pointer. The pointer is usually shaped like an arrow ▏, but it can change to a different shape, depending on the task you're doing. For example, when the computer is busy, the arrow shape turns into an hourglass ⌛, signifying that you should wait for the computer to finish its current task before attempting to start a new task.

FIGURE 5

The Start Menu

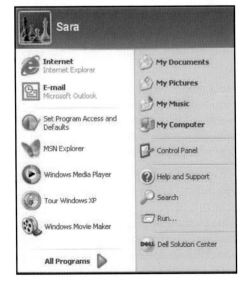

Orientation

MOUSE BASICS

What is a mouse? A mouse is a device used to manipulate items on the screen, such as the controls displayed on the Windows desktop. PC-compatible mice have at least two buttons, typically located on top of the mouse. Some mice also include a scroll wheel mounted between the left and right mouse buttons. Other mice include additional buttons on the top or sides (Figure 6).

Scroll wheel

Left mouse button

Additional buttons

Right mouse button

FIGURE 6

For basic mousing, you need use only the left and right mouse buttons.

How do I use a mouse? Hold the mouse in your right hand as shown in Figure 7. When you drag the mouse from left to right over your mousepad or desk, the arrow-shaped pointer on the screen moves from left to right. If you run out of room to move the mouse, simply pick it up and reposition it. The pointer does not move when the mouse is not in contact with a flat surface.

FIGURE 7

Rest the palm of your right hand on the mouse. Position your index finger over the left mouse button and your middle finger over the right mouse button.

There are several ways you can manipulate on-screen objects. Although you might not be able to manipulate every object in all possible ways, you'll soon learn which mouse actions are allowed for each type of control. The following list describes your repertoire of mouse actions.

Action	How to	Result
Click	Press the left mouse button once, and then immediately release it.	Select an object
Double-click	Press the left mouse button twice in rapid succession without moving the body of the mouse.	Activate an object
Right-click	Press the right mouse button once, and then immediately release it.	Display a shortcut menu
Drag	Hold the left mouse button down while you move the mouse.	Move an object

🖮 TRY IT!

Use your mouse

1. With your computer on and the Windows desktop showing on the screen, move your mouse around on the desk and notice how the mouse movements correspond to the movement of the arrow-shaped pointer.

2. Move the mouse to position the pointer on the Start button.

3. Click the left mouse button to open the Start menu.

4. Click the **Start** button again to close the Start menu.

KEYBOARD BASICS

What are the important features of a computer keyboard? You use the computer keyboard to input commands, respond to prompts, and type the text of documents. An insertion point that looks like a flashing vertical bar indicates where the characters you type will appear. You can change the location of the insertion point by using the mouse or the arrow keys. Study Figure 8 for an overview of important computer keys and their functions.

FIGURE 8

Computer Keyboard

A The **Esc** or "escape" key cancels an operation.

B **Function keys** activate commands, such as Save, Help, and Print. The command associated with each key depends on the software you are using.

C The **Print Screen** key prints the contents of the screen or stores a copy of the screen in memory that you can print or manipulate with graphics software.

D The **Scroll Lock** key's function depends on the software you're using. This key is rarely used with today's software.

E **Indicator Lights** show you the status of three toggle keys: Num Lock, Caps Lock, and Scroll Lock. The Power light indicates whether the computer is on or off.

F The **Backspace** key deletes one character to the left of the insertion point.

G The **Insert** key switches between insert mode and type-over mode.

H The **Home** key takes you to the beginning of a line or the beginning of a document, depending on the software you are using.

I The **Tab** key can move your current typing location to the next tab stop or the next text-entry box.

J The **Caps Lock** key capitalizes all the letters you type when it is engaged, but does not produce the top symbol on keys that contain two symbols. This key is a toggle key, which means that each time you press it, you switch between uppercase and lowercase modes.

K The **Shift** key capitalizes letters and produces the top symbol on keys that contain two symbols.

L You hold down the **Ctrl** key while pressing another key. The result of Ctrl or Alt key combinations depends on the software you are using.

M You hold down the **Alt** key while you press another key.

N The **Enter** key is used to indicate that you have completed a command or want to move your typing position down to the next line.

O The **Delete** key deletes the character to the right of the insertion point.

P The **End** key takes you to the end of a line or the end of a document, depending on the software you are using.

Q The **Page Up** key displays the previous screen of information. The **Page Down** key displays the next screen of information.

R The up, down, right, and left **arrow keys** move the insertion point.

S The **numeric keypad** produces numbers or moves the insertion point, depending on the status of the Num Lock key shown by the status lights.

What do Alt and Ctrl mean? The Alt and Ctrl keys work with the letter keys. If you see <Ctrl X>, Ctrl+X, [Ctrl X], Ctrl-X, or Ctrl X on the screen or in an instruction manual, it means to hold down the Ctrl key while you press X. For example, Ctrl+X is a keyboard shortcut for clicking the Edit menu, and then clicking the Cut option. A keyboard shortcut allows you to use the keyboard rather than the mouse to select menu commands.

What if I make a mistake? Everyone makes mistakes. The first rule is don't panic! Most mistakes are reversible. The hints and tips in Figure 9 should help you recover from mistakes.

FIGURE 9

Most mistakes are easy to fix.

What Happened	What To Do
Typed the wrong thing	Use the Backspace key to delete the last characters you typed.
Selected the wrong menu	Press the Esc key to close the menu.
Opened a window you didn't mean to	Click the X button in the upper-right corner of the window.
Computer has "hung up" and no longer responds to mouse clicks or typed commands	Hold down the Ctrl, Alt, and Delete keys, and then follow instructions to close the program.
Pressed the Enter key in the middle of a sentence	Press the Backspace key to paste the sentence back together

HOW TO START SOFTWARE

How do I start a software program? You can use the Start button to launch just about any software that's installed on your computer. Clicking the Start menu displays a list of recently accessed software. Clicking the All Programs option displays a list of every software program installed on your computer. You can run a program from this list simply by clicking it. Follow the instructions in the TRY IT! box to start Microsoft Word (assuming it is installed on your computer).

TRY IT!

Start Microsoft Word

1. Make sure your computer is on and it is displaying the Windows desktop.

2. Click the **Start** button to display the Start menu.

3. Click **All Programs** to display a list of all software installed on your computer.

4. Click **Microsoft Word**.

5. Wait a few seconds for your computer to display the main screen for Microsoft Word, shown below. Leave Word open for use with the next TRY IT!.

WINDOW CONTROLS

How do I tell the software what I want to do? Word processing, photo editing, and other software designed for use on computers running the Microsoft Windows operating system is referred to as "Windows software." Most Windows software works in a fairly uniform way and uses a similar set of controls.

Each software application appears in a rectangular area called a "window," which includes a title bar, a menu bar, and various controls shown in Figure 10.

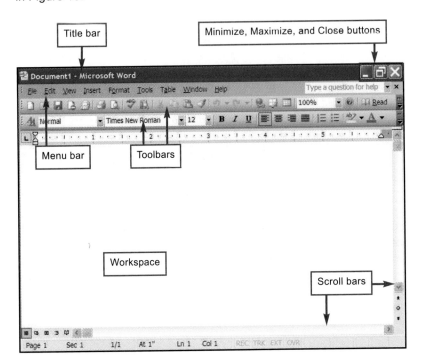

FIGURE 10

The title bar displays the title of the software, the name of the current data file, and the window sizing buttons.

The Minimize button shrinks the window to a button at the bottom of the screen.

The Maximize button stretches the window to fill the screen.

The Close button closes the window and exits the program.

The menu bar displays the titles of menus you can click to select commands.

The toolbar displays a series of tools for accomplishing various tasks.

The scroll bar can be clicked or dragged to see any material that does not fit in the displayed window.

The workspace is the area in which your document is displayed.

If you're unfamiliar with Windows controls, take a few minutes to complete the steps in the TRY IT! box below.

⌨ TRY IT!

Use the menu bar

1. Click **Insert** on the menu bar.

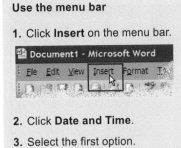

2. Click **Date and Time**.

3. Select the first option.

4. Click the **OK** button. The current date is inserted at the top of the workspace.

Use the toolbar

1. As shown below, click the **Spelling and Grammar** button on the Word toolbar.

2. The computer checks the spelling in your document.

3. You didn't have any misspelled words, so click the **OK** button to end the spell check.

Use the sizing buttons

1. Click the ▬ Minimize button.

2. The Microsoft Word window shrinks down to a button on the taskbar at the bottom of the screen.

⬚ Document1 - Micr...

3. Click the taskbar button to make the Word window appear again. Leave Word open for the next TRY IT!.

Orientation

HELP

How can I get help using software? If you've had problems using software, you're not alone! Everyone has questions at one time or another. Most software offers several sources of help, such as the following:

■ **Message boxes.** When using software, it is important to pay attention to any message boxes displayed on the screen. Make sure you carefully read the options they present. If the box doesn't seem to apply to what you want to do, click its Cancel button to close it. Otherwise, set the options the way you want them, and then click the OK button to continue.

■ **User manual.** Whether you're a beginner or a power user, the manual that comes with software can be an excellent resource. User manuals can contain quick-start guides, tutorials, detailed descriptions of menu options, and tips for using features effectively.

■ **Help menu.** The Help menu provides access to on-screen documentation. Most Windows software offers a standard method for searching through its Help files. Documentation can be accessed through a table of contents, by consulting the index, or by searching for particular words or phrases (Figure 11).

■ **Office Assistant.** Some software includes animated "assistants" that prompt you to type in simple questions (Figure 11). After you've entered a question, the assistant might ask you additional questions to refine your search, or it might display a list of documents that answer your question.

FIGURE 11

Clicking Help on the software menu bar produces a menu of help options, such as the office assistant (below left) or a Help window (below right), where you can use the Contents, Index, or Find tabs to search the Help file for information.

QuickCheck

SECTION A

1. When turning on the components of a desktop computer system, the computer's system [＿＿＿＿＿＿] should be switched on last.

2. Instead of using the on/off switch to turn off your computer, you should use the [＿＿＿＿＿＿] button to initiate a shutdown.

3. Ctrl+X means to hold down the Ctrl key, then press +, then press X. True or false? [＿＿＿＿]

4. The [＿＿＿＿＿＿] key can be used to delete the last character you typed.

5. Most Windows software displays a(n) [＿＿＿＿＿＿] bar that includes options, such as File and Help.

❖ CHECK ANSWERS

Documents, Browsers, and E-mail

To complete assignments for your course, you should be able to work with documents, browsers, and e-mail. Section B begins with how to use word processing software called Microsoft Word to work with documents. Next, it offers a quick overview of the Internet and how to access Web pages using a browser. The section wraps up with e-mail basics.

CREATING DOCUMENTS

How do I create and save a document? To create a document, simply type the text in the workspace provided by the Microsoft Word window. The flashing vertical insertion point (Figure 12) indicates your place in the document. Figure 13 explains how to save a document.

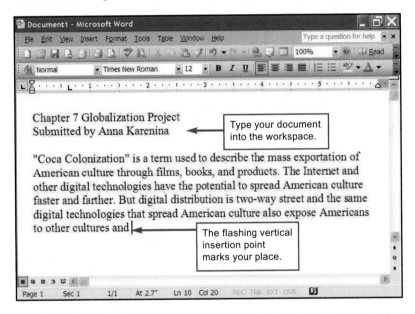

FIGURE 12

When typing text, you can use the following keys to move within a document and make revisions:

■ **Backspace**: Delete the character to the left of the insertion point.

■ **Delete:** Delete the character to the right of the insertion point.

■ **Enter:** End a paragraph and begin a new line.

■ **Arrow keys:** Move the insertion point up, down, right, or left.

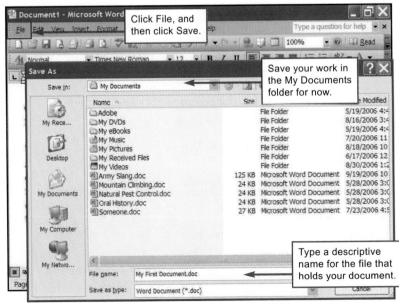

FIGURE 13

It is a good idea to save your document every few minutes, even if it is not finished. When you save a document, use the Save option on the File menu. Your computer is probably configured to save documents in the My Documents folder on the hard disk. No need to change that until you gain more experience. Make sure to enter a descriptive name for the document in the *File name* box. File names can be several words long; just do not use the * / \ " ' : symbols in the file name.

How do I print a document? To print a document, simply click the File menu, and then select Print. Your computer displays a window containing a series of print options. If you want to print a single copy of your document, these settings should be correct, so you can click the OK button at the bottom of the window to send your document to the printer.

Can I send a document to my instructor? You can e-mail a document by using the Send To option on the File menu (Figure 14). To do so, you must know your instructor's e-mail address. You'll learn more about e-mail later in the Orientation, but keep this option in mind because it is a handy way to submit assignments, such as projects and term papers.

How do I find my documents again in the future? If you want to revise a document sometime in the future, simply start Microsoft Word, click File on the menu bar, and then click Open. Your computer should display a list of documents stored in the My Documents folder. Locate the one you want to revise and click it.

What should I do when I'm done? When you're ready to quit, you can close the document by clicking the Close option from the File menu. When you want to close Microsoft Word, you can click the ☒ Close button in the upper-right corner of the screen.

FIGURE 14

The File menu's Send To option produces a submenu of choices for sending mail.

■ Choose *Mail Recipient* to insert your document directly into the body of an e-mail message.

■ Choose *Mail Recipient (as Attachment)* to send the document as a file attached to the e-mail message.

☞ TRY IT!

Create a document

1. Make sure that Microsoft Word is open. (See page O-9 to review how to open Microsoft Word.)

2. Click the workspace to position the insertion point in the upper-left corner, just under the date.

3. Type a paragraph. Refer to Figure 12 for keys to use while typing and revising your work.

4. When the first paragraph is complete, press the **Enter** key to begin a new paragraph.

5. Type a second paragraph of text.

Save a document

1. Click **File** on the Word menu bar.

2. Click **Save**.

3. Make sure the *Save in* box lists My Documents. If not, click the ▾ button and then click My Documents from the list.

4. In the *File name* box, type a name for your document.

5. Click the **Save** button.

6. When the Save As dialog box closes, your document is saved.

Print a document, close it, and exit Word

1. Click **File** on the Word menu bar, and then click **Print**.

2. Make sure the *Page Range* is set to **All**.

3. Make sure *Number of copies* is set to **1**.

4. Click the **OK** button and wait a few seconds for the printer to produce your document.

5. Close the document by clicking **File**, then clicking **Close**. The workspace should become blank.

6. Exit Microsoft Word by clicking the ☒ Close button.

INTERNET AND WEB BASICS

What is the Internet? The Internet is the largest computer network in the world, carrying information from one continent to another in the blink of an eye (Figure 15). The computers connected to this network offer many types of resources, such as e-mail, instant messaging, popular music downloads, and online shopping.

What is the Web? Although some people use the terms "Internet" and "Web" interchangeably, the two are not the same. The Internet refers to a communications network that connects computers all around the globe. The Web—short for World Wide Web—is just one of the many resources available over this communications network.

The World Wide Web is a collection of linked and cross-referenced information available for public access. This information is accessible from Web sites located on millions of computers. The information is displayed as a series of screens called Web pages. You'll use the Web for general research and for specific activities designed to accompany this textbook. To use the Web, your computer must have access to the Internet.

How do I access the Internet? Most computers can be configured to connect to the Internet over telephone or cable television systems. Internet access can be obtained from school computer labs, local service providers, such as your cable television company, and national Internet service providers, such as AOL (America Online), AT&T, and MSN (Microsoft Network).

To expedite your orientation, it is assumed that your computer has Internet access. If it does not, consult your instructor, or ask an experienced computer user to help you get set up.

How do I know if my computer has Internet access? The easiest way to find out if your computer can access the Internet is to try it. You can quickly find out if you have Internet access by starting software called a browser that's designed to display Web pages.

Browser software called Internet Explorer is supplied with Microsoft Windows. Other browsers, such as Netscape, FireFox, and Opera, are also available. Follow the steps in the TRY IT! box to start Internet Explorer.

HOW TO USE A WEB BROWSER AND SEARCH ENGINE

How do I use a browser? A browser lets you enter a unique Web page address called a URL and jump from one Web page to another by using links. Links are usually underlined, and when you position the arrow-shaped mouse pointer over a link, it changes to a hand shape.

FIGURE 15

The Internet communications network stretches around the globe.

TRY IT!

Start your browser

1. Click the [icon] icon located near the Start button.

2. Your computer should soon display a window containing "Microsoft Internet Explorer" in the title bar. (Refer to the next page.)

If your computer displays a *Connect to* box, click the **Dial** button to establish a dial-up connection over your telephone line.

You'll need to cancel the browser command and consult an experienced computer user if:

- Your computer displays a "working off line" message.

- Your computer displays an Internet Connection Wizard box.

You'll learn much more about browsers in Chapter 1. Until you read that material, you can get along quite well using the basic controls shown in Figure 16.

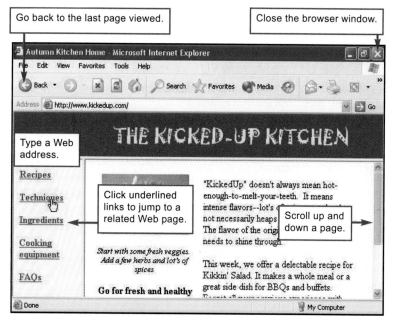

Go back to the last page viewed.

Close the browser window.

Type a Web address.

Click underlined links to jump to a related Web page.

Scroll up and down a page.

FIGURE 16

Using a Browser

A full Web address might look like this:
http://www.kickedup.com
It is not necessary to type the http://, so to access the Kicked-Up Kitchen page shown here, you would type:
www.kickedup.com
When typing a Web address, do not use any spaces and copy upper- and lowercase letters exactly.

How do I find specific information on the Web? If you're looking for information and don't know the Web site where it might be located, you can use a search engine to find it. Follow the steps in the TRY IT! box to "go Googling" by using the Google search engine.

TRY IT!

Use a search engine

1. Make sure the browser window is open.

2. Click the Address box and type:

Address www.google.com

3. Press the **Enter** key. Your browser displays the Web page for the Google search engine.

4. Click the blank search box and then type **national parks**.

Google Advanced Search Preferences

national parks

5. Press the **Enter** key. Google displays a list of Web pages that relate to national parks.

6. Click the underlined **National Park Service** link. Your browser displays the ParkNet home page.

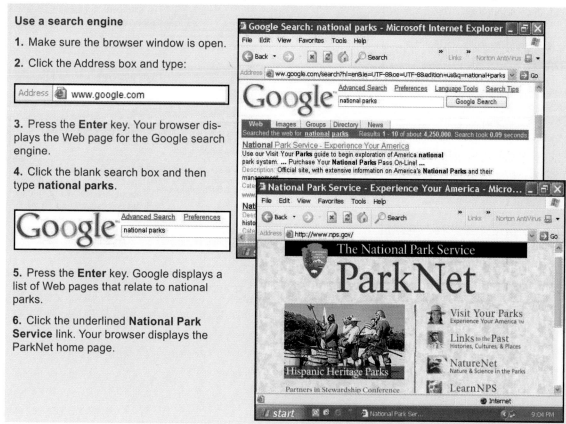

WORKING WITH E-MAIL

What is e-mail? E-mail is a form of communication that relies on computer networks, such as the Internet, to transmit messages from one computer to another. Like regular mail, e-mail messages are sent to a mailbox where they are kept until the recipient retrieves the message. Messages might arrive at their destination within seconds, or might not arrive for a few hours. Once sent, e-mail messages cannot be retrieved.

What do I need to use e-mail? To send and receive e-mail, you need an Internet connection, an e-mail account, and software that enables you to compose, read, and delete e-mail messages. An e-mail account consists of an e-mail address (Figure 17), a password, and a mailbox. You can usually obtain an e-mail account from your Internet service provider, your school, or a Web-based e-mail provider, such as Hotmail, Yahoo! Mail, or GMail.

How do I create and send an e-mail message? Many e-mail systems are available, and each uses slightly different software, making it impossible to cover all options in this short orientation. You might want to enlist the aid of an experienced computer user to help you get started. Chapter 1 provides more detail about e-mail, too. The steps in the TRY IT! box are designed for students who use e-mail software called Outlook Express, which is supplied with Microsoft Windows.

FIGURE 17

E-mail Addresses

An e-mail address consists of a user ID followed by an @ symbol and the name of a computer that handles e-mail accounts. Ask your instructor for his or her e-mail address. It is likely similar to the following:

instructor@school.edu

When typing an e-mail address, use all lowercase letters and do not use any spaces.

TRY IT!

Create and send e-mail

1. Click the 📧 icon located at the bottom of your screen. The Outlook Express window opens.

2. Click the **Create** button to display a form like the one at right.

3. Follow steps 4-6 as shown at right.

7. When your message is complete, click the **Send** button. With most computers, this button places the e-mail in your Outbox.

8. Click the **Send/Recv** button on the toolbar to ship the message from your Outbox over the network to your instructor.

Let me introduce myself

File   Edit   View   Insert   Format   Tools   Message   Help

Send   Cut   Copy   Paste   Undo   Check

To: jedwards@msu.mail.edu

Cc:

Subject: Let me introduce myself

Arial   10   B I U A

Hello -
My name is Grace Gibson and I am a sophomore from Dallas, TX. I plan to become a nurse and because I am fluent in English and Spanish, I hope to work in the Southwest. I play the drums and I march with the school band. This summer I'm planning a trip to Japan, where I will learn about traditional Taiko drumming. That will be a challenge!

I have used computers for e-mail and browsing the Web, but I am n[e]
terminology. I am required to take this course for my nursing major,
something about how computers are used in health care.

start   2 Outlook Express   5:44 PM

4. Click the To box and type your instructor's e-mail address.

5. Click the Subject box and type "Let me introduce myself."

6. Click the empty workspace and type a few lines about yourself. You can use the Backspace and arrow keys to edit, if necessary.

How do I get my mail? As with sending mail, the way you get mail depends on your mail system. In general, clicking the Send/Recv button collects your mail from the network and stores it in your Inbox. Your mail software displays a list of your messages. The new ones are usually shown in bold type. You can click any message to open it, read it, and reply to it, as shown in Figure 18.

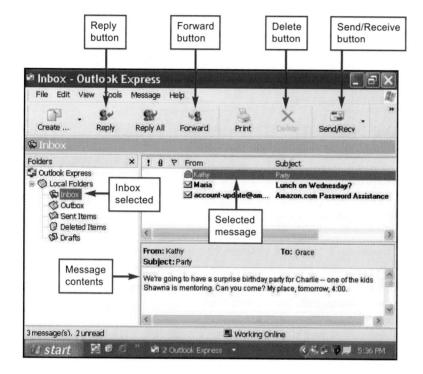

FIGURE 18

Most e-mail software displays a list of your messages. You can:

- Open a message and read it.
- Reply to a message.
- Delete unwanted messages (a good idea to minimize the size of your mailbox).
- Forward a message to someone else.

QuickCheck

SECTION B

1. It is a good idea to [_____] your work every few minutes, even if you are not finished with it.

2. Software called a(n) [_____] helps you access Web pages.

3. If you don't know where to find information, you can use a(n) [_____] engine to produce a list of links to Web pages that might contain the information you seek.

4. The special symbol used in e-mail addresses is [_____].

5. An e-mail [_____] consists of an e-mail address, a password, and a mailbox.

CHECK ANSWERS

Security and Privacy

Today's digital landscape is dotted with a few obstacles that can trip up unwary computer users. As with most other facets of modern life, computing has its share of troublemakers, scam artists, and identity thieves. Section C offers some tips on navigating through the sometimes rough neighborhoods of cyberspace, while keeping your data safe and your identity private.

SECURING YOUR COMPUTER AND DATA

What's at risk if my computer is stolen? A computer can be an attractive target for thieves, but the value of a stolen computer is not so much in the hardware as in the data it contains. With stolen data such as your bank account numbers and PINs, a thief can wipe out your checking and savings accounts. With your credit card numbers, a thief can go on a spending spree. Even worse, a criminal can use stolen data to assume your identity, run up debts, get into legal difficulties, ruin your credit rating, and cause you no end of trouble.

How can I protect my computer data from theft? When you carry a notebook computer, never leave it unattended. To thwart a thief who breaks into your home or dorm room, anchor your computer to your desk with a specially designed lock you can buy at most electronics stores.

If a thief steals your computer, you can make it difficult to access your data by setting up a password. Until the password is entered, your data is off limits. A thief might be able to boot up the Windows desktop, but should not be able to easily look at the data in your folders.

Many new computers are shipped with a standard administrator password that everyone knows. If you are the only person using your computer, you can use the administrator account for your day-to-day computing, but create a secure password (Figure 19) for this account as soon as you can.

Your computer might also include a preset guest account with a nonsecure password such as "guest." You should disable this guest account or assign it a secure password.

FIGURE 19

To create a secure password:

■ Use at least five characters, mixing numbers with letters, as in 2by4s.

■ Do not use your name, the name of a family member, or pet's name.

■ Do not use a word that can be found in the dictionary.

■ Do not forget your password!

TRY IT!

Check the accounts on your computer

1. Click the **Start** button, then select **Control Panel**.

2. Select **User Accounts**. The User Accounts window shown at right displays a list of accounts.

3. If you are working on a school lab computer, close the User Accounts window without making any changes. If you are using your own computer, click the Administrator account and make sure it has a secure password.

User accounts are displayed at the bottom of the window.

AVOIDING VIRUSES

What's so bad about computer viruses? The term "virus" has a technical meaning that you'll learn in Chapter 4, but many people use the term loosely when referring to malicious programs that circulate on disks, in e-mail attachments, and on the Internet. This malware, as it is sometimes called, can steal your data, destroy files, or create network traffic jams. It might display an irritating message to announce its presence, or it might work quietly behind the scenes to spread itself to various files on your computer or mail itself out to everyone in your e-mail address book.

After a virus takes up residence in your computer, it is often difficult to disinfect all your files and make sure it is eliminated. Rather than wait for a virus attack, you should take steps to keep your computer virus free.

How can I keep viruses out of my computer? Back when viruses were less sophisticated, computer users were commonly warned not to download pirated software or open e-mail attachments from unknown senders. These two common sources of viruses still exist, but virus creators have found ways to make pirated software look legitimate and to affix your friends' names to e-mails that carry infected attachments.

Although it is a good idea to avoid pirated software and stay alert when opening e-mail attachments, the best defense against viruses is to install antivirus software such as the packages listed in Figure 20, and configure it to run continuously whenever your computer is on. You should make sure your antivirus software is set up to scan for viruses in incoming files and e-mail messages. At least once a week your antivirus software should run a full system check to make sure every file on your computer is virus free.

As new viruses emerge, your antivirus software needs to update its virus definition file. It gets this update as a Web download. If you've selected the auto update option, your computer should automatically receive updates as they become available.

FIGURE 20

Popular Antivirus Software

Norton AntiVirus

McAfee VirusScan

Kaspersky Anti-Virus

F-Prot

Softwin BitDefender

Panda Antivirus

Trend Micro PC-cillin

TRY IT!

Get familiar with your antivirus software

1. Click the **Start** button, and then select **All Programs**. Look for antivirus software (refer to Figure 20 for a list). Open your antivirus software by clicking it.

Can't find any? If you are using your own computer and it doesn't seem to have antivirus software, you can connect to an antivirus Web site and download it.

2. Each antivirus program has unique features. The figure on the right shows the main screen for Norton AntiVirus software. Explore your antivirus software to make sure it is configured to do the following:

- Scan incoming e-mail

- Run continuously in the background—a feature sometimes called Auto Protect

- Block malicious scripts

3. Check the date of your last full system scan. If it was more than one week ago, you should check the settings that schedule antivirus scans.

4. Check the date when your computer last received virus definitions. If it was more than two weeks ago, you should make sure your antivirus software is configured to receive automatic live updates.

PREVENTING INTRUSIONS

Is it risky to go online? The Internet offers lots of cool stuff—music downloads, movie reviews and trailers, online shopping and banking, consumer information, chat groups, news, sports, weather, and much more. Most Internet offerings are legitimate, but some downloads contain viruses, and shady characters called "hackers" control programs that lurk about waiting to snatch your personal data or infiltrate your computer. The longer your computer remains connected to the Internet, the more vulnerable it is to a hacker's infiltration attempts.

If a hacker gains access to your computer, he or she can look through your files, use your computer as a launching platform for viruses and network-jamming attacks, or turn your computer into a server for pornography and other unsavory material. Hackers have even found ways to turn thousands of infiltrated computers into "zombies," link them together, and carry out coordinated attacks to disrupt online access to Microsoft, Bank of America, and other Internet businesses.

How do hackers gain access to my computer? Intruders gain access by exploiting security flaws in your computer's operating system, browser, and e-mail software. Software publishers are constantly creating patches to fix these flaws. As part of your overall security plan, you should download and install security patches as they become available.

How can I block hackers from infiltrating my computer? Firewall software, such as the packages listed in Figure 21, provides a protective barrier between a computer and the Internet. If your computer is directly connected to the Internet, it should have active firewall software. If your computer connects to a local area network for Internet access, the network should have a device called a router to block infiltration attempts.

When a firewall is active, it watches for potentially disruptive incoming data called "probes." When a probe is discovered, your firewall displays a warning and asks what to do. If the source looks legitimate, you can let it through; if not, you should block it (Figure 22).

Where do I get a firewall? Windows XP includes a built-in firewall. If your computer uses an earlier version of Windows, you can download a third-party firewall.

FIGURE 21

Popular Firewall Software

Tiny Personal Firewall
McAfee Firewall Plus
Zone Alarm Pro
Sygate Firewall Pro
Norton Firewall
Black Ice Defender
Mac OS Firewall
Outpost Firewall

FIGURE 22

When your firewall software encounters new or unusual activity, it asks you what to do.

TRY IT!

Check your computer's firewall

Finding out if your computer has an active firewall requires a little detective work. Try one or more of these three methods. If your computer doesn't seem to have a firewall, you might want to download one and install it.

For non-XP users:

Click the **Start** button, click **All Programs**, and then look through the program list for firewalls such as those in Figure 21. If you find a firewall listed, start it and explore to see if it has been activated.

For Windows XP Service Pack 2 users:

Click the **Start** button, then click **Control Panel**. Double-click the **Security Center** icon and then make sure the Firewall is on.

For Windows XP users:

Click the **Start** button, then click **Control Panel**. Click **Network Connections**. Click the connection you use for Internet access. Under Network Tasks, click **Change Settings for this connection**. Click the **Advanced** tab and look for a check mark in front of the box labeled *Protect my computer and network ...*

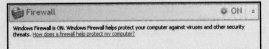

BLOCKING SPYWARE AND POP-UP ADS

Are some Web sites dangerous? When you access Web sites, data is transferred to your computer and displayed by your browser. Most of this data is harmless, but malicious HTML scripts, rogue ActiveX components, and spyware have the potential to search your computer for passwords and credit card numbers, monitor your Web-browsing habits for marketing purposes, block your access to legitimate Web sites, or surreptitiously use your computer as a staging area for illicit activities.

Spyware is the most insidious threat. It often piggybacks on pop-up ads and activates if you click the ad window. Some spyware can begin its dirty work when you try to click the Close button to get rid of an ad.

How can I block spyware? The first line of defense is to never click pop-up ads—especially those with dire warnings about your computer being infected by a virus or spyware! (See Figure 23.) To close an ad, right-click its button on the taskbar at the bottom of your screen, and then select the Close option from the menu that appears. Some browsers can be configured to block spyware and pop-up ads. Your antivirus software might offer similar options. You can also install software specially designed to block spyware and pop-up ads. Figure 24 lists some popular titles.

What other steps can I take to browse the Web safely? Most browsers include security features. You should take some time to become familiar with them. For example, Internet Explorer allows you to specify how you want it to deal with ActiveX components. You can also specify how to deal with HTML scripts, cookies, security certificates, and other Web-based data. If you don't want to be bothered by these details, however, Internet Explorer offers several predefined configurations for Low, Medium, and High security. Most Internet Explorer users set security and privacy options to Medium.

FIGURE 23

Some pop-up ads contain fake warnings about viruses, spyware, and intrusion attempts.

FIGURE 24

Popular Antispyware and Ad-Blocking Software

Webroot SpySweeper
Ad-Aware
Spybot S&D
SpyHunter
SpyRemover
Pest Patrol
Spykiller
Pop-up Defender

⌨ TRY IT!

Check Internet Explorer security and privacy options

1. Start Internet Explorer. Click **Tools** on the menu bar, then select **Internet Options**.

2. Click the **Security** tab. Typically, your security setting should be Medium.

3. Click the **Privacy** tab. Typically, your privacy setting should be Medium.

4. Check the bottom of the window for a Pop-up Blocker option. If your version of Internet Explorer offers this feature, make sure its box contains a check mark so that it is activated.

5. If your version of Internet Explorer does not offer a pop-up blocker, check your antivirus software to see if it can provide protection. Otherwise, you can use the Start button to see if the software listed in Figure 24 has been installed. If your computer seems to have no antispyware or ad-blocking software, you might want to download some and install it.

PROTECTING E-COMMERCE TRANSACTIONS

Is online shopping safe? Online shopping is generally safe. From time to time, shoppers encounter fake storefronts designed to look like legitimate merchants but that are actually set up to steal credit card information. You can avoid these fakes by making sure you enter correctly spelled URLs when connecting to your favorite shopping sites.

How safe is my credit card information when I shop online? Online shopping is no more dangerous than using your credit card for a telephone order or giving it to a server when you've finished eating in a restaurant. Anyone who handles your card can copy the card number, jot down the expiration date, and try to make unauthorized charges.

That's not to say that credit cards are risk free. Credit cards are surprisingly vulnerable both online and off. Thieves can break into merchant computers that store order information. Thieves might even pick up your credit card information from discarded order forms. Despite these risks, we continue to use credit cards.

Many people are concerned about their credit card data getting intercepted as it travels over the Internet. As you wrap up an online purchase and submit your credit card information, it is transmitted from your computer to the merchant's computer. Software called a packet sniffer, designed for legitimately monitoring network traffic, is occasionally used by unscrupulous hackers to intercept credit card numbers and other data traveling over the Internet.

How can I keep my credit card number confidential? When you submit credit card information, make sure the merchant provides a secure connection for transporting data. Typically, a secure connection is activated when you're in the final phases of checking out—as you enter your shipping and credit card information into a form and click a Submit button to send it. A secure connection encrypts your data. Even if your credit card number is intercepted, it cannot be deciphered and used. To make sure you have a secure connection, look for the lock icon in the lower-right corner of your screen. The Address box should also display a URL that begins with shttp:// or https:// (Secure HTTP), or contains ssl (Secure Sockets Layer).

⌨ TRY IT!

Identify a secure connection

1. Start your browser and connect to the site: **www.walmart.com**.

2. Select any item and use the **Add to Cart** option to place it in your online shopping cart.

3. Click the **Proceed to Checkout** button.

4. At the checkout screen, do you see any evidence that you're using a secure connection?

5. Close your browser so that you don't complete the transaction.

AVOIDING E-MAIL SCAMS

What are e-mail scams? From time to time, you hear about con artists who have bilked innocent consumers out of their life savings. The Internet has its share of con artists, too, who run e-mail scams designed to collect money and confidential information from unsuspecting victims. E-mail scams are usually distributed in mass mailings called spam.

What do I need to know about spam? The Internet makes it easy and cheap to send out millions of e-mail solicitations. In the United States, the CAN-SPAM Act requires mass-mail messages to be labeled with a valid subject line. Recipients are supposed to be provided with a way to opt out of receiving future messages. Legitimate merchants and organizations comply with the law when sending product announcements, newsletters, and other messages. Unscrupulous spammers ignore the law and try to disguise their solicitations as messages from your friends, chat room participants, or co-workers (Figure 25).

FIGURE 25

Some e-mail systems use spam filters to flag suspected spam by adding [SPAM] to the subject line. Spam filters are not perfect, however. Some spam is not flagged and occasionally legitimate mail is mistaken for spam.

Is spam dangerous? Many spam messages contain legitimate information, including daily or weekly newsletters to which you've subscribed. Some spam messages, however, advertise illegal products. Others are outright scams to get you to download a virus, divulge your bank account numbers, or send in money for products you'll never receive.

Beware of spam containing offers that seem just too good to be true. For example, you might receive a message from an African businessman who is seeking your help to transfer a large sum of money from his country to yours (Figure 26). These messages are frauds.

FIGURE 26

Many variations of this African money-transfer fraud—complete with deliberate grammatical errors—have circulated on the Internet for years. Victims who respond to these preposterous e-mails have found their bank accounts raided, their credit ratings destroyed, and their reputations ruined. According to the FBI, some victims have even been kidnapped!

What's phishing? Phishing (pronounced "fishing") is a scam that arrives in your e-mailbox looking like official correspondence from a major company, such as Microsoft, PayPal, eBay, MSN, Yahoo!, or America Online. The e-mail message is actually from an illegitimate source and is designed to trick you into divulging confidential information or downloading a virus. Links in the e-mail message often lead to a Web site that looks official, where you are asked to enter confidential information such as your credit card number, Social Security number, or bank account number.

The following are examples of phishing scams you should be aware of:

■ A message from Microsoft with an attachment that supposedly contains a security update for Microsoft Windows. Downloading the attachment infects your computer with a virus.

■ A message from America Online, complete with official-looking logos, that alerts you to a problem with your account. When you click the AOL Billing Center link and enter your account information, it is transmitted to a hacker's computer.

■ A message that's obviously spam, but contains a convenient opt-out link. If you click the link believing that it will prevent future spam from this source, you'll actually be downloading a program that hackers can use to remotely control your computer for illegal activities.

How do I avoid e-mail scams? If your e-mail software provides spam filters, you can use them to block some unsolicited mail from your e-mailbox. Spam filters are far from perfect, however, so don't assume everything that gets through is legitimate. Use your judgment before opening any e-mail message or attachment.

Never reply to a message that you suspect to be fraudulent. If you have a question about its legitimacy, check whether it's on a list of known scams. Never click a link provided in an e-mail message to manage your account information. Instead, use your browser to go directly to the company's Web site and access your account as usual. Microsoft never sends updates as attachments. To obtain Microsoft updates, go to *www.microsoft.com* and click Windows Update or Office Update.

TRY IT!

Arm yourself against e-mail scams

1. Start your browser and connect to the site **www.antiphishing.org**. Scroll down the page and become familiar with the list of recent phishing attacks.

2. Open your e-mail software and find out if it incudes spam filters. You can usually find this information by clicking Help on the menu bar and then typing "spam filter" in the search box.

3. Explore your options for configuring spam filters. If you use Microsoft Outlook for e-mail (shown at right), you can find these settings by clicking **Actions** on the menu bar, pointing to **Junk E-Mail**, then clicking **Junk E-mail Options**.

Spam filters sometimes catch legitimate mail and group it with junk mail. You might want to keep tabs on your spam filters when they are first activated to make sure they are set to a level that eliminates most unwanted spam without catching too much legitimate mail.

Junk E-mail Options

Options | Safe Senders | Safe Recipients | Blocked Senders

Outlook can move messages that appear to be junk e-mail into a special Junk E-mail folder.

Choose the level of junk e-mail protection you want:

○ No Automatic Filtering. Mail from blocked senders is still moved to the Junk E-mail folder.

● Low: Move the most obvious junk e-mail to the Junk E-mail folder.

○ High: Most junk e-mail is caught, but some regular mail may be caught as well. Check your Junk E-mail folder often.

○ Safe Lists Only: Only mail from people or domains on your Safe Senders List or Safe Recipients List will be delivered to your Inbox.

☐ Permanently delete suspected junk e-mail instead of moving it to the Junk E-mail folder

OK | Cancel | Apply

PROTECTING YOUR PRIVACY

How much information has been collected about me? No matter what steps you take to protect your privacy, information about you is stored in many places and has the potential to be consolidated by government agencies, private businesses, and criminals.

Some databases are legitimate—those maintained by credit bureaus and medical insurance companies, for example. By law, you have the right to ask for a copy of these records and correct any errors you find. Many other databases, such as those maintained at e-commerce sites and those illegally acquired by hackers, are not accessible, and you have no way of checking the data they contain.

Can I control who collects information about me? To some extent, you can limit your exposure to future data collection by supplying personal data only when absolutely necessary. When filling out online forms, consider whether you want to or need to provide your real name and address.

You should also be careful about revealing personal information in chat rooms and other online forums. Many chat room participants are not who they appear to be. Some people are just having fun with fantasy identities, but others are trying to con people by telling hard luck stories and faking illnesses. In a chat room, never reveal personal information, such as your full name, address, or phone number. Resist the temptation to meet face to face with chat room participants. Taking simple steps to protect your privacy is an important part of your overall security plan (Figure 27).

TRY IT!

Check your privacy

1. Start your browser and go Googling by connecting to **www.google.com**. Enter your name in the Search box. What turns up?

2. Connect to **www.peopledata.com** and click the **People Search** option. Enter your name and state of residence. Click the **Search** button. Notice all the information that's offered.

3. Connect to **www.ciadata.com** and scroll down the page to view the kind of information anyone can obtain about you for less than $100.

4. Connect to the Federal Trade Commission site:

http://www.ftc.gov/bcp/conline/pubs/credit/crdright.htm

At this site, you can read about your rights to view credit reports.

FIGURE 27

Computer Security Checklist

- Use a password to protect your data in case your computer is stolen.

- Don't leave your computer unattended in public places.

- Run antivirus software and keep it updated.

- Install software service packs and security patches as they become available, but make sure they are legitimate.

- Install and activate firewall software, especially if your computer is directly connected to the Internet by an ISDN, DSL, satellite, or cable connection.

- Do not publish or post personal information, such as your physical address, passwords, Social Security number, or account numbers, on your Web site, your online resume, or other online documents.

- Be wary of contacts you make in public chat rooms.

- Don't click pop-up ads.

- Install and activate antispyware and ad-blocking software.

- Do not reply to spam.

- Ignore e-mail offers that seem too good to be true.

QuickCheck

SECTION C

1. The best defense against viruses is to use a phishing filter before opening e-mail attachments. True or false? [   ]

2. Intruders can access your computer by exploiting [   ] flaws in a computer's operating system, browser, or e-mail software.

3. [   ] is an online threat that compromises your privacy by piggybacking on pop-up ads and collecting personal information.

4. E-mail scams are usually distributed in mass mailings called [   ].

 CHECK ANSWERS

SECTION D

BookOnCD

Studies show that the more you interact with concepts, the faster you'll learn them. The BookOnCD that accompanies your textbook is designed to be an interactive learning environment you can conveniently carry between home and school. This section offers an interactive overview of BookOnCD features.

BOOKONCD BASICS

What is the BookOnCD? The CD packaged with your textbook includes a multimedia version of your textbook with photos that come to life as videos, diagrams that become animations, screenshots that open to guided software tours, and computer-scored activities that will help improve your test scores.

What's the most effective way to use the BookOnCD? If you're used to reading documents and Web pages on your computer screen, you can use the BookOnCD for most of your reading and studying. As you work through a chapter, you'll be able to view the multimedia elements in context and take QuickChecks at the end of each section. If you prefer to read from your printed textbook, you can start the BookOnCD whenever you want to view a multimedia element or work with a computer-scored activity.

How do I start the BookOnCD? To start the BookOnCD and take advantage of its interactive features, follow the instructions in the TRY IT! box below.

FLASH PLAYER

The BookOnCD requires the Macromedia Flash player for displaying screen tours and labs. The Flash player is installed on most computers. If the BookOnCD cannot find your Flash player when it starts, you'll be directed to go online to download and install it.

🖾 TRY IT!

Start the BookOnCD

1. Locate the button on your computer's CD or DVD drive and push it to open the tray.

2. Insert the BookOnCD into the tray, label side up.

3. Push the button on the drive to close it.

4. Wait a few seconds until the BookOnCD has loaded. The main Computer Concepts screen appears, along with the Tracking Options dialog box.

The BookOnCD allows you to save your scores for QuickChecks, practice tests, and other activities, but for this session you do not need to track this data.

5. To disable tracking, make sure the box *Save Tracking data* is empty. If the box contains a check mark, click the box to empty it.

6. Click the **OK** button. The Tracking Options dialog box closes and the BookOnCD is ready for use.

To disable tracking for a session, make sure this box is empty.

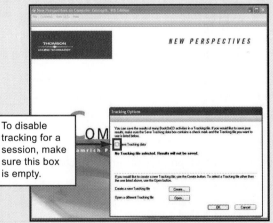

How do I navigate through the book? The BookOnCD menu and toolbar, near the top of the screen, contain tools you can use for navigation. The Next and Back buttons turn one page at a time. To get to the first page of any chapter, you can select it from the Contents menu.

The BookOnCD pages mirror the pages in the printed book, so if you want to take the QuickCheck that's on page 23 of your printed textbook for example, you can use the Go to Page option on the toolbar to jump right to it.

What are the other menu and navigation options? The menu bar includes a Web links menu with options that open your browser and connect to InfoWebLinks, the NP9 Web site, and the Course Technology Web site. The menu bar also includes a Help menu where you can access instructions and troubleshooting FAQs. The Glossary button provides access to definitions for key terms. The Annotation button appears when your instructor has posted comments or lecture notes. If your instructor has not posted annotations, the button will not appear.

How do I exit the BookOnCD? When you have completed a session and want to close the BookOnCD, you can click the ☒ button in the upper-right corner of the title bar, or you can click the File menu and select Exit. Figure 28 helps you locate the Close button and BookOnCD navigation tools.

FIGURE 28

Key features of the BookOnCD menu bar and toolbar.

The Back button displays the previous page.

The Next button displays the next page.

The Contents menu takes you to the first page of any chapter you select.

If you've jumped to a page, you can click the ◐ button to jump back to the page where you started.

To jump to a specific page, enter the page number in the box, then click the ◐ button.

The Close button closes the BookOnCD.

🖵 **TRY IT!**

Open a chapter and navigate the BookOnCD

1. Click **Contents** on the menu bar. The contents menu appears.

2. Click **Chapter 2**.

3. When Chapter 2 appears, click the **Next** button twice until you see page 62.

4. Click the **Back** button twice to go back to the first page of Chapter 2.

5. Click the white box on the right side of Go to Page. Type 68, then click the **Go to Page** ◐ button.

6. Click the ◐ **Go to Page** button. Now you should be back at the first page of Chapter 2.

7. Scroll down the page until you can see the Chapter Contents listing. As shown at right, you can use this list to quickly jump to Sections A, B, C, or D, TechTalk, Issues, Computers in Context, Labs, and End-of-Chapter activities.

8. Click ✳ **Section D** to jump to Section D.

Use the scroll bar to scroll down the page.

The ✳ icons indicate clickable links to sections, labs, and other activities on the CD.

MULTIMEDIA AND COMPUTER-SCORED ACTIVITIES

What kinds of multimedia are included in the BookOnCD?

Figures in your book marked with the ❋ icon morph into multimedia screentours, animations, and videos. A screentour takes you on a guided software tour—even if you don't have the software installed on your computer! Animations and videos visually expand on the concepts presented in the text.

How do I access screentours and other multimedia?

To access multimedia elements, simply click the **CLICK TO START** ❋ icon while using the BookOnCD.

Which activities are computer scored?

Figure 29 lists the BookOnCD activities that are computer scored. You can use these activities to gauge how well you remember and understand the material you read in the textbook.

Suppose you're reading Chapter 3. Work with the TRY IT! below to see how multimedia and computer-scored activities work.

FIGURE 29

BookOnCD Computer-Scored Activities

> **Interactive Summary**
>
> **Interactive Situation Questions**
>
> **Practice Tests**
>
> **Concept Map**
>
> **QuickChecks**
>
> **Lab QuickChecks**

 TRY IT!

Explore multimedia and computer-scored activities

1. Use the **Go to Page** control to jump to page 83.

2. On page 83, Figure 2-29 contains a **CLICK TO START** ❋ icon. Click it to launch the video.

3. If you want to stop the video at any time, click any blank area of the BookOnCD page. To restart the video, click the **CLICK TO START** ❋ icon again.

4. Now, try a computer-scored QuickCheck. Click the **Next** button a few times to go to page 89 and scroll down the page until you can see the entire set of QuickCheck questions.

5. Click the answer box for question 1, and then type your answer. Most answers are a single word. Upper and lower-case have no effect on the correctness of your answer.

6. Press the **Tab** key to jump to question 2, and then type your answer. Don't worry if you don't know the answer, you haven't actually read Chapter 2 yet. Just make a guess for now.

7. When you have answered all the questions, click the ❋ **CHECK ANSWERS** icon. The computer indicates whether your answer is correct or incorrect.

8. Continue to click **OK** to check the rest of your answers.

9. When you've reviewed all your answers, the computer presents a score summary. Click **OK** to close the dialog box

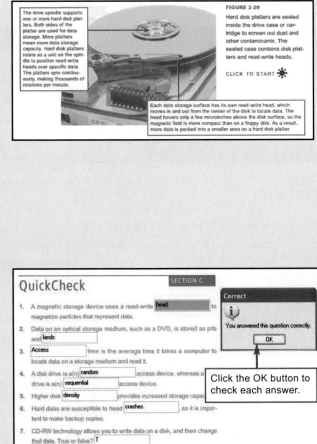

NEW PERSPECTIVES LABS

What about labs? Your textbook gives you access to two kinds of labs. New Perspectives Labs are part of the BookOnCD. Student Edition Labs are located at the NP9 Web site. You'll learn how to access Student Edition Labs in Section E.

New Perspectives Labs give you hands-on experience applying concepts and using software discussed in each chapter. Labs on the BookOnCD are divided into topics, and each topic ends with a QuickCheck so that you can make sure you understand key concepts.

In addition to lab QuickChecks, each New Perspectives Lab also includes a set of assignments located in the Lab section of each chapter. Your instructor might require you to complete these assignments. You can submit them on paper, on disk, or as an e-mail message, according to your instructor's directions.

How do I launch a lab? First, navigate to the lab page using the New Perspectives Labs option from the Chapter Contents list or type in the corresponding page number from the printed book. Click the lab's ✳ icon to start it.

⌨ TRY IT!

Open a New Perspectives Lab

1. Click **Contents** on the BookOnCD menu bar and select **Chapter 1**.

2. Scroll down to the Chapter Contents list and click ✳ **New Perspectives Labs**.

3. When the New Perspectives Labs page appears, click ✳ **Operating a Personal Computer**.

4. The lab window opens. Click the ➡ button to view objectives for Topic 1.

5. Click the ➡ button again to view page 1 of the lab. Read the information on the page, and then continue through the lab, making sure to follow any numbered instructions.

6. After page 8, you will encounter the first QuickCheck question. Click the correct answer, and then click the **Check Answer** button. After you find out if your answer was correct, click the ➡ button to continue to the next question. Complete all the QuickCheck questions for Topic 1.

7. For this TRY IT! you don't have to complete the entire lab. When you are ready to quit, click the ⏏ button.

8. Click the ⏏ button again. Your Lab QuickCheck results are displayed.

9. Click the **OK** button to return to the BookOnCD.

TRACKING YOUR SCORES

Can I save scores from QuickChecks, labs, and other activities? To save your scores, you have to create a Tracking file. The file can be located on a floppy disk, your computer's hard disk, a USB Flash drive, or a network drive where you have permission to store files.

TRY IT!

Create a Tracking file

1. Make sure your BookOnCD is open.

2. Click **File** on the BookOnCD menu bar, then click **Change Tracking Options**.

3. When the Tracking Options dialog box appears, click the **Create** button.

4. When the Create Tracking File dialog box appears, enter the requested data (see illustration above right), then click **Continue**. The Save As dialog box appears.

5. Use the Save As dialog box to specify the location and name for your Tracking file. (See the illustration below right.)

6. After selecting a name and location for your Tracking file, click the **Save** button.

7. Back at the Tracking Options dialog box, make sure there is a check mark in the box labeled *Save Tracking data*, then click the **OK** button. Now your Tracking file is ready to receive your scores.

Complete a Practice Test

To start tracking your scores, you can complete a Practice Test.

1. Click the **Practice Test** button located on the BookOnCD Toolbar.

2. The first question of a 10-question Practice Test appears. Answer the question, then click the **Next** button.

3. Answer the remaining questions, then click the **Check Answers** button.

4. When you see your score summary, click the **OK** button. You can then step through each of your answers or view a study guide.

5. Click the **Study Guide** button. A browser window opens to display each Practice Test question, your answers, and corresponding page numbers in your textbook.

6. Click the ⊠ button on your browser window to close the Study Guide.

7. Click the **Close** button on the Practice Test window to close it and save your scores.

View the contents of your Tracking file

1. Click **File** on the BookOnCD menu bar.

2. Click **View Tracking Report**. Your computer opens your browser and displays a

summary score for the Practice Test you completed. The list of summary scores grows as you save additional Practice Tests, QuickChecks, Interactive Summaries, Interactive Situation Questions, and Lab QuickChecks.

3. To close the Tracking Report, close the browser window by clicking its ⊠ button.

How do I submit scores from my Tracking file? You can use the Submit Tracking Data option on the File menu to send your scores to your instructor. The files are sent over an Internet service called WebTrack. Before you begin, make sure you have the following:

- An Internet connection
- Your instructor's WebTrack address
- Tracking file (If you've stored your data on a USB Flash drive, make sure it is connected; if your data is on a floppy disk, make sure it is inserted in the drive.)

Are the scores erased from my Tracking file when they are sent? No. Your scores remain in your file—a copy is sent to your instructor. If your instructor's computer malfunctions and loses your data, you can resubmit your Tracking file. It is a good idea to back up your Tracking file using the Back Up Tracking File option on the File menu. If your file is damaged or lost, you'll have a copy.

TRY IT!

Send your Tracking data

1. Click **File** on the BookOnCD menu bar, then click **Submit Tracking Data**.

2. Make sure your instructor's Web Track address is correctly displayed in the Tracking Data Destination dialog box, then click **Continue**.

3. Your computer opens a browser window, makes an Internet connection, and contacts the WebTrack server.

4. When the WebTrack screen appears, make sure the information displayed is correct, then click the **Submit** button.

5. When you see a message that confirms your data has been submitted, you can close the browser window by clicking the ⊠ button.

6. Close your BookOnCD before you continue to the next section in the Orientation.

QuickCheck

SECTION D

1. When you use the BookOnCD a(n) [　　　　　　] button appears if your instructor has posted comments or lecture notes.

2. Figures in the book marked with an @ sign morph into multimedia screentours, animations, and videos. True or false? [　　　　　]

3. New Perspectives [　　　　　] are divided into topics and each topic ends with a QuickCheck.

4. To save your scores on computer-scored activities you have to create a [　　　　　] file.

CHECK ANSWERS

SECTION E

NP9 Web Site

The Internet offers access to information that's useful to just about everyone, and New Perspectives students are no exception. Your textbook includes a CoursePort card that allows you to access the New Perspectives NP9 Web site, where you can continue the learning experience you began with your printed textbook and BookOnCD.

WEB SITE RESOURCES

What kinds of Web resources accompany my textbook?

The New Perspectives NP9 Web site—NP9 Web site, for short—includes all sorts of activities and information to help you learn about computers. Figure 30 highlights the features you'll find on the NP9 Web site.

FIGURE 30

NP9 Web Site Features

Detailed Learning Objectives
An expanded version of the Learning Objectives included at the beginning of each chapter.

Chapter Overview
Listen to a 5-minute audio presentation of chapter highlights.

Pre-assessment
Take a short quiz to assess your background in the chapter material.

Interactive Summary
An online version of the Interactive Summary you'll find in the end-of-chapter materials of your printed textbook.

Interactive Situation Questions
An online version of the Interactive Situation Questions you'll find in the end-of-chapter materials of your printed textbook.

Interactive Practice Tests
Each test contains 10 randomly selected questions from the chapter.

Concept Maps
An online version of the concept maps you'll find in the end-of-chapter materials of your printed textbook.

Student Edition Labs
Get hands-on practice with some of the concepts presented in a chapter.

TechTV Videos
Watch a video clip from a recent TechTV show and explore new tech trends.

InfoWebLinks
Follow Web links to find the most current information on equipment, concepts, subject matter, and software you read about in a chapter.

Online Games
Have some fun while refreshing your memory about key concepts that might appear on the next exam.

TechBuzz
Find out about cutting edge technology in the magazine-like TechBuzz section of the Web site.

WEB SITE ACCESS

How do I access the NP9 Web site? You can get to the NP9 Web site in several ways:

- Open your browser and type *www.course.com/np/concepts9*. Your browser will display the main page of the NP9 Web site. From there, you can click links to each chapter's activities and information.

- Open your BookOnCD and click any ✝ link. These links take you directly to the information or activity specified along with the link.

Do I need a password? Yes. The first time you connect to the NP9 Web site, you must create a CoursePort profile. When you have completed the short registration process, you can access the NP9 Web site. Use the New User Registration link to create your CoursePort profile.

⌨ TRY IT!

Access the NP9 Web site

1. Start your browser.

2. Click the address box and type:

Address 🅔 www.course.com/np/concepts9

Make sure to use all lowercase letters, insert no spaces, and use the / slash, not the \ slash.

3. Press the **Enter** key. The CoursePort Login screen is displayed.

4. If you are accessing the NP9 Web site for the first time, click the **New User Registration** link and follow the instructions to create your account.

5. Once you've created a CoursePort account, you can log in by entering your Username and Password, then clicking the **Enter** button.

6. The Welcome screen contains links to activities for each chapter of the textbook. Click the button for Chapter 1 at the top of the screen. Your browser displays links to activities for the first chapter in your textbook.

7. You can always return to the Welcome screen by clicking the Home button on the Chapter toolbar. Click the **Home** button now.

8. Use your browser's ⊠ Close button to exit the NP9 Web site. If you are using a dial-up connection, you might have to manually disconnect from the Internet by double-clicking the 🖳 icon in the lower-right corner of your screen, and then clicking Disconnect.

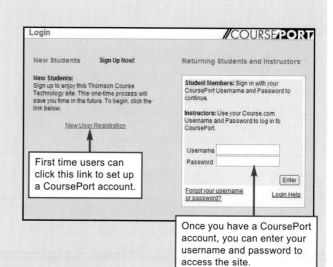

First time users can click this link to set up a CoursePort account.

Once you have a CoursePort account, you can enter your username and password to access the site.

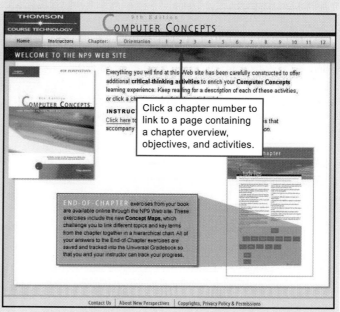

Click a chapter number to link to a page containing a chapter overview, objectives, and activities.

WEB SITE TOUR

How do I use the Chapter Overview and other resources?

The NP9 Web site includes some unique resources and some that are also found on your BookOnCD. You can use the NP9 Web site or BookOnCD to work with end-of-chapter activities, such as the Interactive Summary, Interactive Situation Questions, Practice Tests, and Concept Maps. The InfoWebLinks, which are housed on the Web, can be accessed from the NP9 Web site or from your BookOnCD.

Unique features of the NP9 Web site include the Chapter Overview, Pre-assessment, Tech TV Videos, Online Games, and TechBuzz.

Can I submit scores from Web site activities to my instructor?

You can track your results on many of the NP9 Web site activities through CoursePort's Universal Gradebook. Figure 31 lists the NP9 Web site activities that are trackable.

Follow the steps in the box below to explore the NP9 Web site.

FIGURE 31

Trackable NP9 Web Site Activities

Pre-Assessments

Interactive Summaries

Interactive Situation Questions

Interactive Practice Tests

Concept Maps

Student Edition Labs

Online Games

⌨ TRY IT!

Explore the NP9 Web site

1. Connect to the NP9 Web site and then click the link for **Chapter 1**.

2. Click the **Chapter Overview** link. Listen to the chapter overview for a few seconds, and then use the on-screen buttons to return to the Chapter 1 page.

3. Click the **Interactive Summary** link. Try your hand at answering some of the questions even though you haven't yet completed Chapter 1. Use the on-screen buttons when you are ready to return to the Chapter 1 page and continue your exploration.

4. Click the **TechTV Videos** link. Take a few minutes to watch the video. A project that corresponds to this video is located on the last page of Chapter 1 in your printed textbook. When the video ends, return to the main Web page for Chapter 1.

5. Click the **InfoWeb** link. When you see a list of InfoWebLinks for Chapter 1, click the **Netiquette** link. Read the short overview, and then click the first blue underlined link. Use the **Back** button on your browser window to get back to the Chapter 1 main page of the NP9 Web site.

6. Click the link to the **Lightning** game. Try your hand at a few questions, and then go back to the main Chapter 1 Web page.

7. Click the **TechBuzz** link. This online magazine about technology trends changes every few months so you can keep current with new digital gadgets, computer equipment, and software.

InfoWebLinks provide lots of information to supplement what you've read in the textbook.

Online games, such as Lightning, Don't Tell Me, and Fake Out provide a fun way to review chapter material.

STUDENT EDITION LABS

How do I access the Student Edition Labs? Student Edition Labs help you review the material presented in the textbook and extend your knowledge through dynamic observation and step-by-step practice.

⌨ TRY IT!

Work with Student Edition Labs

1. Make sure you're connected to the NP9 Web site and then click the link for **Chapter 1**.

2. Click the link for **Student Edition Labs**.

3. Click the link for **Chapter 1 Student Edition Labs**. The lab typically takes a few seconds to load, depending on the speed of your Internet connection.

4. Take a few minutes to walk through the section How to Use This Lab.

5. Click the **E-mail** link to start that lab.

6. Complete the first section of the lab, including the Intro, Observe, Practice, and Review activities.

7. When you've completed the review activity, a report containing your results is displayed. Use the Print button to print your report, or return to the NP9 Web site and use the Gradebook link to e-mail your results to your instructor.

8. Exit the lab by clicking the ⊠ button.

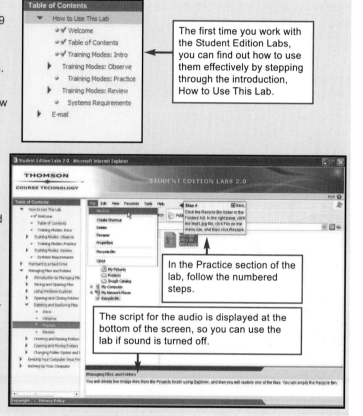

The first time you work with the Student Edition Labs, you can find out how to use them effectively by stepping through the introduction, How to Use This Lab.

In the Practice section of the lab, follow the numbered steps.

The script for the audio is displayed at the bottom of the screen, so you can use the lab if sound is turned off.

QuickCheck
SECTION E

1. To access the NP9 Web site, you need a username and password. True or false? [   ]

2. When you're at the NP9 Web site, you can use the [   ] button to display the Welcome screen.

3. The Chapter [   ] is a 5-minute audio presentation of chapter highlights.

4. The Student Edition [   ] help you review through dynamic observation and step-by-step practice.

✳ CHECK ANSWERS

NEW PERSPECTIVES

9TH EDITION

COMPUTER CONCEPTS

June Jamrich Parsons, Dan Oja

1

Computer, Internet, Web, and E-Mail Basics

TIP

When using the BookOnCD, the ✹ icons are "clickable" to access resources on the CD. The ✝ icons are clickable to access resources on the Web. You can also access Web resources by using your browser to connect directly to the New Perspectives NP9 Web site at: www.course.com/np/concepts9/ch01

COMPUTERS AND THE INTERNET ARE THE CORNERSTONES OF A REVOLUTION

fueled by technology that is dramatically transforming the way we live, work, play, and think. To begin putting this technology into perspective, Chapter 1 helps you get a handle on basic computer, Internet, Web, and e-mail terminology. The end-of-chapter Issue delves into the controversy over e-mail privacy and the Computers in Context section takes a look at the marketing industry's innovative use of emerging technologies.

TAKE A PRE-ASSESSMENT QUIZ

about basic computer terminology and using the Internet, Web, and e-mail. Armed with your results from this quiz, you can focus your study time on concepts that will round out your knowledge of computer basics and improve your test scores.

www.course.com/np/concepts9/ch01

LISTEN TO A CHAPTER OVERVIEW

Get your book and highlighter ready, then connect to the New Perspectives NP9 Web site, where you can listen to an overview that points out the most important concepts for this chapter.

www.course.com/np/concepts9/ch01

BEFORE YOU READ ON, TRY IT

WHAT COMPONENTS ARE INCLUDED IN MY COMPUTER SYSTEM?

Before you begin Chapter 1, take an inventory of your lab, work, or home computer equipment to find their brands, models, and serial numbers. Tuck this information in a safe place. It can come in handy when you need to call technical support, arrange for repair services, or report missing equipment.

1. Fill in the following table for any computer equipment you own, rent, lease, or use.

	Brand	Model	Serial Number
Computer			
Keyboard			
Mouse			
Monitor			
Printer			
Digital camera			
Digital music player			
Internet or network device			
Other (list)			

SECTION A

Computer Basics

Whether you realize it or not, you already know a lot about computers. You've picked up information from commercials and news articles, from books and movies, from conversations and correspondence—perhaps even from using your own computer and trying to figure out why it doesn't always work!

Section A provides an overview that's designed to help you start organizing what you know about computers, give you a basic understanding of how computers work, and get you up to speed with a basic computer vocabulary.

A COMPUTER IS...

How old is the word "computer"? The word "computer" has been part of the English language since 1646, but if you look in a dictionary printed before 1940, you might be surprised to find a computer defined as a *person* who performs calculations! Prior to 1940, machines designed to perform calculations were referred to as calculators and tabulators, not computers. The modern definition and use of the term "computer" emerged in the 1940s, when the first electronic computing devices were developed.

What is a computer? Most people can formulate a mental picture of a computer, but computers do so many things and come in such a variety of shapes and sizes that it might seem difficult to distill their common characteristics into an all-purpose definition. At its core, a **computer** is a device that accepts input, processes data, stores data, and produces output, all according to a series of stored instructions.

Computer **input** is whatever is typed, submitted, or transmitted to a computer system. Input can be supplied by a person, by the environment, or by another computer. Examples of the kinds of input that a computer can accept include words and symbols in a document, numbers for a calculation, pictures, temperatures from a thermostat, audio signals from a microphone, and instructions from a computer program. An input device, such as a keyboard or mouse, gathers input and transforms it into a series of electronic signals for the computer to store and manipulate.

In the context of computing, **data** refers to the symbols that represent facts, objects, and ideas. Computers manipulate data in many ways, and this manipulation is called **processing**. The series of instructions that tell a computer how to carry out processing tasks is referred to as a **computer program**, or simply a "program." These programs form the **software** that sets up a computer to do a specific task. Some of the ways that a computer can process data include performing calculations, sorting lists of words or numbers, modifying documents and pictures, keeping track of your score in a fast-action game, and drawing graphs. In a computer, most processing takes place in a component called the **central processing unit** (CPU), which is sometimes described as the computer's "brain."

> **TIP**
>
> When using the BookOnCD, click any boldface term to see its definition. You can also use the Glossary button at the top of the screen to locate a definition for any term that was introduced in an earlier chapter.

A computer stores data so that it will be available for processing. Most computers have more than one place to put data, depending on how the data is being used. **Memory** is an area of a computer that temporarily holds data waiting to be processed, stored, or output. **Storage** is the area where data can be left on a permanent basis when it is not immediately needed for processing.

Output is the result produced by a computer. Some examples of computer output include reports, documents, music, graphs, and pictures. An output device displays, prints, or transmits the results of processing. Figure 1-1 helps you visualize the input, processing, storage, and output activities of a computer.

FIGURE 1-1

A computer can be defined by its ability to accept input, process data, store data, and produce output, all according to a set of instructions from a computer program.

Computers produce output on devices such as screens and printers.

A computer accepts input from an input device, such as a keyboard, mouse, scanner, or digital camera.

Data is processed in the CPU according to instructions that have been loaded into the computer's memory.

A computer uses disks, CDs, and DVDs to permanently store data.

What's so significant about a computer's ability to store instructions? Take a moment to think about the way you use a simple handheld calculator to balance your checkbook each month. You're forced to do the calculations in stages. Although you can store data from one stage and use it in the next stage, you cannot store the sequence of formulas—the program—required to balance your checkbook. Every month, therefore, you have to perform a similar set of calculations. The process would be much simpler if your calculator remembered the sequence of calculations and just asked you for this month's checkbook entries.

Early "computers" were really no more than calculating devices, designed to carry out a specific mathematical task. To use one of these devices for a different task, it was necessary to rewire its circuits—a job best left to an engineer. In a modern computer, the idea of a **stored program** means that a series of instructions for a computing task can be loaded into a computer's memory. These instructions can easily be replaced by a different set of instructions when it is time for the computer to perform another task.

The stored program concept allows you to use your computer for one task, such as word processing, and then easily switch to a different type of computing task, such as editing a photo or sending an e-mail message. It is the single most important characteristic that distinguishes a computer from other simpler and less versatile devices, such as calculators and pocket-sized electronic dictionaries.

COMPUTER CATEGORIES

Why is it useful to categorize computers? Computers are versatile machines that are able to perform a truly amazing assortment of tasks, but some types of computers are better suited to certain tasks than other types of computers. Categorizing computers is a way of grouping them according to criteria such as usage, cost, size, and capability. Knowing how a computer has been categorized provides an indication of its best potential use.

During the 1940s and 1950s, very few computers existed, and there was really no need to categorize them. Because the main circuitry was usually housed in a closet-sized metal frame, computer techies called these computers "mainframes." The term soon became synonymous with a category of large, expensive computers that were sold to big corporations and government agencies.

In 1968, the term "minicomputer" was used to describe a second computer category. These computers were smaller, less expensive, and less powerful than mainframes, but were, nevertheless, able to provide adequate computing power for small businesses. In 1971, the first microcomputer appeared. A **microcomputer** could be clearly differentiated from computers in other categories because its CPU consisted of a single "chip" called a **microprocessor**.

At one time, then, it was possible to define three distinct categories of computers: mainframes, minicomputers, and microcomputers. Technology has advanced rapidly since then. Today, just about every computer—no matter how large or small—uses one or more microprocessors as its CPU. Therefore, the use of a microprocessor is no longer a distinction between microcomputers and other computer categories. Furthermore, the term "minicomputer" has fallen into disuse. To reflect today's computer technology, the following categories might be more appropriate: personal computers, handheld computers, workstations, videogame consoles, mainframes, supercomputers, and servers.

What is a personal computer? A **personal computer** is a type of microcomputer designed to meet the computing needs of an individual. It typically provides access to a wide variety of computing applications, such as word processing, photo editing, e-mail, and Internet access. Personal computers are available as desktop computers, notebook computers, or tablet computers, as shown in Figure 1-2.

What are the characteristics of desktop computers? A **desktop computer** fits on a desk and runs on power from an electrical wall outlet. A desktop computer's keyboard is typically a separate component, connected to the main unit by a cable. The main unit can be housed in a vertical case (like the one shown in Figure 1-2, top) or a horizontal case. The vertical case is sometimes placed on the floor or in a cubbyhole beneath the desk. The horizontal case can be placed under the display screen to reduce the computer's "footprint" on the desk. The first personal computers were desktop models, and this style remains popular for offices, schools, and homes. Because their components can be manufactured economically, desktop computers typically provide the most computing power for your dollar. The price of an entry-level desktop computer starts at $300 or a bit less, but most consumers select more powerful models that cost between $800 and $1,100.

How do notebook computers differ from desktops? A **notebook computer** (also referred to as a "laptop"), is a small, lightweight personal

FIGURE 1-2

Personal computers are available in desktop, notebook, and tablet configurations.

A desktop computer fits on a desk and features a vertical case (like the one shown) or a horizontal case.

A notebook computer is small and lightweight, giving it the advantage of portability. It can be plugged into an electrical outlet, or it can run on battery power.

A tablet computer is similar in size to a notebook computer, but features a touch-sensitive screen that can be used for input instead of a keyboard.

computer that incorporates screen, keyboard, storage, and processing components into a single portable unit. Notebook computers can run on power supplied by an electrical outlet or a battery. These portable computers are ideal for mobile uses because they are easy to carry and can be used outdoors, in airports, and in classrooms without the need for a nearby electrical outlet. Notebook computers cost a bit more than a desktop computer with similar computing power and storage capacity. The price of an entry-level notebook computer starts at about $600, but consumers often spend between $800 and $1,200 to get the performance they want.

What is a tablet computer? A **tablet computer** is a portable computing device featuring a touch-sensitive screen that can be used as a writing or drawing pad. A "slate" tablet configuration, like the one in Figure 1-2, lacks a keyboard (although one can be attached) and resembles a high-tech clipboard. A "convertible" tablet computer is constructed like a notebook computer, but the screen folds face up over the keyboard to provide a horizontal writing surface. Tablet computers shine for applications that involve handwritten input. Since tablet computers were first introduced in 2002, their price has remained high, starting at about $1,100, but more typically costing $1,400 to $2,300.

What is a handheld? A **handheld computer**, such as a Palm, an iPAQ, a Blackberry, or a PocketPC, features a small keyboard or touch-sensitive screen and is designed to fit into a pocket, run on batteries, and be used while you are holding it. Also called a **PDA** (personal digital assistant), a computer in this category can be used as an electronic appointment book, address book, calculator, and notepad. Inexpensive add-ons make it possible for a handheld computer to send and receive e-mail, use maps and global positioning to get directions, and synchronize information with a personal computer.

PDAs and "smart" cell phones are converging into a single handheld technology that provides keypad input, color screen, digital camera, PDA software, voice communications, text messaging, Web browsing, and e-mail. PDA and smartphone prices start below $100 and range up to $800 for a model with a color screen and integrated cellular phone (Figure 1-3).

With its slow processing speed and small screen, a handheld computer is not powerful enough to handle many tasks, such as sophisticated word processing, photo editing, and financial management, that can be accomplished by desktop, notebook, or tablet personal computers. Yet handhelds provide important computing and communications functions in a mobile package.

TERMINOLOGY NOTE

The term "personal computer" is sometimes abbreviated as "PC." However, the abbreviation "PC" can also refer to a specific type of personal computer that descended from the original IBM PC and runs Windows software. In this book, "PC" refers to IBM PC descendants. It is not used as an abbreviation for the term "personal computer."

INFOWEBLINKS

Learn more about the latest PDA models, prices, software, and accessories by visiting the **PDA InfoWeb**.

www.course.com/np/concepts9/ch01

FIGURE 1-3

Many handheld computers feature a small keyboard, while others accept handwriting input.

What types of computers can be classified as workstations?
The term "**workstation**" has two meanings. Computers advertised as
workstations are usually powerful desktop computers designed for
specialized tasks. A workstation can tackle tasks that require a lot of
processing speed, such as medical imaging and computer-aided design.
Some workstations contain more than one microprocessor, and most have
circuitry specially designed for creating and displaying three-dimensional
and animated graphics. Workstation prices range from $800 to $9,000.
Because of its cost, a workstation, like the one in Figure 1-4, is often
dedicated to design tasks, but is not used for typical microcomputer
applications, such as word processing, photo editing, and accessing the
Web.

A second meaning of the term "workstation" applies to an ordinary personal
computer that is connected to a network. A **computer network** is two or
more computers and other devices connected for the purpose of sharing
data, programs, and hardware. A **LAN** (local area network) is simply a
computer network located within a limited geographical area, such as a
school computer lab or a small business.

Is a PlayStation a computer? A **videogame console**, such as
Nintendo's GameCube, Sony's PlayStation, or Microsoft's Xbox, *is* a
computer, but videogame consoles have not been considered a computer
category because of their history as dedicated game devices that connect
to a TV set and provide only a pair of joysticks for input. Today's videogame
consoles, however, contain microprocessors that are equivalent to any
found in a fast personal computer, and they are equipped to produce
graphics that rival those on sophisticated workstations. Add-ons, such as
keyboards, DVD players, and Internet access, make it possible to use a
videogame console to watch DVD movies, send and receive e-mail, and
participate in online activities, such as multiplayer games. As with handheld
computers, videogame consoles like the one in Figure 1-5 fill a specialized
niche and are not considered a replacement for a personal computer.

What's so special about a mainframe computer? A **mainframe
computer** (or simply a "mainframe") is a large and expensive computer
capable of simultaneously processing data for hundreds or thousands of
users. Mainframes are generally used by businesses or governments to
provide centralized storage, processing, and management for large
amounts of data. Mainframes remain the computer of choice in situations
where reliability, data security, and centralized control are necessary.

The price of a mainframe computer typically starts at several hundred
thousand dollars and can easily exceed $1 million. Its main processing
circuitry is housed in a closet-sized cabinet (Figure 1-6), but after large
components are added for storage and output, a mainframe computer system can fill a good-sized room.

How powerful is a supercomputer? A computer falls into the
supercomputer category if it is, at the time of construction, one of the
fastest computers in the world. Because of their speed, supercomputers
can tackle complex tasks that just would not be practical for other computers. Common uses for supercomputers include breaking codes,
modeling worldwide weather systems, and simulating nuclear explo-
sions. One impressive simulation designed to run on a supercomputer
tracked the movement of thousands of dust particles as they were
tossed about by a tornado.

FIGURE 1-4

A workstation resembles a
desktop computer, but typically
features more processing power
and storage capacity.

FIGURE 1-5

A videogame console includes
circuitry similar to a personal
computer's, but its input and
output devices are optimized
for gaming.

FIGURE 1-6

This IBM z9 109 mainframe
computer weighs 2,672 pounds
and is about 6.5 feet tall.

1

At one time, supercomputer designers focused on building specialized, very fast, and very large CPUs. Today, most supercomputer CPUs are constructed from thousands of microprocessors. Approximately 300 of the 500 fastest supercomputers in the world use microcomputer technology.

What makes a computer a "server"? In the computer industry, the term "server" has several meanings. It can refer to computer hardware, to a specific type of software, or to a combination of hardware and software. In any case, the purpose of a **server** is to "serve" computers on a network (such as the Internet or a LAN) by supplying them with data. A personal computer, workstation, or software that requests data from a server is referred to as a **client**. For example, on a network, a server might respond to a client's request for a Web page. Another server might handle the steady stream of e-mail that travels among clients from all over the Internet. A server might also allow clients within a LAN to share files or access a centralized printer.

INFOWEBLINKS

What's the latest news about supercomputers? Visit the **Supercomputer InfoWeb** to learn more about these amazing machines.

www.course.com/np/concepts9/ch01

Remarkably, just about any personal computer, workstation, mainframe, or supercomputer can be configured to perform the work of a server. That fact should emphasize the concept that a server does not require a specific type of hardware. Nonetheless, computer manufacturers categorize some of their computers as "servers" because they are especially suited for storing and distributing data on a network. Despite impressive performance on server-related tasks, these machines do not include features such as sound cards, DVD players, and other fun accessories, that consumers expect on their desktop computers. Most consumers would not want to buy a server to replace a desktop computer.

PERSONAL COMPUTER SYSTEMS

What's a personal computer system? The term "computer system" usually refers to a computer and all the input, output, and storage devices that are connected to it. At the core of a personal computer system is a desktop, notebook, or tablet computer, which probably looks like one of those in Figure 1-7.

FIGURE 1-7

Personal computer designs run the gamut from drab gray boxes to colorful curvy cases.

Despite cosmetic differences among personal computers, a personal computer system usually includes the following equipment:

■ **System unit.** The **system unit** is the case that holds the main circuit boards, microprocessor, power supply, and storage devices. The system unit for notebook computers holds a built-in keyboard and speakers, too.

■ **Display device.** Most desktop computers use a separate **monitor** as a display device, whereas notebook computers use a flat panel **LCD screen** (liquid crystal display screen) attached to the system unit.

■ **Keyboard.** Most computers are equipped with a keyboard as the primary input device.

■ **Mouse.** A **mouse** is an input device designed to manipulate on-screen graphical objects and controls.

■ **Hard disk drive.** A **hard disk drive** can store billions of characters of data. It is usually mounted inside the computer's system unit. A small external light indicates when the drive is reading or writing data.

■ **CD and DVD drives.** A **CD drive** is a storage device that uses laser technology to work with data on computer or audio CDs. A **DVD drive** can work with data on computer CDs, audio CDs, computer DVDs, or DVD movie disks. Some CD and DVD drives are classified as "read only" devices that cannot be used to write data onto disks. They are typically used to access data from commercial software, music, and movie CDs or DVDs. "Writable" CD and DVD drives, however, can be used to store and access data.

■ **Floppy disk drive.** A **floppy disk drive** is a storage device that reads and writes data on floppy disks.

■ **Sound card and speakers.** Desktop computers have a rudimentary built-in speaker that's mostly limited to playing beeps. A small circuit board, called a **sound card**, is required for high-quality music, narration, and sound effects. A desktop computer's sound card sends signals to external speakers. A notebook's sound card sends signals to speakers that are built into the notebook system unit.

■ **Modem and network cards.** Many personal computer systems include a built-in **modem** that can be used to establish an Internet connection using a standard telephone line. A **network card** is used to connect a computer to a network or cable Internet connection.

■ **Printer.** A computer printer is an output device that produces computer-generated text or graphical images on paper.

FIGURE 1-8

Computer storage media include floppy disks, DVDs and CDs .

FIGURE 1-9

A typical personal computer system includes the system unit and a variety of storage, input, and output devices.

1

What's a peripheral device? The term **peripheral device** designates equipment that might be added to a computer system to enhance its functionality. Popular peripheral devices, such as those in Figure 1-10, include printers, digital cameras, scanners, joysticks, and graphics tablets.

Is a hard disk drive a peripheral device? The word "peripheral" is a relatively old part of computer jargon that dates back to the days of mainframes when the CPU was housed in a giant box and all input, output, and storage devices were housed separately. Technically, a peripheral is any device that is not housed within the CPU.

Although a hard disk drive seems to be an integral part of a computer, by the strictest technical definition, a hard disk drive would be classified as a peripheral device. The same goes for other storage devices and the keyboard, monitor, LCD screen, sound card, speakers, and modem. In the world of personal computers, however, the use of the term "peripheral" varies and is often used to refer to any components that are not housed inside the system unit.

DATA, INFORMATION, AND FILES

Is there a difference between data and information? In everyday conversation, people use the terms "data" and "information" interchangeably. Nevertheless, some computer professionals make a distinction between the two terms. They define data as the symbols that represent people, events, things, and ideas. Data becomes **information** when it is presented in a format that people can understand and use. Most computers store data in a **digital** format as a series of 1s and 0s. Each 1 or 0 is called a **bit**. Eight bits, called a **byte**, are used to represent one character—a letter, number, or punctuation mark.

As a rule of thumb, remember that (technically speaking) data is used by computers; information is used by humans. The bits and bytes that a computer stores are referred to as data. The words, numbers, and graphics displayed for people are referred to as information.

What is a file? A computer file, usually referred to simply as a **file**, is a named collection of data that exists on a storage medium, such as a hard disk, floppy disk, CD, or DVD. Although all files contain data, some files are classified as "data files," whereas other files are classified as "executable files." A **data file** contains data that can be processed—the text for a document, the numbers for a calculation, the specifications for a graph, the frames of a video, the contents of a Web page, or the notes of a musical passage. An **executable file** contains the programs or instructions that tell a computer how to perform a specific task. For example, the word processing program that tells your computer how to display and print text is stored as an executable file.

You can think of data files as passive—the data does not instruct the computer to do anything. Executable files, on the other hand, are active—the instructions stored in the file cause the computer to carry out some action.

How can I tell what's in a file? Every file has a **file name**, which often provides a clue to its contents. A file might also have a **file extension**—sometimes referred to as a "filename extension"—that further describes a file's contents. For example, in Pbrush.exe, "Pbrush" is the file name and "exe" is the file extension. As you can see, the file name is separated from the extension by a period called a "dot." To tell someone the name of the file Pbrush.exe, you would say, "Pbrush dot e-x-e."

FIGURE 1-10

Peripheral devices add to a computer's versatility.

Printer

Digital camera

Scanner

Graphics tablet

Executable files typically have .exe extensions. Data files have a variety of extensions, such as .bmp or .tif for a graphic, .mid for synthesized music, or .htm for a Web page. Chapter 4 provides additional information on file names and file types.

APPLICATION SOFTWARE AND OPERATING SYSTEM BASICS

What is application software? A computer can be "applied" to many tasks, such as writing, number crunching, video editing, and online shopping. **Application software** is a set of computer programs that helps a person carry out a task. Word processing software, for example, helps people create, edit, and print documents. Personal finance software helps people keep track of their money and investments. Video editing software helps people create and edit home movies—and even some professional films.

Is an operating system some type of application software? No. An **operating system** (OS) is essentially the master controller for all the activities that take place within a computer. Operating systems are classified as **system software**, not application software, because their primary purpose is to help the computer system monitor itself in order to function efficiently.

Unlike application software, an operating system does not directly help people perform application-specific tasks, such as word processing. People do, however, interact with the operating system for certain operational and storage tasks, such as starting programs and locating data files.

What are the most popular operating systems? Popular personal computer operating systems include Microsoft Windows and Mac OS. Microsoft Windows Mobile and Palm OS control most handheld computers. Linux and UNIX are popular operating systems for servers.

Microsoft Windows (usually referred to simply as "Windows") is the most widely used operating system for personal computers. As shown in Figure 1-11, the Windows operating system displays on-screen controls designed to be manipulated by a mouse.

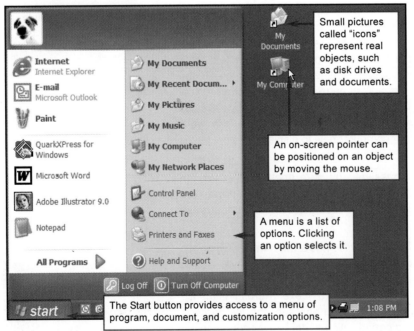

FIGURE 1-11

The Windows operating system displays on-screen icons, menus, buttons, and other graphical controls designed to be manipulated by a mouse.

Is Windows software the same as the Windows operating system?
No. The term "Windows software" refers to any application software designed to run on computers that use the Microsoft Windows operating system. A program called Microsoft Word for Windows is an example of a word processing program—application software—that is referred to as "Windows software."

How does an operating system affect compatibility? Computers that operate in essentially the same way are said to be "compatible." Two of the most important factors that influence compatibility and define a computer's **platform** are the microprocessor and the operating system. Today, two of the most popular personal computer platforms are PCs and Macs.

PCs are based on the design for one of the first personal computer "superstars"—the IBM PC. The "great grandchildren" of the IBM PC are on computer store shelves today—a huge selection of personal computer brands and models manufactured by companies such as IBM, Hewlett-Packard, Toshiba, Dell, and Gateway. The Windows operating system was designed specifically for these personal computers and, therefore, the PC platform is sometimes called the "Windows platform." Most of the examples in this book pertain to PCs because they are so popular.

Macs are based on a proprietary design for a personal computer called the Macintosh, manufactured almost exclusively by Apple Computer, Inc. The stylish iMac is one of Apple's most popular computers, and like other computers in the Mac platform, it uses Mac OS as its operating system.

The PC and Mac platforms are not compatible because of hardware and operating system differences. Consequently, application software designed for Macs does not typically work with PCs and vice versa. When shopping for new software, it is important to read the package to make sure it is designed to work with your computer platform.

INFOWEBLINKS

Apple Computer, Inc. is known for its innovative computer designs. You can learn about its newest computers by connecting to the **Apple Computers InfoWeb.**

www.course.com/np/concepts9/ch01

QuickCheck

SECTION A

1. A computer accepts input, processes data, stores data, and produces [output] according to a series of instructions.

2. The term "microprocessor" is a synonym for the term "microcomputer." True or false? [FALSE]

3. A(n) [notebook] computer is also referred to as a laptop.

4. Most computers include a network card designed to connect a computer to the Internet using standard telephone service. True or false? [ ]

5. Eight [bits] form a byte.

6. PCs and Macs are not considered [compatible] because of hardware and operating system differences.

CHECK ANSWERS

Internet Basics

The Internet has changed society. E-mail and instant messaging have caused a major shift in the way people communicate. Online stores have changed our shopping habits. The ability to easily download music has stirred up controversy about intellectual property. The possibility of unauthorized access to online databases has made us more aware of our privacy and safety. Section B provides a basic overview of the Internet, with an emphasis on how you can connect to it and use it.

INTERNET RESOURCES

How does the Internet work? The **Internet** is a collection of local, regional, national, and international computer networks linked together to exchange data and distribute processing tasks. You can think of the Internet as a network of interconnected communications lines creating a sort of highway system for transporting data. The main routes of the Internet—analogous to interstate highways—are referred to as the **Internet backbone**. Constructed and maintained by major telecommunications companies, including AT&T and Sprint, these telecommunications links can move huge amounts of data at incredible speeds. Data traveling from the United States can arrive in England in less than 60 ms—60 thousandths of a second.

In addition to the backbone, the Internet encompasses an intricate collection of regional and local communications links. These links can include local telephone systems, cable television lines, cellular telephone systems, and personal satellite dishes.

Internet communications links (Figure 1-12) transport data to and from millions of computers and other electronic devices. Amazingly, this data transport works seamlessly between all kinds of platforms—between PCs and Macs and even between personal computers and mainframes. Communication between all the different devices on the Internet is made possible by **TCP/IP** (Transmission Control Protocol/Internet Protocol), a standard set of rules for electronically addressing and transmitting data.

INFOWEBLINKS

Sometimes used as a synonym for the Internet, the term "cyberspace" was coined by science fiction writer William Gibson. Visit the **Cyberspace InfoWeb** for additional background and links to books for sci-fi aficionados.

www.course.com/np/concepts9/ch01

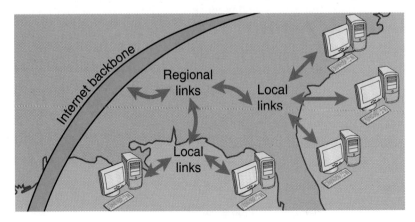

FIGURE 1-12

The Internet backbone connects to regional and local communications links, which provide Internet access to individuals working at their personal computers.

1

Where is all the Internet data stored? The Internet provides access to an amazing volume of data, including corporate Web pages, merchandise catalogs, software, music, college courses, school science projects, telephone directories, library card catalogs, and so on. Although difficult to pin down exact figures, it is estimated that the Internet provides access to more data than is stored in all the academic research libraries in the United States.

Most of the "stuff" that's accessible on the Internet is stored on servers, which are owned and maintained by government agencies, corporations, small businesses, schools, organizations, and even individuals. These servers use special server software to locate and distribute data requested by Internet users.

What kind of resources are available on the Internet? If you're looking for information, if you want to communicate with someone, or if you want to buy something, the Internet offers a good set of resources. Here is a quick overview of Internet resources:

■ **Web sites.** Most people envision Web sites as various locations on the Internet that correspond to a corporation's headquarters, a store, a magazine, or a library. A Web site can provide information or access to other resources, such as search engines and e-mail.

■ **Search engines.** Search engines, such as Google and Yahoo!, help catalog a huge portion of the data stored at Web sites. Without search engines, using the Internet would be like trying to find a book in the Library of Congress by wandering around the stacks.

■ **Downloads and uploads.** Internet servers store all sorts of useful files containing documents, music, software, videos, animations, and photos. The process of transferring one of these files from a remote computer, such as a server, to a local computer, such as your personal computer, is called **downloading**. Sending a file from a local computer to a remote computer is called **uploading** (Figure 1-13).

INFOWEBLINKS

If you'd like to check out some of the resources described in this section, connect to the **Internet Resources InfoWeb**. There you'll find links to examples and to the software that you need to access these useful Internet resources.

www.course.com/np/concepts9/ch01

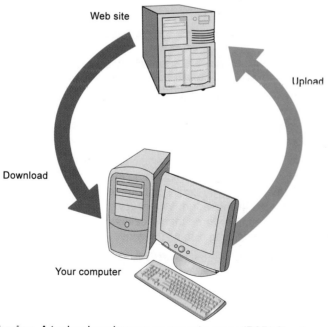

Web site

Upload

Download

Your computer

FIGURE 1-13

Many Web sites provide files that the public can download to personal computers. Uploading, on the other hand, is limited to people who have password access to the site. For a demonstration of how to download a file, click the Start icon.

CLICK TO START

■ **P2P file sharing.** A technology known as **peer-to-peer** (P2P) file sharing makes it possible to access files stored on another Internet user's hard disk—with permission, of course. This technology is the basis for popular music and file exchange sites, such as LimeWire, BitTorrent, and Kazaa.

■ **E-mail.** Also known as "electronic mail," **e-mail** allows one person to send an electronic message to another person or to a group of people listed in a personal address book. A variation of e-mail called a **mailing list server**, or "listserv," maintains a public list of people who are interested in a particular topic. Messages sent to the list server are automatically distributed to everyone on the mailing list.

■ **Bulletin boards.** **Usenet** is a worldwide bulletin board system that contains more than 15,000 discussion forums called **newsgroups**. Newsgroup members post messages to the bulletin board, which can be read and responded to by other group members.

■ **Blogs.** The term **blog**, derived from the phrase "WeB LOG," refers to a personal journal posted on the Web for access by the general public. Blogs can focus on a single topic or cover a variety of issues. A typical blog includes commentary by the author as well as links to additional information. To find blogs, you can use a blog directory, like the one in Figure 1-14.

FIGURE 1-14

Blogs have become a popular way of disseminating information over the Internet. Blog directories, such as this one, provide links to blogs on all sorts of topics.

■ **Chat groups and instant messaging.** A **chat group** consists of several people who connect to the Internet and communicate in a virtual "room" by typing comments to each other. A private version of a chat room, called **instant messaging**, allows two or more people to send typed messages back and forth.

■ **Internet telephony.** Although it is not quite as simple as picking up the telephone, **Internet telephony** allows telephone-style conversations to travel over the Internet to virtually anywhere in the world. When using Internet telephony, the sound quality is sometimes worse than a cellular phone, but the cost is much less than conventional long distance service.

■ **E-commerce.** The Internet is revolutionizing business by directly linking consumers with retailers, manufacturers, and distributors. **E-commerce**, or "electronic commerce," includes activities such as online shopping, electronic auctions, and online stock trading.

■ **Broadcasting.** The Internet carries radio shows and teleconferences that can be broadcast worldwide. Internet radio is popular because broadcasts aren't limited to a small local region. Internet broadcasting technology, referred to as "multicasting," has the potential to increase the use and popularity of Internet broadcasts.

■ **Remote access and control.** Using software, such as Telnet or SSH, and a valid password, it is possible to link two computers so that commands entered on one computer are executed remotely on the other computer. This capability of the Internet and other networks is handy, for example, when a technical support person located in a manufacturer's service center takes remote control of your computer to fix a problem.

INTERNET CONNECTIONS

What are my options for Internet connections? To take advantage of everything the Internet has to offer, you have to establish some sort of communications link between your computer and the Internet. Possibilities include using your existing telephone line, a cable television line, a personal satellite link, wireless or cell phone service, or special high-speed telephone services.

What's the easiest, cheapest way to access the Internet? Many people literally dial up the Internet using an existing telephone line. This type of connection—often referred to as a **dial-up connection**—is relatively simple and inexpensive because the necessary equipment and software are preinstalled on most new computers. A dial-up connection requires a device called a **voiceband modem** (often simply called a "modem"), which converts your computer's digital signals into a type of signal that can travel over telephone lines. Figure 1-15 can help you determine whether a computer has a modem.

FIGURE 1-15

To determine whether a computer has a modem, look for a place to plug in a standard phone cable.

CLICK TO START ✴

To establish a dial-up connection, your computer's modem dials a special access number, which is answered by an Internet modem. Once the connection is established, your computer is "on the Internet." When you complete an Internet session and log off, your modem "hangs up" and the connection is discontinued until the next time you dial in.

Theoretically, the top speed of a dial-up connection is 56 Kbps, meaning that 56,000 bits of data are transmitted per second. Actual speed is usually reduced by distance, interference, and other technical problems, however, so the speed of most 56 Kbps dial-up connections is more like 45 Kbps.

Dial-up modem speed is usable for e-mail, e-commerce, and chat. It is not, however, optimal for applications that require large amounts of data to be quickly transferred over the Internet. Watching an Internet-based video or participating in a teleconference over a 56 Kbps dial-up connection can be like watching a badly organized parade—the sound can be out of sync with the image, and the "show" can be interrupted by lengthy pauses as your computer waits for the next set of video frames to arrive.

Does cable Internet service provide a faster connection?

Many cable TV companies offer Internet access in addition to the traditional roster of movie channels, network television, and specialty channels. This type of Internet access, often referred to as **cable Internet service** is offered to a cable company's customers for an additional monthly charge. Cable Internet service usually requires a **cable modem** (Figure 1-16), a device that changes a computer's signals into a form that can travel over cable TV links.

FIGURE 1-16

A cable modem can be installed by consumers or installed (sometimes for a fee) by the "cable guy." You can usually lease a cable modem from your cable company or purchase one made by a third party—just check to make sure the brand and model are compatible with your cable service.

A cable modem usually connects to the back of your computer using one of the supplied Ethernet or USB cables. Most cable modems are standalone devices set up near a computer, but they can also be integrated into the decoder box for cable television signals.

Cable Internet service is referred to as an **always-on connection** because your computer is, in effect, always connected to the Internet, unlike a dial-up connection that is established only when the dialing sequence is completed. An always-on connection is convenient because you don't have to wait 30–40 seconds for the dial-answer sequence to be completed. A cable modem receives data at about 1.5 Mbps (1.5 million bits per second), which is more than 25 times faster than a dial-up connection. This speed is suitable for most Internet activities, including real-time video, interactive online gaming, and teleconferencing.

What about access provided by a school or business network?

The computers in a school lab or business are usually connected to a LAN that is linked to the Internet. These networked computers offer an always-on connection, similar to cable Internet service. School and business networks do not, however, typically access the Internet through a cable company. Instead they use a high-speed telecommunications link dedicated solely to Internet access.

What other high-speed Internet access options are available?

Many telephone and independent telecommunications companies offer high-speed Internet access over ISDN and DSL lines. **ISDN** (Integrated Services Digital Network) provides data transfer speeds of 64 Kbps or 128 Kbps. With substantial monthly fees and data transfer speeds that are only marginally better than an inexpensive 56 Kbps dial-up connection, ISDN ranks low on the list of high-speed Internet options for most consumers.

DSL (Digital Subscriber Line) is a generic name for a family of high-speed Internet links, including ADSL, SDSL, and DSL lite. Each type of DSL provides different maximum speeds—from twice as fast to approximately 125 times faster than a 56 Kbps dial-up connection. The faster types of DSL require professional installation, but DSL lite can be installed by consumers.

Both ISDN and DSL connections require proximity to a telephone switching station, which can be a problem for speed-hungry consumers in rural areas. Satellite dishes to the rescue! **Satellite Internet service** offers Internet access at an average speed of about 500 Kbps. Monthly fees for a satellite connection are typically more than DSL or cable Internet service, and customers are also required to rent or purchase a satellite dish and pay for its installation.

INTERNET SERVICE PROVIDERS

What's an ISP? To access the Internet, you do not typically connect your computer directly to the backbone. Instead, you connect it to an ISP, such as AOL (America Online), which in turn connects to the backbone. An **ISP** (Internet service provider) is a company that maintains Internet computers and telecommunications equipment in order to provide Internet access to businesses, organizations, and individuals. An ISP that offers dial-up connections, for example, maintains a bank of modems, which communicate with modems in customers' computers.

An ISP works in much the same way as a local telephone company. Just as a telephone company provides a point of access to telephones all over the world, an ISP is a point of access to the Internet. ISP customers arrange for service—in this case, for Internet access—for which they pay a monthly fee. In addition to a monthly fee, an ISP might also charge an installation fee. Dial-up subscribers might also be required to pay per-minute fees for long-distance access.

Do I need an ISP for cable and other fast Internet access? Yes. Your local cable television company serves as your ISP if you subscribe to its cable Internet service. Your telephone company might serve as your ISP for DSL or ISDN service. Small ISPs based in your local area typically offer dial-up service, but might also offer high-speed access. Popular ISPs include AOL, Comcast, SBC, Earthlink, RoadRunner, Cox, Charter, Verizon, NetZero, and CableVision.

How can I find a list of ISPs that provide service in my area? The Yellow Pages typically list ISPs under "Internet." Also, check newspaper ads for new services that are being offered in your area.

If you can get access to a computer that's already connected to the Internet, check *www.thelist.com* for descriptions of national or local ISPs.

Your computer might include a directory of national ISPs. Look for an Internet Connection icon on your desktop, or browse through the options on the Start menu to find the New Connection Wizard (Figure 1-17).

FIGURE 1-17

Computers with the Windows operating system provide access to a list of national ISPs. Look for an Internet Connection icon or click the Start button, select Accessories, Communications, and the New Connection Wizard.

How do I choose an ISP? Selecting an ISP depends on a variety of factors, such as where service is provided; the speed of data transfer; and the cost of equipment, installation, and monthly service. The table in Figure 1-18 summarizes your options in each of these important categories.

FIGURE 1-18

Choosing an ISP

Geographical Coverage	The ISP you select should provide service in the places that you typically use your computer. If your work takes you on the road a lot, you'll want to consider a national ISP that provides local access numbers in the cities you visit. Retirees and students who migrate between locations might also consider a national ISP. For homebodies, a local ISP is usually a very acceptable option. With cable Internet service or DSL service, your computer must remain tethered to your service provider's network, which does not provide Internet access while traveling.
Type of Service	Some ISPs specialize in one type of service. A company that offers dial-up connections might not also offer cable connections. If you want a particular type of service—cable Internet service, for example—you might not have a choice of providers.
Quality of Service	The quality of dial-up and cable Internet services tends to decrease as the number of customers increases. In the case of dial-up connections, too many customers clamoring for modem connections can result in busy signals when you try to connect to your ISP. Cable Internet service works sort of like a lawn sprinkler system that's connected to a small water pump. With only one sprinkler, the water gushes out. Connect 100 sprinklers to the system and the gushing turns into a trickle. Because all the subscribers in your neighborhood use the same data "pipe," as more and more of your neighbors go online, the effective speed of your cable connection can deteriorate. Ask an ISP's current customers what they think of the access speed. Is it consistent, or does it deteriorate during peak usage hours?
Cost of Monthly Service	In the United States and Canada, monthly service fees vary from about $10–$20 per month for dial-up service to $30–$50 per month for cable Internet service. ISP rate plans might offer unlimited access for a flat monthly fee. Other rate plans include a limited number of hours; if you're online for additional hours, you'll pay by the hour. Outside the United States and Canada, many ISPs charge by the minute for Internet access.
Cost of Equipment and Installation	When considering the cost of Internet service, it is important to factor in the cost of equipment and installation. Whereas a modem is relatively inexpensive, a satellite dish costs several hundred dollars. Installation can also be costly—sometimes exceeding $100.
Extra Services	An ISP typically provides a connection to the Internet and an e-mail account. It might also offer useful extra services, such as security enhancements, content filtering, and multiple e-mail accounts so that all members of your family can send and receive their own e-mail messages. Some ISPs, such as AOL, offer a host of proprietary services that are available only to subscribers. These services might include content channels with substantive articles on health, hobbies, investing, and sports; activities specially designed for kids and teens; online shops that comply with high standards for security and customer satisfaction; a variety of voice and text messaging services; and collections of free (and virus-free) software. To find out if proprietary features should influence your ISP choice, talk to subscribers who have similar computer experience; ask them if these features are useful.
Customer Service	Most ISPs are prepared to answer customers' questions over the phone or by e-mail. The critical customer service question is "How long will it take to get a response?" Some national ISPs are notorious for keeping customers on hold for hours, and an e-mail reply can take days. Given a choice, most customers prefer an ISP that can respond quickly. To get an idea of an ISP's response time and expertise, talk to current customers.

USER IDS AND PASSWORDS

Is access to the Internet restricted in any way? Although the Internet is a public network, access to the Internet, or to some parts of the Internet, can be restricted in various ways. For example, an ISP can only be used to access the Internet by its subscribers. Some parts of the Internet—such as military computers—are off limits to the general public. In addition, some parts of Web sites—such as the *New York Times* archives—allow only paying subscribers to access premium content. Many Internet sites encourage memberships and offer perks if you sign up.

User IDs and passwords are designed to provide access for authorized users and to prevent unauthorized access. A **user ID** is a series of characters—letters and possibly numbers—that becomes a person's unique identifier, similar to a Social Security number. A **password** is a different series of characters that verifies the user ID, similar to the way a PIN (personal identification number) verifies your identity when you deposit or withdraw money at an ATM.

Typically, your ISP supplies a user ID and password that you use to connect to the Internet. You will accumulate additional user IDs and passwords from other sources for specific Internet activities, such as reading *New York Times* articles or participating in an online auction. The process of entering a user ID and password is usually referred to as "logging in" or "logging on" (Figure 1-19).

FIGURE 1-19

Typically, when you log in and enter your password, a series of asterisks appears on the screen to prevent someone from looking over your shoulder to discover your password.

Can I choose my own user ID? In some cases, you are allowed to select your user ID, but in other cases, it might be assigned by your service provider. Often a user ID is a variation of your name. Brunhilde Jefferson's user ID might be bjeffe, bjefferson, brunhilde_jefferson, or bjeff0918445.

The rules for creating a user ID are not consistent throughout the Internet, so it is important to read all the instructions carefully before finalizing your ID. For example, spaces might not be allowed in a user ID. Hence, the underline in brunhilde_jefferson is used instead of a space. There might be a length limitation, so Ms. Jefferson might have to choose a short user ID, such as bjeffe.

Some Internet computers don't differentiate between uppercase and lowercase letters, and would consider the user IDs B_Jefferson and b_jefferson to be the same. Other computers are **case sensitive** and differentiate between uppercase and lowercase. On such computers, if Ms. Jefferson selected Brun_Jeff as her user ID, she would not be able to gain access by typing brun_jeff. To avoid such problems, most people stick to lowercase letters for their user IDs.

How do I choose a secure password? Even when you are assigned a "starter" password, you should select a new password immediately, and then change it periodically. Don't share your password with anyone or write it down where it could be found. If your password is discovered, someone could log on and pretend to be you—sending inflammatory e-mail under your name and signing up for memberships at unsavory Web sites.

Your password should be a sequence of characters that is easy for you to remember, but would be difficult for someone else to guess. After all, your password provides protection only if it is secret (Figure 1-20).

FIGURE 1-20

Use these tips to select a secure password.

Do select a password that is at least five characters long

Do try to use both numbers and letters in your password

Do select a password that you can remember

Do consider making a password by combining two or more words or the first letters of a poem or phrase

Do change your password if you think that someone discovered it

Don't select a password that can be found in a dictionary

Don't use your name, nickname, Social Security number, birth date, or name of a close relative

Don't write your password where it is easy to find—under the keyboard is the first place that a password thief will look

Don't let anyone use your password "temporarily" to access Web sites or log on to your ISP

How do I remember my passwords? When you use the Internet, you accumulate a batch of passwords—from your ISP, from online shopping sites, from your online travel agent, and maybe even from your favorite news and information sites. The problem is not remembering *one* password; it's remembering lots of different passwords and their corresponding user IDs.

Your passwords provide the most protection if they are unique, but if you want access to 40 different Internet sites that require passwords, you'll need a really good memory to remember 40 unique passwords and 40 user IDs. You can, of course, resort to writing them down. That practice, however, makes them much more susceptible to thievery.

Instead of using 40 different user IDs and passwords, you need some way to reduce the number of things you have to memorize. First, strive to select a unique user ID that you can use for more than one site. Remember that people with your name who selected user IDs before you might have already taken the obvious user IDs. For example, when John Smith selects a user ID, you can bet that other people have already used johnsmith, jsmith, and john_smith. To keep his user ID unique, John might instead select jsl2wm (the first letters in "John Smith loves 2 watch movies").

Next, select two passwords—one for high security and one for low security. Use your high-security password to protect critical data—for online banking, for managing an online stock portfolio, or for your account at an online bookstore that stores a copy of your billing and credit card information. Change your high-security password periodically in all the places that you use it.

Use your low-security password in situations where you don't really care if your security is compromised. Some places on the Internet want you to establish an account with a user ID and password just to collect basic contact information and put your name on a mailing list. At other sites, your user ID and password provide access to information, but none of your own data (a credit card number, for example) is stored there. It is not necessary to change your low-security password very often.

In addition to protecting access to the Internet, user IDs and passwords also help to screen out unauthorized network users in school labs and businesses. You can even establish a user ID and password on your personal computer to prevent people from browsing through your documents, records, and files.

QuickCheck   SECTION B

1. The main routes of the Internet are referred to as the Internet [   ].

2. Communication between all the different devices on the Internet is made possible by TCP/[   ].

3. The process of transferring a file from a remote computer to a local computer is referred to as [   ].

4. A(n) [   ] is a personal journal posted on the Web for access by the general public.

5. A(n) [   ] modem converts your computer's digital data into signals that can travel over telephone lines.

6. Dial-up, cable Internet, and DSL service are examples of always-on connections. True or false? [   ]

7. ISDN and [   ] service require proximity to a telephone switching station, so they might not be available to rural customers.

8. Quality of [   ] from an Internet service provider can deteriorate as the number of customers increases.

9. [   ] sensitive computers distinguish between upper-case and lowercase letters.

10. When logging on to a computer or network, your [   ] verifies your user ID.

CHECK ANSWERS

SECTION C

Web Basics

Once you have Internet access, you can begin to explore its many resources. The Web is one of the Internet's top attractions, accessed by millions of people every day. It is simple to use, yet provides access to a huge collection of information, including online stores, health information, stock quotes, genealogy data, dictionaries, online courses, music, photos, and videos. Section C provides a basic introduction to the Web. If you're already familiar with the Web, this section should give you a better understanding of how it works. For those of you just embarking onto the Web, this section describes the tools and techniques you need to get started. The Browsing and Searching lab at the end of the chapter provides hands-on experience with two important Web tools—browsers and search engines.

THE WORLD WIDE WEB

What is the Web? One of the Internet's most captivating attractions, the **Web** (short for "World Wide Web") is a collection of files that can be linked and accessed using HTTP. **HTTP** (Hypertext Transfer Protocol) is the communications standard used to transmit Web documents on the Internet.

Many Web-based files produce documents called **Web pages**. Other files contain photos, videos, animations, and sounds that can be incorporated into specific Web pages. Most Web pages contain **links** (sometimes called "hyperlinks") to related documents and media files (Figure 1-21).

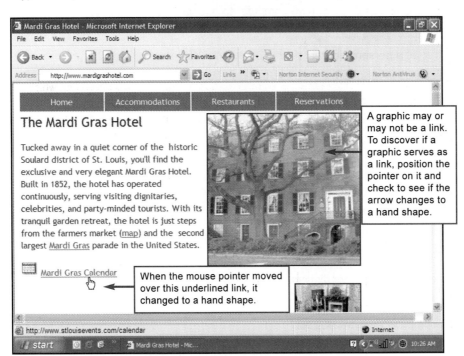

FIGURE 1-21

On most Web pages, underlined text indicates a link, but other objects can serve as links as well. To activate a link, simply click it.

What is a Web site? A collection of Web pages can be grouped into a **Web site**—a sort of virtual "place" in cyberspace. Every day, thousands of people shop at Nordstrom's Web site, an online department store featuring clothing, shoes, and jewelry. Thousands of people visit the Webopedia Web site to look up the meaning of computer terms. At the ABC News Web site, people not only read about the latest news, sports, and weather, but also discuss current issues with other readers. The Web encompasses these and hundreds of thousands of other sites.

Web sites are hosted by corporate, government, college, and private computers all over the world. The computers and software that store and distribute Web pages are called **Web servers**.

What is a URL? Every Web page has a unique address called a **URL** (Uniform Resource Locator, pronounced "You Are ELL"). For example, the URL for the Cable News Network Web site is *http://www.cnn.com*. Most URLs begin with http:// to indicate the Web's standard communications protocol. When typing a URL, the http:// can usually be omitted, so *www.cnn.com* works just as well as *http://www.cnn.com*.

Most Web sites have a main page that acts as a "doorway" to the rest of the pages at the site. This main page is sometimes referred to as a "home page," although this term has another meaning that's discussed later in this chapter. The URL for a Web site's main page is usually short and to the point, like *www.cnn.com*.

The pages for a Web site are typically stored in topic area folders, which are reflected in the URL. For example, the CNN site might include a weather center at *www.cnn.com/weather/* and an entertainment desk at *www.cnn.com/showbiz/*. A series of Web pages are then grouped under the appropriate topic. For example, you might find a page about hurricanes at the URL *www.cnn.com/weather/hurricanes.html,* and you could find a page about El Niño at *www.cnn.com/weather/elnino.html*. The file name of a specific Web page always appears last in the URL—*hurricanes.html* and *elnino.html* are the names of two Web pages. Web page file names usually have an .htm or .html extension, indicating that the page was created with **HTML** (Hypertext Markup Language), a standard format for Web documents. Figure 1-22 identifies the parts of a URL.

FIGURE 1-22

The URL for a Web page indicates the computer on which it is stored, its location on the Web server, its file name, and its extension.

http://www.cnn.com/showbiz/movies.htm

| Web protocol standard | Web server name | Folder name | Document name and file extension |

What are the rules for correctly typing a URL? A URL never contains a space, even after a punctuation mark, so do not type any spaces within a URL. An underline character is sometimes used to give the appearance of a space between words, such as in the URL *www.detroit.com/top_10.html.* Be sure to use the correct type of slash—always a forward slash (/)—and duplicate the URL's capitalization exactly. The servers that run some Web sites are case sensitive. On these servers, typing *www.cmu.edu/Overview.html* (with an uppercase "O") will not locate the Web page that's stored on the Web server as *www.cmu.edu/overview.html* (with a lowercase "o").

BROWSERS

What is a browser? A Web browser—usually referred to simply as a **browser**—is a software program that runs on your computer and helps you access Web pages. Three of today's most popular browsers are Microsoft Internet Explorer (IE), Netscape Navigator (Navigator), and Firefox. A browser window is typically divided into the sections shown in Figure 1-23.

INFOWEBLINKS

The best-selling browsers are updated on a regular basis, and occasionally new browsers challenge the old standbys. For up-to-the-minute information on these important Web tools, tune into the **Browser InfoWeb**.

www.course.com/np/concepts9/ch01

The title bar contains the name of the Web page that is currently displayed and the name of the browser.

The menu bar displays the titles of pull-down menus with options for commands such as saving, printing, copying, navigating, and configuring the browser's settings.

The toolbar contains a series of buttons for frequently used tasks.

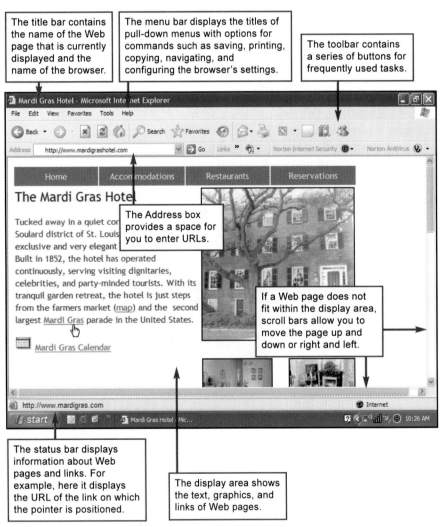

The Address box provides a space for you to enter URLs.

If a Web page does not fit within the display area, scroll bars allow you to move the page up and down or right and left.

The status bar displays information about Web pages and links. For example, here it displays the URL of the link on which the pointer is positioned.

The display area shows the text, graphics, and links of Web pages.

FIGURE 1-23

A browser provides a sort of "window" in which it displays a Web page. The borders of the window contain a set of menus and controls to help you navigate from one Web page to another.

Which features are common to most browsers? Despite small cosmetic differences and some variations in terminology, Web browsers offer a remarkably similar set of features and capabilities. Figure 1-24 provides a quick overview of browser features as shown in Microsoft Internet Explorer, and the Browsing and Searching lab at the end of the chapter shows you how to use them.

FIGURE 1-24

Most browsers provide a standard set of features that allow you to work with Web pages.

1

Navigation buttons. After you look at a sequence of pages, the browser's Back button lets you retrace your steps to view pages you've seen previously. Most browsers also have a Forward button, which—contrary to what you might expect—does not take you to new pages you haven't yet viewed. Instead, the Forward button shows you the page you were viewing before you pressed the Back button.

History list. The Forward and Back buttons keep track of only the pages you have visited since you started your browser; however, they won't help you locate pages you visited in previous sessions. To help you revisit sites from previous sessions, your browser provides a History list. Many browsers allow you to specify how long a URL will remain in the History list. Two or three weeks is usually sufficient.

Search. You can specify what you're looking for on the Web by using the Search button.

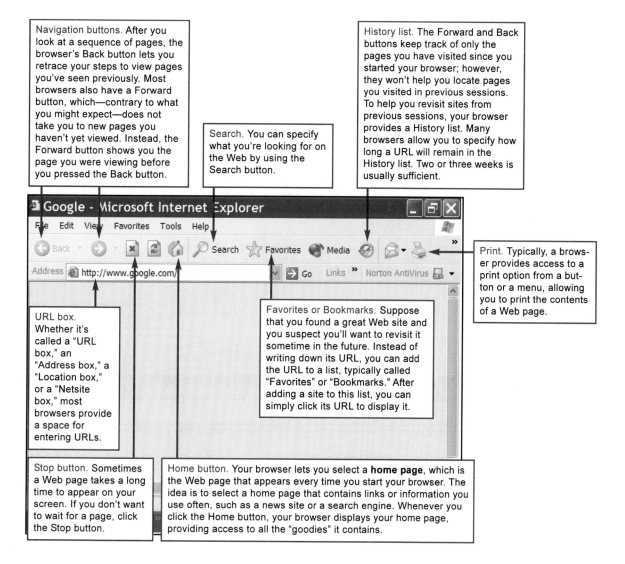

Print. Typically, a browser provides access to a print option from a button or a menu, allowing you to print the contents of a Web page.

URL box. Whether it's called a "URL box," an "Address box," a "Location box," or a "Netsite box," most browsers provide a space for entering URLs.

Favorites or Bookmarks. Suppose that you found a great Web site and you suspect you'll want to revisit it sometime in the future. Instead of writing down its URL, you can add the URL to a list, typically called "Favorites" or "Bookmarks." After adding a site to this list, you can simply click its URL to display it.

Stop button. Sometimes a Web page takes a long time to appear on your screen. If you don't want to wait for a page, click the Stop button.

Home button. Your browser lets you select a **home page**, which is the Web page that appears every time you start your browser. The idea is to select a home page that contains links or information you use often, such as a news site or a search engine. Whenever you click the Home button, your browser displays your home page, providing access to all the "goodies" it contains.

Exactly what does a browser do? A browser fetches and displays Web pages. Suppose that you want to view the Web page located at *www.e-course.com/boxer.html.* You enter the URL into your browser's Address box. When you press the Enter key, the browser contacts the Web server at *www.e-course.com* and requests the *boxer.html* page. The server sends your computer the data stored in *boxer.html.* This data includes two things: the information you want to view, and embedded codes, called **HTML tags**, that tell your browser how to display it. The tags specify details such as the background color, the text color and size, and the placement of graphics. Figure 1-25 shows that a browser assembles a document on your computer screen according to the specifications contained in HTML tags.

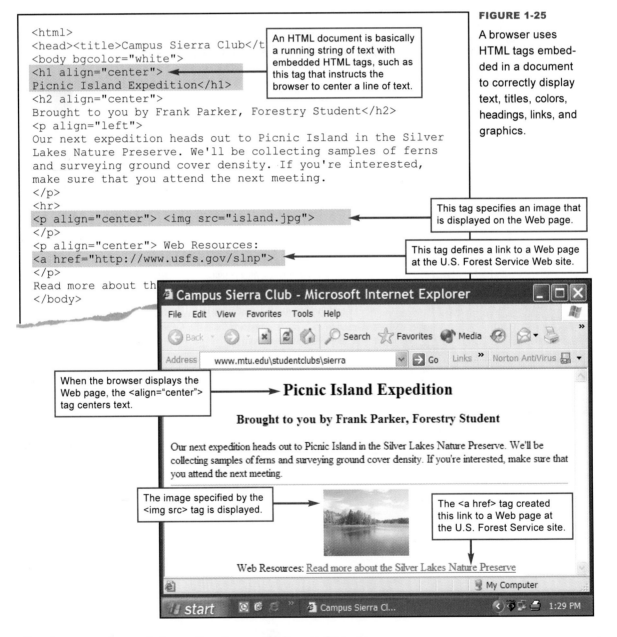

FIGURE 1-25

A browser uses HTML tags embedded in a document to correctly display text, titles, colors, headings, links, and graphics.

Can I copy and save information from a Web page? Most browsers provide a Copy command that allows you to copy a section of text from a Web page, which you can then paste into one of your own documents. To keep track of the source for each text section, you can use the Copy command to record the Web page's URL from the Address box, and then paste the URL into your document (Figure 1-26).

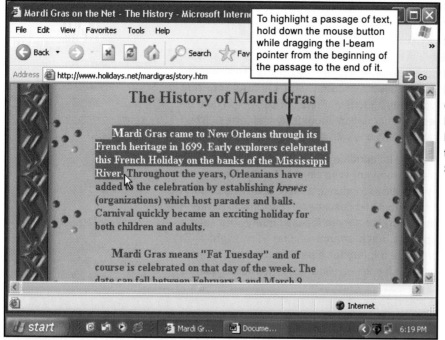

FIGURE 1-26

To copy a passage of text from a Web page, highlight the text, click the Edit menu, then select Copy. Next, switch to your own document and use the Paste option.
For a demonstration of this process, click the Start icon.

CLICK TO START ⚛

SEARCH ENGINES

What is a search engine? The term **search engine** popularly refers to a Web site that provides a variety of tools to help you find information. Search engines such as Google and Yahoo! Search are indispensable tools when it comes to finding information on the Web. Depending on the search engine you use, you can find information by entering a description, filling out a form, or clicking a series of links to drill down through a list of topics and subtopics. Based on your input, the search engine displays a list of Web pages like the one shown in Figure 1-27.

FIGURE 1-27

In response to a query, a search engine produces a list of relevant Web pages, along with a brief description of each page and a link to it.

Search results are typically arranged in order of relevance so that the most promising Web pages should be at the top of the list. A brief description of the page helps you determine whether you want to view it.

Some search sites offer paid links to companies that want to advertise their products or services.

How are search results arranged? If you use two different search engines to search for the same thing, you'll probably get different results. Some search engines give the highest ranks to sites that are accessed most frequently, while others give top ranking to sites in which your key terms appear most frequently. Some search engines sell top billing and some maintain a separate area for paid links.

Exactly what is a query? A **query** describes the information you want to find. It includes one or more keywords and can also include search operators. A **keyword** (sometimes called a "search term") is any word that describes the information you're trying to find. For example, *gorp* could be used as a keyword in a query for information about tasty trail mixes. When entering search terms, separate each one with a space.

Search engines have a tendency to inundate you with possibilities—often finding thousands of potentially relevant Web pages. To receive a more manageable list of results, you need to formulate a more specific search. A **search operator** is a word or symbol that describes a relationship between keywords and thereby helps you create a more focused query. The search operators that you can use with each search engine vary slightly. To discover exactly how to formulate a query for a particular search engine, refer to its Help pages. Most search engines allow you to formulate queries with the search operators described in Figure 1-28.

INFOWEBLINKS

Search engines change at an astonishing rate. Visit the **Search Engine InfoWeb** for a list of popular search engines and their URLs, some comparative statistics, and tips on finding the search engine that's right for you.

www.course.com/np/concepts9/ch01

FIGURE 1-28

Search Operators

AND	When two search terms are joined by AND, both terms must appear on a Web page before it can be included in the search results. The query *railroad AND cars* will locate pages that contain both the words "railroad" and "cars." Your search results might include pages containing information about old railroad cars, about railroad car construction, and even about railroads that haul automobiles ("cars"). Some search engines use the plus symbol (+) instead of the word AND.
OR	When two search terms are joined by OR, either one or both of the search words could appear on a page. Entering the query *railroad OR cars* produces information about railroad fares, railroad routes, railroad cars, automobile safety records, and even car ferries.
NOT	The keyword following NOT must not appear on any of the pages found by the search engine. Entering *railroad NOT cars* would tell the search engine to look for pages that include "railroad" but not the keyword "cars." In some search engines, the minus sign (-) can be used instead of the word NOT.
Quotation Marks	Surrounding a series of keywords with quotation marks indicates that the search engine must treat the words as a phrase. The complete phrase must exist on a Web page for it to be included in the list of results. Entering *"green card"* would indicate that you are looking for information on immigration, not information on the color green, golf greens, or greeting cards.
NEAR	The NEAR operator tells a search engine that you want documents in which one of the keywords is located close to but not necessarily next to the other keyword. The query *library NEAR/15 congress* means that the words "library" and "congress" must appear within 15 words of each other. Successful searches could include documents containing phrases such as "Library of Congress" or "Congress funds special library research."
Wildcards	The asterisk (*) is sometimes referred to as a "wildcard character." It allows a search engine to find pages with any derivation of a basic word. For example, the query *medic** would not only produce pages containing the word "medic," but also "medics," "medicine," "medical," "medication," and "medicinal."
Field Searches	Some search engines allow you to search for a Web page by its title or by any part of its URL. The query *T:Backcountry Recipe Book* indicates that you want to find a specific Web page titled "Backcountry Recipe Book." In this search, the *T:* tells the search engine to look at Web page titles, and the information following the colon identifies the name of the title.

How do I use a topic directory? A **topic directory** is a list of topics and subtopics, such as Arts, Business, Computers, and so on, which are arranged in a hierarchy (Figure 1-29). The top level of the hierarchy contains general topics. Each successive level of the hierarchy contains increasingly specific subtopics. A topic directory might also be referred to as a "category list," an "index," or a "directory."

Reproduced with permission of Yahoo! Inc.   2004 by Yahoo! Inc. YAHOO! and the YAHOO! logo are trademarks of Yahoo! Inc.

FIGURE 1-29

To use a topic directory, simply click a general topic. When a list of subtopics appears, click the one that's most relevant to the information you are trying to locate. If your selection results in another list of subtopics, continue to select the most relevant one until the search engine presents a list of Web pages. You can then link to these pages just as though you had used a keyword query.

CLICK TO START

How do I use a search form to find information? Many search engines provide an advanced search form that helps you formulate a very targeted search. A search form, like the one shown in Figure 1-30, helps you enter complex queries. It might also allow you to search for pages that are written in a particular language, located on a specific Web server, or that were created within a limited range of dates.

FIGURE 1-30

Many search engines provide forms that are designed to simplify the search process. These forms are usually accessible by clicking an Advanced Search link, which often is located on the main page of the search engine Web site.

Can't I just ask a simple question and get an answer? Instead of entering a cryptic query such as *movie+review+"The Producers"*, wouldn't it be nice to enter a more straightforward question like *Where can I find a review of The Producers?* A few search engines specialize in natural language queries, which accept questions written in plain English (Figure 1-31).

FIGURE 1-31

Some search engines accept natural language queries.

QuickCheck   SECTION C

1. HTTP ([   ] Transfer Protocol) is the communications standard for the Web.

2. Every Web page has a unique address called a(n) [   ]. Hint: Use the acronym.

3. A browser assembles a Web page on your computer screen according to the specifications contained in [   ] tags.

4. Google and Yahoo! Search are examples of [   ] engines.

5. The [   ] *railroad AND cars* will locate pages that contain both the words "railroad" and "cars."

6. Search [   ], such as AND and OR, help you create targeted searches.

7. A natural [   ] search engine accepts questions written in plain English.

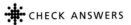 CHECK ANSWERS

D

E-mail Basics

The Internet really took off when people discovered electronic mail. More than 60 billion e-mail messages speed over the Internet each day. E-mail, which is derived from the term "electronic mail," can refer to a single message or to the entire system of computers and software that transmits, receives, and stores e-mail messages. In this section of the chapter, you get some background information about how e-mail works—in particular, the difference between "free" Web-based e-mail and "traditional" store-and-forward e-mail. E-mail labs at the end of the chapter provide hands-on overviews of how to read, compose, send, and reply to e-mail messages.

E-MAIL OVERVIEW

Who can use e-mail? Any person with an e-mail account can send and receive e-mail. An **e-mail account** provides the rights to a storage area, or "mailbox," supplied by an e-mail provider, such as an ISP. Each mailbox has a unique address, which typically consists of a user ID, an @ symbol, and the name of the computer that maintains the mailbox. For example, suppose that a university student named Dee Greene has an electronic mailbox on a computer called rutgers.edu. If her user ID is "dee_greene," her e-mail address would be *dee_greene@rutgers.edu*.

Exactly what is an e-mail message? An **e-mail message** is a document that is composed on a computer and remains in digital, or "electronic," form so that it can be transmitted to another computer. The **message header** includes the recipient's e-mail address and message subject. It might also contain the address of anyone who is receiving a copy of the message, and the name of any file attachments that accompany the message. The body of the e-mail contains your message. The message header and body are usually displayed in a form, as shown in Figure 1-32.

FIGURE 1-32

When you compose an e-mail message, you can begin by entering the address of one or more recipients and the subject of the message. You can also specify one or more files to attach to the message. The body of the e-mail message contains the message itself. When the message is sent, your e-mail software adds the date and your e-mail address to identify you as the sender.

What can I do with basic e-mail? Basic e-mail activities consist of writing, reading, replying to (Figure 1-33), and forwarding messages. Messages can be printed, kept for later reference, or deleted.

FIGURE 1-33

Your e-mail client's Reply button creates a new e-mail message and automatically addresses it to the person who sent the original message. Most e-mail systems also copy the text of the original message into the reply so that everyone has a complete transcript of the messages that were exchanged.

How does forwarding work? After you receive an e-mail message, you can use the Forward feature to pass it on to other people. You might, for example, forward a message that was sent to you but that should be handled by someone else. When you initiate the forwarding process, the original e-mail message is copied into a new message window, complete with the address of the original sender. You can then enter the address of the person to whom you are forwarding the message. You can also add a note about why you are passing the message along.

Some e-mail systems allow you to alter the text of the original message before you forward it. If you do so, include a note explaining your changes, especially if they alter the intent of the original message. You should not forward messages that were intended to be confidential. If you think that such a message needs to be shared with other people, obtain permission from the author of the original message.

What's an e-mail attachment? Originally, e-mail messages were stored in a plain and simple format called "ASCII text." No fancy formatting was allowed—no variation in font type or color, no underlining or boldface, and, of course, no pictures or sounds. Although you cannot insert a digital photo or sound file into a plain ASCII e-mail message, you can send these kinds of files as e-mail attachments.

Any file that travels with an e-mail message is called an **e-mail attachment**. A conversion process called **MIME** (Multi-Purpose Internet Mail Extensions) provides a clever way of disguising digital photos, sounds, and other media as plain ASCII text that can travel over the Internet as e-mail attachments. An electronic message incorporated in the e-mail header provides your e-mail software with the information that allows it to reconstruct the attachment into its original form.

1

Suppose you want to e-mail a photo of your high school reunion to a friend. The photo is stored in a file called Reunion.gif. You can address an e-mail message to your friend, write a short note ("You missed a really fun reunion!"), and then use the Attachment option provided by your e-mail software to specify Reunion.gif as an attachment. Your e-mail software converts Reunion.gif into MIME format and sends it along with your message.

When your friend receives the message, her e-mail software reconstitutes the file into your reunion photo. The way the attachment is displayed depends on your friend's e-mail software. The photo might appear at the end of the e-mail, or it could appear as an attachment icon that has to be double-clicked. With some e-mail systems, the attachment file might have to be downloaded separately and opened using the same software with which it was created.

How does HTML relate to e-mail? Most e-mail software allows you to create e-mail messages in HTML format. HTML messages can contain lots of elaborate formatting that's just not possible with plain ASCII text. By selecting your e-mail software's HTML option, you enter a world of colored, bold, italic, and underlined text; fancy fonts; embedded graphics; and various font sizes. Your e-mail recipients must have HTML-compliant e-mail software. Otherwise, your message will be delivered as plain, unformatted ASCII text. You should also be aware that HTML formatted e-mail messages can distribute viruses and open security holes that leave your computer vulnerable to hackers.

What other e-mail features are available? In addition to attachments and HTML formatting, today's sophisticated e-mail systems typically offer features that help you perform the tasks listed in Figure 1-34.

FIGURE 1-34

E-mail features provide flexibility for sending and receiving messages.

- Maintain an address book and use it to select e-mail addresses instead of entering them every time you compose a message.
- Use the address book to send mail to a "group" that consists of several e-mail addresses.
- Send a "carbon copy" (Cc:) of a message to one or more recipients.
- Send a "blind carbon copy" (Bcc:), which hides the addresses in the Bcc: field from other recipients of the message.
- Assign a priority to a message—high priority is usually indicated by an exclamation point or red text.
- Find a particular message in your list of old mail.
- Enlarge text size for easier reading.
- Sort messages by date received, sender's name, subject, or priority.
- Refuse to accept messages that arrive from a particular e-mail address.
- Automate replies to messages that you receive while on vacation or when you will not be responding to e-mail messages for a few days.
- Automatically fetch mail at specified intervals.
- Check spelling before sending a message.

NETIQUETTE

Is e-mail different from other types of communication? In some respects, e-mail is similar to an old-fashioned letter because its message is conveyed without benefit of the facial expressions, voice inflections, and body gestures that accompany face-to-face conversations. When composing a message, it is important to carefully consider your audience and the message you want to convey.

For example, you might have gotten into the habit of using text messaging shorthand to write messages such as "thnq 4 spking w me 2day. c u 2moro at 10." (Translation: Thank you for speaking with me today. See you tomorrow at 10:00.) Text messaging shorthand recently emerged as a quick and convenient way to communicate when using e-mail, instant messaging, and cell phone text messaging. Although text messaging shorthand works among your friends, it would not be appropriate in other situations, such as confirming the time for a job interview.

By understanding netiquette, you can avoid some of the pitfalls and problems of e-mail communications. **Netiquette** is online jargon for "Internet etiquette." It is a series of customs or guidelines for maintaining civilized and effective communications in online discussions and e-mail exchanges.

■ **Put a meaningful title on the subject line.** The subject line of your message should clearly describe the content of your e-mail message.

■ **Use uppercase and lowercase letters.** An e-mail message that's typed in all uppercase means that you're "shouting."

■ **Check spelling.** Most e-mail software offers a Check Spelling command. Use it.

■ **Be careful what you send.** E-mail is not private, nor is it secure. Treat your messages as though they are postcards that can be read by anyone. Remember that all laws governing copyright, slander, and discrimination apply to e-mail.

■ **Be polite.** Avoid wording that could sound inflammatory or argumentative. If you would not say it face-to-face, don't say it in e-mail.

■ **Be cautious when using sarcasm and humor.** The words in your e-mail arrive without facial expressions or voice intonations, so a sarcastic comment can easily be misinterpreted.

■ **Use smileys and text messaging shorthand cautiously.** **Smileys** are symbols that represent emotions (Figure 1-35). They can help convey the intent behind your words. Smileys and text messaging shorthand should be used only in correspondence with people who understand them.

■ **Use the Bcc function for group mailings.** By placing e-mail addresses for secondary recipients in the Bcc box, the recipients of your message won't have to scroll through a long list of addresses before reaching the "meat" of your message.

■ **Don't send replies to "all recipients."** Use the Reply All command only when there is a very specific need for everyone listed in the To, Cc, and Bcc boxes to receive the message.

■ **Don't send huge attachments.** Try to limit the size of attachments to 50 KB or less. If necessary, use a compression program, such as WinZip, to shrink the attachment.

■ **Explain all attachments.** Attachments can harbor computer viruses. To determine whether an attachment is legitimate, your correspondents will want to know the file name of the attachment, what the attachment contains, and the name of the software you used to create it.

■ **Stay alert for viruses.** Because viruses can tag along with e-mail attachments, don't open an attachment unless it was sent from a reliable source, its purpose is clearly explained in the body of the e-mail, and it was scanned using antivirus software (see Chapter 4).

■ **Notify recipients of viruses.** If you discover that your computer sent out infected attachments, use antivirus software to remove the virus, and then notify anyone to whom you recently sent mail.

INFOWEBLINKS

You can read more about netiquette, smileys, and text messaging shorthand at the **Netiquette InfoWeb**.

www.course.com/np/concepts9/ch01

FIGURE 1-35

Smileys, which are sometimes called "emoticons," are clever symbols that can be added to e-mail messages to convey emotions and take the edge off potentially inflammatory remarks.

"Don't take offense."

"Just kidding!"

"I'm not happy about that."

"I'm perplexed."

"I'm amazed."

SPAM

What is all this junk in my mailbox? One of e-mail's main disadvantages is **spam**—unwanted electronic junk mail about medical products, low-cost loans, and fake software upgrades that arrives in your online mailbox. Today's proliferation of spam is generated by marketing firms that harvest e-mail addresses from mailing lists, membership applications, and Web sites.

Globally, spam accounts for about 70% of all e-mail messages. Legislation to minimize spam exists, but has not met expectations. Although it is impossible to avoid spam, you can reduce it by following these guidelines:

- **Don't reply.** Never reply to spam when you receive it.

- **Don't link.** Don't click links in e-mail messages from unknown senders.

- **Guard your e-mail address.** Provide your e-mail address only to people from whom you want to receive e-mail. Be wary of providing your e-mail address at Web sites, entering it on application forms, or posting it in public places such as online discussion groups.

- **Use spam filters.** If your e-mail client offers a spam filter to block unwanted messages, put it to use. If your e-mail client does not provide a spam filter, you can download and install one from a shareware site on the Web. A **spam filter** automatically routes advertisements and other junk mail to the Deleted Items folder maintained by your e-mail client. Although spam filters can be effective for blocking spam and other unwanted e-mails, it sometimes blocks e-mail messages you want. After activating spam filters, periodically examine your Deleted Items folder to make sure the filters are not overly aggressive.

- **Report spam.** If your e-mail provider offers a way to report spam, use it.

- **Change your e-mail address.** When spam gets out of hand, consider changing your e-mail account so that you have a different e-mail address.

E-MAIL TECHNOLOGY

What is an e-mail system? An **e-mail system** is the equipment and software that carries and manipulates e-mail messages. It includes computers and software called **e-mail servers** that sort, store, and route mail. An e-mail system also includes the personal computers that belong to individuals who send and receive mail. E-mail is based on **store-and-forward technology**—a communications method in which data that cannot be sent directly to its destination is temporarily stored until transmission is possible. This technology allows e-mail messages to be routed to a server and held until they are forwarded to the next server or to a personal mailbox.

Three types of e-mail systems are widely used today: POP, IMAP, and Web-based mail. **POP** (Post Office Protocol) temporarily stores new messages on an e-mail server. When you connect to your ISP and request your mail, it is downloaded from the e-mail server and stored on your computer. **IMAP** (Internet Messaging Access Protocol) is similar to POP, except that you have the option of downloading your mail or leaving it on the server. **Web-based e-mail** keeps your mail at a Web site, instead of transferring it to your computer.

How do I use Web-based e-mail? Before you can use Web-based e-mail, you need an e-mail account with a Web-based e-mail provider. To obtain one, simply connect to the Web-based e-mail provider's Web site and enter the information required to obtain an e-mail address, a user ID, and a password. Armed with these identifiers, you can use a browser to connect to the e-mail Web site from any computer that has access to the

INFOWEBLINKS

U.S. lawmakers enacted the CAN-SPAM Act in an attempt to control the flood of unwanted e-mail. The act allows spam, but requires messages to be labeled so they can be easily filtered out by ISPs or users. For an update on efforts to control spam, connect to the **Spam InfoWeb**.

www.course.com/np/concepts9/ch01

INFOWEBLINKS

One of the biggest advantages of a Web-based e-mail account is that it's free. For descriptions and addresses of the most popular e-mail Web sites, hop over to the **Web-based E-mail InfoWeb**.

www.course.com/np/concepts9/ch01

Internet (Figure 1-36). At the Web site, you can write, read, reply to, and delete e-mail messages. Because most Web-based e-mail providers allocate a limited amount of space to each account, it is important to delete messages when you no longer need them. You don't want your electronic mailbox to overflow and cause some messages to be returned to the senders.

Reproduced with permission of Yahoo! Inc. 2004 by Yahoo! Inc. YAHOO! and the YAHOO! logo are trademarks of Yahoo! Inc.

FIGURE 1-36

If you have a Web-based e-mail account, you can use a browser to access your e-mail messages. Writing, reading, replying to, forwarding, and deleting messages can be accomplished by interacting with a series of Web pages that lists your mail.

How do POP and IMAP work? Most people who use POP or IMAP e-mail have obtained an e-mail account from an ISP. POP mail accounts are more widely available. Such an account provides a mailbox on the ISP's **POP server**—a computer that stores your incoming messages until they can be transferred to your hard disk. Using POP requires **e-mail client software**, such as Microsoft Outlook or QUALCOMM Eudora. This client software, which is installed on your computer, provides an Inbox and an Outbox that allow you to work with your mail, even when your computer is not online.

An Inbox holds incoming messages. When you ask the e-mail server to deliver your mail, all your messages stored on the server are transferred to your computer, stored on your computer's disk drive, and listed as new mail in your Inbox. You can then disconnect from the Internet, if you like, and read the new mail at your leisure.

As shown in Figure 1-37, an Outbox temporarily holds messages you have composed and completed, but haven't transmitted over the Internet. Suppose you want to compose several e-mail messages. You can fire up your e-mail client software, but remain offline while you work on the messages. The ability to compose mail offline is especially useful if you access the Internet over a dial-up connection because the phone line isn't tied up while you compose mail. As you complete a message, it is stored on your

FIGURE 1-37

Outgoing mail can be stored in your Outbox until you connect to the Internet and send it. Incoming mail can be stored on a POP server until it is downloaded to the Inbox on your hard disk.

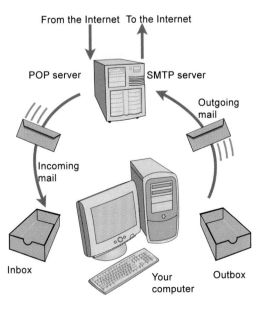

1

computer and listed in the Outbox. When you go online, you can send all the mail being held in your Outbox. Outgoing mail is routed by an **SMTP server** (Simple Mail Transfer Protocol server) instead of a POP server, as Figure 1-37 illustrates.

Does e-mail client software work only for offline e-mail tasks? No. Although you can use your e-mail client software to compose, read, and reply to messages while you're offline, you can also use it while you are online. In fact, this software often provides a setting that bypasses the Outbox and immediately sends messages out over the Internet.

How does POP mail compare to Web-based e-mail? Before answering this question, let's review the important distinctions between the two types of e-mail. First, POP mail requires you to install and use e-mail client software, whereas Web-based e-mail allows you to use a browser as e-mail client software. Second, POP transfers messages to your computer's hard disk, whereas a Web-based e-mail system retains your messages on its server. Both e-mail systems have similar features, allowing you to read, compose, reply to, delete, and forward e-mail messages; maintain an address book; and send attachments. Each system does, however, have unique advantages. Your needs determine which system is better for you.

■ **Control.** POP mail gives you more control over your messages because they are transferred to your computer's hard disk, where you can control access to them. Web-based e-mail maintains your messages on its server, where you have less control over who can access them.

■ **Security.** When messages are stored on your computer, a hard disk drive malfunction could wipe out all your correspondence (along with the rest of your files). A Web-based e-mail provider is rigorous about safeguarding its data, so your mail might be safer than if it was stored on your hard disk.

■ **Travel.** The major advantage of Web-based e-mail is that you can access your messages from any computer connected to the Internet. Therefore, you can get your e-mail when you travel without taking your computer. In contrast, with POP, your computer contains your old mail, your address book, and your e-mail software. Therefore, to use your familiar e-mail tools on the road, you really have to carry your computer with you.

INFOWEBLINKS

What's the latest news about e-mail client software? You'll find descriptions, reviews, and links at the **E-mail Client Software InfoWeb**.

www.course.com/np/concepts9/ch01

QuickCheck SECTION D

1. In an e-mail address, the [   ] symbol separates the user ID from the name of the e-mail server.

2. E-mail attachments are typically converted using [   ], which disguises media and other files as plain ASCII text. Hint: Use the acronym.

3. Unwanted e-mail messages are called [   ].

4. Store-and-[   ] technology stores messages on an e-mail server until they are transmitted to an individual's computer.

5. For many e-mail systems, a(n) [   ] server handles outgoing mail, and a(n) [   ] server handles incoming mail.

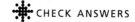 CHECK ANSWERS

TechTalk

The Boot Process

The sequence of events that occurs between the time that you turn on a computer and the time that it is ready for you to issue commands is referred to as the boot process, or "booting" your computer. The term "boot" comes from the word "bootstrap," which describes a small loop on the back of a boot. Just as you can pull on a big boot using a small bootstrap, your computer boots up by first loading a small program into memory, and then it uses that small program to load a large operating system. Your computer's small bootstrap program is built into special ROM (read-only memory) circuitry housed in the computer's system unit. When you turn on a computer, the ROM circuitry receives power and begins the boot process. With a Windows computer, the boot process usually proceeds smoothly and, in a short time, you can begin working with your application software. Sometimes, however, the boot process encounters a problem that must be fixed before you can begin a computing session. You can fix many of the problems a computer might encounter during the boot process. Make sure, however, that you follow the guidelines provided by your school or employer if you encounter equipment problems with computers in school labs or your workplace.

What's the purpose of the boot process? The **boot process** involves a lot of flashing lights, whirring noises, and beeping as your computer performs a set of diagnostic tests called the **power-on self-test** (POST). The good news is that these tests can warn you if certain crucial components of your computer system are not functioning properly. The bad news is that these tests cannot warn you of impending failures. Also, problems identified during the boot process usually must be fixed before you can start a computing session.

The boot process serves an additional purpose—loading the operating system from the hard disk into memory. Without the operating system, a computer's CPU is unable to communicate with any input, output, or storage devices. It can't display information, accept commands, store data, or run any application software. Therefore, loading the operating system is a crucial step in the boot process.

Why doesn't a computer simply leave the operating system in memory? Most of a computer's memory is "volatile" random access memory (RAM), which cannot hold any data when the power is off. Although a copy of the operating system is housed in RAM while the computer is in operation, this copy is erased as soon as the power is turned off.

In addition to RAM, computers have non-volatile memory circuitry, such as ROM and CMOS, which can store data even when the power is off. Typically, ROM and CMOS are not nearly large enough to store an entire operating system.

Given the volatility of RAM and the insufficient size of ROM and CMOS, computer designers decided to store the operating system on a computer's hard disk. During the boot process, a copy of the operating system is copied into RAM where it can be accessed quickly whenever the computer needs to carry out an input, output, or storage operation. The operating system remains in RAM until the computer is turned off (Figure 1-38).

FIGURE 1-38

The bootstrap program copies the operating system into RAM, where it can be directly accessed by the processor to carry out input, output, or storage operations.

Instructions in ROM tell the computer to copy the operating system from disk to RAM.

Hard disk

ROM

RAM

Operating system is available to the processor as needed.

Processor

What is the order of events during the boot process? Six major events happen during the boot process:

1. Power up. When you turn on the power switch, the power light is illuminated, and power is distributed to the computer circuitry.

2. Start boot program. The microprocessor begins to execute the bootstrap program that is stored in ROM.

3. Power-on self-test. The computer performs diagnostic tests of several crucial system components.

4. Identify peripheral devices. The operating system identifies the peripheral devices that are connected to the computer and checks their settings.

5. Load operating system. The operating system is copied from the hard disk to RAM.

6. Check configuration and customization. The microprocessor reads configuration data and executes any customized startup routines specified by the user.

What if I turn on a computer and nothing happens? The first step in the boot process is the power-up stage. Power from a wall outlet or battery activates a small power light. If the power light does not come on when you flip the "on" switch, refer to the checklist in Figure 1-39.

What problems are likely to show up during the power-on self-test? The POST checks your computer's main circuitry, screen display, memory, and keyboard. It can identify when one of these devices has failed, but it cannot identify intermittent problems or impending failures.

The POST notifies you of a hardware problem by displaying an error message on the screen or by emitting a series of beeps. These error messages can help you pinpoint the source of a problem. Unfortunately, many computers display these error messages as numeric codes, such as "1790 Disk 0 Error." You can check the documentation or Web site for your computer to find the specific meaning of numeric error codes.

A **beep code** provides your computer with a way to signal a problem, even if the screen is not functioning. Two short beeps might mean a problem with the keyboard. Three long beeps might mean a problem with the screen display. Beep codes differ from one computer to another, depending on the ROM bootstrap program. The printed or online reference manual for a computer usually explains the meaning of each beep code.

Should I try to fix these problems myself? If a computer displays error messages, emits beep codes, or seems to "freeze up" during the boot process, you can take some simple steps that might fix it. First, turn the computer off. After the computer has powered off, wait five seconds, and then try to start the computer again and hope that the boot process proceeds smoothly. If the boot problem reoccurs, turn the computer off again and check all the cables that run between your computer and peripheral devices, such as the keyboard, mouse, and monitor. After checking the cables, try to boot again. If you still encounter a boot error, contact a technical support person.

FIGURE 1-39

Power-up Checklist

⊕ Make sure the power cable is plugged into the wall and into the back of the computer.

🔋 If you're using a notebook or tablet computer, check batteries or plug into a wall outlet.

🔌 Make sure the wall outlet is supplying power (plug in a lamp and make sure you can turn it on).

⊕ If the computer is plugged into a surge strip, extension cord, or uninterruptible power supply, make sure it is turned on and functioning correctly.

🌀 Can you hear the fan in your desktop computer? If not, the computer's power supply mechanism might have failed.

What's the long list of stuff that appears on my screen during the boot process? After the POST, the bootstrap program tries to identify all devices connected to the computer. On some computers, the settings for each device appear on the screen during the boot process, creating a list of rather esoteric information, as shown in Figure 1-40.

FIGURE 1-40

During the boot process, a computer attempts to identify storage devices, display devices, and other peripheral devices.

```
Award Medallion BIOS v6.0
Copyright (C) 2002-03, Award Software, Inc.

Copyright 2002 by Hewlett Packard, Inc
   Rev. 1.01

Intel(R) Pentium(R) III 500MHz Processor
Memory Test :  1310725 OK

Award Plug and Play BIOS Extension v1.0A
Initialize Plug and Play Cards . . .
PNP Init Completed

Detecting Primary Master        Maxtor 53073H6
Detecting Primary Slave         IOMEGA ZIP 100    ATAPI
Detecting Secondary Master      R/RW 4x4x24
Detecting Secondary Slave       FX482IT
```

On occasion, a device gets skipped or misidentified during the boot process. An error message is not produced, but the device won't seem to work properly. To solve this problem, shut down the computer and reboot. If a device causes persistent problems, check the manufacturer's Web site to see if a new software "patch" will improve its operation.

Do computers have trouble loading the operating system? Problems during the last stages of the boot process are rare, except when a disk has been inadvertently left in the floppy disk drive. Before computers were equipped with hard disk drives, floppy disks were used to store the operating system and application software. As a legacy from these early machines, today's computers first check the floppy disk drive for a disk containing the operating system. If it doesn't find a disk in the drive, it proceeds to look for the operating system on the hard disk. However, if a floppy disk happens to be hanging around in drive A, the computer assumes that you want to boot from it and looks for the operating system on that disk. The error message "Non-system disk or disk error" is the clue to this problem. Remove the floppy disk and press any key to resume the boot process.

How do I know when the boot process is finished? The boot process is complete when the computer is ready to accept your commands. Usually, the computer displays an operating system prompt or a main screen. The Windows operating system, for example, displays the Windows desktop when the boot process is complete.

If Windows cannot complete the boot process, you are likely to see a menu with an option for Safe Mode. **Safe Mode** is a limited version of Windows that allows you to use your mouse, monitor, and keyboard, but no other peripheral devices (Figure 1-41). This mode is designed for troubleshooting, not performing real computing tasks. If your computer enters Safe Mode at the end of the boot process, use the Shut Down command on the Start menu to properly shut down and turn off your computer. You can then turn on your computer again. It should complete the boot process in regular Windows mode. If your computer reenters Safe Mode, consult a technician.

FIGURE 1-41

Windows enters Safe Mode as a response to a problem—usually caused by the device driver software that controls a piece of peripheral equipment. You can also force a computer into Safe Mode by pressing the F8 key during the boot sequence.

When a computer is behaving erratically, does rebooting help? Under some circumstances—such as when a computer has been left on for a few weeks straight—the operating system seems to forget how to handle part of its job. Such problems can be caused by transient "soft errors" in the memory circuits that are supposed to hold the operating system instructions. In other cases, areas of memory that are supposed to be reserved for the operating system somehow get overwritten by snippets of application programs. The end effect is the same—parts of the operating system are missing and can't control a particular input, output, or storage function. As a result, a computer might begin to behave erratically. The remedy for this problem is to restore the operating system back to full functionality. Usually, rebooting does the trick. If not, consider the possibility that your computer might have contracted a virus. (More information on viruses can be found in Chapter 4.)

INFOWEBLINKS

Safe Mode can help technically savvy computer owners identify and fix a number of problems caused by installing new hardware devices. To learn more, check out the **Safe Mode InfoWeb**.

www.course.com/np/concepts9/ch01

QuickCheck   TECHTALK

1. The boot process loads the [   ] system from the hard disk into memory.

2. During the boot process, the [   ] checks your computer's main circuitry, screen display, memory, and keyboard.

3. Windows [   ] Mode provides a limited version of Windows that allows you to troubleshoot, but not use most peripheral devices.

4. If a computer is behaving erratically, rebooting might restore functionality. True or false? [   ]

CHECK ANSWERS

Issue
E-mail Privacy

When you drop an envelope into the corner mailbox, you probably expect it to arrive at its destination unopened, with its contents kept safe from prying eyes. When you make a phone call, you might assume that your conversation will proceed unmonitored by wiretaps or other listening devices. Can you also expect an e-mail message to be read only by the person to whom it is addressed?

In the United States, the Electronic Communications Privacy Act of 2000 prohibits the use of intercepted e-mail as evidence unless a judge approves a search warrant. That doesn't mean the government isn't reading your mail. Heightened security concerns after the September 11, 2001 terrorist attacks resulted in the rapid passage of the Patriot Act, which became law on October 26, 2001. In an effort to assist law enforcement officials, among its other provisions the Patriot Act relaxes the rules for obtaining and implementing search warrants and lowers the Fourth Amendment standard for obtaining a court order to compel an ISP to produce e-mail logs and addresses.

To eavesdrop on e-mail from suspected terrorists and other criminals, the FBI uses commercially available "sniffing" software, which scans through messages entering and leaving an ISP's e-mail system to find e-mail associated with a person who is under investigation. Privacy advocates are concerned because the sniffing software scans all messages that pass through an ISP, not just those messages sent to or received by a particular individual.

Although law enforcement agencies are required to obtain a court order before intercepting e-mail, no

such restriction exists for employers who want to monitor employee e-mail. According to the American Management Association, 33% of U.S. businesses monitor employee e-mail. But this intentional eavesdropping is only one way in which the contents of your e-mail messages might become public. The recipient of your e-mail can forward it to one or more people—people you never intended for it to reach. Your e-mail messages could pop up on a technician's screen in the course of system maintenance, updates, or repairs.

Some Web-based e-mail providers—particularly those that make you look at ads in exchange for free accounts—collect information on how often you log in and might monitor your keystrokes to find out which ads and links you click. E-mail providers claim such information is used internally to deliver the best possible service, prevent fraud, and select the ads for products that you're most likely to buy. Also, keep in mind that e-mail messages—including those you delete from your own computer—can be stored on backups of your ISP's e-mail server.

You might wonder if such open access to your e-mail is legal. The answer in most cases is yes. Although the United States Omnibus Crime Control and Safe Streets Act of 1968 and the Electronic Communications Privacy Act of 1986 prohibit public and private employers from engaging in surreptitious surveillance of employee activity through the use of electronic devices, two exceptions to these privacy statutes exist. The first exception permits an employer to monitor e-mail if one party to the communication consents to the monitoring. An employer must inform employees of this policy before undertaking any monitoring. The second exception permits employers to monitor employees' e-mail if a legitimate business need exists, and the monitoring takes place within the business-owned e-mail system.

Employees generally have not been successful in defending their rights to e-mail privacy because courts have ruled that an employee's right to privacy does not outweigh a company's rights and interests. Courts seem to agree that because a company owns and maintains its e-mail system, it has the right to monitor the messages carried by the system.

Like employees of a business, students who use a school's e-mail system cannot be assured of e-mail privacy. When a CalTech student was accused of sexually harassing a female student by sending lewd e-mail to her and her boyfriend, investigators retrieved all the student's e-mail from the archives of the e-mail server. The student was expelled from the university even though he claimed that the e-mail had been "spoofed" to make it look as though he had sent it, when it had actually been sent by someone else.

Why would an employer want to know the contents of employee e-mail? Why would a school be concerned with the correspondence of its students? It is probably true that some organizations simply snoop on the off chance that important information might be discovered. Other organizations have more legitimate reasons for monitoring e-mail. An organization that owns an e-mail system can be held responsible for the consequences of actions related to the contents of e-mail messages on that system. For example, a school has a responsibility to protect students from harassment. If it fails to do so, it can be sued along with the author of the offending e-mail message. Organizations also recognize a need to protect themselves from false rumors and industrial espionage. For example, a business wants to know if an employee is supplying its competitor with information on product research and development.

Many schools and businesses have established e-mail privacy policies, which explain the conditions under which you can and cannot expect your e-mail to remain private. These policies are sometimes displayed when the computer boots or a new user logs in. Court decisions, however, seem to support the notion that because an organization owns and operates an e-mail system, the e-mail messages on that system are also the property of the organization. The individual who authors an e-mail message does not own all rights related to it. The company, school, or organization that supplies your e-mail account can, therefore, legally monitor your messages.

You should use your e-mail account with the expectation that some of your mail will be read from time to time. Think of your e-mail as a postcard, rather than a letter, and save your controversial comments for face-to-face conversations.

INFOWEBLINKS

You'll find lots more information about e-mail privacy (and lack of it) at the **E-mail Privacy InfoWeb**.

www.course.com/np/concepts9/ch01

What Do You Think?   ISSUE

1. Do you think most people believe that their e-mail is private?   O Yes O No O Not sure

2. Do you agree with CalTech's decision to expel the student who was accused of sending harassing e-mail to another student?   O Yes O No O Not sure

3. Should the laws be changed to make it illegal for employers to monitor e-mail without court approval?   O Yes O No O Not sure

4. Would you have different privacy expectations regarding an e-mail account at your place of work as opposed to an account you purchase from an e-mail service provider?   O Yes O No O Not sure

SAVE RESPONSES

Computers in Context
Marketing

Walking out the gate of ancient Pompeii, you might have come across an eye-catching sign extolling the virtues of a popular tavern in the next town. The sign was a clever bit of marketing designed to target thirsty travelers and drum up business. Throughout the centuries, handbills, newspaper ads, television commercials, radio spots, and mass mail campaigns were all important tools of the marketing industry. Now, computers have opened new vistas for communicating with consumers.

The American Marketing Association defines *marketing* as an organizational function and a set of processes for creating, communicating, and delivering value to customers and for managing customer relationships in ways that benefit the organization and its stakeholders. A person-in-the-street definition might simply be that marketing is an attempt to sell products.

Computers first played a role in marketing as a research tool for quickly crunching numbers from consumer surveys, sales figures, and projections. Statistics derived from that data helped companies focus development efforts on the most promising products and market them effectively. Marketing research data made one fact very clear: even the most effective advertising could not convince everyone to buy a particular product. A costly prime-time television ad, for example, might be seen by millions of viewers, but many of them had no interest at all in the advertised product. To better target potential buyers, marketers turned to direct marketing.

Direct marketing attempts to establish a one-to-one relationship with prospective customers rather than waiting for them to learn about a product from general, impersonal forms of advertising, such as billboards, radio spots, television commercials, and newspaper ads. The first direct marketing techniques included personalized letters, catalogs, and telemarketing. Customer names, addresses, and telephone numbers were mined from extensive computer databases maintained by mailing list brokers. Lists could be tailored in rudimentary ways to fit target markets.

Selling snow tires? Get a list of consumers in northern states. Hawking a new brand of disposable razors? Get a list of men.

"Dear Carmen Smith, you might already have won…" Just about everyone in America has received a personalized sweepstakes mailing. Initially, personalized names were crudely inserted using dot matrix printers, but today high-speed laser printers dash off thousands of personalized letters per hour and use graphics capabilities to affix signatures that appear to have been hand-signed in ink.

Telemarketing is a technique for telephone solicitation. Computerized autodialers make it possible for telemarketers to work efficiently. An autodialer is a device that can dial telephone numbers stored in a list. It can also generate and dial telephone numbers using a random or sequential number generator.

A "smart" autodialer, called a predictive dialer, increases a telemarketer's efficiency even more by automatically calling several numbers at the same time and only passing a call to the marketer when a person answers. If you've picked up the telephone only to hear silence or a disconnect, it was likely an autodialer that connected to more than one person at the same time and dropped your call. Preemptive dialers eliminate telemarketing time that would be otherwise wasted with busy signals, answering machines, and so on.

The Internet opened up dramatic new horizons in direct marketing by providing an inexpensive conduit for collecting information about potential customers and distributing targeted direct marketing. According to author Jim Sterne, "The Internet and the World Wide Web have become the most important new communication media since television, and ones that are fundamentally reshaping contemporary understanding of sales and marketing." Today, a vast amount of information flows over the Internet and marketers are trying to harness that information to most efficiently communicate their message to prospective customers.

Market analysts are interested in consumer opinions about companies and products. Analysts for companies like Ford, Microsoft, and Sony track opinions on the Internet by monitoring message boards, discussion sites, and blogs. Software tools, such as Intelliseek and Cymfony, are similar to Google's Web search technology, but are refined to sift through blogs for conjunctions of words such as "Ford Ranger," ""love," and "dependable" to guess that a blogger is happy with a particular vehicle.

E-commerce Web sites offer a global distribution channel for small entrepreneurs as well as multinational corporations. Consumers can locate e-commerce sites using a search engine. Some search engines allow paid advertising to appear on their sites. Clever marketers use search engine optimization techniques to get their Web sites to the top of search engine lists.

Another way to drive traffic to an e-commerce site is banner advertising that clutters up Web pages with inviting tag lines for free products. Clicking the ad connects consumers to the site. The cost of placing a banner ad depends on the click-through rate—the number of consumers who click an ad. Sophisticated banner ad software displays the banner ad across an entire network and monitors click-through rates. Not only does this software keep track of click throughs for billing purposes, it can automatically adjust the sites that carry each ad to maximize click-through rates.

The word "marketing" combined with "Internet" is often associated with the tidal wave of spam that's currently crashing into everyone's Inbox. These mass spam e-mails, however bothersome, are a very crude form of direct marketing. Typically, spammers use

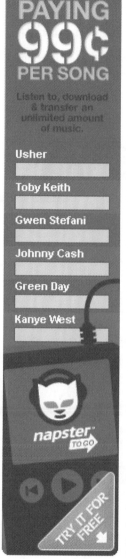

"unscrubbed" mailing lists containing many expired, blocked, and invalid e-mail addresses. This hit-or-miss strategy is cheap. Ten million e-mail addresses can be rented for as low as $100 and server bandwidth provided by e-mail brokers costs about $300 per million messages sent.

Marketing professionals regard massive e-mail spamming with some degree of scorn because most lists don't narrow the focus to the most promising customers. Worse yet, consumers react by installing spam filters. Some spammers try to evade spam filters. More than one Web site offers marketers a free service that analyzes mass e-mail solicitations using a Spam filter simulator. If the solicitation can't get through the filter, the service offers suggestions on what to change so the message slips through.

In contrast to gratuitous spammers, marketing professionals have learned that opt-in mailing lists have much higher success rates. Consumers who have asked for information more often appreciate receiving it and act on it. Opt-in consumers are also more willing to divulge information that develops an accurate profile of their lifestyle so marketers can offer them the most appropriate products.

Most consumers would agree that the marketing industry needs professionals who are socially responsible. In describing the qualifications for marketing professionals, the Bureau of Labor and Statistics states the obvious when it says, "Computer skills are vital because marketing, product promotion, and advertising on the Internet are increasingly common." In preparing for a marketing career, a knowledge of computers, the Web, and the Internet are important. Equally important is preparation in statistical analysis, psychology, and ethics, along with coursework that covers legal and regulatory aspects of the technology-driven marketing industry.

INFOWEBLINKS

You'll find additional information about this Computers in Context topic by visiting the **Computers and Marketing InfoWeb.**

www.course.com/np/concepts9/ch01

Labs

Student Edition Labs

On the Web
Student Edition Labs

To access the Student Edition labs, connect to the New Perspectives NP9 Web site and click the link for Student Edition Labs. The link also provides access to lab assignments.

www.course.com/np/concepts9/ch01

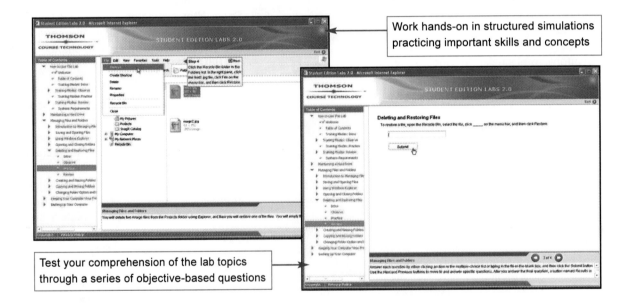

Work hands-on in structured simulations practicing important skills and concepts

Test your comprehension of the lab topics through a series of objective-based questions

E-MAIL

In the E-Mail Student Edition Lab, you will learn the following e-mail skills:

- Composing, replying, and printing e-mail messages
- E-mail organizational and management techniques such as moving messages to a folder and using an address book
- Signing up for and using Web-based e-mail to demonstrate your e-mail skills using your own e-mail account

on the BookOnCD
New Perspectives Labs

To access the New Perspectives labs for Chapter 1, start the BookOnCD and then click the ⚙ icon next to the lab title below.

⚙ OPERATING A PERSONAL COMPUTER

IN THIS LAB YOU'LL LEARN:

How to start a Windows computer

What to do when a computer is in sleep mode

How to deactivate a screen saver

How to select a different screen saver

How to use the Alt, Ctrl, Esc, Num Lock, Caps Lock, Windows, Fn, Backspace, Delete, and arrow keys

The difference between forward and backward slashes

How to start and exit a program

How to close a program that is not responding

When to use the reset button

How to shut down Windows

LAB ASSIGNMENTS

1. Start the interactive part of the lab. Make sure you've enabled Tracking if you want to save your QuickCheck results. Perform each lab step as directed, and answer all the lab QuickCheck questions. When you exit the lab, your answers are automatically graded and your results are displayed.

2. Make a note of the brand and location of the computer you're using to complete these lab assignments.

3. Use the Start button to access your computer's Control Panel folder. Describe the status of your computer's power saver settings.

4. Preview the available screen savers on the computer you use most frequently. Select the screen saver you like the best and describe it in a few sentences.

5. What is the purpose of an Fn key? Does your computer keyboard include an Fn key? Explain why or why not.

6. In your own words, describe what happens when you (a) click the Close button, (b) hold down the Ctrl, Alt, and Del keys, (c) press the reset button, and (d) select the Shut Down option.

⚙ MAKING A DIAL-UP CONNECTION

IN THIS LAB YOU'LL LEARN:

How to connect a computer to your telephone line

How to connect your computer and your phone to the same wall plug

The general procedure for subscribing to an ISP

How to connect to the Internet using ISP-provided software

Why you might need to manually create a dial-up connection

What information is necessary to create a dial-up connection

How to create your own customized dial-up icon

How to use a dial-up icon to connect to your ISP

How to disconnect at the end of an Internet session

LAB ASSIGNMENTS

1. Start the interactive part of the lab. Make sure you've enabled Tracking if you want to save your QuickCheck results. Perform each lab step as directed, and answer all the lab QuickCheck questions. When you exit the lab, your answers are automatically graded and your results are displayed.

2. Make a list of at least five ISPs that are available in your area. If possible, include both local and national ISPs in your list.

3. Suppose that you intend to manually create a dial-up connection icon for AT&T WorldNet. What information do you need, in addition to the following, to create this dial-up connection?

- AT&T's dial-in telephone number
- AT&T's IP address
- Your password

4. List the following information about the Internet connection you typically use: name of ISP, type of Internet connection (dial-up, DSL, cable Internet service, ISDN, satellite Internet service, school network, or business network), connection speed, and monthly fee. (If you don't currently have Internet access, describe the type of connection you would like to use.)

on the BookOnCD
New Perspectives Labs ^{continued}

To access the New Perspectives labs for Chapter 1, start the
BookOnCD and then click the ⚛ icon next to the lab title below.

⚛ BROWSING AND SEARCHING

IN THIS LAB YOU'LL LEARN:

How to work with the URL box, site list, and
History list

How to use links and navigation buttons

How to work with Bookmarks and Favorites lists

What to do if you encounter a "page not found"
message

How to change your home page

How to access a search engine

Where to get help about using a search engine

How to enter a keyword search query

How to use a topic directory

How to use the results list provided by a search
engine

LAB ASSIGNMENTS

1. Start the interactive part of the lab. Make sure
   you've enabled Tracking if you want to save your
   QuickCheck results. Perform each lab step as
   directed, and answer all the lab QuickCheck
   questions. When you exit the lab, your answers
   are automatically graded and your results are
   displayed.

2. Make a note of the brand and location of the
   computer you're using to complete these lab
   assignments.

3. Examine the Favorites or Bookmarks list. How
   many pages are included in this list? Link to three
   of the pages, indicate their URLs, and provide a
   brief description of their contents.

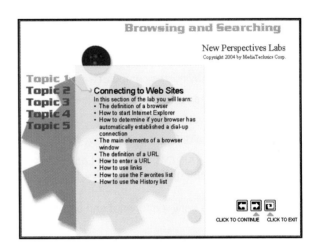

4. Suppose that you want to make your own trail
   mix, but you need a recipe. Enter the query *"trail
   mix" AND recipe* in three different search
   engines. (Refer to the Search Engine InfoWeb
   for a list of popular search engines.) Describe the
   similarities and differences in the results lists the
   three search engines produce.

5. Use the search engine of your choice to determine whether the query

   "Blue book price" Taurus -"used car"

   produces the same results as the query

   Blue book price Taurus -"used car"

   Make sure you enter each query exactly as specified, including the quotation marks (no space after
   the hyphen). Explain the similarities and differences in the query results.

on the BookOnCD
New Perspectives Labs continued

To access the New Perspectives labs for Chapter 1, start the BookOnCD and then click the ⚙ icon next to the lab title below.

⚙ USING E-MAIL

IN THIS LAB YOU'LL LEARN:

How to open a Web-based e-mail account

How to compose an e-mail message

How to reply to a message

How to intersperse your reply within the text of the original message

How to delete a message

How to print a message

How to use your address book

How to add a name to your address book

How to create a group in your address book

How to add an attachment to an e-mail message

How to view an e-mail attachment

LAB ASSIGNMENTS

1. Start the interactive part of the lab. Make sure you've enabled Tracking if you want to save your QuickCheck results. Perform each lab step as directed, and answer all the lab QuickCheck questions. When you exit the lab, your answers are automatically graded and your results are displayed.

2. Using the e-mail software of your choice, send an e-mail message to kendra_hill@cciw.com. In the body of your message, ask for a copy of the "Most Influential Person Survey."

3. Wait a few minutes after sending the message to Kendra Hill, and then check your mail. You should receive a survey from Kendra Hill. Reply to this message and Cc: your instructor. In your reply, answer each question in the survey, interspersing your answers with the original text. Send the reply, following the procedures required by your e-mail provider.

4. Examine the address book offered by your e-mail software. Describe how much information (name, home address, business address, birth date, telephone number, fax number, and so on) you can enter for each person. In your opinion, would this address book be suitable for a business person to use for storing contact information? Why or why not? Send the descriptions and answers to these questions to your instructor in an e-mail.

Interactive Summary

To review important concepts from this chapter, fill in the blanks to best complete each sentence. When using the NP9 BookOnCD or the NP9 Web site, click the Check Answers buttons to automatically score your answers.

A computer is a device that accepts input, [   ] data, stores data, and produces output according to a series of stored instructions. Before a computer processes data, it is temporarily held in [   ]. This data is then processed in the [   ] (CPU). The idea of a [   ] program means that a series of instructions for a computing task can be loaded into a computer's memory.

Computers are grouped into categories, such as personal computers, handhelds, mainframes, super-computers, servers, workstations, and videogame consoles. A [   ] computer is a type of microcomputer designed to meet the needs of an individual. Computers process, store, and transmit data

in [   ] format as a series of 1s and 0s. Each 1 or 0 is called a [   ]. Eight bits, called a [   ], represent one character—a letter, number, or punctuation mark. Data becomes [   ] when it is presented in a format that people can understand and use.

An [   ] system, such as Windows, UNIX, or Mac OS, is essentially the master controller for all activities that take place within a computer. [   ] software is any set of computer programs that helps a person carry out a task. Although "Windows" is the name of an operating system, the term "Windows software" refers to application software designed for computers that run the Windows operating system.

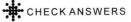 CHECK ANSWERS

The Internet is a collection of local, regional, national, and international computer [   ] that are linked together to exchange data and distribute processing tasks. The main routes of the Internet are referred to as the Internet [   ]. Communication between all the devices on the Internet is made possible by a standard set of rules called [   ]. The Internet hosts a wide variety of activities, such as Web browsing, e-commerce, e-mail, bulletin boards, chat groups, instant messaging, Internet telephony, digital broadcasts, remote access, downloads, uploads, and peer-to-peer file sharing.

Many people access the Internet using a dial-up connection that simply requires a telephone line and a

[   ]. Faster access methods include cable Internet service, ISDN, DSL, and satellite serv-ice. Regardless of the access method, individuals cannot typically connect directly to the Internet backbone and, therefore, need to use an [   ] as an intermediary. Both national ISPs and local ISPs have advantages that cater to different computing lifestyles.

Access to the Internet is not restricted, but access to some areas requires a [   ] and password. Passwords are most secure when they consist of two non-related words or a word and a number. Managing multiple passwords can be simplified by selecting a low-security password and a high-security password, and then applying them as necessary.

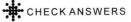 CHECK ANSWERS

Composed of millions of files stored on Web [_____] all over the world, the Web is one of the most popular aspects of the Internet. Many of these Web-based files are documents that a browser displays as Web [_____]. Other files contain photos, videos, animations, and sound clips that can be incorporated into specific Web pages. Web pages also contain [_____] to related documents and media files. Every Web page has a unique address called a [_____]. Most of them begin with "http", which stands for Hypertext [_____] Protocol, the communications standard that's instrumental in ferrying Web documents to all corners of the Internet. A group of Web pages is usually referred to as a Web [_____].

A [_____] is a software program that runs on your computer and helps you access Web pages. It fetches Web pages and interprets HTML [_____] to properly display the page on your computer screen. Current browsers simply fetch information from a given URL, but they do not have the capability to search for information based on your search specifications. A search [_____] provides the tools you need to search for specific information on the Web. These tools include keyword search input areas, advanced search forms, topic directories, and "agents" that understand queries entered as simple questions.

✦ CHECK ANSWERS

E-mail, short for "electronic mail," can refer to a single electronic message or to the entire system of computers and software that transmits, receives, and stores digital e-mail messages. Any person with an e-mail [_____] can send and receive electronic mail. Basic e-mail activities include composing, reading, replying to, sending, forwarding, and deleting messages. More advanced activities include adding attachments, using HTML format, and maintaining an address book. Most e-mail messages are created in a plain and simple format called [_____] text. It is also possible to create messages in [_____] format, which includes underlining, fancy fonts, colored text, and embedded graphics.

E-mail has similarities with and differences from other forms of communications, but it is the differences that spawned a collection of online communications guidelines called [_____].

An e-mail system consists of e-mail servers, which are accessible to e-mail account holders. Today, consumers can choose between three types of e-mail. [_____] mail holds your incoming mail on an e-mail server until you download it to your computer using e-mail [_____] software. [_____] mail gives you the option of downloading your mail or storing it on the e-mail server. [_____]-based mail allows you to use a browser as e-mail client software.

✦ CHECK ANSWERS

Key Terms

Make sure you understand all the boldfaced key terms presented in this chapter. If you're using the NP9 BookOnCD, you can use this list of terms as an interactive study activity. First, try to define a term in your own words, and then click the term to compare your definition with the definition presented in chapter.

Always-on connection, 18
Application software, 12
Beep code, 41
Bit, 11
Blog, 16
Boot process, 40
Browser, 26
Byte, 11
Cable Internet service, 18
Cable modem, 18
Case sensitive, 21
CD drive, 10
Central processing unit (CPU), 4
Chat group, 16
Client, 9
Computer, 4
Computer network, 8
Computer program, 4
Data, 4
Data file, 11
Desktop computer, 6
Dial-up connection, 17
Digital, 11
Downloading, 15
DSL, 19
DVD drive, 10
E-commerce, 16
E-mail, 16
E-mail account, 33
E-mail attachment, 34
E-mail client software, 38
E-mail message, 33
E-mail servers, 37
E-mail system, 37
Executable file, 11
File, 11
File extension, 11
File name, 11
Floppy disk drive, 10
Handheld computer, 7

Hard disk drive, 10
Home page, 27
HTML, 25
HTML tags, 28
HTTP, 24
IMAP, 37
Information, 11
Input, 4
Instant messaging, 16
Internet, 14
Internet backbone, 14
Internet telephony, 16
ISDN, 18
ISP, 19
Keyword, 30
LAN, 8
LCD screen, 10
Links, 24
Macs, 13
Mailing list server, 16
Mainframe computer, 8
Memory, 5
Message header, 33
Microcomputer, 6
Microprocessor, 6
MIME, 34
Modem, 10
Monitor, 10
Mouse, 10
Netiquette, 36
Network card, 10
Newsgroups, 16
Notebook computer, 6
Operating system, 12
Output, 5
Password, 21
PCs, 13
PDA, 7
Peer-to-peer, 15
Peripheral device, 11

Personal computer, 6
Platform, 13
POP, 37
POP server, 38
Power-on self-test (POST), 40
Processing, 4
Query, 30
Safe Mode, 42
Satellite Internet service, 19
Search engine, 29
Search operator, 30
Server, 9
Smileys, 36
SMTP server, 39
Software, 4
Sound card, 10
Spam, 37
Spam filter, 37
Storage, 5
Store-and-forward technology, 37
Stored program, 5
Supercomputer, 8
System software, 12
System unit, 10
Tablet computer, 7
TCP/IP, 14
Topic directory, 31
Uploading, 15
URL, 25
Usenet, 16
User ID, 21
Videogame console, 8
Voiceband modem, 17
Web, 24
Web pages, 24
Web servers, 25
Web site, 25
Web-based e-mail, 37
Workstation, 8

Interactive Situation Questions

Apply what you've learned to some typical computing situations. When using the NP9 BookOnCD or the NP9 Web site, you can type your answers, and then use the Check Answers button to automatically score your responses.

1. Suppose that you walk into an office and see the devices pictured to the right. You would probably assume that they are the screen and keyboard for a [_____] personal computer, [_____], or server.

2. You receive a CD from a friend. It contains a file called EverQuest.exe. Because of the .exe file extension, you assume that the disk contains a(n) [_____] file that is some type of computer program, rather than a data file.

3. You are a musician and you use your Gateway PC to compose music. Your friend, who has an iMac computer, wants you to try the software she uses. If she loans you her composition software, can you use it on your PC? Yes or no? [_____]

4. You are a computer technician hired by Ben and Jerry's Ice Cream to set up a Web site. You know that your site requires a unique [_____] that pinpoints its location on the Internet, and your server will have to use [_____], the standard Internet protocol that transports data between all sorts of computer platforms over the Internet.

5. You want the cheapest Internet connection. You don't mind if the connection is limited to speeds under 56 Kbps and doesn't provide very good video performance. You would probably select an ISP that provides a(n) [_____] connection.

6. You need to select a password for your online bank account. Which of the following passwords would be the LEAST secure: jeff683, hddtmrutc, gargantuan, brickcloset, fanhotshot, or high348? [_____]

7. You want to look at the latest Nike athletic shoes. The URL that will probably get you to Nike's home page is [_____].

8. You want to find some Web pages that contain information about snowboarding competitions. You know that your [_____] can only fetch and display Web pages, so you'll need to connect to a(n) [_____] and enter a query, such as "snowboard competition."

9. If your ISP does not supply you with an e-mail account, you can get a free [_____] e-mail account from a site such as Hotmail or Yahoo!.

10. You receive an e-mail message that contains colored text and underlining. You assume that the person who sent the message had his mail software set for [_____] format.

✷ CHECK ANSWERS

Interactive Practice Tests

Practice tests that consist of 10 multiple-choice, true/false, and fill-in-the-blank questions are available on both the NP9 BookOnCD and the NP9 Web site. The questions are selected at random from a large test bank, so each time you take a test, you'll receive a different set of questions. Your tests are scored immediately, and you can print study guides that help you find the correct answers for any questions that you missed.

56

CHAPTER 1

Projects

An NP9 Project is an open-ended activity that will help you apply the concepts you have learned. Many projects require resources in addition to your textbook, such as current magazines, library materials, or Web access. When you tackle a project, be prepared to use your critical thinking skills, logical analysis, and your creativity.

CRITICAL THINKING

Whether you're taking this course to fulfill a graduation requirement, to improve your career options, or just for fun, take a few minutes to evaluate what you expect to gain from this course. Look through the table of contents of this textbook and select the five sections that you think will be most interesting, and the five sections that seem to be the least relevant to you. Incorporate your thoughts in two or three paragraphs that you e-mail to your instructor.

GROUP PROJECT

Form a group with four or five other students. Each student in the group should ask at least five friends if they have 1) a computer, 2) a cell phone, 3) a portable music player, 4) dial-up Internet access, 5) high speed Internet access. Consolidate the data from all members of your group into an Excel spreadsheet, and then graph it. How do your statistics coincide with nationwide statistics for digital ownership? Graph or write a summary and make sure you site your sources for national statistics.

CYBER CLASSROOM

One of the simplest ways to collaborate on a project is to use e-mail. Most mail clients offer the option to format messages as HTML. With this option on, each recipient can add to the message using a different color text. For this project, your instructor should provide each student with the e-mail addresses of four or five other students who will form a team, and designate a team leader. The team leader should find a news story about a technology issue from a source such as *www.news.google.com* and send it to one of the other students on the team. That student should add his or her opinion and comments, then send the message to another student in the group. Each student should use a different font color and initial their comments. When the message has circulated to all team members, it should be sent to your instructor. Make sure every member of the team is using antivirus software because, as you learned in the chapter, hackers can take advantage of HTML scripts to introduce viruses to unprotected computers.

MULTIMEDIA PROJECT

Screenshots can be useful tools for learning, documentation, and troubleshooting. Any time you need to show someone what's displayed on your computer screen, you can press the Print Screen (PrtScr) key, which stores a copy of the screen into memory. From there, you can paste the screenshot into a document you're creating with a word processor. You can also paste it into a graphics program, such as Microsoft Paint and then edit it. For this project, take a screenshot, and paste it into a Word document. Under the screenshot, enter a description of the software and the purpose of the screen you captured.

RESUME BUILDER

Several Web sites offer career aptitude assessments that claim to help you select a career that's suited to your personality and background. Use a search engine to locate three free Web-based career aptitude tests. Take the tests. If you are asked to sign up, make sure you exercise caution in the amount of personal information you divulge. After completing the tests, compare the results. Do they all point you in a similar career direction? What is your reaction to the results? Which test do you think was the most valid and why? Provide your instructor with your analysis, along with the URLs for the Web sites that provided the tests.

GLOBALIZATION

Although the Internet provides a global communications network, communication between people still depends of finding a common language. For this project, explore the Web and experiment with ways in which technology is being used to close the language gap. You might start at Google or Wikipedia and look at the selection of languages they offer. Chronicle your exploration, making sure to document the Web sites you visited. What are your conclusions about Internet use by non-English speakers?

ISSUE

The Issue section of this chapter focused on how much—or how little—privacy you can expect when using an e-mail account. For this project, you will write a two- to five-page paper about e-mail privacy based on information you gather from the Internet. To begin this project, consult the E-mail Privacy InfoWeb (see page 45) and link to the recommended Web pages to get an in-depth overview of the issue. Next, determine the viewpoint you will present in your paper. You might, for example, decide to present the viewpoint of a student who believes that e-mail should be afforded the same privacy rights as a sealed letter. Or you might present the viewpoint of an employer who wants to explain why your company believes it is necessary to monitor employee e-mail. Whatever viewpoint you decide to present, make sure you can back it up with facts and references to authoritative articles and Web pages. You can place citations to these pages (including the author's name, article title, date of publication, and URL) at the end of your paper as endnotes, on each page as footnotes, or along with the appropriate paragraphs using parentheses. Follow your professor's instructions for submitting your paper by e-mail or as a printed document.

COMPUTERS IN CONTEXT

The Computers in Context section highlighted new technologies used in the marketing industry. Think of a product that you recently bought. Now, suppose you work for the company that produces the product and you've been assigned to create a marketing campaign. Create a table in which the first column contains a short description of every way you can think of to market the product. In the second column of the table, indicate the main technology used to communicate the marketing message. In column 3, indicate which of the methods would be considered direct marketing. In column 4 rank the marketing methods from most expensive (10) to least expensive (1). (You can use the Web to get estimated costs for various types of advertising.) Finally, in column 5 rank the marketing methods from most effective (10) to least effective (1). Submit your table following your instructor's guidelines for format and style.

Study Tips

Study Tips help you to organize and consolidate the information in a unit by making lists, outlines, charts, and sketches. You can use paper and pencil or word processing software to complete most of the Study Tip activities.

1. Make sure you can use your own words to correctly answer each of the orange focus questions that appear throughout the chapter.

2. Use a diagram to explain how a computer makes use of input, processing, storage, memory, output, and the stored program concept.

3. List, briefly describe, and rank (in terms of computing capacity) the characteristics of each computer category described in Section A of this chapter.

4. Diagram, label, and describe each of the components of a basic personal computer system.

5. Describe the difference between a data file and an executable file.

6. Describe the difference between an operating system and application software.

7. Discuss what makes two computer platforms compatible or incompatible.

8. Briefly describe how the Internet works and the significance of TCP/IP.

9. List at least five resources provided by the Internet, and identify those that are most popular.

10. Make a list of the Internet connection technologies presented in this chapter, and specify typical data transport speeds for each.

11. Describe how to select a password that is secure, yet easy to remember. Create five secure passwords and five passwords that might be easy to crack.

12. Make sure you can explain the difference between HTML, HTTP, and hypertext.

13. Make a list of rules you should follow when typing a URL.

14. Describe the difference between a browser and a search engine.

15. Explain the role of MIME as it relates to e-mail attachments.

16. Describe how e-mail is stored and transmitted by POP and SMTP servers.

17. Explain the differences between POP and Web-based e-mail.

18. Define SPAM and list five steps you can take to avoid it.

19. TechTalk: Create a storyboard showing what happens during the boot process.

20. Fill in the blanks on the concept map shown below to show the hierarchy of computer categories described in this chapter:

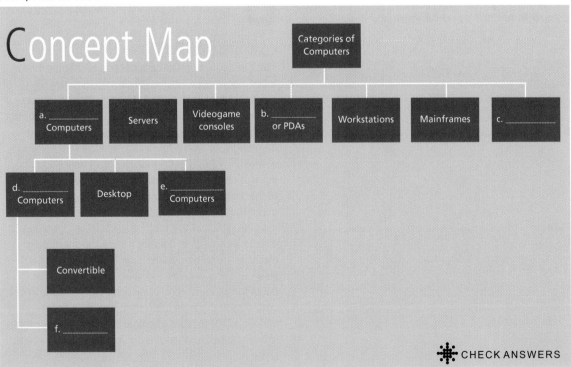

Concept Map

CHECK ANSWERS

Review on the Web

TECHTV VIDEO PROJECT

The TechTV segment *Predicting Big Surf* highlights one of many unique ways to use the Web. After watching this video, write a short description of it. Then, browse around the Web to look for other unique applications. Write a short description of at least three applications you found and then explain whether in your opinion they offer good, solid services or are simply gimmicks.

To work with the Video Projects for this chapter, connect to the New Perspectives NP9 Web site.

www.course.com/np/concepts9/ch01

ONLINE GAMES

Test your comprehension of the concepts introduced in Chapter 1 by playing the NP9 Online Games. At the end of each game, you have three options:

- Submit your results to your instructor using the Universal Gradebook through CoursePort
- Print your results to be submitted to your instructor
- Print a comprehensive study guide complete with page references

To work with the Online Games for this chapter, connect to the New Perspectives NP9 Web site.

www.course.com/np/concepts9/ch01

 LIGHTNING   DON'T TELL ME   FAKE OUT

ONLINE END-OF-CHAPTER ACTIVITIES

The following NP9 Review Activities are also available at the New Perspectives NP9 Web site:

- Interactive Summary
- Interactive Situation Questions
- Interactive Practice Tests
- Concept Map

If you are using the Web site to complete these activities, you can automatically score your answers and share the results with your instructor.

www.course.com/np/concepts9/ch01

2

Computer Hardware

TIP

When using the BookOnCD, the ✻ icons are "clickable" to access resources on the CD. The ✚ icons are clickable to access resources on the Web. You can also access Web resources by using your browser to connect directly to the New Perspectives NP9 Web site at: www.course.com/np/concepts9/ch02

WHETHER YOU ARE SHOPPING FOR A NEW COMPUTER, USING YOUR TRUSTY

laptop, or troubleshooting a system glitch, it is useful to have some background about computer system components and how they work. Chapter 2 begins with the basics of digital gizmos such as chips and system boards. You'll learn how to decipher all the jargon in computer ads, find out why computers offer so many storage options, and discover how to connect accessories to your computer. The chapter concludes with an Issue about recycling and a look at digital warriors.

TAKE A PRE-ASSESSMENT QUIZ

to find out how much you know about bits and bytes, RAM and ROM, processors and storage, printers and monitors. Armed with your results, you can focus your study time to round out your knowledge and improve your test scores.

www.course.com/np/concepts9/ch02

LISTEN TO A CHAPTER OVERVIEW

Get your book and highlighter ready, then connect to the New Perspectives NP9 Web site, where you can listen to an overview that points out the most important concepts for this chapter.

www.course.com/np/concepts9/ch02

BEFORE YOU READ ON, TRY IT

HOW POWERFUL IS MY COMPUTER?

As you read Chapter 2, you'll learn that some computers are more powerful than others because they can store more data and process data faster. To find out how your home, work, or lab computer stacks up, you'll need to know a few of its specifications. Before you begin to read this chapter, check your computer's specifications by doing the following:

1. Start your computer.

2. Click the Start button, then click Control Panel.

3. Double-click the System icon or list item to open the System Properties dialog box.

4. Make sure the General tab is displayed.

5. Record the information about your computer similar to the information provided for the sample computer in the table.

6. Then, just to get an idea of the other equipment you've got attached to your computer, click the Hardware tab near the top of the System Properties dialog box and click the large Device Manager button.

7. Browse through the list. When you're done, close the Device Manager and System Properties dialog boxes by clicking the ☒ buttons.

	Sample Computer	Your Computer
Computer Manufacturer	Dell	
Computer Model	Inspiron 9100	
Processor Manufacturer	Intel	
Processor Type	Pentium 4	
Processor speed	3.2 GHz	
Number of processors	1	
RAM capacity	1 GB	

Data Representation and Digital Electronics

Understanding what makes a computer "tick" can come in handy in today's information age. This information helps you decipher computer ads, troubleshoot equipment problems, and make software work. Although scientists are tinkering with exotic technologies such as quantum computers and molecular computers, just about every computer today is an electronic, digital device based on a concept that's as simple as a basic light switch.

DATA REPRESENTATION

What is data representation? People use computers to work with many kinds of data, including numbers, text, music, photos, and videos. **Data representation** is the process of transforming this diverse data into a form that computers can use for processing. Today, computers typically represent data digitally.

How do computers represent data digitally? Most computers are digital devices. A **digital device** works with discrete—distinct and separate—data, such as the digits 1 and 0. In contrast, an **analog device** works with continuous data. As an analogy, a traditional light switch has two discrete states—on and off—so it is a digital device. A dimmer switch, on the other hand, has a rotating dial that controls a continuous range of brightness. It is, therefore, an analog device (Figure 2-1).

Most computers use the simplest type of digital technology—their circuits have only two possible states. For convenience, let's say that one of those states is "on" and the other state is "off." When discussing these states, we usually indicate the "on" state with 1 and the "off" state with 0. So the sequence "on" "on" "off" "off" would be written 1100. These 1s and 0s are referred to as **binary digits**. It is from this term that we get the word "bit"—*bi*nary dig*it*. Computers use sequences of bits to digitally represent numbers, letters, punctuation marks, music, pictures, and videos.

How does a computer represent numbers? **Numeric data** consists of numbers that might be used in arithmetic operations. For example, your annual income is numeric data, as is your age. The price of a bicycle is numeric data. So is the average gas mileage for a vehicle, such as a car or SUV. Computers represent numeric data using the binary number system, also called "base 2."

The **binary number system** has only two digits: 0 and 1. No numeral like "2" exists in this system, so the number "two" is represented in binary as "10" (pronounced "one zero"). You'll recognize the similarity to what happens when you're counting from 1 to 10 in the familiar decimal system. After you reach 9, you run out of digits. For "ten," you have to use "10"—zero is a placeholder and the "1" indicates "one group of tens."

In binary, you just run out of digits sooner—right after you count to 1. To get to the next number, you have to use the zero as a placeholder and the "1" indicates "one group of 2s." In binary then, you count 0 ("zero"), 1 ("one"), 10 ("one zero"), instead of counting 0, 1, 2 in decimal. If you need to brush up on binary numbers, refer to Figure 2-2 on the next page and to the lab at the end of the chapter.

FIGURE 2-1

A computer is a digital device, more like a standard light switch than a dimmer switch.

Decimal (Base 10)	Binary (Base 2)
0	0
1	1
2	10
3	11
4	100
5	101
6	110
7	111
8	1000
9	1001
10	1010
11	1011
1000	1111101000

FIGURE 2-2

The decimal system uses ten symbols to represent numbers: 0, 1, 2, 3, 4, 5, 6, 7, 8, and 9. The binary number system uses only two symbols: 0 and 1.

The important point to understand is that the binary number system allows computers to represent virtually any number simply by using 0s and 1s, which conveniently translate into electrical "on" and "off" signals. The average gas mileage for an SUV (19) is 10011 in binary, and can be represented by "on" "off" "off" "on" "on."

How can a computer represent words and letters using bits? **Character data** is composed of letters, symbols, and numerals that are not used in arithmetic operations. Examples of character data include your name, address, and hair color. Just as Morse code uses dashes and dots to represent the letters of the alphabet, a digital computer uses a series of bits to represent letters, characters, and numerals. Figure 2-3 illustrates how a computer can use 0s and 1s to represent the letters and symbols in the text "HI!"

FIGURE 2-3

A computer treats the letters and symbols in the word "HI!" as character data, which can be represented by a string of 0s and 1s.

01001000   01001001   00100001

Computers employ several types of codes to represent character data, including ASCII, EBCDIC, and Unicode. **ASCII** (American Standard Code for Information Interchange, pronounced "ASK ee") requires only seven bits for each character. For example, the ASCII code for an uppercase "A" is 1000001. ASCII provides codes for 128 characters, including uppercase letters, lowercase letters, punctuation symbols, and numerals.

A superset of ASCII, called **Extended ASCII**, uses eight bits to represent each character. For example, Extended ASCII represents the uppercase letter "A" as 01000001. Using eight bits instead of seven bits allows Extended ASCII to provide codes for 256 characters. The additional Extended ASCII characters include boxes, circles, and other graphical symbols. An alternative to the 8-bit Extended ASCII code, called **EBCDIC** (Extended Binary-Coded Decimal Interchange Code, pronounced "EB seh dick"), is usually used only by older, IBM mainframe computers.

Unicode (pronounced "YOU ni code") uses sixteen bits and provides codes for 65,000 characters—a real bonus for representing the alphabets of multiple languages. For example, Unicode represents an uppercase "A" in the Russian Cyrillic alphabet as 0000010000010000.

Why do ASCII and Extended ASCII provide codes for 0, 1, 2, 3, 4, 5, 6, 7, 8, and 9? The table in Figure 2-4 illustrates the variety of letters and symbols represented by Extended ASCII. You might wonder why the table contains codes for 0, 1, 2, 3, and so on. Aren't these numbers represented by the binary number system? A computer uses Extended ASCII character codes for 0, 1, 2, 3 to represent numerals that are not used for calculations. For example, you don't typically use your Social Security "number" in calculations, so it is considered character data and represented using Extended ASCII. Likewise, the "numbers" in your street address can be represented by character codes rather than binary numbers.

FIGURE 2-4

The Extended ASCII code uses eight 1s and 0s to represent letters, symbols, and numerals. The first 32 ASCII characters are not shown in the table because they represent special control sequences that cannot be printed. The two "blank" entries are space characters.

(space)	00100000	>	00111110	\	01011100	z	01111010	ÿ	10011000	╢	10110110	╘	11010100	≥	11110010
!	00100001	?	00111111	]	01011101	{	01111011	Ö	10011001	╖	10110111	╒	11010101	≤	11110011
"	00100010	@	01000000	^	01011110	|	01111100	Ü	10011010	╕	10111000	╓	11010110	⌠	11110100
#	00100011	A	01000001	_	01011111	}	01111101	¢	10011011	╣	10111001	╫	11010111	⌡	11110101
$	00100100	B	01000010	`	01100000	~	01111110	£	10011100	║	10111010	╪	11011000	÷	11110110
%	00100101	C	01000011	a	01100001	⌂	01111111	¥	10011101	╗	10111011	┘	11011001	≈	11110111
&	00100110	D	01000100	b	01100010	Ç	10000000	₧	10011110	╝	10111100	┌	11011010	°	11111000
'	00100111	E	01000101	c	01100011	ü	10000001	ƒ	10011111	╜	10111101	█	11011011	·	11111001
(	00101000	F	01000110	d	01100100	é	10000010	á	10100000	╛	10111110	▄	11011100	·	11111010
)	00101001	G	01000111	e	01100101	â	10000011	í	10100001	┐	10111111	▌	11011101	√	11111011
*	00101010	H	01001000	f	01100110	ä	10000100	ó	10100010	└	11000000	▐	11011110	ⁿ	11111100
+	00101011	I	01001001	g	01100111	à	10000101	ú	10100011	┴	11000001	▀	11011111	²	11111101
,	00101100	J	01001010	h	01101000	å	10000110	ñ	10100100	┬	11000010	α	11100000	■	11111110
-	00101101	K	01001011	i	01101001	ç	10000111	Ñ	10100101	├	11000011	ß	11100001	(space)	11111111
.	00101110	L	01001100	j	01101010	ê	10001000	ª	10100110	─	11000100	Γ	11100010		
/	00101111	M	01001101	k	01101011	ë	10001001	º	10100111	┼	11000101	π	11100011		
0	00110000	N	01001110	l	01101100	è	10001010	¿	10101000	╞	11000110	Σ	11100100		
1	00110001	O	01001111	m	01101101	ï	10001011	⌐	10101001	╟	11000111	σ	11100101		
2	00110010	P	01010000	n	01101110	î	10001100	¬	10101010	╚	11001000	µ	11100110		
3	00110011	Q	01010001	o	01101111	ì	10001101	½	10101011	╔	11001001	τ	11100111		
4	00110100	R	01010010	p	01110000	Ä	10001110	¼	10101100	╩	11001010	Φ	11101000		
5	00110101	S	01010011	q	01110001	Å	10001111	¡	10101101	╦	11001011	Θ	11101001		
6	00110110	T	01010100	r	01110010	É	10010000	«	10101110	╠	11001100	Ω	11101010		
7	00110111	U	01010101	s	01110011	æ	10010001	»	10101111	═	11001101	δ	11101011		
8	00111000	V	01010110	t	01110100	Æ	10010010	░	10110000	╬	11001110	∞	11101100		
9	00111001	W	01010111	u	01110101	ô	10010011	▒	10110001	╧	11001111	φ	11101101		
:	00111010	X	01011000	v	01110110	ö	10010100	▓	10110010	╨	11010000	ε	11101110		
;	00111011	Y	01011001	w	01110111	ò	10010101	│	10110011	╤	11010001	∩	11101111		
<	00111100	Z	01011010	x	01111000	û	10010110	┤	10110100	╥	11010010	≡	11110000		
=	00111101	[	01011011	y	01111001	ù	10010111	╡	10110101	╙	11010011	±	11110001		

How does a computer convert music and pictures into codes? Music and pictures are not small, discrete objects like numbers or the letters of the alphabet. To work with music and pictures, they must be digitized. The term **digitize** means to convert raw, analog data into digital format represented by 0s and 1s.

A photograph or drawing can be digitized by treating it as a series of colored dots. Each dot is assigned a binary number according to its color. For example, a green dot might be represented by 0010 and a red dot by 1100, as shown in Figure 2-5. A digital image is simply a list of color numbers for all the dots it contains. In a similar way, music can be digitized by assigning binary codes to notes.

FIGURE 2-5

An image can be digitized by assigning a binary number to each dot.

A red dot might be digitized as 1100.

When a computer works with a series of 1s and 0s, how does it know which code to use? All the "stuff" that your computer works with is stored in files as a long—make that really long—series of 1s and 0s. Your computer needs to know whether to interpret those 1s and 0s as ASCII code, binary numbers, or the code for a picture or sound. Imagine the mess if your computer thought that your term paper, stored as ASCII, was an accounting file that contained a series of numbers stored in binary format. It would never be able to reconstruct the words and sentences of your term paper.

To avoid confusion, most computer files contain a **file header** with information about the code used to represent the file data. A file header is stored along with the file and can be read by the computer, but never appears on the screen. By reading the header information, a computer can tell how a file's contents were coded.

QUANTIFYING BITS AND BYTES

How can I tell the difference between bits and bytes? Computer ads include lots of abbreviations relating to bits and bytes. A few key concepts can help you understand what these abbreviations mean. Even though the word "bit" is an abbreviation for "binary digit," it can be further abbreviated, usually as a lowercase "b." A byte, on the other hand, is composed of eight bits and usually abbreviated as an uppercase "B."

Transmission speeds are typically expressed in bits, whereas storage space is typically expressed in bytes. In Chapter 1, for example, you learned that the speed of most voice band modems is 56 Kbps—56 kilobits per second. In a computer ad, you might see the capacity of a hard disk drive described as 40 GB—40 gigabytes.

What do the prefixes kilo-, mega-, and giga- mean? When working with computers, you'll frequently encounter references such as "50 kilobits per second," "1.44 megabytes," and "2.8 gigahertz." Kilo, mega, giga, and similar terms are used to quantify computer data.

In common usage, "kilo," abbreviated as "K," means a thousand. For example, $50 K means $50,000. In the decimal number system we use on a daily basis, the number 1,000 is 10 to the 3rd power, or 10^3. In the world of computers where base 2 is the norm, a "kilo" is precisely 1,024, or 2^{10}. A **kilobit** (abbreviated Kb or Kbit) is 1,024 bits. A **kilobyte** (abbreviated KB or Kbyte) is 1,024 bytes. Kilobytes are often used when referring to the size of small computer files.

The prefix "mega" means a million, or in the context of bits and bytes, precisely 1,048,576 (the equivalent of 2^{20}). A **megabit** (Mb or Mbit) is 1,048,576 bits. A **megabyte** (MB or MByte) is 1,048,576 bytes. Megabytes are often used when referring to the size of medium to large computer files or to floppy disk capacity.

In computer lingo, the prefix "giga" refers to a billion, or precisely 1,073,741,824. As you might expect, a **gigabit** (Gb or Gbit) is approximately one billion bits. A **gigabyte** (GB or GByte) is one billion bytes. Gigabytes are typically used to refer to RAM and hard disk capacity.

Computers—especially mainframes and supercomputers—sometimes work with huge amounts of data, and so terms such as tera- (trillion), peta- (thousand trillion), and exa- (quintillion) are also handy. Figure 2-6 summarizes the terms commonly used to quantify computer data.

FIGURE 2-6

Quantifying Digital Data

Bit	One binary digit
Byte	8 bits
Kilobit	1,024 or 2^{10} bits
Kilobyte	1,024 or 2^{10} bytes
Megabit	1,048,576 or 2^{20} bits
Megabyte	1,048,576 or 2^{20} bytes
Gigabit	2^{30} bits
Gigabyte	2^{30} bytes
Terabyte	2^{40} bytes
Petabyte	2^{50} bytes
Exabyte	2^{60} bytes

TERMINOLOGY NOTE

What's a kibibyte? Some computer scientists have proposed alternative terminology to dispel the ambiguity in terms such as "mega" that can mean 1,000 or 1,024. They suggest the following prefixes:

Kibi =1,024

Mebi = 1,048,576

Gibi = 1,073,741,824

DIGITAL ELECTRONICS

How does a computer store and transport all those bits? Because most computers are electronic devices, bits take the form of electrical pulses that can travel over circuits, in much the same way that electricity flows over a wire when you turn on a light switch. All the circuits, chips, and mechanical components that form a computer are designed to work with bits. Most of these essential components are housed within the computer's system unit.

What's inside the system unit? If it weren't for the miniaturization made possible by digital electronic technology, computers would be huge, and the inside of a computer's system unit would contain a complex jumble of wires and other electronic gizmos. Instead, today's computers contain relatively few parts. Desktop computers with large system units are designed so that owners can easily upgrade audio, visual, and storage components. Small desktop and notebook computers, on the other hand, usually provide access for expansion and replacement from outside of the case. In Figure 2-7, you can see what's inside a typical desktop computer system unit.

FIGURE 2-7

A computer's system unit typically contains circuit boards, storage devices, and a power supply that converts current from an AC wall outlet into the DC current used by computer circuitry.

Power supply and fan

CD drive

Floppy disk drive

Hard disk drive

Microprocessor located under cooling fan

Cables that transfer data from storage devices to system board

Expansion cards

Main circuit board (system board)

FIGURE 2-8

A computer chip is classified by the number of miniaturized components it contains—from small-scale integration (SSI) of fewer than 100 components per chip to ultra large-scale integration (ULSI) of more than 1 million components per chip.

What's a computer chip? The terms "computer chip," "microchip," and "chip" originated as technical jargon for "integrated circuit." An **integrated circuit** (IC), such as the one pictured in Figure 2-8, is a super-thin slice of semiconducting material packed with microscopic circuit elements, such as wires, transistors, capacitors, logic gates, and resistors.

Semiconducting materials (or "semiconductors"), such as silicon and germanium, are substances with properties between those of a conductor (like copper) and an insulator (like wood). To fabricate a chip, the conductive properties of selective parts of the semiconducting material can be enhanced to essentially create miniature electronic pathways and components, such as transistors.

The assortment of chips inside a computer includes the microprocessor, memory modules, and support circuitry. These chips are packaged in a protective carrier that also provides connectors to other computer components. Chip carriers vary in shape and size—including small rectangular DIPs (dual in-line packages) with caterpillar-like legs protruding from a black, rectangular "body"; long, slim DIMMs (dual in-line memory modules); pincushion-like PGAs (pin-grid arrays); and cassette-like SEC cartridges (single edge contact cartridges). Terms like DIMM and PGA frequently appear in computer ads. Figure 2-9 helps you visualize these components.

INFOWEBLINKS

Find out how thousands of miles of wires and millions of components can be miniaturized to the size of a baby's fingernail by connecting to the **Integrated Circuits InfoWeb.**

www.course.com/np/concepts9/ch02

2

FIGURE 2-9

Integrated circuits can be used for microprocessors, memory, and support circuitry. They are housed within a ceramic carrier. These carriers exist in several configurations, or "chip packages," such as DIPs, DIMMs, PGAs, and SECs.

A DIP has two rows of pins that connect the IC circuitry to a circuit board.

A DIMM is a small circuit board containing several chips, typically used for memory.

A PGA is a square chip package with pins arranged in concentric squares, typically used for microprocessors.

An SEC cartridge houses a circuit board and microprocessor chip.

How do chips fit together to make a computer? The computer's main circuit board, called a **system board**, "motherboard," or "main board," houses all essential chips and provides connecting circuitry between them. If you look carefully at a system board, you'll see that some chips are permanently soldered in place. Other chips are plugged into special sockets and connectors that allow chips to be removed for repairs or upgrades. When multiple chips are required for a single function, such as generating stereo-quality sound, the chips might be gathered together on a separate small circuit board, which can then be plugged into a special slot-like connector. Figure 2-10 on the next page provides a handy guide that can help you identify the components on your computer's system board.

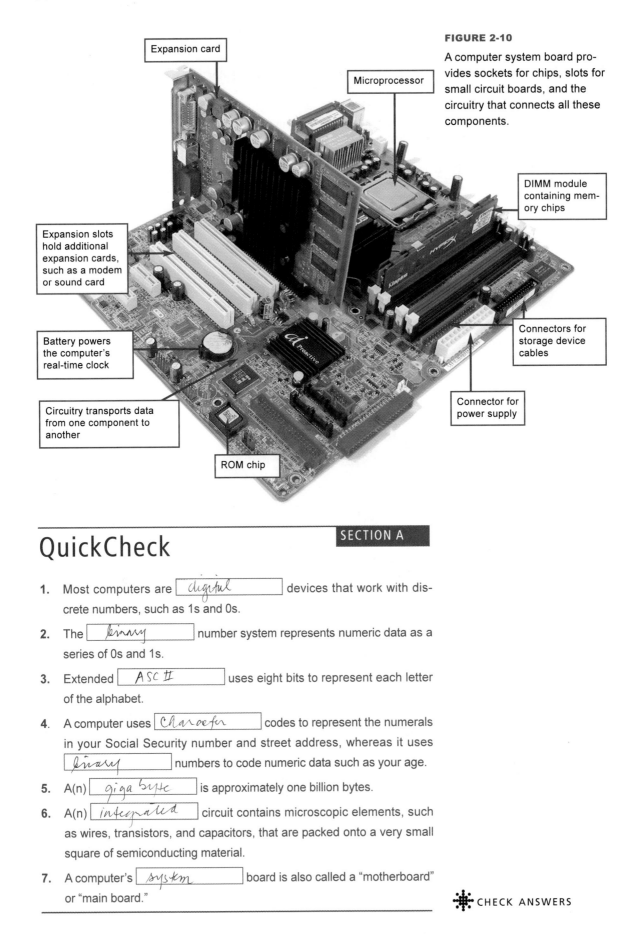

FIGURE 2-10

A computer system board provides sockets for chips, slots for small circuit boards, and the circuitry that connects all these components.

Expansion card

Microprocessor

DIMM module containing memory chips

Expansion slots hold additional expansion cards, such as a modem or sound card

Connectors for storage device cables

Battery powers the computer's real-time clock

Connector for power supply

Circuitry transports data from one component to another

ROM chip

QuickCheck

SECTION A

1. Most computers are ⟨digital⟩ devices that work with discrete numbers, such as 1s and 0s.

2. The ⟨binary⟩ number system represents numeric data as a series of 0s and 1s.

3. Extended ⟨ASCII⟩ uses eight bits to represent each letter of the alphabet.

4. A computer uses ⟨Character⟩ codes to represent the numerals in your Social Security number and street address, whereas it uses ⟨binary⟩ numbers to code numeric data such as your age.

5. A(n) ⟨gigabyte⟩ is approximately one billion bytes.

6. A(n) ⟨integrated⟩ circuit contains microscopic elements, such as wires, transistors, and capacitors, that are packed onto a very small square of semiconducting material.

7. A computer's ⟨system⟩ board is also called a "motherboard" or "main board."

✦ CHECK ANSWERS

2

Microprocessors and Memory

A typical computer ad contains a long list of specifications that describe a computer's components and capabilities. Savvy shoppers understand how these specifications affect computer performance and price. Most computer specifications begin with the microprocessor type and speed. Computer manufacturers want consumers to think that faster is better, but is there a point at which you can pay for speed you won't need? Computer ads also contain information about a computer's memory capacity. Lots of memory can add hundreds of dollars to the cost of a computer. Consumers are right to ask "How much RAM is enough?" Section B explains how microprocessors and memory work, and how they affect computer performance and price.

MICROPROCESSOR BASICS

What exactly is a microprocessor? A **microprocessor** (sometimes simply referred to as a "processor") is an integrated circuit designed to process instructions. It is the most important, and usually the most expensive, component of a computer. Although a microprocessor is sometimes mistakenly referred to as "a computer on a chip," it can be more accurately described as "a CPU on a chip" because it contains—on a single chip—circuitry that performs essentially the same tasks as the central processing unit (CPU) of a classic mainframe computer.

What does it look like? Looking inside a computer, you can usually identify the microprocessor because it is the largest chip on the system board, although it might be hidden under a cooling fan. Most of today's microprocessors are housed in a PGA (pin grid array) chip package, as shown in Figure 2-11.

How does a microprocessor work? Inside the chip carrier, a microprocessor is a very complex integrated circuit, containing as many as 400 million miniaturized electronic components. The miniaturized circuitry in a microprocessor is grouped into important functional areas, such as the ALU and the control unit.

The **ALU** (arithmetic logic unit) is the part of the microprocessor that performs arithmetic operations, such as addition and subtraction. It also performs logical operations, such as comparing two numbers to see if they are the same. The ALU uses **registers** to hold data that is being processed, just as you use a mixing bowl to hold the ingredients for a batch of cookies. The microprocessor's **control unit** fetches each instruction, just as you get each ingredient out of a cupboard or the refrigerator. The computer loads data into the ALU's registers, just as you add all the ingredients to the mixing bowl. Finally, the control unit gives the ALU the green light to begin processing, just as you flip the switch on your electric mixer to begin blending the cookie ingredients.

FIGURE 2-11

Today's microprocessors are typically housed in a PGA chip.

Figure 2-12 illustrates a microprocessor control unit and ALU preparing to add 2 + 3.

Where does the microprocessor get its instructions? The simple answer is that a microprocessor executes instructions provided by a computer program. However, a microprocessor can't follow just any instructions. A program that contains an instruction to "self destruct" won't have much effect because a microprocessor can perform only a limited list of instructions—"self destruct" isn't one of them.

The list of instructions that a microprocessor can perform is called its **instruction set**. These instructions are hard-wired into the processor's circuitry and include basic arithmetic and logical operations, fetching data, and clearing registers. A computer can perform very complex tasks, but it does so by performing a combination of simple tasks from its instruction set.

MICROPROCESSOR PERFORMANCE FACTORS

What makes one microprocessor perform better than another? Computer ads like the one in Figure 2-13 include microprocessor specifications related to its performance. A microprocessor's performance is affected by several factors, including clock speed, word size, cache size, instruction set, and processing techniques.

What do MHz and GHz have to do with computer performance? The speed specifications that you see in a computer ad indicate the speed of the **microprocessor clock**—a timing device that sets the pace for executing instructions. Most computer ads specify the speed of a microprocessor in megahertz or gigahertz. **Megahertz** (MHz) means a million cycles per second. **Gigahertz** (GHz) means a billion cycles per second.

A cycle is the smallest unit of time in a microprocessor's universe. Every action a processor performs is measured by these cycles. It is important, however, to understand that the clock speed is not equal to the number of instructions a processor can execute in one second. In many computers, some instructions occur within one cycle, but other instructions might require multiple cycles. Some processors can even execute several instructions in a single clock cycle.

A specification such as 3.2 GHz means that the microprocessor's clock operates at a speed of 3.2 billion cycles per second. All other things being equal, a computer with a 3.2 GHz processor is faster than a computer with a 1.5 GHz processor or a 933 MHz processor.

Some chipmakers differentiate chips by clock speed whereas other chipmakers use model numbers, called "processor numbers" (PN). Processor numbers do not correspond to a particular clock speed but they can indicate speed relative to other processors within the same family. For example, the Pentium 570 processor has a higher processor number and is faster than the Pentium 550. Processor numbers cannot be compared across product families, however. An Intel M processor 755 is not faster than the Pentium 4 560. Even though 755 is a larger number than 560, the M processor and Pentium 4 are in different processor families. Their processor numbers cannot be compared to each other.

FIGURE 2-12

The control unit fetches the ADD instruction, then loads data into the ALU's registers where it is processed.

Control Unit	
ADD	
ALU	
Register	2
Register	3

FIGURE 2-13

A typical computer ad provides specifications, like those high-lighted in yellow, for processor performance.

- **Intel Pentium EE 840 64-bit dual core processor 3.2 GHz with Hyper-Threading**
- **2 MB L2 cache**
- **2 GB 533 MHz SDRAM (max. 4 GB)**
- **160 GB SATA HD (7200 rpm)**
- **48X CD-RW + 16X DVD+RW/+R with double-layer write capable**
- **3.5" 1.44 MB floppy disk drive**
- **19" LCD TV/monitor**
- **256 MB NVidia AGP graphics card**
- **Sound Blaster PCI sound card**
- **Altec Lansing speakers**
- **U.S. Robotics 56 Kbps modem**
- **Mouse and keyboard**
- **External drive bays: 2 5.25" bays for disk, tape, or CD drives; 1 3.5" bay for a floppy drive**
- **Internal drive bays: 1 HDD bay**
- **8 USB ports: 2 front, 6 back**
- **2 serial, 1 parallel, and 1 video port**
- **1 network port (RJ45 connector)**
- **4 PCI slots and 1 AGP slot**
- **Windows Vista operating system**
- **Home/small business software bundle**
- **3-year limited warranty**

What impact does word size have on performance? Word size refers to the number of bits that a microprocessor can manipulate at one time. Word size is based on the size of registers in the ALU and the capacity of circuits that lead to those registers. A processor with a 32-bit word size, for example, has 32-bit registers, processes 32 bits at a time, and is referred to as a "32-bit processor." Processors with a larger word size can process more data during each processor cycle—a factor that leads to increased computer performance. Today's personal computers typically contain 32-bit or 64-bit processors.

How does the cache size affect performance? Cache (pronounced "cash") is sometimes called "RAM cache" or "cache memory." It is special high-speed memory that allows a microprocessor to access data more rapidly than from memory located elsewhere on the system board. A large cache can increase computer performance. Some computer ads specify cache type and capacity. A **Level 1 cache** (L1) is built into the processor chip, whereas a **Level 2 cache** (L2) is located on a separate chip and takes a little more time to get data to the processor. Cache capacity is usually measured in kilobytes.

How does the instruction set affect performance? As chip designers developed various instruction sets for microprocessors, they tended to add increasingly complex instructions, each requiring several clock cycles for execution. A microprocessor with such an instruction set uses **CISC** (complex instruction set computer) technology. A microprocessor with a limited set of simple instructions uses **RISC** (reduced instruction set computer) technology. A RISC processor performs most instructions faster than a CISC processor. It might, however, require more of these simple instructions to complete a task than a CISC processor requires for the same task. Most processors in today's personal computers use CISC technology.

A processor's ability to handle graphics can be enhanced by adding specialized graphics and multimedia instructions to a processor's instruction set. 3DNow!, MMX, and SSE-3 are examples of instruction set enhancements sometimes mentioned in computer ads. Although instruction set enhancements have the potential to speed up games, graphics software, and video editing, they work only with software designed to utilize these specialized instructions.

Can a microprocessor execute more than one instruction at a time? Some processors execute instructions "serially"—that is, one instruction at a time. With **serial processing**, the processor must complete all steps in the instruction cycle before it begins to execute the next instruction. However, using a technology called **pipelining**, a processor can begin executing an instruction before it completes the previous instruction. Many of today's microprocessors also perform **parallel processing**, in which multiple instructions are executed at the same time. Pipelining and parallel processing enhance processor performance.

To get a clearer picture of serial, pipelining, and parallel processing technology (Figure 2-14), consider an analogy in which computer instructions are pizzas. Serial processing executes only one instruction at a time, just like a pizzeria with one oven that holds only one pizza. Pipelining is similar to a pizza conveyor belt. A pizza (instruction) starts moving along the conveyor belt into the oven, but before it reaches the end, another pizza starts moving along the belt. Parallel processing is similar to a pizzeria with many ovens. Just as these ovens can bake more than one pizza at a time, a parallel processor can execute more than one instruction at a time.

FIGURE 2-14

Microprocessor designers have developed techniques for serial processing, pipelining, and parallel processing.

In serial processing, one instruction is processed at a time.

In pipelining, an instruction can begin to be processed before the previous instruction's processing is complete.

In parallel processing, multiple instructions can be processed at the same time.

TERMINOLOGY NOTE

The term Hyper-Threading, which appears in many computer ads, refers to a technology that enables processors to execute multiple instructions in parallel.

What's a dual core processor? As an alternative to using more than one processor, some computers have a single chip containing the circuitry for two microprocessors. A **dual core processor** is faster than one with a single core. To gain maximum speed, however, your computer's operating system and software should be optimized for dual core processing. Windows supports it, as do some games and graphics software.

With so many factors to consider, how can I compare microprocessor performance? Various testing laboratories run a series of tests to gauge the overall speed of a microprocessor. The results of these tests—called **benchmarks**—can then be compared to the results for other microprocessors. The results of benchmark tests are usually available on the Web and published in computer magazine articles.

TODAY'S MICROPROCESSORS

Which companies produce most of today's popular microprocessors? Intel is the world's largest chipmaker and supplies a sizeable percentage of the microprocessors that power PCs. In 1971, Intel introduced the world's first microprocessor—the 4004. Intel's 8088 processor powered the original IBM PC. Intel introduced the Pentium microprocessor in 1993, and then unveiled the Pentium II in 1997, the Pentium III in 1999, the Pentium 4 in 2000, the Itanium in 2001, and the Itanium2 in 2002. Intel's "budget" Celeron processors are not quite as powerful as the Pentiums, but they do a fine job of running software, and might mean a savings of $100 to $300 on the price of a computer.

AMD (Advanced Micro Devices) is Intel's chief rival in the PC chip market. AMD's Athlon and Opteron processors are direct competitors to Intel's Pentium and Itanium lines. AMD processors are less expensive than comparable Intel models and have a slight performance advantage according to some benchmarks.

Historically, Motorola and IBM were the main chip suppliers for Apple computers, but Apple began a transition to Intel chips in 2005. IBM produces RISC-based POWER processors for servers and other high-performance computers. Transmeta Corporation specializes in chips for mobile computing devices, such as tablet computers.

Which microprocessor is best for my PC? The microprocessor that's "best" for you depends on your budget and the type of work and play you plan to do. The microprocessors marketed with the current crop of computers can handle most business, educational, and entertainment applications (Figure 2-15). You'll want to consider the fastest processor offerings if you typically engage in processing-hungry activities, such as 3-D animated computer games, desktop publishing, multitrack sound recording, or video editing.

Can I replace my computer's microprocessor with a faster one? It is technically possible to upgrade your computer's microprocessor, but computer owners rarely do so. The price of the latest, greatest microprocessor can often get you more than halfway to buying an entirely new computer system. Technical factors also discourage microprocessor upgrades. A microprocessor operates at full efficiency only if all components in the computer can also handle the faster speeds. In many cases, installing a new processor in an old computer can be like attaching a huge outboard engine to a canoe. Safety issues aside, a canoe is not designed to handle all that power, so you can't expect it to go as fast as a high-performance speedboat.

FIGURE 2-15

Today's popular server, desktop, and mobile microprocessors.

Processor	Application
Itanium	Servers
Pentium D	Servers, desktops
Pentium 4	Servers, desktops
Pentium Extreme Edition	Desktops
Celeron	Desktops
Pentium M	Notebooks, PDAs
Mobile Pentium 4	Notebooks, PDAs

AMD▞

Processor	Application
Opteron	Servers
Athlon	Servers, Desktops
Semprom	Desktops
Mobile Athlon	Notebooks, PDAs
Mobile Semprom	Notebooks, PDAs

INFOWEBLINKS

For updates on popular microprocessors, you can connect to the **Microprocessor Update InfoWeb**.

www.course.com/np/concepts9/ch02

RANDOM ACCESS MEMORY

What is RAM? RAM (random access memory) is a temporary holding area for data, application program instructions, and the operating system. In a personal computer, RAM is usually several chips or small circuit boards that plug into the system board within the computer's system unit.

A computer's RAM capacity is invariably included in the list of specifications in a computer ad (Figure 2-16). The amount of RAM in a computer can affect the overall price of a computer system. To understand how much RAM your computer needs and to understand computer ad terminology, it is handy to have a little background on how RAM works and what it does.

Why is RAM so important? RAM is the "waiting room" for the computer's processor. It holds raw data waiting to be processed as well as the program instructions for processing that data. In addition, RAM holds the results of processing until they can be stored more permanently on disk or tape. Let's look at an example. When you use personal finance software to balance your checkbook, you enter raw data for check amounts, which is held in RAM. The personal finance software sends to RAM the instructions for processing this data. The processor uses these instructions to calculate your checkbook balance and sends the results back to RAM. From RAM, your checkbook balance can be stored on disk, displayed, or printed (Figure 2-17).

FIGURE 2-16

A computer ad typically specifies the amount and type of RAM.

2

- Intel Pentium EE 840 64-bit dual core processor 3.2 GHz with Hyper-Threading
- 2 MB L2 cache
- 1 GB 533 MHz SDRAM (max. 4 GB)
- 160 GB SATA HD (7600 rpm)
- 48 X CD-RW + 16 X DVD+RW/+R with double-layer write capable
- 3.5" 1.44 MB floppy disk drive

FIGURE 2-17

RAM is the computer equivalent of the waiting room at an airport or a train station. It holds data waiting to be processed, stored, displayed, or printed.

In addition to data and application software instructions, RAM also holds operating system instructions that control the basic functions of a computer system. These instructions are loaded into RAM every time you start your computer, and they remain there until you turn off your computer.

How does RAM differ from hard-disk storage? People who are new to computers sometimes tend to confuse RAM and hard-disk storage, maybe because both components hold data, because they typically are "hidden" inside the system unit, or because they can both be measured in gigabytes. To differentiate between RAM and hard-disk storage, remember that RAM holds data in circuitry that's directly connected to the system board, whereas hard-disk storage places data on magnetic media. RAM is temporary storage; hard-disk storage is more permanent. In addition, RAM usually has less storage capacity than hard-disk storage.

How does RAM work? In RAM, microscopic electronic parts called **capacitors** hold the bits that represent data. You can visualize the capacitors as microscopic lights that can be turned on or off. A charged capacitor is "turned on" and represents a "1" bit. A discharged capacitor is "turned off" and represents a "0" bit. Each bank of capacitors holds eight bits—one byte of data. A RAM address on each bank helps the computer locate data, as needed, for processing (Figure 2-18).

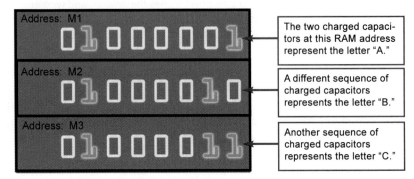

FIGURE 2-18

Each RAM location has an address and uses eight capacitors to hold the eight bits that represent a byte.

In some respects, RAM is similar to a chalkboard. You can use a chalkboard to write mathematical formulas, erase them, and then write an outline for a report. In a similar way, RAM can hold numbers and formulas when you balance your checkbook, and then can hold the outline of your English essay when you use word processing software. RAM contents can be changed just by changing the charge of the capacitors.

Unlike disk storage, most RAM is **volatile**, which means it requires electrical power to hold data. If the computer is turned off or the power goes out, all data stored in RAM instantly and permanently disappears. When someone exclaims, "Rats! I just lost my document," it often means the person was entering the text of a document (which was being held in RAM), and the power went out before the data was saved on disk.

FIGURE 2-19

Minimum RAM requirements are typically displayed on the package of a software product.

How much RAM does my computer need? RAM capacity is expressed in megabytes or gigabytes. Today's personal computers typically feature between 128 MB and 2 GB of RAM. The amount of RAM your computer needs depends on the software you use. RAM requirements are routinely specified on the outside of a software package (Figure 2-19). If you need more RAM, you can purchase and install additional memory up to the limit the computer manufacturer sets. For good basic performance, a computer running Windows software should have at least 256 MB of RAM. Games, desktop publishing, graphics, and video applications tend to run more smoothly with at least 512 MB of RAM.

System Requirements:

- Windows Vista/XP/2000/NT4 Pentium III with 64 MB of RAM

- Windows ME/98(SE)/98, Pentium III with 32 MB of RAM

- 40 MB hard drive space

- CD-ROM drive

- Mouse

- Internet connection (optional)

- Printer (optional)

- Scanner or digital camera with 32-bit twain interface (optional)

Can my computer run out of memory? Suppose that you want to work with several programs and large graphics at the same time. Will your computer eventually run out of memory? The answer is "probably not." Today's personal computer operating systems are quite adept at allocating RAM space to multiple programs. If a program exceeds its allocated space, the operating system uses an area of the hard disk, called **virtual memory**, to store parts of programs or data files until they are needed. By selectively exchanging the data in RAM with the data in virtual memory, your computer effectively gains almost unlimited memory capacity.

Too much dependence on virtual memory can slow down your computer's performance, however, because getting data from a mechanical device, such as a hard disk drive, is much slower than getting data from an electronic device, such as RAM. To minimize virtual memory use, load up your computer with as much RAM as possible.

Do all computers use the same type of RAM? No. RAM components vary in speed, technology, and configuration. Many computer ads provide information on all three aspects of RAM, but consumers who want lots of fast RAM for 3-D gaming and desktop publishing have to wade through a thicket of acronyms and technical jargon. To unlock the meaning of RAM specifications, such as "1 GB 533 MHz SDRAM," you need an understanding of a few more acronyms and abbreviations.

RAM speed is often expressed in nanoseconds or megahertz. One **nanosecond** (ns) is 1 billionth of a second. In the context of RAM speed, lower nanosecond ratings are better because it means the RAM circuitry can react faster to update the data it holds. For example, 8 ns RAM is faster than 10 ns RAM.

RAM speed can also be expressed in MHz (millions of cycles per second). Just the opposite of nanoseconds, higher MHz ratings mean faster speeds. For example, 533 MHz RAM is faster than 400 MHz RAM.

Most of today's personal computers use SDRAM or RDRAM. SDRAM (synchronous dynamic RAM) is fast and relatively inexpensive. Recent innovations, such as dual channel technology and double data rate (DDR) have increased SDRAM speed. RDRAM (rambus dynamic RAM) was first developed for the popular Nintendo 64 game system and then adapted for use in personal computers. RDRAM is more expensive than SDRAM and is usually found in high-performance workstations. RAM is configured as a series of DIPs soldered onto a small circuit board, as shown in Figure 2-20.

FIGURE 2-20

SDRAM is the most popular type of RAM in today's computers. It is typically available on a small circuit board called a DIMM (dual inline memory module). When adding memory to a computer, check with the computer manufacturer to make sure you purchase the correct RAM type and speed.

READ-ONLY MEMORY

How is ROM different from RAM? ROM (read-only memory) is a type of memory circuitry that holds the computer's startup routine. ROM is housed in a single integrated circuit—usually a fairly large, caterpillar-like DIP package—which is plugged into the system board.

Whereas RAM is temporary and volatile, ROM is permanent and non-volatile. ROM circuitry holds "hard-wired" instructions that are a permanent part of the circuitry and remain in place even when the computer power is turned off. This is a familiar concept to anyone who has used a hand calculator that includes various "hard-wired" routines for calculating square roots, cosines, and other functions. The instructions in ROM are permanent, and the only way to change them is to replace the ROM chip.

If a computer has RAM, why does it need ROM too? When you turn on your computer, the microprocessor receives electrical power and is ready to begin executing instructions. As a result of the power being off, however, RAM is empty and doesn't contain any instructions for the microprocessor to execute. Now ROM plays its part. ROM contains a small set of instructions called the **ROM BIOS** (basic input/output system). These instructions tell the computer how to access the hard disk, find the operating system, and load it into RAM. After the operating system is loaded, the computer can understand your input, display output, run software, and access your data.

CMOS MEMORY

Where does a computer store its basic hardware settings?

To operate correctly, a computer must have some basic information about storage, memory, and display configurations. For example, your computer needs to know how much memory is available so that it can allocate space for all the programs you want to run. RAM goes blank when the computer power is turned off, so configuration information cannot be stored there. ROM would not be a good place for this information, either, because it holds data on a permanent basis. If, for example, your computer stored the memory size in ROM, you could never add more memory—well, you might be able to add it, but you couldn't change the size specification in ROM. To store some basic system information, your computer needs a type of memory that's more permanent than RAM, but less permanent than ROM. CMOS is just the ticket.

CMOS memory (complementary metal oxide semiconductor memory), pronounced "SEE moss," is a type of chip that requires very little power to hold data. It can be powered by a small battery that's integrated into the system board and automatically recharges while your computer power is on. The battery trickles power to the CMOS chip so that it can retain vital data about your computer system configuration even when your computer is turned off.

When you change the configuration of your computer system—by adding RAM, for example—the data in CMOS must be updated. Some operating systems recognize such changes and automatically perform the update. You can manually change CMOS settings by running the CMOS setup program, as described in Figure 2-21.

```
                        PhoenixBIOS Setup Utility

   Main    Advanced    Power     Boot     Exit

     System Time:        [10:40:48]                        Item Specific Help
     System Date:        [03/03/2005]
     Language:           [English   (US) ]             <Tab>, <Shift-Tab>, or
                                                       <Enter> selects field.

     Legacy Diskette A:  [1.44 Mb  3.5"]
     Primary Master      [Maxtor  98916H8 - (PM) ]
     Primary Slave       [None]
     Secondary Master    [LG CD-RW CED-8080B- (SM) ]
     Secondary Slave     [LG  DVD-ROM DRD-8120B]


     Installed Memory    512 MB/233 MHz
     Memory Bank 0       512 MB SDRAM
     Memory Bank 1       Not Installed
     Core Version        4.06
     BIOS Revision       4.04  12/07/04

     CPU Type            AMD Athlon (tm)
     CPU Speed/FSB       2200 MHz/300 MHz
     Cache RAM           256 KB

   F1   Help     ↑↓ Select Item      -/+     Change Values    F5   Setup Defaults
   Esc  Exit     ←→ Select Menu      Enter   Select Submenu   F10  Save and Exit
```

FIGURE 2-21

CMOS holds computer configuration settings, such as the date and time, hard disk capacity, number of floppy disk drives, and RAM capacity. To access the CMOS setup program, hold down the F1 key as your computer boots. But be careful! If you make a mistake with these settings, your computer might not be able to start.

If you mistakenly enter the Setup program, follow the on-screen instructions to exit and proceed with the boot process. In Figure 2-21, the Esc (Escape) key allows you to exit the Setup program without making any changes to the CMOS settings.

What information about memory performance is most important? Even though ROM and CMOS have important roles in the operation of a computer, RAM capacity really makes a difference you can notice. The more data and programs that can fit into RAM, the less time your computer will spend moving data to and from virtual memory. With lots of RAM, you'll find that documents scroll faster, games respond more quickly, and many graphics operations take less time than with a computer that has a skimpy RAM capacity.

Most ads specify RAM capacity, speed, and type. Now when you see the specification "512 MB 400 MHz SDRAM (max. 2 GB)" in a computer ad, you'll know that the computer's RAM capacity is 512 megabytes (plenty to run most of today's software), that it operates at 400 megahertz (fairly fast), and that it uses SDRAM (a little slower and less expensive than RDRAM). You'll also have important information about the maximum amount of RAM that can be installed in the computer—2 GB, which is more than enough for the typical computer owner who does a bit of word processing, surfs the Web, and plays computer games.

BUYING A COMPUTER

How do I get the best computer for my money? Different buyers have different needs, so your first step in buying a computer is to assess your budget and think about how you plan to use your computer. Armed with an understanding of the terminology you learned in Sections A and B, you can begin to look at ads and visit online computer stores. The Computer Buyer's Guide InfoWeb is designed to help you get started. Sections C and D provide information about storage and add-on devices that you'll also find useful when shopping for a new computer.

INFOWEBLINKS

The **Computer Buyer's Guide InfoWeb** contains all kinds of tips about how to be a savvy computer shopper. Plus, you'll find worksheets to help assess your needs, compare different computers, and shop for fun accessories.

www.course.com/np/concepts9/ch02

2

QuickCheck   SECTION B

1. The ALU uses ⎡ *registers* ⎤ to hold data as the microprocessor performs arithmetic and logical operations.

2. The ⎡ *control* ⎤ unit in the CPU fetches instructions and coordinates the operation of the entire computer system.

3. Some chipmakers use a ⎡ *processor* ⎤ number, such as 560, to differentiate microprocessors.

4. Microprocessor ⎡ *instruction* ⎤ sets can be classified as CISC or RISC.

5. A microprocessor's ⎡ *clock* ⎤ speed is provided in a specification such as 3.6 GHz.

6. RAM is ⎡ *volatile* ⎤, which means that it cannot hold data when the computer power is off.

7. A computer does not usually run out of RAM because it can use an area of the hard disk called ⎡ *virtual* ⎤ memory.

8. The instructions for loading the operating system into RAM when a computer is first turned on are stored in ⎡ *CMOS* ⎤ memory.

CHECK ANSWERS

Storage Devices

Computer manufacturers typically try to entice consumers by configuring computers with a variety of storage devices, such as a floppy disk drive, hard disk drive, and some sort of CD or DVD drive. What's the point of having so many storage devices? As it turns out, none of today's storage technologies is perfect. One technology might provide fast access to data, but it might also be susceptible to problems that could potentially wipe out all your data. A different technology might be more dependable, but it might have the disadvantage of relatively slow access to data.

Smart shoppers make sure their new computers are equipped with a variety of storage devices. Informed computer owners understand the strengths and weaknesses of each storage technology so that they can use these devices with maximum effectiveness. In this section, you'll learn many secrets that can make you a smart storage technology buyer and owner. The storage technologies you'll learn about are now used in a variety of devices—from digital cameras to player pianos—so an understanding of storage technology can be useful outside the boundaries of personal computing.

STORAGE BASICS

What are the basic components of a data storage system?
A data storage system has two main components: a storage medium and a storage device. A **storage medium** (storage media is the plural) is the disk, tape, CD, DVD, paper, or other substance that contains data. A **storage device** is the mechanical apparatus that records and retrieves data from a storage medium. Storage devices include floppy disk drives, Zip drives, hard disk drives, tape drives, CD drives, and DVD drives. The term "storage technology" refers to a storage device and the media it uses.

How does a storage system interact with other computer components?
You can think of your computer's storage devices as having a direct pipeline to RAM. Data gets copied from a storage device into RAM, where it waits to be processed. After data is processed, it is held temporarily in RAM, but it is usually copied to a storage medium for more permanent safekeeping.

As you know, a computer works with data that has been coded into bits that can be represented by 1s and 0s. When data is stored, these 1s and 0s must be converted into some kind of signal or mark that's fairly permanent, but can be changed when necessary.

Obviously, the data is not literally written as "1" or "0." Instead, the 1s and 0s must be transformed into changes in the surface of a storage medium. Exactly how this transformation happens depends on the storage technology. For example, floppy disks store data in a different way than CD-ROMs. Three types of storage technologies are commonly used for personal computers: magnetic, optical, and solid state.

INFOWEBLINKS

For a table that compares the speeds, costs, and capacities of popular storage devices, and to get an update on the latest computer storage technologies, connect to the **Storage Frontiers InfoWeb**.

www.course.com/np/concepts9/ch02

TERMINOLOGY NOTE

The process of storing data is often referred to as "writing data" or "saving a file" because the storage device writes the data on the storage medium to save it for later use.

The process of retrieving data is often referred to as "reading data," "loading data," or "opening a file."

How does magnetic storage work? Hard disk, floppy disk, and tape storage technologies can be classified as **magnetic storage**, which stores data by magnetizing microscopic particles on the disk or tape surface. The particles retain their magnetic orientation until that orientation is changed, thereby making disks and tapes fairly permanent but modifiable storage media. A **read-write head** mechanism in the disk drive reads and writes the magnetized particles that represent data. Figure 2-22 shows how a computer stores data on magnetic media.

FIGURE 2-22

Before data is stored, particles on the surface of the disk are scattered in random patterns. The disk drive's read-write head magnetizes the particles, and orients them in a positive (north) or negative (south) direction to represent 0 and 1 bits.

2

Data stored magnetically can be easily changed or deleted simply by changing the magnetic orientation of the appropriate particles on the disk surface. This feature of magnetic storage provides lots of flexibility for editing data and reusing areas of a storage medium containing unneeded data.

Data stored on magnetic media such as floppy disks can be altered by magnetic fields, dust, mold, smoke particles, heat, and mechanical problems with a storage device. Placing a magnet on a floppy disk, for example, is a sure way of losing data.

Magnetic media gradually lose their magnetic charge, resulting in lost data. Some experts estimate that the reliable life span of data stored on magnetic media is about three years. They recommend that you refresh your data every two years by recopying it.

How does optical storage work? CD and DVD storage technologies can be classified as **optical storage**, which stores data as microscopic light and dark spots on the disk surface. The dark spots, shown in Figure 2-23, are called **pits**. The lighter, non-pitted surface areas of the disk are called **lands**.

Optical storage gets its name because data is read using a laser light, and it is possible to see the data using a high-powered microscope. The transition between pits and lands is interpreted as the 1s and 0s that represent data. An optical storage device uses a low-power laser light to read the data stored on an optical disk.

The surface of an optical disk is coated with clear plastic, making the disk quite durable and less susceptible to environmental damage than data recorded on magnetic media. An optical disk, such as a CD, is not susceptible to humidity, fingerprints, dust, magnets, or spilled soft drinks, and its useful life is estimated at more than 30 years.

FIGURE 2-23

As seen through an electron microscope, the pits on an optical storage disk look like small craters. Each pit is less than 1 micron (one millionth of a meter) in diameter—1,500 pits lined up side by side are about as wide as the head of a pin.

How does solid state storage work? A variety of compact storage cards can be classified as **solid state storage**, which stores data in a non-volatile, erasable, low-power chip. The chip's circuitry is arranged as a grid, and each cell in the grid contains two transistors that act as gates. When the gates are open, current can flow and the cell has a value that represents a "1" bit. When the gates are closed by a process called Fowler-Nordheim tunneling, the cell has a value that represents a "0" bit. Very little power is required to open or close the gates, which makes solid state storage ideal for battery-operated devices, such as digital cameras. Once the data is stored, it is non-volatile—the chip retains the data without the need for an external power source.

Some solid state storage requires a device called a **card reader** to transfer data to or from a computer (Figure 2-24). Other solid state storage plugs directly into a USB port on a computer's system unit.

Solid state storage provides faster access to data than magnetic or optical storage technology because it includes no moving parts. Solid state storage is very durable—it is virtually impervious to vibration, magnetic fields, or extreme temperature fluctuations. On the downside, the capacity of solid state storage does not currently match that of hard disks, or DVDs. The cost per megabyte of storage—about 16¢—is significantly higher than for magnetic or optical storage.

Can I add storage devices to my computer? Many storage devices—especially those for solid state storage media—simply plug into connectors built into your computer's system unit. You'll learn more about these connectors, including USB, in Section D.

As an alternative, you can install storage devices inside your computer's system unit case in "parking spaces" called **drive bays**. An external drive bay provides access from outside the system unit—a necessity for a storage device with removable media, such as floppy disks, CDs, tapes, and DVDs. Internal drive bays are located deep inside the system unit and are designed for hard disk drives, which don't use removable storage media (Figure 2-25).

FIGURE 2-24

Many solid state card readers have several slots for different types of solid state memory.

FIGURE 2-25

Most notebook computers provide bays for one floppy disk drive, one hard disk drive, and one CD or DVD drive.

An empty drive bay located on the side of a notebook computer

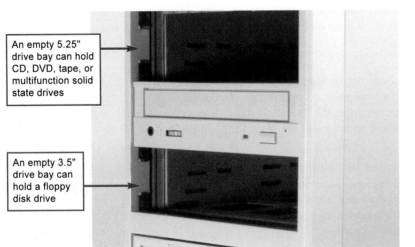

An empty 5.25" drive bay can hold CD, DVD, tape, or multifunction solid state drives

An empty 3.5" drive bay can hold a floppy disk drive

Most desktop computers have several drive bays, some accessible from outside the case, and others—designed for hard disk drives—without any external access. Empty drive bays are typically hidden from view with a face plate.

CLICK TO START

2

Which storage technology is best? Each storage technology has its advantages and disadvantages. If one storage system was perfect, we wouldn't need so many disk and tape drives connected to our computers! To compare storage devices, it is useful to apply the criteria of versatility, durability, speed, and capacity:

■ **Versatility.** Some storage devices can access data from only one type of medium. More versatile devices can access data from several different media. A floppy disk drive, for example, can access only floppy disks, whereas a DVD drive can access computer DVDs, DVD movies, audio CDs, computer CDs, and CD-Rs.

■ **Durability.** Most storage technologies are susceptible to damage from mishandling or other environmental factors, such as heat and moisture. Some technologies are more susceptible than others to damage that could cause data loss. Optical and solid state technologies tend to be more durable than magnetic technologies.

■ **Speed.** Quick access to data is important, so fast storage devices are preferred over slower devices. **Access time** is the average time it takes a computer to locate data on the storage medium and read it. Access time for a personal computer storage device, such as a disk drive, is measured in milliseconds (thousandths of a second). One millisecond (ms) is one-thousandth of a second. Lower numbers indicate faster access times. For example, a drive with a 6 ms access time is faster than a drive with an access time of 11 ms.

Access time is best for random-access devices. **Random access** (also called "direct access") is the ability of a device to "jump" directly to the requested data. Floppy disk, hard disk, CD, and DVD drives are random-access devices, as is solid state storage. A tape drive, on the other hand, must use slower **sequential access** by reading through the data from the beginning of the tape. The advantage of random access becomes clear when you consider how much faster and easier it is to locate a song on a CD (random access) than on a cassette tape (sequential access).

Data transfer rate is the amount of data a storage device can move per second from the storage medium to the computer. Higher numbers indicate faster transfer rates. For example, a CD-ROM drive with a 600 KBps (kilobytes per second) data transfer rate is faster than one with a 300 KBps transfer rate.

■ **Capacity.** In today's computing environment, higher capacity is almost always preferred. Storage capacity is the maximum amount of data that can be stored on a storage medium, and it is measured in kilobytes, megabytes, gigabytes, or terabytes.

FLOPPY DISK TECHNOLOGY

What is floppy disk technology? One of the oldest storage technologies, floppy disks are classified as magnetic storage because data is stored by magnetizing microscopic particles on the disk surface. A **floppy disk** is a round piece of flexible mylar plastic covered with a thin layer of magnetic oxide and sealed inside a protective casing. If you break open the disk casing (something you should never do unless you want to ruin the disk), you would see that the mylar disk inside is thin and literally floppy. Floppy disk technology is used for standard HD DS disks as well as Zip disks.

What is a standard HD DS disk? At one time, just about every personal computer included a floppy disk drive designed for high-density (HD) double-sided (DS) disks. These "standard" floppy disks (Figure 2-26) are still in use. They have a capacity of 1.44 MB—enough space for a 300-

FIGURE 2-26

A standard floppy disk drive reads and writes data on a 3.5" HD DS floppy disk.

page document or one medium-resolution photograph. Floppy disks are also referred to as "floppies" or "diskettes." It is not correct to call them "hard disks" even though they seem to have a "hard" or rigid plastic case. The term "hard disk" refers to an entirely different storage technology.

What are the advantages and disadvantages of HD DS floppy disks? When just about every computer had a floppy disk drive, files could be easily transferred from one computer to another using a floppy disk. Floppies are still used in some school computer labs so that students can transport their data to different lab machines or their personal computers. Today, however, many computers do not have a standard floppy disk drive. File transfers tend to take place using other technologies. Solid state storage media is smaller and more durable for mobile applications. Local computer networks and the Internet have made it easy to share data files without physically transporting them from one place to another.

A standard floppy disk's 1.44 MB capacity is not really sufficient for today's media-intensive applications. Many MP3 music files and photos are too large to fit on a floppy. In the past, floppy disks were extensively used to distribute software. CDs and DVDs offer more capacity for distributing the huge files for today's software applications. Web downloads offer more convenience for smaller files.

Can I protect the data on an HD DS floppy disk? An HD DS floppy disk features a **write-protect window** (Figure 2-27). When you open the window, the disk is "write-protected," which means that a computer cannot write data on the disk. Although it sounds like a useful feature, the write-protect window doesn't do much to protect your data from accidental erasures or changes. Typically when you use a disk, you want to save a new file or modify the data in an existing file. To do so, you must close the write-protect window and the disk is no longer protected. Therefore, when you use a disk and the chance of mistakenly deleting data is highest, you're not likely to have the write-protect feature on.

What is a Zip disk? A Zip disk is a special high-capacity floppy disk, available in 100 MB, 250 MB, and 750 MB versions. Zip disks and their drives, shown in Figure 2-28, are manufactured by Iomega. A Zip drive does not read standard HD DS floppy disks and Zip disks cannot be read by a standard floppy disk drive.

What are the advantages and disadvantages of Zip disks? Zip disks offer portability, simplicity, speed, and security. The storage capacity of Zip disks makes them more useful than standard HD DS floppy disks for storing large music and photo files. The process of reading and writing data is relatively fast and easy. Files on a Zip disk can even be password protected to ensure the security of important data.

Even the highest capacity Zip disks have far less capacity than DVDs or hard disks, however. They cannot substitute for a hard disk as primary storage, nor can they substitute for DVDs for video applications.

How can Zip disks store more data than a standard floppy disk? The amount of data that a disk stores depends on its density. **Disk density** refers to the closeness and size of the magnetic particles on the disk surface. The higher the disk density, the smaller the magnetic particles on the disk surface, and the more data it can store. Think of it this way: Just as you can put more lemons than grapefruit in a basket, you can store more data on a disk coated with smaller particles than one with larger particles. Zip disks store data at a higher density than a standard 3.5" floppy disk.

FIGURE 2-27

When the write-protect window is open, the disk drive cannot add, modify, or delete data from a disk.

FIGURE 2-28

A Zip disk requires a special disk drive, but is transportable and provides more storage capacity than a standard floppy disk.

HARD DISK TECHNOLOGY

Why are hard disk drives so popular? Hard disk technology is the preferred type of main storage for most computer systems for three reasons. First, it provides lots of storage capacity. Second, it provides fast access to files. Third, a hard disk is economical. Incredibly, a hard disk typically stores millions of times more data than a floppy disk, but a hard disk drive might cost only three times as much as a floppy disk drive.

How does a hard disk work? A hard disk is one or more platters and their associated read-write heads. A **hard disk platter** is a flat, rigid disk made of aluminum or glass and coated with magnetic iron oxide particles. Each platter has a read-write head that hovers over the surface to read data, as shown in Figure 2-29.

The drive spindle supports one or more hard disk platters. Both sides of the platter are used for data storage. More platters mean more data storage capacity. Hard disk platters rotate as a unit on the spindle to position read-write heads over specific data. The platters spin continuously, making thousands of rotations per minute.

Each data storage surface has its own read-write head, which moves in and out from the center of the disk to locate data. The head hovers only a few microinches above the disk surface, so the magnetic field is more compact than on a floppy disk. As a result, more data is packed into a smaller area on a hard disk platter.

FIGURE 2-29

Hard disk platters are sealed inside the drive case or cartridge to screen out dust and other contaminants. The sealed case contains disk platters and read-write heads.

CLICK TO START ⊹

Personal computer hard disk platters are typically 3.5" in diameter with storage capacities ranging from 40 to 200 GB. Miniature hard drives, such as the 1.8" drive featured on Apple's iPod digital music player, store 20 to 80 GB. The density of particles on the disk surface provide hard disks with capacities far greater than floppy disks. Also, the access time for a hard disk is significantly faster than for a floppy disk. Hard disk access times of 6 to 11 ms are not uncommon, whereas a floppy takes about half a second to spin up to speed and find data. Hard disk drive speed is sometimes measured in revolutions per minute (rpm). The faster a drive spins, the more rapidly it can position the read-write head over specific data. For example, a 7,200 rpm drive is able to access data faster than a 5,400 rpm drive.

Computer ads typically specify the capacity, access time, and speed of a hard disk drive. So "160 GB 8 ms 7200 RPM HD" means a hard disk drive with 160 gigabyte capacity, access time of 8 milliseconds, and speed of 7,200 revolutions per minute.

You might guess that a hard disk drive would fill one platter before storing data on a second platter. However, it is more efficient to store data at the same locations on all platters before moving the read-write heads to the next location. A vertical stack of storage locations is called a "cylinder"—the basic storage bin for a hard disk drive.

What's all this business about Ultra ATA, EIDE, SCSI, and DMA? Computer ads use these acronyms to describe hard disk drive technology. A hard drive mechanism includes a circuit board called a

TERMINOLOGY NOTE

You often see the terms "hard disk" and "hard disk drive" used interchangeably. You might also hear the term "fixed disk" used to refer to hard disks.

controller that positions the disk and read-write heads to locate data. Disk drives are classified according to their controllers. Popular types of drive controllers include SATA, Ultra ATA, EIDE, and SCSI. Although computer ads often specify the hard drive controller type, consumers don't really have much choice. If you want a 160 GB drive, for example, your hardware vendor is likely to offer only one brand of drive with one type of controller. Figure 2-30 shows a typical controller mounted on a hard disk drive.

FIGURE 2-30

A hard disk controller circuit board is typically mounted in the hard disk drive case.

The storage technology used on many PCs transfers data from a disk, through the controller, to the processor, and finally to RAM before it is actually processed. Computer ads sometimes specify this technology. For example, DMA (direct memory access) technology allows a computer to transfer data directly from a drive into RAM, without intervention from the processor. This architecture relieves the processor of data-transfer duties and frees up processing cycles for other tasks. UDMA (ultra DMA) is a faster version of DMA technology.

What's the downside of hard disk storage? Hard disks are not as durable as many other storage technologies. The read-write heads in a hard disk hover a microscopic distance above the disk surface. If a read-write head runs into a dust particle or some other contaminant on the disk, it might cause a **head crash**, which damages some of the data on the disk. To help prevent contaminants from contacting the platters and causing head crashes, a hard disk is sealed in its case. A head crash can also be triggered by jarring the hard disk while it is in use. Although hard disks have become considerably more rugged in recent years, you should still handle and transport them with care. You should also make sure that you make a backup copy of the data stored on your hard disk in case of a head crash.

Can I use a second hard disk drive to increase storage space? You can increase the storage capacity of your computer by adding a second hard disk drive. A second hard disk drive can also provide backup for your primary drive. Hard disk drives are available as internal or external units. Internal drives are inexpensive and can be easily installed in a desktop computer's system unit. External drives are slightly more expensive and connect to a desktop or notebook computer using a cable.

Removable hard disks or hard disk cartridges offer even more options. They contain platters and read-write heads that can be inserted and removed from the drive much like a floppy disk. Removable hard disks, such as Iomega's REV drive, provide security for data by allowing you to remove the hard disk cartridge and store it separately from the computer.

TAPE STORAGE

What's the purpose of a tape drive? As you have learned, a head crash can easily destroy hard disk data. Protecting the vast amount of data on the hard disk is of particular concern because it would be difficult and time-consuming to reconstruct. A **tape backup** is a copy of the data on a hard disk, which is stored on magnetic tape and used to restore lost data. Tape drive manufacturers produce several types of drives and each requires a specific type of tape. Figure 2-31 shows some of the most popular tape formats for personal computer tape drives.

FIGURE 2-31

A tape cartridge is a removable magnetic tape module similar to a cassette tape. Popular tape drives for personal computers use tape cartridges, but there are several specifications and cartridge sizes, including (from top to bottom) ADR (advanced digital recording), Ditto, Travan, and DDS (digital data storage). Check the tape drive manual to make sure you purchase the correct type of tape for your tape drive.

A tape backup device is relatively inexpensive and can simplify the task of reconstructing lost data. A backup tape can hold the entire contents of a hard disk. If the hard drive fails, that data can be copied from the tape to any functional hard disk.

Tape drives are primarily used on business computers. Unlike CDs and DVDs, a tape backup device is not suitable for everyday storage tasks. To find out why, you need to understand how a tape drive works.

How does a tape drive work? A tape is a sequential, rather than a random-access, storage medium. Essentially, data is arranged as a long sequence of bits that begins at one end of the tape and stretches to the other end. The beginning and end of each file are marked with special "header labels." To locate a file, the tape drive must start at one end of the tape and read through all the data until it finds the right header label. A tape can contain hundreds or—in the case of a mainframe—thousands of feet of tape. Access time is measured in seconds, not in milliseconds as for a hard disk drive.

Tape is simply too slow to be practical as a computer's main storage device. Its pokey nature doesn't, however, diminish its value or effectiveness as a backup device. A backup, simply streams lots of data onto a tape. A sequential device is just fine for this sort of work.

When backing up data, access time is less important than the time it takes to copy data from a hard disk to tape. Manufacturers do not always supply such performance specifications, but a consumer-level tape drive can back up 1 GB in 15-20 minutes. Chapter 4 provides information about the backup process and alternative equipment for backing up personal computer data.

CD AND DVD TECHNOLOGY

Is there a difference between CD and DVD technology?
Today, most computers come equipped with some type of optical drive—a
CD drive or a DVD drive. The underlying technology for CD and DVD
drives is similar, but storage capacities differ.

A computer CD drive is based on the same technology as an audio CD
player. A **CD** (compact disc) was originally designed to hold 74 minutes of
recorded music. This capacity provides 650 MB of storage space for computer data. Later improvements in CD standards increased the capacity to
80 minutes of music or 700 MB of data.

DVD (digital video disc or digital versatile disk) is a variation of CD technology that was originally designed as an alternative to VCRs, but was quickly
adopted by the computer industry to store data. A computer's DVD drive
can read disks that contain computer data as well as disks that contain
DVD movies.

Originally designed to provide enough storage capacity for a full-length
movie, a DVD holds much more data than a CD. The capacity of a DVD is
about 4.7 GB (4,700 MB), compared with 650-700 MB on a CD. A **double
layer DVD** has two recordable layers on the same side and can store 8.5
GB of data. HD-DVDs can store 15 GB; Blu-ray DVDs have 25 GB capacity.

How do CD and DVD drives work? CD and DVD drives contain a spindle that rotates the disk over a laser lens. The laser directs a beam of light
toward the underside of the disk. Dark "pits" and light "lands" on the disk
surface reflect the light differently. As the lens reads the disk, these differences are translated into the 0s and 1s that represent data (Figure 2-32).

Drive spindle spins disk

Laser lens directs a
beam of light to the
underside of the
CD-ROM disk

Laser pickup
assembly senses
the reflectivity of
pits and lands

Tracking mechanism positions a
disk track over the laser lens

FIGURE 2-32

CD and DVD drives use a laser
to read data from the underside
of a disk.

Optical drives use several technologies to write data on CD and DVD disks.
Recordable technology (R) uses a laser to change the color in a dye layer
sandwiched beneath the clear plastic disk surface. The laser creates dark
spots in the dye that are read as pits. The change in the dye is permanent,
so data cannot be changed once it has been recorded.

Rewritable technology (RW) uses "phase change" technology to alter a
crystal structure on the disk surface. Altering the crystal structure creates
patterns of light and dark spots similar to the pits and lands on a CD. The
crystal structure can be changed from light to dark and back again many
times, making it possible to record and modify data much like on a hard
disk.

The suffixes "R" and "RW" denote specific CD and DVD technologies. For
example, CD-R specifies "CD recordable" technology. CD-RW specifies
"CD rewritable" technology.

TERMINOLOGY NOTE

DVDs have two types of
recordable and two types of
rewritable formats. The
recordable formats are
designated as DVD-R and
DVD+R. The rewritable
formats are designated as
DVD-RW and DVD+RW.

What are my choices for CD and DVD media? Several CD and DVD formats are currently popular for use in personal computers:

■ **CD-DA** (compact disc digital audio), more commonly known as "audio CD," is the format for commercial music CDs. Music is typically recorded on audio CDs by the manufacturer, but can't be changed by the consumer.

■ **DVD-Video** (digital versatile disc video) is the format for commercial DVDs that contain feature-length films.

■ **CD-ROM** (compact disc read-only memory, pronounced "cee dee rom") was the original format for storing computer data. Data is stamped on the disk at the time it is manufactured. Data cannot be added, changed, or deleted from these disks.

■ **DVD-ROM** (digital versatile disk read-only memory) contains data stamped onto the disk surface at the time of manufacture. Like CD-ROMs, the data on these disks is permanent, so you cannot add or change data.

■ **CD-R** (compact disc recordable) disks store data using recordable technology. The data on a CD-R cannot be erased or modified once you record it. However, most CD-R drives allow you to record your data in multiple sessions. For example, you can store two files on a CD-R disk today, and add data for a few more files to the disk at a later time.

■ **DVD+R** or **DVD-R** (digital versatile disk recordable) disks store data using recordable technology similar to a CD-R, but with DVD storage capacity.

■ **CD-RW** (compact disc rewritable) disks store data using rewritable technology. Stored data can be recorded and erased multiple times, making it a very flexible storage option.

■ **DVD+RW** or **DVD-RW** (digital versatile disk rewritable) disks store data using rewritable technology similar to CD-RW, but with DVD storage capacity.

Can I use a single drive to work with any CD or DVD media? Most CD drives can read CD-ROM, CD-R, and CD-RW disks, but cannot read DVDs. Most DVD drives can read CD and DVD formats. Storing computer data and creating music CDs requires a recordable or rewritable device. As you can see from the table in Figure 2-33, the most versatile optical storage device is a DVD R/RW/CD-RW combo.

INFOWEBLINKS

For more information about current CD and DVD technology, plus tips on how to handle and clean your CDs, connect to the **CD & DVD InfoWeb**.

www.course.com/np/concepts9/ch02

TERMINOLOGY NOTE

Even though CD-ROM and ROM-BIOS both contain the word "ROM," they refer to quite different technologies. ROM BIOS refers to a chip on the system board that contains permanent instructions for the computer's boot sequence. A CD-ROM drive is an optical storage device that's usually installed in one of the system unit's drive bays.

FIGURE 2-33

CD and DVD Capabilities

	Play Audio CDs	Play DVD Movies	Read CD Data	Read DVD Data	Create Music CDs	Store Data on CDs	Store Data on DVDs
CD-ROM Drive	✔		✔				
CD-R Drive	✔		✔		✔	✔	
CD-RW Drive	✔		✔		✔	✔	
DVD/CD-RW Drive	✔	✔	✔	✔	✔	✔	
DVD R/RW/CD-RW Drive	✔	✔	✔	✔	✔	✔	✔

Are rewritable CD or DVD drives an acceptable replacement for a hard disk? A rewritable CD or DVD drive is a fine addition to a computer system, but is not a good replacement for a hard disk drive. Unfortunately, the process of accessing, saving, and modifying data on a rewritable disk is relatively slow compared to the speed of hard disk access.

The original CD drives could access 150 KB of data per second. The next generation of drives doubled the data transfer rate and were consequently dubbed "2X" drives. Transfer rates seem to be continually increasing. A 52X CD drive, for example, transfers data at 80 Mbps, which is still relatively slow compared to a hard disk drive's transfer rate of 2,560 Mbps.

The speed of a DVD drive is measured on a different scale than a CD drive. A 1X DVD drive is about the same speed as a 9X CD drive. Today's DVD drives typically have 16X speeds for a data transfer rate of 177.28 Mbps.

Is my computer DVD drive the same as the one connected to my TV? Not exactly. Even with the large storage capacity of a DVD, movie files are much too large to fit on a disk unless they are compressed, or shrunk, using a special type of data coding called MPEG-2. The DVD player you connect to your television includes MPEG decoding circuitry, which is not included on your computer's DVD drive. When you play DVD movies on your computer, it uses the CPU as an MPEG decoder. The necessary decoder software is included with Windows or can be located on the DVD itself.

SOLID STATE STORAGE

When would I use solid state storage? Solid state storage is portable, provides fast access to data, and uses very little power, so it is an ideal solution for storing data on mobile devices and transporting data from one device to another. It is widely used in portable consumer devices, such as digital cameras, MP3 music players, notebook computers, PDAs, and cell phones.

A solid state memory card in a digital camera can hold data for hundreds of snapshots. The card can be removed from the camera and inserted into a card reader that's connected to a computer. Once the data is downloaded, the photos can be edited using the computer's graphics software and transmitted through the computer's Internet connection.

Moving data in the other direction, a computer can download MP3 music files and store them on a solid state memory card. That card can be removed from the computer and inserted into a portable MP3 player, so you can hear your favorite tunes while you're on the go.

You can even use solid state storage as you would a floppy disk to transport data from one computer to another—say from your home computer to a computer in your school lab or your workplace.

What are my options for solid state storage? Several types of solid state storage are available to today's consumers (Figure 2-34). A **USB flash drive**, such as Sony's MicroVault, is a portable storage device featuring a built-in connector that plugs directly into a computer's USB port. A USB flash drive requires no card reader, making it easily transportable from one computer to another. Nicknamed "pen drives" or "keychain drives," USB flash drives are about the size of a highlighter pen and so durable that you can literally carry them on your key ring. You can open, edit, delete, and run files stored on a USB flash drive just as though those files were stored on your computer's hard disk.

FIGURE 2-34

Popular Solid State Storage Options

USB flash drive: 32 MB–8 GB capacities

CompactFlash card: 8 MB–8 GB capacities

CompactFlash (CF) cards are about the size of a matchbook and provide high storage capacities and access speeds. CompactFlash cards include a built-in controller that reads and writes data within the solid state grid. The built-in controller removes the need for control electronics on the card reader, so the device that connects to your computer to read the card's data is simply an adapter that collects data from the card and shuttles it to the computer's system unit. With their high storage capacities and access speeds, CompactFlash cards are ideal for use on high-end digital cameras that require megabytes of storage for each photo.

MultiMedia cards (MMC) offer solid state storage in a package about the size of a postage stamp. Initially used in mobile phones and pagers, use of MultiMedia cards has spread to digital cameras and MP3 players. Like CompactFlash cards, MultiMedia cards include a built-in controller, so MMC readers are electronically simple and very inexpensive.

SecureDigital (SD) cards are based on MultiMedia card technology, but feature significantly faster data transfer rates and include cryptographic security protection for copyrighted data and music. SecureDigital cards are popular for storage on digital music players and digital cameras.

SmartMedia cards were originally called "solid state floppy disk cards" because they look much like a miniature floppy disk. Unlike other popular solid state storage, SmartMedia cards do not include a built-in controller, which means that the SmartMedia reader manages the read/write process. These cards are the least durable of the solid state storage media and should be handled with care.

MultiMedia card: 32–2 GB capacities

SecureDigital card: 32 MB–4 GB capacities

SmartMedia card: 32–128 MB capacities

QuickCheck

1. A magnetic storage device uses a read-write _head_ to magnetize particles that represent data.

2. Data on an optical storage medium, such as a DVD, is stored as pits and _lands_ .

3. _access_ time is the average time it takes a computer to locate data on a storage medium and read it.

4. A disk drive is a(n) _random_ access device, whereas a tape drive is a(n) _sequential_ access device.

5. Higher disk _density_ provides increased storage capacity.

6. Hard disks are susceptible to head _crashes_ , so it is important to make backup copies.

7. CD-RW technology allows you to write data on a disk, and then change that data. True or false? _True_

8. A(n) _double layer_ DVD has a capacity of 8.5 GB.

 CHECK ANSWERS

Input and Output Devices

This section provides an overview of the most popular input and output devices for personal computers. It begins with input devices, including keyboards, mice, trackpads, and joysticks. Next, a survey of computer display devices helps you sort out the differences among CRT, LCD, and plasma displays. A guide to printers describes today's most popular printer technologies and provides a handy comparison chart. You'll learn about other peripheral devices in later chapters. You'll also take a look at the computer's expansion bus—the components that carry data to peripheral devices. With an understanding of how the expansion bus works, you'll be able to select, install, and use all kinds of peripherals.

BASIC INPUT DEVICES

What devices can I use to get data into a computer? Most computer systems include a keyboard and pointing device, such as a mouse, for basic data input. Additional input devices, such as scanners, digital cameras, and graphics tablets, are handy for working with graphical input. Microphones and electronic instruments provide input capabilities for sound and music.

What's special about a computer keyboard's design? The design of most computer keyboards is based on the typewriter's QWERTY layout, which was engineered to keep the typewriter's mechanical keys from jamming. In addition to the basic typing keypad, desktop and notebook computer keyboards include a collection of function keys designed for computer-specific tasks. Most desktop computer keyboards also include a calculator-style numeric keypad. They also include an editing keypad with keys such as End, Home, and Page Up, to efficiently move the screen-based insertion point. You can even find tiny keyboards on handheld devices—entering text and numbers is an important part of most computing tasks. Figure 2-35 illustrates a variety of keyboards you might encounter on various computing devices.

FIGURE 2-35

Computer keyboards come in a variety of sizes and styles.

What does a pointing device do? A **pointing device** allows you to manipulate an on-screen pointer and other screen-based graphical controls. The most popular pointing devices for personal computers include mice, trackballs, pointing sticks, trackpads, and joysticks.

How does a mouse work? A standard desktop computer includes a mouse as its primary pointing device. Many computer owners also add a mouse to their notebook computers. A mouse includes one or more buttons that can be "clicked" to input command selections, such as "Start" and "Shut down." To track its position, a computer mouse uses one of two technologies: mechanical or optical (Figure 2-36). Most computer owners prefer the performance of an optical mouse because it provides more precise tracking, greater durability, less maintenance, and more flexibility to use the mouse on a wide variety of surfaces without a mouse pad.

FIGURE 2-36

A mechanical mouse (far left) reads its position based on the movement of a ball that rolls over a mouse pad placed on a desk.

An optical mouse (near left) uses an onboard chip to track a light beam as it bounces off a surface, such as a desk, clipboard, or mouse pad.

When would I use other pointing devices? A **pointing stick**, or "TrackPoint," looks like the tip of an eraser embedded in the keyboard of a notebook computer. It is a space-saving device that you can push up, down, or sideways to move the on-screen pointer. A **trackpad** is a touch-sensitive surface on which you can slide your fingers to move the on-screen pointer. A **trackball** looks like a mechanical mouse turned upside down. You use your fingers or palm to roll the ball and move the pointer. Pointing sticks, trackpads, and trackballs (Figure 2-37) are typically used with notebook computers as an alternative to a mouse.

A **joystick** looks like a small version of a car's stick shift. Moving the stick provides input to on-screen objects, such as a pointer or an action figure in a computer game. Joysticks, like the one pictured in Figure 2-37, can include several sticks and buttons for arcade-like control when playing computer games.

FIGURE 2-37

Alternative Pointing Devices

Pointing stick   Trackpad   Trackball   Joystick

DISPLAY DEVICES

What are my options for display devices? A computer display screen is usually classified as an output device because it typically shows the results of a processing task. Some screens, however, can be classified as both input and output devices because they include touch-sensitive technology that accepts input. Display devices used for output offer three technology options: CRT, LCD, and plasma (Figure 2-38).

A **CRT** (cathode ray tube) display device uses the same sort of bulky glass tube as a standard television. Gun-like mechanisms in the tube spray beams of electrons toward the screen and activate individual dots of color that form an image. CRT display devices, often simply called "monitors," offer an inexpensive and dependable computer display. They are bulky, however, and consume a fair amount of power.

An **LCD** (liquid crystal display) produces an image by manipulating light within a layer of liquid crystal cells. Modern LCD technology is compact in size and lightweight, and provides an easy-to-read display. LCDs are standard equipment on notebook computers. Standalone LCDs, referred to as "LCD monitors" or "flat panel displays," have also become available for desktop computers as a replacement for CRT monitors. The advantages of LCD monitors include display clarity, low radiation emission, portability, and compactness. They are, however, more expensive than CRT monitors.

Plasma screen technology creates an on-screen image by illuminating miniature colored fluorescent lights arrayed in a panel-like screen. The name "plasma" comes from the type of gas that fills fluorescent lights and gives them their luminescence. Like LCD screens, plasma screens are compact, lightweight, and more expensive than CRT monitors.

CRT, LCD, and plasma screens can be equipped with NTSC (standard American television) or HDTV (high-definition television) circuitry so they accept television signals from an antenna or cable. This technology lets you simultaneously view computer data and television on the same display device using split-screen or picture-in-picture format.

Which display technology produces the best image? Image quality is a factor of screen size, dot pitch, width of viewing angle, refresh rate, resolution, and color depth. Screen size is the measurement in inches from one corner of the screen diagonally across to the opposite corner. Typical monitor screen sizes range from 13" to 21". On most monitors, the viewable image does not stretch to the edge of the screen. Instead, a black border makes the image smaller than the size specified. Many computer ads now include a measurement of the **viewable image size** (vis).

Dot pitch (dp) is a measure of image clarity. A smaller dot pitch means a crisper image. Technically, dot pitch is the distance in millimeters between like-colored **pixels**—the small dots of light that form an image. A dot pitch between .26 and .23 is typical for today's monitors.

A monitor's **viewing angle width** indicates how far to the side you can still clearly see the screen image. A wide viewing angle indicates that you can view the screen from various positions without compromising image quality. CRT and plasma screens offer the widest viewing angles. Graphics artists tend to prefer CRT screens, which display uniform color from any angle.

A CRT's **refresh rate** (also referred to as "vertical scan rate") is the speed at which the screen is repainted. The faster the refresh rate, the less the screen flickers. Refresh rate is measured in cycles per second, or Hertz

FIGURE 2-38

Display Device Technology

CRT

LCD

Plasma

INFOWEBLINKS

For up-to-the-minute information on the latest and greatest graphics cards, monitors, and LCD displays, check out the **Display Devices InfoWeb.**

www.course.com/np/concepts9/ch02

(Hz), and is adjustable using the Control Panel settings in Windows. A refresh rate of at least 75 Hz produces a fairly flicker-free display.

The number of colors a monitor can display is referred to as **color depth** or "bit depth." Most PC display devices have the capability to display millions of colors. When set at 24-bit color depth (sometimes called "True Color"), your PC can display more than 16 million colors—and produce what are considered photographic-quality images. Windows allows you to select resolution and color depth. The most popular setting is 24-bit color at 1024 x 768 resolution.

The number of horizontal and vertical pixels that a device displays on a screen is referred to as its **resolution**. The resolution for many early PC displays was referred to as **VGA** (Video Graphics Array). Higher resolutions were later provided by **SVGA** (Super VGA), **XGA** (eXtended Graphics Array), **SXGA** (Super XGA), and **UXGA** (Ultra XGA) (Figure 2-39).

At higher resolutions, text and other objects appear smaller, but the computer can display a larger work area, such as an entire page of a document. The two screens in Figure 2-40 help you compare a display set at 640 x 480 resolution with a display set at 1024 x 768 resolution.

FIGURE 2-39

Common PC Resolutions

VGA	640 x 480
SVGA	800 x 600
XGA	1024 x 768
SXGA	1280 x 1024
UXGA	1600 x 1200

FIGURE 2-40

The screen on the left shows 1024 x 768 resolution. Notice the size of text and other screen-based objects. The screen on the right shows 640 x 480 resolution. Text and other objects appear larger on the low-resolution screen, but you see a smaller portion of the screen desktop.

What are the components of a typical computer display system? In addition to a display device, such as a monitor, a computer display system also requires graphics circuitry that generates the signals for displaying an image on the screen. Graphics circuitry, referred to as "integrated graphics," is built into a computer's system board. Graphics circuitry can also be supplied by a small circuit board called a **graphics card** ("graphics board" or "video card"), like the one in Figure 2-41. Today's fastest graphics cards fit into an AGP expansion slot, which you'll learn about later in this section.

A graphics card typically contains a graphics processing unit (GPU) and special video memory, which stores screen images as they are processed, but before they are displayed. Lots of video memory is the key to lightning-fast screen updating for fast action games, 3-D modeling, and graphics-intensive desktop publishing. In addition to video memory, most graphics cards contain special graphics accelerator technology to further boost performance.

FIGURE 2-41

A graphics card is a small circuit board that plugs into the system board.

PRINTERS

What printer technologies are available for personal computers? Printers are one of the most popular output devices available for personal computers. Today's best-selling printers typically use ink jet or laser technology. Printer technologies for specialized applications include dot matrix, solid ink, thermal transfer, and dye sublimation.

How does an ink jet printer work? An **ink jet printer** has a nozzle-like print head that sprays ink onto paper to form characters and graphics. The print head in a color ink jet printer consists of a series of nozzles, each with its own ink cartridge. Most ink jet printers use CMYK color, which requires only cyan (blue), magenta (pink), yellow, and black inks to create a printout that appears to have thousands of colors. Alternatively, some printers use six or eight ink colors to print midtone shades that create slightly more realistic photographic images.

Ink jet printers, such as the one in Figure 2-42, outsell all other types of printers because they are inexpensive and produce both color and black-and-white printouts. They work well for most home and small business applications. Small, portable ink jet printers meet the needs of many mobile computer owners. Ink jet technology also powers many photo printers, which are optimized to print high-quality images produced by digital cameras and scanners.

How do laser printers compare to ink jet printers? A **laser printer**, such as the one in Figure 2-43, uses the same technology as a photocopier to paint dots of light on a light-sensitive drum. Electrostatically charged ink is applied to the drum and then transferred to paper. Laser technology is more complex than ink jet technology, which accounts for the higher price of laser printers.

A basic laser printer produces only black-and-white printouts. Color laser printers are available, but are somewhat more costly than basic black-and-white models. Laser printers are often the choice for business printers, particularly for applications that produce a high volume of printed material.

FIGURE 2-42

Most ink jet printers are small, lightweight, and inexpensive, yet produce very good-quality color output.

FIGURE 2-43

Laser printers are a popular technology when high-volume output or good-quality printouts are required.

CLICK TO START

What is a dot matrix printer? When PCs first appeared in the late 1970s, dot matrix printers were the technology of choice, and they are still available today. A **dot matrix printer** produces characters and graphics by using a grid of fine wires. As the print head noisily clatters across the paper, the wires strike a ribbon and paper in a pattern prescribed by your PC. Dot matrix printers can print text and graphics—some even print in color using a multicolored ribbon.

Today, dot matrix printers, like the one in Figure 2-44, are used primarily for "back-office" applications that demand low operating cost and dependability, but not high print quality.

2

Print head contains a matrix of thin wires

FIGURE 2-44

Unlike laser and ink jet technologies, a dot matrix printer actually strikes the paper and, therefore, can print multipart carbon forms.

Characters are formed from a pattern of dots created as the wires strike an inked ribbon.

What other printer technologies are available? A **solid ink printer** melts sticks of crayon-like ink and then sprays the liquefied ink through the print head's tiny nozzles. A solid ink printer produces vibrant colors and is sometimes used for professional graphics applications.

A **thermal transfer printer** uses thousands of tiny heating elements to melt the wax from a page-sized ribbon onto specially coated paper or transparency film (the kind used for overhead projectors). This type of printer excels at printing colorful transparencies for presentations, but the fairly expensive per-page costs and the requirement for special paper make it a niche market printer used mainly by businesses.

A **dye sublimation printer** uses technology similar to thermal transfer, but the page-sized ribbon contains dye instead of colored wax. Dye sublimation printers produce excellent color quality—perhaps the best of any printer technology. Although operating costs are high—$3 to $4 per page—these printers are coveted by digital photography enthusiasts.

What features should I look for in a printer? Printers differ in resolution, speed, duty cycle, operating costs, duplex capability, and memory.

■ **Resolution.** The quality or sharpness of printed images and text depends on the printer's resolution—the density of the gridwork of dots that create an image. Printer resolution is measured by the number of dots printed per linear inch, abbreviated as dpi. At normal reading distance, a resolution of about 900 dpi appears solid to the human eye, but a close examination reveals a dot pattern. If you want magazine-quality printouts, 900 dpi is sufficient resolution. If you are aiming for resolution similar to expensive coffee-table books, look for printer resolution of 2,400 dpi or higher.

■ **Print speed.** Printer speeds are measured either by pages per minute (ppm) or characters per second (cps). Color printouts typically take longer than black-and-white printouts. Pages that contain mostly text tend to print more rapidly than pages that contain graphics. Typical speeds for personal computer printers range between 6 and 30 pages per minute.

■ **Duty cycle.** In addition to printer speed, a printer's **duty cycle** determines how many pages a printer is able to churn out. Printer duty cycle is usually measured in pages per month. For example, a personal laser printer has a duty cycle of about 3,000 pages per month (ppm)—that means roughly 100 pages per day. You wouldn't want to use it to produce 5,000 campaign brochures for next Monday, but you would find it quite suitable for printing 10 copies of a five-page outline for a meeting tomorrow.

■ **Operating costs.** The initial cost of a printer is only one of the expenses associated with printed output. Ink jet printers require frequent replacements of relatively expensive ink cartridges. Laser printers require toner cartridge refills or replacements. Dot matrix printers require replacement ribbons. When shopping for a printer, you can check online resources to determine how often you'll need to replace printer supplies and how much they are likely to cost.

■ **Duplex capability.** A printer with duplex capability can print on both sides of the paper. This environment-friendly option saves paper but can slow down the print process, especially on ink-jet printers that pause to let the ink dry before printing the second side.

■ **Memory.** A computer sends data for a printout to the printer along with a set of instructions on how to print that data. **Printer Control Language** (PCL) is the most widely used language for communication between computers and printers, but **PostScript** is an alternative printer language that many publishing professionals prefer. The data that arrives at a printer along with its printer language instructions require memory. A large memory capacity is required to print color images and graphics-intensive documents. Some printers let you add memory to improve printing of such pages.

Figure 2-45 provides comparative information for ink jet, laser, and dot matrix printers. For specific information on a particular brand and model of printer, check the manufacturer's Web site.

INFOWEBLINKS

Before you shop for a printer, take a look at the buying tips in the **Printer Buyer's Guide InfoWeb**.

www.course.com/np/concepts9/ch02

FIGURE 2-45

Printer Comparison

Printer Type	Max. Resolution	Speed	Duty Cycle	Operating Cost	Memory
Ink Jet (B&W) (color graphics)	4800 x 1200	2–7 ppm 1–2 ppm	3,000 ppm	1–7¢/page 6–18¢/page	256 KB–2 MB
Laser (B&W) (color graphics)	2400 dpi	10–20 ppm 2–4 ppm	150,000 ppm	2–4¢/page 2–4¢/page	8–120 MB
Dot Matrix (B&W)	72–360 dpi	5–6 ppm	6,000–60,000 ppm	1.5–2¢/page	2–128 KB

INSTALLING PERIPHERAL DEVICES

Is it difficult to install a new peripheral device? At one time, installing computer peripherals required a screw driver and extensive knowledge of ports, slots, boards, and device drivers. Today, many peripheral devices connect to an external USB (universal serial bus) port and Windows automatically loads their device drivers, making installation as simple as plugging in a table lamp. USB is currently the most popular technology for connecting peripherals.

On most new computer models, USB ports are conveniently located on the front of the system unit for easy access. Many kinds of peripheral devices—including mice, scanners, and joysticks—are available with USB connections. Several types of storage devices, such as USB Flash drives, also use USB connections.

There are still occasions, however, when a simple USB connection is not available. Installing high-end graphics and sound cards for a multimedia or serious gaming computer typically requires you to open the system unit.

Whether you are working with a simple USB connection or more complex equipment, a little information about the computer's data bus will arm you with the information you need to negotiate the steps for installing most peripheral devices.

How does a computer move data to and from peripheral devices? When you install a peripheral device, you are basically creating a connection for data to flow between the device and the computer. Within a computer, data travels from one component to another over circuits called a **data bus**. One part of the data bus runs between RAM and the microprocessor. Other parts of the data bus connect RAM to various storage and peripheral devices. The segment of the data bus that extends between RAM and peripheral devices is called the **expansion bus**. As data moves along the expansion bus, it can travel through expansion slots, cards, ports, and cables.

What's an expansion slot? An **expansion slot** is a long, narrow socket on the system board into which you can plug an expansion card. An **expansion card** is a small circuit board that gives a computer the capability to control a storage device, an input device, or an output device. Expansion cards are also called "expansion boards," "controller cards," or "adapters." Figure 2-46 shows how to plug an expansion card into an expansion slot.

Expansion cards are built for only one type of slot. If you plan to add or upgrade a card in your computer, you must make sure the right type of slot is available on the system board. Most desktop computers provide four to eight expansion slots, some containing factory-installed expansion cards, such as those listed in Figure 2-47.

Expansion slots are classified as these types:

- **ISA** (Industry Standard Architecture) slots are an old technology, used today only for some modems and other relatively slow devices. Many new computers have few or no ISA slots.

- **PCI** (Peripheral Component Interconnect) slots offer fast transfer speeds and a 32-bit or 64-bit data bus. These slots typically house a graphics card, sound card, video capture card, modem, or network interface card.

- **AGP** (Accelerated Graphics Port) slots provide a high-speed data pathway primarily used for graphics cards.

Do notebook computers contain expansion slots? Most notebook computers are equipped with several USB ports and a special type of external slot called a **PCMCIA slot** (Personal Computer Memory

FIGURE 2-46

An expansion card simply slides into an expansion slot and is secured with a small screw. Before you open the case, make sure you unplug the computer and ground yourself—that's technical jargon for releasing static electricity by using a special grounding wristband or by touching both hands to a metal object.

CLICK TO START ✣

FIGURE 2-47

Factory-Installed Expansion Cards

Graphics card provides a path for data traveling to the monitor.

Modem provides a way to transmit data over phone lines or cable television lines.

Sound card carries data out to speakers and headphones or back from a microphone.

Network card allows you to connect your computer to a local area network.

Card International Association). Typically, a notebook computer has only one of these slots, but the slot can hold more than one **PC card** (also called "PCMCIA expansion cards" or "Card Bus cards"). Notebook owners are advised to use the USB ports and PCMCIA slot, rather than opening the notebook's system unit.

What is an expansion port? An **expansion port** is any connector that passes data in and out of a computer or peripheral device. Ports are sometimes called "jacks" or "connectors"—the terminology is inconsistent.

FIGURE 2-48

Expansion Ports

An expansion port is often housed on an expansion card so that it is accessible through an opening in the back of the computer's system unit. A port might also be built into the system unit case of a desktop or notebook computer. The built-in ports supplied with a computer usually include a mouse port, keyboard port, serial port, and USB ports. Figure 2-48 illustrates the major types of expansion ports on a typical desktop computer.

How do I know which cable to use? With so many types of ports, you can expect a corresponding variety of cables. If a cable is supplied with a peripheral device, you can usually figure out where to plug it in by matching the shape of the cable connector to the port. Some manufacturers also color code ports and plugs to make them easy to match. Figure 2-49 on the next page provides information about the computer cables you're most likely to encounter.

Why do some peripheral devices include a disk or CD? Some devices require software, called a **device driver**, to set up communication between your computer and the device. The directions supplied with your peripheral device include instructions on how to install the device driver. Typically, you use the device driver disk or CD one time to get everything set up, and then you can put the disk away in a safe place.

Long-time computer techies probably remember the days when installing a peripheral device meant messing around with little electronic components called dip switches and a host of complex software settings called IRQs. Fortunately, today's PCs include a feature called **Plug and Play** (PnP) that automatically takes care of these technical details. Although it took several years to refine Plug and Play technology, it works quite well for just about every popular peripheral device. If PnP doesn't work, your computer simply won't recognize the device and won't be able to transmit data to it or receive data from it. If you've got a stubborn peripheral device, check the manufacturer's Web site for a device driver update, or call the manufacturer's technical support department.

What's the most important thing to remember about installing peripherals? Installing a peripheral device is not difficult when you remember that it's all about using the expansion bus to make a connection between the system board and a peripheral device. The cable you use must match the peripheral device and a port on the computer. If the right type of port is not available, you might have to add an expansion card. Once the connection is made, PnP should recognize the new device. If not, you'll probably have to install driver software.

FIGURE 2-49

Personal Computer Cables and Connectors

	CONNECTOR	DESCRIPTION	DEVICES
	Serial DB-9	Connects to serial port, which sends data over a single data line one bit at a time at speeds of 56 Kbps.	Mouse or modem
	Parallel DB-25M	Connects to parallel port, which sends data simultaneously over eight data lines at speeds of 12,000 Kbps.	Printer, external CD drive, Zip drive, external hard disk drive, or tape backup device
	USB	Connects to USB port, which sends data over a single data line and can support up to 127 devices. USB-1 carries data at speeds up to 12,000 Kbps; USB-2, at 480,000 Kbps.	Modem, keyboard, joystick, scanner, mouse, external hard disk drive, MP3 player, digital camera
	SCSI C-50F	Connects to SCSI port, which sends data simultaneously over 8 or 16 data lines at speeds between 40,000 Kbps and 640,000 Kbps; supports up to 16 devices.	Internal or external hard disk drive, scanner, CD drive, tape backup device
	IEEE 1394	Connects to the FireWire port, which sends data at 400,000 Kbps.	Video camera, DVD player
	VGA HDB-15	Connects to the video port.	Monitor

QuickCheck

SECTION D

1. Computer _pointing_ devices include mice, trackpads, trackballs, and joysticks.
2. In the context of computer displays, _refresh_ rate refers to the speed at which the screen image is repainted.
3. The number of dots that form an image on a monitor or printer is referred to as _resolution_.
4. A printer with _duplex_ capability can print on both sides of the paper.
5. AGP, PCI, and ISA are types of expansion _slots_.
6. A(n) _USB_ port provides one of the fastest, simplest ways to connect peripherals.
7. Many peripheral devices come packaged with _device_ driver software.

CHECK ANSWERS

TechTalk
How a Microprocessor Executes Instructions

Remarkable advances in microprocessor technology have produced exponential increases in computer speed and power. In 1965, Gordon Moore, co-founder of chipmaker giant Intel Corporation, predicted that the number of transistors on a chip would double every year. Much to the surprise of engineers and Moore himself, "Moore's law" accurately predicted 30 years of chip development. In 1958, the first integrated circuit contained two transistors. Today's processors feature millions of transistors.

What's really fascinating, though, is how these chips perform complex tasks simply by manipulating those ubiquitous bits. How can pushing around 1s and 0s result in professional-quality documents, exciting action games, animated graphics, cool music, e-commerce Web sites, and street maps? To satisfy your curiosity about what happens deep in the heart of a microprocessor, you'll need to venture into the realm of instruction sets, fetch cycles, accumulators, and pointers.

What kind of instructions does a computer execute? A computer accomplishes a complex task by performing a series of very simple steps, referred to as instructions. An instruction tells the computer to perform a specific arithmetic, logical, or control operation.

To be executed by a computer, an instruction must be in the form of electrical signals—those now familiar 1s and 0s that represent "ons" and "offs." In this form, instructions are referred to as **machine code**. They are, of course, very difficult for people to read, so typically when discussing them, we use more understandable mnemonics, such as JMP, M1, and REG1.

An instruction has two parts: the op code and the operands. An **op code**, which is short for "operation code," is a command word for an operation such as add, compare, or jump. The **operands** for an instruction specify the data, or the address of the data, for the operation. Let's look at an example of an instruction from a hypothetical instruction set:

In the instruction JMP M1, the op code is JMP and the operand is M1. The op code JMP means jump or go to a different instruction. The operand M1 stands for the RAM address of the instruction to which the computer is supposed to go. The instruction JMP M1 has only one operand, but some instructions have more than one operand. For example, the instruction ADD REG1 REG2 has two operands: REG1 and REG2.

The list of instructions that a microprocessor is able to execute is known as its instruction set. This instruction set is built into the microprocessor when it is manufactured. Every task that a computer performs is determined by the list of instructions in its instruction set. As you look at the instruction set in Figure 2-50 on the next page, consider that the computer must use instructions such as these for all the tasks it helps you perform—from database management to word processing.

FIGURE 2-50

A Simple Microprocessor
Instruction Set

Op Code	Operation	Example
INP	Input the given value into the specified memory address	INP 7 M1
CLA	Clear the accumulator to 0	CLA
MAM	Move the value from the accumulator to the specified memory location	MAM M1
MMR	Move the value from the specified memory location to the specified register	MMR M1 REG1
MRA	Move the value from the specified register to the accumulator	MRA REG1
MAR	Move the value from the accumulator to the specified register	MAR REG1
ADD	Add the values in two registers; place the result in the accumulator	ADD REG1 REG2
SUB	Subtract the value in the second register from the value in the first register; place the result in the accumulator	SUB REG1 REG2
MUL	Multiply values in two registers; place the result in the accumulator	MUL REG1 REG2
DIV	Divide the value in the first register by the value in the second register; place the result in the accumulator	DIV REG 1 REG2
INC	Increment (increase) the value in the register by 1	INC REG1
DEC	Decrement (decrease) the value in the register by 1	DEC REG1
CMP	Compare the values in two registers. If values are equal, put 1 in the accumulator; otherwise, put 0 in the accumulator	CMP REG1 REG2
JMP	Jump to the instruction at the specified memory address	JMP P2
JPZ	Jump to the specified address if the accumulator holds 0	JPZ P3
JPN	Jump to the specified address if the accumulator does not hold 0	JPN P2
HLT	Halt program execution	HLT

What happens when a computer executes an instruction?

The term **instruction cycle** refers to the process in which a computer executes a single instruction. Some parts of the instruction cycle are performed by the microprocessor's control unit; other parts of the cycle are performed by the ALU. The steps in this cycle are summarized in Figure 2-51.

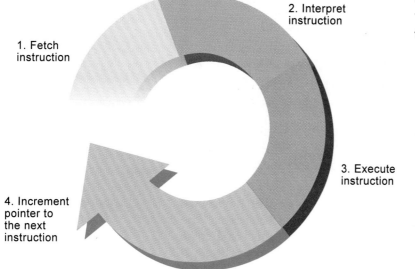

1. Fetch instruction

2. Interpret instruction

3. Execute instruction

4. Increment pointer to the next instruction

FIGURE 2-51

The instruction cycle includes four activities.

What role does the control unit play? The instructions that a computer is supposed to process for a particular program are held in RAM. When the program begins, the RAM address of the first instruction is placed in a part of the microprocessor's control unit called an instruction pointer. The control unit can then fetch the instruction by copying data from that address into its instruction register. From there, the control unit can interpret the instruction, gather the specified data, or tell the ALU to begin processing. Figure 2-52 helps you visualize the control unit's role in processing an instruction.

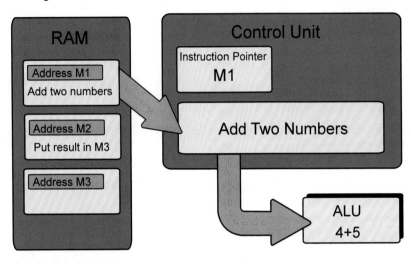

FIGURE 2-52

The control unit fetches instructions, interprets them, fetches data, and tells the ALU which processing operations to perform.

When does the ALU swing into action? The ALU is responsible for performing arithmetic and logical operations. It uses registers to hold data ready to be processed. When it gets the go-ahead signal from the control unit, the ALU processes the data and places the result in an accumulator. From the accumulator, the data can be sent to RAM or used for further processing. Figure 2-53 helps you visualize what happens in the ALU as the computer processes data.

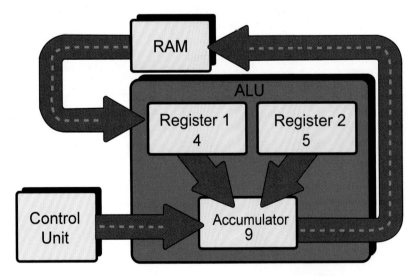

FIGURE 2-53

The ALU uses data from its registers to perform arithmetic and logical operations. The results are placed in another register, called the accumulator.

What happens after an instruction is executed? When the computer completes an instruction, the control unit "increments" the instruction pointer to the RAM address of the next instruction and the instruction cycle begins again. So how does this all fit together? Figure 2-54 on the next page explains how the ALU, control unit, and RAM work together to process instructions.

FIGURE 2-54

The ALU, control unit, and RAM all have a part to play in processing instructions.

QuickCheck

TECHTALK

1. [Machine] code instructions are in the form of 0s and 1s.

2. JMP is an example of a(n) [operation] code.

3. An instruction [pointer] indicates the instruction to be executed.

4. The results of processing are held in a(n) [accumulator].

CHECK ANSWERS

Issue

Computers and the Environment

Manufacturing an average desktop computer with a CRT monitor requires 48 pounds of chemicals and 529 pounds of fossil fuels, according to a United Nations study. That makes producing a computer more materials-intensive than manufacturing an automobile. Extending the lifespan of your computer might be environmentally friendly, but keeping up with technology probably means replacing your computer every few years.

When it is time to replace your computer, is there a way to do it in an environmentally safe way? The National Recycling Coalition estimates that 500 million computers will become obsolete by 2007. In the United States alone, almost eight printer cartridges are discarded every second. A recycling company called GreenDisk estimates that about 1 billion floppy disks, CDs, and DVDs end up in landfills every year.

U.S. landfills already hold more than 2 million tons of computer and electronic parts, which contain toxic substances such as lead, cadmium, and mercury. A computer monitor, for example, can contain up to eight pounds of lead. An Environmental Protection Agency (EPA) report sums up the situation: "In this world of rapidly changing technology, disposal of computers and other electronic equipment has created a new and growing waste stream."

Many computers end up in landfills because their owners are unaware of potential environmental hazards and simply toss them in the garbage. In addition, PC owners typically are not given information on options for disposing of their old machines. Instead of throwing away your old computer, you might be able to sell it; donate it to a local school, church, or community program; have it hauled away by a professional recycling firm; or send it back to the manufacturer. Some artists even accept old computers and use parts in jewelry and craft projects.

With the growing popularity of Internet auctions and dedicated computer reclamation sites, you might be able to get some cash for your old computer. At Web sites such as the Computer Recycle Center at *www.recycles.com*, you can post an ad for your "old stuff." Off the Web, you can find several businesses,

Recycled Computer Creations by Gregory Steele, Marquette, MI

such as Computer Renaissance, that refurbish old computers and sell them in retail stores.

Donating your old computer to a local organization doesn't actually eliminate the disposal problem, but it does delay it. Unfortunately, finding a new home for an old computer is not always easy. Most schools and community organizations have few resources for repairing broken equipment, so if your old computer is not in good working order, it could be more of a burden than a gift. In addition, your computer might be too old to be compatible with the other computers in an organization. It helps if you can donate software along with your old computer. To ensure a legal transfer, include the software distribution disks, manuals, and license agreement. And remember, once you donate the software, you cannot legally use it on your new computer unless it is freeware or shareware.

If you cannot find an organization to accept your computer donation, look in your local Yellow Pages or on the Internet for an electronics recycling firm, which will haul away your computer and recycle any usable materials.

Despite private sector options for selling, donating, or recycling old computers, many governments are worried that these voluntary efforts will not be enough to prevent massive dumping of an ever-growing population of obsolete computers.

Many states have taken legislative action to curtail the rampant disposal of obsolete computer equipment. For example, Massachusetts has banned televisions and computer monitors from its landfills. In Maine it is illegal to dispose of computers or monitors—they have to be recycled in an environmentally sound way. But recycling can be costly—equipment needs to be collected, sorted, disassembled, and shipped to processing or disposal plants.

Basic to the issue of reducing electronic waste is the question of "Who pays?" Should it be the taxpayer, the individual consumer, the retailer, or the computer manufacturer?

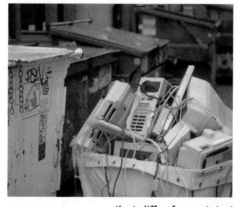

A few years ago, Californians were faced with the prospect of tax hikes to deal with alarming increases in electronic waste, but activists questioned if tax increases were fair to individual taxpayers who generate very little electronic waste. Now, consumers buying computers in California have to pay a recycling fee at the time of purchase.

Other lawmakers propose to make manufacturers responsible for recycling costs and logistics. "Extended producer responsibility" refers to the idea of holding manufacturers responsible for the environmental effects of their products through the entire product life cycle, which includes taking them back, recycling them, or disposing of them. Maryland requires computer manufacturers to ante up an annual fee for electronic waste disposal.

Proposed legislation in Europe would require manufacturers to accept returns of their old equipment free of charge and take appropriate steps to recycle it. The economics of a mandatory take-back program are likely to increase product costs because manufacturers would typically pass on recycling costs to consumers.

Some manufacturers currently participate in voluntary producer responsibility programs. Consumers who buy Hewlett-Packard toner cartridges are provided with a postage-paid shipping box so they can return the cartridges for recycling. Using IBM's PC Recycling Service, consumers can ship any make of computer, including system units, monitors, printers, and optional attachments, to a recycling center for $29.99.

The EPA (Environmental Protection Agency) advocates a national plan in which consumers, retailers, and manufacturers can cooperate to reduce electronic waste. Its Plug-in to eCycling Web site makes the point that "No national infrastructure exists for collecting, reusing, and recycling electronics." With laws that differ from state to state, consumers are often confused about how to dispose of their unwanted computers, monitors, CDs, and ink cartridges.

U.S. Legislators are trying to hammer out the details of an e-waste bill that provides tax incentives for companies that recycle and requires consumers to recycle computers, monitors, and other electronic devices. The United States is not alone in its efforts. Lawmakers in the European Union, Great Britain, Australia, China, and Japan are also addressing ways to manage the electronic waste stream and keep our planet green.

INFOWEBLINKS

You'll find much more information about how you can recycle an old computer by connecting to the **Computer Recycling InfoWeb.**

www.course.com/np/concepts9/ch02

What Do You Think?   ISSUE

1. Have you ever thrown away an old computer or other electronic device?   ○ Yes   ○ No   ○ Not sure

2. Are you aware of any options for recycling electronic equipment in your local area?   ○ Yes   ○ No   ○ Not sure

3. Would it be fair for consumers to pay a recycling tax on any electronic equipment that they purchase?   ○ Yes   ○ No   ○ Not sure

✣ SAVE RESPONSES

Computers in Context
Military

In *Engines of the Mind,* Joel Shurkin writes, "If necessity is the mother of invention, then war can be said to be its grandmother." The military, an early pioneer in computer and communication technologies, continues to be the driving force behind technologies that have revolutionized everyday life. During World War II, the U.S. military initiated a classified research program, called Project PX, to develop an electronic device to calculate artillery firing tables; by hand, each table required weeks of grueling calculations. Project PX produced ENIAC (Electrical Numerical Integrator And Calculator), one of the first general-purpose electronic computers. When ENIAC was completed in 1946, the war was over, but ENIAC's versatile architecture could be used for other calculations, such as designing hydrogen bombs, predicting weather, and engineering wind tunnels. ENIAC's technology evolved into the computers used today.

After Project PX, the military continued to support computer research. Like most large corporations, the military used mainframe computers to maintain personnel, inventory, supply, and facilities records. This data was distributed to terminals at other locations through rudimentary networks. Because all data communication flowed through the mainframe, a single point of failure for the entire system was a possible risk. A malfunction or an enemy "hit" could disrupt command and control, sending the military into chaos. Therefore, the armed forces created the Advanced Research Projects Agency (ARPA) to design a distributed communications system that could continue operating without a centralized computer. The result was ARPANET, which paved the way for the data communications system we know today as the Internet. ARPANET was activated in 1967, but the .mil domain that designates U.S. military Web sites was not implemented until 1984.

The U.S. Department of Defense (DoD) currently maintains two data communications networks: SIPRNet, a classified (secret-level) network, and NIPRNet, which provides unclassified services. The DoD's public Web site, called DefenseLINK, provides official information about defense policies, organizations, budgets, and operations.

Computers and communications technology have also become an integral part of high-tech military operations. U.S. Apache helicopters, for example, are equipped with computer-based Target Acquisition Designation Sights, laser range finder/designators, and Pilot Night Vision Sensors. These arcade-style controls are also used by tank drivers in the U.S. Army's 4th Infantry Division. Each vehicle in this "Digitized Division" is equipped with a Force 21 Battle Command Brigade and Below system, which works like a battlefield Internet to transmit data on the location of friendly and enemy forces from one vehicle to another using wireless communication.

Much like a video game, the Force 21 touch screen shows friendly troops in blue, and a global positioning satellite (GPS) system updates their positions automatically. Enemy troops spotted by helicopters are shown as red icons. To get information on any friendly or enemy vehicle, a soldier can simply touch one of these blue or red icons. To send text messages—much like cell phone and computer instant messaging—a soldier touches the Message button. The built-in GPS system provides location and route information, much like sophisticated mapping programs in luxury cars.

Force 21 computers are installed in shock-resistant cases and equipped with a cooling system that eliminates the need for a fan, which might pull in dust, dirt, or water. The computers run Sun Microsystem's Solaris operating system because it is less vulnerable to viruses and intrusion attacks than Microsoft Windows. To prevent enemy capture and use, Force 21 computers have a self-destruct mechanism that can be triggered remotely.

In addition to pilots and tank drivers, battlefield soldiers will soon be equipped with "wearable" computer and communications equipment. The $2 billion Land Warrior program will provide high-tech "wearable" weaponry, such as the Army's Integrated Helmet Assembly Subsystem. IHAS is a helmet-mounted display screen that a soldier wears over the dominant eye to view graphical data, digital maps, thermal images, intelligence information, and troop locations. The display is updated by a wireless network connection every 30 seconds. Land warrior gear also includes a weapon-mounted video camera, so that soldiers can view and fire around corners and acquire targets in darkness.

The military has also conducted research in computer simulations that are similar to civilian computer games. "Live" military training is dangerous—weapons are deadly and equipment costs millions of dollars. With computer simulations, however, troops can train in a true-to-life environment without physical harm or equipment damage. Flying an F-16 fighter, for example, costs about $5,000 an hour, but flying an F-16 simulator costs only $500 per hour. The military uses simulators to teach Air Force pilots to fly fighter jets, Navy submarine officers to navigate in harbors, and Marine infantry squads to handle urban combat. Military trainers agree that widespread use of computer games helps prepare troops to adapt quickly to simulations.

A 24-year-old preflight student at Pensacola Naval Air Station modified the Microsoft Flight Simulator game to re-create a T-34C Turbo Mentor plane's controls. After logging 50 hours on the simulator, the student performed so well on a real plane that the Navy used his simulation to train other pilots. Today, a growing cadre of computer and communications specialists are needed to create and maintain increasingly complex military systems.

An army once depended on its infantry, but today's high-tech army depends equally on its database designers, computer programmers, and network specialists. Even previously low-tech military jobs, such as mechanics and dietitians, require some computer expertise. Happily, new recruits are finding military computer systems easy to learn, based on their knowledge of civilian technologies, such as the Internet and computer games.

Although most citizens agree that an adequate national defense is necessary, the cost of defense-related equipment, personnel, and research remains controversial. In 1961, President Dwight Eisenhower warned "We must guard against the acquisition of unwarranted influence, whether sought or unsought, by the military-industrial complex." Many socially motivated citizens and pacifists protested diverting tax dollars from social and economic programs to the military-industrial complex Eisenhower cautioned against. In retrospect, however, military funding contributed to many technologies we depend on today. For example, detractors tried to convince the government that Project PX was doomed to failure, but without ENIAC research, computers might not exist today. Skeptics saw no future for the fruits of ARPANET research, but it led to the Internet, which has changed our lives significantly.

INFOWEBLINKS

You'll find lots more information related to this Computers in Context topic at the **Computers and the Military InfoWeb.**

www.course.com/np/concepts9/ch02

2

Labs

On the Web
Student Edition Labs

To access the Student Edition labs, connect to the New Perspectives NP9 Web site and click the link for Student Edition Labs. The link also provides access to lab assignments.

www.course.com/np/concepts9/ch02

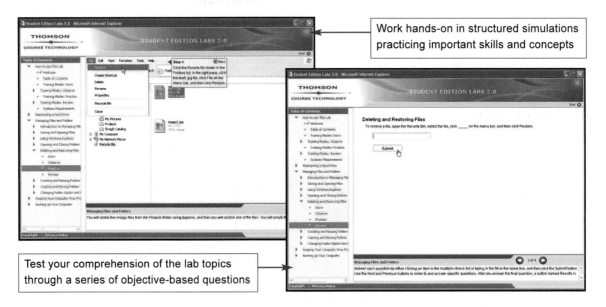

Work hands-on in structured simulations practicing important skills and concepts

Test your comprehension of the lab topics through a series of objective-based questions

BINARY NUMBERS

In the Binary Numbers Student Edition Lab, you will learn the following topics and skills:

- Comparing binary numbers to decimal numbers
- Adding binary numbers manually
- Converting binary numbers to decimal equivalents

PERIPHERAL DEVICES

In the Peripheral Devices Student Edition Lab, you will learn the following topics and skills:

- Identifying commonly used peripheral devices, such as display devices, printers, scanners, digital cameras and storage devices
- Adjusting display properties on a monitor and printer settings on a printer
- Identifying storage devices and their appropriate uses

UNDERSTANDING THE MOTHERBOARD

In the Understanding the Motherboard Student Edition Lab, you will learn the following topics and skills:

- Identifying components of the motherboard, such as integrated circuits, the CPU, RAM, ROM, and expansion slots and cards
- Modifying the way Windows handles virtual memory on a system
- Installing expansion cards into a PC

USING INPUT DEVICES

In the Using Input Devices Student Edition Lab, you will learn the following topics and skills:

- Using a keyboard, including using the function keys and the numeric keypad
- Using a mouse, including double-clicking, right-clicking and dragging objects
- Identifying other input devices, such as touchpads, stylus, microphones, and digital video cameras.

On the BookOnCD
New Perspectives Labs

To access the New Perspectives labs for Chapter 2, start the BookOnCD and then click the ✛ icon next to the lab title below.

✛ WORKING WITH BINARY NUMBERS

IN THIS LAB YOU'LL LEARN:

The difference between the binary number system and the decimal number system

How to count in binary

How to convert decimal numbers into binary numbers

How to convert binary numbers into decimal numbers

How to use the Windows Calculator to convert numbers

How to work with "powers of two"

LAB ASSIGNMENTS

1. Start the interactive part of the lab. Make sure you've enabled Tracking if you want to save your QuickCheck results. Perform each lab step as directed, and answer all the lab QuickCheck questions. When you exit the lab, your answers are automatically graded and your results are displayed.

2. Using paper and pencil, manually convert the following decimal numbers into binary numbers. Your instructor might ask you to show the process that you used for each conversion.

   a. 100   b. 1,000   c. 256
   d. 27   e. 48   f. 112
   g. 96   h. 1,024

3. Using paper and pencil, manually convert the following binary numbers into decimal numbers. Your instructor might ask you to show the process that you used for each conversion.

   a. 100   b. 101   c. 1100
   d. 10101   e. 1111   f. 10000
   g. 1111000 h. 110110

4. Describe what is wrong with the following sequence:

   10 100 110 1000 1001 1100 1110 10000

5. What is the decimal equivalent of 2^0? 2^1? 2^8?

✛ BENCHMARKING

IN THIS LAB YOU'LL LEARN:

Which computer performance factors can be measured by benchmark tests

How to run a test that identifies a computer's processor type, RAM capacity, and graphics card type

How to run benchmarking software that analyzes a computer's processor speed and graphics processing speed

How to interpret the results of a benchmark test

How to compare the results from benchmark tests that were performed on different system configurations

When benchmark tests might not provide accurate information on computer performance

LAB ASSIGNMENTS

1. Start the interactive part of the lab. Make sure you've enabled Tracking if you want to save your QuickCheck results. Perform each lab step as directed, and answer all the lab QuickCheck questions. When you exit the lab, your answers are automatically graded and your results are displayed.

2. If Microsoft Word is available, use the System Info button to analyze the computer you typically use. Provide the results of the analysis along with a brief description of the computer you tested and its location (at home, at work, in a computer lab, and so on).

PROCESSOR BENCHMARKS

Processor	Quake III Arena	PCMark04
"Supernova EE"	548	5198
"Pulsar FX"	551	5020

3. From the Processor Benchmarks table above, which fictional processor appears to be faster at graphics processing? Which processor appears to be better at overall processing tasks?

4. Explain why you might perform a benchmark test on your own computer, but get different results from those stated in a computer magazine, which tested the same computer with the same benchmark test.

5. Use a search engine on the Web to find benchmark ratings for Intel's Pentium 4 processors. What do these ratings show about the relative performance for 1.5 GHz, 2.4 GHz, and 3.8 GHz Pentium 4s?

2

Interactive Summary

To review important concepts from this chapter, fill in the blanks to best complete each sentence. When using the NP9 BookOnCD or the NP9 Web site, click the Check Answers buttons to automatically score your answers.

Most of today's computers are electronic, digital devices that work with data coded as binary digits, also known as __bits__. To represent numeric data, a computer can use the __binary__ number system. To represent character data, a computer uses Extended __ASCII__, EBCDIC, or Unicode. These codes also provide digital representations for the numerals 0 through 9 that are distinguished from numbers by the fact that they are not typically used in mathematical operations. Computers also __represents__ sounds, pictures, and videos into 1s and 0s.

A __bits__ is a single 1 or 0, whereas a __binary__ is a sequence of eight 1s and 0s. Transmission speeds are usually measured in __bits__, but storage space is usually measured in __bytes__ or gigabytes. In the context of computing, the prefix "kilo" means exactly 1,024. Kb stands for __kilobit__, while the abbreviation KB stands for __kilobyte__. The prefix __mega__ means precisely 1,048,576, or about 1 million. The prefix "giga" means about 1 billion; "tera" means about 1 trillion; and "exa" means about 1 quintillion.

The terms "computer chip," "microchip," and "chip" originated as techie jargon for __integrated__ circuits. These chips are made from a super-thin slice of semiconducting material and are packed with millions of microscopic circuit elements. In a computer, these chips include the __microprocessor__, memory modules, and other support circuitry. They are housed inside the computer's system unit on a large circuit board called the __motherboard__.

CHECK ANSWERS

The microprocessor and memory are two of the most important components in a computer. The microprocessor is an __integrated__ circuit, which is designed to process data based on a set of instructions. Its miniaturized circuitry is grouped into important functional areas. The microprocessor's ALU performs arithmetic and __logical__ operations. The __control__ unit fetches each instruction, interprets it, loads data into the ALU's registers, and directs all the processing activities within the microprocessor. In most of today's personal computers, microprocessor performance is measured in __cycle__—the number of cycles per second, or clock rate. Other factors affecting overall processing speed include word size, cache size, instruction set complexity, parallel processing, and pipelining.

RAM is a special holding area for data, program instructions, and the __operating__ system. It stores data on a temporary basis while it waits to be processed. In most computers, RAM is composed of integrated circuits called __SDRAM__ or RDRAM. The speed of RAM circuitry is measured in __nanoseconds__ or in megahertz (MHz). RAM is different from disk storage because it is __temporary__, which means that it can hold data only when the computer power is turned on. Computers also contain __ROM__, which is a type of memory that provides a set of "hard-wired" instructions that a computer uses to boot up. A third type of memory, called __CMOS__, is battery powered and contains configuration settings.

 CHECK ANSWERS

Today's personal computers use a variety of storage technologies, including floppy disks, hard disks, CDs, DVDs, tapes, and flash drives. Each storage device essentially has a direct pipeline to a computer's _____ so that data and instructions can move from a more permanent storage area to a temporary holding area and vice versa.

Magnetic storage technology stores data by magnetizing microscopic particles on the surface of a disk or tape. Optical storage technologies store data as a series of _____ and lands on the surface of a CD or DVD. _____ storage technology stores data by activating electrons in a microscopic grid of circuitry.

A standard 3.5" floppy disk formatted for a PC stores _____ MB of data. Zip disks have a higher disk _____, which provides significantly more storage capacity than a standard floppy disk.

A hard disk provides multiple platters for data storage, and these platters are sealed inside the drive case or cartridge to prevent airborne contaminants from interfering with the read-write heads. These disks are less durable than floppy disks, so it is important to make a _____ copy of the data they contain. Computer ads usually contain information about a hard disk's capacity and its _____ card type: SATA, EIDE, Ultra ATA, or SCSI.

Optical storage technologies, such as CD- and DVD-_____, provide good data storage capacity, but do not allow you to alter the disks' contents. _____ technology allows you to write data on a CD or DVD, but you cannot delete or change that data. _____ technology allows you to write and rewrite data on a CD or DVD.

USB _____ drives provide portable, solid state storage.

✦ CHECK ANSWERS

Most computer systems include a keyboard and some type of _____ device for basic data input. A mouse is standard equipment with most desktop computer systems, but alternatives include pointing _____, trackpads, and trackballs.

For output, most computers include a display device. A _____ produces an image by spraying electrons toward the screen. _____ technology produces an image by manipulating light within a layer of liquid crystal cells. _____ screen technology creates an on-screen image by illuminating miniature fluorescent lights arrayed in a panel-like screen. Image quality for a display device is a factor of screen size, dot _____, _____ of viewing angle, resolution, refresh rate, and color _____. A typical computer display system consists of the display device and a _____ card.

For printed output, most PC owners turn to _____ jet printers, although _____ printers are a popular option when low operating costs and high _____ cycle are important. A dot _____ printer is sometimes used for back-office applications and printing multipart forms.

Installing a peripheral device is not difficult when you remember that it uses the _____ bus to make a connection between the computer's _____ and a peripheral device. The cable you use must match the peripheral device and a _____ on the computer. If the right type of port is not available, you might have to add an _____ card. Once the connection is made, _____ should recognize the new device. If not, you'll probably have to install device _____ software.

✦ CHECK ANSWERS

Key Terms

Make sure you understand all the boldfaced key terms presented in this chapter. If you're using the NP9 BookOnCD, you can use this list of terms as an interactive study activity. First, try to define a term in your own words, and then click the term to compare your definition with the definition presented in the chapter.

Access time, 81
AGP, 97
ALU, 69
Analog device, 62
ASCII, 63
Benchmarks, 72
Binary digits, 62
Binary number system, 62
Cache, 71
Capacitors, 74
Card reader, 80
CD, 86
CD-DA, 87
CD-R, 87
CD-ROM, 87
CD-RW, 87
Character data, 63
CISC, 71
CMOS memory, 76
Color depth, 93
CompactFlash, 89
Control unit, 69
Controller, 84
CRT, 92
Data bus, 97
Data representation, 62
Data transfer rate, 81
Device driver, 98
Digital device, 62
Digitize, 64
Disk density, 82
Dot matrix printer, 94
Dot pitch, 92
Double layer DVD, 86
Drive bays, 80
Dual core processor, 72
Duty cycle, 95
DVD, 86
DVD+R DVD-R, 87
DVD-ROM, 87
DVD+RW DVD-RW, 87
DVD-Video, 87
Dye sublimation printer, 95
EBCDIC, 63
Expansion bus, 97

Expansion card, 97
Expansion port, 98
Expansion slot, 97
Extended ASCII, 63
File header, 65
Floppy disk, 81
Gigabit, 65
Gigabyte, 65
Gigahertz (GHz), 70
Graphics card, 93
Hard disk platter, 83
Head crash, 84
Ink jet printer, 94
Instruction cycle, 101
Instruction set, 70
Integrated circuit, 66
ISA, 97
Joystick, 91
Kilobit, 65
Kilobyte, 65
Lands, 79
Laser printer, 94
LCD, 92
Level 1 cache, 71
Level 2 cache, 71
Machine code, 100
Magnetic storage, 79
Megabit, 65
Megabyte, 65
Megahertz (MHz), 70
Microprocessor, 69
Microprocessor clock, 70
MultiMedia cards, 89
Nanosecond, 75
Numeric data, 62
Op code, 100
Operands, 100
Optical storage, 79
Parallel processing, 71
PC card, 98
PCI, 97
PCMCIA slot, 97
Pipelining, 71
Pits, 79
Pixels, 92

Plasma screen, 92
Plug and Play, 98
Pointing device, 91
Pointing stick, 91
PostScript, 96
Printer Control Language (PCL), 96
RAM, 73
Random access, 81
Read-write head, 79
Recordable technology, 86
Refresh rate, 92
Registers, 69
Resolution, 93
Rewritable technology, 86
RISC, 71
ROM, 75
ROM BIOS, 75
SecureDigital, 89
Semiconducting materials, 66
Sequential access, 81
Serial processing, 71
SmartMedia, 89
Solid ink printer, 95
Solid state storage, 80
Storage device, 78
Storage medium, 78
SVGA, 93
SXGA, 93
System board, 67
Tape backup, 85
Thermal transfer printer, 95
Trackball, 91
Trackpad, 91
Unicode, 63
USB flash drive, 88
UXGA, 93
VGA, 93
Viewable image size, 92
Viewing angle width, 92
Virtual memory, 74
Volatile, 74
Word size, 71
Write-protect window, 82
XGA, 93

Interactive Situation Questions

Apply what you've learned to some typical computing situations. When using the NP9 BookOnCD or the NP9 Web site, you can type your answers, and then use the Check Answers button to automatically score your responses.

2

1. Suppose you're reading a computer magazine and you come across the ad pictured to the right. By looking at the specs, you can tell that the microprocessor was manufactured by which company? [_____]

2. The capacity of the hard disk drive in the ad is [_____] GB and the memory capacity is [_____] GB.

3. The computer in the ad appears to have a(n) [_____] controller card for the hard disk drive.

4. You are thinking about upgrading the microprocessor in your three-year-old computer, which has a 2.6 MHz Pentium microprocessor and 512 MB of RAM. Would it be worthwhile to spend $500 to install a 3.8 GHz Pentium processor? Yes or no? [_____]

5. You're in the process of booting up your computer and suddenly the screen contains an assortment of settings for date and time, hard disk drive, and memory capacity. From what you've learned in this chapter, you surmise that these settings are stored in the [_____] memory, and that they are best left unmodified.

6. You're looking for a portable storage device that you can use to transport a few files between your home computer and your school computer lab. The school lab computers have no floppy disk drives, but do have USB ports. You should be able to transport your files using a USB [_____] drive.

SUP-R GAME DESKTOP MODEL EE2007

- Athlon™ 64 FX-57
- 1 GB 400 MHz SDRAM
- 160 GB UltraATA HD (7200 rpm)
- 16x DVD / 52x36x52x CD-RW Drive
- 3.5" 1.44 MB FDD
- 21" 24 dp monitor
- Dual NVIDIA® GeForce™ 6800 Ultra PCI Express 512MB
- Creative Sound Blaster® Audigy®
- Altec Lansing speakers
- Gigbit Ethernet port
- 3-year limited warranty*
- Windows Vista

$ 1799

7. You want to add a storage device to your computer that reads CD-ROMs, DVD-ROMs, DVD-Videos, and CD-Rs. A DVD/CD-RW will do the job. True or false? [_____]

8. You are a professional graphics designer. A(n) [_____] is likely to give you the best colors from all viewing angles, whereas a(n) [_____] may not show true colors when viewed from some angles.

9. Suppose that you volunteer to produce a large quantity of black-and-white leaflets for a charity organization. It is fortunate that you have access to a(n) [_____] printer with a high duty cycle and low operating costs.

✤ CHECK ANSWERS

Interactive Practice Tests

Practice tests that consist of 10 multiple-choice, true/false, and fill-in-the-blank questions are available on both the NP9 BookOnCD and the NP9 Web site. The questions are selected at random from a large test bank, so each time you take a test, you'll receive a different set of questions. Your tests are scored immediately, and you can print study guides that help you find the correct answers for any questions that you missed.

Projects

An NP9 Project is an open-ended activity that will help you apply the concepts you have learned. Many projects require resources in addition to your textbook, such as current magazines, library materials, or Web access. When you tackle a project, be prepared to use your critical thinking skills, logical analysis, and your creativity.

CRITICAL THINKING

Steve Jobs, co-founder of Apple Computers, coined the idea that computers should be consumer appliances like toasters that could be setup easily, used by anyone, and "democratically priced" so they were affordable to everyone. An opposing philosophy, championed by many PC owners, is that computers should be flexible modular systems that can be easily customized, upgraded, and modified by anyone with a moderate degree of technical savvy. Which philosophy do you personally prefer? What do you think is the preference of the majority of computer shoppers? If you were a computer designer, how would you provide your customers with flexibility while making it approachable for non-techies? Incorporate your ideas in a one-page e-mail message or attachment and submit it to your instructor.

GROUP PROJECT

For this project, work in groups of three or four. The group should select a digital device, such as a printer, scanner, digital camera, Web camera, digital video camera, digital music player, video capture card, digitizing tablet, or accelerated 3-D graphics card. If a member of your group owns the device, that's a plus. Create promotional materials for a tradeshow booth featuring your "product." You might include a product photo, list of specifications, and a short instruction manual. If time permits, your instructor might ask your group to present your sales pitch or a demonstration to the rest of the class.

CYBER CLASSROOM

E-mail the other members of your team a technical support question based on a theoretical problem you're having with your computer. They should try to solve the problem using their current expertise and relevant Web sites. At the end of the project, evaluate your team's success rate based on the difficulty of the problems and the efficiency of their troubleshooting.

MULTIMEDIA PROJECT

Search the Web for "modding" and collect ideas for souping up your computer system unit, keyboard, and mouse. Make sure you check out options for clear lexan and metallic cases, along with lighting options. Download photos from the Web and print them out, keeping track of sources. Using ideas from your collection of photos, sketch out plans for your ultimate modded computer. Submit your plan along with a list of the sources you used to get ideas and images.

RESUME BUILDER

Use the Web and other resources to learn about the computers and other technologies used in your career field or profession of interest to you. Develop the information you find into a format similar to the Computers in Context section of each chapter in this textbook. Make sure you select two photos to accompany your narrative and include a list of relevant InfoWebLinks.

GLOBALIZATION

Computer ownership is growing worldwide and providing access to productivity tools and a global communications infrastructure. For this project, look for statistics and graphs showing the increase in computer ownership over time. How does it compare to telephone, television, and radio ownership? Are any aspects of this data unexpected or surprising? Gather your graphs and analysis into a two- to three-page executive summary.

ISSUE

The Issue section of this chapter focused on the potential for discarded computers and other electronic devices to become a significant environmental problem. For this project, write a two- to five-page paper about recycling computers, based on information you gather from the Internet. To begin this project, consult the Computer Recycling InfoWeb (see page 105) and link to the recommended Web pages to get an in-depth overview of the issue. Next, determine the specific aspect of the issue you will present in your paper. You might, for example, decide to focus on toxic materials that end up in landfills or barriers that discourage shipping old computers across national borders. Whatever aspect of the issue you present, make sure you can back up your discussion with facts and references to authoritative articles and Web pages. Follow your professor's instructions for formatting citations and for submitting your paper by e-mail or as a printed document.

COMPUTERS IN CONTEXT

The Computers in Context section of this chapter focused on computer and communication technologies pioneered by the military and then adopted into civilian use. For this project, research one of two topics:

   The use of notebook computers in combat environments and how design innovations for military use might affect the design of your next computer

   Developments in wearable computers and how soldiers and civilians might use them

To begin the project, survey the material in the Computers and the Military InfoWeb (page 107). Use a Web search engine to locate additional material relevant to the topic you've selected. Then write a two- to four-page paper about your findings and include graphics to illustrate your points. Make sure you cite sources for your material. Follow your professor's instructions for formatting and submitting your paper.

2

Study Tips

Study Tips help you to organize and consolidate the information in a unit by making lists, outlines, charts, and sketches. You can use paper and pencil or word processing software to complete most of the Study Tip activities.

1. Make sure you can use your own words to correctly answer each of the orange focus questions that appear throughout the chapter.

2. Explain the difference between an analog and a digital device. Provide a few examples of your own in addition to the example in the chapter.

3. Describe how the binary number system uses only 1s and 0s to represent numbers.

4. List and briefly describe four codes that computers typically use for character data.

5. Describe the difference between numeric data, character data, and numerals.

6. Make sure you understand the meaning of the following measurement terms, and can indicate what aspects of a computer system they are used to measure: KB, Kb, MB, Mb, GB, KBps, Kbps, MHz, GHz, ms, ns.

7. Create your own diagram of a computer system board, indicating the approximate location of the microprocessor, RAM, and expansion slots.

8. List and describe the factors that affect microprocessor performance.

9. Name two companies that produce microprocessors, and list some of the models that each company produces.

10. List four types of memory and briefly describe how each one works.

11. Describe the advantages and disadvantages of magnetic storage, optical storage, and solid state storage.

12. Create your own diagram to illustrate how the data bus connects RAM, the microprocessor, and peripheral devices.

13. Summarize what you know about how a graphics card can affect a monitor's resolution.

14. Make a table with three columns, labeled Input, Output, and Storage. Page through the chapter and for each device you encounter, place it in one or more of the columns as appropriate.

15. Fill in the blanks on the concept map below to show the hierarchy of system unit components.

Review on the Web

2

TECHTV VIDEO PROJECT

The TechTV segment *Getting Started* demonstrates the basic parts needed to construct a personal computer. While watching the video, make a list of the parts. Use the Web to find an example of each part. Add the manufacturer, model number, and price in your list. Calculate the price of assembling a computer from these parts.

To work with the Video Projects for this chapter, connect to the New Perspectives NP9 Web site.

www.course.com/np/concepts9/ch02

ONLINE GAMES

Test your comprehension of the concepts introduced in Chapter 2 by playing the NP9 Online Games. At the end of each game, you have three options:

- Submit your results to your instructor using the Universal Gradebook through CoursePort
- Print your results to be submitted to your instructor
- Print a comprehensive study guide complete with page references

To work with the Online Games for this chapter, connect to the New Perspectives NP9 Web site.

www.course.com/np/concepts9/ch02

 LIGHTNING   **DON'T TELL ME**   **FAKE OUT**

ONLINE END-OF-CHAPTER ACTIVITIES

The following NP9 Review Activities are also available at the New Perspectives NP9 Web site:

- Interactive Summary
- Interactive Situation Questions
- Interactive Practice Tests
- Concept Map

If you are using the Web site to complete these activities, you can automatically score your answers and share the results with your instructor.

www.course.com/np/concepts9/ch02

3

Computer Software

FOCUS ON THESE LEARNING OBJECTIVES

Describe the components of a typical software package, including executable files, support modules, and data modules

Trace the development of a computer program from its inception as a set of high-level language instructions through its translation into machine language

Describe the differences between system software and application software

Describe the way an operating system manages each computer resource

Identify operating systems for personal computers, PDAs, and servers

Explain the key features and uses for word processing, desktop publishing, and Web authoring software

Describe the major features of spreadsheet software

Describe the key features of database software

List the types of software available for graphics, video, music, education and reference, entertainment, and business

Explain how to install and uninstall software, whether it is supplied on CDs or as a Web download

Describe the differences among new software versions, software patches, and service packs

Describe the rights granted by copyright law, commercial software licenses, shareware licenses, freeware licenses, open source licenses, and public domain software

A detailed list of learning objectives is provided at the New Perspectives NP9 Web site:

www.course.com/np/concepts9/ch03

UNDERSTAND THE CHAPTER CONTENTS

SOFTWARE ESSENTIALLY TRANSFORMS A COMPUTER FROM ONE KIND OF MACHINE TO another—from a drafting station to a typesetting machine; from a flight simulator to a calculator; from a filing system to a music remixing machine. In Chapter 3 you'll find out what makes your computer's operating system and applications software tick. You'll also find out how to install software and navigate the legalities of your software's license agreement.

3

TAKE A PRE-ASSESSMENT QUIZ

Find out how much you know about installing and using software. Armed with your results from this quiz, you can focus your study time on concepts that will round out your knowledge of computer software and improve your test scores.

www.course.com/np/concepts9/ch03

LISTEN TO A CHAPTER OVERVIEW

Get your book and highlighter ready, then connect to the New Perspectives NP9 Web site, where you can listen to an overview that points out the most important concepts for this chapter.

www.course.com/np/concepts9/ch03

BEFORE YOU READ ON, TRY IT

IS MY SOFTWARE UP TO DATE?

Chapter 3 introduces you to basic concepts about computer software. Before you begin reading, take a glance at the software installed on your home, work, or school computer. Want to know if your software is up to date? You can use the "About" feature of any software package to find its version number and discover if a service pack (SP) has been installed.

1. Start your computer.

2. Click the Start button.

3. Click the All Programs option to display a list of installed software.

4. Point to items in the list that have a ▸ symbol to see a sublist of software programs.

5. As you read through the list of installed software, jot down the names of any that you're not familiar with. When you read the chapter, you might find out what they do.

6. Look for Internet Explorer in the list of programs.

7. Click Internet Explorer to open the program.

8. Click the Help menu, then click About Internet Explorer. A dialog box appears. It contains a version number like 6.0 and an update version like SP2. You'll learn the significance of version numbers and service packs when you read the chapter.

9. Click the OK button to close the About Internet Explorer window, then click the ✕ button to close the Internet Explorer program.

10. Explore the About dialog box for other software on your computer. Does it provide more or less information than the Internet Explorer Dialog box?

TIP

When using the BookOnCD, the ✱ icons are "clickable" to access resources on the CD. The ✱ icons are clickable to access resources on the Web. You can also access Web resources by using your browser to connect directly to the New Perspectives NP9 Web site at: www.course.com/np/concepts9/ch03

A

Software Basics

Computer software determines the types of tasks a computer can help you accomplish. Some software helps you create documents, while other software helps you edit home videos, prepare your tax return, or design the floor plan for a new house. But how does software transform your computer into a machine that can help with so many tasks? Section A delves into the characteristics of computer software and explains how it works.

SOFTWARE: THE INSIDE STORY

What is software? As you learned in Chapter 1, the instructions that tell a computer how to carry out a task are referred to as a computer program. These programs form the software that prepares a computer to do a specific task, such as document production, video editing, graphic design, or Web browsing. Software is usually distributed on CDs or DVDs, as shown in Figure 3-1. It also can be made available as a Web download.

What kinds of files are included in a typical software product? Whether it's on a CD or downloaded from the Web, today's software is typically composed of many files. You might be surprised by the number of files that are necessary to make software work. For example, the eVideo-In Pro software includes numerous files with extensions such as .exe, .dll, and .hlp, as shown in Figure 3-2.

FIGURE 3-1

In popular usage, the term "software" usually refers to one or more computer programs and any additional files that are provided to carry out a specific type of task.

FIGURE 3-2

The files required by the eVideo-In Pro software contain user-executable programs, support programs, and data.

At least one of the files included in a software package contains an executable program designed to be launched, or started, by users. On PCs, these programs are stored in files that typically have .exe file extensions and are sometimes referred to as "executable files" or "user-executable files." When using a Windows PC, you can start an executable file by clicking its icon, selecting it from the Start menu, or entering its name in the Run dialog box.

Other files supplied with a software package contain programs that are not designed to be run by users. These "support programs" contain instructions for the computer to use in conjunction with the main user-executable file. A support program can be "called," or activated, by the main program as needed. In the context of Windows software, support programs often have file extensions such as .dll and .ocx.

In addition to program files, many software packages also include data files. As you might expect, these files contain any data that is necessary for a task, but not supplied by the user, such as Help documentation, a word list for an online spell checker, synonyms for a thesaurus, or graphics for the software's toolbar icons. The data files supplied with a software package sport file extensions such as .txt, .bmp, and .hlp. Figure 3-3 illustrates the relationship between the various files distributed with a typical software package.

TERMINOLOGY NOTE

The term "software" was once used for all non-hardware components of a computer. In this context, software referred to computer programs and to the data the programs used. It could also refer to any data that existed in digital format, such as documents or photos. Using today's terminology, however, the documents and photos you create are usually classified as "data" rather than as "software."

3

FIGURE 3-3

The main executable file provides the primary set of instructions for the computer to execute and calls various support programs and data files as needed.

Why does software require so many files? The use of a main user-executable file plus several support programs and data files offers a great deal of flexibility and efficiency for software developers. Support programs and data files from existing programs can usually be modified by developers for other programs without changing the main executable file. This modular approach can significantly reduce the time required to create and test the main executable file, which usually contains a long and fairly complex program. The modular approach also allows software developers to reuse their support programs in multiple software products and adapt preprogrammed support modules for use in their own software.

Modular programming techniques are of interest mainly to people who create computer programs; however, these techniques affect the process of installing and uninstalling software, discussed later in this chapter. It is important, therefore, to remember that computer software typically consists of many files that contain user-executable programs, support programs, and data.

PROGRAMMERS AND PROGRAMMING LANGUAGES

Who creates computer software? **Computer programmers** write computer programs that become the components of a computer software product. The finished software product is then distributed by the programmers or by **software publishers**—companies that specialize in marketing and selling commercial software.

At one time, businesses, organizations, and individuals had to write most of the software they used. Today, however, most businesses and organizations purchase commercial software (also referred to as "off-the-shelf software") to avoid the time and expense of writing their own. Individuals rarely write software for their personal computers, preferring to select from thousands of software titles available in stores, from catalogs, and on the Internet. Although most computer owners do not write their own software, working as a computer programmer for a government agency, business, or software publisher can be a challenging career.

How does a programmer "write" software? Most software provides a task-related environment, which includes a screen display, a means of collecting commands and data from the user, the specifications for processing data, and a method for displaying or outputting data. Figure 3-4 illustrates a very simple software environment that converts a Fahrenheit temperature to Celsius and displays the result.

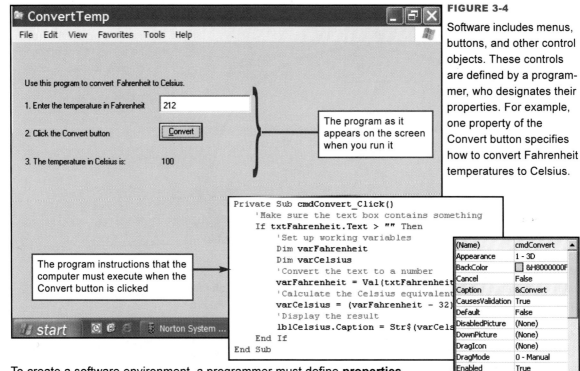

FIGURE 3-4

Software includes menus, buttons, and other control objects. These controls are defined by a programmer, who designates their properties. For example, one property of the Convert button specifies how to convert Fahrenheit temperatures to Celsius.

The program as it appears on the screen when you run it

The program instructions that the computer must execute when the Convert button is clicked

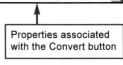

Properties associated with the Convert button

To create a software environment, a programmer must define **properties** for each element in the environment, such as where an object appears, its shape, its color, and its behavior. For the example shown in Figure 3-4, the programmer must define many properties for the Convert button, including:

- Its height: 375

- Its label (caption): Convert

- The button font: MS Sans Serif

- What happens when you click it: Subtract 32 from Fahrenheit, divide by 1.8, and then display the answer

A **programming language** (sometimes referred to as a "computer language") provides the tools a programmer uses to create software and produce a lengthy list of instructions, called **source code**, which defines the software environment in every detail—what it looks like, how the user enters commands, and how it manipulates data. Most programmers today prefer to use a **high-level language**, such as C++, Java, Ada, COBOL, or Visual Basic. These languages have some similarities to human languages and produce programs that are fairly easy to test and modify.

HOW SOFTWARE WORKS

How does a computer process a program? A computer's microprocessor understands only **machine language**—the instruction set that is "hard wired" within the microprocessor's circuits. Therefore, instructions written in a high-level language must be translated into machine language before a computer can use them. Figure 3-5 gives you an idea of what happens to a high-level instruction when it is converted into machine language instructions.

FIGURE 3-5

A simple instruction to add two numbers becomes a long series of 0s and 1s in machine language.

3

High-level Language Instruction	Machine Language Equivalent	Description of Machine Language Instructions
Answer=FirstNumber+SecondNumber	10001000 00011000 010000000	Load FirstNumber into Register 1
	10001000 00010000 00100000	Load SecondNumber into Register 2
	00000000 00011000 00010000	Perform ADD operation
	10100010 00111000	Move the number from the accumulator to the RAM location called Answer

How are instructions converted to machine language? The process of translating instructions from a high-level language into machine language can be accomplished by two special types of programs: compilers and interpreters. A **compiler** translates all the instructions in a program as a single batch, and the resulting machine language instructions, called **object code**, are placed in a new file (Figure 3-6). Most of the program files on a distribution CD for commercial software are compiled so that they contain machine language instructions that are ready for the processor to execute.

FIGURE 3-6

A compiler converts high-level instructions into a new file containing machine language instructions.

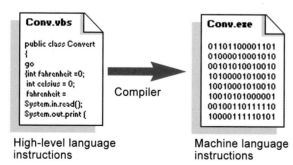

High-level language instructions   Compiler   Machine language instructions

As an alternative to a compiler, an **interpreter** converts one instruction at a time while the program is running. An interpreter reads the first instruction, converts it into machine language, and then sends it to the microprocessor. After the instruction is executed, the interpreter converts the next instruction, and so on (Figure 3-7 on the next page).

FIGURE 3-7

An interpreter converts high-level instructions into machine language instructions while the program is running.
An interpreted program runs more slowly than a compiled program because the translation process happens while the program is running.

CLICK TO START

So how does software work? Assume that a video editing program, such as eVideo-In Pro, is installed on your computer, which is running Windows. Figure 3-8 illustrates how the files included in this software package interact when you edit videos.

FIGURE 3-8

The main executable file loads into RAM when the program runs, and can call various other files as needed.

1. When you start the eVideo-In Pro software, the instructions in the file eVidpro.exe are loaded from disk into RAM and then sent to the microprocessor.

2. eVidpro.exe is a compiled program, so its instructions are immediately executed by the processor.

3. As processing begins, the eVideo-In Pro window opens and the graphical controls for video editing tasks appear. The program waits for you to select a control by clicking it with the mouse.

4. Based on your selection, eVidpro.exe follows its instructions and performs the actions you specify. Many of the instructions for these actions are included in the main executable file. If not, eVidpro.exe calls a support program, such as Sftrans.dll.

5. If you access eVideo-In Pro Help, eVidpro.exe loads the data file eVidpro.hlp into the processor.

6. eVidpro.exe continues to respond to the controls you select until you click the Close button, which halts execution of the program instructions, closes the program window, and releases the space the program occupied in RAM for use by other programs or data.

APPLICATION SOFTWARE AND SYSTEM SOFTWARE

How is software categorized? Software is categorized as application software or system software. When you hear the word "application," your first reaction might be to envision a financial aid application or a form you fill out to apply for a job, a club membership, or a driver's license. The word "application" has other meanings, however. One of them is a synonym for the word "use." A computer certainly has many uses, such as creating documents, crunching numbers, drawing designs, and editing photographs.

Each use is considered an "application," and the software that provides the computer with instructions for each use is called **application software**, or simply an "application." The primary purpose of application software is to help people carry out tasks using a computer.

In contrast, the primary purpose of **system software**—your computer's operating system, device drivers, programming languages, and utilities—is to help the computer carry out its basic operating functions. Figure 3-9 illustrates the division between system software and application software. You'll learn more about these software categories in Sections B and C.

FIGURE 3-9

Software can be classified into categories.

3

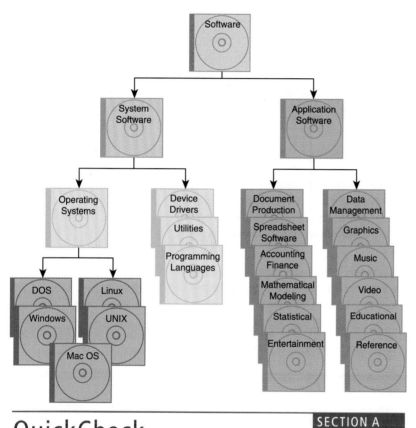

QuickCheck

SECTION A

1. When using a Windows PC, you can start a(n) [executable] file by clicking its icon, selecting it from the Start menu, or entering its name in the Run dialog box.

2. A programming language provides tools for creating a lengthy list of instructions called [source] code.

3. Instructions that are written in a(n) [high]-level language must be translated into machine language before a computer can use them.

4. As a program is running, a(n) [interpreter] converts one instruction at a time into machine language.

5. Computer software can be divided into two major categories: [application] software and system software.

CHECK ANSWERS

SECTION B

Operating Systems and Utilities

An operating system is an integral part of virtually every computer system. It fundamentally affects how you can use your computer. Can you run two programs at the same time? Can you connect your computer to a network? Does your computer run dependably? Does all your software have a similar "look and feel," or do you have to learn a different set of controls and commands for each new program you acquire?

To answer questions like these, it is helpful to have a clear idea about what an operating system is and what it does. Section B provides an overview of operating systems and compares some of the most popular operating systems for personal computers. It also highlights some of today's most popular utility software supplied by operating systems and third-party vendors.

OPERATING SYSTEM OVERVIEW

What is an operating system? Chapter 1 explained that an operating system (abbreviated OS) is a type of system software that acts as the master controller for all activities that take place within a computer system. It is one of the factors that determines your computer's compatibility and platform. Most personal computers are sold with a preinstalled operating system, such as Windows or Mac OS.

What does an operating system do? Your computer's operating system and application software are organized similar to the chain of command in an army. You issue a command using application software. Application software tells the operating system what to do. The operating system tells the device drivers, device drivers tell the hardware, and the hardware actually does the work. Figure 3-10 illustrates this chain of command for printing a document or photo.

FIGURE 3-10

A command to print a document is relayed through various levels of software, including the operating system, until it reaches the printer.

2. The word processing application signals the operating system that a document must be sent to the printer.

Printer Driver

1. You issue the Print command while using application software, such as a word processor.

4. The device driver controls the printer as it prints the document.

3. The operating system communicates the document data to the device driver for the printer.

The operating system interacts with application software, device drivers, and hardware to manage a computer's resources. In the context of a computer system, the term **resource** refers to any component that is required to perform work. For example, the processor is a resource. RAM, storage space, and peripherals are also resources. While you interact with application software, your computer's operating system is busy behind the scenes with tasks such as those listed in Figure 3-11 on the next page.

Manage memory

Manage processor resources

Keep track of storage resources

Ensure that input and output proceed in an orderly manner

Establish basic elements of the user interface

FIGURE 3-11

Operating System Tasks

3

How does the operating system manage processor resources? Chapter 2 explained how the control unit directs activities within the microprocessor. The operating system also controls the microprocessor—just at a slightly higher level. Every cycle of a computer's microprocessor is a resource for accomplishing tasks.

Many activities—called "processes"—compete for the attention of your computer's microprocessor. Commands are arriving from programs you're using, while input is arriving from the keyboard and mouse. At the same time, data must be sent to the display device or printer, and Web pages are arriving from your Internet connection. To manage all these competing processes, your computer's operating system must ensure that each one receives its share of microprocessor cycles.

Ideally, the operating system should be able to help the microprocessor switch tasks so that, from the user's vantage point, everything seems to be happening at the same time. The operating system also must ensure that the microprocessor doesn't "spin its wheels" waiting for input while it could be working on some other processing task.

A computer can take advantage of performance-enhancing technologies, such as multitasking, multithreading, and dual core or multiple processors, if its operating system and programs support them.

Multitasking provides process and memory management services that allow two or more tasks, jobs, or programs to run simultaneously. Most of today's operating systems, including the OS on your personal computer, offer multitasking services.

Within a single program, **multithreading** allows multiple parts, or threads, to run simultaneously. For example, one thread for a spreadsheet program might be waiting for input from the user while other threads perform a long calculation in the background. Multithreading can speed up performance on single or multiple processor computers.

Many new computers include dual core processors or multiple processors. An operating systems **multiprocessing** capability supports a division of labor among all the processing units.

Why does an operating system manage memory? A microprocessor works with data and executes instructions stored in RAM—one of your computer's most important resources. When you want to run more than one program at a time, the operating system has to allocate specific areas of memory for each program, as shown in Figure 3-12.

FIGURE 3-12

The operating system allocates a specific area of RAM for each program that is open and running. The operating system is itself a program, so it requires RAM space, too.

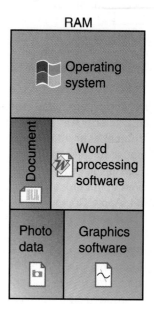

RAM

When multiple programs are running, the OS must ensure that instructions and data from one area of memory don't "leak" into an area allocated to another program. If an OS falls down on the job and fails to protect each program's memory area, data can get corrupted, programs can "crash," and your computer displays error messages, such as "General Protection Fault" or "Program Not Responding." Your PC can sometimes recover from memory leak problems if you use the Ctrl+Alt+Del key sequence to close the corrupted program.

How does the OS keep track of storage resources? Behind the scenes, an operating system acts as a filing clerk that stores and retrieves files from your disks and CDs. It remembers the names and locations of all your files and keeps track of empty spaces where new files can be stored. Chapter 4 explores file storage in more depth and explains how the operating system affects the way you create, name, save, and retrieve files.

TERMINOLOGY NOTE

The term "buffer" is technical jargon for a region of memory that holds data waiting to be transferred from one device to another.

Why does the operating system get involved with peripheral devices? Every device connected to a computer is regarded as a resource. Your computer's operating system communicates with device driver software so that data can travel smoothly between the computer and these peripheral resources. If a peripheral device or driver is not performing correctly, the operating system makes a decision about what to do—usually it displays an on-screen message to warn you of the problem.

Your computer's operating system ensures that input and output proceed in an orderly manner, using "buffers" to collect and hold data while the computer is busy with other tasks. By using a keyboard buffer, for example, your computer never misses one of your keystrokes, regardless of how fast you type or what else is happening in your computer at the same time.

FIGURE 3-13

A graphical user interface (top) features menus and icons that you can manipulate with the click of a mouse. A command-line interface (bottom) requires you to memorize and type commands.

How does the operating system affect the user interface? A **user interface** can be defined as the combination of hardware and software that helps people and computers communicate with each other. Your computer's user interface includes a display device, mouse, and keyboard that allow you to view and manipulate your computing environment. It also includes software elements, such as menus and toolbar buttons. The operating system's user interface defines the "look and feel" for all its compatible software. For example, application software that runs under Windows uses a standard set of menus, buttons, and toolbars based on the operating system's user interface.

Most computers today feature a graphical user interface. Abbreviated "GUI" (sometimes pronounced as "gooey"), a **graphical user interface** provides a way to point and click a mouse to select menu options and manipulate graphical objects displayed on the screen. GUIs were originally conceived at the prestigious Xerox PARC research facility. In 1984, Apple Computer turned the idea into a commercial success with the launch of its popular Macintosh computer, which featured a GUI operating system and applications. Graphical user interfaces didn't really catch on in the PC market until 1992 when Windows 3.1 became standard issue on most PCs, replacing a **command-line interface** that required users to type memorized commands to run programs and accomplish tasks (Figure 3-13).

Where is the operating system stored? In some computers—typically handhelds and videogame consoles—the entire operating system is small enough to be stored in ROM. For nearly all personal computers, servers, workstations, mainframes, and supercomputers, the operating system program is quite large, so most of it is stored on a hard disk. The operating system's small **bootstrap program** is stored in ROM and supplies the instructions needed to load the operating system's core into memory when the system boots. This core part of the operating system, called the **kernel**, provides the most essential operating system services, such as memory management and file access. The kernel stays in RAM all the time your computer is on. Other parts of the operating system, such as customization utilities, are loaded into RAM as they are needed.

Do I ever interact directly with the OS? Although its main purpose is to control what happens "behind the scenes" of a computer system, many operating systems provide helpful tools, called operating system utilities, that you can use to control and customize your computer equipment and work environment. Utilities, like those listed below, are typically accessed by using a GUI, such as the familiar Windows desktop.

- **Launch programs.** When you start your computer, Windows displays graphical objects, such as icons, the Start button, and the Programs menu, which you can use to start programs.

- **Manage files.** Another useful utility, called Windows Explorer, allows you to view a list of files, move them to different storage devices, copy them, rename them, and delete them.

- **Get help.** Windows offers a Help system you can use to find out how various commands work.

- **Customize the user interface.** The Control Panel, accessible from the Start menu, provides utilities that help you customize your screen display and work environment.

- **Configure equipment.** The Control Panel also provides access to utilities that help you set up and configure your computer's hardware and peripheral devices (Figure 3-14).

FIGURE 3-14

Many Windows utilities can be accessed from the Control Panel. You'll find it by clicking the Start button. If it does not appear on the Start menu, click Settings and then Control Panel.

Are different operating systems needed for different computing tasks? One operating system might be better suited to some computing tasks than others. To provide clues to their strengths and weaknesses, operating systems are informally categorized and characterized using one or more of the following terms:

A **single-user operating system** expects to deal with one set of input devices—those that can be controlled by one user at a time. Operating systems for handheld computers and many personal computers fit into the single-user category. DOS is an example of a single-user operating system.

A **multiuser operating system** allows a single computer—often a mainframe—to deal with simultaneous input, output, and processing requests from many users. One of its most difficult responsibilities is to schedule all the processing requests that a centralized computer must perform. IBM's OS/390 is one of the most popular mainframe multiuser operating systems.

A **network operating system** (also referred to as a "server operating system") provides communications and routing services that allow computers to share data, programs, and peripheral devices. Novell NetWare, for example, is almost always referred to as a network operating system. The difference between network services and multiuser services can seem a little hazy—especially because operating systems such as UNIX, Linux, and Sun Microsystem's Solaris offer both. The main difference, however, is that multiuser operating systems schedule requests for processing on a centralized computer, whereas a network operating system simply routes data and programs to each user's local computer, where the actual processing takes place.

A **desktop operating system** is one that's designed for a personal computer—a desktop, notebook, or tablet computer. The computer you use at home, at school, or at work is most likely configured with a desktop operating system, such as Windows or Mac OS. Typically, these operating systems are designed to accommodate a single user, but might also provide networking capability. Today's desktop operating systems invariably provide multitasking capabilities.

Some operating system vendors characterize their products as "home" or "professional" versions. The home version usually has fewer network management tools than the professional version.

WINDOWS, MAC OS, UNIX, LINUX, AND DOS

What's the best-selling operating system? **Microsoft Windows** is installed on more than 80% of the world's personal computers. The number and variety of programs that run on Windows are unmatched by any other operating system, a fact that contributes to its dominant position as the most widely used desktop operating system. Since its introduction in 1985, Windows has evolved through several versions, listed in Figure 3-15.

FIGURE 3-15

Windows Timeline

2006 Windows Vista
Featured 64-bit support, enhanced security, and more flexible file management. Also more powerful search capabilities and live icons that show document thumbnails.

2001 Windows XP
Featured an updated user interface, used the Windows 2000 32-bit kernel, and supported FAT32 and NTFS file systems.

2000 Windows Me
The last Windows version to use the original Windows kernel that accesses DOS.

2000 Windows 2000
Billed as a "multipurpose network OS for businesses of all sizes" and featured enhanced Web services.

1998 Windows 98
Increased stability was a big feature of this Windows version, which also included the Internet Explorer browser.

1995 Windows 95
Featured a revised user interface. Supported 32-bit processors, TCP/IP, dial-up networking, and long file names.

1993 Windows NT
Provided management and security tools for network servers and the NTFS file system.

1992 Windows for Workgroups
Provided peer-to-peer networking, e-mail, group scheduling, and file and printer sharing.

1992 Windows 3.1
Introduced program icons and the file folder metaphor.

1990 Windows 3.0
Introduced graphical controls.

1987 Windows 2.0
Introduced overlapping windows and expanded memory access.

1985 Windows 1.0
Divided the screen into "windows" that allowed users to work with several programs at the same time.

The first versions of Windows, including Windows 3.1, were sometimes referred to as "operating environments" rather than operating systems because they required DOS to supply the operating system kernel. Windows operating environments primarily supplied a point-and-click user interface, complete with graphical screen displays and mouse input. Windows operating environments evolved into today's comprehensive operating systems, which do not require the DOS kernel.

The Windows operating system gets its name from the rectangular work areas that appear on the screen-based desktop. Each work area (or "window") can display a different document or program, providing a visual model of the operating system's multitasking capabilities (Figure 3-16).

INFOWEBLINKS

You'll find lots of current information about Windows at the **Microsoft Windows InfoWeb**.

www.course.com/np/concepts9/ch03

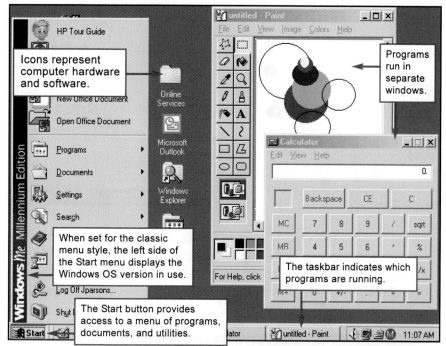

FIGURE 3-16

If you find a Start button sporting the Windows logo in the lower-left corner of the screen, it is a good bet that the computer is running some version of Windows.

The graphical user interface for Windows Me (shown at left) features many similarities and some cosmetic differences when compared to the interface for Windows XP (shown below).

3

Microsoft currently offers several types of operating systems. Home, Professional, and Workstation editions are designed for personal computers. Server editions are designed for LAN, Internet, and Web servers. Embedded editions are designed for handheld devices, such as PDAs and mobile phones. Figure 3-17 categorizes Windows offerings.

FIGURE 3-17

Microsoft offers several versions of Windows, designed for different computing tasks and equipment.

Personal Computers

Windows Vista
Windows XP Home Edition
Windows XP Professional
Windows XP Tablet PC Edition
Windows 2000 Professional
Windows Me
Windows 98

LAN, Internet, and Web Servers

Windows Server 2005
Windows Server 2003
Windows 2000 Server

PDAs, Mobile Phones, and Non-personal Computer Devices

Windows Mobile OS
Pocket PC OS 2002
Pocket PC OS 2000
Windows CE
Windows XP Embedded

Is Mac OS similar to Windows? Although **Mac OS** was developed several years before Windows, both operating systems base their user interfaces on the graphical model pioneered at Xerox PARC. Like Windows, Mac OS has been through a number of revisions, including OS X "Tiger" (X meaning version 10), released in 2004.

A quick comparison of Figures 3-16 and 3-18 shows that both Mac and Windows interfaces use a mouse to point and click various icons and menus. Both interfaces feature rectangular work areas to reflect multitasking capabilities. Both operating systems provide basic networking services. A decent collection of software is available for computers that run Mac OS, although the selection is not as vast as the Windows collection. Many of the most prolific software publishers produce one version of their software for Windows and another, similar version for Mac OS.

INFOWEBLINKS

The **Apple InfoWeb** links you to the official site for Apple Computer, Inc.

www.course.com/np/concepts9/ch03

FIGURE 3-18

The Apple logo at the top of the screen is your clue that a computer is running Mac OS.

The Apple logo provides access to a menu.

Two different programs can run in two separate windows.

Menus and other on-screen objects are manipulated by using a mouse.

Icons represent computer hardware components and software.

Are UNIX and Linux the same? The **UNIX** operating system was developed in 1969 at AT&T's Bell Labs. It gained a good reputation for its dependability in multiuser environments, and many versions of it became available for mainframes and microcomputers. UNIX provides the foundation for Apple's Mac OS X Tiger, giving Macs an industrial-strength stability.

In 1991, a young Finnish student named Linus Torvalds developed the **Linux** (pronounced LIH nucks) operating system. Linux was inspired by and loosely based on a UNIX derivative called MINIX, created by Andrew Tanenbaum.

Linux is rather unique because it is distributed along with its source code under the terms of a General Public License (GPL), which allows everyone to make copies for their own use, to give to others, or to sell. This licensing policy has encouraged programmers to develop Linux utilities, software, and enhancements. Linux is primarily distributed over the Web.

Although Linux is designed for microcomputers, it shares several technical features with UNIX, such as multitasking, virtual memory, TCP/IP drivers, and multiuser capabilities. These features make Linux a popular operating system for e-mail and Web servers as well as for local area networks. Linux has been gaining popularity as a desktop operating system, and some new personal computers now come configured with Linux instead of Windows or Mac OS. Linux typically requires a bit more tinkering than the Windows and Mac desktop operating systems. The comparatively limited number of programs that run under Linux also discourages many nontechnical users from selecting it as the OS for their desktop and notebook computers.

Several Web sites offer a Linux "distribution," which is a package that contains the Linux kernel, system utilities, applications, and an installation routine. Beginner-friendly Linux distributions include Mandrakelinux, Linspire, College Linux, and Xandros Desktop. Most of these distributions include a GUI module that provides a user interface similar to the one pictured in Figure 3-19.

INFOWEBLINKS

If you're interested in exploring the world of "open source" operating systems, start your journey at the **Linux InfoWeb**.

www.course.com/np/concepts9/ch03

3

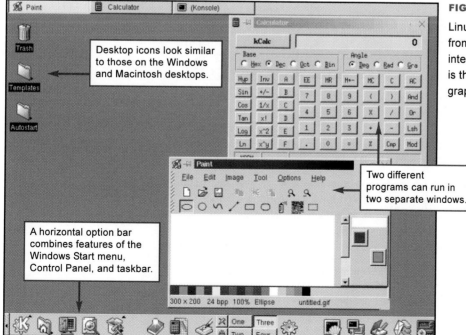

FIGURE 3-19

Linux users can choose from several graphical interfaces. Pictured here is the popular KDE graphical desktop.

Desktop icons look similar to those on the Windows and Macintosh desktops.

Two different programs can run in two separate windows.

A horizontal option bar combines features of the Windows Start menu, Control Panel, and taskbar.

Why do I keep hearing about DOS? Old-timers in the computer industry sometimes reminisce about DOS. It was the first operating system that many of them used, and its cryptic command-line user interface left an indelible impression. **DOS** (which rhymes with "toss") stands for Disk Operating System. It was developed by Microsoft—the same company that later produced Windows—and introduced on the original IBM PC in 1982. Although IBM called this operating system PC-DOS, Microsoft marketed it to other companies under the name MS-DOS.

After more than 20 years, remnants of DOS still linger in the world of personal computers because it provided part of the operating system kernel for Windows versions 3.1, 95, 98, and Me.

During the peak of its popularity, thousands of software programs were produced for computers running DOS. You can occasionally find some of these programs on the Internet, and run them using the MS-DOS Prompt option (Windows 98, Me, NT, and 2000) or the Command Prompt option (Windows XP) on the Windows Start menu. DOS also offers handy troubleshooting utilities, such as Ping, Tracert, Copy *, msconfig, and netstat used by tech-savvy computer users. DOS programs look rather unsophisticated by today's standards, so for many of today's computer owners, DOS and DOS software are nothing more than footnotes in the history of the computer industry.

INFOWEBLINKS

If you want to find out more about this venerable operating system, connect to the **DOS InfoWeb.**

www.course.com/np/concepts9/ch03

HANDHELD AND TABLET OPERATING SYSTEMS

What are the options for handheld operating systems? Three operating systems dominate the realm of handheld computers: Palm OS, Windows Mobile OS, and Symbian OS shown in Figure 3-20.

FIGURE 3-20

From left to right, Palm OS, Windows Mobile OS, and Symbian OS are popular PDA and smartphone operating systems.

Palm OS is produced by PalmSource, a spinoff of the company that produced some of the first commercially successful PDAs. Palm OS is currently used for popular PDAs such as palmOne Zire and Sony CLIE. It also powers Fossil's wristwatch PDA and smartphones from manufacturers such as palmOne, Samsung, and Kyocera.

Windows Mobile OS is an operating system built on the Microsoft Windows CE technology. As a cousin to Windows XP, Windows Mobile OS sports some features similar to those found on the Windows desktop. Windows Mobile OS is the operating system for a variety of PDAs, phone-enabled PDAs, and smartphones.

Symbian OS is a multitasking, multithreaded operating system popular on Ericsson and Nokia smartphones. Symbian can be easily programmed with languages such as C++, Visual Basic, or Personal Java, and so some interesting third-party freeware and shareware is available.

Are operating systems for handheld devices similar to desktop operating systems? Operating systems for handheld and desktop devices provide many similar services, such as scheduling processor resources, managing memory, loading programs, managing input and output, and establishing the user interface. But because handheld devices tend to be used for less sophisticated tasks, their operating systems are somewhat simpler and significantly smaller.

By keeping the operating system small, it can be stored in ROM. Without the need to load the OS from disk into RAM, a handheld device's operating system is ready almost instantly when the unit is turned on. Operating systems for handheld devices provide built-in support for touch screens, handwriting input, wireless networking, and cellular communications.

FIGURE 3-21

Handwriting recognition is one of the main services a tablet computer OS provides.

What about operating systems for tablet computers? Windows XP Tablet Edition is the operating system supplied with just about every tablet computer. Its main feature is handwriting recognition, which accepts printed input from the touch-sensitive screen and then converts it into ASCII text, as shown in Figure 3-21.

UTILITIES

What are utilities? In general, **utility software** (often referred to simply as "utilities") is a type of system software that's designed to perform a specialized task, such as system maintenance or security. As you learned earlier in the chapter, your computer's operating system supplies a variety of utilities that help you manage files, get help, customize the user interface, and so on.

What are third-party utilities? Utility software that doesn't come packaged with an operating system is often referred to as a third-party utility. Many third-party utilities are designed for the same tasks handled by operating system utilities, while others handle completely different tasks.

Why would I want third party utilities? Most operating systems supply a variety of built-in utilities, but computer owners typically also use utilities from third-party vendors for one of two reasons. Operating system utilities are sometimes not as dependable as third-party utilities designed by companies that specialize in system maintenance or security. Additionally, some operating system utilities are not as full featured as third-party versions.

For example, although Windows supplies a file compression utility that reduces file size for quick transmission or efficient storage, many computer owners prefer to use third-party utilities, such as WinZip, WinAce, IZArc, QuickZip, or PKZIP, that offer a variety of compression options. FTP utilities, such as WSFTP, are popular even though many Web sites offer automated downloads.

What are the most popular utilities? In past years, antivirus software, such as Norton AntiVirus and McAfee VirusScan, was a popular category of third-party utilities. With the recent influx of nuisance ads, intrusion attempts, and spam, utilities such as pop-up ad blockers, personal firewalls, and spam filters have also become best sellers.

Other security-related utilities include file-encryption software, such as PGP, that scrambles file contents for storage or transmission. For people nervous about the trail of Web sites they leave behind, utilities like 12Ghosts Wash remove Internet history lists, files, and graphics from locations that can be scattered in many parts of the hard disk. Filtering software, such as NetNanny, is used by parents to block their children from objectionable Web sites.

Computer owners like to customize their screen-based desktops with screensavers that display clever graphics when the machine is idle. "Skins" that customize the look and feel of media players and DVD burners are also popular (Figure 3-22).

Acrobat Reader is a long-time favorite utility that transforms all kinds of files into a portable format that can be created and read by any computer on which it is installed. Acrobat is especially handy for distributing documents created using expensive desktop publishing software that's not likely to be installed on many people's computers.

Another popular category of utility software is system utilities, such as Norton System Works, and System Mechanic PowerToys. These utilities can track down and fix disk errors, repair corrupted files, and give your PC a performance-enhancing tune-up.

A final group of utilities worth mentioning is designed for backing up and cleaning up hard disks, and shredding files so they can't be recovered. Utilities such as Recover My Files, VirtualLab, and R-Undelete can help you recover files deleted by mistake.

Where can I get utilities? The big-name antivirus and system utilities are commercial packages that you can purchase in any store that carries computers or office supplies. They can also be purchased online. Many other utilities can be downloaded for free and used on a trial basis for a short period of time. To continue using useful utilities, you can make an online payment as instructed in the Readme file or pop-up registration menu that appears at the end of the trial period.

FIGURE 3-22

Skins that change the appearance of Windows Media Player are an example of popular utilities.

QuickCheck

SECTION B

1. An operating system manages a computer's [*Resources*], such as RAM, storage space, and peripherals.

2. To run more than one program at a time, the operating system must allocate specific areas of [*memory*] for each program.

3. A graphical [*user*] interface provides a way to point and click a mouse to select menu options and manipulate objects that appear on the screen.

4. The core part of an operating system is called its [*kernel*].

5. A desktop operating system, such as Windows, is designed for personal computers. True or false? [*T*]

6. Handheld devices, such as PDAs and smartphones typically feature multiuser operating systems. True or false? [*F*]

CHECK ANSWERS

C

SECTION

Application Software

Most computers include some basic word processing, e-mail, and Internet access software, but computer owners invariably want additional software to increase their computers' productivity, business, learning, or entertainment capabilities. Section C provides an overview of the vast array of application software that's available for personal computers.

DOCUMENT PRODUCTION SOFTWARE

How can my computer help me with my writing? Whether you are writing a 10-page paper, generating software documentation, designing a brochure for your new startup company, or laying out the school newspaper, you will probably use some form of **document production software**. This software assists you with composing, editing, designing, printing, and electronically publishing documents. The three most popular types of document production software are word processing, desktop publishing, and Web authoring (Figure 3-23).

Word processing software, such as Microsoft Word, has replaced typewriters for producing many types of documents, including reports, letters, memos, papers, and manuscripts. Word processing software gives you the ability to create, spell-check, edit, and format a document on the screen before you commit it to paper.

Desktop publishing software (abbreviated DTP) takes word processing software one step further by helping you use graphic design techniques to enhance the format and appearance of a document. Although today's word processing software offers many page layout and design features, DTP software products, such as QuarkXPress and Adobe InDesign, have sophisticated features to help you produce professional-quality output for newspapers, newsletters, brochures, magazines, and books.

Web authoring software helps you design and develop customized Web pages that you can publish electronically on the Internet. Only a few years ago, creating Web pages was a fairly technical task that required authors to insert HTML tags, such as <a href="contents.htm">. Now Web authoring software products, such as Microsoft FrontPage and Macromedia Dreamweaver, help nontechnical Web authors by providing easy-to-use tools for composing the text for a Web page, assembling graphical elements, and automatically generating HTML tags.

How does document production software help me turn my ideas into sentences and paragraphs? Document production software makes it easy to let your ideas flow because it automatically handles many tasks that might otherwise distract you. For example, you don't need to worry about fitting words within the margins. A feature called "word wrap" determines how your text will flow from line to line by automatically moving words down to the next line as you reach the right margin. Imagine that the sentences in your document are ribbons of text; word wrap bends the ribbons. Changing the margin size just means bending the ribbon in

FIGURE 3-23

Popular document production software includes Microsoft Word, QuarkXPress, and Macromedia Dreamweaver.

3

INFOWEBLINKS

This InfoWeb is your guide to today's best-selling **Document Production Software**.

www.course.com/np/concepts9/ch03

different places. Even after you type an entire document, adjusting the size of your right, left, top, and bottom margins is simple (Figure 3-24).

FIGURE 3-24

Document production software makes it easy to get your ideas down on your screen-based "paper." Start the video to see word wrap and the spelling checker in action.

CLICK TO START

Document production software automatically tries to fit your text within the margins using word wrap.

What if I'm a bad speller? Most document production software includes a **spelling checker** that marks misspelled words in a document. You can easily correct a misspelled word as you type, or you can run the spelling checker when you finish entering all the text. Some software even has an autocorrecting capability that automatically changes a typo, such as "teh," to the correct spelling ("the").

Although your software's spelling checker helps you correct misspellings, it cannot guarantee an error-free document. A spelling checker works by comparing each word from your document to a list of correctly spelled words that is stored in a data file called a **spelling dictionary**. If the word from your document is in the dictionary, the spelling checker considers the word correctly spelled. If the word is not in the dictionary, the word is counted as misspelled. Sounds okay, right? But suppose your document contains a reference to the city of "Negaunee." This word is not in the dictionary, so the spelling checker considers it misspelled, even though it is spelled correctly. Proper nouns and scientific, medical, and technical words are likely to be flagged as misspelled, even if you spell them correctly, because they do not appear in the spelling checker's dictionary.

Now suppose that your document contains the phrase "a pear of shoes." Although you meant to use "pair" rather than "pear," the spelling checker will not catch your mistake because "pear" is a valid word in the dictionary. Your spelling checker won't help if you have trouble deciding whether to use "there" or "their," "its" or "it's," or "too" or "to." Remember, then, that a spelling checker cannot substitute for a thorough proofread.

Can document production software improve my writing? Because word processing software tends to focus on the writing process, it offers several features that can improve the quality of your writing. These features may not be available in desktop publishing software or Web authoring software, which focus on the format of a document.

Your word processing software is likely to include a **thesaurus**, which can help you find a synonym for a word so that you can make your writing more varied and interesting. A **grammar checker** "reads" through your document and points out potential grammatical trouble spots, such as incomplete sentences, run-on sentences, and verbs that don't agree with nouns.

Your word processing software might also be able to analyze the reading level of your document using a standard **readability formula**, such as the Flesch-Kincaid reading level. You can use this analysis to find out if your writing matches your target audience, based on sentence length and vocabulary.

Can document production software help me break bad writing habits? Most word processing, DTP, and Web authoring software includes a **Search and Replace** feature. You can use this feature to hunt down mistakes that you typically make in your writing. For example, you might know from experience that you tend to overuse the word "typically." You can use Search and Replace to find each occurrence of "typically," and then you can decide whether you should substitute a different word, such as "usually" or "ordinarily."

How do I get my documents to look good? The **format** for a document refers to the way that all the elements of a document—text, pictures, titles, and page numbers—are arranged on the page. The final format of your document depends on how and where you intend to use it. A school paper, for example, simply needs to be printed in standard paragraph format—perhaps double spaced and with numbered pages. Your word processing software has all the features you need for this formatting task. A brochure, newsletter, or corporate report, on the other hand, might require more ambitious formatting, such as columns that continue on noncontiguous pages and text labels that overlay graphics. You might consider transferring your document from your word processing software to your desktop publishing software for access to more sophisticated formatting tools. For documents that you plan to publish on the Web, Web authoring software usually provides the most useful set of formatting tools.

The "look" of your final document depends on several formatting factors, such as font style, paragraph style, and page layout. A **font** is a set of letters that share a unified design. Font size is measured as **point size**, abbreviated pt. (One point is about 1/72 of an inch.) Figure 3-25 illustrates several popular fonts included with document production software.

3

INFOWEBLINKS

You can add to your font collection by downloading font files from the **Font InfoWeb**.

www.course.com/np/concepts9/ch03

Times New Roman Font	8 pt.
Times New Roman Font	10 pt.
Times New Roman Font	12 pt.
Times New Roman Font	16 pt.
Times New Roman Font	**16 pt. Bold**
Times New Roman Font	16 pt. Green
Arial Font	16 pt.
Comic Sans MS	16 pt.
Georgia Font	**16 pt. Bold Gold**
Dotto	24 pt. Orange

FIGURE 3-25

You can vary the font style by selecting character formatting attributes, such as bold, italics, underline, superscript, and subscript. You can also select a color and size for a font. The font size for the text in a typical paragraph is set at 8, 10, or 12 pt. Titles can be as large as 72 pt.

Paragraph style includes the alignment of text within the margins and the space between each line of text. **Paragraph alignment** refers to the horizontal position of text—whether it is aligned at the left margin, aligned at the right margin, or **fully justified** so that the text is aligned evenly on both the right and left margins. Your document will look more formal if it is fully justified, like the text in this paragraph, than if it has an uneven or "ragged" right margin. **Line spacing** (also called **leading**, pronounced "LED ing") refers to the vertical spacing between lines. Documents are typically single spaced or double spaced, but word processing and DTP software allow you to adjust line spacing in 1 pt. increments.

Instead of individually selecting font and paragraph style elements, document production software typically allows you to define a **style** that lets you apply several font and paragraph characteristics with a single click. For example, instead of applying bold to a title, changing its font to Times New Roman, centering the text, and then adjusting the font size to 18 pt., you can define a Document Title style as 18 pt., Times New Roman, centered, bold. You can then apply all four style characteristics at once simply by selecting the Document Title style (Figure 3-26).

FIGURE 3-26

By defining a style, you can apply multiple font attributes with a single click.

CLICK TO START

Page layout refers to the physical position of each element on a page. In addition to paragraphs of text, these elements might include:

- **Headers and footers.** A **header** is text that you specify to automatically appear in the top margin of every page. A **footer** is text that you specify to automatically appear in the bottom margin of every page. You might put your name and the document title in the header or footer of a document so that its printed pages won't get mixed up with those of another printed document.

- **Page numbers.** Word processing and DTP software automatically number the pages of a document according to your specifications, usually placing the page number within a header or footer. A Web page, no matter what its length, is all a single page, so Web authoring software typically doesn't provide page numbering.

- **Graphical elements.** Photos, diagrams, graphs, and charts can be incorporated in your documents. **Clip art**—a collection of drawings and photos designed to be inserted in documents—is a popular source of graphical elements.

- **Tables.** A **table** is a grid-like structure that can hold text or pictures. For printed documents, tables are a popular way to produce easy-to-read columns and rows of data and to position graphics. It may sound surprising, but for Web pages, tables provide one of the few ways to precisely position text and pictures. As a result, Web page designers make extensive and very creative use of tables.

Most word processing software is page-oriented meaning that it treats each page as a rectangle that can be filled with text and graphics. Text automatically flows from one page to the next. In contrast, most DTP software is frame-oriented, allowing you to divide each page into several rectangular-shaped **frames** that you can fill with text or graphics. Text flows from one frame to the next, rather than from page to page (Figure 3-27).

Attack on Everest
by Janell Chalmers

Mountain climbing was once the domain of professional explorers, whose bodies and minds were honed to a long assault against weather, ice, and rock. Expeditions attacked Mount Everest ~~til 1953~~

Wrapping text around a frame adds interest to the layout.

guide, Tenzing Norkay, reached the summit. Hillary was knighted for this accomplishment.

Sir Edmund Hillary would be amazed to discover that today Mount Everest has become something of a tourist destination. Guided "adventure" tours head toward the summit like cruise ships plying

"Because it's there."
George Mallory

Caribbean ports. This $65,000 trek is not without risk. In 1996 a sudden storm killed eight climbers.

Back in 1923, British mountaineer George Mallory was asked, why climb Everest? His reply, "Because it's there." A new answer to this question, "Because we can" may be largely attributable to new high-tech mountain gear. Nylon, polypropylene and Gore-Tex clothing provide light, yet warm protection from the elements. New, high-tech ultraviolet lenses protect eyes from dangerous "snowblindness."

An other gear makes the mountain seem less

FIGURE 3-27

DTP frames give you exact control over the position of elements on a page, such as a figure and a caption on top of it.

CLICK TO START ✦

One frame holds the centered title and author's byline. This text is linked to the text in subsequent frames.

"Guide lines" that do not appear on printouts help align text and graphical elements.

Text can link to frames on the next page or on any page of the document.

Does document production software increase productivity?
Word processing software, in particular, provides several features that automate tasks and allow you to work more productively. For example, suppose that you want to send prospective employers a letter and your resume. Instead of composing and addressing each letter individually, your software can perform a **mail merge** that automatically creates personalized letters by combining the information in a mailing list with a form letter. Some additional capabilities of word processing software include:

- Automatically generating a table of contents and an index for a document

- Automatically numbering footnotes and positioning each footnote on the page where it is referenced

- Providing document templates and document wizards that show you the correct content and format for a variety of documents, such as business letters, fax cover sheets, and memos

- Exporting a document into HTML format

SPREADSHEET SOFTWARE

What is a spreadsheet? A **spreadsheet** uses rows and columns of numbers to create a model or representation of a real situation. For example, your checkbook register is a type of spreadsheet because it is a numerical representation of the cash flowing in and out of your bank account. Today, **spreadsheet software**, such as Microsoft Excel, provides tools to create electronic spreadsheets. It is similar to a "smart" piece of paper that automatically adds up the columns of numbers you write on it. You can use it to make other calculations, too, based on simple equations that you write or more complex, built-in formulas. As an added bonus, spreadsheet software helps you turn your data into a variety of colorful graphs. It also includes special data-handling features that allow you to sort data, search for data that meets specific criteria, and print reports.

Spreadsheet software was initially popular with accountants and financial managers who dealt with paper-based spreadsheets, but found the electronic version far easier to use and less prone to errors than manual calculations. Other people soon discovered the benefits of spreadsheets for projects that require repetitive calculations—budgeting, maintaining a grade book, balancing a checkbook, tracking investments, calculating loan payments, and estimating project costs.

Because it is so easy to experiment with different numbers, spreadsheet software is particularly useful for **what-if analysis**. You can use what-if analyses to answer questions such as "What if I get an A on my next two economics exams? But what if I get only Bs?" "What if I invest $100 a month in my retirement plan? But what if I invest $200 a month?"

What does a computerized spreadsheet look like? You use spreadsheet software to create an on-screen **worksheet**. A worksheet is based on a grid of columns and rows. Each **cell** in the grid can contain a value, label, or formula. A **value** is a number that you want to use in a calculation. A **label** is any text used to describe data. For example, suppose that your worksheet contains the value $486,000. You could use a label to identify this number as "Income" (Figure 3-28).

INFOWEBLINKS

For links to today's best-selling spreadsheet software, connect to the **Spreadsheet InfoWeb**.

www.course.com/np/concepts9/ch03

FIGURE 3-28

In a worksheet, each column is lettered and each row is numbered. The intersection of a column and row is called a cell. Each cell has a unique cell reference, or "address," derived from its column and row location. For example, A1 is the cell reference for the upper-left cell in a worksheet because it is in column A and row 1. You can select any cell and make it the active cell by clicking it. Once a cell is active, you can enter data into it.

You can format the labels and values on a worksheet in much the same way as you would format text in a word processing document. You can change fonts and font size, select a font color, and select font styles, such as bold, italic, and underline.

How does spreadsheet software work? The values contained in a cell can be manipulated by formulas placed in other cells. A **formula** works behind the scenes to tell the computer how to use the contents of cells in calculations. You can enter a simple formula in a cell to add, subtract, multiply, or divide numbers. More complex formulas can be designed to perform just about any calculation you can imagine. Figure 3-29 illustrates how a formula might be used in a simple spreadsheet to calculate savings.

3

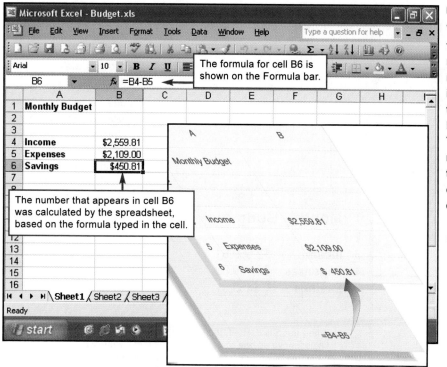

FIGURE 3-29

When a cell contains a formula, it displays the result of the formula rather than the formula itself. To view and edit the formula, you use the Formula bar.

You can think of the formula as working "behind the scenes" to perform calculations and then display the result.

CLICK TO START

FIGURE 3-30

Functions are special formulas provided by spreadsheet software.

A formula, such as =D4-D5+((D8/B2)*110), can contain **cell references** (like D4 and D5), numbers (like 110), and **mathematical operators**, such as the multiplication symbol (*), the division symbol (/), the addition symbol, and the subtraction symbol. Parts of a formula can be enclosed in parentheses to indicate the order in which the mathematical operations should be performed. The operation in the innermost set of parentheses—in this case, (D8/B2)— should be performed first.

You can enter a formula "from scratch" by typing it into a cell, or you can use a built-in preset formula called a **function**, provided by the spreadsheet software. To use a function, you simply select one from a list, as shown in Figure 3-30, and then indicate the cell references of any values you want to include in the calculation.

What happens when I modify a worksheet? When you change the contents of any cell in a worksheet, all the formulas are recalculated. This **automatic recalculation** feature ensures that the results in every cell are accurate for the information currently entered in the worksheet.

Your worksheet is also automatically updated to reflect any rows or columns that you add, delete, or copy within the worksheet. Unless you specify otherwise, a cell reference is a **relative reference**—that is, a reference that can change from B4 to B3, for example, if row 3 is deleted and all the data moves up one row.

If you don't want a cell reference to change, you can use an absolute reference. An **absolute reference** never changes when you insert rows or copy or move formulas. Understanding when to use absolute references is one of the key aspects of developing spreadsheet design expertise. Figure 3-31 and its associated tour provide additional information about relative and absolute references.

FIGURE 3-31

As shown in the examples, relative references within a formula can change when you change the sequence of a worksheet's rows and columns. An absolute reference is "anchored" so that it always refers to a specific cell.

CLICK TO START

	A	B	C
1	Monthly Budget		
2			
3			
4	Income	$2,559.81	
5	Expenses	$2,109.00	
6	Savings	$450.81	
7			
8			
9			
10			
11			

Two blank rows

The original formula =B4-B5 uses relative references.

	A	B	C
1	Monthly Budget		
2			
3	Income	$2,559.81	
4	Expenses	$2,109.00	
5	Savings	$450.81	
6			
7			
8			
9			
10			
11			

When row 3 is deleted, the Income and Expenses values move up one row, which means these values have new cell references. The formula changes to =B3-B4 to reflect the new cell references.

How will I know which formulas and functions to use when I create a worksheet? To create an effective and accurate worksheet, you typically must understand the calculations and formulas that are involved. If, for example, you want to create a worksheet that helps you calculate your final grade in a course, you need to know the grading scale and understand how your instructor plans to weight each assignment and test.

Most spreadsheet software includes a few templates or wizards for pre-designed worksheets, such as invoices, income-expense reports, balance sheets, and loan payment schedules. Additional templates are available on the Web. These templates are typically designed by professionals and contain all the necessary labels and formulas. To use a template, you simply plug in the values for your calculation.

"NUMBER CRUNCHING" SOFTWARE

Aside from spreadsheets, what other "number crunching" software is available? Spreadsheet software provides a sort of "blank canvas" on which you can create numeric models by simply "painting" values, labels, and formulas. The advantage of spreadsheet software is the flexibility it provides—flexibility to create customized calculations according to your exact specifications. The disadvantage of spreadsheet software is that—aside from a few predesigned templates—you are responsible for entering formulas and selecting functions for calculations. If you don't know the formulas or don't understand the functions, you're out of luck.

In contrast to the "blank canvas" approach provided by spreadsheet software, other "number crunching" software works more like "paint by numbers." It provides a structured environment dedicated to a particular number crunching task, such as statistical analysis, mathematical modeling, or money management.

Statistical software helps you analyze large sets of data to discover relationships and patterns. Products such as SPSS and Statsoft STATISTICA are helpful tools for summarizing survey results, test scores, experiment results, or population data. Most statistical software includes graphing capability so that you can display and explore your data visually.

Mathematical modeling software provides tools for solving a wide range of math, science, and engineering problems. Students, teachers, mathematicians, and engineers, in particular, appreciate how products such as Mathcad and Mathematica help them recognize patterns that can be difficult to identify in columns of numbers (Figure 3-32).

INFOWEBLINKS

For more information about popular "number crunching" software, take a look at the **Numeric Software InfoWeb**.

www.course.com/np/concepts9/ch03

FIGURE 3-32

Mathematical modeling software helps you visualize the product of complex formulas. Here the points from a sphere are graphed onto a plane, to demonstrate the principles behind the Astronomical Clock of Prague.

Money management software offers a variety of tools for tracking monetary transactions and investments. In this software category, **personal finance software**, such as Microsoft Money and Intuit Quicken, is designed to keep records of income, expenses, assets, and liabilities using a simple checkbook-like user interface. This software also automates routine financial tasks, such as budgeting, investing, check writing, and bill paying. Many personal financial software products provide direct links to online banking services, so you can use them to check account balances, transfer funds, and pay bills.

Personal financial software produces reports and graphs that show you where your money goes. For example, you can analyze various aspects of your cash flow, such as how much you spent on entertainment last month and how that compares to the previous month.

Tax preparation software is a specialized type of personal finance software designed to help you gather your annual income and expense data, identify deductions, and calculate tax payments. Popular products, such as Intuit TurboTax, even accept data directly from personal finance software to eliminate hours of tedious data entry.

DATABASE SOFTWARE

What is a database? The term "database" has evolved from a specialized technical term into a part of our everyday vocabulary. In the context of modern usage, a **database** is simply a collection of data that is stored on one or more computers. A database can contain any sort of data, such as a university's student records, a library's card catalog, a store's inventory, an individual's address book, or a utility company's customers. Databases can be stored on personal computers, LAN servers, Web servers, mainframes, and even handheld computers.

What is database software? Database software helps you enter, find, organize, update, and report information stored in a database. Microsoft Access, FileMaker Pro, and askSam are three of the most popular examples of database software for personal computers. Oracle and MySQL are popular server database software packages. For PDAs, popular choices include HanDBase, Mobile DB, dBNow, and JFile.

How does a database store data? Database software stores data as a series of records, which are composed of fields that hold data. A **record** holds data for a single entity—a person, place, thing, or event. A **field** holds one item of data relevant to a record. You can envision a record as a Rolodex or index card and a series of records as a table (Figure 3-33).

INFOWEBLINKS

For more information about popular database software, connect to the **Database Software InfoWeb**.

www.course.com/np/concepts9/ch03

TERMINOLOGY NOTE

Database software is also referred to as database management software (DBMS).

FIGURE 3-33

A single database record is similar to a Rolodex card or an index card. A series of records is usually depicted in table format.

Song Title	Performer	Composer	CD	Date	Record Label	Length
Seven Years	Norah Jones	Lee Alexander	Come Away with Me	02/01/2002	Blue Note	2:24
Shoot the Moon	Norah Jones	Jesse Harris	Come Away with Me	02/01/2002	Blue Note	3:57
Summertime	Janis Joplin	George Gershwin	Greatest Hits	08/31/1999	Sony	3.28
Summertime	Sarah Vaughan	George Gershwin	Compact Jazz	06/22/1987	Polygram	4:34

Some database software provides tools to work with more than one collection of records, as long as the records are somehow related to each other. For example, MTV might maintain a database pertaining to jazz music. One series of database records might contain data about jazz songs. It could contain fields such as those shown in Figure 3-33. Another series of records might contain biographical data about jazz performers, including name, birth date, and home town. It might even include a field for the performer's photo.

These two sets of records can be related by the name of the performing artist, as shown in Figure 3-34.

JAZZ PERFORMERS

Performer	Birth Date	Home Town
Ella Fitzgerald	04/25/1918	Newport News, VA
Norah Jones	03/30/1979	New York, NY
Billie Holiday	04/07/1915	Baltimore, MD
Lena Horne	06/17/1917	Brooklyn, NY

JAZZ SONGS

Song Title	Performer	Composer	CD	Date	Record Label	Length
Seven Years	Norah Jones	Lee Alexander	Come Away with Me	02/01/2002	Blue Note	2:24
Shoot the Moon	Norah Jones	Jesse Harris	Come Away with Me	02/01/2002	Blue Note	3:57
Summertime	Janis Joplin	George Gershwin	Greatest Hits	08/31/1999	Sony	3.28
Summertime	Sarah Vaughan	George Gershwin	Compact Jazz	06/22/1987	Polygram	4:34

FIGURE 3-34

The two sets of records are related by the Performer field. The relationship allows you to select Norah Jones from the Jazz Performers records and jump to any records in the Jazz Songs records that Norah Jones performed.

3

How do I create records? Database software provides the tools you need to define fields for a series of records. Figure 3-35 shows a simple form you might use to specify the fields for a database.

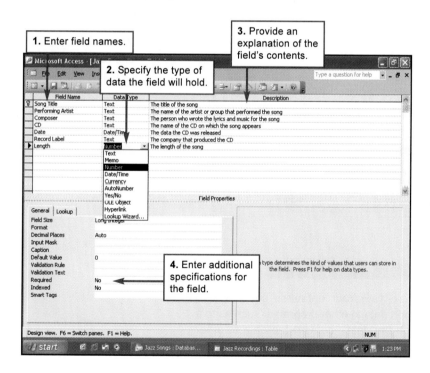

FIGURE 3-35

Database software provides tools for specifying fields for a series of records.

CLICK TO START

When can I enter data? After you've defined fields for a series of records, you can enter the data for each record. Your database software provides a simple-to-use data entry form that allows you to easily fill in the data for each field. Instead of typing data into a database, you can also import data from a commercial database, such as a customer mailing list. You can even download databases from the Web, and then import the data into fields you have defined with your database software.

How do I locate specific data? Many databases contain hundreds or thousands of records. If you want to find a particular record or a group of records, scrolling through every record is much too cumbersome. Instead, you can enter a query to perform a search, and the computer will quickly locate the records you seek.

Most database software provides one or more methods for making queries. A **query language**, such as SQL (Structured Query Language), provides a set of commands for locating and manipulating data. To locate all performances of *Summertime* before 1990 from a Jazz Songs database, you might enter a query such as:

Select * from JazzSongs where SongTitle = 'Summertime' and Date < '1990'

In addition to a formal query language, some database software provides **natural language query** capabilities. To make such queries, you don't have to learn an esoteric query language. Instead, you can simply enter questions, such as:

Who performed Summertime before 1990?

As an alternative to a query language or a natural language query, your database software might allow you to **query by example** (QBE), simply by filling out a form with the type of data you want to locate. Figure 3-36 illustrates a query by example for *Summertime* performances before 1990.

TERMINOLOGY NOTE

You encountered the term "query" in Chapter 1 in the context of search engines, which allow you to search through a database of information pertaining to the content of Web pages.

A query is a set of keywords and operators that describe information you want to find.

FIGURE 3-36

When you query by example, your database software displays a blank form on the screen, and you enter examples of the data that you want to find.

How can I use search results? Your database software can typically help you print reports, export data to other programs (such as to a spreadsheet where you can graph the data), convert the data to other formats (such as HTML so that you can post the data on the Web), and transmit data to other computers.

Whether you print, import, copy, save, or transmit the data you find in databases, it is your responsibility to use it appropriately. Never introduce inaccurate information into a database. Respect copyrights, giving credit to the person or organization that compiled the data. You should also respect the privacy of the people who are the subject of the data. Unless you have permission to do so, do not divulge names, Social Security numbers, or other identifying information that might compromise someone's privacy.

GRAPHICS SOFTWARE

What kind of software do I need to work with drawings, photos, and other pictures? In computer lingo, the term **graphics** refers to any picture, drawing, sketch, photograph, image, or icon that appears on your computer screen. **Graphics software** is designed to help you create, manipulate, and print graphics. Some graphics software products specialize in a particular type of graphic, while others allow you to work with multiple graphics formats. If you are really interested in working with graphics, you will undoubtedly end up using more than one graphics software product.

Paint software (sometimes called "image editing software") provides a set of electronic pens, brushes, and paints for painting images on the screen. A simple program called Microsoft Paint is included with Windows. More sophisticated paint software products include JASC Paint Shop Pro and Procreate Painter. Many graphic artists, Web page designers, and illustrators use paint software as their primary computer-based graphics tool.

Photo editing software, such as Adobe Photoshop, includes features specially designed to fix poor-quality photos by modifying contrast and brightness, cropping out unwanted objects, and removing "red eye." Photos can also be edited using paint software, but photo editing software typically offers tools and wizards that simplify common photo editing tasks.

Drawing software provides a set of lines, shapes, and colors that can be assembled into diagrams, corporate logos, and schematics. The drawings created with tools such as Adobe Illustrator and Macromedia Freehand tend to have a "flat" cartoon-like quality, but they are very easy to modify, and look good at just about any size. Figure 3-37 illustrates a typical set of tools provided by drawing software.

FIGURE 3-37

Drawing software provides tools for creating and manipulating graphics.

3-D graphics software provides a set of tools for creating "wireframes" that represent three-dimensional objects. A wireframe acts much like the framework for a pop-up tent. Just as you would construct the framework for the tent and then cover it with a nylon tent cover, 3-D graphics software can cover a wireframe object with surface texture and color to create a graphic of a 3-D object (Figure 3-38 on the next page).

FIGURE 3-38

3-D graphics software provides tools for creating a wireframe that represents a 3-D object. Some 3-D software specializes in engineering-style graphics, while other 3-D software specializes in figures.

CAD software (computer-aided design software) is a special type of 3-D graphics software designed for architects and engineers who use computers to create blueprints and product specifications. AutoCAD is one of the best-selling professional CAD products. TurboCAD is a low-cost favorite. Scaled-down versions of professional CAD software provide simplified tools for homeowners who want to redesign their kitchens, examine new landscaping options, or experiment with floor plans.

Presentation software supplies the tools you need for combining text, photos, clip art, graphs, animations, and sound into a series of electronic slides, like those in Figure 3-39. You can display electronic slides on a color monitor for a one-on-one presentation or use a computer projection device for group presentations. You can also output the presentation as overhead transparencies, paper copies, or 35 mm slides. Popular presentation software products include Microsoft PowerPoint and Harvard Graphics.

FIGURE 3-39

A computer-based presentation consists of a series of slides, created with presentation software.

CLICK TO START

MUSIC SOFTWARE

Why would I need music software? You don't have to be a musician or composer to have a use for music software. Many types of music software are available. You might be surprised to find how many of them come in handy.

It is possible—and easy—to make your own digital voice and music recordings, which you store on your computer's hard disk. Windows and Mac OS operating system utilities usually supply the necessary **audio editing software**—Sound Recorder on PCs (Figure 3-40) and iTunes on Macs.

FIGURE 3-40

Audio editing software, such as Sound Recorder, provides controls much like those on a tape recorder. Menus offer additional digital editing features, such as speed control, volume adjustments, clipping, and mixing.

Audio editing software typically includes playback as well as recording capabilities. A specialized version of this software called karaoke software integrates music files and on-screen lyrics—everything you need to sing along with your favorite tunes.

Music can be stored in a variety of digital formats on a computer or on a portable audio player, such as Apple's iPod. Digital music formats, such as MP3 and AAC, are not the same formats used to store music on commercial audio CDs. These file formats take up much less storage space than on the original CD.

A variety of software allows you to convert music from commercial CDs for use on computers and portable audio players. **CD ripper software** pulls a track off an audio CD and stores it in "raw" digital format on your computer's hard disk. **Audio encoding software** (sometimes called an "audio format converter") converts the raw audio file into a format such as MP3 or AAC. After the file is converted, you can listen to it on your computer, or you can transfer it to a portable MP3 player.

Ear training software targets musicians and music students who want to learn to play by ear, develop tuning skills, recognize notes and keys, and develop other musical skills. **Notation software** is the musician's equivalent of a word processor. It helps musicians compose, edit, and print the notes for their compositions. For non-musicians, **computer-aided music software** is designed to generate unique musical compositions simply by selecting the musical style, instruments, key, and tempo. **MIDI sequencing software** and software synthesizers are an important part of the studio musician's toolbox. They're great for sound effects and for controlling keyboards and other digital instruments.

TERMINOLOGY NOTE

Some CD ripper software also includes audio encoding software so that ripping and encoding seem to happen within a single operation.

INFOWEBLINKS

At the **Music Software InfoWeb**, you'll find detailed information on popular software in this category.

www.course.com/np/concepts9/ch03

VIDEO EDITING AND DVD AUTHORING SOFTWARE

What can video editing software do? The popularity of computer-based video editing can be attributed to video editing software, such as Windows Movie Maker and Apple iMovie, now included with Windows computers and Macs. **Video editing software** provides a set of tools for transferring video footage from a camcorder to a computer, clipping out unwanted footage, assembling video segments in any sequence, adding special visual effects, and adding a sound track. Despite an impressive array of features, video editing software is relatively easy to use, as explained in Figure 3-41.

INFOWEBLINKS

Learn more about Apple iMovie and Adobe Premiere at the **Video Editing Software InfoWeb**.
www.course.com/np/concepts9/ch03

FIGURE 3-41

Video editing software, such as Adobe Premiere, helps you import a series of video clips from a camera or VCR, arrange the clips in the order of your choice, add transitions between clips, and add an audio track.

With the growing popularity of writable DVD drives, desktop video authors now want to transfer their productions to DVDs and watch them on standard DVD players connected to television sets or projectors. **DVD authoring software** offers tools for creating DVDs with Hollywood-style menus. Just like commercial movies, desktop videos can now include menu selections such as Play Movie, Scene Selection, and Special Features. You can use the remote control for your DVD player to scroll through and select menu options. Examples of DVD authoring software include Sonic DVDit!, ULead DVD MovieFactory, Apple iDVD, and Adobe EncoreDVD.

SOFTWARE SUITES

What is a software suite? A **software suite** is a collection of application software sold as a single package. Office suites, such as Microsoft Office, Star Office, Open Office, and WordPerfect Office, include applications to boost basic productivity: word processing, spreadsheet, and e-mail software. Graphics suites, such as Adobe Creative Suite, Macromedia Studio MX, and CorelDRAW Graphics Suite, typically include paint, draw, and Web graphics tools. Media suites such as InterVideo MediaOne provide tools for creating music CDs and video DVDs. Figure 3-42 on the next page lists the components of several popular software suites.

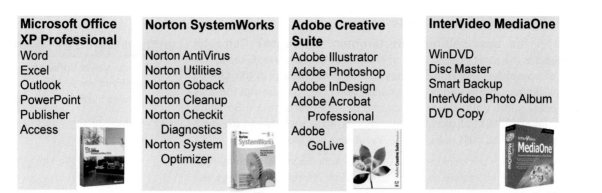

Microsoft Office XP Professional
Word
Excel
Outlook
PowerPoint
Publisher
Access

Norton SystemWorks
Norton AntiVirus
Norton Utilities
Norton Goback
Norton Cleanup
Norton Checkit
  Diagnostics
Norton System
  Optimizer

Adobe Creative Suite
Adobe Illustrator
Adobe Photoshop
Adobe InDesign
Adobe Acrobat
  Professional
Adobe
  GoLive

InterVideo MediaOne
WinDVD
Disc Master
Smart Backup
InterVideo Photo Album
DVD Copy

FIGURE 3-42

Software suites are available in many application categories, such as productivity, antivirus, graphics, and media.

What are the advantages and disadvantages of software suites? Purchasing a software suite is usually much less expensive than purchasing the applications separately. Another advantage is usability. Because all the applications in a suite are produced by the same software publisher, they tend to use similar user interfaces and provide an easy way to transport data from one application to another.

The disadvantage of a software suite is that it might include applications you don't need. If that is the case, you should calculate the price of the applications you *do* need and compare that to the cost of the suite.

EDUCATIONAL AND REFERENCE SOFTWARE

How can I use my computer for learning new things? Educational software helps you learn and practice new skills. For the youngest students, educational software, such as MindTwister Math and 3-D Froggy Phonics, teaches basic arithmetic and reading skills. Instruction is presented in game format, and the levels of play are adapted to the player's age and ability.

For older students and adults, software is available for such diverse educational endeavors as learning languages, training yourself to use new software, learning how to play the piano or guitar, improving keyboarding skills, and even learning managerial skills for a diverse workplace. Exam preparation software is available for standardized tests such as the SAT, GMAT, and LSAT. Web-based distance education software tools, such as WebCT and BlackBoard, help instructors keep track of student progress and provide students with interactive study and testing activities.

What's reference software? Reference software provides a collection of information and a way to access that information. This type of software includes massive amounts of data—unlike database software, which is shipped without any data. The reference software category spans a wide range of applications—from encyclopedias to medical references, from map software to trip planners, and from cookbooks to telephone books. The options are as broad as the full range of human interests.

Because of the quantity of data it includes, reference software is generally shipped on a CD or DVD, or can be accessed on the Web. Encyclopedias are the most popular software packages in this category. Bestsellers include Microsoft Encarta and Britannica's CD. An encyclopedia on CD-ROM or the Web has several advantages over its printed counterpart. Finding information is easier, for example. Also, electronic formats take up less space on your bookshelf and include interesting video and audio clips. A single CD is cheaper to produce than a shelf full of hard-bound printed books. These lower production costs translate to more affordable products and allow an average person to own a comprehensive encyclopedia.

INFOWEBLINKS

What can you learn on your computer? Check out the **Educational and Reference Software InfoWeb**.
www.course.com/np/concepts9/ch03

3

ENTERTAINMENT SOFTWARE

What's the best-selling entertainment software? Computer games are the most popular type of entertainment software. Over $7 billion of computer and video games are sold each year in the United States alone. Contrary to popular belief, teenage boys are not the only computer game enthusiasts. According to the Entertainment Software Association, 35% of all gamers are under 18, 43% are between the ages of 18 and 49, and 19% are over 50. About 43% are women.

Computer games are generally classified into subcategories, such as role-playing, action, adventure, puzzles, simulations, sports, and strategy/war games, as described in Figure 3-43.

INFOWEBLINKS

The **Entertainment Software InfoWeb** is your link to the best game sites on the Internet.

www.course.com/np/concepts9/ch03

FIGURE 3-43

Game Categories

Type of Game	Description	Examples
Role-playing	Based on a detailed story line—often one that takes place in a medieval world populated with dastardly villains and evil monsters—the goal is to build a character into a powerful entity that can conquer the bad guys and accumulate treasure.	Diablo, EverQuest, Icewind Dale, Planescape
Action	Like arcade games, action games require fast reflexes as you maneuver a character through a maze or dungeon.	Quake, Doom, Unreal Tournament, Enter the Matrix, Tomb Raider
Adventure	Similar to role-playing games except that the focus is on solving problems rather than building a character into a powerful wizard or fighter.	Myst, The Longest Journey, Return to Monkey Island
Puzzle	Include computerized versions of traditional board games, card games, and Rubik's cube-like challenges.	Tetris, Lemmings
Simulation	Provide a realistic setting, such as the cockpit of an airplane. Players must learn to manipulate controls using the keyboard, joystick, or special-purpose input device. A great way to get your adrenaline pumping without expenses or risks.	Flight Simulator, NASCAR Racing, Mech Warrior
Sports	Place participants in the midst of action-packed sports events, such as a football game, baseball game, hockey final, soccer match, or golf tournament. Most sports games offer arcade-like action and require quick reflexes.	NBA Live, MVP Baseball, SimGolf
Strategy	Players (one player might be the computer) take turns moving characters, armies, and other resources in a quest to capture territory.	Age of Empires, Sim City, Warcraft

How do multiplayer games work? Multiplayer games provide an environment in which two or more players can participate in the same game. Even some of the earliest computer games, like Pong, supplied joysticks for two players. Today's multiplayer games are a far cry from those simplistic games. Now numerous players can use Internet technology to band together or battle one another in sophisticated virtual environments.

Large-scale multiplayer games, such as Battlefield 1942 and EverQuest, operate on multiple Internet servers, each one with the capacity to handle thousands of players at peak times. A new twist in online multiplayer games is "persistent metaworlds," in which objects remain even when play ends. If one player drops an object, for example, it will be there when other players pass by.

Are computer games rated like movies and music? Since it was established in 1994, the Entertainment Software Rating Board (ESRB) has rated more than 12,000 video and computer games. Rating symbols can usually be found in the lower-right corner of the game box. In past years, about 50% of the rated games received an "Everyone" rating. About 35% received a "Teen" rating, and about 15% received a "Mature" rating.

INFOWEBLINKS

Who rates software and how do they do it? Find out at the **Software Ratings InfoWeb**.

www.course.com/np/concepts9/ch03

BUSINESS SOFTWARE

Do businesses use specialized software? The term "business software" is a broad term that describes vertical and horizontal market software, which helps businesses and organizations accomplish routine or specialized tasks.

What is vertical market software? Vertical market software is designed to automate specialized tasks in a specific market or business. Examples include patient management and billing software that is specially designed for hospitals, job estimating software for construction businesses, and student record management software for schools. Today, almost every business has access to some type of specialized vertical market software designed to automate, streamline, or computerize key business activities.

What is horizontal market software? Horizontal market software is generic software that just about any kind of business can use. **Payroll software** is a good example of horizontal market software. Almost every business has employees and must maintain payroll records. No matter what type of business uses it, payroll software must collect similar data and make similar calculations to produce payroll checks and W-2 forms. Accounting software and project management software are additional examples of horizontal market software. **Accounting software** helps a business keep track of the money flowing in and out of various accounts. **Project management software** is an important tool for planning large projects, scheduling project tasks, and tracking project costs.

What is groupware? Groupware is a type of horizontal market software, designed to help several people collaborate on a single project using LAN or Internet connections. It usually provides the capability to maintain schedules for group members, automatically select meeting times for the group, facilitate communication by e-mail or other channels, distribute documents according to a prearranged schedule or sequence, and allow multiple people to contribute to a single document.

QuickCheck   SECTION C

1. Various kinds of ⌊*documents*⌋ production software provide tools for creating and formatting printed and Web-based materials.

2. A spelling checker will find an error in "The sailor tied a complex not." True or false? ⌊*F*⌋

3. ⌊*spreadsheet*⌋ software provides a sort of "blank canvas" on which you can create numeric models by simply "painting" values, labels, and formulas.

4. ⌊*database*⌋ software stores data as a series of records and allows you to establish relationships between different types of records.

5. CD ⌊*ripper*⌋ software transfers files from an audio CD to your computer's hard disk.

6. ⌊*DVD*⌋ authoring software allows you to add Hollywood-style menus to digital videos.

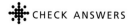 CHECK ANSWERS

3

D

Buying and Installing Software

It's surprising how quickly your collection of software can grow as you discover new ways to use your computer for school, work, and play. Before you can use software, you have to install it on your computer. As you read this section, you'll find out how to install software from CDs or from downloads. After you've used your software for a while, you might want to upgrade it to a new version. From time to time, you might want to eliminate some of the software on your computer. Section D discusses how to acquire, upgrade, and remove software. The section ends with a discussion of software copyrights—important information that will help you understand the difference between legal and illegal software copying.

BUYING SOFTWARE

Where can I get software? Software is sold in some surprising places. You might find graphics software at your local art supply store. Your favorite beauty salon might carry Cosmopolitan's makeup and hairstyle makeover software. You might even find homeopathic medicine software on sale at a health food store. Of course, software is also available from traditional sources, including office stores, computer superstores, electronics superstores, and discount stores as well as local computer stores. You can buy software from mail-order catalogs, the software publisher's Web site, and software download sites.

What's included in a typical software package? The key "ingredients" necessary to install new software are the files that contain the programs and data. These files might be supplied on **distribution media**—one or more CDs or DVDs that are packaged in a box, along with an instruction manual. The files might also be supplied as an Internet download that contains program modules and the text of the instruction manual.

How do I know if a software program will work on my computer? Tucked away at the software publisher's Web site or printed on the software package (Figure 3-44) you'll find **system requirements**, which specify the operating system and minimum hardware capacities necessary for a software product to work correctly.

FIGURE 3-44

System requirements typically can be found on the software box or posted on the download site.

System Requirements

Operating Systems: Windows 95/98/2000/Me/XP/Vista
Processor: Pentium class computer
Memory: 16 MB or more
Hard Disk Space: 10 MB free
Network Protocol: TCP/IP
Network Connection: 10/100 Ethernet LAN/WAN,
cable modem, DSL router, ISDN router, or dial-up modem

eCourse Internet Works
2006 eCourseWare Corp. All rights reserved. eCourse is a registered trademark of eCourseWare Corp.

INSTALLATION BASICS

Why is it necessary to install most software? When you **install** software, the new software files are placed in the appropriate folders on your computer's hard disk, and then your computer performs any software or hardware configurations necessary to make sure the program is ready to run. During the installation process, your computer usually performs the following activities:

- Copies files from distribution media or downloads files to specified folders on the hard disk

- Uncompresses files that have been distributed in compressed format

- Analyzes the computer's resources, such as processor speed, RAM capacity, and hard disk capacity, to verify that they meet or exceed the minimum system requirements

- Analyzes hardware components and peripheral devices to select appropriate device drivers

- Looks for any system files and players, such as Internet Explorer or Windows Media Player, that are required to run the program but are not supplied on the distribution media or download

- Updates necessary system files, such as the Windows Registry and the Windows Start menu, with information about the new software

Are all files for the software provided on the distribution media? With Windows and other operating systems, application software programs share some common files. These files are often supplied by the operating system and perform routine tasks, such as displaying the Print dialog box, which allows you to select a printer and specify how many copies of a file you want to print. These "shared" files are not typically provided on the new software's distribution media or download because the files should already exist on your computer. The installation routine attempts to locate these files. It then notifies you if any files are missing, and provides instructions for installing them.

Are all the files for the new software installed in the same folder? Most executable files and data files for new software are placed in the folder you specify. Some support programs for the software, however, might be stored in other folders, such as Windows\System. The location for these files is determined by the software installation routine. Figure 3-45 maps out the location of files for a typical Windows software installation.

FIGURE 3-45

When you install software, its files might end up in different folders. Files for the eVideo-In Pro software are installed in two folders.

Distribution CDs

Windows\System

File name	Size	Type
eVidmdbg.dll	20 KB	Support Program
eVidodec32.dll	92 KB	Support Program
eVidwave.dll	37 KB	Support Program
Version.dll	24 KB	Support Program
eVidpodbc.dll	955 KB	Support Program
eVidgain.dll	116 KB	Support Program
eVgateway.ocx	42 KB	Support Program

Program Files\ eVideo-In Pro

File name	Size	Type
eVidpro.exe	5,500 KB	Main Executable Program
eVidpro.hlp	275 KB	Help File
eVidcore.hlp	99 KB	Help File
eVidcore.dll	1,425 KB	Support Program
eVidpro.dll	1,517 KB	Support Program
Readme.doc	65 KB	Data File
eVdplugin.dll	813 KB	Support Program
eVdtrans.dll	921 KB	Support Program

3

INSTALLING FROM DISTRIBUTION MEDIA

How do I install software from distribution media?

Installation procedures vary, depending on a computer's operating system. Take a look at the installation process on a computer running Windows.

Windows software typically contains a **setup program** that guides you through the installation process. Figure 3-46 shows you what to expect when you use a setup program.

FIGURE 3-46

Installing from Distribution Media

1 Insert the first distribution CD or DVD. The setup program should start automatically. If it does not, look for a file called Setup.exe and then run it.

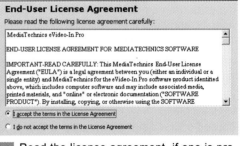

2 Read the license agreement, if one is presented on the screen. By agreeing to the terms of the license, you can proceed with the installation.

○ **Full Installation**
○ **Custom Installation**

3 Select the installation option that best meets your needs. If you select a full installation, the setup program copies all files and data from the distribution medium to the hard disk of your computer system. A full installation gives you access to all features of the software.

If you select a custom installation, the setup program displays a list of software features for your selection. After you select the features you want, the setup program copies only the selected program and data files to your hard disk. A custom installation can save space on your hard disk.

4 Follow the prompts provided by the setup program to specify a folder to hold the new software program. You can use the default folder specified by the setup program or a folder of your own choosing, You can also create a new folder during the setup process.

5 If the software includes multiple distribution CDs, insert each one in the specified drive when the setup program prompts you.

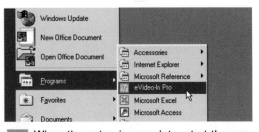

6 When the setup is complete, start the program you just installed to make sure it works.

INSTALLING DOWNLOADED SOFTWARE

Is the installation process different for downloaded software? The installation process is slightly different for Windows software that you download. Usually all the files needed for the new software are **zipped** to consolidate them into one large file, which is compressed to decrease its size and reduce the download time. As part of the installation process, this downloaded file must be reconstituted, or **unzipped**, into the original collection of files (Figure 3-47).

FIGURE 3-47

Installing Downloaded Software

1. At the distribution Web site, locate any information pertaining to installing the software. Read it. You might also want to print it.

2. Click the download link.

3. If you are downloading from a trusted site and have antivirus software running, click the Open button in the File Download dialog box.

4. Wait for the download to finish. Typically, the setup program included in the download starts automatically.

5. Use the setup program to specify a folder to hold the new software program. You can use the default folder specified by the setup program or a folder of your own choosing. You can also create a new folder during the setup process.

6. Wait for the setup program to uncompress the downloaded file and install the software in the selected directory. During this process, respond to license agreement and other prompts. When the installation is complete, test the software to make sure it works.

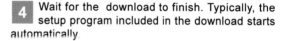

Downloadable software can be provided in several different formats. Some automatically install themselves, but others require manual procedures. A downloadable file typically is set up as a **self-installing executable file**, **self-executing zip file**, or **non-executing zip file** (Figure 3-48).

FIGURE 3-48

Downloadable File Formats

Self-installing Executable Files

Under the most automated installation system, the process of downloading new software automatically initiates the entire installation process.

The software download is packaged as one large file with an .exe extension. This file automatically unzips itself and starts the setup program. You simply follow the setup program prompts to acknowledge the license agreement, indicate the folder for the software files, and complete the installation.

Self-executing Zip Files

Downloaded files with .exe extensions do not always install themselves. Some are simply self-executing zip files, which automatically unzip the software's files, but do not automatically start the setup program.

To install software from a self-executing zip file, you start the executable file to unzip the files for the new software. One of these files will be the Setup.exe program. Next, you manually start the setup program and follow its prompts to complete the installation.

Non-executing Zip Files

If you download software and it arrives as one huge file with a .zip extension, you must locate this file on your hard disk and then use Windows XP or a program such as WinZip to unzip it.

After unzipping the file, you must run the setup program to acknowledge the license agreement, indicate the folder for the software files, and complete the installation.

SOFTWARE UPDATES

What's a software update? Software publishers regularly update their software to add new features, fix bugs, and update its security. Types of software updates (also called "upgrades"), include new versions, patches, and service packs.

Periodically software publishers produce new versions of their software designed to replace older versions. To keep these updates straight, each version carries a version or revision number. For example, version 1.0 might be replaced by a newer version 1.1 or version 2.0. Updating to a new version usually involves a fee, but it is typically less costly than purchasing the new version off the shelf.

A **software patch** is a small section of program code that replaces part of the software you currently have installed. The term **service pack**, which usually applies to operating system updates, is a set of patches that correct problems and address security vulnerabilities. Software patches and service packs are usually free.

How do I get updates? If you have registered your software—usually by connecting to the publisher's Web site during or after an installation—you might receive an e-mail notice when an update is available. Alternatively, you can check the publisher's Web site from time to time.

You can usually download updates from the software publisher's Web site, unless the program files are too large to feasibly transmit over your Internet connection. For large programs, you might have to request a CD by mail.

Some software provides an Automatic Update option that periodically checks the software publisher's Web site for updates, downloads updates automatically, and installs them without user intervention. The advantage of Automatic Update is convenience. The disadvantage is that changes can be made to your computer without your knowledge.

When should I update my software? It is always a good idea to install patches and service packs when they become available. The revised code they contain often addresses security vulnerabilities and the sooner you patch up those holes, the better.

Version updates are a slightly different story. Many savvy computer owners like to wait for a few weeks or months after new software versions become available. The reason they wait is to find out how other users like the new version. If Internet chatter indicates some major flaws, it can be prudent to wait until the publisher is able to address them with patches.

Is installing a software update different from installing the original version? A new version update usually installs in a similar way as you installed the original version, by activating a setup program, displaying a license agreement, and adding updated entries to your computer's Start menu.

Patches and service packs are usually distributed over the Internet and automatically install themselves when you download them.

To combat piracy, many software publishers require users to type in a validation code to complete an installation. A **validation code** is a long sequence of numbers and letters that's typically supplied separately from the software itself. It is not the serial number that you sometimes see in the About dialog box—that number can exist electronically even if the software is a pirated copy. Validation codes are not part of the software. Instead they can usually be found on distribution media or CD packaging. They might also be sent to you via e-mail.

To use a validation code, you simply enter it when instructed during the installation process.

When I install an update, what happens to the old version? The result of an update depends on several factors. Most patches and service pack installations cannot be reversed. A new version installation typically overwrites the old version, but you might have the option to keep the old version just in case you have trouble with the new one and need to revert back to the previous version. The documentation for the update should explain your options for retaining or overwriting old versions.

UNINSTALLING SOFTWARE

How do I get rid of software? With some operating systems, such as DOS, you can remove software simply by deleting its files. Other operating systems, such as Windows and Mac OS, include an **uninstall routine**, which deletes the software's files from various folders on your computer's hard disk. The uninstall routine also removes references to the program from the desktop and from operating system files, such as the file system and, in the case of Windows, the Windows Registry (Figure 3-49).

FIGURE 3-49

To uninstall any Windows application software, first look for an Uninstall option listed on the same menu you use to start the program. If that option is not available, use Add/Remove Programs from the Control Panel.

SOFTWARE COPYRIGHTS AND LICENSES

Is it legal to copy software? After you purchase a software package, you might assume that you can install it and use it in any way you like. In fact, your "purchase" entitles you to use the software only in certain prescribed ways. In most countries, computer software, like a book or movie, is protected by a copyright. A **copyright** is a form of legal protection that grants the author of an original "work" an exclusive right to copy, distribute, sell, and modify that work, except under special circumstances described by copyright laws. These exceptions include:

■ The purchaser has the right to copy software from distribution media or a Web site to a computer's hard disk in order to install it.

■ The purchaser can make an extra, or backup, copy of the software in case the original copy becomes erased or damaged, unless the process of making the backup requires the purchaser to defeat a copy protection mechanism designed to prohibit copying.

■ The purchaser is allowed to copy and distribute sections of a software program for use in critical reviews and teaching.

Most software displays a **copyright notice**, such as "© 2006 eCourse," on one of its screens. This notice is not required by law, however, so programs without a copyright notice are still protected by copyright law. People who circumvent copyright law and illegally copy, distribute, or modify software are sometimes called software pirates, and their illegal copies are referred to as pirated software.

What is a software license? In addition to copyright protection, computer software is often protected by the terms of a software license. A **software license**, or "license agreement," is a legal contract that defines the ways in which you may use a computer program. For personal computer software, you will find the license on the outside of the package, on a separate card inside the package, on the CD packaging, or in one of the program files.

Typically, computer owners purchase the right to use software that is distributed under a **single-user license** that limits use of the software to only one person at a time. Schools, organizations, and businesses sometimes purchase a **site license**, **multiple-user license**, or **concurrent-use license**, which allows more than one person to use the software.

Most legal contracts require signatures before the terms of the contract take effect. This requirement becomes unwieldy with software—imagine having to sign a license agreement and return it before you can use a new software package. To circumvent the signature requirement, software publishers typically use two techniques to validate a software license: shrink-wrap licenses and installation agreements.

When you purchase computer software, the distribution media are usually sealed in an envelope, plastic box, or shrink wrapping. A **shrink-wrap license** goes into effect as soon as you open the packaging. Figure 3-50 explains more about the mechanics of a shrink-wrap license.

A **EULA** (end-user license agreement) is displayed on-screen when you first install software. After reading the software license on the screen, you can indicate that you accept the terms of the license by clicking a designated button—usually labeled "OK," "I agree," or "I accept." If you do not accept the terms, the software does not load and you will not be able to use it.

INFOWEBLINKS

To read the actual text of software copyright laws, connect to the **Software Copyright InfoWeb**.

www.course.com/np/concepts9/ch03

TERMINOLOGY NOTE

A site license is generally priced at a flat rate and allows software to be used on all computers at a specific location.

A multiple-user license is priced per user and allows the allocated number of people to use the software at any time.

A concurrent-use license is priced per copy and allows a specific number of copies to be used at the same time.

FIGURE 3-50

When software has a shrink-wrap license, you agree to the terms of the software license by opening the package. If you do not agree with the terms, you should return the software in its unopened package.

network
ASSOCIATES

Who's watching your network

IMPORTANT

Opening this package constitutes your acceptance of the terms and conditions of the license agreement in this box. Please read the license agreement before opening this sealed package.

NAI-01-0002-2(G)

Software licenses are often lengthy and written in "legalese," but your legal right to use the software continues only as long as you abide by the terms of the software license. Therefore, you should understand the software license for any software you use. To become familiar with a typical license agreement, you can read through the one in Figure 3-51.

Software License Agreement

Important - READ CAREFULLY: This License Agreement ("Agreement") is a legal agreement between you and eCourse Corporation for the software product, eCourse GraphWare ("The SOFTWARE"). By installing, copying, or otherwise using the SOFTWARE, you agree to be bound by the terms of this Agreement. The SOFTWARE is protected by copyright laws and international copyright treaties. The SOFTWARE is licensed, not sold.

GRANT OF LICENSE. This Agreement gives you the right to install and use one copy of the SOFTWARE on a single computer. The primary user of the computer on which the SOFTWARE is installed may make a second copy for his or her exclusive use on a portable computer.

OTHER RIGHTS AND LIMITATIONS. You may not reverse engineer, decompile, or disassemble the SOFTWARE except and only to the extent that such activity is expressly permitted by applicable law.

The SOFTWARE is licensed as a single product; its components may not be separated for use on more than one computer. You may not rent, lease, or lend the SOFTWARE.

You may permanently transfer all of your rights under this Agreement, provided you retain no copies, you transfer all of the SOFTWARE, and the recipient agrees to the terms of this Agreement. If the software product is an upgrade, any transfer must include all prior versions of the SOFTWARE.

You may receive the SOFTWARE in more than one medium. Regardless of the type of medium you receive, you may use only one medium that is appropriate for your single computer. You may not use or install the other medium on another computer.

WARRANTY. eCourse warrants that the SOFTWARE will perform substantially in accordance with the accompanying written documentation for a period of ninety (90) days from the date of receipt. TO THE MAXIMUM EXTENT PERMITTED BY APPLICABLE LAW, eCourse AND ITS SUPPLIERS DISCLAIM ALL OTHER WARRANTIES AND CONDITIONS EITHER EXPRESS OR IMPLIED, INCLUDING, BUT NOT LIMITED TO, IMPLIED WARRANTIES OF MERCHANTABILITY, FITNESS FOR A PARTICULAR PURPOSE, TITLE, AND NON-INFRINGEMENT, WITH REGARD TO THE SOFTWARE PRODUCT.

FIGURE 3-51

When you read a software license agreement, look for answers to the following questions:

Am I buying the software or licensing it?

When does the license go into effect?

Under what circumstances can I make copies?

Can I rent the software?

Can I sell the software?

What if the software includes a distribution CD and a set of distribution floppy disks?

Does the software publisher provide a warranty?

Can I loan the software to a friend?

Are all software licenses similar? Copyright laws have fairly severe restrictions on copying, distributing, and reselling software; however, a license agreement might offer additional rights to consumers. The licenses for commercial software, shareware, freeware, open source, and public domain software specify different levels of permission for software use, copying, and distribution.

Commercial software is typically sold in computer stores or at Web sites. Although you "buy" this software, you actually purchase only the right to use it under the terms of the software license. A license for commercial software typically adheres closely to the limitations provided by copyright law, although it might give you permission to install the software on a computer at work and on a computer at home, provided that you use only one of them at a time.

Shareware is copyrighted software marketed under a "try before you buy" policy. It typically includes a license that permits you to use the software for a trial period. To use it beyond the trial period, you must pay a registration

---

fee. A shareware license usually allows you to make copies of the software and distribute them to others. If they choose to use the software, they must pay a registration fee as well. These shared copies provide a low-cost marketing and distribution channel. Registration fee payment relies on the honor system, so unfortunately many shareware authors collect only a fraction of the money they deserve for their programming efforts. Thousands of shareware programs are available, encompassing just about as many applications as commercial software.

Freeware is copyrighted software that—as you might expect—is available for free. Because the software is protected by copyright, you cannot do anything with it that is not expressly allowed by copyright law or by the author. Typically, the license for freeware permits you to use the software, copy it, and give it away, but does not permit you to alter it or sell it. Many utility programs, device drivers, and some games are available as freeware.

Open source software makes the uncompiled program instructions—the source code—available to programmers who want to modify and improve the software. Open source software may be sold or distributed free of charge in complied form, but it must, in every case, also include the source code. Linux is an example of open source software, as is FreeBSD—a version of UNIX designed for personal computers.

Public domain software is not protected by copyright because the copyright has expired, or the author has placed the program in the public domain, making it available without restriction. Public domain software may be freely copied, distributed, and even resold. The primary restriction on public domain software is that you are not allowed to apply for a copyright on it.

QuickCheck   `SECTION D`

1. System [requirements] specify the operating system and minimum hardware capacities required for software to work correctly.

2. During the [installation] process, your computer performs many tasks, including updating the Windows Registry and Start menu.

3. The [set-up] program typically asks for your consent to the license agreement and confirms the folder into which you want files copied.

4. The files for downloaded software are usually zipped into one large compressed file. True or false? [True]

5. A software [patch] is a small section of program code that replaces part of the software you currently have installed.

6. You can uninstall software using the [Control] Panel's Add/Remove Programs option.

7. Linux is an example of [open] source software.

8. [Public] domain software is not copyrighted, making it available for use without restriction, except that you cannot apply for a copyright on it.

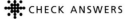 CHECK ANSWERS

TechTalk
The Windows Registry

To many computer owners, the Windows Registry is simply a mysterious "black box" that is mentioned occasionally in articles about computer troubleshooting. Certainly, it is possible to use a computer without intimate knowledge of the Registry; however, the Registry is the "glue" that binds together many of the most important components of a PC—the computer hardware, peripheral devices, application software, and system software. After reading this TechTalk section, you should have a basic understanding of the Registry and its role in the operation of a computer system.

3

Why does Windows need the Registry? Reflect back for a moment on what you know so far about how a computer works. You know that you use menus, dialog boxes, and other controls provided by application software to direct the operations a computer carries out. For some operations—particularly those involving hardware—the application software communicates with the operating system. The operating system might communicate with device drivers or, in some cases, it can directly communicate with a peripheral device.

To act as an intermediary between software and peripheral devices, Windows needs information about these components—where they are located, what's been installed, how they are configured, and how you want to use them. CMOS memory holds the most essential data about your computer's processing and storage hardware, but the **Windows Registry** keeps track of your computer's peripheral devices and software so that the operating system can access the information it needs to coordinate computer system activities. Figure 3-52 lists some of the items the Registry tracks.

Where can I find the Registry? The contents of the Registry are stored in multiple files in the Windows folder of your computer's hard disk and combined into a single database when Windows starts. Although each version of Windows uses a slightly different storage scheme, the basic organization and function of the Registry are similar in all versions.

Windows 95, 98, and Me store the entire contents of the Registry in two files: System.dat and User.dat. System.dat includes configuration data for all the hardware and software installed on a computer. User.dat contains user-specific information, sometimes called a "user profile," which includes software settings and desktop settings. Windows 2000, XP, and Vista divide Registry data among about two dozen files.

What does the Registry look like? The Registry has a logical structure that appears as a hierarchy of folders, similar to the directory structure of your hard disk, as shown in Figure 3-53.

FIGURE 3-52

Items Tracked by the Windows Registry

User preferences for desktop colors, icons, pointers, shortcuts, and display resolution

Sounds that are assigned to various system events, such as clicking and shutting down

The capability of your CD-ROM drive for playing audio CDs and autorunning computer CDs

The options that appear on a shortcut menu when you right-click an object

The computer's network card settings and protocols

The locations of uninstall routines for all installed software

FIGURE 3-53

The Windows Registry is organized as a hierarchy of folders and files.

There are six main folders in the Registry, and their names begin with HKEY. Each folder contains data that pertains to a particular part of a computer system, as described in Figure 3-54.

FIGURE 3-54

Registry Folder Contents

Folder	Contents
HKEY_CLASSES_ROOT	This folder contains data that associates file extensions with a particular application and a list of desktop shortcuts to programs.
HKEY_CURRENT_USER	Information for the current user is transferred here from the HKEY_USERS folder.
HKEY_LOCAL_MACHINE	This folder contains computer-specific information about hardware configuration and software preferences. This information is used for all users who log on to this computer.
HKEY_USERS	This folder contains individual preferences for each person who uses the computer.
HKEY_CURRENT_CONFIG	This folder links to the section of HKEY_LOCAL_MACHINE appropriate for the current hardware configuration.
HKEY_DYN_DATA	This folder points to the part of HKEY_LOCAL_MACHINE that maintains data for Plug and Play devices. This data is dynamic and can change as devices are added and removed from the system.

What does the Registry data look like? The Registry contains thousands of esoteric-looking data entries, such as those shown in Figure 3-55.

FIGURE 3-55

The Registry entries for Display Settings specify such settings as DPI, display fonts, and resolution.

Can I make changes to the Registry? You change the Registry indirectly whenever you install or remove software or hardware. The setup program for your software automatically updates the Registry with essential information about the program's location and configuration. Device drivers and the Windows Plug and Play feature provide similar update services for hardware.

You can also make changes to the Windows Registry by using the dialog boxes for various configuration routines provided by the operating system and application software. For example, if you want to change the desktop colors for your user profile, you can do so by selecting the Settings option from the Start menu, clicking Control Panel, and then selecting the Display option. Any changes you make to settings in the Display Properties dialog box (Figure 3-56) will be recorded in the Windows Registry.

3

FIGURE 3-56

Changes that you make when using the Display Properties dialog box automatically update the corresponding entries in the HKEY_CURRENT_CONFIG folder of the Registry.

QuickCheck

TECHTALK

1. The Windows Registry contains settings and preferences for the peripheral devices and software that are installed on a computer. True or false? [T]

2. The Registry is stored in the [Windows] folder.

3. In the hierarchy of Registry folders, each folder name begins with [HKey].

4. The [Set-up] program automatically updates the Registry when you install software.

 CHECK ANSWERS

Issue
Software Piracy

Software is easy to steal. You don't have to walk out of a Best Buy store with a $495 DVD Workshop software box under your shirt. You can simply borrow your friend's DVD Workshop distribution CDs and install a copy of the program on your computer's hard disk. It seems so simple that it couldn't be illegal. But it is.

Piracy takes many forms. End-user piracy includes friends loaning distribution disks to each other and installing software on more computers than the license allows. Although it is perfectly legal to lend a physical object, such as a sweater, to a friend, it is not legal to lend digital copies of software and music because, unlike a sweater that can be worn by only one person at a time, copies of digital things can be simultaneously used by many people.

Counterfeiting is the large-scale illegal duplication of software distribution media, and sometimes, even its packaging. According to Microsoft, many software counterfeiting groups are linked to organized crime and money-laundering schemes that fund a diverse collection of illegal activities, such as smuggling, gambling, extortion, and prostitution. Counterfeit software is sold in retail stores and through online auctions—often the packaging looks so authentic that buyers have no idea they have purchased illegal goods.

Internet piracy uses the Web as a way to illegally distribute unauthorized software. In "Net" jargon, the terms "appz" and "warez" (pronounced as "wares" or "war EZ") refer to pirated software. Some warez has even been modified to eliminate serial numbers, registration requirements, expiration dates, or other forms of copy protection. The Business Software Alliance (BSA) estimates that more than 800,000 Web sites illegally sell or distribute software.

In many countries, including the United States, software pirates are subject to civil lawsuits for monetary damages and criminal prosecution, which can result in jail time and stiff fines. Nonetheless, software piracy continues to have enormous impact. According to a BSA and IDC 2005 Piracy Study, $59 billion was spent on software worldwide, but software worth $90 billion was installed during the year. That means software worth a whopping $31 billion was pirated.

A small, but vocal, minority of software users, such as members of GNU (which stands for "Gnu's Not UNIX"), believes that data and software should be freely distributed. Richard Stallman writes in the GNU Manifesto, "I consider that the golden rule requires that if I like a program I must share it with other people who like it. Software sellers want to divide users and conquer them, making each user agree not to share with others. I refuse to break solidarity with other users in this way. I cannot in good conscience sign a nondisclosure agreement or a software license agreement."

Is software piracy really damaging? Who cares if you use a program without paying for it? Software piracy is damaging because it has a negative effect on the economy. Software production makes a major contribution to the United States economy, employing more than 2 million people and accounting for billions of dollars in corporate revenue. It fuels economic development in countries such as India, China, and Malaysia. A BSA economic impact study concluded that lowering global piracy from an average of 36% to only 26% would add more that 1 million jobs and $400 billion in worldwide economic growth.

Decreases in software revenues can have a direct effect on consumers, too. When software publishers are forced to cut corners, they tend to reduce customer service and technical support. As a result, you, the consumer, get put on hold when you call for technical support, find fewer free technical support sites, and encounter customer support personnel who are only moderately knowledgeable about their products. The bottom line—software piracy negatively affects customer service.

As an alternative to cutting support costs, some software publishers might build the cost of software piracy into the price of the software. The unfortunate result is that those who legitimately license and purchase software pay an inflated price. The BSA and IDC reported about 35% of the software currently in use is pirated. Vietnam, Ukraine, and China have the world's highest piracy rates—92% of the software used in Vietnam is believed to be pirated. The figure is 91% in Ukraine and 90% in China. In Russia the piracy rate is 87%. In the United States, an estimated 21% of software is pirated. In Japan, the rate is 28%.

Piracy Rates by Region (as percent of total in use)

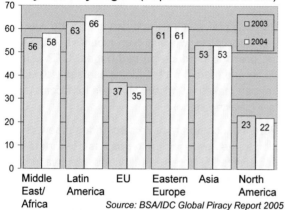

Source: BSA/IDC Global Piracy Report 2005

Although the rate of business software piracy might be declining, total piracy appears to be growing by one or two percentage points each year. Analysts fear that the Internet is a major factor in piracy growth. As Internet access becomes available to subscribers in countries such as China, piracy could skyrocket. To make matters worse, increased access to high-speed Internet connections makes it much easier to quickly download large software files.

As a justification of high piracy rates, some observers point out that people in many countries simply might not be able to afford software priced for the U.S. market. This argument could apply to China, where the

average annual income is equivalent to about U.S. $3,500, and in North Korea, where the average income is only U.S. $900. A Korean who legitimately purchases Microsoft Office for U.S. $250 would be spending more than one-quarter of his or her annual income.

Many countries with a high incidence of software piracy, however, have strong economies and respectable per capita incomes. To further discredit the theory that piracy stems from poverty, India—which has a fairly large computer-user community, but a per capita income of only U.S. $1,600—is not among the top 10 countries with high rates of software piracy.

If economic factors do not account for the pervasiveness of software piracy, what does? The incidence of piracy seems to be higher among small business and individual users than corporations and government agencies. Two-thirds of college and university students see nothing unethical about swapping or downloading digital copyrighted software, music, and movie files without paying for them and more than half of the respondents believe it is acceptable to do so in the workplace.

Some analysts suggest that people need more education about software copyrights and the economic implications of piracy. Other analysts believe that copyright enforcement must be increased by implementing more vigorous efforts to identify and prosecute pirates.

INFOWEBLINKS

You can read the GNU Manifesto and other thought-provoking articles about software piracy by going to the **Copyright and Piracy InfoWeb**.

www.course.com/np/concepts9/ch03

3

What Do You Think?   ISSUE

1. Do you believe that software piracy is a serious issue?   ○ Yes ○ No ○ Not sure

2. Do you know of any instances of software piracy?   ○ Yes ○ No ○ Not sure

3. Do you think that most software pirates understand that they are doing something illegal?   ○ Yes ○ No ○ Not sure

4. Should software publishers try to adjust software pricing for local markets?   ○ Yes ○ No ○ Not sure

SAVE RESPONSES

Computers in Context

Journalism

In the ancient world, news spread by word of mouth, relayed by bards and merchants who traveled from town to town—in essence, the first reporters to "broadcast" the news. The news business is all about gathering and disseminating information as quickly as possible. Technology has played a major role in news reporting's evolution from its bardic roots to modern 24-hour "live" news networks.

Johann Gutenberg's printing press (ca. 1450), the first technological breakthrough in the news business, made it feasible to publish news as printed notices tacked to walls in the town square. As paper became more economical, resourceful entrepreneurs sold broadsheets to people eager for news, and the concept of a newspaper was born. The first regularly published newspapers appeared in Germany and Holland in 1609, and the first English newspaper, the *Weekly News*, was published in 1622.

But the news spread slowly. In the early 1800s, it took four weeks for newspapers in New York to receive reports from London. With the advent of the telegraph in 1844, however, reporters from far-flung regions could "wire" stories to their newspapers for publication the next day. The first radio reporters in the 1920s offered live broadcasts of sports events, church services, and variety shows. Before the 1950s, black-and-white newsreels shown in movie theaters provided the only visual imagery of news events, but television gave viewers news images on a nightly basis.

Technology has benefited print journalism, too. For decades, typesetters transferred reporters' handwritten stories into neatly set columns of type. Today, reporters use computers and word processing software to tap out their stories and run a preliminary check of spelling and grammar.

Stories are submitted by computer network to editors, who also use word processing software to edit stories to fit time and space constraints. The typesetting process has been replaced by desktop publishing software and computer to plate (CTP) technology. Digital pages produced with desktop publishing software are sent to a raster image processor (RIP), which converts the pages into dots that form words and images. After a page has been

RIPed, a platesetter uses lasers to etch the dots onto a physical plate, which is then mounted on the printing press to produce printed pages. CTP is much faster and more flexible than typesetting, so publishers can make last-minute changes to accommodate late-breaking stories.

Personal computers have also added a new dimension to the news-gathering process. Reporters were once limited to personal interviews, observation, and fact gathering at libraries, but can now make extensive use of Internet resources and e-mail. Web sites and online databases provide background information on all sorts of topics. Other resources include newsgroups and chat rooms, where reporters can monitor public opinion on current events and identify potential sources.

Most major networks maintain interactive Web sites that offer online polls and bulletin boards designed to collect viewers' opinions. Although online poll respondents are not a representative sample of the

population, they can help news organizations gauge viewer opinions and determine whether news coverage is comprehensive and effective.

E-mail has changed the way reporters communicate with colleagues and sources. It's often the only practical method for contacting people in remote locations or distant time zones, and it's useful with reluctant sources, who feel more comfortable providing information under the cloak of anonymous Hotmail or Yahoo! accounts. "Vetting" e-mail sources—verifying credentials such as name, location, and occupation—can be difficult, however, so reporters tend not to rely on these sources without substantial corroboration.

For broadcast journalism, digital communications play a major role in today's "live on the scene" television reporting. Most news organizations maintain remote production vans, sometimes called "satellite news gathering (SNG) trucks," that travel to the site of breaking news, raise their antennas, and begin to broadcast. These complete mobile production facilities include camera control units, audio and video recording equipment, and satellite or microwave transmitters.

On-the-scene reporting no longer requires a truck full of equipment, however. Audiovisual editing units and video cameras have gone digital, making them easier to use and sized to fit in a suitcase. A new breed of "backpack journalists" carry mini-DV cameras, notebook computers, and satellite phones. Jane Ellen Stevens, a pioneer backpack journalist specializing in science and technology, has reported since 1997 from remote locations, such as a space camp in Russia.

Backpack journalists can connect their minicams to notebook computers with a FireWire cable, transfer their video footage to the hard disk, and then edit the footage using consumer-level video editing software.

The resulting video files, compressed for transmission over a satellite phone, are sent to newsroom technicians, who decompress and then broadcast them—all in a matter of seconds.

One drawback of backpack journalists' use of minicams and compression is that the video quality usually isn't as crisp as images filmed with studio cameras. News organizations with high standards were once hesitant to use this lower quality video, but have found that viewers would rather see a low-quality image now than a high-quality image later. To many viewers, a few rough edges just make the footage seem more compelling, more "you are there."

A memorable tour de force in SNG was the brainchild of David Bloom, an NBC reporter embedded with the U.S. Army 3rd Infantry Division during Operation Iraqi Freedom. He helped modify an M-88 tank recovery vehicle into a high-tech, armored SNG vehicle. The $500,000 "Bloommobile" featured a gyrostabilized camera that could produce jiggle-free video as the tank blasted over sand dunes at 50 mph. Tragically, Bloom died while covering the conflict, but many viewers vividly remember his exhilarating reports as the Bloommobile raced down desert roads, trundled along with army supply convoys, and narrowly escaped enemy fire.

Computers, the Internet, and communications technology make it possible to instantly broadcast live reports across the globe, but live reporting is not without controversy. A reporter who arrives at the scene of a disaster with microphone in hand has little time for reflection, vetting, and cross-checking, so grievous errors, libelous images, or distasteful video footage sometimes find their way into news reports.

Jeff Gralnick, former executive producer for ABC News, remarks, "In the old days, we had time to think before we spoke. We had time to write, time to research and time to say, 'Hey, wait a minute.' Now we don't even have the time to say, 'Hey, wait a nanosecond.' Just because we can say it or do it, should we?" Technology has given journalists a powerful arsenal of tools for gathering and reporting the news, but has also increased their accountability for accurate, socially responsible reporting.

INFOWEBLINKS

You'll find lots more information related to this topic at the **Computers and Journalism InfoWeb**.

www.course.com/np/concepts9/ch03

Labs

On the Web
Student Edition Labs

To access the Student Edition labs, connect to the New Perspectives NP9 Web site and click the link for Student Edition Labs. The link also provides access to lab assignments.

www.course.com/np/concepts9/ch03

Work hands-on in structured simulations practicing important skills and concepts

WORD PROCESSING

In the Word Processing Student Edition Lab, you will learn the following topics and skills:

- Opening, saving, and printing a document
- Moving the insertion point and entering and editing text
- Moving and deleting blocks of text
- Inserting graphics and formatting your document
- Checking your document for spelling errors

SPREADSHEETS

In the Spreadsheets Student Edition Lab, you will learn the following topics and skills:

- Entering labels, values, and formulas
- Selecting and naming ranges
- Inserting functions
- Formatting a worksheet
- Creating a chart

DATABASES

In the Databases Student Edition Lab, you will learn the following topics and skills:

- Entering and editing data
- Understanding the relationships between tables
- Sorting data
- Creating an index
- Creating queries

- Applying filters
- Creating and modifying reports

ADVANCED SPREADSHEETS

In the Advanced Spreadsheets Student Edition Lab, you will learn the following topics and skills:

- Sorting and filtering lists and creating subtotals
- Using conditional formatting, data validation, Goal Seek and macros
- Creating PivotTables
- Protecting and documenting a worksheet

PRESENTATION SOFTWARE

In the Presentation Software Student Edition Lab, you will learn the following topics and skills:

- Adding text, graphics, animations, and sound to slides
- Using slide layouts and design templates
- Understanding the slide master
- Previewing, viewing, and printing a presentation

INSTALLING AND UNINSTALLING SOFTWARE

In the Installing and Uninstalling Software Student Edition Lab, you will learn the following topics and skills:

- Installing software from a distribution CD
- Installing downloaded software
- Understanding the differences between upgrades, updates, and patches
- Uninstalling software applications

USING WINDOWS

In the Using Windows Student Edition Lab, you will learn the following topics and skills:

- Identifying common elements of Windows software
- Working with the taskbar and Start menu
- Using menus, toolbars, and dialog boxes

On the BookOnCD
New Perspectives Labs

To access the New Perspectives labs for Chapter 3, start the BookOnCD and then click the ✤ icon next to the lab title below.

✤ USING THE WINDOWS INTERFACE

IN THIS LAB YOU'LL LEARN:

Why the standard Windows controls make it easy to learn new Windows software

How ToolTips or ScreenTips help you identify icons and toolbar buttons

How to use the Maximize, Minimize, Restore, and Close buttons, scroll bars, and toolbars

How to navigate through a series of menus

Which menus are common to most Windows applications

The meaning of menu conventions, such as the ellipsis and triangle

How to use standard dialog box controls, such as option buttons, spin boxes, tabs, check boxes, and lists

How to take a screenshot and print it

LAB ASSIGNMENTS

1. Start the interactive part of the lab. Make sure you've enabled Tracking if you want to save your QuickCheck results. Perform each lab step as directed, and answer all the lab QuickCheck questions. When you exit the lab, your answers are automatically graded and your results are displayed.

2. Draw a sketch or print a screenshot of the Windows desktop on any computer you use. Use ToolTips (or ScreenTips) to identify all the icons on the desktop and the taskbar.

3. Use the Start button and Accessories menu to start an application program called Paint. (If Paint is not installed on your computer, you can use any application software, such as a word processing program.) Draw a sketch or print a screenshot of the Paint (or other application) window and label the following components: window title, title bar, Maximize/Restore button, Minimize button, Close button, menu bar, toolbar, and scroll bar.

4. Look at each of the menu options the Paint software (or other application) provides. Make a list of those that seem to be standard Windows menu options.

5. Draw a sketch of Paint's Print dialog box (or other application's Print dialog box). Label the following parts: buttons, spin bar, pull-down list, option button, and check boxes.

✤ INSTALLING AND UNINSTALLING SOFTWARE

IN THIS LAB YOU'LL LEARN:

How to use a setup program to install Windows application software from a distribution CD

The difference between typical, compact, and custom installation options

How to specify a folder for a new software installation

How to install downloaded software

How to install an upgrade

How to uninstall a Windows application

What happens, in addition to deleting files, when you uninstall a software application

How to locate the program that will uninstall a software application

Why you might not want to delete all of the files associated with an application

LAB ASSIGNMENTS

1. Start the interactive part of the lab. Make sure you've enabled Tracking if you want to save your QuickCheck results. Perform each lab step as directed, and answer all the lab QuickCheck questions. When you exit the lab, your answers are automatically graded and your results are displayed.

2. Browse the Web and locate a software application that you might like to download. Use information supplied by the Web site to answer the following questions:

   a. What is the name of the program and the URL of the download site?

   b. What is the size of the download file?

   c. According to the instructions, does the download file appear to require manual installation, is it a self-executing zip file, or is it a self-installing executable file?

3. On the computer you typically use, look through the list of programs (click Start, then select Programs to see a list of them). List the names of any programs that include their own uninstall routines.

4. On the computer you typically use, open the Control Panel and then open the Add/Remove Programs dialog box. List the first 10 programs that are currently installed on the computer.

3

Interactive Summary

To review important concepts from this chapter, fill in the blanks to best complete each sentence. When using the NP9 BookOnCD or the NP9 Web site, click the Check Answers buttons to automatically score your answers.

_____ consists of computer programs and data files that work together to provide a computer with the instructions and data necessary for carrying out a specific type of task, such as document production, video editing, graphic design, or Web browsing. Computer _____ write the programs that become the components of a computer software product. To understand how software is installed and uninstalled, it is important for computer owners to recognize that today's software typically consists of many files.

To create a software environment, a programmer must define the _____ for each element in the environment, such as where an object appears, its shape, its color, and its behavior. A computer program-

ming _____ provides the tools a programmer uses to create software. Most programmers today prefer to use _____ languages, such as C, C++, Java, Ada, COBOL, and Visual Basic. A computer's microprocessor understands only _____ language, however, so a program that is written in a high-level language must be compiled or interpreted before it can be processed. A _____ translates all the instructions in a program as a single batch, and the resulting machine language instructions, called _____ code, are placed in a new file. An alternative method of translation uses an _____ to translate instructions one at a time while the program runs.

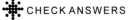 CHECK ANSWERS

A computer's software is like the chain of command in an army. _____ software tells the operating system what to do. The operating system tells the device drivers, device drivers tell the hardware, and the hardware actually does the work. The operating system interacts with application software, device drivers, and hardware to manage a computer's _____. In addition, many operating systems also influence the "look and feel" of your software, or what's known as the user _____.

The core part of an operating system is called the _____. In addition to this core, many operating systems provide helpful tools, called _____, that you can use to control and customize your computer equipment and work environment. Operating systems are informally categorized

and characterized using one or more of the following terms: A _____ operating system expects to deal with one set of input devices—those that can be controlled by one person at a time. A _____ operating system is designed to deal with input, output, and processing requests from many users. A _____ operating system provides process and memory management services that allow two or more programs to run simultaneously. A _____ operating system is one that's designed for a personal computer—either a desktop or notebook computer. Popular desktop operating systems include Windows 95/98/Me/XP and Mac OS. Popular _____ operating systems include Windows NT/2000, Linux, and UNIX. Operating systems for PDAs are typically smaller than PC operating systems and can fit in _____.

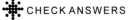 CHECK ANSWERS

Document [_____] software assists you with composing, editing, designing, printing, and electronically publishing documents. The three most popular types of document production software include word processing, desktop publishing, and Web authoring. [_____] software is similar to a "smart" piece of paper that automatically adds up the columns of numbers you write on it. You can use it to make other calculations, too, based on simple equations that you write or more complex, built-in formulas. Because it is so easy to experiment with different numbers, this type of software is particularly useful for [_____] analyses. [_____] software helps you store, find, organize, update, and report information stored in one or more tables. When two sets of records are [_____], database software allows you to access data from both tables at the same time. [_____] software, includ-

ing paint, photo editing, drawing, 3-D, and presentation software, is designed to help you create, manipulate, and print images.

Music and video editing software, educational and reference software, and entertainment software round out the most popular categories of personal computer software. A software [_____] is a "bundled" collection of application software sold as a single package.

For businesses, [_____] market software is designed to automate specialized tasks in a specific market or business. [_____] market software is generic software that can be used by just about any kind of business. [_____] is a type of horizontal market software designed to help several people collaborate on a single project using LAN or Internet connections.

CHECK ANSWERS

When you [_____] software, the new software files are placed in the appropriate folders on your computer's hard disk, and then your computer performs any software or hardware configurations that are necessary to make sure the program is ready to run. The [_____] files and data files for the software are placed in the folder you specify. Some [_____] programs for the software, however, might be stored in different folders, such as Windows\System. Windows software typically contains a [_____] program that guides you through the installation process.

To install application software from a [_____] CD, simply place the CD in the drive and wait for the setup program to begin. The installation process is slightly different for application software that you download. Usually all the files needed for the new software are consolidated into one large file, which is [_____] to decrease its size and reduce the download time. This large, downloaded file must be reconstituted, or [_____], into the origi-

nal collection of files as a first step in the installation process. A self-installing [_____] file automatically unzips the downloaded file and starts the setup program. A self-executing [_____] file automatically unzips the software's files, but does not automatically start the setup program.

Free software updates include [_____] and service packs that contain code to fix bugs and security vulnerabilities. Some updates require a validation code.

A [_____] is a form of legal protection that grants the author of an original "work" the right to copy, distribute, sell, and modify that work, except under special circumstances described by copyright laws. A software [_____] is a legal contract that defines the ways in which you may use a computer program. Licenses for commercial, shareware, freeware, open source, and public domain software provide consumers with different sets of rights pertaining to copying and distribution.

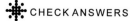 CHECK ANSWERS

Key Terms

Make sure you understand all the boldfaced key terms presented in this chapter. If you're using the NP9 BookOnCD, you can use this list of terms as an interactive study activity. First, try to define a term in your own words, and then click the term to compare your definition with the definition presented in the chapter.

Absolute reference, 144
Application software, 125
Automatic recalculation, 144
Bootstrap program, 129
Cell, 142
Cell references, 143
Clip art, 141
Command-line interface, 128
Commercial software, 163
Compiler, 123
Computer programmers, 122
Concurrent-use license, 162
Copyright, 162
Copyright notice, 162
Database, 146
Desktop operating system, 130
Distribution media, 156
DOS, 134
EULA, 162
Field, 146
Font, 139
Footer, 140
Format, 139
Formula, 143
Frames, 141
Freeware, 164
Fully justified, 140
Function, 143
Grammar checker, 139
Graphical user interface, 128
Graphics, 149
Groupware, 155
Header, 140
High-level language, 123
Install, 157
Interpreter, 123

Kernel, 129
Label, 142
Leading, 140
Line spacing, 140
Linux, 133
Mac OS, 132
Machine language, 123
Mail merge, 141
Mathematical operators, 143
Microsoft Windows, 130
Multiple-user license, 162
Multiprocessing, 127
Multitasking, 127
Multithreading, 127
Multiuser operating system, 130
Natural language query, 148
Network operating system, 130
Non-executing zip file, 160
Object code, 123
Open source software, 164
Page layout, 140
Palm OS, 134
Paragraph alignment, 140
Paragraph style, 140
Point size, 139
Programming language, 123
Properties, 122
Public domain software, 164
Query by example, 148
Query language, 148
Readability formula, 139
Record, 146
Relative reference, 144
Resource, 126
Search and Replace, 139
Self-executing zip file, 160

Self-installing executable file, 160
Service pack, 160
Setup program, 158
Shareware, 163
Shrink-wrap license, 162
Single-user license, 162
Single-user operating system, 130
Site license, 162
Software license, 162
Software patch, 160
Software publishers, 122
Software suite, 152
Source code, 123
Spelling checker, 138
Spelling dictionary, 138
Spreadsheet, 142
Style, 140
Symbian OS, 134
System requirements, 156
System software, 125
Table, 141
Thesaurus, 139
Uninstall routine, 161
UNIX, 133
Unzipped, 159
User interface, 128
Utility software, 135
Validation code, 161
Value, 142
What-if analysis, 142
Windows Mobile OS, 134
Windows Registry, 165
Worksheet, 142
Zipped, 159

Software Key Terms

3

Interactive Situation Questions

Apply what you've learned to some typical computing situations. When using the NP9 BookOnCD or the NP9 Web site, you can type your answers, and then use the Check Answers button to automatically score your responses.

1. While using several programs at the same time, your computer displays an error message that refers to a general protection fault. You recognize this problem as a potential [_____] leak and decide to close the corrupted program using Ctrl+Alt+Del.

2. You've volunteered to create some graphics for a nonprofit organization, but you'll need a variety of graphics software tools for the organization's computer. Your first choice is to consider a graphics [_____] that bundles together paint, draw, and Web graphics software.

3. Suppose that you've been hired to organize a professional skateboard competition. When you consider how you'll need to use computers, you realize that you must collect information on each competitor and keep track of every competitive event. With at least two types of related records, you'll probably need to use [_____] software.

4. Imagine that you just purchased a new software package. You insert the distribution CD, but nothing happens. No problem—you can manually run the [_____] program, which will start the install routine.

5. You are preparing to download a new software program from the Web. The download consists of one huge file with an .exe extension. You recognize this as a self-[_____] executable file that will automatically unzip itself and start the installation routine.

6. You download an open source software program from the Web. You assume that the download includes the uncompiled [_____] code for the program as well as the [_____] version.

✦ CHECK ANSWERS

Interactive Practice Tests

Practice tests that consist of 10 multiple-choice, true/false, and fill-in-the-blank questions are available on both the NP9 BookOnCD and the NP9 Web site. The questions are selected at random from a large test bank, so each time you take a test, you'll receive a different set of questions. Your tests are scored immediately, and you can print study guides that help you find the correct answers for any questions that you missed.

CLICK ✦ TO START

Projects

An NP9 Project is an open-ended activity that will help you apply the concepts you have learned. Many projects require resources in addition to your textbook, such as current magazines, library materials, or Web access. When you tackle a project, be prepared to use your critical thinking skills, logical analysis, and your creativity.

CRITICAL THINKING

Have you heard about the "24-hour rule" for software that says you can legally use any software for free for 24 hours without paying for it? How about your right to use "abandoned" software that's no longer supported or that was created by a company now out of business? Both the 24-hour rule and the concept of abandoned software are urban legends and have no basis in copyright law. Does it seem to you that most people don't have the facts about copyrights? How strong a factor is that in the proliferation of software piracy? What are your thoughts about the connection between knowing the copyright rules and following them? Put your thoughts in order, write them up, and send them to your instructor.

CYBERCLASSROOM

Some productivity packages, such as Microsoft Word, include features designed for group collaboration. Learn how to use revision marks. Create a document at least three paragraphs long about your favorite computer software and circulate it to all team members as an e-mail attachment for comment using revision marks.

MULTIMEDIA PROJECT

Find a photo from one of your old albums or at an antique store. Scan the photo into digital format. Use graphics software to improve the photo quality. Your instructor might run a contest to see which students can most dramatically improve their original photos.

GROUP PROJECT

Form a group with at least two of your classmates. Now imagine that your college (or business) has decided to negotiate with software publishers to offer students (or employees) a bundled software package at a greatly discounted price. Your group's job is to select the 15 software products for the bundle. Your group must make sure the software effectively meets the major needs of the students at your school (or employees in your workplace). Use Internet resources to look at the range of software available and make your selections. Make sure you take advantage of group members' expertise and experience with software products. Arrange your final list into categories like those on page 121.

RESUME BUILDER

Use the Web and other resources to compile a list of the software used in your current or future career field. Are there standard packages that job applicants need to know how to use? If so, what can you find out about those packages on the Web? If your career field does not use any standard software packages, explain why you think that is the case.

Also, make a list of the software packages you're familiar with. Use the software classification system on page 121 to classify your list. As you consider your school and career goals for the next year, list at least five additional software packages you would like to learn. Explain why they would be helpful. Submit your lists to your instructor by e-mail.

GLOBALIZATION

Computer games are big business. They are exported worldwide and accessed by communities of online players around the globe. For this project gather information about the most internationally popular computer games. Try some of them yourself to see what they're all about. What effect, if any, would you expect these games to have on individual players living in the cultures of 1) industrialized countries, 2) Middle-eastern countries, and 3) developing countries? Summarize your ideas in one or two pages.

ISSUE

The Issue section of this chapter focused on copyrights and software piracy. For this project, you will write a two- to five-page paper about this issue based on information you gather from the Internet. To begin this project, consult the Copyright and Piracy InfoWeb (see page 165), and link to the recommended Web pages to get an in-depth overview of the issue. Armed with this background, select one of the following viewpoints and statements and argue for or against it:

- Free software advocates: As an enabling technology, software should be freely distributed, along with its modifiable source code.
- Librarians: Copyright laws, especially the Digital Millennium Copyright Act, minimize the needs of the public and go too far in their efforts to protect the rights of software authors.
- Software Publishers Association: Strong copyright laws and enforcement are essential for companies to publish and support high-quality software.

COMPUTERS IN CONTEXT

The Computers in Context section of this chapter focused on computer and communications technology used by reporters and journalists. Technology has had a major effect on "backpack journalists" who use small-scale digital devices to gather and report the news. For this project, use a Web search engine to collect information on the advantages and disadvantages of backpack journalism. In your research, you should explore technical issues, such as the cost of equipment, video quality, and transmission capabilities. Also explore ethical issues pertaining to on-the-spot news reporting.

Summarize your research in a two-four page paper. Make sure you cite sources for your material. Follow your professor's instructions for formatting and submitting your paper.

3

Study Tips

Study Tips help you to organize and consolidate the information in a unit by making lists, outlines, charts, and sketches. You can use paper and pencil or word processing software to complete most of the Study Tip activities.

1. Make sure you can use your own words to correctly answer each of the orange focus questions that appear throughout the chapter.

2. Make sure you can list and describe the three types of files that are typically supplied on a software distribution disk.

3. Explain the difference between a compiler and an interpreter and between source code and object code.

4. List three types of system software, and at least five categories of application software.

5. Make sure you can list and describe the four main resources that an operating system manages.

6. Explain the term "memory leak," and describe what you can do if one occurs on your PC.

7. Describe the difference between a graphical user interface and a command-line user interface.

8. Describe five tasks for which you must interact directly with the operating system.

9. Study the figures of Windows, Mac OS, and Linux in Section B. If you were to start an unfamiliar computer, describe how you would identify its operating system.

10. Discuss the pros and cons of using Linux as a desktop operating system.

11. Describe the strengths of word processing, DTP, and Web authoring software.

12. Explain how a spelling checker works and why it is not a substitute for proofreading.

13. Draw a sketch of a simple worksheet and label the following: columns, rows, cell, active cell, values, labels, formulas, and Formula bar.

14. Explain the difference between an absolute reference and a relative reference, giving an example of each.

15. List five types of "number crunching" software that you can use instead of spreadsheet software.

16. Describe how you would use each of the six types of graphics software described in this chapter.

17. Explain the purpose of a software patch and describe how it differs from a service pack.

18. Describe the process of installing software from a distribution CD, and contrast it with the process of installing downloaded software.

19. Explain the differences between commercial software, shareware, open source software, freeware, and public domain software.

20. Arrange the items in Figure 3-52 so that the Registry items you would change most frequently are at the top of the list.

21. Fill in the blanks on the concept map below to show the hierarchy of system software described in this chapter:

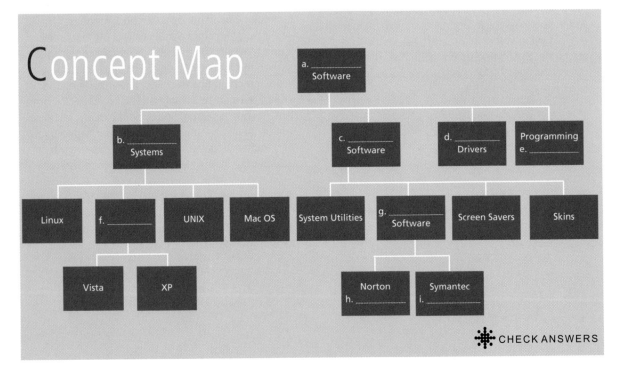

Concept Map

a. _____ Software

b. _____ Systems

c. _____ Software

d. _____ Drivers

Programming e. _____

Linux

f. _____

UNIX

Mac OS

System Utilities

g. _____ Software

Screen Savers

Skins

Vista

XP

Norton h. _____

Symantec i. _____

CHECK ANSWERS

Review on the Web

TECHTV VIDEO PROJECT

The TechTV segment *Software Vending Machines* highlights an innovative way to get software into the hands of consumers. After watching the video, write a short description of how this technology works. Next, suppose you are asked to invest in this company. What do you see as the advantages and disadvantages of this technology? Do alternative technologies exist that might be more effective? Discuss your thoughts on these questions.

To work with the Video Projects for this chapter, connect to the New Perspectives NP9 Web site.

www.course.com/np/concepts9/ch03

3

ONLINE GAMES

Test your comprehension of the concepts introduced in Chapter 3 by playing the NP9 Online Games. At the end of each game, you have three options:

- Submit your results to your instructor using the Universal Gradebook through CoursePort
- Print your results to be submitted to your instructor
- Print a comprehensive study guide complete with page references

To work with the Online Games for this chapter, connect to the New Perspectives NP9 Web site.

www.course.com/np/concepts9/ch03

 LIGHTNING   **DON'T TELL ME**   **FAKE OUT**

ONLINE END-OF-CHAPTER ACTIVITIES

The following NP9 Review Activities are also available at the New Perspectives NP9 Web site:

- Interactive Summary
- Interactive Situation Questions
- Interactive Practice Tests
- Concept Map

If you are using the Web site to complete these activities, you can automatically score your answers and share the results with your instructor.

www.course.com/np/concepts9/ch03

4

File Management, Virus Protection, and Backup

FOCUS ON THESE LEARNING OBJECTIVES

Create valid names for files and folders, plus demonstrate that you can construct and trace file paths

Demonstrate how to use file management features of application software and operating system utilities

Describe how a computer physically stores data on disks, but represents this storage system with a logical model

Explain how file viruses, boot sector viruses, macro viruses, Trojan horses, worms, bots, and Denial of Service attacks affect files and disrupt computer operations

Describe how a computer owner can use antivirus software to avoid, find, and remove viruses

Demonstrate that you can implement a viable backup and restore plan

Compare the advantages and disadvantages of using tapes, floppy disks, a second hard disk, CDs, Zip disks, networks, and Web sites for backups

A detailed list of learning objectives is provided at the New Perspectives NP9 Web site:

www.course.com/np/concepts9/ch04

UNDERSTAND THE CHAPTER CONTENTS

✳ **SECTION A: FILE BASICS**

File Names, Extensions, and Formats
File Locations, Folders, and Paths
File Sizes and Dates

✳ **SECTION B: FILE MANAGEMENT**

Application-based File Management
File Management Utilities
File Management Metaphors
Windows Explorer
File Management Tips
Physical File Storage

✳ **SECTION C: COMPUTER VIRUSES**

Viruses
Trojan Horses
Worms
Bots
Combating Malicious Code
Virus Hoaxes

✳ **SECTION D: DATA BACKUP**

Backup and Restore Procedures
Backup Devices
Network and Internet Backup
Backup Software
Boot and Recovery Disks

✳ **TECHTALK: FILE FORMATS**

✳ **ISSUE: COMPUTER CRIME**

✳ **COMPUTERS IN CONTEXT: LAW ENFORCEMENT**

✳ **STUDENT EDITION LABS**

Maintaining a Hard Drive
Managing Files and Folders
Keeping Your Computer Virus Free
Backing Up Your Computer

✳ **NEW PERSPECTIVES LABS**

Working with Windows Explorer
Backing Up Your Computer

✳ **REVIEW ACTIVITIES**

Interactive Summary
Key Terms
Interactive Situation Questions
Interactive Practice Tests
Projects
Study Tips and Concept Map
Review on the Web

TIP

When using the BookOnCD, the ✳ icons are "clickable" to access resources on the CD. The ✝ icons are clickable to access resources on the Web. You can also access Web resources by using your browser to connect directly to the New Perspectives NP9 Web site at: www.course.com/np/concepts9/ch04

YOUR IMPORTANT DOCUMENTS, MUSIC COLLECTIONS, AND DIGITAL PHOTOS

are stored in files on your computer's hard disk and other storage media, such as CDs and DVDs. This chapter begins with some basic information about how a computer keeps track of files, then explains how you can organize your files for easy access and how to protect them from viruses and equipment failures.

4

TAKE A PRE-ASSESSMENT QUIZ

to find out how much you know about computer file management, viruses, and backup. Armed with your results, you can focus your study time on concepts that will round out your knowledge of computer files and improve your test scores.

www.course.com/np/concepts9/ch04

LISTEN TO A CHAPTER OVERVIEW

Get your book and highlighter ready, then connect to the New Perspectives NP9 Web site, where you can listen to an overview that points out the most important concepts for this chapter.

www.course.com/np/concepts9/ch04

BEFORE YOU READ ON, TRY IT

IS MY COMPUTER'S HARD DISK GETTING FULL?
Chapter 4 is all about files—how to create them, where to store them, and how to keep them safe. Your computer's hard disk stores a high percentage of the programs you use and the data files you create. You might wonder if your hard disk is getting full. To find out, you can use the My Computer icon.

1. Start your computer and make sure you can see the Windows desktop.

2. Double-click the My Computer icon. If that icon is not on your desktop, click the Start button and click My Computer from the menu that appears.

3. Right-click Local disk (C:) to display the pop-up menu.

4. Click Properties.

5. A Local Disk Properties dialog box should appear containing statistics about your computer's hard disk.

6. Using the blanks on the figure to the right, jot down the statistics for used space, free space, and capacity, and then sketch in the slices of the pie chart for your computer.

7. Also jot down the file system used by your computer in the blank provided. You'll learn the significance of the file system when you read the chapter.

Local Disk (C:) Properties

General | Tools | Hardware | Norton | Sharing | Quota

Type: Local Disk
File system: _____

Used space: _____ bytes ____ GB
Free space: _____ bytes ____ GB

Capacity: _____ bytes ____ GB

Drive C   Disk Cleanup

☐ Compress drive to save disk space
☑ Allow Indexing Service to index this disk for fast file searching

OK Cancel Apply

A

File Basics

The term "file" was used for filing cabinets and collections of papers long before it became part of the personal computer lexicon. Today, computer files in digital format offer a compact and convenient way to store documents, photos, videos, and music. Most computer files can be easily duplicated and quickly transferred over computer networks, making them much easier to share and distribute than paper files. Computer files have several characteristics, such as a name, format, location, size, and date. To make effective use of computer files, you'll need a good understanding of these file basics, and that is the focus of Section A.

FILE NAMES, EXTENSIONS, AND FORMATS

What is a computer file? As you learned in Chapter 1, a computer file—or simply a "file"— is defined as a named collection of data that exists on a storage medium, such as a disk, CD, DVD, or tape. A file can contain a group of records, a document, a photo, music, a video, an e-mail message, or a computer program.

When you use word processing software, the text you enter for a document is stored as a file. You can give the file a name, such as *A History of Film Noir*. A music file, such as *Bach Brandenberg Concertos* that you download over the Internet is stored as a file, too.

What are the rules for naming files? Every file has a name and might also have a file extension. When you save a file, you must provide a valid file name that adheres to specific rules, referred to as **file-naming conventions**. Each operating system has a unique set of file-naming conventions. Figure 4-1 lists the file naming conventions for the current versions of Windows.

Is there a maximum length for file names? DOS and Windows 3.1 limited file names to eight characters. With that limitation, it was often difficult to create descriptive file names. A file name such as HseBud06 might be used for a file containing a household budget for 2006. With such cryptic file names, it was not always easy to figure out what a file contained. As a result, files were sometimes difficult to locate and identify. Today, most operating systems allow you to use long file names.

Current versions of Windows support file names up to 255 characters long. That limitation includes the entire file path—drive letter, folders, file name, and extension—which you'll learn about later in the chapter. A file name limitation of 255 characters gives you the flexibility to use descriptive file names so that you can easily identify what a file contains.

Why are certain characters not allowed in a file name? If an operating system attaches special significance to a symbol, you might not be able to use it in a file name. For example, Windows uses the colon (:) character to separate the device letter from a file name or folder, as in *C:Music*. A file name that contains a colon, such as *Report:2007,* is not valid because the operating system would become confused about how to interpret the colon. When you use Windows applications, avoid using the symbols : * \ < > | " / and ? in file names.

FIGURE 4-1

Windows File-naming Conventions

Case sensitive	No
Maximum length of file name	File name and extension cannot exceed 255 characters
Spaces allowed	Yes
Numbers allowed	Yes
Characters not allowed	* \ : < > | " / ?
File names not allowed	Aux, Com1, Com2, Com3, Com4, Con, Lpt1, Lpt2, Lpt3, Prn, Nul

What are reserved words? Some operating systems also contain a list of **reserved words** that are used as commands or special identifiers. You cannot use these words alone as a file name. You can, however, use these words as part of a longer file name. For example, under Windows, the file name *Nul* would not be valid, but you could name a file something like *Nul Committee Notes.doc* or *Null Set.exe*.

In addition to *Nul*, Windows users should avoid using the following reserved words as file names: *Aux*, *Com1*, *Com2*, *Com3*, *Com4*, *Con*, *Lpt1*, *Lpt2*, *Lpt3*, and *Prn*.

What else should I know about creating file names? Some operating systems are case sensitive, but not those you typically work with on personal computers. Feel free to use uppercase and lowercase letters in file names that you create on PCs and Macs.

You can also use spaces in file names. That's a different rule than for e-mail addresses where spaces are not allowed. You've probably noticed that people often use underscores or periods instead of spaces in e-mail addresses such as Madi_Jones@msu.edu. That convention is not necessary in file names, so a file name such as Letter to Madi Jones is valid.

Are file extensions important? As explained in Chapter 1, a file extension is an optional file identifier that is separated from the main file name by a period, as in *Paint.exe*. With some operating systems, such as Windows, file extensions work like tickets that admit people to different plays, movies, or concerts. If you have the right ticket, you get in. If a file has the right extension for a particular application program, you'll see it in the list of files you can open with that software. For example, files with a .doc extension appear in the Open and Save As lists when you're working with Microsoft Word software.

A file extension is usually related to the **file format**, which is defined as the arrangement of data in a file and the coding scheme used to represent the data. Files containing graphics are usually stored using a different file format than files containing text. Hundreds of file formats exist, and you'll encounter many of them as you use a variety of software. Most software stores files in a **native file format** unless you specify otherwise. As an example, Microsoft Word stores document files in DOC format, whereas Adobe Acrobat stores document files in PDF format.

When using a software application such as Microsoft Word to open a file, the program displays any files that have the file extension for its native file format, as shown in Figure 4-2.

FIGURE 4-2

The next time you use software, take note of the file extensions that appear when you look at the list of files in the Open dialog box. If you don't see any file extensions, you've discovered the results of a Windows setting that can hide (but not erase) file extensions.

If Windows is set to hide file extensions, you can view them by opening Windows Explorer, selecting the Tools menu, selecting Folder Options, then changing the "Hide file extensions" option.

CLICK TO START

Files with native file extension are displayed in the Open, Save, and Save As dialog boxes.

FILE LOCATIONS, FOLDERS, AND PATHS

How do I designate a file's location? To designate a file's location, you must first specify where the file is stored. As shown in Figure 4-3, each of a PC's storage devices is identified by a device letter—a convention that is specific to DOS and Windows. The floppy disk drive is usually assigned device letter A and is referred to as "drive A." A device letter is usually followed by a colon, so drive A could be designated as A: or as 3.5" Floppy (A:).

The main hard disk drive is usually referred to as "drive C." Additional storage devices can be assigned letters D through Z. Although most PCs stick to the standard of drive A for the floppy disk drive and drive C for the hard disk drive, the device letters for CD, Zip, and DVD drives are not standardized. For example, the CD-writer on your computer might be assigned device letter E, whereas the CD-writer on another computer might be assigned device letter R.

What's the purpose of folders? An operating system maintains a list of files called a **directory** for each storage disk, tape, CD, or DVD. The main directory of a disk is referred to as the **root directory**. On a PC, the root directory is identified by the device letter followed by a backslash. For example, the root directory of the hard disk would be C:\. You should try to avoid storing your data files in the root directory of your hard disk; instead, store them in a subdirectory.

A root directory can be subdivided into smaller lists. Each list is called a **subdirectory**. When you use Windows, Mac OS, or a Linux graphical file manager, these subdirectories are depicted as **folders** because they work like folders in a filing cabinet to store related items, such as documents, sound clips, and photos for a school project or music collection. Each folder has a name, so you can easily create a folder called *Documents* to hold reports, letters, and so on. You can create another folder called *My Music* to hold your MP3 files. Folders can be created within other folders. You might, for example, create a *Jazz* folder within the *My Music* folder to hold your jazz collection and another folder named *Reggae to* hold your reggae collection.

A folder name is separated from a drive letter and other folder names by a special symbol. In Microsoft Windows, this symbol is the backslash (\ ). For example, the folder for your reggae music (within the *My Music* folder on drive C) would be written as *C:\ My Music\Reggae*.

Imagine how hard it would be to find a specific piece of paper in a filing cabinet that was stuffed with a random assortment of reports, letters, and newspaper clippings. By storing a file in a folder, you assign it a place in an organized hierarchy of folders and files.

A computer file's location is defined by a **file specification** (sometimes called a **path**), which includes the drive letter, folder(s), file name, and extension. Suppose that you have stored an MP3 file called *Marley One Love* in the *Reggae* folder on your hard disk. Its file specification would be as follows:

C:\My Music\Reggae\Marley One Love.mp3

| Drive letter | Primary folder | Secondary folder | File name | File extension |

FIGURE 4-3

The Windows operating system labels storage devices with letters, such as A: and C:.

Name	Type
Hard Disk Drives	
Local Disk (C:)	Local Disk
Devices with Removable Storage	
3½ Floppy (A:)	3½-Inch Floppy Disk
DVD/CD-RW Drive (D:)	CD Drive
Network Drives	
files on 'Mtcnas' (H:)	Network Drive

FILE SIZES AND DATES

What's the significance of a file's size? A file contains data, stored as a group of bits. The more bits, the larger the file. **File size** is usually measured in bytes, kilobytes, or megabytes. Knowing the size of a file can be important. Compared to small files, large files fill up storage space more quickly, require longer transmission times, and are more likely to be stripped off e-mail attachments by a mail server. Your computer's operating system keeps track of file sizes and supplies that information when you request a listing of files.

Is the file date important? Your computer keeps track of the date that a file was created or last modified (Figure 4-4). The **file date** is useful if you have created several versions of a file and want to make sure you know which version is the most recent. It can also come in handy if you have downloaded several updates of a software package, such as an MP3 player, and you want to make sure you install the latest version.

Name ▲	Size	Type	Date Modified
Folder Settings		File Folder	4/17/2006 2:56 PM
My Music		File Folder	12/6/2006 4:57 PM
My Pictures		File Folder	12/6/2006 4:57 PM
My Webs		File Folder	7/13/2006 5:00 PM
Temp		File Folder	3/26/2006 3:16 PM
ABC.doc	33 KB	Microsoft Word Document	9/16/2006 6:59 PM
Application Letter.doc	24 KB	Microsoft Word Document	7/16/2006 6:22 PM
Home Inventory.mdb	360 KB	Microsoft Office Access Application	4/21/2005 1:21 PM
Jazz Recordings.mdb	176 KB	Microsoft Office Access Application	3/31/2005 1:23 PM

File size   File date

FIGURE 4-4

File sizes and dates can provide information that is useful when working with files.

4

QuickCheck

SECTION A

1. Windows file-naming [   ] are different than for Linux.

2. When using Windows, you cannot use a reserved word, such as Aux, as a file name. True or false? [   ]

3. Microsoft Word uses DOC as its [   ] file format.

4. On a computer running Windows, the hard disk letter is usually designated as [   ].

5. The root directory of a disk can be divided into smaller lists called [   ], that are depicted as folders.

6. A file's location is defined by a file path, which includes the drive letter, one or more [   ], file name, and extension.

7. A file's [   ] can be important information when you are planning to transmit it to another computer over a network.

 CHECK ANSWERS

B

SECTION

File Management

File management encompasses any procedure that helps you organize your computer-based files so that you can find and use them more efficiently. Depending on your computer's operating system, you can organize and manipulate your files from within an application program or by using a special file management utility the operating system provides. Section B offers an overview of application-based and operating system-based file management.

APPLICATION-BASED FILE MANAGEMENT

How does a software application help me manage files?

Applications, such as word processing software or graphics software, typically provide a way to open files and save them in a specific folder on a designated storage device. An application might also have additional file management capabilities, such as deleting, copying, and renaming files. Take a look at an example of the file management capabilities in a typical Windows application—Microsoft Word.

Suppose you want to write a letter to the editor of your local newspaper about the rising tide of graffiti in your neighborhood. You would open your word processing software and type the document. As you type, the document is held in RAM. At some point, you'll want to save the document. To do so, you click File on the menu bar, and then select the Save As option. The Save As dialog box, shown in Figure 4-5, opens and allows you to specify a name for the file and its location on one of your computer's storage devices.

1. Begin by clicking this arrow button to display a list of storage devices. Double-clicking any device displays its folders.

2. Select a storage device and folder to indicate where you want the file to be stored.

3. Type a name for the file.

4. Click the Save button.

FIGURE 4-5

The Save As dialog box is used to name a file and specify its storage location.

FILE MANAGEMENT UTILITIES

How does the operating system help me manage files?
Although most application software gives you access to commands you can use to save, open, rename, and delete individual files, you might want to work with groups of files or perform other file operations that are inconvenient within the Open or Save dialog boxes.

Most operating systems provide **file management utilities** that give you the "big picture" of the files you have stored on your disks and help you work with them. For example, Windows provides a file management utility that can be accessed from the My Computer icon or from the Windows Explorer option on the Start menu. On computers with Mac OS, the file management utilities are called the Finder and Spotlight. These utilities, shown in Figure 4-8, help you view a list of files, find files, move files from one place to another, make copies of files, delete files, discover file properties, and rename files.

TERMINOLOGY NOTE

Utilities called desktop search tools help you also find and access information stored in e-mails, Web pages, and contact lists in addition to data and program files. Desktop search tools are offered by third-party vendors such as Google and Yahoo! They are also being added to operating system utilities.

FIGURE 4-8

The Windows file management utility can be tailored to show files as icons (top) or as a list (middle).
Mac OS provides a file management utility called the Finder (bottom).

What's the difference between the Save option and the Save As option? Most Windows applications provide a curious set of options on the File menu. In addition to the Save As option, the menu contains a Save option. The difference between the two options is subtle, but useful. The Save As option allows you to select a name and storage device for a file, whereas the Save option simply saves the latest version of a file under its current name and at its current location.

A potentially confusing aspect of these options occurs when you try to use the Save option for a file that doesn't yet have a name. Because you can't save a file without a name, your application displays the Save As dialog box, even though you selected the Save option. The flowchart in Figure 4-6 will help you decide whether to use the Save or Save As command.

What other options are available in the Save As dialog box? The Save As dialog box displayed by Windows applications allows you to do more than just save a file. You can use it to rename a file, delete a file, or create a folder, as shown in Figure 4-7.

FIGURE 4-6

Should I use the Save or Save As command?

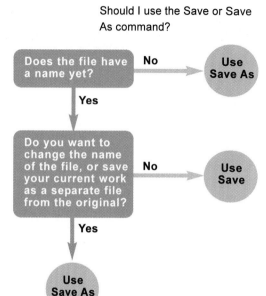

FIGURE 4-7

The Save As dialog box not only helps you name a file and designate its destination drive, but also allows you to rename files, delete files, create folders, and rename folders.

CLICK TO START

FILE MANAGEMENT METAPHORS

How can a file management utility help me visualize my computer's file storage? File management utilities often use some sort of **storage metaphor** to help you visualize and mentally organize the files on your disks and other storage devices. These metaphors are also called **logical storage models** because they are supposed to help you form a mental (logical) picture of the way in which your files are stored.

What storage metaphors are typically used for personal computers? After hearing so much about files and folders, you might have guessed that the filing cabinet is a popular metaphor for computer storage. In this metaphor, each storage device of a computer corresponds to one of the drawers in a filing cabinet. The drawers hold folders and the folders hold files.

Another storage metaphor is based on a hierarchical diagram that is sometimes referred to as a "tree structure." In this metaphor, a tree represents a storage device. The trunk of the tree corresponds to the root directory. The branches of the tree represent folders. These branches can split into small branches representing folders within folders. The leaves at the end of a branch represent the files in a particular folder. Figure 4-9 illustrates the tree lying on its side so that you can see the relationship to the metaphor shown in the next figure, Figure 4-10.

The tree structure metaphor offers a useful mental image of the way in which files and folders are organized. It is not, however, particularly practical as a user interface. Imagine the complexity of the tree diagram from Figure 4-9 if it were expanded to depict branches for hundreds of folders and leaves for thousands of files.

For practicality, storage metaphors are translated into more mundane screen displays. Figure 4-10 shows how Microsoft programmers combined the filing cabinet metaphor with the tree structure metaphor in the Windows Explorer file management utility.

FIGURE 4-9

You can visualize the directory of a disk as a tree on its side. The trunk corresponds to the root directory, the branches to folders, and the leaves to files.

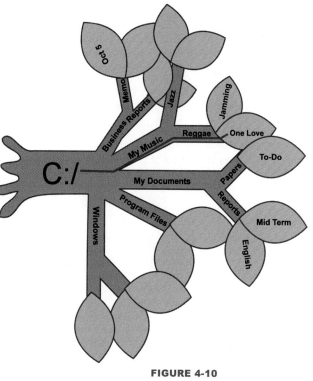

FIGURE 4-10

Windows Explorer borrows folders from the filing cabinet metaphor and places them in a hierarchical structure similar to a tree on its side.

4

WINDOWS EXPLORER

How do I use a file management utility? As an example of a file management utility, take a closer look at **Windows Explorer**, a utility program bundled with the Windows operating system and designed to help you organize and manipulate the files stored on your computer.

The Windows Explorer window is divided into two "window panes." The pane on the left side of the window lists each of the storage devices connected to your computer, plus several important system objects, such as My Computer, My Network Places, and the Desktop.

An icon for a storage device or other system object can be "expanded" by clicking its corresponding plus-sign icon. Expanding an icon displays the next level of the storage hierarchy—usually a collection of folders.

A device icon or folder can be "opened" by clicking directly on the icon rather than on the plus sign. Once an icon is opened, its contents appear in the pane on the right side of the Windows Explorer window. Figure 4-11 illustrates how to manipulate the directory display.

FIGURE 4-11

Windows Explorer makes it easy to drill down through the levels of the directory hierarchy to locate a folder or file.

CLICK TO START ✛

The left pane displays your computer's hierarchy of storage devices and folders.

The minus-sign icon can be used to collapse a device or folder to hide levels of the hierarchy.

The plus-sign icon can be used to expand a device or folder to display the next level of the hierarchy.

The right pane displays the folders and files contained in the device or folder that is currently open in the left pane.

Any device or system object can be opened by clicking it.

Can I work with more than one file or folder at a time? To work with a group of files or folders, you must first select them. You can accomplish this task in several ways. You can hold down the Ctrl key as you click each item. This method works well if you are selecting files or folders that are not listed consecutively. As an alternative, you can hold down the Shift key while you click the first item and the last item you want to select. By using the Shift key method, you select the two items that you clicked and all the items in between. Windows Explorer displays all the items you selected by highlighting them. After a group of items is highlighted, you can use the same copy, move, or delete procedure that you would use for a single item.

What can I do with the folders and files that are listed in Windows Explorer? In addition to locating files and folders, Windows Explorer provides a set of procedures (shown in Figure 4-12 on the next page) that help you manipulate files and folders in the following ways:

■ **Rename.** You might want to change the name of a file or folder to better describe its contents.

■ **Copy.** You can copy a file from one device to another—for example, from a floppy disk in drive A to the hard disk in drive C. You can also make a copy of a document so that you can revise the copy and leave the original intact.

■ **Move.** You can move a file from one folder to another or from one storage device to another. When you move a file, it is erased from its original location, so make sure you remember the new location of the file. You can also move entire folders and their contents from one storage device to another storage device, or move them to a different folder.

■ **Delete.** You can delete a file when you no longer need it. You can also delete a folder. Be careful when you delete a folder because most file management utilities also delete all the files within a folder.

FIGURE 4-12

Windows Explorer helps you delete, copy, move, and rename files.

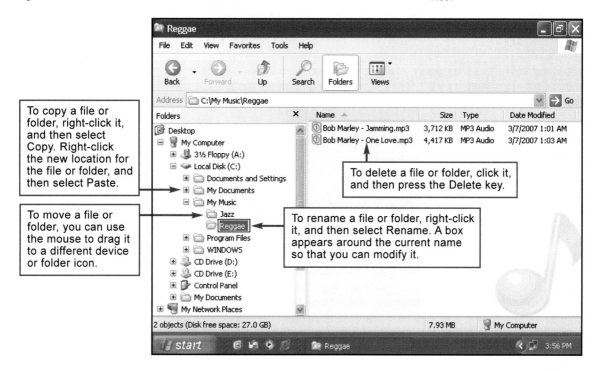

To copy a file or folder, right-click it, and then select Copy. Right-click the new location for the file or folder, and then select Paste.

To move a file or folder, you can use the mouse to drag it to a different device or folder icon.

To delete a file or folder, click it, and then press the Delete key.

To rename a file or folder, right-click it, and then select Rename. A box appears around the current name so that you can modify it.

4

FILE MANAGEMENT TIPS

A file management utility provides tools and procedures to help you keep track of your program and data files, but these tools are most useful when you have a logical plan for organizing your files and when you follow some basic file management guidelines. The following tips pertain to managing files on your own computer. When working with files on lab computers, follow the guidelines from your instructor or lab manager.

■ **Use descriptive names.** Give your files and folders descriptive names, and avoid using cryptic abbreviations.

■ **Maintain file extensions.** When renaming a file, keep the original file extension so that you can easily open it with the correct application software.

■ **Group similar files.** Separate files into folders based on subject matter. For example, store your creative writing assignments in one folder and your MP3 music files in another folder.

■ **Organize your folders from the top down.** When devising a hierarchy of folders, consider how you want to access files and back them up. For example, it is easy to specify one folder and its subfolders for a backup. If your important data is scattered in a variety of folders, however, making backups is more time consuming.

■ **Consider using the My Documents default directory.** Windows software typically defaults to the *My Documents* folder for storing data files. You might want to use *My Documents* (Figure 4-13) as your main data folder, and add subfolders as necessary to organize your files.

■ **Do not mix data files and program files.** Do not store data files in the folders that hold your software—on Windows systems, most software is stored in subfolders of the *Program Files* folder.

■ **Don't store files in the root directory.** Although it is acceptable to create folders in the root directory, it is not a good practice to store programs or data files in the root directory of your computer's hard disk.

■ **Access files from the hard disk.** For best performance, copy files from floppy disks or CDs to your computer's hard disk before accessing them.

■ **Follow copyright rules.** When copying files, make sure you adhere to copyright and license restrictions.

■ **Delete or archive files you no longer need.** Deleting unneeded files and folders helps keep your list of files from growing to an unmanageable size.

■ **Be aware of storage locations.** When you save files, make sure the drive letter and folder name specify the correct storage location.

■ **Back up!** Back up your folders regularly.

PHYSICAL FILE STORAGE

Is data stored in specific places on a disk? So far, you've seen how an operating system such as Windows can help you visualize computer storage as files and folders. This logical storage model, however, has little to do with what actually happens on your disk. The structure of files and folders you see in Windows Explorer is called a "logical" model because it is supposed to help you create a mental picture. The **physical storage model** describes what actually happens on the disks and in the circuits. As you will see, the physical model is quite different from the logical model.

Before a computer can store a file on a disk, CD, or DVD, the storage medium must be formatted. The **formatting** process creates the equivalent of electronic storage bins by dividing a disk into **tracks** and then further dividing each track into **sectors**. Tracks and sectors are numbered to provide addresses for each data storage bin. The numbering scheme depends on the storage device and the operating system. On floppy, Zip, and hard disks, tracks are arranged as concentric circles; on CDs and DVDs, one or more tracks spiral out from the center of the disk (Figure 4-14).

FIGURE 4-13

Windows XP supplies a series of default folders, including *My Documents*, that many users find convenient for storing their data.

- 🖳 My Computer
  - ⊞ 💾 3½ Floppy (A:)
  - ⊟ 💽 Local Disk (C:)
    - ⊟ 📁 Documents and Settings
      - ⊞ 📁 Administrator
      - ⊞ 📁 All Users
      - ⊞ 📁 Default User
      - ⊟ 📁 Jane Allson
        - ⊞ 📁 Application Data
        - 📁 Cookies
        - 📁 Desktop
        - ⊞ ⭐ Favorites
        - ⊞ 📁 Local Settings
        - ⊟ 📁 My Documents
          - 📁 MIDI music
          - 🎵 My Music
          - 🖼 My Pictures

FIGURE 4-14

A process called formatting prepares the surface of a disk to hold data.

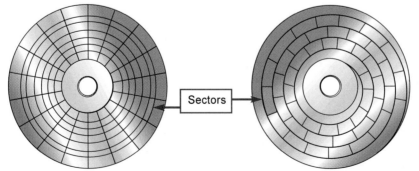

Disks are divided into tracks and wedge-shaped sectors—each side of a floppy disk typically has 80 tracks divided into 18 sectors. Each sector holds 512 bytes of data.

On a typical CD, a single track is about three miles long and is divided into 336,000 sectors. Each sector holds 2,048 bytes of data.

How does a disk get formatted? Today, most floppy, Zip, and hard disks are preformatted at the factory; however, computer operating systems provide **formatting utilities** you can use to reformat some storage devices—typically floppy and hard disks. Formatting utilities are also supplied by the companies that manufacture hard disk drives, writable CD and DVD drives, and CD/DVD recording software.

When you use a formatting utility, it erases any data that happens to be on the disk, and then prepares the tracks and sectors necessary to hold data. You might consider reformatting some of your old floppy disks (instead of just deleting the files they contain) if you really want to make them blank before you reuse them. The screen tour associated with Figure 4-15 demonstrates how to use Windows to format a floppy disk.

FIGURE 4-15

Windows includes a floppy disk formatting utility, which can be accessed from the A: (Floppy disk) icon in the My Computer window or Windows Explorer.

CLICK TO START

4

How does the operating system keep track of a file's location? The operating system uses a **file system** to keep track of the names and locations of files that reside on a storage medium, such as a hard disk. Different operating systems use different file systems. Most versions of Mac OS use the Macintosh Hierarchical File System (HFS). Ext2fs (extended 2 file system) is the native file system for Linux. Windows NT, 2000, XP, and Vista use a file system called **NTFS** (New Technology File System). The file system for Windows 3.1 was called FAT16. Windows 95, 98, and Me use a file system called **FAT32**.

To speed up the process of storing and retrieving data, a disk drive usually works with a group of sectors called a **cluster** or a "block." The number of sectors that form a cluster varies, depending on the capacity of the disk and the way the operating system works with files. A file system's primary task is to maintain a list of clusters and keep track of which are empty and which hold data. This information is stored in a special index file. If your computer uses the FAT32 file system, for example, this index file is called the **File Allocation Table** (FAT). If your computer uses NTFS, it is called the **Master File Table** (MFT).

Each of your disks contains its own index file so that information about its contents is always available when the disk is in use. Unfortunately, storing this crucial file on disk also presents a risk because if the index file is damaged by a hard disk head crash or corrupted by a virus, you'll generally lose access to all the data stored on the disk. Index files become damaged all too frequently, so it is important to back up your data.

When you save a file, your PC's operating system looks at the index file to see which clusters are empty. It selects one of these empty clusters, records the file data there, and then revises the index file to include the new file name and its location.

A file that does not fit into a single cluster spills over into the next contiguous (meaning adjacent) cluster, unless that cluster already contains data. When contiguous clusters are not available, the operating system stores parts of a file in noncontiguous (nonadjacent) clusters. Figure 4-16 helps you visualize how an index file, such as the MFT, keeps track of file names and locations.

Master File Table

File	Cluster	Comment
MFT	1	Reserved for MFT files
DISK USE	2	Part of MFT that contains list of empty sectors
Bio.txt	3, 4	Bio.txt file stored in clusters 3 and 4
Jordan.wks	7, 8, 10	Jordan.wks file stored noncontiguously in clusters 7, 8, and 10
Pick.wps	9	Pick.wps file stored in cluster 9

FIGURE 4-16

Each colored cluster on the disk contains part of a file. Bio.txt is stored in contiguous clusters. Jordan.wks is stored in noncontiguous clusters. A computer locates and displays the Jordan.wks file by looking for its name in the Master File Table.

When you want to retrieve a file, the OS looks through the index for the file name and its location. It moves the disk drive's read-write head to the first cluster that contains the file data. Using additional data from the index file, the operating system can move the read-write heads to each of the clusters containing the remaining parts of the file.

What happens when a file is deleted? When you click a file's icon and then select the Delete option, you might have visions of the read-write head somehow scrubbing out the clusters that contain data. That doesn't happen. Instead, the operating system simply changes the status of the file's clusters to "empty" and removes the file name from the index file. The file name no longer appears in a directory listing, but the file's data remains in the clusters until a new file is stored there. You might think that this data is as good as erased, but it is possible to purchase utilities that recover a lot of this "deleted" data—law enforcement agents, for example, use these utilities to gather evidence from deleted files on the computer disks of suspected criminals.

To delete data from a disk in such a way that no one can ever read it, you can use special **file shredder software** that overwrites "empty" sectors with random 1s and 0s. You might find this software handy if you plan to donate your computer to a charitable organization, and you want to make sure your personal data no longer remains on the hard disk.

Can deleted files be undeleted? The Windows Recycle Bin and similar utilities in other operating systems are designed to protect you from accidentally deleting hard disk files you actually need. Instead of marking a file's clusters as available, the operating system moves the file to the Recycle Bin folder. The "deleted" file still takes up space on the disk, but does not appear in the usual directory listing.

Files in the Recycle Bin folder can be undeleted so that they again appear in the regular directory. The Recycle Bin can be emptied to permanently delete any files it contains.

How does a disk become fragmented? As a computer writes files on a disk, parts of files tend to become scattered all over the disk. These **fragmented files** are stored in noncontiguous clusters. Drive performance generally declines as the read-write heads move back and forth to locate the clusters containing the parts of a file. To regain peak performance, you can use a **defragmentation utility**, such as Windows Disk Defragmenter, to rearrange the files on a disk so that they are stored in contiguous clusters (Figure 4-17).

FIGURE 4-17

Defragmenting a disk helps your computer operate more efficiently. Consider using a defragmentation utility at least once a month to keep your computer running in top form.

4

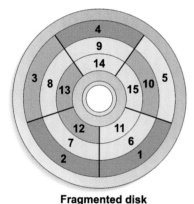

Fragmented disk

On the fragmented disk (left), the purple, orange, and blue files are stored in noncontiguous clusters.

When the disk is defragmented (right), the sectors of data for each file are moved to contiguous clusters.

Defragmented disk

QuickCheck

1. The _____ option on an application's File menu allows you to save the latest version of a file under its current name and at its current location.

2. A storage _____, such as a filing cabinet or tree, helps you visualize and mentally organize your computer files.

3. Windows _____ is utility software provided by the operating system and designed to help you organize and manipulate files.

4. A hard disk stores data in concentric _____, which are divided into wedge-shaped _____.

5. File _____ software overwrites deleted files with random 1s and 0s.

CHECK ANSWERS

C

Computer Viruses

Viruses are one of the biggest threats to the security of your computer files. In 1981, there was one known computer virus. Today, the count exceeds 100,000. Between 900 and 1,300 new viruses appear every month. Viruses are spreading more rapidly than ever. The Michelangelo virus infected 75,000 computers in seven months; the Melissa virus reached 3.5 million computers in 10 hours; and a virus called I-love-you took only three hours to reach 72 million. Today, MyDoom, Sasser, and Rbot infestations affect hundreds of millions of computers despite vigorous eradication efforts. Computer viruses invade all types of computers, including mainframes, servers, personal computers, and even handheld computers. To defend your computer against viruses, you should understand what they are, how they work, and how to use antivirus software.

VIRUSES

What kind of code can attack my computer? The term **malicious code** (sometimes called "malware") refers to any program or set of program instructions designed to surreptitiously enter a computer and disrupt its normal operations. Many types of malicious code, including viruses, worms, and Trojan horses, are created and unleashed by individuals referred to as "hackers" or "crackers."

The term "hacker" originally referred to a highly skilled computer programmer. Today, however, the terms "hacker" and "cracker" usually refer to anyone who uses a computer to gain unauthorized access to data, steal information, distribute viruses, or crash computer systems. Spreading a computer virus is a crime in many countries, including the United States.

What is a computer virus? A **computer virus** is a set of program instructions that attaches itself to a file, reproduces itself, and spreads to other files. It can corrupt files, destroy data, display an irritating message, or otherwise disrupt computer operations. A common misconception is that viruses spread themselves from one computer to another. They don't. Viruses can replicate themselves only on the host computer.

How do viruses spread? Viruses spread when people distribute infected files by exchanging disks and CDs, sending e-mail attachments, exchanging music on file-sharing networks, and downloading software from the Web. To avoid viruses, be cautious of floppy disks, homemade CDs, and Web sites that contain games and other supposedly fun stuff. Check these files with antivirus software before you copy or use them.

Many computer viruses infect files executed by your computer—files with extensions such as .exe, .com, or .vbs. When your computer executes an infected program, it also executes the attached virus instructions. These instructions then remain in RAM, waiting to infect the next program your computer runs or the next disk it accesses.

Are there different kinds of viruses? A virus can be classified as a file virus, boot sector virus, or macro virus. A **file virus** infects application programs, such as games. A **boot sector virus** infects the system files your computer uses every time you turn it on. These viruses can cause widespread damage to your computer files and recurring problems. A

TERMINOLOGY NOTE

The term "computer virus" is often used to refer to any malicious code or software that invades a computer system.

Technically, however, viruses differ from other types of malware, such as Trojan horses, worms, and bots. You'll learn the differences as you read this section of the chapter.

INFOWEBLINKS

The old saying "know thy enemy" applies to viruses and worms. To learn more details about current threats, visit the **Virus Descriptions InfoWeb**.
www.course.com/np/concepts9/ch04

macro virus infects a set of instructions called a "macro"—a miniature program that usually contains legitimate instructions to automate document and worksheet production. When you view a document containing an infected macro, the macro virus duplicates itself into the general macro pool, where it is picked up by other documents.

What's so bad about viruses? In addition to replicating itself, a virus might deliver a **payload**, which could be as harmless as displaying an annoying message or as devastating as corrupting the data on your computer's hard disk. A **trigger event**, such as a specific date, can unleash some viruses. For example, the Michelangelo virus triggers on March 6, the birthday of artist Michelangelo.

Viruses that deliver their payloads on a specific date are sometimes referred to as "time bombs." Viruses that deliver their payloads in response to some other system event are referred to as "logic bombs."

A key characteristic of viruses is their ability to "lurk" in a computer for days or months, quietly replicating themselves. While this replication takes place, you might not even know that your computer has contracted a virus; therefore, it is easy to inadvertently spread infected files to other people's computers.

TROJAN HORSES

What is a Trojan horse? A **Trojan horse** (sometimes simply called a "Trojan") is a computer program that seems to perform one function while actually doing something else. Trojan horses are notorious for stealing passwords using a **keylogger**—a type of program that records your keystrokes. For example, one Trojan horse arrives as an e-mail attachment named Picture.exe, which leads you to believe you've received some type of graphics software. If you open this file, however, it searches for America Online (AOL) user information and tries to steal your login and e-mail passwords. Trojan horses can also generate official-looking forms that are actually fake to collect your credit card, banking, or PayPal account numbers (Figure 4-18).

Security Measures

As part of our continuing commitment to protect your account and to reduce the instance of fraud on our website, we are undertaking a period review of our member accounts.

Before signing in, please confirm that you are the owner of this account.

Please fill in the correct information to verify your identity.

Full Name

Card & expiration date

Your card number

3-digit validation code on back of card (cw2)

ATM PIN-Code

Click Once To Continue

Image Copyright © F-Secure Corporation

FIGURE 4-18

A Trojan horse called Padodor watches your browser window for text strings such as "Sign in" and "Log in." It then displays a fake login screen like the one shown here to collect your credit card numbers and ATM PIN code.
Messages that demand your PayPal account number, your AOL password, or your ATM PIN are additional examples of Trojan horses currently making the rounds.

Many Trojan horses have **backdoor** capability, which allows unauthorized access to victims' computers. A backdoor allows remote hackers to download and execute files on your computer, upload a list of other infected computers, and use your computer as a relay station for breaking into other computers.

How is a Trojan horse different from a virus? Technically, a Trojan horse is not the same as a virus. Unlike a virus, a Trojan horse is not designed to make copies of itself. Unlike a virus that inserts itself into program code, most Trojan horses are standalone programs.

Some Trojan horses contain a virus, however, which can replicate and spread. Other Trojan horses are carried by worms. Virus experts use the term **blended threat** to describe threats that combine more than one type of malicious program. Common blended threats include Trojan-horse/virus combinations and worm/virus combinations.

Can I tell if my computer has a Trojan horse? If a Trojan horse has delivered a virus to your computer, you'll discover it when the virus delivers its payload. If the Trojan horse is a keylogger designed to collect your keystrokes and send them to a hacker, you might never discover your computer has been compromised unless you scan it with antivirus software. Although your keystroke log is being sent to a hacker by e-mail, the Trojan horse has its own e-mail client and the messages going to the hackers will not appear in the outbox of your regular e-mail program.

WORMS

What's a worm? With the proliferation of network traffic and e-mail, worms have become a major concern in the computing community. Unlike a virus, which is designed to spread from file to file, a **worm** is designed to spread from computer to computer. Most worms take advantage of communications networks—especially the Internet—to travel within e-mail and TCP/IP packets, jumping from one computer to another. Some worms simply spread throughout a network. Others also deliver payloads that vary from harmless messages to malicious file deletions.

How do worms spread? Mass-mailing worms have become especially troublesome. A **mass-mailing worm** spreads by sending itself to every address in the address book of an infected computer. Mass-mailing worms such as Klez, Netsky, MyDoom, Sasser, and Bagle (also called Beagle) have made headlines and caused havoc on personal computers, LANs, and Internet servers.

To make these worms difficult to track, the "From" line of the infected message sometimes contains a **spoofed address** of a randomly selected person—a valid address—from the address book rather than the address of the computer that actually sent the mail.

Mass-mailing worms often include an attachment that contains the worm. Opening the attachment unleashes the worm. Some mass-mailing worms contain a Web link that installs a worm, Trojan horse, or virus. Sasser and other mass-mailing worms, however, require no user interaction to infect a computer.

The conventional wisdom for avoiding e-mail-borne infections is not to open suspicious attachments—especially those with executable file extensions, such as .exe. Most computer owners recognize that an attachment called Amazing Photo.exe that arrives from an unknown sender probably contains a virus.

Hackers, however, have become proficient at using "social engineering" techniques to make e-mail messages and their attachments seem legitimate. For example, a virus called Bofra looks like a message from your e-mail postmaster. Opening the attachment to view the undelivered mail triggers the worm (Figure 4-19).

FIGURE 4-19

Hackers use many tricks to get you to open e-mail attachments that contain worms. Here a seemingly legitimate message about undelivered mail includes an attachment infested with the MyDoom worm. The message looks legitimate and has no particular characteristics that would warn you of the virus it harbors. In a situation like this one, you have to depend on your antivirus software to detect the malicious attachment.

4

Other examples of social engineering are fake messages that appear to be from banks, Microsoft, Amazon, ISPs, and other commonly visited Web sites. A fake message from PayPal, for example, indicates that a charge has been made to your credit card. Clicking the link for more information takes you to a Web site that downloads a worm to your computer (Figure 4-20). If you're uncertain about any e-mail that seems to arrive from a reputable organization, open your browser and manually type in the organization's Web site address. Once you have connected to the legitimate Web site, you can verify the message and take actions as necessary.

FIGURE 4-20

You might be tempted to click the link to find out why PayPal charged your account $175. Don't do it! This worm is an example of social engineering techniques used to make infected e-mail messages look legitimate.

Worms can also be distributed in HTML scripts. Chapter 1 explained that you can set your e-mail software to use HTML format, which provides a variety of font colors, types, and sizes for your messages. Unfortunately, e-mail that's in HTML format can harbor worms hidden in program-like scripts that hackers embed in the HTML tags. These worms are difficult to detect—even for antivirus software. As a result, many people stick with plain-text, non-HTML e-mail.

Although e-mail is currently the primary vehicle used to spread worms, hackers have also devised ways to spread worms over file-sharing networks, such as Kazaa. Some worms are designed to spread over instant messaging links. Worms such as Cabir and Symbos_skulls can even infect mobile phones.

BOTS

What is a bot? Any software that can automate a task or autonomously execute a task when commanded to do so is called an intelligent agent. Because an intelligent agent behaves somewhat like a robot, it is often called a **bot**.

Good bots perform a variety of helpful tasks. They scan the Web to assemble data for search engines, such as Google. Some bots offer online help, while others monitor chat groups for prohibited behavior and language. Individuals can set up bots to track the best airfares or watch online databases for job openings in a specified career field.

Good bots have been overshadowed by mounting publicity about bad bots launched and controlled by hackers. Bad bots were originally called remote access Trojan horses because they allow hackers to essentially sneak into a computer and control it without the owner's knowledge or authorization.

Bot-infested computers are sometimes referred to as zombies because they carry out instructions from a malicious leader. Bad bots, such as Agobot, Mytob, Rbot, and Zotob, can be used to steal passwords, copy confidential data, launch attacks on other computers, and generate spam anonymously. They become an even greater threat when formed into botnets.

What's a botnet? Like a spider in its web, the person who controls many bot-infested computers can link them together into a network called a **botnet**. Botnets as large as 400,000 computers have been discovered by security experts.

Botmasters who control botnets use the combined computing power of their zombie legions for many types of nefarious tasks. For example, an estimated 66% of spam circulating around the Internet is sent through botnets. Botmasters even rent out their botnets to professional spammers who pay between three and six cents per week for each bot they use. Botnets can also be used to carry out Denial of Service attacks against other computers, such as the highly publicized Mytob attack on CNN, ABC, and the New York Times a few years ago.

Some hackers have used the computation power of botnets to create a powerful virtual supercomputer for breaking into encrypted data. Security experts are concerned about the potential for large botnets to launch destructive worms. A virus or worm launched from a single computer can spread relatively quickly, but antivirus publishers can typically identify such threats and distribute updates before damage is widespread. If a worm or virus is launched from a large botnet, however, it will spread much faster and can potentially do much more damage.

What are the similarities and differences between bots, viruses, and worms? Bots use some of the same delivery methods as worms, such as legitimate-looking e-mail messages that contain infected attachments and e-mail links that direct you to a Web site that automatically downloads malicious code (Figure 4-21).

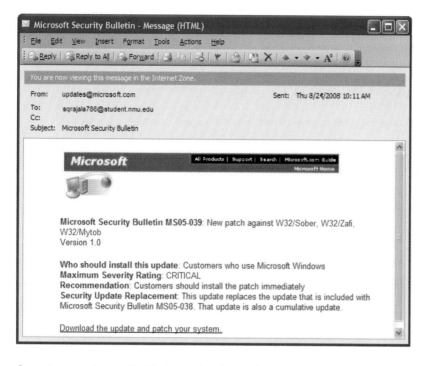

FIGURE 4-21

As with worms, bots can be delivered in e-mail messages that appear to be legitimate. If you click the link in this e-mail message, it installs the Mytob bot on your computer. Microsoft never puts links to software patches in e-mail messages.

Security experts say that bots are harder to detect than viruses or worms. They rarely damage files on your computer or show any noticeable signs of their existence. That stealthiness is by design because as soon as you discover a bot, you would take steps to remove it and the botmaster would have one less zombie to control.

What makes my computer vulnerable to bots? Bots often gain access through operating system security holes that you have not patched. Think of your computer as a watering can. When everything is working, water flows out of the sprinkler, just like data flows out of your computer. Suppose, however, that your watering can has a manufacturing defect and water also leaks out of the bottom. That's essentially what happens when your operating system has a security hole—data can flow into and out of your computer in ways it is not supposed to. You can patch your watering can with a little epoxy. You can also plug up operating system security holes with software patches.

To keep your computer from being exploited in a botnet, make sure you install operating system security patches as they become available and keep your antivirus software up to date.

Are bots more dangerous than viruses? Before widespread use of the Internet, viruses were the biggest threat to computer security. They spread relatively slowly because they depended on people to inadvertently transfer them from disk to disk. As the popularity of the Internet and e-mail grew, hackers found a way to cut a much wider and faster path of destruction using network-borne worms. Today, however, bots have become the biggest threat because of their ability to form botnets that can launch widescale Denial of Service attacks and distribute mountains of spam.

Looking toward the future, experts predict an increase of blended threats that combine worm-like distribution with virus and bot payloads. Worms and bots that spread through channels other than e-mail are likely to become more prevalent, too. Figure 4-22 highlights some landmarks and trends in the development of malicious code.

FIGURE 4-22

Malicious Code Trends

Date	Threats	Trends
1981	Cloner	The first known virus begins to spread. Cloner infects files on disks formatted for Apple II computers. The prevalence of disk-borne viruses continues well into the1990s with Jerusalem (1987), Michelangelo (1992), and others.
1988	Internet Worm	The first major worm attack over the Internet sets the stage for today's prolific crop of mass-mailing worms.
1998	Back Orifice	First Trojan horse designed to allow a remote hacker to gain unauthorized access to a computer.
1999	Melissa	Macro viruses, such as Melissa and Laroux, are prevalent for several years and cause trouble by infecting Microsoft Word and Excel files.
2000	Love Letter	One of the fastest spreading mass-mailing worms of all time. Followed by Sobig, Blaster, and MyDoom (2004).
2001	Code Red	Worms designed for Denial of Service attacks gather steam. Code Red, which targeted the White House, is followed by Blaster (2001) and Slammer (2003).
2002	Klez	Klez is a mass-mailing worm that is particularly difficult to eradicate. Because the "From" address is spoofed, it is almost impossible to locate infected computers.
2003	Mimail	Social engineering takes center stage and users are confused by fake e-mails from seemingly legitimate companies, such as PayPal, Microsoft, and Wells Fargo.
2004	Sasser Netsky Xombe MyDoom, Zafi Bagle	Worms, such as Sasser, begin to emerge that infect computers without user interaction, such as opening an infected e-mail attachment. Mass-mailing worms are still most prevalent. Worms that spread over instant messaging and handheld devices begin to emerge.
2005	Mytob Zotob Rbot	Bots become one of the biggest security problems. Arriving as e-mail attachments, links embedded in e-mail messages, or from infected banner ads, bots install themselves on unprotected computers, which can then be controlled by unauthorized hackers and commandeered into botnets that launch spam and Denial of Service attacks.

What kind of damage is caused by malicious code? The current crop of viruses, Trojan horses, bots, and worms cause various problems, ranging from displaying harmless messages to bringing down Web sites. The list of malware activities below illustrates why everyday computer users and security specialists are concerned.

Network traffic jam. When worms and bots are active, they generate traffic on LANs and the Internet. Service deteriorates as download time increases for files, Web pages, and e-mail messages.

Denial of Service. A **Denial of Service attack** (DoS) is designed to generate a lot of activity on a network by flooding its servers with useless traffic—enough traffic to overwhelm the server's processing capability and essentially bring all communications to a halt. Successful DoS attacks have been launched against Microsoft, the White House, and the controversial Internet ad agency DoubleClick.

Browser reconfiguration. Some worms block users from accessing certain Web sites and can change your home page setting. They can also set up a redirection routine that downloads malicious code from an infected Web site, even when you enter a legitimate Web address.

Delete and modify files. Many viruses are designed to delete files on a personal computer's hard disk. Some malicious code modifies the

Windows Registry and can cause system instability. Viruses, called **ransomware**, encrypt documents and other files, then demand payment for the decryption key.

Access confidential information. Trojan horses are notorious for using backdoors to steal passwords and credit card numbers. Worms can also scan files and Web sites for e-mail addresses.

Performance degradation. Malicious code requires system resources to send mail and scan files. While a virus or worm is active, your computer might seem to perform slower than normal.

Disable antivirus and firewall software. Malicious programs called **retro viruses** are designed to attack antivirus software by deleting the files that contain virus descriptions or corrupting the main executable virus-scanning program. One antivirus vendor calls them "anti-antivirus viruses."

COMBATING MALICIOUS CODE

How can I avoid viruses and worms? Keeping viruses, Trojan horses, bots, and worms out of your computer is preferable to trying to eliminate these pesky programs after they have taken up residence. When malicious code infiltrates your computer, it can be difficult to eradicate. Certain viruses are particularly tenacious—just the process of booting up your computer can trigger their replication sequence or send them into stealth mode to avoid detection.

These are the top three steps you can take to prevent your computer from becoming infected:

☑ Use antivirus software on every computing device you own.

☑ Keep software patches and operating system service packs up to date.

☑ Do not open suspicious e-mail attachments.

What is antivirus software? **Antivirus software** is a type of utility software that can look for and eradicate viruses, Trojan horses, bots, and worms. This essential software is available for handheld computers, personal computers, and servers. Popular antivirus software for personal computers includes McAfee VirusScan, Norton AntiVirus, and F-Secure Anti-Virus.

How does antivirus software work? Antivirus software uses several techniques to find viruses. As you know, some viruses attach themselves to an existing program. The presence of such a virus often increases the length of the original program. The earliest antivirus software simply examined the programs on a computer and recorded their length. A change in the length of a program from one computing session to the next indicated the possible presence of a virus.

To counter early antivirus software, hackers became more cunning. They created viruses that insert themselves into unused portions of a program file without changing its length. Antivirus software developers fought back. They designed software that examines the bytes in an uninfected application program and calculates a checksum. A **checksum** is a number calculated by combining the binary values of all bytes in a file. Each time you run an application program, antivirus software calculates the checksum and compares it with the previous checksum. If any byte in the application program has changed, the checksum will be different, and the antivirus software assumes that a virus is present.

INFOWEBLINKS

If you don't have antivirus software for your computer, you should get it. Use the **Antivirus Software InfoWeb** to link to Web sites where you can purchase and download antivirus software.

www.course.com/np/concepts9/ch04

4

Today's viruses, Trojan horses, bots, and worms are not limited to infecting program files, so modern antivirus software attempts to locate them by searching your computer's files and memory for virus signatures. A **virus signature** is a section of program code, such as a unique series of instructions, that can be used to identify a known malicious program, much as a fingerprint is used to identify an individual.

When should I use antivirus software? The short answer is "all the time." Most antivirus software allows you to specify what to check and when to check it. You can, for example, fire it up only when you receive a suspicious e-mail attachment, or you can set it to look through all the files on your computer once a week. The best practice, however, is to keep your antivirus software running full-time in the background so that it scans all files the moment they are accessed and checks every e-mail message as it arrives. The scanning process requires a short amount of time, which creates a slight delay in downloading e-mail and opening files. The wait is worth it, however, when you can feel confident that the files you open have been scanned for viruses.

How often should I get an update? The information antivirus software uses to identify and eradicate viruses, Trojan horses, bots, and worms is stored in one or more files usually referred to as "virus definitions." New viruses and variations of old viruses are unleashed just about every day. To keep up with these newly identified pests, antivirus software vendors provide virus definition updates, which are usually available as Web downloads (Figure 4-23). You should check your antivirus vendor's Web site for the latest updates of antivirus software every few days or when you hear of a new virus making headlines.

How reliable is antivirus software? Considering the number of existing viruses and the number of viruses debuting every month, antivirus software is surprisingly reliable. Viruses try to escape detection in many ways. **Multi-partite viruses** (pronounced multi-PAR-tite) are able to infect multiple types of targets. For example, a multi-partite virus might combine the characteristics of a file virus (which hides in .exe files) and a boot sector virus (which hides in the boot sector). If your antivirus software looks for that particular virus only in .exe files, the virus could escape detection by hiding in the boot sector as well.

Polymorphic viruses mutate to escape detection by changing their signatures. **Stealth viruses** remove their signatures from a disk-based file and temporarily conceal themselves in memory. Antivirus software can find stealth viruses only by scanning memory.

Unfortunately, antivirus software is not 100% reliable. On rare occasions, it might not identify a virus, or it might conclude that your computer has a virus when one does not actually exist. Despite these rare mistakes, the protection you get is worth the required investment of time and money. Remember that without antivirus software, your computer is susceptible to all the nasty little programs that can cause damage to your files and irritate the friends and colleagues whose computers you infect.

VIRUS HOAXES

What's a virus hoax? Some virus threats are very real, but you're also likely to get e-mail messages about "viruses" that don't really exist. A **virus hoax** usually arrives as an e-mail message containing dire warnings about a supposedly new virus on the loose (Figure 4-24 on the next page).

TERMINOLOGY NOTE

Because today's antivirus software scans for virus signatures, it is sometimes referred to as "virus scanning software."

FIGURE 4-23

It is important to get regular updates for your antivirus software. Some antivirus vendors feature an electronic update service that you can set to automatically download and install updated virus definitions.

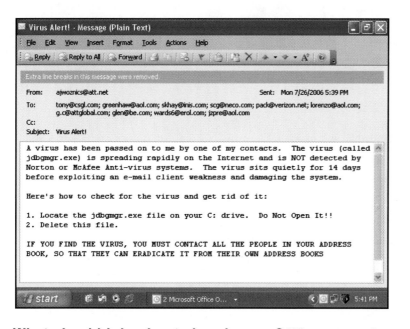

FIGURE 4-24

A virus hoax tends to contain telltale characteristics, such as:

- Warns of a "new" or "dangerous" virus spreading on the Internet.
- Contains a long list of people in the To: or Cc: boxes.
- Cites some "authority" to make you think the alert is official.
- Includes some technical jargon that supposedly explains the virus attack.
- Provides instructions, such as reformatting your computer's hard disk drive or deleting a file, for eradicating the virus. The instructions can cause more damage than the virus itself!
- Urges you to send the e-mail message to everyone in your address book.

What should I do about virus hoaxes? When you receive an e-mail message about a virus, don't panic. Many of them are hoaxes. If you are uncertain, check one of the many antivirus Web sites. There you can look up the alleged virus by name to see if it is a real threat or a hoax.

If the virus is a real threat, the antivirus Web site can provide information to determine whether your computer has been infected. You can also find instructions for eradicating the virus and updating the list of virus definitions your computer's antivirus software uses. If the virus threat is a hoax, you can ignore it. Under no circumstances should you forward virus hoax messages to other people.

INFOWEBLINKS

Some Web sites specialize in tracking hoaxes. For links to these sites, visit the **Hoax InfoWeb**.

www.course.com/np/concepts9/ch04

QuickCheck   SECTION C

1. The key characteristic of a virus is that it can replicate itself. True or false? [   ]

2. Many Trojan horses have [   ] capability, which allows unauthorized access to victims' computers.

3. Many mass-mailing worms are difficult to trace because they contain [   ] addresses.

4. Social [   ] is a technique used by hackers to make e-mail messages and their attachments seem legitimate.

5. A group of computers called a(n) [   ] under the direction of a hacker can distribute spam and launch Denial of Service attacks.

6. A virus [   ] is a section of the virus program, such as a unique series of instructions, that can be used to identify a known virus.

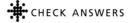 CHECK ANSWERS

Data Backup

SECTION D

Computer experts universally recommend that you make backups of your data. It sounds pretty basic, right? Unfortunately, this advice tells you what to do, not how to do it. It fails to address some key questions, such as: Do I need special backup equipment and software? How often should I make a backup? How many of my files should I back up? What should I do with the backups?

In this section you'll find the answers to your questions about backing up data that's stored on a personal computer. You'll begin by looking at how to devise a backup plan that's right for you, and then review your equipment and software options. Along the way, you should pick up lots of practical tips to keep your data safe.

BACKUP AND RESTORE PROCEDURES

Why do I need to make backups? Have you ever mistakenly copied an old version of a document over a new version? Has your computer's hard disk drive gone on the fritz? Did a virus wipe out your files? Has lightning "fried" your computer system? These kinds of data disasters are not rare; they happen to everyone. You can't always prevent them, so you need a backup plan that helps you recover data that's been wiped out by operator error, viruses, or hardware failures.

How do I make a backup? A **backup** is a copy of one or more files that has been made in case the original files become damaged. A backup is usually stored on a different storage medium from the original files. For example, you can back up files from your hard disk to a different hard disk, a writable CD or DVD, tape, floppy disk, or Web site. The exact steps you follow to make a backup depend on your backup equipment, the software you use to make backups, and your personal backup plan. That said, the list in Figure 4-25 gives you a general idea of the steps in a typical backup session.

FIGURE 4-25

These are the steps in a typical backup session.

CLICK TO START

1. Insert the disk, CD, or tape on which you'll store the backup.

2. Start your backup software.

3. Select the folders and files you want to back up.

4. Give the "go ahead" to start copying data.

5. Feed in additional disks, CDs, or tapes if prompted to do so.

6. Clearly label each disk, CD, or tape.

7. Test your backup.

8. Store your backup in a safe place.

How do I restore data? In technical jargon, you **restore** data by copying files from a backup to the original storage medium or its replacement. As with the procedures for backing up data, the process you use to restore data to your hard disk varies, depending on your backup equipment and software. It also depends on exactly what you need to restore.

After a hard disk crash, for example, you'll probably need to restore all your backup data to a new hard disk. On the other hand, if you inadvertently delete a file or mistakenly copy one file over another, you might need to restore only a single file from the backup. Most software designed to back up and restore data allows you to select which files you want to restore. A typical session to restore data follows the steps in Figure 4-26.

What's the best backup plan? A good backup plan allows you to restore your computing environment to its pre-disaster state with a minimum of fuss. Unfortunately, no single backup plan fits everyone's computing style or budget. You must devise your own backup plan that's tailored to your particular computing needs.

The list in Figure 4-27 outlines factors you should consider as you formulate your own backup plan.

FIGURE 4-26

These are the steps in a typical restore session.

1. Start the software you used to make the backup.
2. Select the file or files you want to restore.
3. Insert the appropriate backup disk or tape.
4. Wait for the files to be copied from the backup to the hard disk.

FIGURE 4-27

Backup Tips

- Decide how much of your data you want, need, and can afford to back up.
- Create a realistic schedule for making backups.
- Make sure you have a way to avoid backing up files that contain viruses.
- Find out what kind of boot disks you might need to get your computer up and running after a hard disk failure or boot sector virus attack.
- Make sure you can test your restore procedure so that you can successfully retrieve the data you've backed up.
- Find a safe place to store your backups.
- Decide what kind of storage device you'll use to make backups.
- Select software to handle backup needs.

Do I have to back up every file? A **full-system backup** contains a copy of every program, data, and system file on a computer. The advantage of a full-system backup is that you can easily restore your computer to its pre-disaster state simply by copying the backup files to a new hard disk. A full-system backup takes a lot of time, however, and automating the process requires a large-capacity tape backup device or a second hard disk drive.

A workable alternative to a full system backup is a "selective" backup that contains only your most important data files. A backup of these files ensures that your computer-based documents and projects are protected from many data disasters. You can back up these files on floppy disks, Zip disks, removable hard disks, an external hard disk, CDs, or DVDs. The disadvantage of this backup strategy is that because you backed up only data files, you must manually reinstall all your software before restoring your data files.

If your strategy is to back up your important data files, the procedure can be simplified if you've stored all these files in one folder or its subfolders. For example, Windows users might store their data files in folders contained in the *My Documents* folder. A folder called *My Documents\Music* might hold MP3 files, a *My Documents\Reports* folder can hold reports, a *My Documents\Art* folder can hold various graphics files, and so on. With your data files organized under the umbrella of a single folder, you are less likely to omit an important file when you make backups.

Some applications, such as financial software, create files and update them without your direct intervention. If you have the option during setup, make sure these files are stored under the My Documents umbrella. Otherwise, you must discover the location of the files and make sure they are backed up with the rest of your data.

FIGURE 4-28

Back up these files in addition to your documents, graphics, and music files.

In addition to data files you create, a few other types of data files might be important to you. Consider making backups of the files listed in Figure 4-28.

Internet connection information. Your ISP's phone number and IP address, your user ID, and your password are often stored in an encrypted file somewhere in the *Windows\System* folder. Your ISP can usually help you find this file.

E-mail folders. If you're using POP e-mail software, your e-mail folder contains all the e-mail messages you've sent and received, but not deleted. Check the Help menu on your e-mail program to discover the location of these files.

E-mail address book. Your e-mail address book might be stored separately from your e-mail messages. To find the file on a Windows computer, use the Search or Find option on the Start menu to search for "Address Book."

Favorite URLs. If you're attached to the URLs you've collected in your Favorites or Bookmarks list, you might want to back up the file that contains this list. To find the file, search your hard disk for "Favorites" or "Bookmarks."

Downloads. If you paid to download any files, you might want to back them up so that you don't have to pay for them again. These files include software, which usually arrives in the form of a compressed .exe file that expands into several separate files as you install it. For backup purposes, the compressed .exe file should be all you need.

What about backing up the Windows Registry? Windows users often hear a variety of rumors about backing up the Windows Registry. The Registry, as it is usually called, is an important group of files the Windows operating system uses to store configuration information about all the devices and software installed on a computer system. If the Registry becomes damaged, your computer might not be able to boot up, launch programs, or communicate with peripheral devices. It is a good idea to have an extra copy of the Registry in case the original file is damaged.

As simple as it sounds, backing up the Registry can present a bit of a problem because the Registry is always open while your computer is on. Some software that you might use for backups cannot copy open files. If you use such software, it might never back up the Registry. Windows users whose backup plans encompass all files on the hard disk must make sure their backup software provides an option for including the Windows Registry. Even if a full-system backup is not planned, many experts recommend that you at least copy the Registry to a separate folder on the hard disk or to a floppy disk. If you do so, you should update this copy whenever you install new software or hardware.

INFOWEBLINKS

For more detailed information on backup techniques, such as backing up the Registry, take a look at the **Backup Techniques InfoWeb**.

www.course.com/np/concepts9/ch04

How do I avoid backing up files that contain viruses?
Viruses can damage files to the point that your computer can't access any data on its hard disk. It is really frustrating when you restore data from a backup only to discover that the restored files contain the same virus that wiped out your data. If your antivirus software is not set to constantly scan for viruses on your computer system, you should run an up-to-date virus check as the first step in your backup routine.

How often should I back up my data? Your backup schedule depends on how much data you can afford to lose. If you're working on an important project, you might want to back up the project files several times a day. Under normal use, however, most people schedule a once-a-week backup. If you work with a To Do list, use it to remind yourself when it is time to make a backup.

Where should I store my backups? Store your backups in a safe place. Don't keep them at your computer desk because a fire or flood that damages your computer could also wipe out your backups. In addition, a thief who steals your computer might also scoop up nearby equipment and media. Storing your backups at a different location is the best idea, but at least store them in a room apart from your computer.

BACKUP DEVICES

How do I choose a backup device? The backup device you select depends on the value of your data, your current equipment, and your budget. Most computer owners use what they have—a writable CD drive, Zip drive, or floppy disk drive. If you have several backup options available, use the table in Figure 4-29 to evaluate the strengths and weaknesses of each one.

FIGURE 4-29

Storage Capacities and Costs of Backup Media

	Device Cost	Media Cost	Capacity	Comments
Floppy disk	$30 (average)	25¢	1.44 MB	Low capacity means that you have to wait around to feed in disks
Zip disk	$100 (average)	$9	750 MB	Holds much more than a floppy but a backup still requires multiple disks
External hard disk	$200 (average)	N/A	250 GB (average)	Fast and convenient, but might hold only one backup
Removable hard disk	$130 (average)	$50	35 GB (average)	Fast, limited capacity, but disks can be removed and locked in a secure location
CD-R	$40 (average)	15¢	680 MB	Limited capacity, can't be reused, long shelf life
CD-RW	$50 (average)	25¢	680 MB	Limited capacity, reusable, very slow
Writable DVD	$100 (average)	25¢	4.7 GB	Good capacity, reasonable media cost, higher capacity coming soon
Tape	$2,000 (average)	$80	200 GB (average)	Most convenient but expensive for capacity equal to today's hard drives
USB Flash drive	$15–$500	N/A	32 MB–4 GB	Convenient and durable, but high-capacity models are expensive
Web site	N/A	$15.00 per month	1 GB	Transfer rate depends on your Internet connection; security and privacy of your data might be a concern

What's the easiest way to back up my important data?
Today, most computers are equipped with a writable CD or DVD drive with
adequate storage capacity for a typical computer owner's data files. An
easy way to back up your important data is simply copying selected files to
a writable CD or DVD. No special software is necessary for this task. The
software supplied with your CD or DVD writer includes a formatting routine
that prepares a disk to hold data and allows you to select the files you want
to copy, or "burn," as a backup (Figure 4-30).

FIGURE 4-30

Use the software supplied with
your CD or DVD drive to format
disks and copy files.

What are the limitations of CDs and DVDs? The major disadvantage of backing up your data on CDs and DVDs is that the writing
process is slow—slower than writing data to tape or a removable hard disk.
Further, although it is feasible to back up your entire system on a series of
CDs or DVDs, you would have to use special backup software, monitor the
backup process, and switch disks occasionally. CDs and DVDs are more
practical for backing up a select group of important data files.

Unfortunately, if you simply back up data files, the process of restoring a
crashed computer is cumbersome. You must load the operating system,
device drivers, and application software from original distribution disks
before copying your data from CDs or DVDs to your computer's hard disk.

Can I use floppy disks and Zip disks to back up my data?
Floppy disks are inexpensive and many computers include a floppy disk
drive. The 1.44 MB capacity of a floppy disk is suitable for storing several
documents, but does not provide enough capacity for digital photos or
most MP3 music files. If you have no other means to back up your data, at
least copy your e-mail address book and important document files to floppy
disks.

Zip disks with 100 MB or 250 MB capacity are sufficient for backups of documents and most digital graphics files. Several 750 MB Zip disks might be
enough for backing up all your data files and could be feasible for a full-
system backup if you have not installed lots of application software.

Can I back up to a second hard disk? A second hard disk drive is a good backup option—especially if it has equivalent capacity to your main hard disk. This capacity allows the backup process to proceed unattended because you won't have to swap disks or CDs. Speed-wise, a hard disk is faster than tape, CD, or DVD drives. Unfortunately, like your computer's main hard disk, a backup hard disk is susceptible to head crashes, making it one of the least reliable storage options.

Internal hard disk drives are inexpensive, but they are not desirable backup devices because they are susceptible to electrical damage and any other catastrophe that besets your computer. External hard disk drives, like the one shown in Figure 4-31, are preferred for backups because they can be disconnected from your computer and stored in a safe place. An internal hard disk drive with removable disks is also an acceptable option because the disks can be removed for safe storage.

What about using a tape drive for backups? Tape drives are typically used in business computing situations, when a full-system backup is desirable. Tape drives with the capacity to back up today's high capacity hard disks are fairly expensive, but they can be conveniently left unattended as the backup proceeds.

NETWORK AND INTERNET BACKUP

Can I store backup files on a network server? If your computer is connected to a local area network, you might be able to use the network server as a backup device. Before entrusting your data to a server, check with the network administrator to make sure you are allowed to store a large amount of data on the server. Because you might not want strangers to access your data, you should store it in a password-protected, non-shared folder. You also should make sure the server will be backed up on a regular basis so that your backup data won't be wiped out by a server crash.

Can I store my backups on the Internet? Several Web sites offer fee-based backup storage space. When needed, you can simply download backup files from the Web site to your hard disk. These sites are practical for backups of your data files, but space limitations and download times make them impractical for a full-system backup. Experts suggest that you should not rely on a Web site as your only method of backup. If a site goes out of business or is the target of a Denial of Service attack, your backup data might not be accessible.

BACKUP SOFTWARE

What does backup software do? To make a backup, you can use **backup software**—a set of utility programs designed to back up and restore files. Backup software usually includes options that make it easy to schedule periodic backups, define a set of files that you want to regularly back up, and automate the restoration process.

Backup software differs from most copy routines because it typically compresses all the files for a backup and places them in one large file. Under the direction of backup software, this file can spread across multiple tapes if necessary. The file is indexed so that individual files can be located, uncompressed, and restored.

Where can I get backup software? Backup software is supplied with most tape drives and other backup devices. Some versions of Windows include Microsoft Backup software, which you can usually find by

FIGURE 4-31

An external hard disk drive typically connects to your computer's USB port. The drive can easily be disconnected when not in use and stored in a safe place.

4

INFOWEBLINKS

Interested in using a Web site for your backup? You can evaluate several of these sites by following the links at the **Web-based Backup InfoWeb**.

www.course.com/np/concepts9/ch04

INFOWEBLINKS

For current links to backup software information, reviews, and manufacturers, visit the **Backup Software InfoWeb**.

www.course.com/np/concepts9/ch04

clicking the Start button, and then selecting Accessories and System Tools. You can also purchase and download backup software from companies that specialize in data protection software.

Whatever backup software you use, remember that it needs to be accessible when it comes time to restore your data. If the only copy of your backup software exists on your backup media, you will be in a Catch-22 situation. You won't be able to access your backup software until you restore the files from your backup, but you won't be able to restore your files until your backup software is running! Make sure you keep the original distribution CD for your backup software or a disk-based copy of any backup software you downloaded from the Web.

How do I use backup software? Backup software provides tools for scheduling backup dates and selecting the files you want to back up. The scheduling feature allows you to automate the backup process and reduces the chance that you'll forget to make regular backups. Backup software can also save time and storage space by offering options for full, differential, or incremental backups.

What is a full backup? A **full backup** makes a fresh copy of every file in the folders you've specified for the backup. In contrast to a full-system backup, a full backup does not necessarily contain every file on your computer. A full backup might contain only your data files, for example, if those are the files you want to regularly back up.

What is a differential backup? A **differential backup** makes a backup of only those files that were added or changed since your last full backup session. After making a full backup of your important files, you can make differential backups at regular intervals. If you need to restore all your files after a hard disk crash, first restore the files from your full backup, and then restore the files from your latest differential backup.

What is an incremental backup? An **incremental backup** makes a backup of the files that were added or changed since the last backup—not necessarily the files that changed from the last full backup, but the files that changed since any full or incremental backup. After making a full backup of your important files, you can make your first incremental backup containing the files that changed since the full backup. When you make your second incremental backup, it will contain only the files that changed since the first incremental backup. To restore files from an incremental backup, files from a full backup are restored first, followed by files from each incremental backup, starting with the oldest and ending with the most recent. The video associated with Figure 4-32 describes the difference between full, differential, and incremental backups.

FIGURE 4-32

Full, incremental, and differential backups each take a slightly different approach to backing up files.

CLICK TO START

How many backups do I need? Most experts recommend that you keep more than one set of backups. If you use recordable CDs or DVDs for your backups, then you simply burn a new disk each time you back up. If you are using rewritable media, such as removable hard disks, tapes, or CD-RWs, then you can reuse your backups—typically by rotating three backup disks or tapes.

To maintain a rotating backup, use one disk or tape for the first backup, and then use a different disk or tape for the next backup. Use another disk or tape for the third backup. For the fourth backup, you can overwrite the data on the first backup; for the fifth backup, overwrite the data on the second backup, and so on. So that you know which backup is the most recent, write the date of the backup on the disk or tape label.

How can I be sure that my backup works? If your computer's hard disk crashes, you do not want to discover that your backups are blank! To prevent such a disastrous situation, it is important to enable the "read after write" or "compare" option backup software provides. These options force the software to check the data in each sector as it is written to make sure it is copied without error. You should also test your backup by trying to restore one file. Try it with one of your least important data files, just in case your backup is faulty.

BOOT AND RECOVERY DISKS

What is a boot disk? If your computer's hard disk is out of commission, you might wonder how it can access the operating system files needed to carry out the boot process. If your hard disk fails or a virus wipes out the boot sector files on your hard disk, you will not be able to use your normal boot procedure.

A **boot disk** is a floppy disk or CD containing the operating system files needed to boot your computer without accessing the hard disk. A bare-bones boot disk simply loads the operating system kernel. You can make a boot disk using My Computer or Windows Explorer, as shown in Figure 4-33. The boot disk you create, however, boots DOS, not Windows.

FIGURE 4-33

To create an MS-DOS boot disk, insert a blank floppy disk in drive A. Open My Computer or Windows Explorer, and then right-click the Drive A icon. Select Format and check the box labeled Create an MS-DOS startup disk.

4

A more sophisticated boot disk—sometimes referred to as a **recovery CD**—loads hardware drivers and user settings as well as the operating system. Recovery CDs are sometimes included with new computer systems. Some computer manufacturer Web sites offer a download that creates a recovery CD. The operating system might also supply a method for creating recovery CDs. For example, the Windows XP Backup utility creates a set of **Automated System Recovery** disks (Figure 4-34).

Backup Utility - [Untitled]

Job   Edit   View   Tools   Help

| Welcome | Backup | Restore and Manage Media | Schedule Jobs |

Welcome to the Backup Utility Advanced Mode

If you prefer, you can switch to Wizard Mode to use simplified settings for backup or restore.

Backup Wizard (Advanced)
The Backup wizard helps you create a backup of your programs and files.

Restore Wizard (Advanced)
The Restore wizard helps you restore your data from a backup.

Automated System Recovery Wizard
The ASR Preparation wizard helps you create a two-part backup of your system: a floppy disk that has your system settings, and other media that contains a backup of your local system partition.

FIGURE 4-34

Windows XP includes an Automated System Recovery Wizard that helps you create a boot disk containing your system settings.

The contents and capabilities of recovery CDs vary. Some are designed to restore your computer to its "like new" state and wipe out all your data. Others attempt to restore user settings, programs, and data. Before you depend on a recovery CD, make sure you know what it contains and how to use it in case of a system failure.

QuickCheck   SECTION D

1. When backing up selected files, rather than making a full backup, you should make a copy of the Windows [＿＿＿＿＿＿＿＿] and keep it updated every time you install new hardware or software.

2. The backup process is simplified if you store all your important data files in a single [＿＿＿＿＿＿＿].

3. One of the best devices for home backup is a(n) [＿＿＿＿＿＿＿] hard disk drive.

4. A(n) [＿＿＿＿＿＿＿] backup copies only those files that have changed since your last backup session.

5. A(n) [＿＿＿＿＿＿＿] CD helps restore a computer system by loading hardware drivers and user settings as well as the operating system.

 CHECK ANSWERS

TechTalk
File Formats

As you learned earlier in the chapter, the way data is stored in a file is referred to as its file format (or file type) and is indicated by its file extension. Most computer users quickly catch on to the basic idea that a file extension provides a clue as to which application software is needed to open the file. For example, files with .doc extensions typically can be opened using Microsoft Word.

Although a basic understanding of file formats might be sufficient for computer "newbies," a more in-depth understanding can come in handy. This TechTalk is designed to take your current knowledge of file formats in the Windows environment to the next level so that you'll become more adept at using and manipulating the files stored on your computer.

Why should I know about file formats? Some operating systems do a fairly good job of shielding users from the intricacies of file formats. For example, Windows uses a file association list to link a file extension to its corresponding application software. This handy feature allows you to open a data file without first opening an application, simply by double-clicking the file from within Windows Explorer or selecting it from the Documents list that's accessible from the Start menu.

Of course, your application software also shields you from the messy task of searching through directories to find the files it will open. When you use the Open dialog box, most applications automatically comb through the files on a specified device and in a specified folder to display only those that have the "right" file extensions.

With all this help from the operating system and your application software, it might seem that knowing about file formats is unimportant. You might, however, find it useful to understand file formats so that you can easily accomplish tasks such as those listed in Figure 4-35.

What determines a file's format? Although a file extension is a good indicator of a file's format, it does not really define the format. You could use the Rename command to change a QuickTime movie called Balloons.mov to Balloons.doc. Despite the .doc extension, the file is still in QuickTime format because the data elements in the file are arranged in a specific configuration unique to QuickTime.

The format of a file might include a header, data, and possibly an end-of-file marker. You might recall that file headers were defined in Chapter 2. A file header is a section of data at the beginning of a file that contains information about a file—typically the date it was created, the date it was last updated, its size, and its file type.

A file header should not be confused with the headers appearing at the top of each page in a document created with a word processor. Instead, envision a file header as a hidden Post-It note that's attached to the beginning of a file. Although it is hidden to users, computers can read the information in a file header to determine the file's format.

4

FIGURE 4-35

Understanding file formats helps you perform the following tasks:

- Figure out the correct format for e-mail attachments that you send to friends or colleagues.

- Find the right player software for music and media files that you download from the Web.

- Discover how to work with a file that doesn't seem to open.

- Convert files from one format to another.

The remaining contents of a file depend on whether it contains text, graphics, audio, or multimedia data. A text file, for example, might contain sentences and paragraphs interspersed with codes for centering, boldfacing, and margin settings. A graphics file might contain color data for each pixel, followed by a description of the color palette. The file format dictates the arrangement of this data. Figure 4-36 illustrates the layout for a Windows bitmap file and contrasts it with the layout of a GIF file.

Bitmap File Format	GIF File Format
File header	File header
Bitmap header	Logical screen descriptor
Color palette	Global color table
Bitmap data	Local image descriptor
	Local color table
	Image data
	End-of-file character

FIGURE 4-36

Although bitmap and GIF file formats contain graphics, the file layouts differ.

Which file formats am I most likely to encounter? A software program typically consists of at least one executable file with an .exe file extension. It might also include a number of support programs with extensions such as .dll, .vbx, and .ocx. Configuration and startup files usually have .bat, .sys, .ini, and .bin extensions. In addition, you'll find files with .hlp and .tmp extensions. Files with .hlp extensions hold the information for a program's Help utility. Files with .tmp extensions are temporary files. When you open a data file with software applications, such as word processors, spreadsheets, and graphics tools, your operating system makes a copy of the original file and stores this copy on disk as a temporary file. It is this temporary file that you work with as you view and revise a file.

INFOWEBLINKS

The **File Formats InfoWeb** provides a list of file extensions and their corresponding software.

www.course.com/np/concepts9/ch04

To the uninitiated, the file extensions associated with programs and the operating system might seem odd. Nevertheless, executable and support files—even so-called temporary files—are crucial for the correct operation of your computer system. You should not manually delete them unless they become corrupted. The table in Figure 4-37 lists the file extensions typically associated with the operating system and executable files.

FIGURE 4-37

OS and Executable Extensions

Type of File	Description	Extension
Batch file	A sequence of operating system commands executed automatically when the computer boots	.bat
Configuration file	Information about programs the computer uses to allocate the resources necessary to run them	.cfg .sys .mif .bin .ini
Help	The information displayed by on-screen Help	.hlp
Temporary file	A sort of "scratch pad" that contains data while a file is open, but is discarded when you close the file	.tmp
Support program	Program instructions executed along with the main .exe file for a program	.ocx .vbx .vbs .dll
Program	The main executable files for a computer program	.exe .com

The list of data file formats is long, but becoming familiar with the most popular formats and the type of data they contain is useful. Figure 4-38 provides this information in a convenient table. Where noted, a file format is associated with a particular software program.

FIGURE 4-38

Data File Extensions

Type of File	Extension
Text	.txt .dat .rtf .doc (Microsoft Word and WordPad) .wpd (WordPerfect)
Sound	.wav .mid .mp3 .au .ra (RealAudio)
Graphics	.bmp .pcx .tif .wmf .gif .jpg .png .eps .ai (Adobe Illustrator)
Animation/video	.flc .fli .avi .mpg .mov (QuickTime) .rm (RealMedia) .wmv (Windows Media Player)
Web pages	.htm .html .asp .vrml
Spreadsheets	.xls (Microsoft Excel) .wks (Lotus 1-2-3) .dif
Database	.mdb (Microsoft Access)
Miscellaneous	.pdf (Adobe Acrobat) .ppt (Microsoft PowerPoint) .zip (WinZip) .pub (Microsoft Publisher) .qxp (QuarkExpress)

How do I know which files a program will open? A software application can open files that exist in its native file format, plus several additional file formats. For example, Microsoft Word opens files in its native DOC (.doc) format, plus files in formats such as HTML (.htm or .html), Text (.txt), and Rich Text Format (.rtf). Within the Windows environment, you can discover which formats a particular software program can open by looking at the *Files of type* list in the Open dialog box, as shown in Figure 4-39.

FIGURE 4-39

An application's *Files of type* list usually displays the file formats a program can open. You can also look for an Import option on the File menu.

Why can't I open some files? Suppose you receive an e-mail attachment called Cool.tif. "Aha!" you say to yourself, "My Photoshop software ought to open that file." You try—several times—but all you get is an error message. When a file doesn't open, one of three things probably went wrong:

- The file might have been damaged—a techie would call it "corrupted"—by a transmission or disk error. Although you might be able to use file recovery software to repair the damage, it is usually easier to obtain an undamaged copy of the file from its original source.

- Someone might have inadvertently changed the file extension. While renaming the Cool file, perhaps the original .bmp extension was changed to .tif. If you have a little time, you can change the file extension and try to open the file. If a file contains a graphic, chances are that it should have the extension for one of the popular graphics formats, such as .bmp, .gif, .jpg, .tif, or .png. Otherwise, you should contact the source of the file to get accurate information about its real format.

- Some file formats exist in several variations, and your software might not have the capability to open a particular variation of the format. You might be able to open the file if you use different application software. For example, Photoshop might not be able to open a particular file with a .tif file extension, but Corel Paint Shop Pro might open it.

What if all my software fails to open a particular file format? Although a computer might be able to discover a file's format, it might not necessarily know how to work with it. Just as you might be able to identify a helicopter, you can't necessarily fly it without some instructions. Your computer also requires a set of instructions to use most file formats. These instructions are provided by software. To use a particular file format, you must make sure your computer has the corresponding software.

Suppose you download a file with an .rm extension and none of your current software works with this file format. Several Web sites provide lists of file extensions and their corresponding software. By looking up a file extension in one of these lists, you can find out what application software you'll need to find, buy, download, and install.

Many files downloaded from the Web require special "player" or "reader" software. For example, PDF text files require software called Acrobat Reader, MP3 music files require software called an MP3 player, and RM video files require the RealMedia Player software. Typically, you can follow a link from the Web page that supplied your file download to find a site from which you can download the necessary player or reader software.

How do I know what kinds of file formats I can send to my friends, colleagues, and instructor? Unless you know what application software is installed on your friends' computers, you won't know for certain whether they can open a particular file you've sent. There's a good chance, however, that your friends can open files saved in common file formats represented by the extensions listed in Figure 4-40. You should check with the recipient before sending files in less common, proprietary formats, such as Adobe Illustrator's AI format and QuarkExpress's QXP format.

Is it possible to convert a file from one format to another? Perhaps you created a Word document on your PC, but you need to convert it into a format that's usable by your colleague who owns a Mac. Or suppose you want to convert a Word document into HTML format so that you can post it on the Web. You might also want to convert a Windows bitmap (.bmp)

FIGURE 4-40

Extensions for Common File Formats

.bmp	.tif
.gif	.doc
.txt	.wav
.jpg	.mid
.htm	.html
.xls	.rtf
.mp3	.aac
.wmv	.wma

graphic into GIF format so that you can include it on a Web page. The easiest way to convert a file from one format to another is to find an application program that works with both file formats. Open the file using that software, and then use the Export option, or the Save As dialog box, to select a new file format, assign the file a new name, and save it (Figure 4-41).

FIGURE 4-41

An easy way to convert a file from one format to another is to open it with an application that supports both file formats, and then use the Save As dialog box to select an alternative file format.

CLICK TO START

4

Many file formats convert easily to another format, and the resulting file is virtually indistinguishable from the original. Some conversions, however, do not retain all the characteristics of the original file. When you convert a DOC file into HTML format, for example, the HTML page does not contain any of the headers, footers, superscripts, page numbers, special characters, or page breaks that existed in the original DOC file.

When you need a conversion routine for an obscure file format, or if you need to convert between many different file formats, consider specialized conversion software, available through commercial or shareware outlets.

INFOWEBLINKS

Conversion software runs the gamut from simple shareware to "industrial-strength" commercial packages. The **Conversion Software InfoWeb** will help you compare what's available.

www.course.com/np/concepts9/ch04

QuickCheck

TECHTALK

1. A file _____ is a section of data at the beginning of a file that contains information about the file type.

2. File extensions such as .ocx, .vbx, .vbs, and .dll typically indicate _____ programs.

3. The _____ file format for Microsoft Word is DOC.

4. Conversion software can help you transform one file type into a different file type. True or false? _____

CHECK ANSWERS

Issue

Computer Crime

It doesn't take any special digital expertise to master-mind some computer crimes. Setting fire to a computer doesn't require the same finesse as writing a stealthy virus, but both can have the same disastrous effect on data. "Old-fashioned" crimes, such as arson, that take a high-tech twist because they involve a computer can be prosecuted under traditional laws.

Traditional laws do not, however, cover the range of possibilities for computer crimes. Suppose a person unlawfully enters a computer facility and steals back-up tapes. That person might be prosecuted for breaking and entering. But would common breaking and entering laws apply to a person who uses an off-site terminal to "enter" a computer system without authorization? And what if a person copies a data file without authorization? Has that file really been "stolen" if the original remains on the computer?

Many countries have computer crime laws that specifically define computer data and software as personal property. These laws also define as crimes the unauthorized access, use, modification, or disabling of a computer system or data. But laws don't necessarily stop criminals. If they did, we wouldn't have to deal with malicious code and intrusions.

Computer Crime Gambits

Data diddling: Unauthorized alterations to data stored on a computer system, such as a student changing grades stored in a school's computer.
Identity theft: Unauthorized copying of personal information, such as credit card numbers, passwords, Social Security numbers, and bank account PINs.
Salami shaving: Redirecting small, unnoticeable amounts of money from large amounts.
Denial of Service: An attempt to disrupt the operations of a network or computer system, usually by flooding it with data traffic.
Information theft: Unauthorized access to a computer system, such as military or government computers, to gain restricted information.
Virus distribution: Launching viruses, worms, and Trojan horses.
Vandalism: Intentional defacement of Web sites.

Computer crimes—costly to organizations and individuals—include a variety of gambits, such as virus distribution, data diddling, identity theft, and salami shaving.

One of the first computer crime cases involved a worm unleashed on the ARPANET in 1988 that quickly spread through government and university computer systems. The worm's author, Robert Morris, was convicted and sentenced to three years' probation, 400 hours of community service, and a $10,000 fine. This relatively lenient sentence was imposed because Morris claimed he had not intended to cripple the entire network.

A 1995 high-profile case involved a computer hacker named Kevin Mitnick, who was accused of breaking into dozens of corporate, university, government, and personal computers. Although vilified in the media, Mitnick had the support of many hackers and other people who believed that the prosecution grossly exaggerated the extent of his crimes. Nonetheless, Mitnick was sentenced to 46 months in prison and ordered to pay restitution in the amount of $4,125 during his three-year period of supervised release. The prosecution was horrified by such a paltry sum—an amount that was much less than its request for $1.5 million in restitution.

Forbes reporter Adam L. Penenberg took issue with the 46-month sentence imposed by Judge Marianne Pfaelzer and wrote, "This in a country where the average prison term for manslaughter is three years. Mitnick's crimes were curiously innocuous. He broke into corporate computers, but no evidence indicates that he destroyed data. Or sold anything he copied. Yes, he pilfered software—but in doing so left it behind. This world of bits is a strange one, in which you can take something and still leave it for its rightful owner. The theft laws designed for payroll sacks and motor vehicles just don't apply to a hacker."

In 2005 a German teenager confessed to creating the Sasser computer worm that was blamed for shutting down British Airways and Delta Airlines flight check-ins, hospitals and government offices in Hong Kong, part of Australia's rail network, Finnish banks, British Coast Guard stations, and millions of other computers worldwide. The teen was given a suspended sentence of 21 months and was required to perform 30 hours of community service. Microsoft paid a $250,000 reward to the two people who tipped off German police to the virus author's identity. The teen now holds a job at a computer company that creates antivirus software.

Officials also made two arrests in connection with the Blaster worm. A 24-year-old Romanian citizen and an American teenager apparently downloaded copies of the worm source code, altered it slightly, and sent their versions back out again. The Romanian was allegedly angered by his treatment by one of his professors. The American teenager was just trying to see what he could get away with.

Under Romanian law, distributing a virus can mean a 15-year prison sentence. The U.S. Patriot Act and the Cyber-Security Enhancement Act carry even stiffer penalties—anywhere from 10 years to life in prison.

A CNET reporter questions the harshness of such penalties: "What bothers me most is that here in the United States, rapists serve, on average, 10 years in prison. Yet if, instead of assaulting another human being, that same person had released a virus on the Net, the criminal would get the same or an even harsher sentence."

Law makers hope that stiff penalties will deter cyber criminals. U.S. Attorney John McKay is quoted as saying, "Let there be no mistake about it, cyber-hacking is a crime. It harms persons, it harms individuals, it harms businesses. We will investigate, track down, and prosecute cyber-hackers."

These cases illustrate our culture's ambivalent attitude toward computer hackers. On the one hand, they are viewed as evil cyberterrorists who are set on destroying the glue that binds together the Information Age. From this perspective, hackers are criminals who must be hunted down, forced to make restitution for damages, and prevented from creating further havoc.

From another perspective, hackers are viewed more as Casper the Friendly Ghost in our complex cyber-machines—as moderately bothersome entities whose pranks are tolerated by the computer community, along with software bugs and hardware glitches. Seen from this perspective, a hacker's pranks are part of the normal course of study that leads to the highest echelons of computer expertise. "Everyone has done it," claims one hacking devotee, "even Bill Gates (founder of Microsoft) and Steve Jobs (founder of Apple Computer)."

Which perspective is right? Are hackers dangerous cyberterrorists or harmless pranksters? Before you make up your mind about computer hacking and cracking, you might want to further investigate several landmark cases by following links at the Computer Crime InfoWeb.

INFOWEBLINKS

Who's in the cybercrime news? How are cybercriminals caught? The **Computer Crime InfoWeb** provides answers to these questions and more.

www.course.com/np/concepts9/ch04

What Do You Think?   ISSUE

1. Should a computer virus distribution sentence carry the same penalty as manslaughter?   ○ Yes ○ No ○ Not sure

2. Should it be a crime to steal a copy of computer data while leaving the original data in place and unaltered?   ○ Yes ○ No ○ Not sure

3. Should hackers be sent to jail if they cannot pay restitution to companies and individuals who lost money as the result of a prank?   ○ Yes ○ No ○ Not sure

4. Do you think that a hacker would make a good consultant on computer security?   ○ Yes ○ No ○ Not sure

                                                         ⁜ SAVE RESPONSES

Computers in Context
Law Enforcement

Sirens wail. Blue lights strobe the night. A speeding car slows and pulls off to the side of the road. It looks like a routine traffic stop, but the patrol car is outfitted with a mobile data computer. The police officers on this high-tech force have already checked the speeding car's license plate number and description against a database of stolen cars and cars allegedly used in kidnapping and other crimes.

Mounted in the dashboard of marked and unmarked police cars, a mobile data computer resembles a notebook computer with its flat-panel screen and compact keyboard. Unlike a consumer-grade notebook, however, the computers in police cruisers use hardened technology designed to withstand extreme conditions, such as high temperatures in parked vehicles. The dashboard-mounted computer communicates with an office-based server using a wireless link, such as short-range radio, CDPD (cellular digital packet data) technology, or Wi-Fi. With this wireless link, police officers can access data from local, state, and national databases.

One national database, the National Crime Information Center (NCIC), is maintained by the FBI and can be accessed by authorized personnel in local, state, and federal law enforcement agencies. The system can process more than 2.4 million queries per day related to stolen vehicles, wanted criminals, missing persons, violent gang members, stolen guns, and members of terrorist organizations. The officers who pulled over the speeding car received information from the NCIC that the car was

stolen, so they arrested the car's occupant and took him to the police station for booking.

At the police station, digital cameras flash and the suspect's mug shot is automatically entered into an automated warrants and booking system. The system stores the suspect's complete biographical and arrest information, such as name, aliases, addresses, Social Security number, charges, and arrest date. The system also checks for outstanding warrants against the suspect, such as warrants for other thefts. Booking agents can enter those charges into the system, assign the new inmate to a cell, log his personal items, and print a photo ID or wrist band.

Automated warrants and booking systems have been proved to increase police productivity. New York City's system handles more than 300,000 bookings per year, with gains in productivity that have put nearly 300 officers back into action investigating crimes and patrolling neighborhoods.

As part of the booking process, the suspect is fingerprinted. A standard fingerprint card, sometimes called a "ten-print card," contains inked prints of the fingers on each hand, plus name, date of birth, and other arrest information. Now, however, instead of using ink, a biometric scanning device can electronically capture fingerprints. Text information is entered using a keyboard and stored with digital fingerprint images.

The fingerprint information can be transmitted in digital format from local law enforcement agencies to the FBI's Automated Fingerprint Identification System (AFIS). This biometric identification methodology uses digital imaging technology to analyze fingerprint data. Using sophisticated algorithms, AFIS can classify arriving prints for storage or search the collection of 600 million fingerprint cards for matching prints.

Conventional crimes, such as car theft, are often solved by using standard investigative techniques with information from computer databases. To solve cybercrimes, however, often the special skills of computer forensic investigators are required.

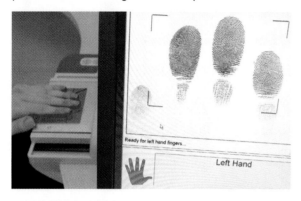

Left Hand

Computer forensics is the scientific examination and analysis of data located on computer storage media, conducted to offer evidence of computer crimes in court. Computer crimes can be separated into two categories. The first includes crimes that use computers, such as transmitting trade secrets to competitors, reproducing copyrighted material, and distributing child pornography. The second includes crimes targeted at computers, such as Denial of Service attacks on servers, Web site vandalism, data theft, and destructive viruses. Computer forensics can be applied to both categories.

Whether investigators suspect that a computer is the origin of a cyber attack or contains evidence, the first step in the forensic process is to use disk imaging software to make an exact replica of the information stored on the hard disk. The disk image is collected on a write-once medium that cannot be altered with "planted" evidence, and the forensic scientist begins analyzing the disk image data with simple search software that looks through files for keywords related to the crime. In the case of the "Gap-Toothed Bandit" who was convicted for robbing nine banks, analysis of the disk image revealed word processing files containing notes he handed to tellers demanding money.

Criminals typically attempt to delete files with incriminating evidence, but a good forensic scientist can retrieve data from deleted files with undelete software or data recovery software. Temporary Internet or cache files can also yield evidence, pointing law enforcement officers to Web sites the suspect visited that might be fronts for illegal activity.

When a computer is a target of a cyber attack, forensic investigators use three techniques to track the source. The first option is to make an immediate image of the server's hard disk and look through its log files for evidence of activity coming from unauthorized IP addresses. A second technique is to monitor the intruder by watching login attempts, changes to log files, and file access requests. Sophisticated intruders might be able to detect such monitoring, however, and cover their tracks. A third technique is to create a "honeypot"—an irresistible computer system or Web site containing fake information that allows investigators to monitor hackers until identification is possible.

Despite the many techniques and tools available to forensic investigators, they have three main constraints. First, they must adhere to privacy regulations and obtain warrants to set up wiretaps or gather information from ISPs about their customers. Second, they must scrupulously document their procedures so that the evidence they produce cannot be discredited in court as "planted" or fabricated. Third, forensic investigators must examine a wide range of alternatives pertaining to the crime, such as the chance that an IP or e-mail address used to commit a cybercrime doesn't belong to an innocent bystander being spoofed by the real hacker.

Privacy, documentation, and evidentiary constraints cost forensic investigators time, and failure to adhere to strict standards can sometimes allow criminals to avoid conviction and penalties. But even within these constraints, careful forensic investigation is an important aspect of catching and convicting high-tech criminals.

4

INFOWEBLINKS

For more information about police and FBI technology, connect to the **Computers in Law Enforcement InfoWeb**.

www.course.com/np/concepts9/ch04

Labs

Student Edition Labs

On the Web
Student Edition Labs

To access the Student Edition labs, connect to the New Perspectives NP9 Web site and click the link for Student Edition Labs. The link also provides access to lab assignments.

www.course.com/np/concepts9/ch04

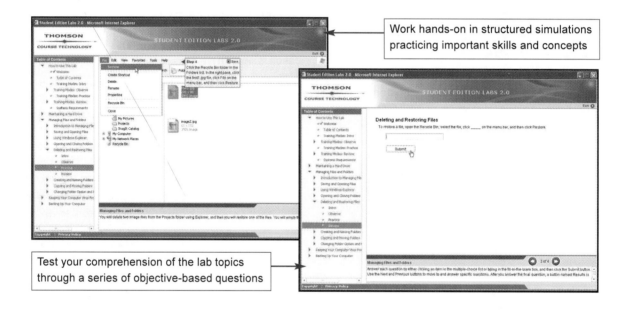

Work hands-on in structured simulations practicing important skills and concepts

Test your comprehension of the lab topics through a series of objective-based questions

MAINTAINING A HARD DRIVE

In the Maintaining a Hard Drive Student Edition Lab, you will learn the following topics and skills:

- Defragmenting a hard disk
- Running ScanDisk
- Detecting system and program failure
- Freeing up disk space

MANAGING FILES AND FOLDERS

In the Managing Files and Folders Student Edition Lab, you will learn the following topics and skills:

- Using Windows Explorer to manage files and folders
- Deleting and restoring files
- Creating, naming, copying, and moving folders
- Changing folder options and properties

KEEPING YOUR COMPUTER VIRUS FREE

In the Keeping Your Computer Virus Free Student Edition Lab, you will learn the following topics and skills:

- Using antivirus software
- Virus detection and prevention

BACKING UP YOUR COMPUTER

In the Backing Up Your Computer Student Edition Lab, you will learn the following topics and skills:

- Creating a backup
- Creating an incremental backup
- Backing up the Windows Registry
- Scheduling backup jobs
- Restoring an entire backup

On the BookOnCD
New Perspectives Labs

To access the New Perspectives labs for Chapter 4, start the BookOnCD and then click the ✵ icon next to the lab title below.

✵ WORKING WITH WINDOWS EXPLORER

IN THIS LAB YOU'LL LEARN:

How to access Windows Explorer

How to expand and collapse the directory structure

How to rename or delete a file or folder

The basic principles for creating an efficient directory structure for your files

How to create a folder

How to select a single file or a group of files

How to move files from one folder to another

LAB ASSIGNMENTS

1. Start the interactive part of the lab. Make sure you've enabled Tracking if you want to save your QuickCheck results. Perform each lab step, and answer all the lab QuickCheck questions.

2. Use Windows Explorer to look at the directory of the hard disk or floppy disk that currently contains most of your files. Draw a diagram showing the hierarchy of folders. Write a paragraph explaining how you could improve this hierarchy, and draw a diagram to illustrate your plan.

3. On a blank floppy disk or USB Flash drive, create three folders: Music, Web Graphics, and Articles. Within the Music folder, create four additional folders: Jazz, Reggae, Rock, and Classical. Within the Classical folder, create two more folders: Classical MIDI and Classical MP3. If you have Internet access, go on to #4.

4. Use your browser software to connect to the Internet, and then go to a Web site, such as *www.zdnet.com* or *www.cnet.com*. Look for a small graphic (remember, the capacity of a floppy disk is only 1.44 MB!) and download it to your Web Graphics folder. Next, use a search engine to search for "classical MIDI music." Download one of the compositions to the Music\Classical\Classical MIDI folder. Open Windows Explorer and expand all the directories for drive A. Open the Music\Classical\Classical MIDI folder and make sure your music download appears. Capture a screenshot. Follow your instructor's directions to submit this screenshot as a printout or an e-mail attachment.

✵ BACKING UP YOUR COMPUTER

IN THIS LAB YOU'LL LEARN:

How to start the Windows Backup utility

How to use the Backup Wizard

How to create a backup job

Which files to select for a backup job

How to back up the Windows Registry

The advantages and disadvantages of using a password to protect your backup data

The implications of compressing your backup data

How to restore data from an entire backup job

How to restore a single file from a backup

LAB ASSIGNMENTS

1. Start the interactive part of the lab. Make sure you've enabled Tracking if you want to save your QuickCheck results. Perform each lab step as directed, and answer all the lab QuickCheck questions. When you exit the lab, your answers are automatically graded and your results are displayed.

2. Describe where most of your data files are stored, and estimate how many megabytes of data (not programs) you have in all these files. Next, take a close look at these files and estimate how much data (in megabytes) you cannot afford to lose. Finally, explain what you think would be the best hardware device for backing up this amount of data.

3. Draw a sketch or capture a screenshot of the Microsoft Backup window's toolbar. Use ToolTips, ScreenTips, or the window's status bar to find the name of each toolbar button. Use this information to label the buttons on your sketch or screenshot.

4. Assume that you will use Microsoft Backup to make a backup of your data files. Describe the backup job you would create—specify the folders you must include. It is not necessary to list individual files unless they are not within one of the folders you would back up. Make sure you indicate whether you would use password protection, the type of compression you would select, and how you would handle the Windows Registry.

4

Interactive Summary

To review important concepts from this chapter, fill in the blanks to best complete each sentence. When using the NP9 BookOnCD or the NP9 Web site, click the Check Answers buttons to automatically score your answers.

A computer [ ] is a named collection of data that exists on a storage medium, such as a hard disk, floppy disk, CD, DVD, or tape. Every file has a name and might also have a file extension. The rules that specify valid file names are called file-naming [ ]. These rules typically do not allow you to use certain characters or [ ] words in a file name. A file [ ] is usually related to a file format—the arrangement of data in a file and the coding scheme used to represent the data. A software program's [ ] file format is the default format for storing files created with that program.

A file's location is defined by a file [ ] (sometimes called a "path"), which includes the storage device, folder(s), file name, and extension. In Windows, storage devices are identified by a drive letter, followed by a [ ]. An operating system maintains a list of files called a directory for each storage disk, tape, CD, or DVD. The main directory of a disk is sometimes referred to as the [ ] directory, which can be subdivided into several smaller lists called subdirectories that are depicted as [ ].

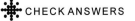 CHECK ANSWERS

File [ ] encompasses any procedure that helps you organize your computer-based files so that you can find and use them more effectively. [ ]-based file management uses tools provided with a software program to open and save files. Additional tools might also allow you to create new folders, rename files, and delete files. The Save and Save As dialog boxes are examples of these file management tools.

Most operating systems provide file management [ ] that give you the "big picture" of the files you have stored on your disks. The structure of folders that you envision on your disk is a logical model, which is often represented by a storage [ ], such as a tree structure or filing cabinet. Windows Explorer is an example of a file management utility provided by an operating system. Windows Explorer allows you to find, rename, copy, move, and delete files and folders. In addition, it allows

you to perform these file management activities with more than one file at a time.

The way that data is actually stored is referred to as the [ ] storage model. Before a computer stores data on a disk, CD, or DVD, it creates the equivalent of electronic storage bins by dividing the disk into [ ], and then further dividing the disk into [ ]. This dividing process is referred to as [ ]. Each sector of a disk is numbered, providing a storage address that the operating system can track. Many computers work with a group of sectors, called a [ ], to increase the efficiency of file storage operations. An operating system uses a file system to track the physical location of files. The file system for Windows 95, 98, and Me is called FAT32; for Windows NT, 2000, XP, and Vista, it is called [ ].

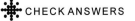 CHECK ANSWERS

A computer virus is a set of program instructions that attaches itself to a file, reproduces itself, and spreads to other files. You might encounter several types of viruses. A virus that attaches itself to an application program, such as a game utility, is known as a [＿＿＿＿＿] virus. A boot [＿＿＿＿＿] virus infects the system files your computer uses every time you turn it on. A [＿＿＿＿＿] virus infects a set of instructions that automates document and worksheet production.

A Trojan horse is a computer program that seems to perform one function while actually doing something else. Such programs are notorious for stealing [＿＿＿＿＿], although some delete files and cause other problems.

A [＿＿＿＿＿] is a program designed to spread from computer to computer. Most take advantage of communications networks—especially the Internet—to travel within e-mail and TCP/IP packets, jumping from one computer to another. Today, mass

[＿＿＿＿＿] worms, such as MyDoom, are one of the most common threats to computer networks. Many worms are designed to trigger Denial of [＿＿＿＿＿] attacks that flood networks and block access to servers.

[＿＿＿＿＿] are automated agents that lurk in your computer waiting for a hacker to send instructions.

Viruses can slip into your computer from a variety of sources, such as floppy disks, homemade CDs, and Web sites that contain games and other supposedly fun stuff. E-mail [＿＿＿＿＿] are another common source of viruses. HTML-formatted e-mail is susceptible to viruses and worms hidden in program-like "scripts" that are embedded in HTML tags.

[＿＿＿＿＿] software can help prevent viruses from invading your computer system and can root out viruses that take up residence. This software typically scans for a virus [＿＿＿＿＿] and is sometimes referred to as virus scanning software.

 CHECK ANSWERS

A backup is a copy of one or more files that has been made in case the original files become damaged. For safety, a backup is usually stored on a different storage medium from the original files. A good backup plan allows you to [＿＿＿＿＿] your computing environment to its pre-disaster state with a minimum of fuss.

No single backup plan fits everyone's computing style or budget. Your personal backup plan depends on the files you need to back up, the hardware you have available to make backups, and your backup software. In any case, it is a good idea to back up the Windows [＿＿＿＿＿] and make sure your files are free of [＿＿＿＿＿]. Backups should be stored in a safe place, away from the computer.

Backups can be recorded on floppy disks, writable CDs and DVDs, networks, Web sites, a second hard disk, or tapes. Many computer owners depend on writable CDs for backups, and use My Computer or Windows [＿＿＿＿＿] to simply select files and copy files to the backup. [＿＿＿＿＿] drives and backup software are typically used in business situations when a full-system backup is desirable. Backup software differs from most copy routines because it [＿＿＿＿＿] all the files for a backup into one large file.

In addition to file backups, you should have a [＿＿＿＿＿] disk containing the operating system files and settings needed to start your computer without accessing the hard disk.

CHECK ANSWERS

Key Terms

Make sure you understand all the boldfaced key terms presented in this chapter. If you're using the NP9 BookOnCD, you can use this list of terms as an interactive study activity. First, try to define a term in your own words, and then click the term to compare your definition with the definition presented in the chapter.

Antivirus software, 205
Automated System Recovery, 216
Backdoor, 200
Backup, 208
Backup software, 213
Blended threat, 200
Boot disk, 215
Boot sector virus, 198
Bot, 202
Botnet, 202
Checksum, 205
Cluster, 195
Computer virus, 198
Defragmentation utility, 197
Denial of Service attack, 204
Differential backup, 214
Directory, 186
FAT32, 195
File Allocation Table, 195
File date, 187
File format, 185
File management utilities, 190
File-naming conventions, 184
File shredder software, 196
File size, 187
File specification, 186
File system, 195

File virus, 198
Folders, 186
Formatting, 194
Formatting utilities, 195
Fragmented files, 197
Full backup, 214
Full-system backup, 209
Incremental backup, 214
Keylogger, 199
Logical storage models, 191
Macro virus, 199
Malicious code, 198
Mass-mailing worm, 200
Master File Table, 195
Multi-partite viruses, 206
Native file format, 185
NTFS, 195
Path, 186
Payload, 199
Physical storage model, 194
Polymorphic viruses, 206
Ransomware, 205
Recovery CD, 216
Reserved words, 185
Restore, 209
Retro viruses, 205
Root directory, 186

Sectors, 194
Spoofed address, 200
Stealth viruses, 206
Storage metaphor, 191
Subdirectory, 186
Tracks, 194
Trigger event, 199
Trojan horse, 199
Virus hoax, 206
Virus signature, 206
Windows Explorer, 192
Worm, 200

Interactive Situation Questions

Apply what you've learned to some typical computing situations. When using the NP9 BookOnCD or the NP9 Web site, you can type your answers, and then use the Check Answers button to automatically score your responses.

1. Suppose you are using Microsoft Word and you want to open a file. When your software lists the documents you can open, you can expect them to be in Word's [   ] file format, which is DOC.

2. Can you use a Windows application, create a document, and store it using the file name I L*ve NY ? Yes or no? [   ]

3. When you want to work with several files—to move them to different folders, for example—it would be most efficient to use a file management utility, such as Windows [   ].

4. When specifying a location for a data file on your hard disk, you should avoid saving it in the [   ] directory.

5. Your computer seems to be taking longer to store and retrieve files. You use a(n) [   ] utility to rearrange the files in contiguous clusters.

6. You have an old computer that you will donate to a school, but you want to make sure its hard disk contains no trace of your data. To do so, you should use file [   ] software that overwrites "empty" sectors with random 1s and 0s.

7. You receive e-mail from PayPal asking you to renew your account by entering your current user ID and password. You assume that a hacker is using

[   ] engineering to make a Trojan horse appear to be a legitimate message.

8. You receive an e-mail message that says, "Your computer has contracted a virus. You can remove it by using the program attached to this message." Would you assume that this message is a hoax? Yes or no? [   ]

9. You just finished making a full system backup on a set of DVDs. Before you depend on this backup, you should test it to make sure you can successfully [   ] the data in the event of a hard disk crash.

10. Your hard disk crashed for some unknown reason. Now when you switch on the computer power, all you get is an "Error reading drive C:" message. You use a(n) [   ] CD that contains the operating system files and device drivers needed to start your computer without accessing the hard disk. ✛ CHECK ANSWERS

Interactive Practice Tests

Practice tests that consist of 10 multiple-choice, true/false, and fill-in-the-blank questions are available on both the NP9 BookOnCD and the NP9 Web site. The questions are selected at random from a large test bank, so each time you take a test, you'll receive a different set of questions. Your tests are scored immediately, and you can print study guides that help you find the correct answers for any questions that you missed.

CLICK ✛ TO START

Projects

An NP9 Project is an open-ended activity that will help you apply the concepts you have learned. Many projects require resources in addition to your textbook, such as current magazines, library materials, or Web access. When you tackle a project, be prepared to use your critical thinking skills, logical analysis, and your creativity.

CRITICAL THINKING

Viruses and other nuisances are becoming an overwhelming burden on the computer community, even with laws in place that make it illegal to spread viruses. Antivirus software is helpful, and some computer scientists are considering the pros and cons of distributing "good" viruses that hunt down and destroy malicious code anywhere on the Internet. But the white hats are running into opposition. One antivirus publisher has been sued by a software distributor who believes its product should not have been classified as a virus. Who should be able to specify which programs are viruses? Who should be able to hunt down and destroy other programs on the Internet or on your hard disk? Organize your thoughts into a one-page document and e-mail it to your instructor.

GROUP PROJECT

Keeping files and folders organized is a skill worth developing. Work with one or two other people to streamline the organization of folders and files on a computer storage device, such as a hard disk or flash drive. The storage device should contain at least 100 files. You can have the computer generate a listing of the files by connecting to *www.support.microsoft.com*, searching for article 196158, and following the instructions you find there for "How to Create a Text File List of the Contents of a Folder." Once you have a document containing the list, you can edit it to indicate how you would rearrange the files into a better structure of folders. Use a series of indents or Microsoft Word's outlining function to show the hierarchy of files and folders. Annotate your list by indicating the kinds of files you expect to be stored in each folder.

CYBERCLASSROOM

A backup plan is important and getting one in writing is the first step to making it happen. For this project, you'll write up a backup plan and get it critiqued by other team members.

Create an e-mail message that describes your backup equipment and plan along with the date of your last backup. In the subject line, include your name and the title "Original Backup Plan." Send the message to other members of your team and solicit comments and questions.

Based on the feedback you receive, use a word processor to revise your backup plan so it gives you improved protection against losing files. Using copy and paste, add the text of your Original Backup Plan and all the comments you received from your team. Your final document should contain your Revised Backup Plan, your Original Backup Plan, and your team's comments. Send this document to your instructor as an e-mail attachment.

MULTIMEDIA PROJECT

Suppose you are a reporter for a local television station. Your assignment is to create a 90-second story about virus hoaxes for your local TV news show. The basic objectives of the story are (1) to remind people not to panic when they receive e-mail about viruses and (2) to provide a set of concrete steps that a person could take to discover whether a virus threat is real or a hoax. Of course, the network wants the story to be interesting, so you have to include a human-interest angle. Write the script for the story, and include notes about the visuals (screenshots, URLs, checklists) that will appear. Follow your professor's instructions for submitting your script as an e-mail attachment or as a printed document.

RESUME BUILDER

In the digital job marketplace, one way to make a distinctly bad impression is to inadvertently send a prospective employer an e-mail message or resume that's infected with a virus. For this project, you should use your own computer. If you use a lab computer, check with your instructor or lab manager before you begin.

To start the project, make sure you have antivirus software installed on your computer and then activate a full system scan for viruses.

Next, check to see if your computer is vulnerable to Internet intrusions. Connect to *www.grc.com* and select the Shields Up! test or connect to *http://www.dslreports.com/scan.* Print your results. If you find security holes, don't panic! Work with your instructor and technical support team to determine which ones need to be closed or patched.

Finally, connect to the site, such as *www.microsoft.com,* that provides patches and service packs for your computer's operating system. Use the utilities at that site to find out if you have the most recent patches for your operating system.

When you've completed the project activities, write a short summary of the results and submit it to your instructor.

GLOBALIZATION

The Web is plagued by e-mail scams, viruses, worms, bots, and intruders. Cyberspace criminals can easily cross international borders, for example, by launching a virus from an Eastern European country that affects computers in countries such as China, England, Canada, and the United States. For this project, research the origins of viruses and other Internet-borne hacking. What are the problems with hunting down these cross-border hackers? Is the international community working on deterrents? Summarize your findings into a two-page document and submit it to your instructor. Make sure you include a list of your sources.

ISSUE

The Issue section of this chapter focused on cybercrime. For this project, write a two- to five-page opinion paper about the "right to hack," based on information that you gather from the Internet. To begin this project, consult the Computer Crime InfoWeb (see page 225), and link to the recommended Web pages to get an in-depth overview of the issue. Armed with this background, select one of the following statements and argue for or against it:

- People have the "right" to hone their computing skills by breaking into computers.
- A person who creates a virus is perfectly justified in releasing it if the purpose is to make everyone aware of these security breaches.
- Computer crimes are no different from other crimes, and computer criminals should be held responsible for the damage they cause.

Whatever viewpoint you decide to present, make sure you back it up with facts and references to authoritative articles and Web pages. Follow your professor's instructions for submitting your paper by e-mail or as a printed document.

COMPUTERS IN CONTEXT

The Computers in Context section focused on computer use in law enforcement. For this project, use Web-based resources to search for cases in which computer forensic evidence was used in a criminal or civil investigation. Write a paragraph about the case's particulars, including a description of the alleged criminal activity. Next, create a list of elements, such as e-mail messages, attachments, files, and server logs, that were the focus of the forensic investigation. Follow up with a summary of the outcome. Was the suspect found guilty? Was a penalty imposed? Finally, state your opinion of how forensic evidence affected the case. Was it key evidence required to make the case, or did it simply support other physical evidence? Was the computer forensic evidence solid or open to interpretation and challenges from the defense? Make sure you include the URLs used for your research, and check with your professor for instructions on submitting this project on disk, by e-mail, or in print.

4

Study Tips

Study Tips help you to organize and consolidate the information in a unit by making lists, outlines, charts, and sketches. You can use paper and pencil or word processing software to complete most of the Study Tip activities.

1. Make sure you can use your own words to correctly answer each of the orange focus questions that appear throughout the chapter.

2. Make a list of five file names that are valid under the file-naming conventions for your operating system. Also create a list of five file names that are not valid, and explain the problem with each one.

3. Pick any five files on the computer that you typically use, and write out the full path for each one.

4. Describe the difference between the Save and the Save As options provided by an application.

5. In your own words, describe the difference between a logical storage model and a physical storage model.

6. Explain the kinds of file management tasks that might best be accomplished using a file management utility such as Windows Explorer, instead of the Save As or Open dialog box provided by a software application.

7. Explain the differences between an operating system and a file system.

8. Describe the difference between a sector and a cluster.

9. Make sure that you can describe what happens in the MFT or FAT when a file is stored or deleted.

10. Describe the characteristics of viruses, Trojan horses, worms, bots, mass-mailing worms, Denial of Service attacks, and blended threats.

11. List the extensions of files that might typically harbor a virus.

12. Explain how multi-partite, stealth, polymorphic, and retro viruses work.

13. Explain how antivirus software works, and how it is able to catch new viruses that are created after the software is installed on your computer.

14. Describe the various types of boot disks that might help you recover from a hard disk crash.

15. Discuss the pros and cons of each type of backup hardware.

16. Make a list of backup tips that you think would help people devise a solid backup plan.

17. TechTalk: Make a list of at least 20 file extensions you find on the computer you use most often. Group these extensions into the following categories: system files, graphics files, sound files, text files, other.

18. Fill in the blanks in the concept map below that illustrates the hierarchy of malicious code.

Review on the Web

TECHTV VIDEO PROJECT

The TechTV segment *Five Tips to Detect Phishing* highlights some of the tricks used by online scam artists to snag your confidential information. Sorting out legitimate communications from phishing attacks is not easy. After watching the video, use a search engine to find out more about phishing scams and ways to avoid them. If your search engine can find Mailfrontier's phishing quiz, use it to gauge your phishing savvy. Summarize what you've learned about phishing by creating your own list of guidelines to avoid being fooled by phishing attacks.

To work with the Video Projects for this chapter, connect to the New Perspectives NP9 Web site.

www.course.com/np/concepts9/ch04

4

ONLINE GAMES

Test your comprehension of the concepts introduced in Chapter 4 by playing the NP9 Online Games. At the end of each game, you have three options:

- Submit your results to your instructor using the Universal Gradebook through CoursePort
- Print your results to be submitted to your instructor
- Print a comprehensive study guide complete with page references

To work with the Online Games for this chapter, connect to the New Perspectives NP9 Web site.

www.course.com/np/concepts9/ch04

TECHBUZZ

The TechBuzz article at the New Perspectives NP9 Web site features new trends in digital hardware gadgets and gizmos that you can use in conjunction with your computer. As you look at technology trends and as you consider your own lifestyle, what do you expect will be the most useful digital device for you in the next year? What about in the next five years? Before you answer these questions, you might want to browse the Web to find additional information about hardware trends. When you report about the gadgets that will be most useful to you, discuss them in the context of your own lifestyle, and then expand your discussion to the broader population of consumers in your country and others. Submit your summary, making sure you cite your sources.

www.course.com/np/concepts9/techbuzz

ONLINE END-OF-CHAPTER ACTIVITIES

The following NP9 Review Activities are also available at the New Perspectives NP9 Web site:

- Interactive Summary
- Interactive Situation Questions
- Interactive Practice Tests
- Concept Map

If you are using the Web site to complete these activities, you can automatically score your answers and share the results with your instructor.

www.course.com/np/concepts9/ch04

5

Internet and LAN Technology

FOCUS ON THESE LEARNING OBJECTIVES

Describe the characteristics of various networks

Diagram Shannon's model of a communications network

List the types of cables and other links typically used for data communications networks

Make a list of network devices, explain the role of each one, and indicate whether they are typically used on the Internet or with LANs

Describe the role of communications protocols and list some protocols associated with the Internet and LANs

Explain the difference between packet switching and circuit switching technology

Draw a conceptual diagram illustrating the Internet backbone, NAPs, NSPs, routers, and ISPs

Explain when and why you might use Ping and Traceroute utilities

Explain the differences between static IP addresses, dynamic IP addresses, private IP addresses, and domain names

Describe the advantages and disadvantages of dial-up, cable, DSL, ISDN, and fixed wireless Internet access

Explain when and why it is important to implement security measures, such as antivirus software, firewalls, and Network Address Translation

A detailed list of learning objectives is provided at the New Perspectives NP9 Web site:

www.course.com/np/concepts9/ch05

UNDERSTAND THE CHAPTER CONTENTS

❋ **SECTION A: NETWORK BUILDING BLOCKS**

Network Advantages and Challenges
Network Classifications
Geographic Scope: PANs, NANs, LANs, MANs, and WANs
Organizational Structure: Client/Server and Peer-to-Peer
Physical Topology
Network Links
Analog and Digital Signals
Bandwidth
Communications Protocols

❋ **SECTION B: LOCAL AREA NETWORKS**

LAN Standards
Ethernet
Wi-Fi
HomePNA and HomePLC Networks

Installing a LAN
Using a LAN

❋ **SECTION C: INTERNET TECHNOLOGY**

Background
Internet Structure
ISP Infrastructure
Internet Protocols
IP Addresses
Domain Names

❋ **SECTION D: INTERNET ACCESS**

Dial-up Connections
Cable Internet Service
DSL, ISDN, and Dedicated Lines
Wireless Internet Services
LAN Internet Access
Mobile Internet Access
Internet Connection Roundup

❋ **TECHTALK: INTERNET ACCESS SECURITY**

❋ **ISSUE: FREE WI-FI**

❋ **COMPUTERS IN CONTEXT: EDUCATION**

❋ **STUDENT EDITION LABS**

Networking Basics
Connecting to the Internet
Wireless Networking

❋ **NEW PERSPECTIVES LABS**

Tracking Packets
Securing Your Connection

❋ **REVIEW ACTIVITIES**

Interactive Summary
Key Terms
Interactive Situation Questions
Interactive Practice Tests
Projects
Study Tips and Concept Map
Review on the Web

TIP

When using the BookOnCD, the ❋ icons are "clickable" to access resources on the CD. The ⊥ icons are clickable to access resources on the Web. You can also access Web resources by using your browser to connect directly to the New Perspectives NP9 Web site at: www.course.com/np/concepts9/ch05

TODAY, COMPUTING IS ALL ABOUT GETTING CONNECTED—ACCESSING THE

Internet from home or your local Starbucks; hooking into the school network from your dorm room, apartment, or the campus commons; and checking your e-mail from your notebook computer, PDA, or cell phone. To take advantage of the benefits offered by computer networks, a little background information comes in handy. Chapter 5 explains what makes networks tick and offers some pointers for setting up, connecting to, and using networks.

TAKE A PRE-ASSESSMENT QUIZ

Take the pre-assessment quiz to find out how much you know about computer network technologies such as Ethernet, Wi-Fi, and TCP/IP. Armed with your results, you can focus your study time on network concepts that will round out your knowledge and improve your test score.

www.course.com/np/concepts9/ch05

LISTEN TO A CHAPTER OVERVIEW

Get your book and highlighter ready, then connect to the New Perspectives NP9 Web site, where you can listen to an overview that points out the most important concepts for this chapter.

www.course.com/np/concepts9/ch05

BEFORE YOU READ ON, TRY IT

HOW FAST AND DEPENDABLE IS MY INTERNET CONNECTION?

Chapter 5 introduces computer networks and explains how handy they are for sharing files and accessing the Internet at home, at school, or in a business. You can access the Internet in various ways—using your phone line, your cable TV connection, or a personal satellite dish. Is your Internet connection fast enough for activities such as downloading DVDs and playing online multiplayer games? You can discover the speed of your Internet connection by doing the following steps.

1. Make sure your computer is on and click the Start button.

2. Point to Accessories, then click Command Prompt from the list. This action opens what's called a "DOS box."

3. Type Ping www.google.com and then press the Enter key.

4. Your computer makes four attempts to access the Google Web site and measures the time required for each attempt. Fill in the blanks below with the Ping statistics for your computer. When you read the chapter, you'll learn how those statistics stack up for videoconferencing, Voice over IP, and online multiplayer gaming.

5. Click the ☒ button to close the DOS box.

```
Command Prompt                                    _ □ x
Microsoft Windows XP [Version 5.1.2600]
(C) Copyright 1985-2001 Microsoft Corp.

C:\Documents and Settings>ping www.google.com

Pinging www.l.google.com [64.233.161.99] with 32 bytes of data:

Reply from 64.233.161.99: bytes=32 time=92ms TTL=240
Reply from 64.233.161.99: bytes=32 time=92ms TTL=240
Reply from 64.233.161.99: bytes=32 time=86ms TTL=240
Reply from 64.233.161.99: bytes=32 time=84ms TTL=240

Ping statistics for 64.233.161.99:
    Packets: Sent = 4, Received = 4, Lost = 0 (0% loss),
Approximate round trip times in milli-seconds:
    Minimum = 84ms, Maximum = 92ms, Average = 88ms

C:\Documents and Settings>_
```

PING STATISTICS FOR MY COMPUTER

Packets sent: _____

Packets received: _____

Packets lost: _____

Round trip minimum: _____ms

Round trip maximum: _____ms

Round trip average: _____ms

SECTION A
Network Building Blocks

Today, networks are everywhere and network technology is evolving rapidly. Just when you think you have dial-up under control, along come cable access and Wi-Fi. Just as you get comfortable with your school's campus-wide network, everyone is issued notebook computers that use wireless connections. Although network technology continues to evolve, it is based on a set of fairly stable concepts. If you understand these network building blocks, working with new network technologies will be a piece of cake.

NETWORK ADVANTAGES AND CHALLENGES

Why are computer networks advantageous? In the early years of the personal computer's popularity, networks were scarce. Most personal computers functioned as standalone units, and computing was essentially a solitary activity in which one person interacted with a limited set of software tools, such as a word processor, spreadsheet, database, and games.

Some computer engineers, however, had the foresight to anticipate that personal computers could be networked to provide advantages not available with standalone computers. One of the most significant network ideas was conceived by Bob Metcalfe in 1976. His plan for transporting data between computers, shown in Figure 5-1, has become a key element in just about every computer network, including the Internet.

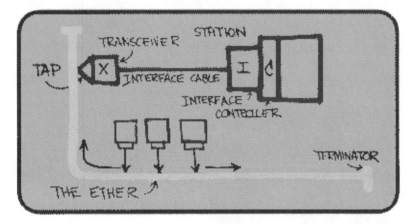

FIGURE 5-1

In 1976, Bob Metcalfe drew this diagram of a network technology, which he called "Ethernet."

Today, the pervasiveness of networks has dramatically changed the face of computing by offering **shared resources**—hardware, software, and data made available for authorized network users to access. Networks offer the following advantages:

■ **Sharing networked hardware can reduce costs.** In an office environment, for example, a single expensive color printer can be purchased and attached to a network, instead of the costly alternative of purchasing color printers for each employee who wants to generate color printouts.

■ **Sharing networked hardware can provide access to a wide range of services and specialized peripheral devices.** A network can allow multiple users to access Internet services through a single Internet connection. Networked peripheral devices, such as scanners, photo printers, plotters, high-capacity storage devices, and computer-aided manufacturing (CAM) equipment, can be accessed by any authorized network users.

■ **Sharing networked software can reduce costs.** Although purchasing and installing a single software copy for an entire network might be technically possible, it is typically not allowed under the terms of a single-user license agreement. However, software site licenses for network use are usually less expensive than purchasing single-user versions of a product for each network user.

■ **Sharing data on a network is easy.** To transfer data between standalone computers, a file is usually copied to some type of removable storage media, and then carried or mailed to the other computer where it is copied onto the hard disk. Networks can provide authorized users with access to data stored on network servers or workstations.

■ **Networks enable people to work together regardless of time and place.** Using groupware and other specialized network application software, several people can work together on a single document, communicate by e-mail and instant messaging, and participate in online conferences and Webcasts (Figure 5-2).

TERMINOLOGY NOTE

Throughout this chapter, the term "workstation" means a personal computer connected to a network.

FIGURE 5-2

An Internet teleconference links participants from multiple geographical locations.

5

Do networks have disadvantages? The primary disadvantage of networks is their vulnerability to unauthorized access. Whereas a standalone computer is vulnerable to on-premises theft or access, network computers are vulnerable to unauthorized access from many sources and locations.

Through unauthorized use of a network workstation, intruders can access data stored on the network server or other workstations. Networks connected to the Internet are vulnerable to intrusions from remote computers in distant states, provinces, or countries. Wireless networks can be tapped from a specially equipped "snooping" computer in a car that's being driven by a hacker.

Networks are also more vulnerable than standalone computers to malicious code. Whereas the most prevalent threat to standalone computers is disk-borne viruses, networks are susceptible to an ever-increasing number of worms, Trojan horses, and blended threats.

Most computer owners are enthusiastic about the benefits provided by networks and believe that those benefits outweigh the risks of intrusions and viruses—especially if their computers can be protected by security tools, such as antivirus software and firewalls. You'll learn more about network security threats and countermeasures later in this chapter.

NETWORK CLASSIFICATIONS

Are there different kinds of networks? In the past, a great diversity of network technologies existed as engineers pioneered various ideas to make data transport faster, more efficient, and more secure. Today, networks are becoming more standardized, but some diversity remains necessary to accommodate networking environments that range from simple household networks to complex global banking networks.

How are networks classified? It would be nice if networks could be neatly classified and we could define a "personal computer network," for example, as consisting of technologies X, Y, and Z. Networks, however, exist in many variations because each one is constructed from a collection of technologies. The network you use in a school lab might be referred to as an "Ethernet," but at the same time it might also be called a "fiber-optic network," and it could further be described as a "local area network." The network you use at home might also be referred to as a "local area network," but it might use HomePLC technology instead of fiber optics and might not be classified as Ethernet.

To understand network classifications and make sense of the network options available for your computer, think of a network as composed of several layers of technology. The technology from a single layer is often used in casual conversation to classify a network, even though it does not provide a complete description of the technologies used in all layers.

Network layers important for classification are described in Figure 5-3. The remainder of Section A explains the components of these network layers in more detail.

FIGURE 5-3

Network Technology Layers

Geographical scope	The area in which network devices are located	WAN, MAN, LAN, NAN, PAN
Organizational structure	The hierarchy of devices connected to a network	Client/server, peer-to-peer
Physical topology	The physical layout and relationship between network devices	Star, bus, ring, mesh, tree
Network links	The technologies for cables and signals that carry data	Twisted-pair cable, coaxial cable, fiber-optic cable, RF signals, microwaves, infrared light, power line, phone line
Bandwidth	The capacity of a network for carrying data	Broadband, narrowband
Communications protocols	The transportation standards that provide an orderly way to package data and make sure data is not corrupted in transit	TCP/IP, SPX/IPX (Novell networks), NetBEUI/NetBIOS (Microsoft networking), AppleTalk

GEOGRAPHIC SCOPE: PANS, NANS, LANS, MANS, AND WANS

Why is geographic scope important? Localized networks typically include a small number of computers, which can be connected using basic equipment. As the area of network coverage expands, the number of workstations grows, specialized devices are sometimes required to boost signals, and the diversity of devices requires sophisticated management tools and strategies. From a geographic perspective, networks can be classified as PANs, NANs, LANs, MANs, and WANs.

What are the options? **PAN** (personal area network) is a term sometimes used to refer to the interconnection of personal digital devices within a range of about 30 feet (10 meters) and without the use of wires or cables. For example, a PAN could be used to wirelessly transmit data from a notebook computer to a PDA or portable printer.

A **NAN** (neighborhood area network) provides connectivity within a limited geographical area, usually spread over several buildings. These networks are becoming popular as local coffee shops and computer hobbyists offer wireless Internet connections.

A **LAN** (local area network) is a data communications network that typically connects personal computers within a very limited geographical area—usually a single building. LANs use a variety of wired and wireless technologies, standards, and protocols. School computer labs and home networks are examples of LANs.

A **MAN** (metropolitan area network) is a public high-speed network capable of voice and data transmission within a range of about 50 miles (80km). Examples of MANs that provide data transport services include local Internet service providers, cable television companies, and local telephone companies.

A **WAN** (wide area network) covers a large geographical area and usually consists of several smaller networks, which might use different computer platforms and network technologies. The Internet is the world's largest WAN. Networks for nationwide banks and multi-location "superstores" can also be classified as WANs.

ORGANIZATIONAL STRUCTURE: CLIENT/SERVER AND PEER-TO-PEER

How are networks structured? A typical organizational chart diagrams the hierarchy of personnel in a business. In a hierarchical business, the president at the top of the chart is the main decision maker. In a "flattened," decentralized chart, decisions are shared among peers. Like a business, networks also have an organizational structure that provides a conceptual model of the way data is stored and transported. The two most prevalent network organizational structures are client/server and peer-to-peer.

What is the difference between a client/server network and a peer-to-peer network? A **client/server network** contains one or more computers configured with server software and other computers, configured with client software, that access the servers. The server provides a centralized repository for data and a transfer point through which data traffic flows. Web sites, retail point-of-sale networks, school registration systems, online databases, and Internet-based multiplayer games typically use a client/server organizational structure.

A **peer-to-peer network** (sometimes called P2P) treats every computer as an "equal" so that workstations can store network data, which can be transported directly to other workstations without passing through a central server. P2P technology forms the basis for file-sharing networks, such as Kazaa and Microsoft Networking provided with Windows. Figure 5-4 contrasts the client/server structure with the peer-to-peer structure.

FIGURE 5-4

In a client/server network, a server is the most important resource. In a peer-to-peer network, every computer is treated as an equal resource.

5

Client/server

Peer-to-peer

PHYSICAL TOPOLOGY

How are the devices on a network physically arranged?
Each connection point on a network is referred to as a **node**. A network node typically contains one of the following devices:

- Server: A computer responsible for storing data and programs

- Workstation: A personal computer connected to a network

- Networked peripheral: A device, such as a printer or scanner, directly connected to a network rather than to a workstation

- Network device: An electronic device that broadcasts network data, boosts signals, or routes data to its destination

The arrangement of devices in a network is referred to as its **physical topology**. Figure 5-5 illustrates star, ring, bus, mesh, and tree topologies; the pathways shown between nodes can be linked by physical cables or wireless signals.

What are the advantages of each topology?
A network arranged as a **star topology** features a central connection point for all workstations and peripherals. The central connection point is not necessarily a server—more typically it is a network device called a **hub**, which is designed to broadcast data to workstations and peripherals. Some hubs are also repeaters. A **repeater** can boost the strength of the signal that carries data over any network topology when the distance between two nodes exceeds the range of their connecting links.

Many home networks are arranged in a star topology. The advantage of this topology is that any link can fail without affecting the rest of the network. Its primary disadvantage is that it requires quite a bit of cable to link all the devices—a disadvantage that disappears with wireless networks. Although the failure of a link does not affect the rest of the network, you can see from Figure 5-5 that a device with a failed link would be cut off from the network and unable to receive data.

A **ring topology** connects all devices in a circle, with each device having exactly two neighbors. Data is transmitted from one device to another around the ring. This topology minimizes cabling, but failure of any one device can take down the entire network. Ring topologies, once championed by IBM, are infrequently used in today's networks.

A **bus topology** uses a common backbone to connect all network devices. The backbone functions as a shared communication link, which carries network data. The backbone stops at each end of the network with a special device called a "terminator." Bob Metcalfe's 1976 network plan was based on a bus topology. However, bus networks work best with a limited number of devices. Bus networks with more than a few dozen computers are likely to perform poorly, and if the backbone cable fails, the entire network becomes unusable.

A **mesh topology** connects each network device to many other network devices. Data traveling on a mesh network can take any of several possible paths from its source to its destination. These redundant data pathways make a mesh network very robust. Even if several links fail, data can follow alternative functioning links to reach its destination—an advantage over networks arranged in a star topology. The original plan for the Internet was based on mesh topology.

FIGURE 5-5

Network Topologies

Star topology

Ring topology

Bus topology

Mesh topology

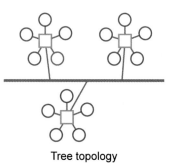

Tree topology

A **tree topology** is essentially a blend of star and bus networks. Multiple star networks are connected into a bus configuration by a backbone. Tree topologies offer excellent flexibility for expansion—a single link to the backbone can add an entire group of star-configured devices. This link can be accomplished using the same type of hub that is used as the central connection point in a star network. Most of today's school and business networks are based on tree topologies.

How **Can various networks be interconnected?** Yes. Two similar networks can be connected by a device called a **bridge**, which simply transfers data without regard to its format. Networks that use different topologies and technologies can be interconnected by using gateways. **Gateway** is a generic term for any device or software code used to join two dissimilar networks by converting data sent from one network into a format compatible to the receiving network. A gateway can be implemented completely in software, completely in hardware, or as a combination of the two.

The most commonly used gateway is a **router**, an electronic device that joins two or more networks. For example, a home network can use a router and a DSL or cable modem to join the home's LAN to the Internet's WAN. A router acts as a LAN's access point to a larger network and can include bridging or conversion capabilities to interact with dissimilar networks. A router accepts incoming data transmissions and distributes them to devices attached to its local network. It also shuttles data from a local network to other networks, as shown in Figure 5-6.

Data addressed to computers in external networks

Router

Data sent from LAN workstations

Hub

LAN workstations

FIGURE 5-6

A router typically connects a LAN to a WAN and filters transmissions between them. The router forwards messages destined for other networks (orange), but keeps local messages (green) within the network.

NETWORK LINKS

What connects the nodes of a network? Data can travel from one network device to another over a cable or through the air. A **communications channel**, or "link," is a physical path or a frequency for a signal transmission. For example, Channel 12 on your TV tuner is a specific frequency used to broadcast audiovisual data for a television station. This data might also be carried over another channel, such as coaxial cable, as part of a cable TV system.

Data in a **wired network** travels from one device to another over cables. Data in a **wireless network** travels through the air, eliminating the need for cables.

What are popular network cabling options? If you install your own home network, it is likely to require twisted-pair cables to connect network devices, such as workstations and hubs. A **twisted-pair cable** is a popular, inexpensive cable designed for telephone and network installations. It typically contains four pairs of copper wires. Each pair of wires is independently insulated and then twisted together, which gives this cable its name. Twisted-pair cables are frequently used in school labs and small business LANs as well as home networks.

When purchasing twisted-pair cable, you have shielding and category options. Shielded twisted-pair cable (STP) contains shielding, which reduces signal noise that might interfere with data transmitted over unshielded cable (UTP). Cable categories (abbreviated as CAT) indicate carrying capacity. CAT 1 is sufficient for telephone cabling, whereas CAT 5 provides more capacity for networking. Twisted-pair cables typically terminate with plastic RJ-11 plugs like those on standard phones, or wider RJ-45 plugs (Figure 5-7).

INFOWEBLINKS

Make your own fiber-optic cable with duct tape and flashlights? You'll find some fun facts as well as solid technical information at the **Fiber Optics InfoWeb**.

www.course.com/np/concepts9/ch05

FIGURE 5-7

Twisted-pair cable is popular for LANs. Some LANs use RJ-11 phone plugs (shown) while others use RJ-45 plugs.

Coaxial cable, often called "coax cable" (pronounced CO ax), consists of a copper wire encased in a nonconducting insulator, a foil shield, a woven metal outer shield, and a plastic outer coating. It is the cable of choice for cable television because its high capacity simultaneously carries signals for hundreds of television channels, with additional capacity for carrying cable modem signals. If you use a cable modem, you'll probably use a coaxial cable to connect it to the cable wall outlet. A coaxial cable is typically terminated with metal BNC or F-type connectors, as shown in Figure 5-8.

FIGURE 5-8

Coaxial cable is a common component of cable television systems. Some networks use the large BNC connectors shown here, while others use slimmer F-type connectors.

Fiber-optic cable is a bundle of extremely thin strands of glass. Each strand, called an optical fiber, is much thinner than a human hair. A fiber-optic cable usually consists of a strong inner support wire, multiple strands of optical fiber (each covered by a plastic insulator), and a tough outer covering (Figure 5-9). Unlike twisted-pair and coaxial cables, fiber-optic cables do not conduct or transmit electrical signals. Instead, miniature lasers convert data into pulses of light that flash through the cables. Fiber-optic cables are an essential part of the Internet backbone and are increasingly found on business and campus networks.

FIGURE 5-9

Fiber-optic cables have good carrying capacity, but are costly and require special installation tools and techniques.

USB, serial, parallel, SCSI, and FireWire cables can also be pressed into service as communications channels. They are typically used to transport data between a computer and a network or communications device. For example, you might use a USB cable to connect your computer to a cable modem or a serial cable to connect your computer to a voiceband modem. Some home networks allow you to make use of existing electrical wiring, using special adapters that connect computers to electrical wall outlets.

What are the options for wireless networks? Most wireless LANs transport data as **RF signals** (radio frequency signals). RF signals—commonly called "radio waves"—are sent and received by a **transceiver** (a combination of a transmitter and a receiver) that is equipped with an antenna. Every network workstation, peripheral device, and hub is equipped with a transceiver, which sends and receives data (Figure 5-10).

Microwaves (the waves themselves, not your oven!) provide another option for transporting data. Like radio waves, microwaves are electromagnetic signals, but they behave differently. Microwaves can be aimed in a single direction and have more carrying capacity than radio waves. However, microwaves cannot penetrate metal objects and work best for "line-of-sight" transmission when a clear path exists between the transmitter and receiver. Microwave installations typically provide data transport for large corporate networks.

Radio and microwave transmissions cannot bend around the surface of the Earth to reach far-flung towers, so Earth-orbiting **communications satellites** play an important role in long-distance communications. A signal can be relayed from a ground station to a communications satellite. On board the satellite, a **transponder** receives a signal, amplifies it, and then retransmits the signal back to a ground station on Earth. Satellite dishes provide a way for people in remote areas to connect personal computers to the Internet.

Today most people are familiar with remote controls that use **infrared light** beams to change television channels. Infrared can also carry data signals, but only for short distances and with a clear line of sight. Its most practical use seems to be for transmitting data between devices connected to a PAN.

ANALOG AND DIGITAL SIGNALS

What's the difference between analog and digital signals? When data is transmitted it usually takes the form of an electromagnetic signal. You can think of these signals as waves that ripple through cables or through the air. Digital signals are transmitted as bits using a limited set of frequencies. Analog signals can assume any value within a specified range of frequencies. Figure 5-11 helps you visualize the difference between digital and analog waves.

Are digital signals better than analog signals? At its most primitive level, digital equipment must be sensitive to only two frequencies—one that represents 1s and one that represents 0s. In contrast, analog equipment such as a telephone or a microphone, must be sensitive to a wide range of audible frequencies, or else it will not be able to pick up and transport very high or very low sounds. The beauty of digital signals is that they require simple circuitry and are easy to "clean up" after being affected by noise.

To understand how digital waves might get cleaned up, suppose that a computer network uses different voltages to transmit 0s and 1s. A "perfect" 0 is sent as -5 volts and a perfect 1 is sent as +5 volts. What if, during trans-

FIGURE 5-10

Wireless LANs transport data between transceivers installed in hubs, workstations, and peripheral devices.

Wireless hub

Wireless network card for workstation

FIGURE 5-11

Digital and Analog Wave Forms

The signals carried on a digital channel are depicted as a stepped wave.

An analog signal is depicted as a smooth wave.

5

mission, some interference changes the voltage of a "perfect" 1 to +3 volts? When the signal is received, the receiving device realizes that +3 volts is not one of the two valid voltages. It "guesses" that a 1 bit (+5 volts) was actually transmitted, and "cleans" the signal by reestablishing its voltage to +5.

In contrast, suppose that interference changes a 1,200 Hz wave in an analog transmission to a 1,233 Hz wave. The receiving device cannot determine whether the 1,233 Hz signal is an error or just one of the many analog values that were originally sent. The 1,233 Hz signal, therefore, remains part of the transmission, even if it is the result of static. Most modern networks carry digital signals rather than analog signals.

BANDWIDTH

What's bandwidth? Networks must move data and move it quickly. **Bandwidth** is the transmission capacity of a communications channel. Just as a four-lane freeway can carry more traffic than a two-lane street, a high-bandwidth communications channel can carry more data than a low-bandwidth channel. For example, the coaxial cable that brings you more than 100 channels of cable TV has a higher bandwidth than your home telephone line. The bandwidth of a digital channel is usually measured in bits per second (bps). The bandwidth of an analog channel is typically measured in hertz (Hz).

To better grasp the significance of bandwidth in a communications network, imagine a dial-up connection's 56 Kbps bandwidth as a narrow bike path that allows a limited amount of slow traffic. A 1.5 Mbps connection through your cable TV company is equivalent to a two-lane highway. A typical LAN, such as a college computer lab, might provide 100 Mbps bandwidth—equivalent to a 260-lane expressway.

High-bandwidth communications systems, such as cable TV and DSL, are sometimes referred to as **broadband**, whereas systems with less capacity, such as the telephone system, are referred to as **narrowband**.

COMMUNICATIONS PROTOCOLS

How does data travel over a network? In 1948, Claude Shannon, an engineer at the prestigious Bell Labs, published an article describing a communications system model applicable to today's voice and data networks.

In Shannon's model, data from a source, such as a network workstation, is encoded and sent over a communications channel to a destination, such as a network printer, storage device, server, or workstation. When data arrives at its destination, it is decoded. Transmission can be disrupted by interference called "noise," which has the potential to corrupt data, making it erroneous or unintelligible (Figure 5-12). Networks use protocols to set standards for encoding and decoding data, guiding data to its destination, and mitigating the effects of noise.

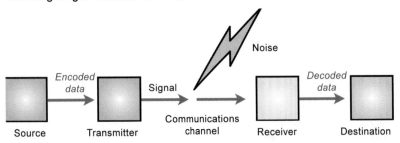

TERMINOLOGY NOTE

Hz is an abbreviation for hertz, which refers to the number of times a wave oscillates, or peaks, per second. Telephone signals are transmitted in the 1,200 Hz range. Many wireless networks transmit a 2.4 GHz signal that peaks 2.4 billion times per second.

FIGURE 5-12

A communications system basically sends information from a source to a destination. Although the path between the source and destination might appear to be straight in the diagram, the data can pass through several devices, which convert it to electrical, sound, light, or radio signals; beam it up to satellites; route it along the least congested links; or clean up parts of the signal that have been distorted by noise.

What is a protocol? In general, a "protocol" is a set of rules for interacting and negotiating. In some respects, it is like signals between the pitcher and catcher in a baseball game. Before the ball is thrown, the catcher and pitcher use hand signals to negotiate the speed and style of the pitch.

In the context of networks, the term "protocol," or **communications protocol**, refers to a set of rules for efficiently transmitting data from one network node to another. Just as a pitcher signals the catcher in baseball, two computers on a network might negotiate their communications protocols through a process called **handshaking**. The transmitting device sends a signal that means "I want to communicate." It then waits for an acknowledgement signal from the receiving device. The two devices "negotiate" a protocol that both can handle. The sounds you hear as two modems or fax machines connect are examples of handshaking.

The best-known communications protocol is probably TCP/IP—popular because it is the protocol that regulates Internet data transport. Figure 5-13 lists some popular communications protocols for computer networks.

What can protocols do? Protocols perform several important network functions, including:

- Dividing messages into packets
- Affixing addresses to packets
- Initiating transmission
- Regulating the flow of data
- Checking for transmission errors
- Acknowledging receipt of transmitted data

What's a packet? When you send a file or an e-mail message, you might suppose that it is transmitted as an entire unit to its destination. This is not the case. Your file is actually chopped up into small pieces called packets. A **packet** is a "parcel" of data that is sent across a computer network. Each packet contains the address of its sender, the destination address, a sequence number, and some data. When packets reach their destination, they are reassembled back into the original message according to the sequence numbers (Figure 5-14).

FIGURE 5-13

Network Protocols

Protocol	Main Use
TCP/IP	Internet
NetBIOS/ NetBEUI	Microsoft networks
AppleTalk	Macintosh networks
IPX/SPX	Novell networks

FIGURE 5-14

Before transmission, communications software divides messages into packets. Upon arriving at their destination, packets are reassembled into the original message.

Why not just send an entire message? Some communications networks, such as the telephone system, use a technology called **circuit switching**, which essentially establishes a dedicated, private link between one telephone and another for the duration of a call. This type of switching provides callers with a direct pipeline over which streams of voice data can flow. Unfortunately, circuit switching is rather inefficient. For example, when someone is "on hold," no communication is taking place—yet the circuit is reserved and cannot be used for other communications.

A more efficient alternative to circuit switching is **packet switching** technology, which divides a message into several packets that can be routed independently to their destination. Messages divided into equal-size pack-

5

ets are easier to handle than an assortment of small, medium, large, and huge files.

Packets from many different messages can share a single communications channel, or "circuit." Packets are shipped over the circuit on a "first come, first served" basis. If some packets from a message are not available, the system does not need to wait for them. Instead, the system moves on to send packets from other messages. The end result is a steady stream of data (Figure 5-15).

FIGURE 5-15

Packet switching networks (left) provide a more efficient communications system than circuit switching networks (right).

Each circuit dedicates an entire channel to one sender and one receiver.

A single line can carry packets from many devices.

Packet switching can even work for tasks once performed by circuit switching networks, for example, by carrying voice conversations. This technology, called **Voice over IP** (VoIP) or "Internet telephony" uses Internet packets to send voices. It can be used instead of land-based or cell phone service and allows you to play games, for example, and chat about your moves—all while you are online.

How are packets routed to their destinations? Every device on a network has an address. Every packet that travels over a network includes the address of its destination device, similar to the way a letter contains the address of a house or mailbox. Communications protocols specify the proper format for addresses within a particular type of network. When a packet reaches a network node, a router examines the address and sends the packet along to its destination or to another router that's closer to the packet's destination.

INFOWEBLINKS

At the **Voice over IP InfoWeb**, you'll find links to software downloads and more information about using the Internet as a voice channel.

www.course.com/np/concepts9/ch05

QuickCheck   SECTION A

1. Networks offer shared [   ], such as printers, software applications, and storage space.

2. Most school computer labs are examples of [   ], whereas the Internet is a WAN. Hint: Use the abbreviation.

3. The central point of connection in a network is often a hub or router. True or false? [   ]

4. A(n) [   ] switching network divides messages into small parcels and handles them on a "first come, first served" basis, whereas a(n) [   ] switching network establishes a dedicated connection between two devices.

 CHECK ANSWERS

SECTION B

Local Area Networks

LANs used to be a fairly esoteric and quirky technology that required certified technicians to "magically" keep all the connections up and running. As network technology stabilized, LANs became a must-have tool for small business. Today, everyone has jumped onto the LAN bandwagon. Small networks are popping up in homes, apartments, and dorm rooms. The key attraction: A LAN allows several computers to share a high-speed Internet connection. Section B provides some general background on LANs and specific details on how to set one up. For information about connecting a LAN to the Internet, refer to Section D.

LAN STANDARDS

What are LAN standards? LAN technologies are standardized by the Institute of Electrical and Electronics Engineers (IEEE) *Project 802 - Local Network Standards*. IEEE standards are available for most types of commercial networks. An IEEE designation number, such as IEEE 802.3, is sometimes used to refer to a network standard in articles and advertisements. When you're shopping for equipment to connect your computer to a network, these designation numbers help you identify compatible network technologies. Historically, several LAN standards have experienced popularity, including ARCnet, Token Ring, and FDDI.

What is ARCnet? Introduced in 1977, **ARCnet** (Attached Resource Computer network) is one of the oldest, simplest, and least expensive LAN technologies. The original ARCnet standard supported transmission rates of 2.5 Mbps. Later versions of ARCnet offered 20 and 100 Mbps transmission rates. A special advantage of ARCnet permits twisted-pair, coax, and fiber-optic cables to be mixed on the same network to connect up to 255 workstations. Although no longer popular for LANs, ARCnet technology is now deployed for applications such as industrial control, building automation, transportation, robotics, and casino gaming.

What is Token Ring technology? A **Token Ring network**, defined by the IEEE 802.5 standard, passes data around a ring topology using a signal called a "token" to control the flow of data. When the token is available, a network device attaches a packet to the token to be carried to its destination. After delivering the packet, the token returns to the sending device, announces a successful delivery, and becomes available to circulate and pick up additional packets (Figure 5-16). The original Token Ring standard carried data at 4 Mbps. In 1989, the speed was increased to 16 Mbps.

Token Ring technology was intensively marketed by IBM. Some Token Ring networks are still operational. However, new network technologies offer faster and less expensive solutions, and by 1999 it was clear that Token Ring was headed for gradual extinction.

5

FIGURE 5-16

To send data on a Token Ring network, a workstation must wait for the token to become available. A packet is then attached to the token and travels around the network until it reaches its destination.

#21
This workstation attached a packet to the token.
TOKEN
To #23
TOKEN

TOKEN
To #23
To #23
TOKEN
#22

#23
This workstation sees its address on the packet and detaches the data from the token.

What is the FDDI standard? **FDDI** (Fiber Distributed Data Interconnect) offers 100 Mbps speeds over fiber-optic cables. As defined by the IEEE 802.8 standards, an FDDI network supports up to 500 devices, cabled as a dual ring—the second ring provides redundancy in case the first ring fails. Like Token Ring networks, FDDI uses a token to control data transmission. Typically, the FDDI ring links network devices, such as servers and routers. Workstations do not connect directly to the ring, but instead connect by twisted-pair cable to a router, as shown in Figure 5-17.

FDDI networks became a popular campus network technology and made some inroads into small businesses. By 1999, however, FDDI was losing ground to less expensive technologies that offered faster data transfer rates.

So what are the current LAN standards? Today, most LANs are configured with Ethernet technology and use compatible Wi-Fi standards in applications that require wireless access. When you connect your computer to a home, school, or workplace network, it will probably use Ethernet or Wi-Fi standards, so these technologies are worth a more detailed look.

ETHERNET

How does Ethernet work? In 1980, Bob Metcalfe's 1976 concept for Ethernet became commercially available. **Ethernet**, defined by IEEE 802.3, simultaneously broadcasts data packets to all network devices. A packet is accepted only by the device to which it is addressed (Figure 5-18).

FIGURE 5-17

FDDI networks connect routers and servers using a double ring topology. Workstations connect to a router rather than to the ring.

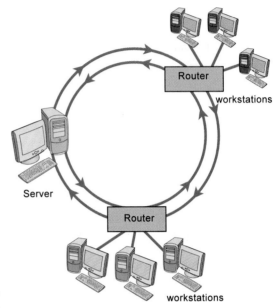

FIGURE 5-18

On an Ethernet, a packet is broadcast to every device, but is accepted only by the device to which it is addressed.

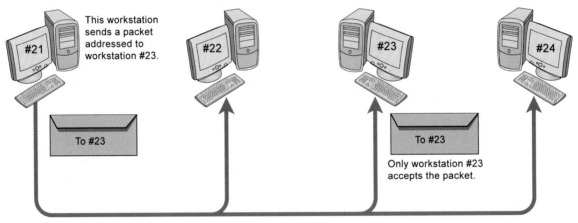

This workstation sends a packet addressed to workstation #23.

To #23

Only workstation #23 accepts the packet.

The packet is broadcast to every device.

An integral part of Ethernet technology relies on **CSMA/CD** protocol (Carrier Sense Multiple Access with Collision Detection). CSMA/CD takes care of situations in which two network devices attempt to transmit packets at the same time. A "collision" occurs and the signals do not reach their destination. CSMA/CD protocol detects the collision, deletes the colliding signals, resets the network, and prepares to retransmit the data. The two devices wait for random time periods before retransmitting to prevent a collision from reoccurring (Figure 5-19).

FIGURE 5-19

On an Ethernet, data travels on a "first come, first served" basis. If two workstations attempt to send data at the same time, a collision occurs. That data must be resent.

CLICK TO START

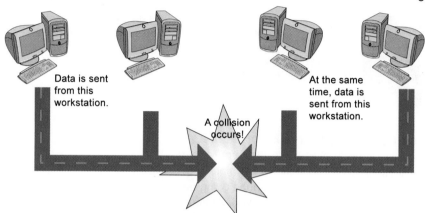

Data is sent from this workstation.

At the same time, data is sent from this workstation.

A collision occurs!

How fast is an Ethernet network? The original Ethernet standard carried data over a coaxial cable bus topology at 10 Mbps. Today, the term "Ethernet" refers to a family of LAN technologies that offer various data transmission rates over fiber-optic and twisted-pair cables arranged in a bus or star topology. Of the Ethernet variations shown in Figure 5-20, Fast Ethernet is currently the most popular for small to medium LANs, like those you might find in homes and small businesses.

Ethernet Standard	IEEE Designation	Speed	Cable
10BaseT Ethernet	IEEE 802.3	10 Mbps	CAT 3 or CAT 5
Fast Ethernet	IEEE 802.3u	100 Mbps	CAT 5 or fiber-optic
Gigabit Ethernet	IEEE 802.3z	1000 Mbps	CAT 5 or fiber-optic
10 Gig Ethernet	IEEE 802.3ae	10 Gbps	Fiber-optic

FIGURE 5-20

Ethernet Standards

What equipment is required for a home Ethernet? Workstations and other devices that connect to an Ethernet require Ethernet circuitry, which can be built into the main board or added as an Ethernet card. An **Ethernet card** is a type of network interface card (NIC), or network adapter, designed to support Ethernet protocols. Many desktop, notebook, and tablet computers include a preinstalled Ethernet card. Ethernet circuitry is also included in some printers and other peripheral devices.

Add-on Ethernet cards for desktop computers fit into a slot inside the system unit. Add-on Ethernet cards for notebook and tablet computers are designed to fit in a PCMCIA slot. The cost of add-on Ethernet cards, such as those shown in Figure 5-21, can be as low as $15.

In addition to Ethernet cards, a home Ethernet network requires some type of link between network nodes—typically CAT 5 twisted-pair cable. These cables link workstations and peripherals to a central connection point called

FIGURE 5-21

Ethernet Cards

5

an Ethernet hub. Today, most Ethernet hubs also serve as routers. Ethernet hubs are available in many configurations offering various numbers of ports. Your hub should have enough ports to accommodate the number of devices you plan to connect to the network. A five-port or an eight-port hub is typical for home networks. A 16-port hub, such as the one in Figure 5-22, might be used in a small business.

FIGURE 5-22

An Ethernet hub or combination hub/router features a collection of ports for connecting servers, workstations, and peripheral devices.

What additional equipment is needed for large Ethernet installations? Large Ethernets typically stretch over a sizable geographic area and connect hundreds or thousands of workstations. A simple step up from a basic single-hub network is to connect several hubs using an **uplink port**. A repeater can boost signals between distant workstations. A bridge can be used to connect two smaller Ethernet segments. Enterprise devices called concentrators allow network builders to add modules containing Ethernet ports to a rack-like case. Equipment for large networks can become quite specialized and beyond the scope of this textbook.

Why is Ethernet so popular? Despite challenges from other technologies, Ethernet has emerged as the leading LAN technology. It is currently used in approximately 85% of LANs worldwide. Ethernet's success is attributable to several factors:

■ Ethernet networks are easy to understand, implement, manage, and maintain.

■ As a nonproprietary technology, Ethernet equipment is available from a variety of vendors, and market competition keeps prices low.

■ Current Ethernet standards allow extensive flexibility in network topology to meet the needs of small and large installations.

Ethernet 802.3 standards pertain to wired networks. Ethernet's cousin, Wi-Fi, provides standards for popular wireless networking options.

INFOWEBLINKS

Ethernet is definitely cool. See what the "Ether" is all about at the **Ethernet InfoWeb**.

www.course.com/np/concepts9/ch05

WI-FI

What is Wi-Fi? Wi-Fi refers to a set of wireless networking technologies defined by IEEE 802.11 standards that are compatible with Ethernet. A Wi-Fi network transmits data as radio waves over predefined frequencies, much like cordless telephones. Wi-Fi networks operate at 2.4 or 5 GHz, as shown in Figure 5-23.

FIGURE 5-23

Wi-Fi Standards

IEEE Designation	Frequency	Speed	Range	Pros/Cons
IEEE 802.11b	2.4 GHz	11 Mbps	100–300 feet	Original standard
IEEE 802.11a	5 GHz	54 Mbps	25–75 feet	Not compatible with 802.11b, g, or n
IEEE 802.11g	2.4 GHz	54 Mbps	100–150 feet	Faster than, but compatible with, 802.11b
IEEE 802.11n	2.4/5 GHz	200 Mbps	100–150 feet	Faster but compatible with b and g

What are the pros and cons of Wi-Fi? The big attraction of Wi-Fi is the absence of wires and cables running through walls and between floors. Wireless networks are especially desirable for notebook and tablet computers that don't otherwise need to be tethered to electrical outlets.

Wi-Fi is similar to cordless telephones in that it uses unlicensed frequencies, such as 2.4 GHZ and 5 GHz. Whereas the frequencies used for broadcast TV, radio, and cable TV require a license from the FCC (Federal Communications Commission), Wi-Fi networks require no license.

When compared to wired networks, Wi-Fi has three disadvantages: slow transmission rates, susceptibility to interference, and lack of security. The fastest Wi-Fi standards operate at a maximum speed of 200 Mbps, but actual throughput is about half the maximum speed.

In a typical office environment, Wi-Fi's range varies from 25 to 150 feet, although considerably more range is possible with additional equipment. Thick cement walls, steel beams, and other environmental obstacles can, however, drastically reduce this range to the point that signals cannot be reliably transmitted. Wi-Fi signals can also be disrupted by interference from electronic devices operating at the same frequency, such as 2.4 GHz cordless telephones.

Wi-Fi signals that travel through the air are easy to intercept by any suitably equipped sending or receiving devices within the network's range of service. One threat to wireless network users is called an "evil twin." Users think they are logging onto a legitimate network, but its signals are being jammed by hackers who can extract passwords and credit card information from unsuspecting users.

A practice called "war driving" or "LAN-jacking" occurs when hackers cruise around with a Wi-Fi-equipped notebook computer set up in "promiscuous mode" to search for Wi-Fi signals coming from home and corporate Wi-Fi networks. War drivers can access and use unsecured Wi-Fi networks to hack into files and gain unauthorized access to larger, wired networks.

Preventing Wi-Fi signal interception is difficult, but encrypting transmitted data using **WEP** (Wired Equivalent Privacy) is an essential step in making your data useless to intruders. The WEP algorithm has been broken, however, so although it is adequate for a typical home network, corporations must establish additional security measures. Despite security concerns and other potential drawbacks, Wi-Fi is becoming increasingly popular in corporate, school, and home networks.

What equipment is required for a Wi-Fi network? As with a wired Ethernet network, every workstation and network peripheral requires network interface circuitry, which can be built in or added as a Wi-Fi card. A **Wi-Fi card** includes a transmitter, receiver, and antenna to transmit signals. Wi-Fi cards for notebook or tablet computers can plug into a PCMCIA slot or USB port. Wi-Fi capability can be added to a desktop computer as a Wi-Fi card that fits into a system unit slot with the antenna protruding out of the back or as a small box that connects to a USB port. Yet another option is to use a wireless adapter to convert a standard Ethernet port into a wireless port. Figure 5-24 illustrates various Wi-Fi cards.

A **wireless access point** performs the same function as a hub or router in a wired Ethernet network by broadcasting signals to any devices with compatible Wi-Fi cards. Many wireless access points also include ports for connecting wired devices and a cable modem (Figure 5-25).

INFOWEBLINKS

For the latest information on Wi-Fi equipment and pricing, check out the **Wireless LAN InfoWeb**.

www.course.com/np/concepts9/ch05

FIGURE 5-24

Wi-Fi Cards

FIGURE 5-25

A wireless access point provides a central point for data transmitted over a Wi-Fi network.

Are any alternative wireless networking technologies available? **Bluetooth** is a short-range wireless network technology that's designed to make its own connections between electronic devices, without wires, cables or any direct action from a user. Unlike Wi-Fi, Bluetooth is not typically used to connect a collection of workstations. Instead, Bluetooth connectivity replaces the short cables that would otherwise tether a mouse, keyboard, or printer to a computer. Bluetooth can also be used to link devices in a PAN, connect home entertainment system components, and to synchronize PDAs with desktop base stations.

Bluetooth is built into some peripheral devices and can be added to personal computers using a variety of add-on cards. The cool feature of Bluetooth-enabled devices is that they automatically find each other and strike up a conversation without any user input at all. Bluetooth operates at the same 2.4 GHz frequency as Wi-Fi, but offers peak transmission rates of only 1 Mbps over a range of about 30 feet (Figure 5-26).

HOMEPNA AND HOMEPLC NETWORKS

What's HomePNA? A **HomePNA network** utilizes existing telephone wiring to connect network devices. The HomePNA network standard uses a special NIC and cable to connect each computer to a standard telephone wall jack. The NICs contain circuitry that eliminates the need for hubs. When your computer is connected to a HomePNA network, you can typically use the phone to make a call and send information over the network at the same time because the network frequency is different from the voice frequency. You cannot, however, make a voice call while a dial-up Internet connection is active.

What's HomePLC? A **HomePLC network**, or "power line network," uses a special NIC to connect a computer to a standard electrical outlet. Data, transmitted as low-frequency radio waves, travels along the electrical wiring until it reaches another network device. Unfortunately, power line fluctuations caused by fluorescent lights, baby monitors, dimmer switches, amateur band radios, air-conditioning units, or other major appliances can disrupt the signal and cause momentary loss of network connections.

How do LAN technologies compare? LANs operate at different speeds, over various distances, and provide unique advantages and disadvantages. Figure 5-27 compares the LAN standards presented in this section.

FIGURE 5-26

Bluetooth technology is used for wireless keyboards and mice, but it is also the technology used for devices like Motorola's Bluetooth headset that clips to a motorcycle helmet so you don't miss important cell calls.

INFOWEBLINKS

For the latest information on HomePNA and HomePLC networks, connect to the **Home Network InfoWeb**.

www.course.com/np/concepts9/ch05

FIGURE 5-27

LAN Technology Comparison

Network Type	Advantages	Disadvantages	Speed
Ethernet	Inexpensive; reliable; standard technology; fast	Unsightly cables; might require running cables through walls, ceilings, and floors	10 Mbps, 100 Mbps, 1 Gbps, 10 Gbps
Wi-Fi	No cables required	Each device requires a transceiver, which adds costs; signals can be intercepted; susceptible to interference from large metal objects and other wireless devices	11 Mbps (802.11b) 54 Mbps (802.11a and 802.11g) 200 Mbps (802.11n)
Bluetooth	Inexpensive; reliable; built into many popular devices	Slow; limited range; little security	1 Mbps (Bluetooth 1.0) 3 Mbps (Bluetooth 2.0)
HomePLC	No cables required; uses any standard electrical outlet	Susceptible to electrical interference; very slow	14 Mbps
HomePNA	No cables required; uses existing telephone wiring	Requires telephone jacks near computers	128 Mbps

INSTALLING A LAN

How do I set up a simple LAN? Setting up a small LAN is easy. Equipment for HomePLC and HomePNA LANs is typically sold in kit form, with detailed instructions on setup procedures. To set up an Ethernet or Wi-Fi LAN, most consumers purchase parts from a computer, electronics, or office store, and follow the setup instructions provided with the hub or router. Figure 5-28 provides an overview of Ethernet and Wi-Fi setup.

INFOWEBLINKS

Your basic shopping list for a simple Ethernet LAN is at the **Building a LAN InfoWeb**.

www.course.com/np/concepts9/ch05

FIGURE 5-28

Installing a LAN

1. To begin, determine if the computers and peripherals you'll connect to the network contain built-in network circuitry. If not, install network cards. Install Ethernet cards for the devices you intend to connect using cables; Wi-Fi cards for devices slated for wireless connections.

CLICK TO START

2. Place the hub or router in a central location and plug it into a surge-protected outlet.

If you are planning to link your LAN to the Internet, connect the hub or router to your Internet connection. (More details on the options for Internet connections are presented in Section D.)

3. For wired connections, run cables from the hub or router to the NIC in each device.

Turn on network devices one at a time. Windows should automatically detect the NICs and establish a connection to the network.

Use the Windows Start menu to access Control Panel. From there, select the Network Setup Wizard to complete the installation process.

5

USING A LAN

How do I access network resources?
If you use Windows, it automatically detects the network any time you turn on a workstation. Depending on your network setup, you might be asked to log in by entering a user ID and password. Once access is established, you can use any shared resources for which you have been given authorization.

You can access shared data on other workstations in a variety of ways. For example, you can use My Computer to access shared resources listed under the My Network Places icon or NetHood folder in Windows Explorer. Resources on other computers are listed as folders or drives; their names might indicate the computer on which they reside. Figure 5-29 shows a NetHood listing of available network resources.

FIGURE 5-29

Windows Explorer lists drives and folders that network users designate as shared. This example shows Jane Cook's directory listing. She can access any of the items listed in the NetHood folder by clicking them just as she would click to open her own drives, folders, and files.

On some networks, NetHood cannot find all the shared drives and folders, so some might not be listed. If you want to access a shared resource that is not listed, you can use the Map Network Drive tool. **Drive mapping** assigns a drive letter to a storage device located on a network workstation (Figure 5-30).

FIGURE 5-30

In this drive mapping example, a server's drive C is mapped as drive F by a workstation. After the mapping is complete, the server's hard disk appears in the workstation's directory as drive F and can be used just as though it were a drive connected directly to the workstation.

CLICK TO START

How do I specify which resources can be shared by other workstations?
If your computer is part of a network, you can typically specify which of your drives and folders can be accessed from other network workstations. For security reasons, however, it is not advisable to allowed shared access to the root directory of your C: drive.

You can allow other network users to view and edit files in the folders you've designated as shared, or you can limit access only to viewing. Figure 5-31 explains how to use Windows to designate a folder as shared.

What if my network connection stops working? Network connections can quit functioning for a variety of reasons. As shown in Figure 5-32, you can use the Windows Network Connections tool for basic troubleshooting. You can also use this tool to temporarily disable a connection, create new connections, change security settings, and see your network connection status—its speed and how long it has been connected.

FIGURE 5-31

To make a folder on your computer available to other network users, right-click the folder name from Windows Explorer or My Computer. Use the pop-up menu to select Sharing and Security. Using the dialog box shown at left, check the box for *Share this folder on the network.* If you want to allow users to edit the files in the shared folder, click the next check box, too.

FIGURE 5-32

The Network Connection tool, accessed from Control Panel, helps troubleshoot connection problems.

QuickCheck

1. A(n) [＿＿＿＿＿＿] LAN simultaneously broadcasts data packets over all network links and uses CSMA/CD protocol to handle collisions.

2. Today's most popular wireless LAN technology is compatible with Ethernet and called [＿＿＿＿＿＿].

3. [＿＿＿＿＿＿] is a short-range technology used for PANs.

4. A Home [＿＿＿＿＿＿] network uses existing telephone wiring, whereas a Home [＿＿＿＿＿＿] uses power lines.

✦ CHECK ANSWERS

SECTION C

Internet Technology

To most people, the Internet seems like old hat. Even people who haven't used the Internet know a lot about it from watching the news, reading magazines, and watching movies. Using the Internet is actually pretty easy. Browsing Web sites, shopping at the Net mall, sending e-mail, and chatting online? No problem. But what makes the Internet "tick"? How can one network offer so much information to so many people? Section C pulls back the curtain and gives you a glimpse of what happens behind the scenes on the Net.

BACKGROUND

How did the Internet get started? The history of the Internet begins in 1957 when the Soviet Union launched Sputnik, the first man-made satellite. In response to this display of Soviet superiority, the U.S. government resolved to improve its scientific and technical infrastructure. One of the resulting initiatives was the Advanced Research Projects Agency (ARPA).

ARPA swung into action with a project designed to help scientists communicate and share valuable computer resources. The ARPANET, created in 1969, connected computers at UCLA, Stanford Research Institute, University of Utah, and University of California at Santa Barbara (Figure 5-33). In 1985, the National Science Foundation (NSF) used ARPANET technology to create a similar, but larger, network, linking not just a few mainframe computers, but entire LANs at each site. Connecting two or more networks creates an "inter-network" or "internet." The NSF network was an internet (with a lowercase "i"). As this network grew throughout the world, it became known as the Internet (with an uppercase "I").

Early Internet pioneers—mostly educators and scientists—used primitive command-line user interfaces to send e-mail, transfer files, and run scientific calculations on Internet supercomputers. Finding information was not easy. Without search engines, Internet users relied on word of mouth and e-mail to keep informed about new data and its location. "The data you need is on the Stanford computer in a file called Chrome.txt." was typical of messages between colleagues.

How did the Internet become so popular? In the early 1990s, software developers created new user-friendly Internet access tools, and Internet accounts became available to anyone willing to pay a monthly subscription fee. Today, the Internet connects computers all over the globe and supplies information to people of all ages and interests.

How big is the Internet today? With an estimated 200 million nodes and 500 million users, the Internet is huge. Although exact figures cannot be determined, it is estimated that Internet traffic exceeds 100 terabytes each week—about 100 trillion bytes. That's approximately 10 times the amount of data stored in the entire printed collection of the U.S. Library of Congress.

FIGURE 5-33

An original diagram of the ARPANET included four nodes, depicted as circles.

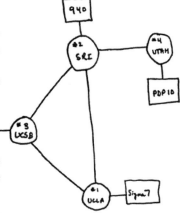

TERMINOLOGY NOTE

A few years ago, Wired News announced it would no longer capitalize the word "Internet," a move supported by National Public Radio and several prominent linguists. Most style guides, however, still recommend that you capitalize references to the global communications network called the Internet.

INTERNET STRUCTURE

How is the Internet structured? Surprisingly, the Internet is not "owned" or operated by any single corporation or government. It is a data communications network that grew over time in a somewhat haphazard configuration as networks connected to other networks.

In Chapter 1 you learned that the Internet backbone provides the main high-speed routes for data traffic. At one time, the topology of the Internet backbone and interconnected networks might have resembled a spine with ribs connected along its length. Today, however, it more resembles a map of interstate highways with many junctures and redundant routes.

How does the backbone tie the Internet together? The Internet backbone consists of high-speed fiber-optic links connecting high-capacity routers that direct network traffic. Backbone links and routers are maintained by **network service providers** (NSPs), such as AT&T, MCI, Qwest, Sprint, and UUNET. NSP equipment and links are tied together by **network access points** (NAPs), so that, for example, data that begins its journey on an AT&T link can cross over to a Sprint link, if necessary, to reach its destination.

Large ISPs connect directly to backbone routers. Smaller ISPs typically connect to a larger ISP to gain Internet access and supply it to their customers. Figure 5-34 shows a simplified, conceptual diagram of the Internet backbone and its components.

5

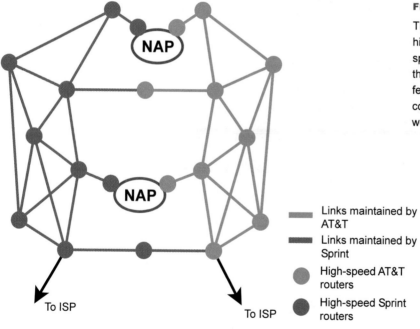

FIGURE 5-34

The Internet backbone includes high-speed routers and high-speed fiber-optic links. Parts of the backbone maintained by different communications companies are connected at network access points (NAPs).

Is it possible to track data as it travels over the Internet? You can track the route of data you send using Internet utilities, such as Ping and Traceroute. An Internet utility called **Ping** (Packet Internet Groper) sends a signal to a specific Internet address and waits for a reply. If a reply arrives, Ping reports that the computer is online and displays the elapsed time, or **latency**, for the round-trip message. Ping is useful for finding out whether a site is up and running.

Ping is also useful for determining whether a connection offers adequate speed for videoconferencing, Voice over IP, or online computer games. If you want to play online multiplayer games, it is best to have a ping rate of 100 ms (milliseconds) or less. Good quality Voice over IP and videoconferencing require ping rates of 200 ms or less.

Ping also shows whether packets were lost in transmission. Packets can become lost when signal interference or network congestion overwhelms Internet servers and routers. Lost packets can cause jitter in Voice over IP communications and videoconferencing. Too many lost packets during an online gaming session can cause the game to stutter or stall. And if packets don't arrive in the correct order, your game character might seem to act randomly for a few seconds.

A utility called **Traceroute** records a packet's path—including intermediate routers—from your computer to its destination. Figure 5-35 contains a Traceroute report.

INFOWEBLINKS

Would you like a color map showing your data's path through cyberspace? Check out the **Traceroute Utilities InfoWeb**.

www.course.com/np/concepts9/ch05

A list of routers indicates the path of the packet sent by Traceroute.

The trace timed out before the packet arrived at its destination—all in all, a "bad" connection.

Latency between 757 ms and 3378 ms indicates a very "slow" round-trip.

FIGURE 5-35

In this example, Traceroute is used to monitor an Internet connection between a small lakeside cabin in northern Michigan and the HotWired Web site. The satellite connection has extremely high latency and timed out before the Web site could be accessed.

How fast does data travel over the Internet? Using Ping or Traceroute, you can discover how long data is in transit from point A to point B. On average, data within North America usually arrives at its destination in less than 100 ms after it is sent. Overseas transmission usually requires a little more time.

ISP INFRASTRUCTURE

What kinds of network devices are part of an ISP? An ISP operates network devices that handle the physical aspects of transmitting and receiving data from your computer. For example, an ISP that offers telephone modem connections must maintain a bank of modems that answer when your computer dials the ISP's access number.

Many ISPs operate e-mail servers to handle incoming and outgoing mail for their subscribers and some also have Web servers for subscriber Web sites. An ISP might also operate a server that translates an address, such as *www.google.com*, into a valid, numeric Internet address, such as 208.50.141.12. You'll learn more about this topic later in the chapter. ISPs can also maintain servers for chat groups, instant messaging, music file sharing, FTP, and other file transfer services (Figure 5-36 on the next page).

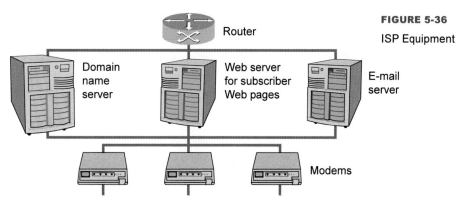

FIGURE 5-36

ISP Equipment

How does my computer fit into the structure of the Internet? Your computer connects to the Internet in one of two ways (Figure 5-37). It can link directly to an ISP using a device such as a voice-band modem, cable modem, satellite dish, or DSL modem. Or, if your computer is part of a LAN, an Internet connection can be provided by a LAN link. Section D provides detailed information on linking computers and networks to the Internet.

INTERNET PROTOCOLS

What protocols are used by the Internet? TCP/IP is a combination of protocols; working together, TCP and IP serve as the primary protocols responsible for message transmission on the Internet. **TCP** (Transmission Control Protocol) breaks a message or file into packets. **IP** (Internet Protocol) is responsible for addressing packets so that they can be routed to their destination. From a practical perspective, TCP/IP provides a protocol standard for the Internet that is easy to implement, public, free, and extensible.

Is TCP/IP limited to the Internet? No. TCP/IP is also used on LANs and WANs. A local area network that uses TCP/IP is called an **intranet**. Intranets are popular with businesses that want to store information as Web pages but not provide them for public access. An intranet that provides private, external access is called an **extranet**.

Is TCP/IP the only Internet protocol? No. Several other protocols are used with TCP/IP on the Internet. Figure 5-38 briefly describes some of them.

FIGURE 5-37

Your computer can connect to the Internet as a standalone device or part of a LAN.

FIGURE 5-38

Protocols Used on the Internet

Protocol	Name	Function
HTTP	Hypertext Transfer Protocol	Exchanges information over the Web
FTP	File Transfer Protocol	Transfers files between local and remote host computers
POP	Post Office Protocol	Transfers mail from an e-mail server to a client Inbox
SMTP	Simple Mail Transfer Protocol	Transfers e-mail messages from client computers to an e-mail server
IMAP	Internet Mail Access Protocol	An alternative to POP
TELNET	Telecommunication Network	Allows users who are logged on to one host to access another host
SSL	Secure Sockets Layer	Provides secure data transfer over the Internet

IP ADDRESSES

Does the Internet use a special addressing scheme? The "IP" part of TCP/IP defines the format for the addresses that identify computers on the Internet. As a result, these addresses are referred to as **IP addresses**; however, you might also see them referred to as "TCP/IP addresses" or "Internet addresses."

An IP address is a series of numbers, such as 204.127.129.1. When written, an IP address is separated into four sections by periods for the convenience of human readers (Figure 5-39). The number in each section cannot exceed 255. Each section is called an **octet** because in binary it is represented by eight bits. An entire IP address requires 32 bits.

204.	127.	129.	1
Octet	Octet	Octet	Octet

FIGURE 5-39

Each section of an IP address, called an octet, can contain a number from 0–255.

Does each octet correspond to part of a URL? Although an IP address, such as 216.247.67.77, might correspond to a URL, such as *http://www.mediatechnics.net*, the octets do not map to the parts of a URL. That means the first octet, 216, does not correspond to *http://*. Nor does the second octet, 247, map to *www*. Instead, IP address octets designate specific networks and subnetworks. Octets 216.247, for example, designate a network called Interland that hosts the MediaTechnics Web site.

Do I need a permanent IP address? A computer can have a permanently assigned **static IP address** or a temporarily assigned **dynamic IP address**. As a general rule, computers on the Internet that act as servers use static IP addresses. Typically, ISPs, Web sites, Web hosting services, and e-mail servers are constantly connected to the Internet and require static addresses.

Theoretically, the IP addressing scheme provides approximately 4.3 billion unique addresses—a meager number considering the growing demands of today's information-hungry consumers. Happily, you don't need a static IP address to engage in client (as opposed to server) activities, such as surfing the Web, sending and receiving e-mail, listening to Internet radio, or participating in chat groups. A "temporary" dynamic IP address suffices for these activities.

When do I get a dynamic IP address? Every ISP controls a unique pool of IP addresses, which can be assigned as needed to subscribers. ISPs assign dynamic IP addresses for most dial-up connections and some DSL, ISDN, or cable Internet service connections.

When you use a dial-up connection, for example, your ISP assigns a temporary IP address to your computer for use as long as it remains connected. When you end a session, that IP address goes back into a pool of addresses that can be distributed to other subscribers when they log in.

INFOWEBLINKS

Want to know how to find your current IP address? It's easy. You can find out how at the **IP Address InfoWeb**.

www.course.com/np/concepts9/ch05

Your computer is rarely assigned the same IP address it had during a previous dial-up session. As a dial-up "nomad" with no permanent address, you can't feasibly run a Web site or perform other server-related activities from your computer because your previous IP address—the one that your customers recorded in their Favorites lists and the one that appears in search engines—does not remain assigned to your computer after you log off.

The address situation for DSL, ISDN, and cable Internet service subscribers varies, depending on the ISP. You might be assigned a static IP address; you might be given a dynamic address each time you connect; or you might be allocated a semi-permanent address that lasts for several months. If you want to operate a server over a DSL, ISDN, or cable Internet connection, ask your ISP about its method of address allocation and its policies on allowing server activities.

DOMAIN NAMES

What's a domain name? Although IP addresses work for communication between computers, people find it difficult to remember long strings of numbers. Therefore, many Internet servers also have an easy-to-remember name, such as *nike.com*. The official term for this name is "fully qualified domain name" (FQDN), but most people just refer to it as a **domain name**. By convention, you should type domain names using all lowercase letters.

A domain name is a key component of URLs and e-mail addresses. It is the Web server name in a URL and the e-mail server name in an e-mail address. For example, in the URL *www.msu.edu/infotech*, the domain name is *msu.edu*. In the e-mail address *jbillings@msu.edu*, the domain name is also *msu.edu*.

A domain name ends with an extension that indicates its **top-level domain**. For example, in the domain name *msu.edu*, *edu* indicates that the computer is maintained by an educational institution. Some of the most commonly used top-level domains are listed in Figure 5-40.

Domain	Description
biz	Unrestricted use; usually for commercial businesses
com	Unrestricted use; usually for commercial businesses
edu	Restricted to North American educational institutions
gov	Restricted to U.S. government agencies
info	Unrestricted use
int	Restricted to organizations established by international treaties
mil	Restricted to U.S. military agencies
net	Unrestricted use; traditionally for Internet administrative organizations
org	Unrestricted use; traditionally for professional and nonprofit organizations

FIGURE 5-40

Top-level Domains

Country codes also serve as top-level domains. Canada's top-level domain is ca; the United Kingdom's is uk; Australia's is au. A domain with growing popularity is tv. Originally assigned to the small Polynesian island of Tuvalu, the tv domain is marketed by a professional management team and is available for a fee to media-related Web sites.

How are domain names related to IP addresses? Every domain name corresponds to a unique IP address that has been entered into a huge database called the **Domain Name System** (DNS). Computers that host this database are referred to as **domain name servers**. A domain name, such as *travelocity.com*, must be converted into an IP address before any packets can be routed to it. For example, when you type the URL *www.travelocity.com* into your browser, the browser's first step is to contact a domain name server to get the IP address for the Travelocity Web server, as shown in Figure 5-41.

FIGURE 5-41

A domain name request is routed through your ISP to your designated domain name server, which searches through its database to find a corresponding IP address. The IP address can then be attached to packets, such as requests for Web pages.

ISP

www.travelocity.com

www.travelocity.com

Domain name server

151.193.165.126

You enter the URL: www.travelocity.com on your computer.

The Domain Name System is based on a distributed database. Amazingly, this database is not stored as a whole in any single location; instead, it exists in parts all over the Internet. Your Internet connection is set up to access one of the many domain name servers that reside on the Internet. When you enter a domain name or URL, it is sent to your designated domain server, which can do one of three things:

- It can send back the IP address that corresponds to the domain name.

- If your domain name server does not have a record of the domain name, it can contact another domain name server and request the IP address.

- It can send back the address for a domain name server that is more likely to have the IP address of the domain name you requested.

The servers in the Domain Name System are quite efficient and typically manage to supply IP addresses in a matter of milliseconds.

Do I need my own domain name? For client-style Internet activities, such as Web browsing, e-mail, and chat, you do not need your own domain name. You might, however, want a domain name if you plan to operate your own Web server or if you establish a Web site using servers provided by a Web site hosting service.

Suppose you decide to set up a Web site called Rocky Mountain Photos. If you would like people to access your site by typing *www.rockymtnphotos.com*, you must obtain the *rockymtnphotos.com* domain name. In contrast, if your Web site is set up on a Web server supplied by your ISP, your own domain name might not be necessary because you use the domain of the ISP's Web server. For example, if you set up your Rocky Mountain Photos on AOL's Hometown Web server, your URL might be *hometown.aol.com/rockymtnphotos*.

How do I get a domain name? An organization called **ICANN** (Internet Corporation for Assigned Names and Numbers) is recognized by the United States and other governments as the global organization that coordinates technical management of the Internet's Domain Name System. It supervises several for-profit Accredited Domain Registrars, which handle domain name requests.

INFOWEBLINKS

Where can you register a domain name? What are the current fees? These questions are answered at the **Domain Name InfoWeb**.

www.course.com/np/concepts9/ch05

The first step in registering a domain name is to find out whether the name is available. By connecting to an Accredited Domain Registrar Web site, you can enter a domain name, as shown in Figure 5-42.

FIGURE 5-42

The first step in registering a domain name is to find out whether the name is currently in use or reserved for future use.

If a domain name is not available, consider using a different top-level domain, such as biz instead of com.

After you've found an available domain name you like, you can continue the registration process by filling out a simple online form.

CLICK TO START

Is a fee required to obtain a domain name? You can register a domain name for a minimal annual fee—currently between $10 and $50, depending on the registration service.

Some domain names are not currently in use, yet they are not available because they are reserved. Internet entrepreneurs have made a business of registering high-profile domain names with the intention of reselling them. For example, the domain name *message.com* is "for sale" for the tidy sum of $750,000; *drugstore.net* has a price tag of $200,000. To obtain one of these domain names, you must purchase it from the seller. After you pay for the name, you can register it for the standard annual fee.

QuickCheck   SECTION C

1. Network _____ providers, such as AT&T and UUNET, maintain links and routers on the Internet backbone.

2. A utility called _____ checks whether a network computer is online and displays the elapsed time for a round-trip message.

3. The _____ protocol breaks a message or file into packets; _____ is responsible for addressing packets so that they can be routed to their destination. Hint: Use acronyms.

4. Internet servers typically have a(n) _____ IP address.

5. An Internet address, such as *msu.edu*, is called a fully qualified _____ name.

CHECK ANSWERS

SECTION D

Internet Access

One of the most challenging aspects of the Internet is selecting a connection. Although most people begin with a dial-up connection, many soon explore high-speed Internet access options. Home-based LANs and wireless Internet access have become very popular. In this section of the chapter, you'll discover why online interactive game players shun satellite Internet connections. You'll learn why DSL and cable Internet service might leave your computer open to hackers who cruise the Internet searching for user IDs, passwords, and launching points for bothersome viruses. To learn how to close up network security holes, when you complete Section D read on to the TechTalk.

DIAL-UP CONNECTIONS

How does a dial-up connection work? A dial-up connection uses **POTS** (plain old telephone service) to transport data between your computer and your ISP. To understand how it works, you'll need a little background on telephone communications.

The telephone communications system uses a tiered network to transport calls locally, cross-country, and internationally. At each level of the network, a switch creates a connection so that a call eventually has a continuous circuit to its destination. The first tier of this network uses a star topology to physically connect each telephone in a city to a switch in what's called a "switching station," "local switch," or "central office."

The second tier of the telephone network links several local switching stations. Connections then fan out to switches maintained by many different local and long-distance telephone companies, as shown in Figure 5-43.

FIGURE 5-43

The telephone system connects your telephone to a local switch. Local switches are connected to other nearby local switches and to long-haul communications links.

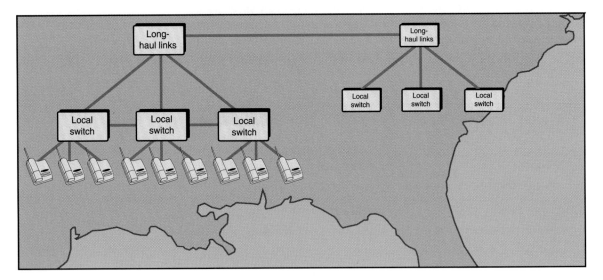

When you use a dial-up connection, your computer's modem essentially places a regular telephone call to your ISP. Your call is routed through the telephone company's local switch and out to the ISP. When the ISP's computer "answers" your call, a dedicated circuit is established between you and your ISP—just as though you had made a voice call and someone at the ISP had "picked up" the phone. The circuit remains connected for the duration of your call and provides a communications link that carries data between your computer and the ISP. As your data arrives at the ISP, a router sends it out over the Internet. Figure 5-44 illustrates the path of your data when you use a dial-up connection.

FIGURE 5-44

When you use an ISP to access the Internet, your data travels through the local telephone switch to your ISP, which sends it onto the Internet.

To the Internet

ISP's modem

ISP's router

Telephone wall jack

Your computer and modem

How does a modem work? The signals that represent data bits exist in your computer as digital signals. The telephone system, however, expects to work with human voices, so the "stuff" that it carries must be in the format of analog audio tones. It's as though you are trying to move a bunch of ice cubes through a tube. If the cubes won't fit through the tube, you can melt them into water, which can flow through the tube. A voiceband modem—usually referred to simply as a "modem"—converts the signals from your computer into signals that can travel over telephone lines. A modem transmits a 1,070 Hz tone for a 0 and a 1,270 Hz tone for a 1.

The word "modem" is derived from the words "modulate" and "demodulate." In communications terminology, **modulation** means changing the characteristics of a signal, as when a modem changes a digital pulse into an analog audio signal. **Demodulation** means changing a signal back to its original state, as when a modem changes an audio signal back to a digital pulse (Figure 5-45).

INFOWEBLINKS

If you're curious about the latest modem technology, speed, and prices, check out the **Modem InfoWeb**.

www.course.com/np/concepts9/ch05

FIGURE 5-45

When you transmit data, your modem modulates the signal that carries your data. A modem at the other end of the transmission demodulates the signal.

5

Digital signal

Analog audio signal

Digital signal

Your computer generates a digital signal.

Your modem changes the digital signal into an analog audio signal.

The receiving modem converts the analog signal back into a digital signal.

When your computer's modem initiates a connection, it sends a signal that is equivalent to picking up the receiver of a telephone to get a dial tone. It then dials the ISP by emitting a series of tones—the same tones you'd produce if you punched in the ISP's number using a phone keypad. The modem then waits for the ISP's modem to answer the call. After the ISP's modem answers, the two modems begin to negotiate communications protocols, such as transmission rate. The series of beeps, tones, and whooshing sounds you hear when you connect to your ISP is the sound of your modem "talking" to the ISP's modem. When the negotiation, or "handshaking," is complete, data transmission can begin.

Why doesn't new digital telephone technology eliminate the need for a modem? Although telephone companies went digital long ago, their digital switches kick into action only after your call arrives at the local switching station. The technology between your telephone and your local switch would be recognizable to Alexander Graham Bell. The "local loop," as it is sometimes called, is designed to carry analog voice signals.

To transport data over this local loop, the digital signals from your computer must be converted into analog tones that can travel over the telephone lines to your local switch. When these signals arrive at the local switch, they are converted into digital signals—but not in the same digital format as they originated from your computer—so that they can be sent over the digital section of the telephone network. With all this conversion, it seems amazing that data actually reaches its destination!

Can I talk and send data at the same time? When your computer is connected to your ISP over a dial-up connection, data is transmitted over the same frequencies normally used for voice conversations. If you have only one telephone line, you cannot pick up your telephone receiver, dial your friend, and carry on a voice conversation while you are sending data. Some modems use technology similar to call waiting that allows you to remain connected to your ISP and temporarily suspend data transfers while answering a voice call.

How fast is a modem? When modems were a new technology, their speed was measured as **baud rate**—the number of times per second that a signal in a communications channel varies or makes a transition between states. An example of such a transition is the change from a signal representing a 1 bit to a signal representing a 0 bit. A 300-baud modem's signal changes state 300 times each second, but—and this is the tricky part—each baud doesn't necessarily carry one bit. So a 300-baud modem might be able to transmit more than 300 bits per second.

To help consumers make sense of modem speeds, they are now measured in bits per second. (If you're a stickler for details, you'll realize that bps is actually a measure of capacity, but everyone calls it "speed.") Since 1998, most modems use a standard called V.90 to provide a theoretical maximum speed of 56 Kbps. Actual data transfer speeds are affected by factors such as the quality of your local loop connection to the telephone switch. Even with a "perfect" connection, a 56 Kbps modem tops out at about 44 Kbps. Slightly faster speeds are possible with V.92 and V.44 modems (Figure 5-46).

FIGURE 5-46

Modems with V.92/V.44 technology are gradually replacing the V.90 standard.

Many Internet connection methods provide faster **downstream** (the data you receive) transmission rates than **upstream** (the data you send) rates. Dial-up connections are no exception; 44 Kbps is a typical downstream speed for a 56 Kbps modem. Upstream, the data rate drops to about 33 Kbps or less.

CABLE INTERNET SERVICE

How does cable Internet service work? The cable television system was originally designed for remote areas where TV broadcast signals could not be received in an acceptable manner with an antenna. These systems were called "community antenna television," or CATV. The CATV concept was to install one or more large, expensive satellite dishes in a community, catch TV signals with these dishes, and then send the signals over a system of cables to individual homes.

The satellite dish "farm" at which television broadcasts are received and retransmitted is referred to as the **head-end**. From the head-end, a cabling system branches out and eventually reaches consumers' homes.

The topology of a CATV system looks a lot like the physical topology for a computer network. And that is just what is formed when your cable TV company becomes your Internet provider. A router and high-speed connection from the head-end to the Internet provide the potential for Internet connectivity over every cable in the system. Your computer becomes part of a neighborhood LAN like the one depicted in Figure 5-47.

FIGURE 5-47

Cables from the CATV head-end branch out to neighborhoods where customer computers are grouped into small networks. The cable that comes from the pole to a customer's home is referred to as a "drop."

5

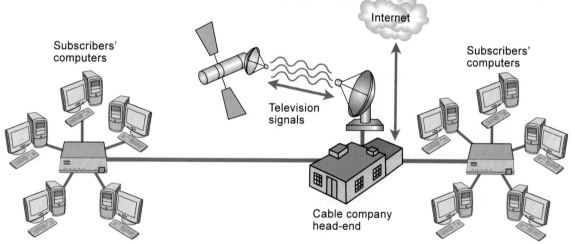

Subscribers' computers
Internet
Television signals
Subscribers' computers
Cable company head-end

Are television and data signals carried over the same cable? The lowest-capacity coaxial cable the CATV system uses has a far greater carrying capacity than POTS lines. Cable Internet service plans offer speeds up to 6 Mbps. To offer both television and Internet access, the cable's bandwidth is divided among three activities. As shown in Figure 5-48, a CATV cable must provide bandwidth for television signals, incoming data signals, and outgoing data signals.

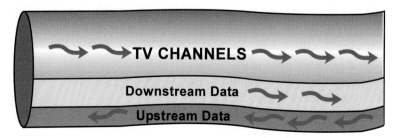

TV CHANNELS
Downstream Data
Upstream Data

FIGURE 5-48

A CATV cable has enough band-width to support TV channels and data flowing downstream as well as data flowing upstream.

How do I set up cable Internet service? When you configure your computer for cable Internet service, you are essentially connecting to an Ethernet-style LAN that connects a neighborhood of cable subscribers. The two requirements for this type of connection are circuitry to handle Ethernet protocols and a cable modem, which converts your computer's signal into one that can travel over the CATV network.

Some cable modems include Ethernet circuitry, and they can be connected directly to your computer's USB port. If the cable modem does not contain Ethernet circuitry, your computer must be equipped with an Ethernet card. Figure 5-49 shows how to connect a cable modem to a desktop computer's Ethernet card.

INFOWEBLINKS

For an in-depth look at cable modem technology, connections, bandwidth, and security, follow the links at the **Cable Modem InfoWeb**.

www.course.com/np/concepts9/ch05

FIGURE 5-49

If your home has only one CATV cable outlet, you need to use a splitter to link your cable modem and television. If you have multiple cable outlets, you can connect your cable modem directly to any one of them.

A standard coaxial cable connects the cable modem to your cable TV wall outlet or a splitter.

Cable modem

An Ethernet card is installed in a slot on your computer's system board.

A cable connects the Ethernet card to the cable modem.

Unlike a dial-up connection that's connected only for the duration of your call, cable Internet service provides an **always-on connection** that is "on" whenever your computer is powered up—whether or not you are online using a browser, an e-mail client, FTP, or other Internet utility. With an always-on connection, you might have the same IP address for days or even months, depending on your ISP. Because your computer is connected to the Internet for long periods of time, an always-on connection is particularly vulnerable to hackers. Gaining access to unprotected computers allows hackers to steal data, launch virus attacks, and send e-mail from your account.

What's the significance of becoming part of a "neighborhood network"? When your cable connection is up and running, your computer becomes part of a neighborhood data network that includes any of your neighbors who subscribe to cable Internet service. Two issues become significant: bandwidth and security.

The cable you share with your neighbors has a certain amount of bandwidth. As more and more neighbors use the service, it might seem to get slower and slower. As an analogy, consider the luggage conveyor belt in an airport, which moves at a constant speed. If you have three pieces of luggage and you are the only passenger on the plane, your bags arrive one right after another. However, if you just arrived on a full 747, your bags are intermixed with those of hundreds of other passengers, and it takes longer to collect them.

Your cable company's network carries packets at a constant speed. However, if many of your neighbors are sending and receiving packets at the same time, those packets seem to arrive more slowly.

As for the security issue, in the early days of cable Internet service, some cable Internet subscribers were unpleasantly surprised when they happened to open Windows Network Neighborhood, only to be greeted with a list of their neighbors' computers! When you have an Ethernet card in your PC, Windows automatically takes inventory of any LANs during bootup, and looks for any computers on the network that have file and printer sharing activated, and then lists them in the My Network Places or NetHood window, as shown in Figure 5-50.

FIGURE 5-50

If your PC is part of a network and has file and printer sharing activated, other network users might be able to access your files by opening the My Network Places or NetHood window.

Today, most cable companies use DOCSIS-compliant cable modems that block "crossover" traffic between subscribers. **DOCSIS** (Data Over Cable Service Interface Specification) is a security technology that filters packets to certain ports, including the port Windows uses for networking. DOCSIS secures your computer from your neighbors, but it does not close up all the security holes that are opened when you use an always-on connection.

DSL, ISDN, AND DEDICATED LINES

What other options are available for high-speed Internet access? Although the standard equipment provided by telephone companies limits the amount of data you can transmit and receive over a voiceband modem, the copper wire that runs from your wall jacks to the switching station actually has a fair amount of capacity. Several services, such as DSL, ISDN, and dedicated lines take advantage of this capacity to offer high-speed digital communications links for voice and data.

What is DSL? DSL (digital subscriber line) is a high-speed, digital, always-on, Internet access technology that runs over standard phone lines. It is one of the fastest Internet connections that's affordable to individual consumers. Several variations of this technology exist, including ADSL (asymmetric DSL, with downstream speed faster than upstream speed), SDSL (symmetric DSL, with the same upstream and downstream speed), HDSL (high-rate DSL), VDSL (very high speed DSL), and DSL lite.

TERMINOLOGY NOTE

The acronym xDSL refers to the entire group of DSL technologies (including symmetric DSL, HDSL, and so on), but xDSL is not a separate variation of DSL.

DSL is digital, so data doesn't need to be changed into analog form and then back to digital as it does when you use a dial-up connection. Data is transmitted over your local loop in pure digital form, bypassing the bottleneck of analog-to-digital-to-analog conversion and escaping the requirement to use the narrow bandwidth allocated to voice transmissions. The result is fast data transmission over standard copper telephone cable.

A DSL connection can simultaneously carry voice and data, if permitted by your DSL provider. You can then use your DSL line for voice calls instead of your POTS line. The digital data and analog voice signals travel over the DSL line to the local switching station. There the voice signals are transferred to the telephone company's regular lines. The data signals are interpreted by special equipment called a **DSLAM** (DSL Access Multiplexor) and routed over high-speed lines to a DSL provider or directly to the Internet.

In many areas, DSL is a joint venture between the telephone company and the DSL provider. The telephone company is responsible for the physical cabling and voice transmission. The DSL provider is responsible for data traffic. Figure 5-51 illustrates how DSL handles voice and data.

INFOWEBLINKS

Nationwide, DSL vendors are grouping and regrouping. How might this affect your Internet access? You'll find up-to-date consumer information at the **DSL InfoWeb**.

www.course.com/np/concepts9/ch05

FIGURE 5-51

Voice and data signals travel over DSL to a special device at the local telephone switching station, where they are divided and routed to an ISP or to the regular telephone network.

The speed of a DSL connection varies according to the characteristics of your telephone line, the equipment at your local switch, and your distance from the switching station. Most DSL modems are rated for 1.5 Mbps downstream. A DSL signal deteriorates over distance, however, which limits dependable DSL service to customers who live within three "cable" miles of a switching station. When shopping for a DSL connection, you should inquire about actual speed, find out if the upstream rate differs from the downstream rate, and check your distance from the switching station.

FIGURE 5-52

In a typical DSL installation, a twisted-pair cable connects your computer's Ethernet card to a DSL modem, which is plugged into a wall jack.

How do I install DSL? Most DSL installations require trained service technicians. Your DSL provider requests your local telephone company to designate a telephone line for the DSL connection. This line might utilize unused twisted pairs in your current telephone line, or it might require a new line from the nearest telephone pole to the telephone box outside your house. This line is connected to a DSL switch at the phone company's local switching office.

Next, a technician from the DSL provider makes a service call to run cables and install a DSL wall jack, if necessary. The technician usually installs a **DSL modem**, which manages the interface between your computer and a DSL line. If the modem includes Ethernet circuitry, a USB cable connects the modem to your PC. Other types of DSL modems connect to your computer's Ethernet card (Figure 5-52).

Is ISDN faster than DSL? ISDN (Integrated Services Digital Network) connections move data at speeds of 64 Kbps or 128 Kbps—not as fast as DSL or cable Internet service but faster than a dial-up connection. As with DSL, ISDN is an all-digital service with the potential to simultaneously carry voice and data. A device called an **ISDN terminal adapter** connects a computer to a telephone wall jack and translates the computer's digital signals into signals that can travel over the ISDN connection.

ISDN service is typically regarded as a high-speed Internet connection option for businesses that maintain small LANs. The service is usually obtained from a local telephone company or a dedicated ISDN service provider. ISDN availability and pricing vary from place to place.

What is a dedicated line? T1, T3, and T4 services are dedicated, leased lines that offer fast, high-capacity data transmission. Speed ranges from 1.544 Mbps to 274 Mbps. T3 and T4 lines provide many of the links on the Internet backbone. T1, T3, and T4 lines are leased from the telephone company and are not usually shared by other customers. These high-speed services are usually too expensive for individuals.

WIRELESS INTERNET SERVICES

What are my options for wireless Internet access? There are two primary options for connecting your home PC or LAN to the Internet: satellite Internet service or fixed wireless Internet service.

How does satellite Internet service work? Most people are familiar with services that provide access to television programming over a personal satellite dish. Many companies that provide satellite TV also offer Internet access.

Satellite Internet service uses a geosynchronous or low-Earth satellite to transmit computer data directly to and from a satellite dish, or "base station," owned by an individual. A satellite Internet modem connects the satellite dish to a computer, as shown in Figure 5-53.

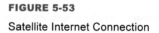

FIGURE 5-53

Satellite Internet Connection

What are the pros and cons of satellite Internet service? In many rural areas, satellite Internet service is the only alternative to a dial-up connection. Satellite service typically offers 1,000-1,500 Kbps downstream speed but only 35–128 Kbps upstream.

On the downside, satellite data transport is subject to latency delays of one second or more, which occur as your data is routed between your computer and a satellite that orbits 22,200 miles above the Earth. Latency might not pose much of a problem for general Web surfing and downloading MP3 files, but it can become a showstopper for interactive gaming that requires quick reactions. Satellite transmission and reception can be blocked by adverse weather conditions, such as rain and snow, which makes this type of data transport less reliable than most wired options.

As with cable Internet service, satellite data transport speeds might seem to decline when other users subscribe to the service because the satellite's bandwidth is shared among all users. Equipment and installation costs for satellite Internet service are often higher than for dial-up, ISDN, DSL, or cable Internet service.

What is fixed wireless Internet service? **Fixed wireless Internet service** is designed to offer Internet access to homes and businesses by broadcasting RF data signals over areas large enough to cover most cities and outlying areas. Wireless technologies such as WiMAX have less latency than satellite Internet service and can offer connection speeds suitable for online gaming and teleconferencing. **WiMAX** is an Ethernet-compatible network technology that is essentially wide-area Wi-Fi, with a range of 30 miles and data transmission rates of 70 Mbps.

How do I set up a fixed wireless connection? Wireless service providers are usually local or regional businesses that you can find in the telephone book under Internet Service Providers. Your wireless service provider typically supplies you with a wireless modem that you'll connect to your computer. The modem includes a transceiver to send and receive signals to a wireless point of access, usually located on a nearby communications tower. Subscribers on the outlying edges of the network's range might also require an antenna mounted on a window or roof and line-of-sight range to the WiMAX tower.

LAN INTERNET ACCESS

How can I connect to the Internet through a LAN? A LAN provides a cost-effective way to share one Internet connection among several computers. School computer labs and businesses usually provide Internet access over LANs.

LAN Internet access is also feasible for home networks. A single cable Internet, DSL, ISDN, or satellite connection can be cabled into your home LAN and accessed by all its workstations. Before connecting multiple computers to a single Internet connection, check with your service provider. Some have restrictions on sharing connections.

To establish LAN Internet access, you need:

- An operational wired or wireless LAN

- A router or a hub with router capabilities

- A high-speed Internet connection, such as DSL, ISDN, or cable Internet

- A modem that corresponds to your Internet connection type

A LAN, such as your home Ethernet or Wi-Fi network, can easily be connected to the Internet in several ways, illustrated in Figure 5-54.

Typically, routers are configured to automatically distribute IP addresses to LAN workstations using DHCP (Dynamic Host Configuration Protocol). Most Windows computers are configured to request an IP address using DHCP, so the computer and router can work together to establish a connection for each computer.

Networks typically use always-on connections, so it is important to implement security measures to protect data on network servers and workstations. Refer to the TechTalk at the end of this chapter for information on Internet access security.

INFOWEBLINKS

The **Satellite InfoWeb** dishes out lots of goodies about satellite Internet access—the technology, service providers, prices, and even reviews from disgruntled computer game players.

www.course.com/np/concepts9/ch05

FIGURE 5-54

Connecting a LAN to the Internet

Connect a device (D) containing modem and routing circuitry directly to the outlet for DSL, ISDN, or satellite service.

Connect a hub/router (H/R) to a cable, DSL, ISDN, or satellite modem (M).

Connect a hub (H) to a router (R) and the router to a cable, DSL, ISDN, or satellite modem (M).

MOBILE INTERNET ACCESS

Can I access Internet services using mobile devices? When you are not using a computer with access to your home Internet connection, you can use a mobile Internet connection to surf the Web and check your e-mail. Devices such as cell phones, PDAs, notebook computers, and tablet computers can be easily configured for mobile Internet access. Currently, the two most popular options for mobile Internet access are Wi-Fi hotspots and cellular phone service.

What is a Wi-Fi hotspot? A **Wi-Fi hotspot** is wireless broadband Internet service offered in public locations such as Starbucks, Borders Books & Music, FedEx Kinko's, libraries, schools, and airports (Figure 5-55). Any Wi-Fi equipped device that enters a hotspot can gain access to the network's services. Some Wi-Fi hotspots offer free service; others require a service plan or one-time use fee. A company that maintains Wi-Fi hotspots is sometimes referred to as a **WISP** (wireless ISP). U.S.-based WISPs include T-Mobile, Verizon, Sprint, and AT&T Wireless.

What are Wi-Fi hotspot advantages and disadvantages? In a typical scenario, you might take your notebook computer—equipped with a Wi-Fi card—to your local Starbucks cafe. You buy a cup of cappuccino, sit down in a comfortable chair, and switch on your computer. Windows networking utilities automatically sense a Wi-Fi network and establish a connection using your T-Mobile account. You can then surf the Web, just as though you were at home using a connection supplied by your desktop ISP.

Wi-Fi hotspot technology offers the convenience of broadband Internet access outside your home. Theoretically, Wi-Fi networks can pump data through at 56 Mbps. However, hotspot providers such as Verizon advertise peak speeds of only 1.5 Mbps. Actual speed can vary depending on your distance from the access point, the number of people logged in, and interference from other networks. The biggest advantage of Wi-Fi hotspots is that you're using your notebook computer with its large screen, full keyboard, sophisticated software, and all your data. With some other wireless options, such as PDAs, you're limited to a small screen, cell phone keypad, and small amount of storage space.

Wi-Fi hotspot availability is currently limited. Many small towns have no hotspots, and in big cities coverage is localized. On the bright side, hotspot coverage is expanding. Web sites such as *www.wi-fihotspotlist.com* help you find Wi-Fi hotspots in a specific city. Another drawback is that Wi-Fi service plans are not interchangeable. You cannot, for example, access a T-Mobile hotspot if you have a Verizon Wi-Fi Access service plan. Access plans can be expensive, too. Daily plans for 24 hours of access run $4-$6. Monthly unlimited access costs about the same as basic cell phone service.

How can I use my cell phone service to access the Internet? You can subscribe to a WAP plan offered by your cellular phone provider, as explained in the following paragraphs, or you can use a cellular-ready modem with your notebook computer (described later in this section).

What is WAP? **WAP** (Wireless Access Protocol) is a communications protocol that provides Internet access from handheld devices, such as cell phones and PDAs. WAP-enabled devices contain a microbrowser that simplifies Web and e-mail access on a small, low-resolution screen (Figure 5-56). You can obtain WAP-enabled devices and services from many mobile telecommunications providers, such as T-Mobile, Verizon, Cingular, and CellularOne.

FIGURE 5-55

Starbucks Wi-Fi hotspots offer wireless Internet access to customers with T-Mobile accounts.

FIGURE 5-56

The advantage of WAP-enabled devices is their portability. The disadvantage is their small, low-res screens. Although various schemes for scrolling over a full-sized Web page have been tried, most WAP users stick to Web sites specially designed for small screen devices.

5

What kind of services are available from handheld devices?
Cell phones and PDAs might not have huge screens, full-size keyboards, or full-featured application software, but in addition to Internet browsing they offer an expanding array of useful services.

■ **Short message service (SMS).** Also known as text messaging, SMS allows cell phone and PDA users to enter short messages and send them to other cell phones where they are displayed on screen. People with hearing disabilities make extensive use of SMS. Text messaging uses less airtime than a voice message. Innovative uses include using SMS to pay for merchandise purchased from vending machines.

■ **Multimedia messaging (MMS).** Camera phones can take still photos and/or videos that can be sent to other mobile phones or to e-mail addresses. Camera phones make it easy to snap a picture while shopping to get your friend's opinion. Cell phone photos have even been used to solve crimes. Despite a ban on photography, "cellcerting" has become popular as concert-goers snap shots of live action so their friends can participate. Camera phones have been banned from many gyms, however, because of privacy concerns. Picture messaging and video messaging usually require activation and incur additional service charges.

■ **Music fingerprinting.** With music fingerprinting technology, songs can be identified from an audio snippet captured on your cell phone. Suppose you're listening to a song on the radio. You missed the introduction and don't know the song title. Just key in GraceNote or 411-Song, hold your cell phone to the music source, and in a few seconds you'll know the name of the song and have an opportunity to buy it.

■ **Games.** You can download wireless versions of popular Activision, NBA, and Xbox games. Multiplayer games are even in the works—but make sure you have unlimited air time before you get into lengthy battles!

■ **City guides.** Use your cell phone to access information about restaurants and find the nearest ATM, gas station, or mall.

■ **E-mail.** Exchange e-mail messages with personal computer users as well as other cell phone users. Your cellular service provider usually supplies an e-mail account for your use, since you might not be able to access your desktop POP or Web-based e-mail account from the cell phone.

■ **News, sports, stocks, and weather.** You can subscribe to personalized content through your cellular provider or third party. You'll get sports scores as the game progresses, and you can watch the stock ticker from your online trading account.

What are my options for handheld devices? When shopping for a handheld device to access the Internet, you should consider screen size, keypad functionality, and network connection options. Color screens—the bigger the better—are essential for a look similar to your desktop browser. A 26-letter keypad sure beats double- and triple-thumbing to enter text. And why have one device for Wi-Fi hotspots and another device for cellular access? PDAs such as Hewlett-Packard's iPAQ 6315 (Figure 5-57) offer cellular, Wi-Fi, and Bluetooth connectivity.

Cellular service providers offer dual-band, tri-band, and quad-band phones. The "band" refers to the radio frequency used to transmit calls. Cellular service in major U.S. cities tends to use the 1,900 MHz band. Many rural areas are covered by 850 MHz service. You benefit from a dual-band phone if you use your phone outside big cities. If you plan to use your phone in Europe, you might consider a tri-band phone that also works in the 900 MHz band or a quad-band phone that adds 1,800 MHz capability.

TERMINOLOGY NOTE

The term "smartphone" refers to a cell phone that includes computer capabilities, such as e-mail, Web browsing, and gaming. The term is occasionally used to refer to PDAs with cellular access, but more often they are referred to as "smartphone/PDAs."

FIGURE 5-57

HP's iPAQ PDA offers a large color screen and clip-on keyboard. It can connect to Wi-Fi hotspots and GSM/GPRS cellular networks using quad-band frequencies in the U.S. and Europe. This PDA also offers Bluetooth connectivity to printers and other PAN devices.

What are my options for cellular service? Cellular technology is evolving rapidly and generates a real alphabet soup of acronyms, such as G1, AMPS, CDMA, GSM, and GPRS. First-generation (G1) cell phones are analog, operate in the 800 MHz band, and offer few features beyond voice communications. Second-generation (G2) cell phones offer digital voice service, e-mail, and limited Internet access, but have slow data transmission speeds. An in-between generation, sometimes called G2.5, combines second-generation technology with GPRS (general packet radio service) to provide always-on network connections and broadband data transmission speeds. G3 cell phones offer always-on broadband connections with speeds up to 2 Mbps.

Within each generation are technology subcategories. With the exception of GPRS, which is often combined with GSM, a cellular service provider's network typically offers only one technology. Figure 5-58 can help you understand technologies that might be mentioned in cell phone advertising.

FIGURE 5-58

Cellular Network Technologies

Generation	Service		Features
G1	AMPS	(advanced mobile phone service)	Analog voice service No data service
G2	CDMA	(code division multiple access)	Digital voice service 9.6 Kbps–14.4 Kbps speed Enhanced calling features, such as caller ID No always-on data connection
	TDMA	(time division multiple access)	
	PDC	(personal digital cellular)	
	GSM	(global system for mobile communications)	
G2.5	GPRS	(general packet radio service)	Adds always-on data transfers at 171.2 Kbps to CDMA, TDMA, and GSM networks
G3	W-CDMA	(wide-band code division multiple access)	Superior digital voice service Always-on data service at 2 Mbps speed Broadband multimedia data services
	UTMS	(universal mobile telecommunications system)	
	CDMA-2000	(time division synchronous code-division multiple access)	
	EDGE	(enhanced data for global evolution)	

Can I connect my notebook computer to my cell phone service? Some cell phones connect to your computer and act as a wireless modem to transmit data over the Internet. Another option is to purchase a cellular-ready modem packaged as a PC card that slips easily into the PCMCIA port of a notebook or tablet computer.

With either method, data transfer speeds using basic cell phone service, top out at 14.4 Kbps or less—only a fraction of the speed of a dial-up connection. Some cellular carriers, however, offer special data transfer services that match or exceed 56 Kbps dial-up speeds. These services are fairly expensive. For example, one company charges $80 per month for its nationwide talk plan and high-speed data service.

Cell phone and notebook combinations are practical only for mobile computer users who want to use their notebook computers in areas not serviced by Wi-Fi hotspots.

INTERNET CONNECTION ROUNDUP

What's the best Internet connection for my PC? The best Internet connection depends on your budget, what's available in your area, and what you do while connected. For fixed Internet access, cable Internet service is usually the first choice, when available. If cable Internet service is not available, or proves slower or less dependable than expected, the next choice would be DSL or fixed wireless service, if available. For mobile access, Wi-Fi offers the best alternative.

If several Internet connection services are offered in your area, the table in Figure 5-59 can help you evaluate their requirements, costs, advantages, and disadvantages.

FIGURE 5-59

Internet Access Options

	Dial-up	ISDN	DSL	Cable	Satellite	WiMAX	Wi-Fi
Downstream speed (max)	56 Kbps	128 Kbps	384 Kbps–1.5 Mbps	1.5–6 Mbps	500 Kbps	268 Mbps	11, 56, or 200 Mbps
Upstream speed (max)	33 Kbps	128 Kbps	128 Kbps–1.5 Mbps	256–768 Kbps	40–60 Kbps	70 Mbps	11, 56, or 200 Mbps
Downstream speed (avg)	44 Kbps	128 Kbps	1 Mbps	1 Mbps	400 Kbps	70 Mbps	11, 56, or 200 Mbps
Latency	100–200 ms	10–30 ms	10–20 ms	10–20 ms	1–3 seconds	10-50 ms	3-4 ms
Image file (2 MB) download time	6 minutes	2 minutes	20 seconds	20 seconds	40 seconds	2 seconds	10 seconds
Short video (72 MB) download time	4 hours	78 minutes	12 minutes	12 minutes	25 minutes	10 seconds	5 minutes
Requirements	Telephone line, ISP, voiceband modem	Computer must be located within 3 miles of local telephone switch	Computer must be located within 3 miles of local telephone switch	CATV service that provides Internet access	Clear view of southern sky	WiMAX modem, line-of-sight to WiMAX tower for distances > 10 miles	Wi-Fi equipped computer or PDA, access to Wi-Fi hotspot
Monthly fee	$10–$30	$50–$100	$30–$200	$30–$50	$35–$80	$0–$30	$0–$50
Installation cost	$0	$0–$300	$0–$200	$0–$50	$200–$300	$50–$150	$0–$50

QuickCheck   SECTION D

1. Many types of Internet connections offer faster [   ] transmission rates than [   ] transmission rates.

2. [   ] connections, such as DSL or ISDN, are particularly vulnerable to security breaches.

3. [   ] provides high-speed Internet access over standard phone lines and comes in symmetric and asymmetric versions.

4. Satellite Internet service is the best Internet service for gamers because of its high latency. True or false? [   ]

5. Many Starbucks offer Wi-Fi [   ].

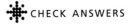 CHECK ANSWERS

TechTalk
Internet Access Security

Whether you work with a standalone computer or a LAN, Internet connections pose two kinds of risks: malicious code and intrusions. As you learned in Chapter 4, to deal with malicious code, such as viruses and worms, it is important to run antivirus software on standalone computers and all network workstations. To prevent intrusions, you need to take additional precautions. This TechTalk explains the most important steps you can take to secure your Windows-based computer from intrusions.

Should I worry about intrusions when using a standalone computer? A standalone computer with an always-on DSL, ISDN, or cable Internet connection is particularly susceptible to intrusions. Without any visible sign or warning, hackers can infiltrate your computer to obtain personal information or use your computer as a launching pad for attacks on other machines. If you have an always-on connection, you should take steps to secure your computer from intrusions (Figure 5-60).

How do I secure a standalone computer? One of the easiest steps to enhance your computer's security is to turn it off when you aren't using it. When your computer is turned off, it is not vulnerable to intrusions. Putting your computer into sleep mode or activating a screen saver is not sufficient protection. Your computer must be shut down and turned off.

You should also keep your computer up-to-date with the latest Windows security patches and service packs. Hackers look for holes or vulnerabilities in Windows and Internet Explorer and work out ways to exploit them to gain unauthorized access to computers. As Microsoft develops security patches, they are posted at *www.microsoft.com/security*. Check the site frequently to download the most recent patches.

You can also use Windows Automatic Updates to periodically check for patches. To configure Automatic Updates, go to Control Panel, select System, and select a setting from the Automatic Updates tab (Figure 5-61). When updates are available, you'll see the New Updates icon on the taskbar:

In addition to updating security patches, you should configure your computer to run **firewall software**, which is designed to analyze and control incoming and outgoing packets. This software helps keep your computer secure in several ways. It makes sure that incoming information was actually requested and is not an unauthorized intrusion. It blocks activity from suspicious IP addresses and—best of all—it reports intrusion attempts so that you can discover whether any hackers are trying to break into your computer.

FIGURE 5-60

Standalone Computer Security Checklist

✔ Turn your computer off when not in use.

✔ Make sure operating system security patches and service packs are up to date.

✔ Disable file and printer sharing.

✔ Check security settings in Internet Explorer.

✔ Enable the Internet Connection Firewall.

FIGURE 5-61

To configure your computer for Automatic Updates, use Control Panel's System icon.

5

How can I get firewall protection? Windows XP includes firewall software called Internet Connection Firewall (ICF) or Windows Firewall. To activate and configure it, use Control Panel's Network Connections option (Figure 5-62 left). For earlier Windows versions or non-Windows operating systems, Tiny Personal Firewall and BlackICE are popular personal firewall products.

FIGURE 5-62

Activating Windows Internet Connection Firewall (left) and setting Internet Explorer security options (right) is easy.

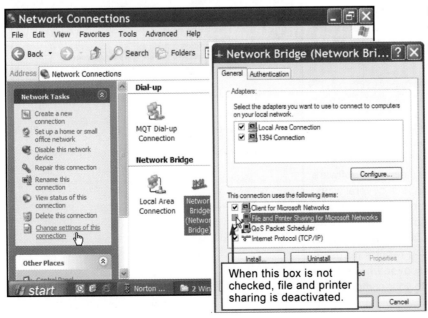

What other Windows security options should I use? You should also check your browser's security options. With Internet Explorer, the Medium setting allows maximum flexibility for browsing while providing a good level of protection from intrusions. To check this setting, open Internet Explorer and select Internet Options from the Tools menu (Figure 5-62 right).

If your computer is not connected to a LAN or used for access to a public Wi-Fi network, you should deactivate file and printer sharing. Figure 5-63 demonstrates this procedure for Windows XP.

FIGURE 5-63

When you turn off file and printer sharing, your files and printer cannot be accessed by other network users.

When this box is not checked, file and printer sharing is deactivated.

What about LAN security? Many security measures for LANs are the same as for standalone computers. You should not, however, deactivate file and printer sharing, which would defeat the purpose of having a network. Nor should you activate ICF. Instead, use firewall software designed for networks. LAN managers should establish user IDs and passwords for all users and close all "backdoors," such as default passwords. In addition to the precautions listed in Figure 5-64, LAN managers also should consider using Network Address Translation to add another layer of security.

What is Network Address Translation? A LAN requires a device with routing capabilities, and that device can become part of a network's security defenses. **Network Address Translation** (NAT) is a way to configure a network so that workstations are hidden from Internet intruders. Here's how it works. Your ISP typically assigns an IP address to your high-speed connection. This address is visible to the rest of the Internet. Within your LAN, however, workstations can be assigned private Internet addresses.

When the IP addressing scheme was devised, three ranges of addresses were reserved for internal or "private" use: 10.0.0.0—10.255.255.255, 172.16.0.0—172.31.255.255, and 192.168.0.0—192.168.255.255. These **private IP addresses** cannot be routed over the Internet. If you assign private IP addresses to your workstations, they are essentially hidden from hackers, who see only the IP address for your router.

You might wonder how you can transmit and receive data from a workstation with a nonroutable address. Your router maintains a NAT table that keeps track of the private IP addresses assigned to each workstation. For outgoing packets, the router substitutes its own address for the address of the workstation. When a response to a packet arrives, the router forwards it to the appropriate workstation. In that way, only the router's address is publicly visible. The router should, of course, be protected by antivirus software and firewall software.

Is it possible to secure connections for remote users? Sales representatives and telecommuters often have to access corporate networks by using a remote connection from home or a customer's office. It is possible to secure these remote connections by setting up **virtual private network** (VPN) access to a remote access server that uses Point-to-Point Tunneling Protocol or Layer Two Tunneling Protocol.

To initiate a VPN connection, dial your ISP as usual. After the connection is established, a second connection to the remote access server creates an encrypted channel for data transmission. Windows XP and several standalone products provide VPN software. Figure 5-65 illustrates how a VPN operates.

QuickCheck `TECHTALK`

1. An important security measure for a standalone computer is putting it into sleep mode when not in use. True or false? [____]

2. Windows Internet Connection [____] blocks activity from suspicious IP addresses.

3. A(n) [____] private network provides secure remote access to corporate networks.

FIGURE 5-64

Network Workstation Security Checklist

✔ Make sure operating system security patches and service packs are up to date.
✔ Install a router and NAT.
✔ Check security settings in Internet Explorer.
✔ Install firewall software.
✔ Control access by using passwords.
✔ Close all "backdoors."

FIGURE 5-65

Virtual Private Network

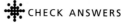 CHECK ANSWERS

Issue

Free Wi-Fi

How would you like high-speed Internet access that requires no cables, no modem, and best of all—no subscription fees? Free community wireless access in cities as diverse as San Francisco, Miami, New York, Prague, and Amsterdam is made possible by free WLANs (wireless LANs). Dubbed "renegade WLANs" by some members of the press, these free networks are operated by public-spirited individuals who like to tinker with technology and want to provide a useful community service. Free WLAN operators typically subscribe to a DSL or cable provider for high-speed Internet access. They pay their monthly fees, but instead of limiting access to their own personal use, they distribute their connections to friends, neighbors, and just about anyone who passes by with the right computer equipment.

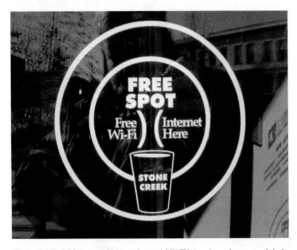

Free WLANs are based on Wi-Fi technology, which uses the 802.11 networking standard to create wireless Ethernet-compatible LANs. The technology itself is not inherently renegade. It is used for many mainstream applications. Wi-Fi networks are popular in corporations and universities where users are mobile and the flow of information typically requires broadband capacity.

The 802.11 standard uses an unlicensed telecommunications spectrum, so it is perfectly legal to set up an antenna to transmit and receive Wi-Fi signals without obtaining a broadcast license or paying any fees to the Federal Communications Commission. Not only is it legal, setting up a Wi-Fi antenna is simple and inexpensive. A basic Wi-Fi antenna can be created with a few wires and an empty Pringles container. Fancier antennas require a ravioli can—really!

Using a Wi-Fi network is even cheaper and easier than setting one up. Many notebook computers have built-in Wi-Fi transceivers and software. If a transceiver is not built into your computer, you can add one for less than $100. With a Wi-Fi-ready computer, you can literally walk down the street, and your computer will look for and connect to any available Wi-Fi network.

Some free WLAN advocates envision a nationwide web of interconnected Wi-Fi networks that will form "a seamless broadband network built by the people, for the people." In this vision of a world connected by free WLANs, libraries can offer Internet access to people in low income neighborhoods. Local schools could get wired without exorbitant cabling expenses. Parents, kids, and grandparents, as well as corporate executives, could exchange e-mail and instant messages from locations that include the kitchen table, the corner coffee shop, and the Little League field.

But some broadband providers, such as AT&T and Time Warner Cable, fear that every user of a free wireless network is one less paying customer. According to one industry analyst, "The telecom industries are addicted to the one-wire, one-customer philosophy." Sharing an Internet connection that is intended for single-user access does not coexist with this philosophy. Most subscriber agreements contain wording that limits use of a broadband connection to one user and perhaps immediate family members. Although wording varies from one provider to another, most agreements expressly prohibit subscribers from using their connections for commercial purposes. Some free WLAN operators don't believe that sharing is commercial use. "I'm sharing it with people," says one free WLAN provider, "I'm not selling it. I'm not making a profit off it."

Whether or not free WLANs are legal, their benefits are tempered by several potentially negative repercussions. For example, tightening up subscriber agreements to eliminate the sharing loophole could affect many broadband subscribers who currently operate private wired or wireless networks that link several computers to a single Internet connection. Broadband providers could force private network operators to purchase more expensive multiuser licenses—an option that might be too expensive for many home networks.

Most free WLANs are operated as a hobby. Some operators are very conscientious, but others have a laid-back attitude toward quality of service: If no one gets charged, no one can complain when the network doesn't work. Consequently, free WLAN access can be unreliable. If broadband providers threaten to pull out of areas where free WLANs are popular, community members might have to choose between unreliable free WLAN service offered by hobbyists and more reliable, but more costly, services supplied by for-profit providers.

The wisdom of unregulated network availability is called into question by the proliferation of free WLANs. A publicly accessible LAN that requires no passwords or accounts can be used anonymously for a variety of illegal and dangerous activities. Like drug dealers who use public telephones to avoid taps and traces, terrorists and other criminals can simply walk into a free WLAN zone, tap into the Internet, and walk away without leaving a trace.

Widespread distribution of free WLANs can reduce the bandwidth available to paying customers. If your neighbor sets up a free WLAN that becomes popular with customers in a nearby coffee house, your previously sedate network neighborhood might suddenly become an overcrowded metropolis with major Internet access traffic jams.

Despite possible repercussions, the free WLAN movement appears to be growing and becoming more controversial. Some industry analysts expect a battle similar to the one that ensued when Napster's peer-to-peer music-sharing network was attacked by the music industry. The free WLAN controversy could pit a group of telecommunications giants against a rag-tag alliance of free WLAN advocates. The outcome has the potential to affect broadband subscribers everywhere.

5

INFOWEBLINKS

The **Free WLAN InfoWeb** provides more details about Wi-Fi technology and renegade LANs.

✢

www.course.com/np/concepts9/ch05

What Do You Think?   ISSUE

1. Have you ever accessed a free WLAN?   ◯ Yes   ◯ No   ◯ Not sure

2. Do you believe that pirate WLANs can survive alongside for-profit broadband ISPs?   ◯ Yes   ◯ No   ◯ Not sure

3. Are broadband providers justified in limiting the terms of their service agreements to "one subscription, one customer"?   ◯ Yes   ◯ No   ◯ Not sure

✦ SAVE RESPONSES

Computers in Context
Education

The first educational application of computers emerged in the 1960s, when huge mainframes with clunky interfaces introduced students to computer-aided instruction (CAI). Based on operant conditioning research by B. F. Skinner and Ivan Pavlov—remember dogs salivating when a bell rings?—CAI uses basic drill and practice: The computer presents a problem, the student responds, and the computer evaluates the response. Studies in the 1970s indicated that CAI systems, such as PLATO (Programmed Logic for Automated Teaching Operations), improved student test scores, but students found the mainframe's monochrome display and the CAI's regimented drill format boring. Recent incarnations of CAI, such as an "alien invader" style elementary math program, use snazzy graphics and arcade formats to grab learners' attention.

Educators looking for ways to harness computers' interactive and programmable nature arrived at the idea of computer-based training (CBT). CBT is formatted as a series of tutorials, beginning with a pretest to see whether students have the prerequisite skills and ending with a CAI-style drill and practice test to determine whether students can move on to the next tutorial segment. Today, CBT is a popular approach to learning how to use computer software.

Another educational approach, called computer-aided learning (CAL), uses the computer more as a source of information than an assessment mechanism. Students using CAL make decisions about their level of expertise, what material is relevant, and how to pace their own learning. Exploratory CAL environments include Seymour Papert's Logo programming language; students can investigate geometry concepts by using Logo to program a graphical turtle on-screen.

In addition to CAI, CBT, and CAL, simulations have become a popular educational tool. The computer mimics a real-world situation through a narrative description or with graphics. Students are given options and respond with a decision or an action. The computer evaluates each response and determines its consequences. Oregon Trail, a simulation popular with elementary school students, describes events that beset a group of pioneers traveling in a wagon train. Students respond to each event, while learning bits of history, money-handling skills, conservation, and decision making.

Most educators believe that computers can help create an individualized and interactive learning environment, which can make learning more effective and efficient. Although 99% of American public schools have computers and 93% of students use them in some way, these statistics can be deceiving. The reality falls far short of the ideal situation—every student having access to a computer throughout the school day.

The challenge is to figure out how to achieve the computers' potential in an educational setting when supplying computers for every student is often cost prohibitive. Compromise solutions have been tried with varying degrees of success. Some schools have installed learning labs where students go for scheduled lab time. In elementary schools, often a few computers are placed in special work areas of classrooms and used for small group projects or individual drill and practice. Some schools have relegated most computers to the library, where they are connected to the Internet and used for research. In some classrooms, a single computer can be used as an effective presentation device.

A few schools without the budget for enough desktop computers have opted for inexpensive PDAs instead. "Students need to use technology just as you and I do, not just one hour a day," says one teacher in support of PDAs. Students use standard PDA software for educational tasks: tracking nutritional intake for health class, collecting data from experiments in biology class, graphing functions in math class, translating phrases for French class, and maintaining to-do lists. The biggest drawback to more widespread educational use of PDAs, however, is a lack of software specifically designed for education.

As another option, some schools—primarily colleges—have confronted the problem of computer access by requiring all incoming first-year students to purchase notebook computers. Many colleges, for example, provide Internet connections in dorm rooms and library study carrels or offer campuswide Wi-Fi service. Students can tote their notebook computers to class and take notes. They can contact instructors via e-mail, use the Internet as a research resource, and run educational software.

Another educational use of computers can be seen in distance education (DE) courses (also called "distance learning"). Historically, distance education meant correspondence study or courses delivered by radio or television, but the meaning has been broadened to encompass any educational situation in which students and instructors aren't in the same place. Therefore, most DE courses today require students to have access to a computer and an Internet connection. DE courses are offered to K-12 students, college students, military personnel, business people, and the general public. Most students who choose DE courses do so because they want to learn at their own pace, at a convenient time, and in a location close to home. Single parents who must deal with the realities of child care, working professionals who cannot relocate to a college town, and physically disabled students find distance education handy. Distance education has the potential of increasing the pool of students for a course by making it financially feasible; for example, an advanced Kanji

course could be offered at a midwestern university with only 10 on-campus Japanese majors if enough distance education students can boost enrollment.

The Internet hosts a wide variety of DE courses, both credit-earning and noncredit courses. Several course management systems (CMSs), such as Blackboard and WebCT, help teachers prepare and manage DE courses. These systems are popular with degree-granting institutions that offer credit-earning DE courses in their course catalogs (subject to the usual course fees and requirements).

Course management software typically runs from a server maintained by a school system, college, or university. Using Web browsers, teachers access the CMS to post an online syllabus, develop Web pages with course content, create a database of questions for online assessment, manage e-mail, set up online discussion groups, and maintain a gradebook. Students using Internet-connected computers and standard Web browsers can access course materials, submit assignments, interact with other students, and take tests.

Computers and the Internet have opened opportunities for life-long learning. Prospective students can use a search engine to easily find non-credit courses and tutorials for a wide range of topics, including pottery, dog grooming, radio astronomy, desktop publishing, and drumming. Some tutorials are free, and others charge a small fee. Several Web sites, such as Barnes & Noble University and Online-Learning.com, offer a good choice of fee-based or free courses. In a society that promotes learning as a lifelong endeavor, the Internet has certainly made it possible for students of all ages to pursue knowledge and skills simply by using a computer and an Internet connection.

INFOWEBLINKS

You'll find lots more information related to this Computers in Context topic at the **Computers and Education InfoWeb.**

www.course.com/np/concepts9/ch05

5

Labs

Student Edition Labs

On the Web
Student Edition Labs

To access the Student Edition labs, connect to the New Perspectives NP9 Web site and click the link for Student Edition Labs. The link also provides access to lab assignments.

www.course.com/np/concepts9/ch05

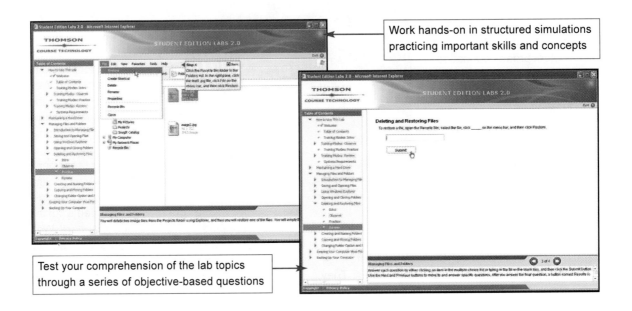

Work hands-on in structured simulations practicing important skills and concepts

Test your comprehension of the lab topics through a series of objective-based questions

NETWORKING BASICS

In the Networking Basics Student Edition Lab, you will learn the following topics and skills:

- Network architecture, hardware, and software
- Network protocols and utilities
- Networked resources
- Network security

CONNECTING TO THE INTERNET

In the Connecting to the Internet Student Edition Lab, you will learn the following topics and skills:

- Establishing an Internet connection
- Connecting to the Internet using dial-up, DSL, cable, and wireless
- Installing ISP software
- Creating Internet connections manually

WIRELESS NETWORKING

In the Wireless Networking Student Edition Lab, you will learn the following topics and skills:

- Implementing wireless networks
- Wireless security

on the BookOnCD
New Perspectives Labs

To access the New Perspectives labs for Chapter 5, start the BookOnCD and then click the ✣ icon next to the lab title below.

✣ TRACKING PACKETS

IN THIS LAB YOU'LL LEARN:

How Ping and Traceroute work

How to use the Ping and Tracert utilities supplied by Windows

How to interpret Ping and Tracert reports to determine the speed and reliability of your Internet connection

How to access and use a graphical Traceroute utility

How to find and use Web-based Ping and Traceroute utilities

The advantages and disadvantages of Web-based Ping and Traceroute utilities

How to access the Internet Traffic Report Web site and interpret its data and graphs

How to use Internet traffic data, Ping, and Traceroute to pinpoint problems with your Internet connection

LAB ASSIGNMENTS

1. Start the interactive part of the lab. Perform each lab step as directed, and answer all the lab QuickCheck questions.

2. Use the Ping utility that's supplied by Windows to ping *www.abcnews.com*. Record the IP address for the ABC News site, plus the minimum, maximum, and average times. For each time, indicate whether it would be considered poor, average, or good.

3. Use the Tracert utility that's supplied by Windows to trace a packet between your computer and *www.excite.com*. Print the Traceroute report listing transmission times. Circle any pings on the report that indicate high latency.

4. Locate a Web-based Ping utility and use it to ping *www.gobledegok.com*. Indicate the URL for the Web site where you found the Ping utility. Explain the ping results.

5. Connect to the Internet Traffic Report Web site, make a note of the date and time, and then answer the following questions:

    a. What is the traffic index for Asia?

    b. How does the index for Asia compare with the traffic index for North America?

    c. During the previous 24 hours in Europe, what was the period with the worst response time?

✣ SECURING YOUR CONNECTION

IN THIS LAB YOU'LL LEARN:

How to use Windows utilities, online utilities, and firewall software to check the security of your Internet connection

Why an unauthorized intruder might want to gain access to your computer

The significance of communications ports as an intrusion risk factor

How a Trojan horse can open up ports on your computer to provide intruders with full access to your computer system

How to use the Windows Netstat utility to check your computer's open ports

How to use an online utility to get a hacker's view of your computer

Why Windows file and printer sharing can make your computer files vulnerable

What features to look for in personal firewall software

How to use firewall software, add packet filtering rules, and interpret firewall reports

LAB ASSIGNMENTS

1. Start the interactive part of the lab. Make sure you've enabled Tracking if you want to save your QuickCheck results. Perform each lab step as directed, and answer all the lab QuickCheck questions. When you exit the lab, your answers are automatically graded and your results are displayed.

2. Use the Netstat utility to scan any computer that you typically use. Write out the Netstat report or print it. To print the report, copy it to Paint or Word, and then print. Explain what the Netstat report tells you about that computer's security.

3. Connect to the *grc.com* site and access the Shields Up! tests. Test the shields and probe the ports for the same computer you used for Assignment 2. Explain the similarities and differences between the Shields Up! report and the Netstat report for this computer. Which report indicates more security risks? Why?

4. In the lab, you learned which dialog boxes to use for disabling Windows file and printer sharing, plus a technique for unbinding TCP from file and printer sharing. Without actually changing the settings, use the dialog boxes to determine whether file and printer sharing is active or disabled on your computer. Also, discover whether file and printer sharing is bound to TCP on your computer. Report your findings and indicate whether these settings are appropriate for network access and security.

5

Interactive Summary

To review important concepts from this chapter, fill in the blanks to best complete each sentence. When using the NP9 BookOnCD or the NP9 Web site, click the Check Answers buttons to automatically score your answers.

Computer networks offer several advantages, including shared [＿＿＿＿＿＿], such as hardware, software, and data. Networks can be classified by geographical scope as PANs, [＿＿＿＿＿＿], MANs, NANs, and WANs. Organizationally, they can be classified as client/[＿＿＿＿＿＿] or peer-to-peer. Physical network topologies include star, bus, [＿＿＿＿＿＿], mesh, and tree.

The central connection device in a star network is called a [＿＿＿＿＿＿]. A device called a [＿＿＿＿＿＿] amplifies and regenerates signals so that they can retain the necessary strength to reach their destination. Two similar networks can be connected by a device called [＿＿＿＿＿＿]. Two dissimilar networks can be connected using a hardware or software [＿＿＿＿＿＿], such as a router.

Data is transmitted over a variety of communications channels, including twisted-pair cables, coaxial cable, fiber-optic cable, RF signals, microwaves, infrared light, and laser light. The transmission capacity of a channel is called [＿＿＿＿＿＿]. High-capacity communications systems, such as cable TV, are sometimes referred to as [＿＿＿＿＿＿], whereas systems with less capacity, such as the telephone system, are referred to as [＿＿＿＿＿＿]. The transmission capacity of a digital channel is usually measured in [＿＿＿＿＿＿] per second (bps).

The rules for orderly communications are established by communications [＿＿＿＿＿＿], such as TCP/IP. A [＿＿＿＿＿＿] is a parcel of data that is sent across a computer network. Most computer networks use [＿＿＿＿＿＿] switching technology that allows data from several different sources to share a single communications channel.

✦ CHECK ANSWERS

A LAN (local [＿＿＿＿＿＿] network) connects computers, called workstations, within a limited geographical area. Today, most LANs are based on the Ethernet standard, which uses CSMA/CD to detect [＿＿＿＿＿＿]. A basic Ethernet network requires an Ethernet card in each workstation. Network devices are typically connected by CAT 5 cables, which converge at a centrally located Ethernet [＿＿＿＿＿＿].

Ethernet's wireless cousin, called [＿＿＿＿＿＿], is specified under IEEE 802.11 standards. A wireless [＿＿＿＿＿＿] point performs the same functions as a hub or router in a wired Ethernet. Because airborne signals from a wireless network are easy to intercept, it is essential to provide a basic level of security using [＿＿＿＿＿＿] encryption.

An alternative wireless technology, which is called [＿＿＿＿＿＿], transmits data over a short distance and is typically used for PANs. For home networks, HomePNA uses existing telephone wiring and Home [＿＿＿＿＿＿] uses existing electrical wiring.

Setting up a small LAN is easy. After the hardware and connections are in place, Windows detects the network any time you turn on a workstation. Workstation users can use drive [＿＿＿＿＿＿] to assign drive letters to storage devices located on other workstations and to designate files and folders to be shared with other network users.

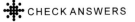 CHECK ANSWERS

The Internet has its roots in a network called [_____], which was developed in 1969. Gradually this network grew until it spanned the globe. In the early 1990s, user-friendly Internet access tools, such as graphical browsers, attracted millions of people to the Internet.

Network [_____] providers, such as MCI, UUNET, and AT&T, supply high-speed links for the Internet backbone. The acronym [_____] refers to points where equipment and links from these companies intersect. Internet [_____] direct data to the proper path according to its address.

An Internet utility called [_____] helps you discover whether a host, such as a Web server, is "alive." This utility also reports the elapsed time, called [_____], for a packet to travel from your computer to the host and back. Another utility, called [_____], records the path of a packet as it travels from your computer to its destination.

Most people access the Internet through an [_____], which provides modems, e-mail servers, domain name servers, and routers. The Internet protocol called [_____] breaks a message into packets and then attaches an IP address. A computer can have a permanently assigned [_____] IP address or a temporary [_____] IP address. In addition to an IP address, many Internet servers also have a corresponding [_____] name, which is tracked by a large database called the [_____] Name System.

✦ CHECK ANSWERS

5

Dial-up connections use POTS to transport data between your computer and your ISP over a "local loop" that carries [_____], not digital, signals. A modem [_____] your computer's digital signal so that it can travel over telephone lines. To restore a signal to its original state, it must be [_____]. Like many other Internet access technologies, a dial-up connection's [_____] transmission rate is usually faster than the [_____] rate.

A cable modem provides Internet access over the same [_____] cables that carry television signals from the cable company's head-end to your home. Some cable modems connect to a port provided by an [_____] card, whereas other cable modems connect to a USB port.

DSL connections are similar to cable connections in several ways, except that a DSL connection uses specially conditioned telephone lines that carry [_____] signals over the local loop. A similar, but slower, service is called [_____].

[_____] connections, such as DSL and cable, are active any time your computer is turned on. With such a connection, security becomes an issue.

[_____] Internet service provides another high-speed Internet access method, but it has higher latency than [_____], which is essentially wide-area Wi-Fi.

LANs can also provide Internet connections. Typically, a [_____] connects the LAN to a single DSL, cable, or T1 Internet connection that can be shared by all the LAN workstations.

Mobile Internet access is available from Wi-Fi [_____] and cellular services. Notebook computers equipped with Wi-Fi capability and a compatible service plan can gain access to network services, such as an Internet connection. Cellular devices use [_____] protocol to handle e-mail and Web browsing on devices with small, low-res screens.

✦ CHECK ANSWERS

Key Terms

Make sure you understand all the boldfaced key terms presented in this chapter. If you're using the NP9 BookOnCD, you can use this list of terms as an interactive study activity. First, try to define a term in your own words, and then click the term to compare your definition with the definition presented in the chapter.

Always-on connection, 270
ARCnet, 249
Bandwidth, 246
Baud rate, 268
Bluetooth, 254
Bridge, 243
Broadband, 246
Bus topology, 242
Circuit switching, 247
Client/server network, 241
Coaxial cable, 244
Communications channel, 243
Communications protocol, 247
Communications satellites, 245
CSMA/CD, 251
Demodulation, 267
DOCSIS, 271
Domain name, 263
Domain name servers, 264
Domain Name System, 264
Downstream, 269
Drive mapping, 256
DSL modem, 272
DSLAM, 272
Dynamic IP address, 262
Ethernet, 250
Ethernet card, 251
Extranet, 261
FDDI, 250
Fiber-optic cable, 244
Firewall software, 279
Fixed wireless Internet service, 274
Gateway, 243
Handshaking, 247
Head-end, 269
HomePLC network, 254
HomePNA network, 254

Hub, 242
ICANN, 264
Infrared light, 245
Intranet, 261
IP, 261
IP addresses, 262
ISDN terminal adapter, 273
LAN, 241
Latency, 259
MAN, 241
Mesh topology, 242
Microwaves, 245
Modulation, 267
NAN, 241
Narrowband, 246
Network access points, 259
Network Address Translation, 281
Network service providers, 259
Node, 242
Octet, 262
Packet, 247
Packet switching, 247
PAN, 241
Peer-to-peer network, 241
Physical topology, 242
Ping, 259
POTS, 266
Private IP addresses, 281
Repeater, 242
RF signals, 245
Ring topology, 242
Router, 243
Shared resources, 238
Star topology, 242
Static IP address, 262
TCP, 261
Token Ring network, 249

Top-level domain, 263
Traceroute, 260
Transceiver, 245
Transponder, 245
Tree topology, 243
Twisted-pair cable, 244
Uplink port, 252
Upstream, 269
Virtual private network, 281
Voice over IP, 248
WAN, 241
WAP, 275
WEP, 253
Wi-Fi, 252
Wi-Fi card, 253
Wi-Fi hotspot, 275
Wired network, 243
Wireless access point, 253
Wireless network, 243
WISP, 275
WiMAX, 274

Interactive Situation Questions

Apply what you've learned to some typical computing situations. When using the NP9 BookOnCD or the NP9 Web site, you can type your answers, and then use the Check Answers button to automatically score your responses.

1. You're installing a LAN and you decide to go with Ethernet. You'll typically use Category [____] cables to connect each workstation to a(n) [_____].

2. You're finally ready to get a high-speed Internet connection. Because the cable modem provided by your CATV company contains Ethernet circuitry, you can simply connect the modem to your computer's [_____] port (shown in the photo at right).

3. Your Internet access seems very slow one day. You might be able to use a networking utility called [_____] to discover the source of the slowdown.

4. Suppose that you decide to open a little Web store to sell handcrafted pottery. Your Web site will need a(n) [_____] IP address, and you'll want to register a(n) [_____] name.

5. Imagine that your computer contains a 56 Kbps modem that uses the V.90 standard. You can expect about 44 Kbps [_____] speed and about 33 Kbps as the maximum [_____] speed.

6. Suppose you have installed a cable modem on a standalone PC. To secure your computer, you should first use Control Panel's Network Connections icon to turn off file and printer

[_____]. You should also activate Internet Connection [_____] software.

7. You install an 802.11b network, but it seems to stop working at various times. To begin troubleshooting, you look for any devices, such as cordless phones, that use the [____] GHz frequency.

8. Your PC is connected to a LAN, and you want to regularly access a file that's stored on one of the LAN workstations. You'd like to access that computer's hard disk as though it were connected to your own computer, so you decide to [_____] the workstation's hard disk drive as drive F.

9. You arrive at work and one of your co-workers tells you that the "router is down." You can surmise that your workstation will not be able to access the [_____] until the router is fixed.

✦ CHECK ANSWERS

Interactive Practice Tests

Practice tests that consist of 10 multiple-choice, true/false, and fill-in-the-blank questions are available on both the NP9 BookOnCD and the NP9 Web site. The questions are selected at random from a large test bank, so each time you take a test, you'll receive a different set of questions. Your tests are scored immediately, and you can print study guides that help you find the correct answers for any questions that you missed.

CLICK ✦ TO START

Projects

An NP9 Project is an open-ended activity that will help you apply the concepts you have learned. Many projects require resources in addition to your textbook, such as current magazines, library materials, or Web access. When you tackle a project, be prepared to use your critical thinking skills, logical analysis, and your creativity.

CRITICAL THINKING

The Internet offers e-mail, e-commerce, chat groups, and a vast assortment of information. How do you use the Internet? What advantages does it provide for you? What are your pet peeves about the Internet as it currently works (privacy, safety, ads, false information, etc.)? What would be your ideal Internet? Incorporate your answers in a one- or two-page document and follow your instructor's guidelines for submitting it as a printed document or using e-mail.

CYBERCLASSROOM

Each member of your team should Ping Google and record results. Exchange your results with other students in your team to find out who has the fastest connection. How many members of the group have a connection fast enough to play online interactive multiplayer games? The member of your team with the fastest connection should summarize the team's data and submit it to your instructor.

MULTIMEDIA PROJECT

The speed of your Internet connection will affect the download time for media, such as photos and videos. Use Ping to find the speed of your Internet connection, then experiment with viewing five different short videos on news or entertainment Web sites. How does the performance of each video relate to the kind of Internet connection you have? Were you able to view all the videos you wanted to see, or did some require additional software? If so, what software? All in all, how would you rate the quality and convenience of Web-based video? Compile your findings into a well-organized PowerPoint presentation. Slide 1 should provide a brief description of your computer and Internet connection. Slide 2 should include a screen shot of your Ping statistics. Slides 3 through 7 should describe each of the videos you viewed, including their URLs and your evaluation of the video quality. The final slide should include your overall evaluation of the quality and convenience of Web-based video. Follow your instructor's guidelines for submitting and/or presenting your project.

GROUP PROJECT

Form a group with three or four other students. Suppose you are all living in adjacent dorm rooms and decide to create a LAN to connect your computers. For this project, first describe the number, type, and location of the computers that will form your network. Next, decide what type of network technology you want to use: Ethernet, HomePNA, Wi-Fi, HomePLC, or a mixture. Create a diagram showing the location of each computer, the wiring path (for Ethernet), the location of electrical outlets (for HomePLC), the location of telephone outlets (for HomePNA), or potential signal interference (for wireless). Create a shopping list of the network components you need to purchase, and then use the Web to locate prices for each item on your list. Make sure you supply your instructor with the URLs for sites where you found pricing information.

RESUME BUILDER

The Internet provides resources for career development. Think about your ideal job and make a table that lists (in the first column) the top 10 qualifications and skills you'll need to be a successful applicant. In the second column, indicate whether you currently possess each qualification or skill. For those you need to develop in the future, indicate how you plan to obtain them, for example from a college course, on-the-job training, or self-paced study. Find out if you can develop any of these skills and qualifications using online resources, such as online courses. Provide URLs for any Internet resources that you find. Follow your instructor's guidelines for submitting your career development table as an e-mail attachment or as a printed document.

GLOBALIZATION

Worldwide, communications capabilities are growing at a rapid pace. Nonetheless, there exists among countries a great disparity in communications capabilities. What you take for granted in your country might not be available to the average person in, say, Greece. On the other hand, you might discover that people in Finland, for example, make far greater use of cell phones than the people in your country. For this project, use library and Internet resources to gather information about the communications options that are available throughout the world. You should consider which technologies are available and the number of people who use each technology. Your research can include any of the following: land-based phones, cellular phones, premium phone services such as ISDN and ADSL, Internet access, broadcast television, and cable television. Once you have gathered these facts, consider how they might affect the lifestyles, politics, and economies of various regions. Suppose that you are organizing a high school debate about global communications technology. As the organizer, you must devise a controversial question on which the debate will be based. You should also write three "pro" and "con" paragraphs just to make sure that both sides of the issue will have substantial material to debate. For this project, write the controversial debate question, your "pro" and "con" paragraphs, and a short bibliography of your sources.

ISSUE

The Issue section of this chapter focuses on the use of Wi-Fi technology to build wireless LANs that provide free Internet access. For this project, write a two- to five-page paper that examines one aspect of the free WLAN controversy. You might explore Wi-Fi technology to learn more about how it works. You might look for examples of free WLANs and try to find what motivates their operators. Or you might research how broadband providers are reacting to free WLANs. To begin this project, consult the Free WLAN InfoWeb (see page 283) to get an overview of the controversy. Using that information as background, choose the focus for your paper and continue your research. As you write your paper, make sure you can back up your statements with facts and references to authoritative articles and Web pages. Follow your professor's instructions for submitting your paper by e-mail or as a printed document.

5

COMPUTERS IN CONTEXT

The Computers in Context section focuses on the many ways computers and Internet technology are used in education. For this project, identify a topic you'd like to learn more about, such as a hobby or your academic major. Under the heading "Topic Description," write a brief description of your topic, why it interests you, and what you would like to learn about it. Next, use a search engine, such as Google, to locate online tutorials about your topic. Under the heading "Available Tutorials," write a brief description of your search results. Indicate the number of tutorials you found on the topic, provide the URLs for at least three tutorials, and write a short description of each one. Take one of the free tutorials. Under the heading "Evaluation," describe the format for the tutorial, its ease of use, and what you learned.

Study Tips

Study Tips help you to organize and consolidate the information in a unit by making lists, outlines, charts, and sketches. You can use paper and pencil or word processing software to complete most of the Study Tip activities.

1. Make sure you can use your own words to correctly answer each of the orange focus questions that appear throughout the chapter.

2. Make a list of the advantages and another list of the disadvantages of creating and using a computer network.

3. Describe the characteristics of PANs, NANs, LANS, MANs, and WANs, plus provide an example of each.

4. Create a list of network devices mentioned in this chapter. Write a brief description of each one, and indicate whether it would typically be part of the Internet, a LAN, or both.

5. Draw diagrams of star, ring, bus, mesh, and tree network topologies. Make sure that you can trace the route of data over an Ethernet. Discuss how collisions are detected and/or avoided.

6. Make a list of network cabling options and wireless options. Explain the advantages/disadvantages of each.

7. Explain the difference between an analog signal and a digital signal. Why do most modern communications systems use digital signals?

8. Draw a diagram of Shannon's communications model. Apply this model to an Internet dial-up connection by indicating which real-world devices would exist at various points in the model to originate data, encode it, transmit signals, and so on.

9. Make a list of the LAN standards in Section B. For each one, indicate the type of technology it uses, its maximum speed, and the devices available to set up network communications.

10. Draw a diagram of the Internet that includes the following devices connected in a technically correct configuration so that data can flow from the personal computer to the Web server: personal computer, voiceband modem, ISP modem, e-mail server, ISP router, domain name server, two backbone routers, backbone repeater, and Web server.

11. Make sure that you can list the Internet access methods in which upstream transmission rates differ from downstream rates.

12. List the options for wireless Internet access and explain their strengths and weaknesses.

13. Study the Internet Access Options table in Figure 5-59. Add a statement for each column summarizing the strengths and weaknesses of each option.

14. TechTalk: Make a list of security concerns that are related to Internet access. Describe the steps that you would take to (a) secure an individual connection or (b) secure a network connection.

15. Fill in the blanks on the concept map shown below to show the hierarchy of Internet access options.

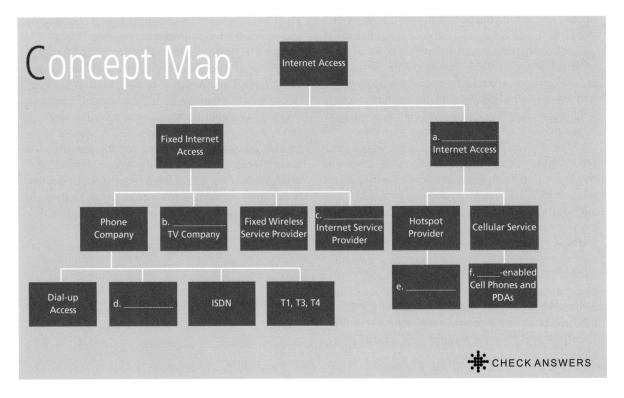

Concept Map

CHECK ANSWERS

Review on the Web

TECHTV VIDEO PROJECT

The TechTV video clip *Free Wi-Fi Blankets San Francisco* highlights a growing trend in many cities. After watching the video clip, write a short summary and explain why San Francisco is ideally suited for this technology. Next, use a Wi-Fi hotspot locator on the Web to get lists of hotspots in three of your favorite cities. Can you tell how many of these hotspots are free and how many require a service plan? Write a summary of your findings.

To work with the Video Projects for this chapter, connect to the New Perspectives NP9 Web site.

www.course.com/np/concepts9/ch05

ONLINE GAMES

Test your comprehension of the concepts introduced in Chapter 5 by playing the NP9 Online Games. At the end of each game, you have three options:

- Submit your results to your instructor using the Universal Gradebook through CoursePort
- Print your results to be submitted to your instructor
- Print a comprehensive study guide complete with page references

To work with the Online Games for this chapter, connect to the New Perspectives NP9 Web site.

www.course.com/np/concepts9/ch05

 LIGHTNING   **DON'T TELL ME**   **FAKE OUT**

ONLINE END-OF-CHAPTER ACTIVITIES

The following NP9 Review Activities are also available at the New Perspectives NP9 Web site:

- Interactive Summary
- Interactive Situation Questions
- Interactive Practice Tests
- Concept Map

If you are using the Web site to complete these activities, you can automatically score your answers and share the results with your instructor.

www.course.com/np/concepts9/ch05

5

6

Web Pages, Web Sites, and E-commerce

FOCUS ON THESE LEARNING OBJECTIVES

Describe the roles that HTML, XHTML, HTTP, URLs, browsers, and Web servers play in bringing Web pages to your desktop

Explain why cookies are useful in an environment that is based on a stateless protocol, and provide some concrete examples of their use

Identify some Web page design tools and discuss their advantages and disadvantages

Describe how HTML tags, cascading style sheets, links, buttons, hot spots, frames, forms, and tables are used in the design and creation of Web pages

Identify the elements that typically form a Web page

Explain how to test and post Web pages

Describe how DHTML, XML, and XSL technologies work to enhance Web pages

List some advantages and disadvantages of using JavaScript, VBScript, Java applets, and ActiveX controls

Discuss why e-commerce has become so popular with consumers and merchants

List some threats to the security of credit card numbers and other sensitive data during e-commerce transactions

Describe how the following e-commerce technologies work: shopping carts, SSL, one-time-use credit cards, electronic wallets, and person-to-person payment systems

A detailed list of learning objectives is provided at the New Perspectives NP9 Web site:

www.course.com/np/concepts9/ch06

UNDERSTAND THE CHAPTER CONTENTS

TIP

When using the BookOnCD, the ✳ icons are "clickable" to access resources on the CD. The ✚ icons are clickable to access resources on the Web. You can also access Web resources by using your browser to connect directly to the New Perspectives NP9 Web site at: www.course.com/np/concepts9/ch06

WHEN THE INTERNET WAS FIRST DEVELOPED, ONLY A HANDFUL OF SCIENTISTS and science fiction writers envisioned it as an interlinked network of information that would one day attract billions of visitors to a virtual global village. Today, the Web is one of the most popular services the Internet offers. Although you might already be adept at navigating the Web, this chapter provides background information about how the Web works that can help you use it efficiently and avoid pitfalls such as viruses and spyware.

TAKE A PRE-ASSESSMENT QUIZ

Take the pre-assessment quiz to find out how much you know about Web technology, e-commerce, and creating Web sites. Armed with your results, you should be able to focus your study time on concepts that will round out your knowledge of the Web and improve your test scores.

www.course.com/np/concepts9/ch06

LISTEN TO A CHAPTER OVERVIEW

Get your book and highlighter ready, then connect to the New Perspectives NP9 Web site, where you can listen to an overview that points out the most important concepts for this chapter.

www.course.com/np/concepts9/ch06

BEFORE YOU READ ON, TRY IT

WHAT'S MY BROWSER STATUS?

Chapter 6 focuses on the World Wide Web, or "Web" for short. The most important software tool for accessing the Web is called a browser. To learn about the browser on your computer, do the following steps:

1. Make sure your computer is on and displaying the Windows desktop.

2. Which browser do you typically use to access the Web? _____
If you don't know, look for browser icons on your desktop. Popular browsers include Internet Explorer, Netscape Navigator, Firefox, and Opera.

3. What is the URL that your browser uses as your home page? _____
To find your browser's home page, start your browser. The home page is the first page displayed and the one displayed when you click the Home button.

4. What is the version number for the browser your are using? _____
To find your browser's version number, click Help and then click About. Your browser's version number should be displayed in a dialog box. After you write down the version number, close the dialog box.

5. Are you using the most recent version of your browser? _____

To find the most recent version for your browser, go to its Web site, for example *www.mozilla.org/products/firefox*, *www.microsoft.com/windows/ie*, *www.netscape.com*, or *www.opera.com*. You should be able to locate a download link that will display the latest version number. Unless you want to download the most recent version of your browser and have permission to do so, exit the download area and close your browser.

Web Technology

In 1990, a British scientist named Tim Berners-Lee developed specifications for URLs, HTML, and HTTP. He hoped that these technologies would help researchers share information by creating access to a sort of "web" of electronic documents. Berners-Lee's free Web software appeared on the Internet in 1991, but the Web didn't take off until 1993 when Marc Andreessen and his colleagues at the University of Illinois created Mosaic, a graphical browser. Andreessen later formed his own company and produced a browser called Netscape, which put the Web into the hands of millions of Web "surfers." In this section of the chapter, you'll peel back the layers of Web technologies to take a look at what happens "behind" your browser window.

THE WEB, THE NET, AND HYPERTEXT

What's the difference between the Web and the Internet?
The Internet is basically a collection of computers and cables that form a communications network, similar in many ways to the telephones and cables that form the telephone system. The Internet is designed to carry computer data, just as the telephone network is designed to carry conversations. The Internet carries a variety of data, including e-mail, videoconferences, and instant messages. The Internet also carries text, graphical, and audio data that form Web pages.

In the words of Tim Berners-Lee, "The Web is an abstract (imaginary) space of information. On the Net, you find computers—on the Web, you find documents, sounds, videos, and information. On the Net, the connections are cables between computers; on the Web, connections are hypertext links." In other words, the Internet is a communications system, and the Web is an interlinked collection of information that flows over that communications system.

What is hypertext and what does it have to do with the Web?
Two of the most important elements of the Web—Hypertext Transfer Protocol (HTTP) and Hypertext Markup Language (HTML)—contain "hypertext" in their names. A **hypertext** is a group of interlinked files. Hypertext is a key concept for understanding today's Web, but the idea of hypertext originated much earlier than the Web or even the Internet. In 1945, an engineer named Vannevar Bush wrote the article "As We May Think," which described a microfilm-based machine called the Memex that linked associated information or ideas through "trails." The idea resurfaced in the mid-1960s when Harvard graduate Ted Nelson coined the term "hypertext" to describe a computer system that could store literary documents, link them according to logical relationships, and allow readers to comment and annotate what they read. Nelson sketched the diagram in Figure 6-1 to explain his idea of a computer-based "web" of "links."

FIGURE 6-1

Ted Nelson's early sketch of project Xanadu—a distant relative of the Web—used the terms "links" and "web."

LINKS are connections between documents which the user may follow.

DOCUMENTS contain a series of POINTERS into the changing web of data.

Expanding Tissue of Text, Data, and Graphics

On today's Web, many aspects of hypertext have become a reality. A typical Web page is based on a document stored in a file and identified by a unique address called a URL. To access any one of these documents, you can type its URL. You can also click an underlined word or phrase called a **hypertext link** (or simply a "link") to access related Web pages.

HTTP and HTML are two of the major ingredients that define the Web. If you add URLs, browsers, and Web servers to this recipe, you'll have a pretty complete menu of the basic technologies that make the Web work.

How does the Web work? A Web server stores data for Web pages that form a Web site. One way to store data for a Web page is as a file called an **HTML document**—a plain text, or ASCII, document with embedded HTML tags. Some of these tags specify how the document is to be displayed when viewed in a browser. Other tags contain links to related document, graphics, sound, and video files that are also stored on Web servers.

As an alternative to HTML documents, Web servers can store Web page data in other types of files, such as databases. Data from product databases, college course schedules, and music catalogs can be assembled into HTML format "on the fly" in response to Web page requests.

To "surf" the Web, you use Web client software called a browser. When you type a URL into the browser's Address box, you are requesting HTML data for a specific Web page. Your browser creates a request for the data by using the HTTP "GET" command. For example, when you enter the URL *www.e-course.com/tutorial*, your browser generates an HTTP request like "GET www.e-course.com/tutorial." Your request goes out over the Internet, where it is routed to the correct Web server.

In the meantime, the Web server has been "listening" for incoming HTTP requests. When your request arrives, the Web server examines it, locates the Web page data you requested, and sends it to your computer. When your request is fulfilled, the server moves on to service other requests. If additional elements are needed for the Web page your browser is displaying—a graphic, for example—your browser must issue a new request to the server for that element. Figure 6-2 illustrates how a Web server and browser interact to display a Web page stored as an HTML document.

TERMINOLOGY NOTE

The terms URL (Uniform Resource Locator), HTTP (Hypertext Transfer Protocol), and HTML (Hypertext Markup Language) were introduced in Chapter 1.

6

FIGURE 6-2

Web browsers and Web servers exchange HTTP messages.

CLICK TO START

1. A browser sends a request to a server using HTTP.

GET document.html

2. The server receives the browser's request and locates the requested HTML document.

HTTP

document.html

4. The browser starts displaying the Web page according to HTML tags embedded in the document.

3. The HTML document is shipped to the browser using HTTP, and then the server waits for requests from other browsers.

HTML AND XHTML

What is HTML? HTML is a set of specifications for creating HTML documents that a browser can display as a Web page. HTML is called a **markup language** because authors mark up their documents by inserting special instructions, called HTML tags, that specify how the document should appear when displayed on a computer screen or printed.

Tim Berners-Lee developed the original HTML specifications in 1990. These specifications were revised several times by the **World Wide Web Consortium** (W3C), but many of the early revisions did not gain widespread acceptance. HTML 3.2, introduced in 1997, was the first widely adopted revision of the original HTML specifications. HTML version 4.0 was introduced in late 1997, and HTML 4.01 in 1999.

XHTML is the follow-up version to HTML 4. Rather than calling it HTML 5, the W3C preferred to name it XHTML 1.0 to reflect its extensibility. XHTML includes all HTML 4 tags, but it can be extended by adding customized tags. Today's Web operates according to XHTML standards, even though people commonly refer to the technology simply as HTML.

How do HTML tags work? In an HTML document, HTML tags, such as <hr /> and <b>, are enclosed in angle brackets. These tags are instructions for the browser. When your browser displays a Web page on your computer screen, it does not show the tags or angle brackets. Instead, it attempts to follow the tags' instructions. Figure 6-3 illustrates how the <hr /> tag produces a horizontal rule on a Web page.

INFOWEBLINKS

The W3C is a worldwide organization that formulates standards for the Web. Learn more by connecting to the **W3C InfoWeb**.

www.course.com/np/concepts9/ch06

FIGURE 6-3

An <hr /> tag in an HTML document (top) produces a Web page (bottom) that contains a horizontal line called a "rule."

The <hr /> tag is called a **self-closing tag**, which is a single tag that includes a closing "/" symbol. A space between the "hr" and "/" is included for maximum compatibility with various browsers.

Unlike the self-closing <hr /> tag, most HTML tags work in pairs. An opening tag begins an instruction, which stays in effect until a closing tag appears. Closing tags always contain a slash. For example, the following sentence contains opening and closing bold tags:

<b>Caterpillars</b> love sugar.

When displayed by a browser, the word "Caterpillars" will be bold, but the other words in the sentence will not be bold.

HTML is not a case-sensitive language, but XHTML style requires tags to be lowercase so that they work on case-sensitive servers. Notice, too, that in self-closing tags such as <hr />, the slash comes at the end of the tag, whereas in a closing tag such as </b>, the slash comes at the beginning.

In addition to formatting, HTML tags can be used to specify how to incorporate graphics on a page. Some people are surprised to learn that HTML documents contain no graphics. Of course, graphics do appear on many of the Web pages displayed in your browser window, so how do they get there? The <img src> tag specifies the name and location of the graphics file to be displayed as part of a Web page. Figure 6-4 illustrates how graphics are incorporated into a Web page.

TERMINOLOGY NOTE

A self-closing tag is sometimes referred to as a "one-sided tag" because it is only needed on one side of the material you are formatting.

FIGURE 6-4

An <img src> tag in an HTML document (top) produces a graphic when your browser displays the Web page (bottom).

6

The HTML document contains no graphics. Instead, it contains references to files that hold graphics.

This graphic is stored in the file library.jpg.

This graphic was inserted by the <img src> tag.

HTML tags do more than make a Web page look pretty. They also produce links that connect you to other Web documents. The <a href> tag specifies the information your browser needs to display links that allow you to jump to related Web pages. Figure 6-5 illustrates <a href> tags that produce links to two Web pages.

FIGURE 6-5

<a href> tags in an HTML document produce underlined links when your browser displays the Web page.

Xtreme.txt - Notepad

File Edit Format View Help

```
<html>|
<head><title> XtremeSport </title></head>
<body>
<font size="+4"> Mort's XtremeSport Report </font>
<br /><br />
The gang is heading out to Philly next week for the X Games.
This year's Games are going to be awesome. Look for really
heavy competition from the vert riders.
Check the <a href="http://www.expn.com/xgamesched.htm">
Official Schedule of Events </a>so you don't miss these
guys.
BTW, it looks like they got to have more volunteers to
collect tickets and do general gopher stuff. You get in
free.
Hey. If your cash tank is running on empty, take a look at
the <a href="http://www.expn.com/volunteers.htm">
volunteers info</a>.
If you can't get enough action at the Games, the annual Tube
Film Festival will be going down at the Prince Music
Theatre. Skip the party scene one night for the
brilliant lineup of short flicks about action sports.
</body>
</html>
```

xgamesched.htm

```
<html>
<head> <title> Schedule of
<body>
<font size="+2"> Schedule of
Monday
10:00 Opening Ceremony
11:00 Preliminary Competition
```

volunteers.htm

```
<html>
<head> <title> Volunteers
<body>
<font size="+2"> Be a volunte
Want to get involved in the gam
you can still get a chance to s
```

The <a href> HTML tag contains the URL for the linked page. Text between the <a href> and </a> tags (such as "volunteers info" in Figure 6-6) appears as an underlined link when the Web page is displayed in a browser.

<a href = "http://www.expn.com/volunteers.htm">volunteers info</a>
URL for linked page   Text for underlined link

FIGURE 6-6

The components of the <a href> tag (left) specify the location of the linked page and the underlined text to display as the link (below).

So HTML documents look a lot different from Web pages, right? Exactly. An HTML document is like a screenplay, and your browser is like a director who makes a screenplay come to life by assembling cast members and making sure they deliver their lines correctly. As the HTML screenplay unfolds, your browser must follow the instructions in an HTML document to display the lines of text on your computer screen in the right color, size, and position. If the screenplay calls for a graphic, your browser must collect it from the Web server and display it. Although the HTML screenplay exists as a permanent file, the Web page you see on your computer screen exists only for the duration of the "performance."

Technically speaking, you can distinguish HTML documents—the "screenplay"—from Web pages—the performance. However, in everyday conversation, the term "Web page" is often used for the HTML document as well as the Web page displayed on screen.

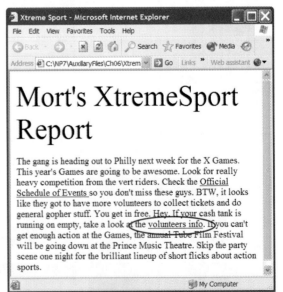

Can I see the HTML tags used to create a Web page? Your browser is designed to display nicely formatted Web pages, not a messy source document filled with HTML tags. However, if you are curious about how a page is constructed or you would like to duplicate the features of a Web page, you can view the source document and its HTML tags by using a menu option on your browser. Figure 6-7 explains.

FIGURE 6-7

Most browsers include a menu option for viewing an HTML source document and the HTML tags it contains. This example illustrates how to view source HTML while using Internet Explorer.

CLICK TO START

What are the most commonly used HTML tags? HTML includes hundreds of tags. For convenience, these tags can be classified into four groups. **Formatting tags** change the appearance of text and work in much the same way as the formatting options in a word processor that create bold and italic text, adjust text size, change text color, arrange text in table format, or center text on a page. **Link tags** specify where and how to display links to other Web pages and e-mail addresses. **Media tags** specify how to display media elements, such as graphics, sound clips, or videos. **Operational tags** specify the basic setup for a Web page, provide ways for users to interact with a page, and offer ways for Web pages to incorporate information derived from databases.

WEB BROWSERS

Why do I need a browser to access the Web? In Chapter 1, you learned that a Web browser—usually referred to simply as a "browser"—is a software program that runs on your computer and helps you access Web pages. Technically, a browser is the client half of the client/server software that facilitates communication between a personal computer and a Web server. The browser is installed on your computer, and Web server software is installed on servers connected to the Internet.

Your browser plays two key roles. First, it uses HTTP to send messages to a Web server—usually a request for a specific HTML document. Second, when it receives an HTML document from a Web server, your browser interprets the HTML tags to display the requested Web page.

6

What are some of today's most popular browsers? Netscape Navigator version 1.0 was published in December 1994. "Netscape," as it is generally called, quickly became the most popular browser on both Macintosh and PC platforms. Numerous revisions added pioneering features, such as frames, plug-ins, and JavaScript support. Netscape is currently published by Netscape Communications, a subsidiary of AOL.

In 1998, Netscape source code became open source software, managed by an organization known as Mozilla. The organization's main product, a browser called Mozilla, was all but ignored by most computer owners. In 2004, however, a new version of Mozilla, dubbed Firefox, rapidly gained popularity because it offered effective security features.

Internet Explorer (IE) version 1.0 was published by Microsoft in August 1995. The program code for the original IE 1.0 browser was licensed from a Netscape spin-off called Spyglass, which provided IE with many of the same features as Netscape. Until IE 4.0 appeared in 1997, however, Microsoft's browser was unable to match Netscape's popularity. Today, IE has supplanted Netscape as the dominant browser across Mac and PC platforms. It is also available for Linux and several versions of UNIX. AOL's browser is a slightly modified version of IE.

Before Firefox, Opera was one of the few alternatives to IE and Netscape. First published in December 1996, Opera began as a Norwegian phone company project to develop a small and fast browser for computers with meager memory and processing resources. Unlike IE and Netscape, which descended from Mosaic, Opera was written from scratch; as a result, it has some unique features, such as page zoom and a multidocument display. Versions of Opera are available for Windows, Linux, UNIX, and Mac OS.

Should I upgrade my browser when new versions become available? It is a good idea to upgrade when a new version of your browser appears. Both IE and Netscape updates are free. Therefore, you can get up-to-date browser functionality simply by spending a few minutes downloading and installing an update.

The problem with using an old version of a browser is that some Web pages depend on new HTML features supported only by the latest browser versions. Without the latest upgrade, you might encounter errors when your browser tries to display a page, but cannot interpret some of the HTML. In other cases, your browser might display the Web page without errors, but you will not see all the intended effects.

Another important reason to upgrade is for increased security. As hackers discover and take advantage of security holes, browser publishers try to patch the holes. Upgrades usually contain patches for known security holes, although new features might sometimes open new holes.

FIGURE 6-8

Today's popular browsers from top to bottom: Netscape Navigator, Internet Explorer, Opera, and Firefox.

HELPER APPLICATIONS, PLUG-INS, AND PLAYERS

Why do I have to download software to view some Web pages? Native file formats for early browsers were typically limited to documents in HTML format and graphics files in GIF and JPEG formats. Today, browsers work with additional file formats to provide more features in displayed pages, but they might not have built-in support for proprietary file formats commonly used on the Web, such as PDF, QuickTime, and Flash.

If you click a link that leads to a file stored in a format your browser cannot handle, you can usually download software necessary to read the file format. For example, you might be directed to the Adobe Web site to download the Acrobat Reader software that handles PDF files. To display an animation, you might need Macromedia's Flash software. For movies, you might need the QuickTime player. The software your browser calls upon to read non-native file formats can take the form of a helper application, plug-in, or player.

What is a helper application? A **helper application** (sometimes called a "browser add-on") is a program that extends a browser's ability to work with file formats. Most helper applications can be downloaded from the Web. The process of installing a helper application creates an association between the browser and a file format, such as PDF, SWF, or MOV. Whenever your browser encounters one of these file formats, it automatically runs the corresponding helper application, which in turn opens the file.

Is a plug-in the same as a helper application? A **plug-in** is a type of helper application, pioneered by Netscape developers, that can be activated from an <embed> tag inserted in an HTML document. For example, <embed src = "sample.swf"> instructs a browser to activate the plug-in that works with the SWF file format, which can in turn open the sample.swf file. Recent versions of Internet Explorer, however, do not respond to the <embed> tag and, therefore, are not able to use Netscape-style plug-ins. Instead, IE uses ActiveX components, which are activated by the <object> tag. Aside from this technical distinction, today's helper applications and plug-ins are very similar from the user's perspective.

The current trend is to use the term **player** to refer to any helper application or plug-in that helps a browser display a particular file format. Figure 6-9 shows a list of players installed for use with Internet Explorer.

INFOWEBLINKS

For information about the most popular players, connect to the **Browser Players InfoWeb**.

www.course.com/np/concepts9/ch06

FIGURE 6-9

You can usually find a list of players installed for use with your browser. If you use Internet Explorer, look for a Manage Add-ons option on the Tools menu. Your browser's list of players might include a PDF reader and spyware detectors used by your antivirus software.

6

HTTP

How does HTTP work? HTTP is a protocol that works with TCP/IP to get Web resources to your desktop. A Web resource can be defined as any chunk of data that has a URL, such as an HTML document, a graphic, or a sound file.

HTTP includes commands called "methods" that help your browser communicate with Web servers. GET is the most frequently used HTTP method. The GET method is typically used to retrieve the text and graphics files necessary for displaying a Web page. This method can also be used to pass a search query to a file server.

HTTP transports your browser's request for a Web resource to a Web server. Next, it transports the Web server's response back to your browser.

An HTTP exchange takes place over a pair of sockets. A **socket** is an abstract concept that represents one end of a connection. Although a packet switching network doesn't actually make point-to-point connections between network nodes, many people find it handy to visualize network connections as a communication line with a doorway-like "socket" at each end.

In an HTTP exchange, your browser opens a socket on your PC, connects to a similar open socket at the Web server, and issues a command, such as "send me an HTML document." The server receives the command, executes it, and sends a response back through the socket. The sockets are then closed until the browser is ready to issue another command. Figure 6-10 demonstrates the messages that flow between your browser and a Web server to retrieve an HTML document.

FIGURE 6-10

HTTP messages flow between a browser and a Web server.

CLICK TO START ✦

1. The URL in the browser's Address box contains the domain name of the Web server that your browser contacts.

Address   www.infoweblinks.com/np/chapter6.html

2. Your browser opens a socket and connects to a similar open socket at the Web server.

Get np/chapter6.htm HTTP/1.1

3. Next, your browser generates and sends an HTTP message through the socket.

4. The server sends back the requested HTML document through the open sockets.

HTTP/1.1 200 OK
Date: Fri 23 Dec 2006
Content-Type: text.htm
Content-Length: 1354
<html>
<body>
<h1> NP InfoWebs</h1>

5. After sending the response, the server closes its socket and the browser closes its socket.

Does a browser have to request each Web page element separately? Yes. HTTP is classified as a **stateless protocol**, which maintains no record of previous interactions and handles each request based entirely on information that comes with it. HTTP generally allows only one request and response per session. As a result, your browser can request an HTML document during a session, but as soon as the document is sent, the session is closed, and the Web server "forgets" that your browser ever made a request. To make additional requests—for example, to request a graphic that's supposed to be displayed on a Web page—your browser must open another session. You can understand, then, that to assemble a complex Web page with several graphics, buttons, and sounds, your browser makes many HTTP requests to the Web server.

What if a Web server cannot find the file a browser requested? A Web server's response to a browser's request includes an **HTTP status code** that indicates whether the browser's request could be fulfilled. The status code 200 means that the request was fulfilled—the requested HTML document, graphic, or other resource was sent. Anyone who surfs the Web has encountered the "404 Not Found" message. Your browser displays this message when a Web server sends a 404 status code to indicate that the requested resource does not exist. HTTP status codes are summarized in Figure 6-11.

FIGURE 6-11

HTTP Status Codes

Code	Message	Description
200	OK	The request succeeded, and the resulting resource, such as a file or script output, has been sent.
301	Moved Permanently	The resource has been moved.
302	Moved Temporarily	The resource is temporarily not available.
303	See Other	The resource has moved to another URL and should be automatically retrieved by the client.
404	Not Found	The requested resource doesn't exist.
500	Server Error	An unexpected server error, such as encountering a scripting error, has occurred.

WEB SERVERS

How does a Web server understand HTTP requests? A Web server is configured to include HTTP software. This software is always running when the server is "up" and ready to fulfill requests. One of the server's ports is dedicated to listening for HTTP requests. When a request arrives, the server software analyzes the request and takes whatever action is necessary to fulfill it.

Why does a Web server need a special port for HTTP requests? The computer that runs Web server software might have other software running on it as well. For example, a computer might operate as a Web server, as an e-mail server, and as an FTP (File Transfer Protocol) server all at the same time! To efficiently handle these diverse duties, a computer devotes one port to HTTP requests, one port to handling e-mail, and another port to FTP requests. Traditionally, port 80 is devoted to HTTP traffic, port 25 deals with SMTP e-mail traffic, and port 21 handles FTP.

6

The way that a computer allocates one port to each service helps explain how it is possible for a Web server to be "down" when the computer is still up and running. A computer runs separate software for each service it offers. As long as the right software is running, the service is available. Suppose, however, that a server encounters a bug in the HTTP software and stops working. That server is no longer able to fulfill HTTP requests, even though it can continue to deal with e-mail and FTP.

Can a Web server handle more than one request at a time?
Just as a multiple-outlet strip can accept many electrical plugs, a single port on a Web server can connect to many sockets that carry requests from browsers. The number of socket connections that a port can handle depends on the server's memory and operating system, but at minimum, hundreds of requests can be handled at the same time.

Some large-volume sites, such as Yahoo! and Amazon.com, have more traffic than any single Web server can handle. These sites tend to use a group of multiple servers, also known as a **server farm**, to handle the thousands of requests that come in each second (Figure 6-12).

FIGURE 6-12

Large-volume Web sites often use a server farm to handle thousands of simultaneous Web page requests.

Is a Web server the same as a Web site? Not necessarily. Most Web server software can be configured so that the server responds to requests addressed to more than one IP address or domain name. In such a case, one computer running one Web server program can act like multiple Web sites. This type of shared hosting is typically supplied to small Web sites that don't have enough traffic to justify the cost of operating their own Web servers.

Similarly, very large Web sites with lots of traffic often configure multiple Web servers to respond to requests for the same IP address or domain name. When you connect to *www.hotmail.com*, for example, you are usually redirected to one of several identically configured file servers.

What happens when traffic exceeds the capacity of Web servers? In a classic example of demand exceeding capacity, the first online Victoria's Secret lingerie show frustrated thousands of shoppers as images appeared at a snail's pace and eventually the servers crashed. During the first months of the conflict in Iraq, the U.S. Army home page, which typically takes 4 seconds to load on a high-speed connection, averaged more than 80 seconds at peak times because the site was inundated with traffic from family members of Army personnel and others interested in information about the unfolding war.

Excessive demand can occur when special circumstances attract people to a Web site or when a worm launches a denial-of-service attack. When traffic exceeds capacity, a Web server can take a long time to fulfill Web page requests—some requests might even time out and produce a "page not found" error. If you experience excessive delays from a Web site, try again at another time, when traffic might be lighter.

COOKIES

What is a "cookie"? A **cookie** is a small chunk of data generated by a Web server and stored in a text file on your computer's hard disk. Figure 6-13 contains an example.

Cookie: jqstudent@sarasota.fl.us/

SITESERVER ID=9022591d2390f3b8639aa3c7cf1ca8f5 sarasota.fl.us/
0 642859008 31887777 2868194304 29411026 *

FIGURE 6-13

A cookie is created by a Web server and stored on your computer's hard disk.

Cookies allow a Web site to store information on a client computer for later retrieval. Web sites use cookies to:

■ Monitor your path through a site to keep track of the pages you viewed or the items you purchased.

■ Gather information that allows a Web server to present ad banners targeted to products you previously purchased at that Web site.

■ Collect personal information you type into a Web page form and retain it for the next time you visit the Web site.

Why do Web sites use cookies? In many respects, cookies are a "fix" for the problems caused by HTTP's stateless protocol. Cookies are frequently used to remind a Web server who you are each time your browser makes a request.

Suppose that you use your browser to visit a popular online music store. You search for your favorite bands, listen to some sample tracks, and select a few CDs you want to purchase. After browsing through 20 or 30 pages, you eventually go to the checkout counter where you see a list of the CDs you selected. You fill out a form that requests your name, shipping address, and payment information.

Although you might have been browsing at the music site for 30 minutes or more, from the perspective of the site's server, that activity could just as well have been carried out by several people, each one spending only a few seconds at the site. Because HTTP is a stateless protocol, each time you connect to a different page, the server regards it as a new visit.

Cookies allow the music site's server to identify you so that your requests won't get mixed up with those of other people visiting the site. Cookies also enable the server to keep track of your activity and compile a list of your purchases.

How do cookies work? When your browser connects to a site that uses cookies, it receives an HTTP "Set-cookie" message from the Web server. This cookie message contains some information that your browser stores on your computer's hard disk. The cookie information can include a customer number, a shopping cart number, a part number, or any other data. In addition, the cookie usually contains the date the cookie expires and the domain name of the host that created the cookie. A server that creates a cookie can request it the next time you connect to one of its Web pages.

Are cookies safe and private? Cookies are a relatively safe technology. A cookie is data, not a computer program or script. Although a cookie is sent to your computer and stored there, it cannot be executed to activate a virus or worm.

INFOWEBLINKS

At the **Cookies InfoWeb**, you'll find links to a collection of articles that focus on cookie technology, including how they affect security and privacy.

www.course.com/np/concepts9/ch06

6

Cookies have several important privacy features. First, cookies don't use your name for identification purposes. Instead, a Web server sends your browser a randomly generated number, which is saved in the cookie and used to identify you and keep track of your activity on the site. Your name is not associated with your cookies unless you entered it into a form, which is then transferred to the cookie.

The second privacy feature of cookies is that they can contain only as much information as you disclose while using the Web site that sets the cookie. A cookie cannot rummage through your hard disk to find the password for your e-mail account, the number for your checking account, or the PIN for your credit card. However, if you enter your credit card number in the process of making an online purchase, it is possible for the cookie to store that number. Most reputable Web sites do not store such sensitive information in cookies—a site's privacy policy often supplies information on this important privacy and security topic.

The third privacy characteristic is that a cookie can be accessed only by the site that created it. For example, if the *www.cduniverse.com* server creates a cookie that contains your preference for rap music, no other Web site should be able to access this cookie and send you junk mail about discount rap CDs. Unfortunately, this aspect of cookie privacy can be defeated—you'll learn more about this topic in the e-commerce section.

Does my computer have to accept cookies? Most browsers include security settings that block cookies (Figure 6-14). Unfortunately, on many Web sites, cookies are the only mechanism available for tracking your activity or remembering your purchases. If you turn off cookies, you probably won't be able to make online purchases, you'll have to manually enter your user IDs and passwords, and you won't be able to take advantage of targeted marketing (such as when a music Web site keeps track of your favorite bands and shows you their new CDs).

A more sophisticated approach to cookie security is provided by **P3P** (Platform for Privacy Preferences Project), which defines a standard set of security tags that become part of the HTTP header for every cookie. This header, called a **Compact Privacy Policy**, describes how a Web site uses cookie data. Based on your security preferences, your browser can use this header data to decide whether to accept the cookie. Compact Privacy Policy headers are supported by recent versions of most browsers.

P3P standards do not ensure your privacy. Although your browser might supply some personal data to a company because the Compact Privacy Policy promised not to distribute or sell that data to other businesses, several months later, the policy might change.

How long do cookies stay on my computer? A Web developer can program a cookie to "time out" after a designated period of time. When a cookie reaches the end of its predefined lifetime, your Web browser simply erases it.

FIGURE 6-14

Most browsers allow you to block cookies, but doing so might make it impossible to shop at some Web sites.

You can also delete cookies, but first you must discover where they are stored. Netscape stores cookies in one large file called *Cookies.txt* on a PC or in *Magiccookie* on a Macintosh. IE stores each cookie in a separate file. Refer to your browser documentation to discover which folder holds your cookies. Most browsers allow you to delete unwanted cookies, as shown in Figure 6-15.

FIGURE 6-15

Internet Explorer typically stores cookies as individual files on your computer's hard disk. You can view a list of cookies stored on your computer and delete those you no longer want.

QuickCheck

SECTION A

1. A hypertext [_____] can be specified by a Web page author using the <a href> tag.

2. The protocol that delivers Web resources to your desktop is called [_____].

3. The followup version to HTML 4 is called [_____] to reflect its extensibility.

4. A Web [_____] is the client half of the client/server software that provides access to information on the Web.

5. Some file formats, such as QuickTime and Flash, require browser plug-ins. True or false? [_____]

6. HTTP is a(n) [_____] protocol, so each time you connect to a different page, the Web server regards it as a new connection.

7. A(n) [_____] is a small chunk of data generated by a Web server and stored as a text file on your computer's hard disk.

CHECK ANSWERS

SECTION B

Basic Web Page Authoring

So you want to make your own Web pages? No problem. With today's Web-related software tools, creating a basic Web page has never been easier. In this section of the chapter, you'll learn about the components of a Web page and discover some tips for incorporating graphics, creating menus, adding navigation buttons, and posting your finished pages to a Web server.

WEB PAGE AUTHORING TOOLS

What tools can I use to create Web pages? You have several choices when it comes to Web page authoring tools. You can use a text editor, HTML conversion tools, online Web authoring tools, or Web authoring software.

How do I use a text editor? The most difficult—and some would say old-fashioned—way to create Web pages is to use a text editor, such as Notepad. A **text editor** is similar to word processing software. Unlike word processing software, however, a text editor creates an ASCII document with no hidden formatting codes. When you use a text editor to create an HTML document, you simply type the HTML tags along with the text that you want the browser to display on a Web page.

When saving the document you create with a text editor, make sure you specify an .html or .htm file extension so that browsers recognize it as an HTML document. If you want to create Web pages using a text editor, like the one shown in Figure 6-16, you need a good HTML reference book.

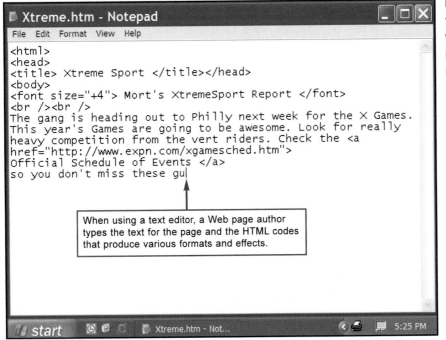

FIGURE 6-16

The most "primitive" Web page authoring tool is a simple text editor, such as Notepad.

What is an HTML conversion tool? An HTML conversion tool adds HTML tags to a document, spreadsheet, or other text-based file to create a file that can be displayed by a browser. For example, Microsoft Word allows you to create a standard DOC file and then use the File menu's Save As Web Page option to convert the document into HTML format. You might also find HTML conversion capabilities in your spreadsheet, presentation, or desktop publishing software. To discover if an application has an HTML option, check the File, Save As, or Export menus. Converting a document into HTML format sometimes produces an unusual result, however, because some of the features and formatting in your original document might not be possible within the world of HTML.

What kind of Web authoring tools can I find online? A third option for budding Web page authors is to use a set of online Web page authoring tools. These template-like tools are provided by some ISPs and other companies that host Web pages for individuals and businesses. Working with these tools is quite simple—you type, select, drag, and drop elements onto a Web page. These simple tools are great for beginners, but they sometimes omit features included with more sophisticated authoring tools.

What's Web authoring software? A fourth option for creating Web pages is a special category of software called **Web authoring software**, which provides tools specifically designed to enter and format Web page text, graphics, and links (Figure 6-17). Popular Web authoring products include Microsoft FrontPage and Macromedia Dreamweaver.

Some Web authoring software has features that help you manage an entire Web site, as opposed to simply creating Web pages. Web site management tools can automatically link pages within a site. They are also capable of checking all the external links at a site to make sure they still link to valid Web pages—that's a valuable feature for today's constantly changing Web!

INFOWEBLINKS

For help in selecting software to design your own Web pages, connect to the **Web Authoring Tools InfoWeb**.

www.course.com/np/concepts9/ch06

6

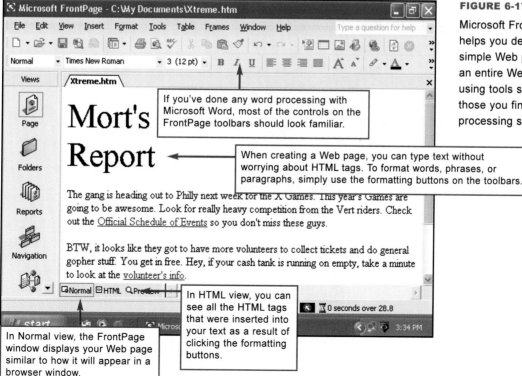

FIGURE 6-17

Microsoft FrontPage helps you design a simple Web page or an entire Web site using tools similar to those you find in word processing software.

BASIC WEB PAGE COMPONENTS

What are the components of a Web page? A Web page consists of text, links, and media elements, such as graphics, sound, and video. These components can be displayed and combined in various ways to create unique, eye-catching pages.

The HTML document for a Web page is divided into two sections: the head and the body. If you create an HTML document using a text editor, you must manually enter the tags that begin and end these two sections. If you use Web authoring software, these tags are automatically entered for you. Figure 6-18 outlines the sections of an HTML document.

The **head section** begins with the <head> HTML tag and contains information that defines some global properties for the document. Information in the head section of an HTML document can include the following:

- The Web page title that appears in the title bar of the browser window

- Global formatting information

- Information about the page that can be used by search engines

- Scripts that add interactivity to the Web page

The **body section** of an HTML document begins with the <body> HTML tag. It contains the text you want the browser to display, the HTML tags that format the text, plus a variety of links—including links to graphics, sounds, and videos. Most Web pages use headers to break up the text into organized sections. A **Web page header** (casually referred to as a "heading") is simply a subtitle displayed in a font that is a different size or color from the normal text in the paragraphs that appear on the page. HTML supports six predefined levels of headings, with H1 using the largest font and H6 using the smallest font. Figure 6-19 illustrates the basic components of a typical Web page.

FIGURE 6-18

The framework for an HTML document consists of two sections: the head and the body.

```
<html>
<head>
<title>
This text appears on the
title bar of the browser
window
</title>
</head>

<body>
This text is displayed in
the browser window as
the Web page
</body>

</html>
```

FIGURE 6-19

Most Web pages feature similar elements.

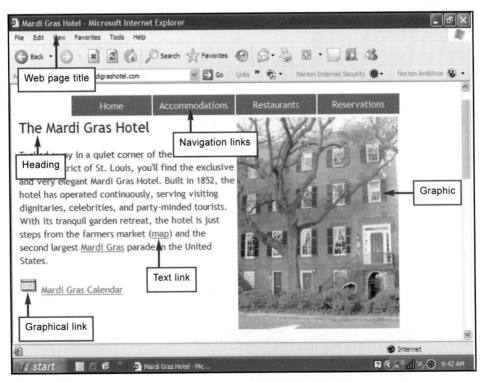

FORMATS, STYLES, AND STYLE SHEETS

How do I format the text on a Web page? When working with Web authoring software, you can simply highlight the text you want to format, and then select formatting attributes from a list.

When you create Web pages with a text editor, you can format text by inserting HTML tags, such as <font size="4" face="Arial" color= "#121212">. Figure 6-20 lists some formatting tags typically used in an HTML document.

FIGURE 6-20

HTML Formatting Tags

Tag	Use
<font size="xxx">	Specify a font size by inserting a number between the quotes
<font color="color">	Specify a color name or number between the quotes
<b>	Bold text
<i>	Italicize text
<u>	Underline text
<align="direction">	Specify paragraph alignment by inserting right, center, or left between the quotes
<bgcolor="color">	Specify a background color for the entire page

What is a style? In the world of Web pages, a style is essentially the same as in the world of word processing. It is a combination of attributes—such as bold, italic, green, and Arial—that specifies the way text is displayed. You can use styles for emphasis and decoration. Just don't get carried away with all the possibilities for colors, sizes, and fonts. Avoid dark or garish background colors. Choose a base font that is easy to read for paragraphs of text. Also, use a consistent set of styles for headers.

What is a style sheet? A style sheet—officially referred to as a **cascading style sheet** (CSS)—acts as a template that can control the layout and design of a Web page. Style sheets, like the one in Figure 6-21, work with HTML tags and make it easy to globally change one or more formats on a Web page without modifying individual HTML tags.

Suppose you are creating a Web page and you plan to include 20 key terms in a bold green 12-point font. You could specify this font style 20 times—one time for each key term. Using a style sheet, however, you can simply define the style as h2 one time at the beginning of the HTML document, and then apply it by using a single HTML tag (if you are using a text editor) or by selecting the style from a list (if you are using Web authoring software). If you later decide to make all these key terms a different color, you can change only the initial definition for the style, and then the change will "cascade" through the entire page.

Rather than define styles in each HTML document for a Web site, you can set up an **external style sheet** that contains formatting specifications for a group of Web pages. All these Web pages can use this external style sheet by means of a link placed in their head sections.

Are style sheets universally supported by all browsers? The main disadvantage of style sheets is that some of their features are not uniformly supported by all browsers. For example, an HTML document that uses style sheets might be displayed differently in Firefox than in IE. If you decide to use style sheets for the Web pages you create, it is important to preview your pages using the browsers that visitors to your Web site might use.

FIGURE 6-21

Styles can be defined in the head section or as a separate document. Here, the head section defines the font used throughout the document for the text in normal paragraphs (p) and in heading 2 (h2).

```
<head>

p { font-size: 12pt;
font-family: Garamond, serif; }

h2 { color: green;
font-weight: bold;
font-size: 12pt;}

</head>
```

6

WEB PAGE GRAPHICS, SOUND, AND ANIMATION

How are graphics incorporated into Web pages? As you learned in Section A, the HTML document that your browser receives does not actually contain any graphics. Instead, it contains an <img src> HTML tag that references a graphic. When displaying a Web page, your browser retrieves the specified graphic and displays it with the rest of the page.

If you use a text editor to create a Web page, you must manually enter the complete tag, such as <img src="truck.gif">, which includes the file name for the graphic. When using Web page authoring software, you can use a menu option to select the graphic from a list of files stored on your computer. Figure 6-22 illustrates how to select a graphic when creating a Web page with FrontPage software.

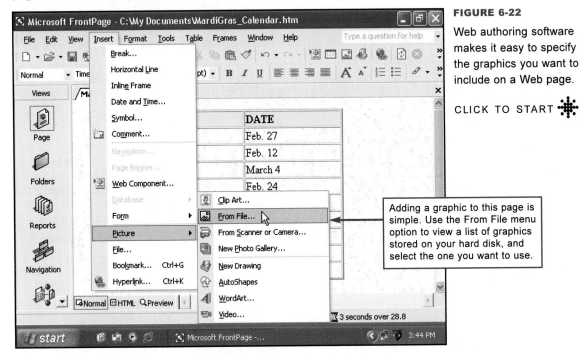

FIGURE 6-22

Web authoring software makes it easy to specify the graphics you want to include on a Web page.

CLICK TO START

Adding a graphic to this page is simple. Use the From File menu option to view a list of graphics stored on your hard disk, and select the one you want to use.

Can I use any graphic format on a Web page? Most of the graphics used for Web pages are stored in GIF, JPEG, or PNG format. All three graphics formats use compression techniques to store graphical images in a relatively small number of bytes. Keeping graphics files size small helps Web pages download swiftly and appear quickly in the browser window. The size of the graphic file on the page should be large enough to view clearly without overwhelming the text on the page. You'll learn more about graphics formats and their use on the Web in Chapter 7.

How do I include sound? You can include sound files in the foreground or background of a Web page. The <a href> tag creates a foreground link that visitors can click to hear the sound. The HTML looks like this:

<a href="FileName.wav"> Click here for music </a>

A second method, commonly referred to as "background sound," uses the <embed> tag to attach a sound file that starts to play as soon as a browser displays the Web page. The Web page can show a pop-up window containing sound controls, or the music can play completely in the background. The HTML looks like this:

<embed src="FileName.wav">

What about video and animation? Videos and animations can add dynamic elements to Web pages. They can be added to Web pages using the simple <embed> tag, the <a href> tag, or the more complex <object> tag.

An **animated GIF** is a graphics file that consists of a sequence of frames or related images. Animated GIFs, such as the one shown in Figure 6-23, are supported by most browsers and offer one of the easiest ways to add simple animation to a Web page.

FIGURE 6-23

When an animated GIF is displayed, your browser cycles through the frames, resulting in a simple repeating animation. In this example, the spacecraft spins to illustrate its operation in space.

CLICK TO START

Flash animation is a proprietary technology developed by Macromedia that requires client software for viewing. Many computer owners have downloaded the Flash client, making it one of the most popular animation formats. Flash with its SWF file format provides more flexibility than animated GIFs and can be used for more complex animations.

Popular video formats, such as QuickTime, MPEG, and AVI, are used for Web-based and disk-based video playback. Variations of these formats are specially designed to handle the communications details for Web playback. To play video, your computer needs corresponding player software, usually specified at the Web site.

LINKS, BUTTONS, AND HOT SPOTS

How do links work? Typically, a link appears on a Web page as underlined blue text, but a link can be any color, might not be underlined, and could look like a graphic or a button. Remember from Chapter 1 that the arrow-shaped pointer changes to a pointing hand when it moves over any text or graphics link in the browser window.

The HTML that indicates a link (Figure 6-24) specifies two elements: a destination and a label.

FIGURE 6-24

The link destination specifies a URL—usually the Web page that appears as a result of clicking the link. The link label is the underlined text that appears on the Web page as the clickable link.

<a href = "http://www.e-course.com/instructions.html" > Click for instructions. </a>

Link destination

Link label that appears on the Web page

The <a href> link tag also allows a Web page author to specify whether the linked page will appear in the current browser window or a new browser window. You've probably encountered Web page links that create a new window. When used effectively, new windows help you easily return to previous pages. Too many new windows, however, can clutter your screen.

How can I turn a graphic into a link? Instead of a text label, you can use an image as a clickable link. These graphical links can connect to other Web pages or graphics. You might have encountered graphical links called "thumbnails" that expand in size when clicked. Graphical links can even look like buttons, complete with labels and icons.

Suppose you want to create a Web page that displays a photograph of a sports car. You want your Web page visitors to be able to click the sports car to see a list of its features. The HTML tag might look like the one in Figure 6-25.

FIGURE 6-25

This link shows an image of a sports car from the file *sports car.jpg*. When clicked, this graphical link displays the information contained in the file named *features.html*.

`<a href = "http://www.cars.com/features.html">`	`<img src =`	`"sports car.jpg">`	`</a>`
Link destination	HTML graphics tag	File name for graphic	

What kinds of links can I add to a page? Text and graphics links can specify a variety of destinations.

- An **internal link** (also called a "local link" or "page link") links to other pages at the same Web site. Web page authors typically use these links for navigation within a Web site.

- An **external link** (also called a "remote link") links to pages outside the Web site. You can create links to any Web site in the world, but it is a good idea to check the site's policies on external links. A site might ask that you create links only to its main page rather than to a specific page within the site.

- An **intrapage link** (also called an "anchor link") is a type of link used to jump to a different location within the current Web page. These links are handy for a long page that's divided into sections. User group FAQs are often structured as a long page of questions and answers. The page begins with a list of questions. Each question is linked to its answer, which appears farther down the page.

- A **mailto link** automatically opens a preaddressed e-mail form that can be completed and sent. These links are often used as a method for contacting the Webmaster who maintains the site or a customer service representative.

How do "hot spots" work? While browsing the Web, you've probably encountered graphics divided into several clickable areas. These images might be maps that allow you to click a region to view a list of local attractions, businesses, or dealers. You might even come across a Web site with a photo on the main page that is divided into areas representing different parts of the Web site.

A clickable map, photo, or diagram (Figure 6-26) is referred to as an **image map**, and each link within the image map is sometimes referred to as a **hot spot**. Hot spots are defined by a set of HTML tags that specify the coordinates and destination page for each clickable area. A Web authoring tool makes it easy to drag over an area of an image, and then use menus and dialog boxes to specify the destination page for each hot spot.

FIGURE 6-26

Using Web page authoring software, hot spots can be defined by dragging over areas of the graphic. Here hot spots define areas of the moon. When the image map is complete, clicking one of these hot spots produces information about that area of the moon.

What is a broken link? A nonfunctioning link is called a **broken link**. A Web page link works only as long as a file with the corresponding URL exists on the server. If the requested file has been deleted or its name changed, the link will not function properly (Figure 6-27).

It is the responsibility of Web page authors to periodically check links on their Web pages to make sure they work. To test links, an author can manually click through them or use the link checking feature of Web authoring software. Broken links must be removed or edited to reflect the correct URL for a destination page.

HTML FORMS

What is an HTML form? An **HTML form** (usually referred to simply as a "form") is a series of fill-in blanks created using the HTML <form> and <input> tags. Forms are used to collect user input for e-commerce orders, site registrations, opinion polls, and so on.

What happens to the data that's entered into a form? The information you enter into an HTML form is held in the memory of your computer, where your browser creates temporary storage bins that correspond to the input field names designated by the form's HTML tags. Your address, in the form shown in Figure 6-28, might be temporarily held in a memory location that's called "Customer Address." When you click a Submit button, your browser gathers the data from memory and sends it to a specially designated program on an HTTP server, where it can be processed and stored.

FIGURE 6-27

When a broken link points to a nonexistent HTML document, your browser typically produces a 404 Not Found error. When a broken link points to a nonexistent graphic or other non-HTML file, your browser usually displays one of the broken link icons, shown below.

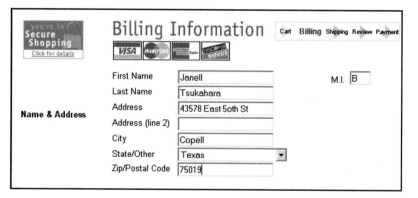

FIGURE 6-28

HTML forms are typically used to collect payment and shipping information at the "check-out counter" of e-commerce Web sites.

What happens to form data after it arrives at a server? The HTTP message containing your data also contains the name of a small CGI or ASP program called a "script" that accepts the form data after it arrives at the server. **CGI** (Common Gateway Interface) is a set of specifications or standards for how servers can handle a variety of HTTP requests. Using these specifications, programmers and Web page authors can write CGI scripts that run on a server to handle form data submitted as HTTP messages. These scripts can be written using a variety of programming and scripting languages, such as Perl, C, C++, C#, and Java.

ASP (Active Server Pages) is a server-side technology developed by Microsoft as an alternative to CGI. ASP scripts, like CGI scripts, run on a server and deal with form data submitted as HTTP messages. ASP scripts can be written in VBScript, Perl, REXX, or JScript—Microsoft's version of JavaScript.

The CGI or ASP script that accepts data from a form specifies how the server should deal with the data. In an e-commerce environment, the data is typically part of a purchase transaction, so it is processed to calculate the total price of an order and then stored in the company's database.

TABLES AND FRAMES

Why are tables such an integral part of many Web pages?

A **Web page table** (usually referred to simply as a "table") is a grid of cells that can be used as a layout tool for specifying the placement of text and graphics on a Web page. Tables are an important part of Web page design because HTML does not include a formatting feature for multiple columns. Without tables, authors would have very little control over the position of text and graphics displayed in the browser window. The effectiveness of tables is clear in Figure 6-29, where one Web page uses tables and the other page does not.

FIGURE 6-29

The Web page displayed at left uses a table to position graphics and text. Without a table, the Web page at right simply displays text and graphics in a single column.

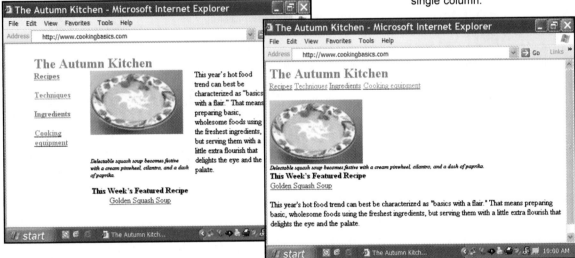

How flexible are tables?

The cells of a table can contain text or graphics, but all the columns and rows in a table do not have to be the same size—they can be sized according to the material they contain. This feature of tables makes them a flexible layout tool. Many Web page designers put the entire contents of a Web page into a single table.

Tables are easy to create—especially when using Web authoring software or word processing software that converts documents into HTML format. You simply define the number of columns and rows for a table, and then specify the size for each row and column. You can merge two or more cells to create a larger cell, or you can subdivide a cell to make it smaller.

FIGURE 6-30

Expert Web designers suggest using frames sparingly and making sure that frames close when linking to other sites.

CLICK TO START

What's a frame?

An **HTML frame** (or simply "frame") is part of a Web page that scrolls independently of other parts of the page so that titles and menus remain visible while you scroll through text and graphics. Frames also allow your browser to display multiple documents at the same time. Frames have fallen out of favor—in part because some Web designers littered Web pages with frames that remained visible after visitors linked to other sites.

A typical use of frames, shown in Figure 6-30, is to display a stationary banner at the top of a page and a set of links on the left side of the screen that do not move as you scroll through the main text on the Web page.

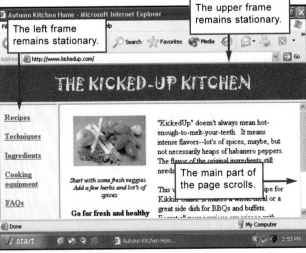

TESTING AND POSTING WEB PAGES

How do I get my Web pages on the Internet? Creating a Web page is not the end of the publishing process. You also must test your pages, transfer them to a Web server, and test all your links, as explained by the steps in the following list:

1. Test each page locally. When you complete the first draft of a Web page, you must test it to verify that every element is displayed correctly by any browsers that visitors to your Web page might use. You can accomplish this task without connecting to the Web. Simply open a browser, and then enter the local file name for the HTML document you created for your Web page. Repeat this process for any other browsers you expect visitors to use. One caution: Your hard disk drive is much faster than a dial-up connection, so the text and graphics for your Web page are displayed faster during your local test than for someone viewing your page over the Internet. Figure 6-31 shows you how to test Web pages offline.

FIGURE 6-31

You can open Web pages offline if they are stored on your computer's hard disk.

You can type the entire path for the file in your browser's Address box. If you stored the file on your computer's hard disk, the path will begin with C:\.

The page you've selected will appear in your browser window. Test the page by making sure all the graphics appear and formats are applied correctly to the text.

If you don't remember the file name, use the Open option on your browser's File menu to view the Open dialog box. Click the Browse button to view a list of files and select one.

2. Transfer pages to a Web server. Whether you're publishing a single page, a series of pages, or an entire Web site, you must put your pages on a Web server—a process called "posting." Although Web server software is available for your home computer, you probably will not want to leave your computer on continuously with a live dial-up, DSL, or cable link to the Internet. Instead, you should look for a site that will "host" your pages by providing space for your HTML files on a Web server.

Some universities allocate space for student Web pages and resumes. ISPs, such as America Online and AT&T WorldNet, also offer space for subscriber Web pages. If you are setting up a site for your business, consider a Web hosting service that, for a monthly fee, provides space on a reliable Web server in a secure data center.

6

The process of posting a Web page consists of transferring from your computer to the hard disk of a Web server the file containing your HTML document and all associated media files, such as graphics, sound, and video files. To accomplish the transfer for pages you've created using a text editor or word processor, you can use a file transfer utility, such as WSFTP. Web authoring software usually provides a menu option that automates the process of posting HTML documents and associated media files.

Regardless of the posting tool you use, it is necessary to follow the posting procedure required by your hosting service. You need to obtain a password that allows you to save files on the server, and you need to know the URL for the server and folder that will hold your files.

3. Test all pages and links. After you post your pages on a Web server, make sure you can access each page, and then test the links between your pages as well as the links to pages on other sites.

4. Update your site to keep it current. Periodically, you should review the information on your Web pages and verify that the links still connect to existing Web pages. You can easily change your pages and then test them offline before reposting them. You might encounter "Under Construction" signs at some Web sites, but they aren't usually necessary. You should handle your construction and revision work offline.

INFOWEBLINKS

Before you post Web pages, take a good look at them. For hints about creating effective Web pages and avoiding design disasters, check the links at the **Web Page Design Tips InfoWeb**.

www.course.com/np/concepts9/ch06

QuickCheck   SECTION B

1. A text editor, such as Notepad, creates a(n) [   ] document to which you can manually add HTML tags.

2. Some Web [   ] software not only offers tools for creating Web pages, but also includes Web site management tools for checking external links.

3. The [   ] section of an HTML document can contain information that defines global formatting and scripts.

4. A(n) [   ] style sheet acts as a template that controls the formats for Web page headers, fonts, and colors.

5. The three graphics formats most commonly used for Web pages are GIF, [   ], and PNG.

6. For Web-based animation, the most popular technology is [   ].

7. Clicking a(n) [   ] link automatically opens a pre-addressed e-mail form.

8. A clickable area of an image map is called a(n) [   ].

9. Many Web page authors and designers use tables as a layout tool for positioning the elements of a Web page. True or false? [   ]

10. After creating Web pages, you have to [   ] them on a Web server before they can be accessed by others.

CHECK ANSWERS

SECTION C

Web Page Extensions, Scripts, and Programs

Originally, Web pages were static, unchanging, and maybe a little boring. After a page was downloaded and displayed in your browser window, that was it. The only way to change it was to download an update to the entire page. Suppose, for example, that a Web designer wants a star to appear next to any item you select from a list displayed on a Web page. With basic HTML, the only way to accomplish that feat is to make the list item a hot spot, and link it to a copy of the same page in which a star appears next to the selected item.

Basic HTML does not provide much flexibility in two key areas. First, it does not allow Web pages to change in appearance after they are downloaded and displayed, and it does not provide a convenient way for users to interact with Web pages. To address these deficiencies, technologies such as Web page extensions, scripts, and programming tools are now available. With these tools, Web page design goes far beyond basic HTML. Students who plan careers as Web page designers need to learn how to use them. For people who simply browse the Web, a basic grasp of these tools is also valuable for understanding usability, security, and privacy issues.

DHTML

What is DHTML? **DHTML** (Dynamic HTML) is typically used to describe the combination of HTML tags, cascading style sheets, and scripts that enables Web page authors to animate the pages they create. DHTML allows the appearance of a Web page to change after it's loaded into the browser, without any additional communication with the Web server for an update.

DHTML is sometimes described as "animating HTML." For example, after a Web page appears in the browser window, a chunk of text can change color, or a graphic can move from one location to another in response to some user action, such as a mouse click or mouseover. The term **mouseover** refers to Web page changes—such as the appearance of a pop-up menu—that occur when a mouse passes over a Web page hot spot. Mouseovers don't require a user click to initiate action (Figure 6-32).

FIGURE 6-32

DHTML effects usually activate as a result of a mouseover. In this example, moving the mouse over the Chapter 4 button changes the color of the button and displays a pop-up overview of the chapter.

CLICK TO START

6

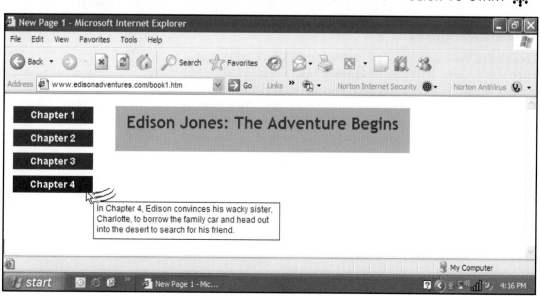

Is DHTML a replacement for HTML? DHTML is not a replacement for HTML. In fact, DHTML is not a language at all. It is simply a term used to describe a method for using HTML in combination with a few other technologies to make Web pages more, well, dynamic.

Do all browsers support DHTML? All of today's popular personal computer browsers support DHTML. However, each browser supports DHTML somewhat differently. As a result, the tags and scripts that a Web page author uses for dynamic effects to be displayed by the Firefox browser could differ from the tags required to achieve the same effects with Internet Explorer.

If you ever noticed a message such as "This site is best when viewed with Internet Explorer," you might have encountered a Web page that includes DHTML effects that work only when the page appears in the Internet Explorer browser window. When you encounter these Web pages, it might be possible to obtain information from the site regardless of the browser you use. You just might not be able to see all the dynamic effects if you are not using the recommended browser.

XML AND XSL

What is XML? XML (Extensible Markup Language) is a method for putting structured data, such as spreadsheet cells or database records, into a text file. As with HTML, XML uses tags and attributes to mark up the contents of a file. Whereas HTML tags, such as <b>, focus on the format or appearance of a document, XML tags essentially define fields of data. For example, XML tags, such as <part number>, <price>, and <weight>, explicitly identify a particular kind of information—much like a field heading in a database.

As the name suggests, XML is extensible, which means that individual users and groups of users can create their own tags and even their own markup languages. A series of specialized tags pertaining to sports, for example, can be formalized as a markup language and used to record data, store it, and then exchange it in a variety of formats, such as Web pages and printed documents. Figure 6-33 lists some markup languages created with XML.

How does XML work? Suppose an automobile manufacturing group wants a standard way to store and exchange information about car features and prices. The group can specify new tags, such as <dealer_price> and <suggested_retail_price>, which can be inserted into XML documents along with corresponding data.

Of course, these new tags must be defined somewhere, so the XML specifications provide for **DTD files** (Document Type Definition files), which contain the tags used in an XML file. DTD files can exist in the same location as the XML file or on a server elsewhere on the Web. This flexibility makes it possible for an entire industry to define and use the same tags by referencing a DTD file on a known server. The tool for reading XML documents is referred to as an **XML parser** and is included in all of today's popular browsers.

What is XSL? XSL (Extensible Stylesheet Language) is a technology that's similar to XML, but can be used to create customized tags that control the display of data in an XML document. The files containing the definitions for new XSL tags can be stored in the same location as the XML file, or they can be referenced from a server anywhere on the Internet. XSL and XML work well together to produce customized, flexible, and platform-independent Web pages.

INFOWEBLINKS

To learn more about DHTML, XML, and XSL, you can access the **Beyond HTML InfoWeb**.

www.course.com/np/concepts9/ch06

FIGURE 6-33

XML Applications

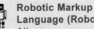

Real Estate Transaction Standard (RETS) Designed to allow realtors and county clerks to access real estate transaction information.

Green Building XML Helps architects, engineers, and builders obtain and calculate energy efficiency data for construction projects.

Robotic Markup Language (RoboML) Allows researchers, designers, and manufacturers to communicate and archive data used by human-robot interface agents.

OpenGIS Geography Markup Language Designed for geographers and mapmakers to record and exchange topographic details and coordinate reference points.

SportsML Helps recruiters, sportswriters, and coaches record and exchange sports scores, schedules, standings, and statistics for a wide variety of competitions.

DocBook Enables authors and technical writers to create and store the contents of books and papers about computer hardware and software.

Chemical Markup Language Helps researchers record, exchange, and display chemical information, particularly at the molecular level.

JAVASCRIPT AND VBSCRIPT

Is it possible to add programs to a Web page? Standard HTML provides a way to display text and graphics on a Web page and link to other Web pages, but because it isn't a programming language, HTML does not provide a way to perform complicated tasks or respond to user actions. Scripting languages, such as JavaScript and VBScript, allow a Web designer to embed simple program instructions, called "scripting statements," directly into the text of an HTML document. A series of these scripting statements is called a **script**. Scripting statements are not displayed by the browser; instead, they instruct the browser to perform specific actions or respond to specific user actions.

How would a Web page author use a scripting language? Scripting languages allow Web pages to become more interactive and incorporate activities that would otherwise require a computer program. Scripts enable e-commerce sites to verify credit card information. They also make it possible to create interactive Web pages, such as loan payment calculators. Scripts work with cookies to deliver custom Web pages, such as those Amazon.com generates each time you return to the site. Scripts don't replace normal HTML—they extend and enhance it.

What are the most popular scripting languages? JavaScript and **VBScript** are the most popular scripting languages. Alternatives include PerlScript, Python, REXX, and Awk.

How do scripts work? Scripts can run on the client or the server. A **client-side script** consists of scripting statements embedded in an HTML document. The statements are executed by the browser, which must have the capability to deal with that scripting language. Most of today's browsers can handle JavaScript, but only IE has the built-in capability to execute VBScript.

A **server-side script** consists of statements that run on the server. Server-side scripts accept data submitted by a form, process that data, and then generate a custom HTML document that is sent to the browser for display. Because the server-side script is interpreted on the server, the browser receives only straight HTML code. The browser does not receive scripts that it must process, which eliminates many of the compatibility problems with client-side scripting.

What's a scripting error? If you've used the Web a lot, you have almost certainly encountered your share of JavaScript error messages, similar to the one in Figure 6-34.

6

FIGURE 6-34

A JavaScript error means that your browser cannot execute the instructions in a Java script. The Windows XP error message might contain a prompt asking if you want to debug the problem. A JavaScript error can be corrected only by the programmer, so your response to this prompt is "no."

A **scripting error** occurs when a browser or server cannot execute one or more statements in a script. In some cases, scripting errors occur when one of the statements does not adhere to the rules of the scripting language. Usually, these "syntax errors" are caused by a careless Web page author who neglects to test pages before posting them. In other cases, scripting errors occur because the browser that's trying to run the script does not support one of the commands.

Some browsers do not include support for a particular scripting language. For example, Opera and Netscape version 6 do not support VBScript. If support for a scripting language is missing, you can download a player, provided one is available for your browser. For example, IE6 users might find it necessary to download and install a Java plug-in to correctly display Web pages that include JavaScript.

Whatever the cause, if you encounter a scripting error message, you can sometimes close the error message dialog box and continue to access information from the Web site. In some instances, the script is tied to a key aspect of the Web site, and you might have to use a different browser to view its pages.

JAVA APPLETS

What's a Java applet? Java, a high-level programming language developed by Sun Microsystems, has become a popular programming tool for Web-based projects. Small Java applications are called **Java applets**.

How do applets work? A programmer or Web page author can use the Java programming language to write Java applet source code, which is stored in a file with a .java file extension. This source code is compiled into a format called **bytecode** with a .class file extension. A reference to this bytecode file is included in an HTML document using the <applet> HTML tag. When an HTML document contains an <applet> tag, your browser downloads the specified bytecode file and then executes the applet using a **Java Virtual Machine** (JVM). Figure 6-35 helps you visualize this process.

FIGURE 6-35

Programmers can create Java applet source code, compile it, and then include it in an HTML document, where it is executed by a browser.

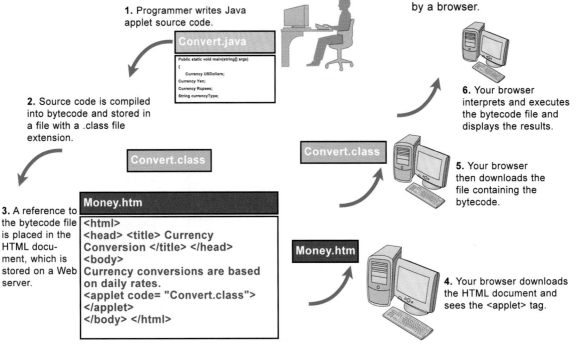

1. Programmer writes Java applet source code.

Convert.java

```
Public static void main(string[] args)
{
    Currency USDollars;
Currency Yen;
Currency Rupees;
String currencyType;
```

2. Source code is compiled into bytecode and stored in a file with a .class file extension.

Convert.class

3. A reference to the bytecode file is placed in the HTML document, which is stored on a Web server.

Money.htm

```
<html>
<head> <title> Currency
Conversion </title> </head>
<body>
Currency conversions are based
on daily rates.
<applet code= "Convert.class">
</applet>
</body> </html>
```

Convert.class

Money.htm

6. Your browser interprets and executes the bytecode file and displays the results.

5. Your browser then downloads the file containing the bytecode.

4. Your browser downloads the HTML document and sees the <applet> tag.

What's the difference between Java applets and JavaScript?
Although their names would lead you to believe that they are similar, Java applets and JavaScript are two very different technologies. The table in Figure 6-36 summarizes their differences.

FIGURE 6-36

Java Applet and JavaScript Comparison

Java Applets	JavaScript
Must be compiled into bytecode	Not compiled
Stored as a separate file or embedded in HTML document	Entire script stored with HTML document
Referenced using the <applet> or <object> HTML tags	Referenced using the <script> HTML tag
Requires the browser to use a Java Virtual Machine	Requires a JavaScript interpreter
Programmers and Web page authors must use Java programming tools	No special programming tools required

How safe are Java applets?
A Java applet is a program that your browser downloads and runs on your computer. You might wonder if a Java applet could contain a virus that would take up residence in your computer system or a worm that would spread over your network. The technology for Java applets was designed with security in mind. The applets you download from the Web have the following restrictions:

- They cannot open, modify, delete, or create files on your computer.

- They cannot make any network connections except to the originating site.

- They cannot start other programs.

You can see from this list that applets are prohibited from the activities that characterize viruses and worms. Because they cannot attach themselves to files (thereby modifying them), delete files on your hard disk, mail themselves to people in your address book, and so on, applets are considered a fairly safe technology.

A more troublesome aspect of Java applets is that they are sometimes blocked by network firewalls. When an applet is blocked, your browser might display a Security Exception error message, or you might see the broken graphics link icon. If you encounter such problems on your network, you should refer to your personal firewall documentation or consult your network manager.

6

INFOWEBLINKS

Maybe you're interested in adding Java applets to your Web pages. You'll find links to online tutorials at the **Java Applets InfoWeb**.

www.course.com/np/concepts9/ch06

ACTIVEX CONTROLS

What is an ActiveX control? Sometimes when you connect to a Web site, you might see a dialog box containing a security warning, such as the one in Figure 6-37. To better understand what this warning means, you need some background information about ActiveX controls.

FIGURE 6-37

Web surfers who use Internet Explorer sometimes encounter the Security Warning dialog box.

An **ActiveX control** is a compiled computer program that can be referenced from within an HTML document, downloaded, installed on your computer, and executed within the browser window. ActiveX controls can be used on the server side, too. Programmers and Web page authors use programming languages, such as C++ and Visual Basic, to create these controls, which can be applied in a wide variety of ways to make Web pages interactive and provide the functionality many consumers expect after using full-featured applications, such as word processing, graphics, and entertainment software.

How do ActiveX controls differ from Java applets? ActiveX controls are installed on your computer's hard disk, whereas Java applets are simply downloaded into memory and run. The advantage of installing an ActiveX control is that it is available locally the next time you want to use it. Java applets cannot be installed on your computer—they are downloaded every time they are used and therefore might seem to operate more slowly than ActiveX controls.

Another key difference between the two technologies is that Java applets work on many computer platforms, but ActiveX controls are designed only for the Windows platform. ActiveX plug-ins are available for some versions of Firefox, Netscape, and Opera, however, ActiveX components work most reliably on Windows PCs using the IE browser. ActiveX, which is a Microsoft technology, is currently not supported by non-Windows operating systems, such as Linux or Mac OS.

INFOWEBLINKS

ActiveX controls are used in all sorts of Windows software—not just Web-based applications. You can get the scoop on ActiveX controls, including how they affect security, by linking to the **ActiveX InfoWeb**.

www.course.com/np/concepts9/ch06

Are ActiveX controls safe? Most ActiveX controls are safe. However, an ActiveX control is a full-fledged program, which gives it the potential to include routines that alter or delete data on your computer's hard disk. If you use IE as your browser, you can adjust its security settings so that it never downloads any ActiveX controls; it downloads and installs only those controls with signed digital certificates; or it downloads and installs any ActiveX controls. Figure 6-38 shows IE options for ActiveX security settings.

Use the slider bar to select a security level. Medium security is typically recommended.

The Custom Level button allows you to change settings for each security item.

When security is set at Medium, unsigned ActiveX controls are not downloaded.

FIGURE 6-38

Internet Explorer allows you to select a level of security for Web browsing. To access the dialog box, select Tools from the menu bar, then select Internet Options. The Medium setting gives you a good level of security, and allows your browser to use signed ActiveX controls, which are usually safe.

What is a "signed" ActiveX control? ActiveX controls include digital certificates to increase their security. A **digital certificate** is an electronic attachment to a file, such as an ActiveX control, that verifies the identity of its source. It is similar to a check cashing card or the stamp you get on your hand when a bouncer checks your ID at the entry to a club. In the world of ActiveX controls, a digital certificate means that the control was created by an identifiable person or company, which can be held accountable for its contents.

An individual programmer, a Web author, or a company can apply for a digital certificate through a **certificate authority** such as VeriSign. Applicants must provide information to verify their identities. The certificate authority then confirms this information before issuing a certificate. Most certificates must be renewed annually. The fee for an individual certificate is free. Corporate certificates are $3,000.

A digital certificate can be electronically attached to any ActiveX control the applicant creates. That control is then referred to as "signed"—it is as though the programmer signed his or her name to it. The certificate authority never reviews the ActiveX control itself, so a digital certificate does not ensure that the control is virus-free. Instead, a certificate provides consumers with the name of the person who created the control—the theory being that malicious programmers would not put their names on certificates that travel with an ActiveX control infected with a virus or worm.

INFOWEBLINKS

The **Digital Certificates InfoWeb** explains their use in monitoring ActiveX controls and in verifying consumer and merchant identities in an e-commerce transaction.

www.course.com/np/concepts9/ch06

6

How does a digital certificate work? Suppose you connect to a Web page that includes an ActiveX control, and your browser's security setting is Medium—the recommended setting for the average Web surfer. When your browser encounters the HTML tag that references a signed ActiveX control, it displays a warning message to alert you that an ActiveX component is trying to install itself. Your browser reads the digital certificate, displays the name of the person or company that signed it, and verifies that the component was not altered since it was signed.

After examining this information, you can decide whether you want your browser to download and install the ActiveX control. To avoid viruses, you should not accept ActiveX controls that are unsigned, signed with "weird" names, or have been changed since they were created. Figure 6-39 shows an example of a valid digital certificate.

FIGURE 6-39

A valid digital certificate contains the certificate holder's name. To ensure that the certificate is legitimate, you can click the underlined links to connect to the certificate holder's Web site and the Web site of the certificate authority.

QuickCheck

1. If you want to put structured data, such as spreadsheet cells, into an HTML document, you can use [_____] tags to identify the contents of each field. Hint: Use the acronym.

2. To create interactive Web pages, such as loan payment calculators and online tests, developers can insert [_____] into HTML documents.

3. A(n) [_____] applet is stored as a bytecode and activated by an <applet> HTML tag.

4. A(n) [_____] control is a compiled program that can be referenced from within an HTML document, downloaded, installed on your computer, and executed.

5. A digital [_____] carries an electronic signature to verify the source of a program, file, script, or control.

CHECK ANSWERS

SECTION D

E-commerce

One of the most popular activities on the Web is shopping. Online shopping has the same allure as catalogs—you can shop at your leisure, anonymously, and in your pajamas. But the economics of the Web provide opportunities that go beyond retail catalogs. Even small businesses and individual artists can post Web pages that display their wares. The Internet was opened to commercial use in 1991. Since then, thousands of businesses have set up shop at Web sites. This section of the chapter focuses on e-commerce and the technologies a typical shopper might encounter on the Web.

E-COMMERCE BASICS

What is e-commerce? Chapter 1 introduced e-commerce as Internet activities that include online shopping, electronic auctions, online banking, and online stock trading. Although the experts don't always agree on its definition, the term **e-commerce** typically refers to business transactions that are conducted electronically over a computer network. It encompasses all aspects of business and marketing processes enabled by Internet and Web technologies.

E-commerce wares include many kinds of physical products, digital products, and services. Physical products offered at e-commerce sites include such goods as clothing, shoes, skateboards, and cars. Most of these products can be shipped to buyers through the postal service or a parcel delivery service.

Increasingly, e-commerce goods include digital products, such as news, music, video, databases, software, and all types of knowledge-based items. The unique feature of these products is that they can be transformed into bits and delivered over the Web. Consumers can get them immediately upon completing their orders, and no one pays shipping costs.

E-commerce merchants also peddle services, such as arranging trips, online medical consultation, and distance education. Some of these services can be carried out by computers. Others require human agents. Services can be delivered electronically, as in the case of a distance education course, or they might produce some physical product, such as a cruise ship ticket.

Who is the typical e-commerce customer? The demographics of e-commerce have not yet stabilized. Whereas the typical e-commerce consumer in 1995 was a 30-something white male, in recent years, females and teens have entered the online shopping fray in droves.

Most of the e-commerce activities Web surfers enjoy are classified as **B2C** (business-to-consumer) e-commerce. In the B2C model, businesses supply goods and services to individual consumers. In the **C2C** (consumer-to-consumer) model, consumers sell to each other. This model includes wildly popular online auctions and rummage sales. Figure 6-40 lists some popular B2C and C2C activities. **B2B** (business-to-business) e-commerce involves one enterprise buying goods or services from another enterprise. **B2G** (business-to-government) e-commerce aims to help businesses sell to governments.

FIGURE 6-40

B2C and C2C e-commerce offer consumers many types of goods and services.

Online storefronts sell a variety of goods, such as clothing, books, toys, music, food, sports gear, and electronics.

Online auctions provide consumers with a worldwide market for antiques, collectibles, and other new and used items.

Online schools offer credit and noncredit courses, tutorials, and even college degrees.

Online ticket and reservation systems provide concert and event tickets plus air, hotel, and car reservations.

Online information services sell subscriptions to news archives, databases, and online magazines.

6

How profitable is e-commerce? E-commerce enhances traditional business models by offering efficiency and opportunities for automation, computerization, and digitization. As with a traditional "brick and mortar" business, profit in an e-commerce business is the difference between income and expenses.

One of the advantages of e-commerce is its ability to increase profit margins by cutting costs. For example, a typical catalog order placed over the phone costs the merchant $2.50, whereas an online transaction costs about 35 cents. A hotel reservation made online costs the innkeeper 80% less than a booking by phone. A withdrawal or deposit costs the bank about a dollar when handled by a teller, about 25 cents on an ATM, and only a penny on the Web.

E-commerce merchants also gain income by hosting advertising space for marketers, who are creating increasingly hard-to-avoid styles of online advertisements, such as banner and pop-up ads. A **banner ad** is an advertisement, typically embedded at the top of a Web page. A **pop-up ad**, such as the one in Figure 6-41, is an advertisement that appears in a separate window when you connect to a Web page. When you click a banner or pop-up ad, your browser connects directly to the advertiser's Web site, where you can find product information and make a purchase.

Banner and pop-up ads earn revenue for hosting merchants based on **click-through rate**—the number of times that site visitors click the ad to connect to the advertiser's site. The hosting merchant is paid a small fee for each click through. Click-through rates have declined in recent years because most consumers simply ignore the ads or install **ad-blocking software** to prevent ads from appearing on their screens. Recent versions of Internet Explorer include a configurable feature to block pop-up ads.

E-commerce has matured from its early days, when investors were happy to throw money at any e-commerce scheme, through a "dot-com bust," when sites with flawed business models closed down. Today, e-commerce is rebuilding its image, based on more realistic business plans and responsible management.

Is e-commerce popular worldwide? North America accounts for about half of all e-commerce activity, and Western Europe and Asian Pacific regions account for most of the rest. The low volume of e-commerce activity in Africa, Eastern Europe, and Russia can be attributed to several factors, including lack of Internet access, language barriers, depressed economies, shipping limitations, and merchant policies.

Today's e-commerce model is aimed at English speakers with Internet access and a credit card. Although a handful of Web sites offer language alternatives, non-English speakers have difficulty using search engines and reading product descriptions. In regions where electricity and telephone service are not available, Internet access is simply not possible (Figure 6-42). Many e-commerce merchants do not accept checks or cash and might not accept credit cards issued by non-U.S. banks. Even if cash payment is accepted, the price of goods remains beyond the budget of many people in developing countries.

FIGURE 6-41

Pop-up ads appear as separate windows.

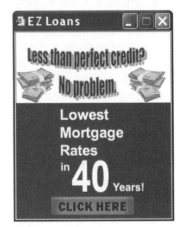

FIGURE 6-42

In some regions of the world, e-commerce obstacles include language barriers, economic factors, and even lack of electrical service.

ONLINE SHOPPING

What makes online shopping so special? E-commerce offers some unique advantages over brick-and-mortar stores and mail-order catalogs. Customers can easily search for specific merchandise. They can configure products online, see actual prices, and build an order over several days. Customers can easily compare prices between multiple vendors.

Merchants are always looking for ways to attract customers. The Web and its search engines give merchants a way to be found by customers without expensive, national advertising. Even small merchants can reach a global market. Web technology also allows merchants to track customer preferences and produce individually tailored marketing.

How does an e-commerce store work? E-commerce seems simple from the perspective of a shopper who connects to an online store, browses the electronic catalog, selects merchandise, and then pays for it. The screentour in Figure 6-43 walks you through a typical shopping session.

FIGURE 6-43

In a typical shopping session, you connect to an online storefront and use navigation controls to browse through the merchant's catalog. As you browse, you can drop items into your electronic shopping cart. At the checkout counter, you enter the information necessary to pay for the items you selected.

CLICK TO START ✣

6

Behind the scenes, an e-commerce site uses several technologies to display merchandise, keep track of shoppers' selections, collect payment data, attempt to protect customers' privacy, and prevent credit card numbers from falling into the wrong hands.

An e-commerce site's domain name, such as *www.amazon.com*, acts as the entry to the online store. A Web page at this location—sometimes referred to as an "electronic storefront"—welcomes customers and provides links to various parts of the site. The goods and services for sale appear in a customer's browser window.

An e-commerce site usually includes some mechanism for customers to select merchandise and then pay for it. Customer orders might be processed manually in a small business. Most high-volume e-commerce businesses, however, use as much automation as possible; their order-processing systems automatically update inventories, and then print packing slips and mailing labels.

SHOPPING CARTS

What's an online shopping cart? If you've done any shopping online, you've probably used an **online shopping cart**—a cyberspace version of the metal cart you wheel around a store and fill up with merchandise.

How do shopping carts work? As mentioned earlier, HTTP is a stateless protocol, which fulfills a single request for a Web resource and then immediately forgets about it. Under these circumstances, you might wonder how it is possible for an online retail store to remember the items you put in your shopping cart.

Most shopping carts work because they use cookies to store information about your activities on a Web site. Cookies work with shopping carts in one of two ways, depending on the e-commerce site. An e-commerce site might use cookies as a storage bin for all the items you load into your shopping cart, as shown in Figure 6-44.

FIGURE 6-44

Shopping cart items can be stored in a cookie.

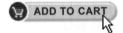

1. When you click the Add to Cart button, the merchant's server sends a message to your browser to add that item number to the cookie, which is stored on your computer.

ITEM #B7655

VIEW CART

2. When you check out, the server asks your browser for all the cookie data that pertains to your shopping cart items.

3. Your browser sends those cookies along with a request for an order summary.

Your order:

1 Blender $29.95

1 Wok $38.49

4. The Web server uses the cookies to produce a Web page listing the items you want to purchase.

Some e-commerce sites use cookies simply as a way to uniquely identify each shopper. These sites generate a unique ID number that is stored along with your item selections in a server-side database (Figure 6-45).

FIGURE 6-45

Shopping cart items can be stored in a server-side database.

Order for CART #2098-2

1 Blender   B7655 $29.95

1 Wok   GJK4-31 $38.49

1. When you connect to a merchant's site, the server assigns you a unique shopping cart ID number and sends it to your browser in a cookie.

WEB SERVER

CART # 2098-2

DATABASE

CART # 2098-2

ITEM # B7655

3. The Web server stores this number and your merchandise selection in the merchant's server-side database.

WEB SERVER
CART # 2098-2

2. When you select an item to purchase, your browser reads your shopping cart ID number from the cookie, and then sends this number to the merchant's Web server.

BUY IT

4. When you check out, your browser sends your shopping cart number to the server, which retrieves all your selections from the merchant's database.

TRANSACTION PRIVACY AND SECURITY

Is it safe to shop online? Online shoppers are justifiably worried that personal information and credit card numbers supplied in the course of an e-commerce transaction might be hijacked and used inappropriately. Web sites can surreptitiously collect data about your browsing and purchasing habits. Credit card numbers can be stolen and used without authorization.

How does e-commerce affect my privacy? Online merchants are eager to get the attention of prospective customers, but they sometimes use spyware that has the potential to compromise your privacy. **Spyware** is any technology that surreptitiously gathers information. In the context of the Web and e-commerce, spyware secretly gathers information and relays it to advertisers or other interested parties. Web-based marketers use several spyware techniques, including ad-serving cookies and clear GIFs.

What is an ad-serving cookie? When you connect to a Web site, you expect it to store an innocuous cookie on your computer's hard disk. Some Web sites, however, feature banner ads supplied by third-party marketing firms. If you click the ad, this third party can create an **ad-serving cookie** (Figure 6-46) and use it to track your activities at any site containing banner ads from that third party. The marketing firms that distribute ad-serving cookies claim that this data is simply used to select and display ads that might interest you, but privacy advocates are worried that shopper profiles can be compiled, sold, and used for unauthorized purposes.

FIGURE 6-46

Ad-serving cookies can be created and stored on your computer's hard disk without your knowledge.

What is a clear GIF? A **clear GIF** or "Web bug" is typically a 1x1 pixel graphic on a Web page. Clear GIFs can be used to set cookies to third-party Web sites. Unlike ad-serving cookies, you don't have to click a banner ad to receive a GIF-activated cookie. Simply viewing the page that contains a clear GIF sets the cookie. Cookies created with clear GIFs have the same uses and potential for misuse as ad-serving cookies.

Can I do anything about spyware? Ad-blocker software and anti-spyware are designed to block ad-serving cookies, clear GIFs, and other spyware—some even block banner and pop-up ads altogether. These products are becoming quite popular, despite their tendency to slightly slow your browser's response time.

INFOWEBLINKS

For more information about software you can install to block ads, ad-serving cookies, and clear GIFs, check out the **Ad Blocker InfoWeb**.

www.course.com/np/concepts9/ch06

6

Can credit card numbers get intercepted? Many shoppers worry that their credit card numbers might get intercepted while traveling over the Internet. A **packet sniffer** (officially called a "protocol analyzer") is a computer program that monitors data as it travels over networks. Most network devices read only the packets addressed to them and ignore the packets addressed to other devices. However, a packet sniffer can observe and open any packet traveling on the network. Packet sniffers have legitimate uses in system maintenance, but hackers can also use them to pilfer data as it travels from customers' computers to e-commerce sites.

To protect your data from packet-sniffing hackers, you should engage in electronic transactions only over a secure connection. A **secure connection** encrypts the data transmitted between your computer and a Web site. Even if a hacker can capture the packets containing your payment data, this data must be decrypted before it can be used for illicit purposes. Technologies that create secure connections include SSL and S-HTTP.

What is SSL? **SSL** (Secure Sockets Layer) is a protocol that encrypts data traveling between a client computer and an HTTP server. This encryption protocol creates what's called an "SSL connection" using a specially designated port—typically Port 443 rather than Port 80, which is used for unsecured HTTP communication. Web pages that provide an SSL connection start with *https:* instead of *http:*.

What is S-HTTP? **S-HTTP** (secure HTTP) is an extension of HTTP that simply encrypts the text of an HTTP message before it is sent. Although SSL and S-HTTP both use encryption techniques to securely transmit data, they are technically different. Whereas SSL creates a secure connection between a client and a server over which any amount of data can be sent securely, S-HTTP is simply designed to encrypt and then transmit an individual message.

How do I know if a connection is secure? Your browser helps you identify when you are using a secure connection. Figure 6-47 explains.

> **TERMINOLOGY NOTE**
>
> Secure connections differ from secure Web sites. A secure connection encrypts the data transmitted between your computer and a Web site. A secure Web site, such as an online banking site, uses password security to prevent unauthorized access to pages on the site.

FIGURE 6-47

Secure connections are indicated by a dialog box, URL, and taskbar icon.

When a secure connection is about to be activated, your browser usually displays a dialog box.

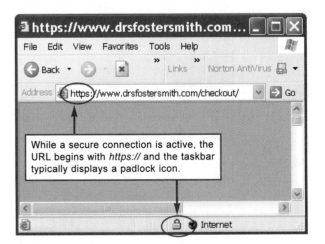

While a secure connection is active, the URL begins with *https://* and the taskbar typically displays a padlock icon.

What is the danger of a database break-in? An increasing number of businesses report that their customer databases have been accessed without authorization. In some cases, thousands of credit card numbers are stolen. Security-conscious e-commerce merchants protect their databases by limiting access and encrypting data. Unfortunately, not all businesses follow these practices. Even when databases seem secure, hackers might find security holes and retrieve sensitive data.

As a consumer, you cannot prevent database break-ins, but you can take steps to ensure that the credit card number stored in a merchant's database is of little use to a hacker. Several credit card companies offer one-time-use credit card numbers, which allow consumers to make purchases while keeping their actual card numbers hidden.

A one-time-use credit card number works for a single online purchase. Your credit card company tracks the purchases you incur with one-time-use numbers and adds the charges to your monthly credit card statement. One-time-use numbers cannot be used twice, so even if a hacker steals the number, it will not be accepted for any online or offline purchases.

Should I worry about dishonest employees? An online break-in into the database of a merchant or credit card processing service is a fairly high-tech crime, but your credit card number can be compromised by low-tech methods as well. If a merchant collects your credit card number instead of routing it directly to a credit card processing service, a dishonest employee who works for the merchant might be able to obtain your card number while processing your order. Individual consumers can't do much to prevent this type of theft, but the likelihood of it occurring is low—you take a similar risk every time you pay for a meal by allowing a waiter to take your credit card back to a cashier station or give your credit card number over the phone.

What is a fake storefront? A fake storefront appears to be an online store, but is in fact a fraudulent Web site, designed exclusively for the purpose of collecting credit card numbers from unwary shoppers. These sites might have all the trappings of a real e-commerce site—they might even offer a secure connection for transmitting your credit card number. When your data is received, however, it is stored in a database that belongs to a hacker, who can use the data for illegitimate transactions. Figure 6-48 explains how you can avoid fake storefronts.

TERMINOLOGY NOTE

In banking jargon, a one-time-use credit card number is called a controlled payment number. Banks and credit card companies offer this service under many different names, such as Citibank's Virtual Accounts and Discover Card's Deskshop.

INFOWEBLINKS

Connect to the **Safeguarding Your Credit Card InfoWeb** for tips on this important aspect of e-commerce.

www.course.com/np/concepts9/ch06

6

FIGURE 6-48

The URLs for fake storefronts often differ from the real thing by a single character. For example, hackers might create a fake storefront using the URL *www.ediebauer.com*— similar to the legitimate store at *www.eddiebauer.com.* To protect yourself from fake storefronts, make sure to type the URL correctly. Better yet, type the store name—Eddie Bauer, for example—in a search engine such as Google, and use the link provided to reach the site's home page.

Can hackers steal credit card numbers from my hard disk? If your computer is connected with an always-on network connection, such as DSL or cable Internet service, unwanted intruders could find their way into the files stored on your computer's hard disk. If your credit card number exists in any file—for example, in an order confirmation sent to you in an e-mail message—a hacker could find it. As explained in Chapter 5, to block intruders from accessing your computer's hard disk, you should install firewall software.

What is an electronic wallet? An **electronic wallet** (also called a "digital wallet") is software that stores billing and shipping information that a customer submits when finalizing an e-commerce purchase. Electronic wallets, such as Microsoft Passport and Yahoo! Wallet, might also hold a digital certificate that verifies your identity.

You can create an electronic wallet by subscribing at the wallet provider's site. After you create your electronic wallet, it pops up on your screen when you make a purchase at a participating merchant's site (Figure 6-49).

FIGURE 6-49

An electronic wallet can transfer your billing and shipping information to a participating site's e-commerce Web server when you check out.

CLICK TO START

How does an electronic wallet work? The data for an electronic wallet can be stored on your computer or on a server maintained by a wallet provider—usually a financial institution, such as a bank or credit card company. Server-side wallets are sometimes referred to as "thin wallets" because they don't require much storage space on your computer.

A wallet requires client-side and server-side software. The client-side software resides on your computer—usually in the form of a browser plug-in. The server-side wallet software resides on an HTTP server that the merchant maintains. Many "brands" of wallets exist, and a merchant's server can collect data only from a compatible wallet.

When you proceed to an online checkout, software on the merchant's server sends an HTTP message to your PC that looks for and activates compatible wallet software. By clicking a Submit button, your payment data is transferred from your electronic wallet to the server.

How safe is an electronic wallet? Most wallets implement **SET** (Secure Electronic Transaction)—a security method that relies on cryptography and digital certificates to ensure that transactions are legitimate as well as secure. Even if a hacker gains access to your wallet file from your computer or a server, the data it contains will be difficult to decode. Of course, you don't have to decode the contents of your electronic wallet before using it, so you might wonder if a hacker could simply copy your wallet and use the whole encrypted file just as you do. Your wallet is protected by a password, which acts as a PIN to prevent unauthorized use.

Electronic wallets have several vulnerabilities, however. Security analysts were stunned to discover that it is possible to steal credit card numbers from an electronic wallet simply by getting the victim to open an e-mail message. Hackers might also be able to snag data as it flows from an electronic wallet to a merchant's site by using Trojan horse technology to collect your wallet password. Consumers should carefully study current security bulletins before trusting their data to electronic wallets.

What is a person-to-person payment? A **person-to-person payment** (sometimes called an "online payment" or a P2P payment) offers an alternative to credit cards. It can be used to pay for online auction items and to wire money over the Internet. An online service called PayPal pioneered person-to-person payments. PayPal's model has since been copied by several other service providers.

How does a person-to-person payment work? The process begins when you open an account at a person-to-person payment service. Some services require you to deposit money in your account—just as though you were opening a bank account. Other services allow you to supply your credit card number, which is billed only as you make purchases. You receive a user ID and password that enable you to access your account to make purchases and deposit additional funds. Money can be sent to anyone who has an e-mail account, as shown in Figure 6-50.

Is person-to-person payment safe? The major advantage of person-to-person payments is that the payment service is the only entity that sees your credit card number—merchants, auction dealers, and other payment recipients never receive your credit card number and, therefore, can't misuse it or store it on an unsecured computer. Currently, however, the person-to-person payment industry is in its infancy, and companies are still scrambling to offer reliable, long-term service to customers. Consumer advocates recommend using these services with caution and keeping your account balances low.

FIGURE 6-50

Using a person-to-person payment service.

1. To use a person-to-person payment service, simply log in to your account, enter the recipient's e-mail address, and indicate the payment amount.

2. The recipient immediately receives an e-mail notification of your payment.

3. The recipient connects to the payment site to "pick up" the money by transferring the funds to his or her checking or payment account, requesting a check, or sending the funds to someone else.

6

QuickCheck   SECTION D

1. Examples of B2C e-commerce include online auctions and wholesale clearance sites where businesses sell goods to each other. True or false? [   ]

2. A clear [   ] or Web bug can be used to set cookies to a third-party site.

3. A padlock icon at the bottom of your browser window indicates an S-HTTP or [   ] connection. Hint: Use the acronym.

4. A packet [   ] is a computer program that monitors data as it travels over networks and is sometimes used by hackers to intercept packets.

5. Most electronic [   ] use SET cryptography and digital certificates.

✦ CHECK ANSWERS

TechTalk

Encryption

At one time, encryption was synonymous with spies, secret agents, and an assortment of cloak-and-dagger activities. The average person's exposure to encryption was pretty much limited to Captain Midnight decoder rings and pig Latin. Today, the situation is different. Encryption is one of the most important technologies for maintaining your privacy and the security of important information, such as your credit card number. This TechTalk is designed to provide a basic background in encryption, which you can apply when participating in e-commerce and other online activities.

Is encryption the same as coding? In the context of computers, the word "code" is bantered about in a variety of ways. Programmers write computer code to create software. ASCII and EBCDIC codes are used to represent the letters of the alphabet. These codes, however, are not the same as encryption. Encryption transforms a message in such a way that its contents are hidden from unauthorized readers. Encryption is designed to keep messages secret. Its purpose, therefore, is quite different from simple coding schemes, such as ASCII and EBCDIC, which are designed to transform data into formats that are publicly known and shared.

How does encryption work? An original message—one that has not yet been encrypted—is referred to as **plaintext** or "cleartext." An encrypted message is referred to as **ciphertext**. The process of converting plaintext into ciphertext is called **encryption**. The reverse process—converting ciphertext into plaintext—is called **decryption**. In an e-commerce transaction, for example, your credit card number exists as plaintext, which is encrypted into ciphertext for its journey over a secure connection to the merchant. When the ciphertext arrives at its destination, it is decrypted back into the original plaintext credit card number.

Messages are encrypted by using a cryptographic algorithm and key. A **cryptographic algorithm** is a specific procedure for encrypting or decrypting a message. A **cryptographic key** (usually just called a "key") is a word, number, or phrase that must be known to encrypt or decrypt a message.

For example, Julius Caesar made extensive use of an encryption method called simple substitution, which could have been used to turn the plaintext message "Do not trust Brutus" into GRQRWWUXVWEUXWXV. The cryptographic algorithm was to offset the letters of the alphabet. The key was 3. Anyone who knew this algorithm and key could set up a transformation table like the one in Figure 6-51 to encrypt or decrypt messages for Caesar.

FIGURE 6-51

The algorithm for Caesar's encryption technique was to offset the letters of the alphabet—in this case by three letters. A simple transformation table was used to encrypt or decrypt a message. For example, if a "G" appears in the encrypted message, it would be a "D" in the original unencrypted message.

Ciphertext letters:

D E F G H I J K L M N O P Q R S T U V W X Y Z A B C

Equivalent plaintext letters:

A B C D E F G H I J K L M N O P Q R S T U V W X Y Z

What's the difference between strong and weak encryption?
Caesar's simple substitution key is an example of **weak encryption** because it is easy to decrypt even without the algorithm and key. Unauthorized decryption is sometimes referred to as "breaking" or "cracking" a code. You could crack Caesar's code in several ways. For example, you could discover the key by making 25 different transformation tables, each with a different offset (assuming that the encryption method uses the letters of the alphabet in sequence and not at random). You could also analyze the frequency with which letters appear—in English documents, E, T, A, O, and N appear most frequently—and you can piece together the message by guessing the remaining letters.

Strong encryption is loosely defined as "very difficult to break." Of course, with continuous advances in technology, strong encryption is a moving target. For example, several encryption methods that were considered "impossible" to break 10 years ago have recently been cracked by using networks of personal computers. The encryption methods used for most e-commerce transactions are considered "strong" but not unbreakable.

How long does it take to "break" strong encryption?
Encryption methods can be broken by the use of expensive, specialized, code-breaking computers. The cost of these machines is substantial, but not beyond the reach of government agencies, major corporations, and organized crime. Encryption methods can also be broken by standard computer hardware—supercomputers, mainframes, workstations, and even personal computers. These computers typically break codes using a **brute-force method**, which consists of trying all possible keys (Figure 6-52).

The length of a computer-readable encryption key is measured in bits. A bit, as you know, can be a 1 or a 0. Unlike the PIN example in which each digit could be one of 10 possible numbers, in a computer-readable encryption key, each digit can be one of two possible numbers: 0 or 1. Figuring out how many numbers you must try to break a computer code requires a calculation using powers of two rather than powers of 10. A 32-bit key, therefore, could be one of about 4.2 billion (2^{32}) numbers. Surprisingly, it would be possible to try all these numbers and discover the key in less than a day by using an average personal computer.

To discover a 40-bit key, you would have to try about 1 trillion possible combinations—a week's worth of processing time on a personal computer. 56-bit and 64-bit encryption—once thought to be unbreakable by any computer in the private sector—require a lot of computing power, but have been broken by combining the power of many personal computers connected over the Internet. 128-bit encryption and 256-bit encryption are probably secure for several years. Most encryption today uses a 128-bit key.

Another way to understand how the length of a key affects the strength of encryption is to consider this guideline: Beginning with a 40-bit key, each additional bit doubles the time it would take to discover the key. If a personal computer takes one week to crack a 40-bit key, it takes two weeks to crack a 41-bit key, four weeks to crack a 42-bit key, and eight weeks to crack a 43-bit key. A 128-bit key takes $2^{(128-40)}$ times longer to crack than a 40-bit key—that's 309,485,009,821,345,068,724,781,056 times longer!

FIGURE 6-52

Is your PIN secure?

6

Suppose that a criminal steals an ATM card. The card cannot be used, however, without the correct PIN. A four-digit PIN could be one of 10,000 possible combinations.

If you're mathematically inclined, you'll realize that each digit of the PIN could be one of 10 possibilities: 0, 1, 2, 3, 4, 5, 6, 7, 8, or 9, so 10^4 or 10x10x10x10 possible PINs exist.

To discover a PIN by brute force, a criminal must try, at most, 10,000 possibilities. Although it would take a person quite a long time to figure out and try all 10,000 possibilities, a computer could polish them off as quickly as the ATM would accept them.

What's public key encryption? Caesar's encryption method is an example of symmetric key encryption, which is also called "secret key" or "conventional" encryption. With **symmetric key encryption**, the key used to encrypt a message is also used to decrypt the message.

Symmetric key encryption is often used to encrypt stationary data, such as corporate financial records. It is not, however, a very desirable encryption method for data that's on the move. The person who encrypts the data must get the key to the person who decrypts the data, without the key falling into the wrong hands. On a computer network, key distribution is a major security problem because of the potential for a packet sniffer to intercept the key.

To eliminate the key-distribution problem, Whitfield Diffie and Martin Helman introduced a concept called **public key encryption** (PKE). It uses asymmetric key encryption, in which one key is used to encrypt a message, but another key is used to decrypt the message. Figure 6-53 illustrates how public key encryption works.

FIGURE 6-53

Public key encryption uses two keys. A public key is used to encrypt a message. A private key is used to decrypt the message.

1. James sends the *public* key to JoBeth, but he keeps a *private* key.

2. JoBeth uses the public key to encrypt a message, which she sends back to James.

4. James can decrypt the message using his *private* key.

3. If the message and public key are intercepted by Draco, he cannot decrypt the message because he does not have the private key.

Public key encryption is a crucial technology on the Web, particularly for e-commerce. When you use an SSL connection to transmit your credit card number, the server sends a public key to your browser. Your browser uses this public key to encrypt the credit card number. After it's encrypted, no one—not even you—can use this public key to decrypt the message. The encrypted message is sent to the Web server, where the private key is used to decrypt it.

Public key encryption is not perfect. The mathematics of PKE make it easier to crack than symmetric key encryption. To get a level of security equal to 80-bit symmetrical encryption requires a 1024-bit public encryption key! As a result of these huge keys, PKE encryption and decryption usually require lots of processing time—about 1000 times more than for symmetric encryption. For this reason, PKE is best used for short messages, such as e-commerce transactions and e-mail.

What are the most commonly used encryption methods? **RSA** (named for its inventors—Ron Rivest, Adi Shamir, and Leonard Adelman) is the most commonly used public key encryption algorithm. In addition to being the technology used for SSL connections, RSA is used to encrypt the data in most digital certificates. **DES** (Data Encryption Standard) is an encryption method based on an algorithm developed by IBM and the U.S. National Security Agency. It uses 56-bit symmetric key encryption. Although it was once the cornerstone of government encryption, DES is being replaced by AES, which offers stronger encryption. **AES** (Advanced Encryption Standard) is an encryption standard that uses three key sizes of 128, 192, or 256 bits. It is based on the Rijndael (pronounced "rain doll") encryption algorithm.

What kind of encryption can I use on my computer? When you engage in an e-commerce transaction, secure connections that encrypt your data are provided by the e-commerce site. In most cases, this is all the encryption necessary for the transaction. Even if you were to further encrypt your data, it is unlikely that the e-commerce server would be equipped to handle the decryption. You might, however, want to encrypt other data, such as your e-mail messages or your data files.

When personal computer users want to encrypt e-mail or other documents, they turn to Phillip Zimmerman's **PGP** (Pretty Good Privacy) software. In addition to encrypting data files, this software lets you digitally sign a message, which verifies to the recipient that you are the sender and that no tampering is involved.

PGP is a type of public key encryption. When you first use PGP, the software generates a private key and a public key. You must keep your private key hidden. You e-mail the public key to the people you have authorized to send encrypted messages to you.

The people who receive your public key can store it in their PGP programs, which they then use to encrypt messages. When they send these messages to you, you can decrypt them using your private key. PGP software is available as a free download from several Web sites. Figure 6-54 contains an example of a public key generated by PGP.

INFOWEBLINKS

For additional resources on using ciphertext to protect data, including PGP software that you can use on your PC, connect to the **Encryption InfoWeb**.

www.course.com/np/concepts9/ch06

6

-----BEGIN PGP PUBLIC KEY BLOCK-----

Version: 5.0

```
mQCNAi44C30AAAEEAL1r6BylvuSAvOKIk9ze9yCK+ZPPbRZrpXIRFBbe
+U8dGPMb9XdJS4L/cy1fXr9R9j4EfFsK/rgHV6i2rE83LjWrmsDPRPSaizz+
EQTIZi4AN99jiBomfLLZyUzmHMoUoE4shrYgOnkc0u101ikhieAFje77j/F3
596pT6nCx/9/AAURtCRBbmRyZSBCYBNhcmQgPGFiYWNhcmRAd2Vsb
C5zZi5jYS51cz6JAFUCBRAuOA6O7zYZz1mqos8BAXr9AgCxCu8CwGZR
dpfSs65r6mb4MccXvvfxO4TmPi1DKQj2FYHYjwYONk8vzA7XnE5aJmk5J
/dChdvfIU7NvVifV6AF=GQv9
```

-----END PGP PUBLIC KEY BLOCK-----

FIGURE 6-54

PGP software generates a huge public key. Each person's public key is unique. You can e-mail this key to anyone who might want to send you an encrypted message.

QuickCheck

1. In an e-commerce transaction, your credit card number exists as [_____], which is encrypted into [_____].

2. [_____] key encryption uses the same key to encrypt a message as it does to decrypt the message.

3. [_____] key encryption uses one key to encrypt a message, but another key to decrypt the message.

4. [_____] is public key encryption software that is popular with personal computer owners who want to encrypt e-mail and data files. Hint: Use the acronym.

CHECK ANSWERS

Issue
Censorship on the Web

The Internet offers instant access to information across national and cultural borders, but along with helpful information the Internet hosts a disturbing amount of unsavory material. Militias and hate groups use Web sites to recruit new members and spread their views. Hundreds of pornographic sites make a business of selling lewd images and their come-ons can be accessed by anyone—even children. In chat rooms on innocent topics, the conversation can deteriorate into X-rated banter. Pedophile and bestiality sites that cater to warped sexual habits pop up in search engine lists. International terrorists use Web sites as recruiting tools and for boasting about suicide bombings. Criminals, anarchists, and dissenters post guidebooks and tips on how to do all kinds of illegal activities, from making suitcase bombs to spreading computer viruses.

Some concerned netizens advocate cyber censorship to curtail irresponsible Web sites, blogs, and discussion groups. Cyber censorship typically means blocking access to Web sites, but it can also mean closing sites and removing them from host servers. Censorship advocates are opposed by free speech supporters who believe that the right to free expression should be unshackled by any laws or regulations.

The controversy over censorship is not new. Guidelines from the pre-Internet era also shape the cyber-censorship-vs-free-speech debate.

In most cases, words are acceptable, whereas actions can be punishable. Writing a mystery novel that describes how the main character cultivates botulism and then uses it to poison one of the other characters is acceptable. Actually carrying out such as act would be against the law. This concept was applied to cyberspace when the U.S. Supreme Court upheld a law that pornography featuring real children was illegal, but ruled that child pornography featuring computer-generated children is not illegal because children were not harmed when it was created.

Cyberlaw is not yet totally consistent on the words vs. deeds precedent, however. In some cases, words are punishable. For example, the Digital Millennium Copyright Act makes it illegal to even disseminate information on defeating software, CD, and DVD copy restrictions.

A second censorship guideline hinges on local standards of morality. Local communities can apply their own standards to determine whether material is obscene. Therefore, a raunchy magazine that you might find on a supermarket newsstand in New York City might be limited to adult bookstore shelves in a conservative Tennessee community.

Local standards, however, are difficult to sort out on the Internet where a Web surfer in Tennessee can easily access Web sites, bulletin boards, and chat groups that originate from anywhere in the world. Judges upheld the conviction of two sysops whose California-based porn site distributed obscene material to individuals in Tennessee. The sysops claimed that the Internet required a more flexible definition of "community" to account for the Internet's global accessibility; otherwise Web sites would be forced to eliminate all materials objected to by anyone. Judges denied that claim, saying that technology could be used to filter out objectionable material based on age and location information provided by member registration data.

Underlying a group of decisions on cyber censorship, the U.S. Supreme Court seems to support the concept of cyberzones that limit net access to certain materials in a way similar to how the adult sections of street-corner newsstands restrict children from browsing through certain magazines. As now-retired Justice O'Connor explained, "Cyberspace is malleable. Thus, it is possible to construct barriers in cyberspace and use them to screen for identity, making cyberspace more like the physical world and, consequently, more amenable to zoning laws." As an example, AOL is trying to develop a family-friendly Internet portal by enforcing policies against offensive speech, but has been criticized by free-speech advocates for its policies. AOL responds that it is a private company and members who disagree with AOL terms of use are free to terminate their subscriptions.

In some countries, however, cyber citizens have no choice but to use a government-controlled ISP. In many countries, free speech is not a basic right conferred to all citizens. Many dictatorial regimes want their citizens to receive news from the outside world only after it has been screened by a government censor. Officials in more than 20 countries use sophisticated tools to block Web sites, filter e-mail, and censor discussion groups.

China has some of the most rigorous Internet censorship in the world. The "Great Firewall of China" as it is sometimes called, blocks Internet content by preventing IP addresses of objectionable sites from being routed through its gateways into China. The system also selectively engages in DNS poisoning, a technique that tricks a DNS server into believing it has received authentic information when, in reality, it has not. So Web surfers in China who attempt to access the Electronic Frontier Foundation's Web site that advocates free speech, might

instead see a Chinese government site on social responsibility. In addition to blocking Web sites, the Chinese government filters e-mail, message boards, chat rooms, and blogs.

In Iran, government censors monitor political and news Web sites, and block access to many pornographic Web sites, anonymizer tools, sites with gay and lesbian content, politically sensitive sites, and women's rights sites. If you tried to access *Rolling Stone* magazine's Web site from Saudi Arabia, you would find that access has been denied. The Saudi government claims it censors the Internet to preserve Islamic culture and heritage. That argument in many ways reflects the concept of cyberzones that conform to local standards of ethics and morality. Even free-speech activists at the OpenNet Initiative (ONI) seem to agree, "We do think that information should be free," states one ONI technician, "but we do need to find a balance for respect for sovereign states to preserve their own culture."

Despite such cultural sensitivity, technology giants, such as Microsoft, Yahoo!, and Cisco Systems have been criticized for providing foreign governments with tools for blocking culturally objectionable sites. Critics question whether companies in a free society should aid foreign governments' attempts to censor cyberspace.

For some people it is astonishing to realize that ideas such as liberty, equality, and womens rights would be subject to the same censorship attempts as pornography and hate speech. The solution to online censorship is still evolving as free speech comes into balance with cultural, ethical, and moral concerns in the global realm of cyberspace.

6

INFOWEBLINKS

You'll find more fascinating Internet myths and substantive articles about disinformation at the **Web Censorship** InfoWeb.

www.course.com/np/concepts9/ch06

What Do You Think?   ISSUE

1. Should governments be allowed to block access to Web sites based on local religions, politics, and customs?   ○ Yes ○ No ○ Not sure

2. Do you believe that a privately-held Internet Service Provider like AOL has the right to censor the data posted on Web sites it hosts?   ○ Yes ○ No ○ Not sure

3. Should companies like Microsoft, Yahoo!, and Cisco Systems provide blocking technology to foreign governments?   ○ Yes ○ No ○ Not sure

4. Would you use filtering software that was preprogrammed to block pornographic and nuisance Web sites?   ○ Yes ○ No ○ Not sure

SAVE RESPONSES

Computers in Context
Fashion Industry

Fashion is big business. Worldwide, clothing sales generate more than $200 billion in revenue. Shoes, accessories, and jewelry bump this industry's revenue even higher. Competition is tough as designers, manufacturers, and retailers compete for customer dollars. In the fashion industry, trends change quickly. As the saying goes, "Today's style is tomorrow's markdown." Fashion industry players look for every competitive advantage. It is no surprise that technology plays a major role in this glitzy industry.

Fashion begins with designers, such as Miuccia Prada, John Galliano, and Ralph Lauren. Their runway extravaganzas set off fashion trends that eventually work their way to retail stores. Fashion runways went high-tech in 1999 when lingerie manufacturer Victoria's Secret produced a Webcast watched by over 1 million viewers. Now, with inexpensive digital technology, even haute couture wannabes can stage their own online runway shows. Young designers without the cash to stage elaborate runway shows can turn to companies such as Nouveau Media, a video production company that creates "Fashion Video Shorts." These digital runway videos can be produced on DVDs and displayed on TV monitors in retail stores, broadcast as commercials, or posted on Web sites.

Although runway fashions are typically conceived with a sketch and stitched by hand, designs are adapted for the ready-to-wear market by using computer-assisted design (CAD) tools, such as pattern-making software. Garments are constructed by sewing together sections of fabric that form arms, fronts, backs, collars, and so forth. The set of templates used to cut fabric sections is called a pattern. Pattern-making is a tricky 3D challenge because flat pieces of fabric eventually become garments shaped to conform to curved body contours. Pattern making software helps designers visualize how flat pieces fit together and drape when sewn. Once a master pattern is complete, pattern-making software automatically generates a set of patterns for each garment size.

Fashion requires fabric, and computers play a major role in fabric design and manufacturing. Computer software, such as ArahWeave, lets fabric designers experiment with colors, yarns, and weaves while viewing detailed, realistic on-screen samples. Fabric designs can be stored in a variety of formats for weaving machines. A few older mechanical weaving machines are controlled by punched cards. Digital fabric designs can be transferred to punched cards with a dedicated card punch machine. Most of today's weaving mills use computerized machinery that directly accepts digital input to control threads and patterns. Networks tie looms to CAD stations and to the Internet. Fabric designs can be stored in XML format, transmitted to a fabric manufacturer over the Internet, and used directly by computerized weaving machines.

Clothing production, warehousing, and shipping are also highly automated. Benetton's high-tech facility at Castrette, Italy can produce over 110 million garments per year. Its automated distribution center uses a workforce of only 24 people to handle 40,000 boxes of merchandise daily. Radio frequency identification (RFID) tags—sometimes called "smart labels"—can be attached to individual garments or to packing boxes as an important tool for controlling inventory.

RFID technology uses an inexpensive, tiny computer chip with built-in antenna and the capacity to store between 64 and 128 bits of data about a garment—its SKU number, size, model, dye lot, manufacturing date, and so on. Tags can be attached to a garment or its label. An RFID reader that can retrieve data from tags is used to track merchandise from the manufacturing plant through the distribution chain to the retailer. RFID tags are becoming popular for all types of merchandise. Businesses that use them can save time and money. For example, RFID tags can reduce the time it takes to do a physical inventory by a factor of 10. Privacy advocates, however, are worried because these tags remain active even after you bring your merchandise home. Could a thief circle your house with an RFID scanner to find out what's inside? Could a stalker follow your movements by tracking the RFID tag embedded in your sweater? After customers protested a plan to attach RFID tags to every sweater, Benetton currently uses the tags only on shipping cartons.

In response to competition from offshore companies, U.S. clothing manufacturers pioneered Quick Response (QR)—a business model for compressing supply chains to quickly obtain raw materials, such as fabric, yarn, buttons, and zippers. Sophisticated software tools, such as the Sourcing Simulator, simplify QR planning.

Online shopping has become routine, but one drawback of catalog and online ordering is the cost associated with restocking returned merchandise. Can an online customer find out how a garment will fit and look before ordering it? In 1998, Lands' End introduced "My Virtual Model" technology that allows shoppers to create a custom model of themselves by choosing from a variety of hair colors and styles, face shapes, and body types. The model can "try on" clothes to show online customers how they would look when wearing the garments.

More recently, Lands' End toured the country with a body-scanning device to collect actual measurements from thousands of customers. Body-scanning devices use cameras and lasers to capture approximately 300,000 data points that can be pieced together into a 3D image.

Body scanners are also helping the fashion industry by collecting research data. Sizing standards fell by the wayside when "vanity sizing" added an inch or two to a garment so that consumers can feel good about themselves by fitting into smaller sizes. In the U.S. clothing industry, a comprehensive study of body shapes and sizes can help standardize sizing and eliminate much of the trial and error involved in finding apparel that fits. Collecting data from body scans is part of this ongoing research effort.

No discussion of fashion and computers would be complete without highlighting wearable technology. Clothing that contains digital devices has made its way out of the laboratory and onto store shelves. For example, Burton Snowboards, electronic fabric manufacturer SOFTswitch, and Apple teamed up to create the limited-edition Burton Amp, a jacket with integrated iPod controls designed for snowboarders to control music from the sleeves of their jackets without fumbling with zippers, gloves, and small control buttons.

Another "wearable," originally popular with secret service agents, is the SCOTTeVEST, a jacket with pockets for cell phone, PDA, MP3 player, and built-in wiring to connect these devices into a personal area network (PAN). Available as a jacket or vest and in men's and women's sizes, the jacket can now be purchased by civilians.

With a growing emphasis on the use of technology in fashion design and manufacturing, fashion degree programs at colleges and technical schools have added courses such as computer-aided fashion design, computer-based pattern drafting, pattern grading and computer-aided drafting, and wearable computers.

6

INFOWEBLINKS

You'll find information related to this Computers in Context topic at the Computers and Fashion InfoWeb.

www.course.com/np/concepts9/ch06

Labs

Student Edition Labs

On the Web
Student Edition Labs

To access the Student Edition labs, connect to the New Perspectives NP9 Web site and click the link for Student Edition Labs. The link also provides access to lab assignments.

www.course.com/np/concepts9/ch06

> Work hands-on in structured simulations practicing important skills and concepts

PROTECTING YOUR PRIVACY ONLINE

In the Protecting Your Privacy Online Student Edition Lab, you will learn the following topics and skills:

- How cookies work
- Deleting cookies using a browser
- Adjusting your cookie settings in Internet Explorer

CREATING WEB PAGES

In the Creating Web Pages Student Edition Lab, you will learn the following topics and skills:

- Starting a Web page
- Formatting paragraphs and text on a Web page
- Using graphics and backgrounds on a Web page
- Linking to other Web pages
- Using tables on a Web page

GETTING THE MOST OUT OF THE INTERNET

In the Getting the Most Out of the Internet Student Edition Lab, you will learn the following topics and skills:

- Customizing your Web browser
- Searching the Web

- Online job hunting
- Online travel reservations
- Building Web communities

E-COMMERCE

In the E-Commerce Student Edition Lab, you will learn the following topics and skills:

- Paying with electronic cash
- Ensuring security in an e-commerce transaction
- Technical components of an e-commerce Web site
- Developing an e-commerce Web site

WEB DESIGN PRINCIPLES

In the Web Design Principles Student Edition Lab, you will learn the following topics and skills:

- Designing the site structure
- Designing the site look and feel
- Designing for readability
- Using hypertext and images effectively

on the BookOnCD
New Perspectives Labs

To access the New Perspectives labs for Chapter 6, start the BookOnCD and then click the ✳ icon next to the lab title below.

✳ BROWSER SECURITY SETTINGS

IN THIS LAB YOU'LL LEARN:

How to adjust the security settings for Internet Explorer

The significance of Internet, Local Intranet, Trusted, and Restricted security zones

How to add sites to a security zone and adjust security zone settings

Why ActiveX controls pose a potential security threat and how to adjust ActiveX control security settings

Why downloads pose a potential security threat to your computer and how to activate the recommended download security settings

Why Java applets pose a potential security threat to your computer

The significance of Java permission levels

How to activate the recommended Java security settings

LAB ASSIGNMENTS

1. Perform each lab step as directed, and answer all the lab QuickCheck questions.

2. Check the Internet zone security setting on the computer you typically use. Indicate whether the setting is High, Medium, Medium-low, Low, or Custom. Describe how this setting handles ActiveX controls, downloads, and Java applets.

3. On the computer you typically use, find out whether any Web sites are listed in the Trusted or Restricted zones. Would you make changes to the list of sites for these zones? Explain why or why not.

4. Activate the Prompt setting for the Download ActiveX controls security setting. After you have done so, use your browser to connect to *http://www.infoweblinks.com/np6/samples/active x.htm*, where you should encounter an ActiveX control security alert. Use your computer's Print Screen (PrtSc or PrtScrn) key to capture a screenshot of the warning. Paste the screenshot into Paint and then print it. Would you accept this ActiveX control? Why or why not?

✳ WORKING WITH COOKIES

IN THIS LAB YOU'LL LEARN:

How Web servers use cookies

Why cookies might pose a threat to your privacy

How to locate cookies stored on your computer

How to view the contents of a cookie

How to delete a single cookie created by Internet Explorer

How to delete all the cookies stored on your computer

How to limit the space allocated to cookies created by Internet Explorer

How to block cookies

What a session cookie is

How to set cookie prompts and use the cookie prompt dialog box

How to take advantage of P3P and Compact Privacy Policies

The differences between first-party and third-party cookies

How to "opt out" of receiving third-party cookies

LAB ASSIGNMENTS

1. Perform each lab step as directed, and answer all the lab QuickCheck questions.

2. Use Windows Explorer to look at the cookies stored on your computer. Indicate how many cookies are currently stored. Examine the contents of one cookie, and indicate whether you think it poses a threat to your privacy.

3. Indicate the name and version of the browser you typically use. To find this information, open your browser, and then select the About option from the Help menu. Next, look at the cookie settings your browser provides. Describe how you would adjust these settings to produce a level of privacy protection that is right for your needs.

4. Adjust your browser settings so that you are prompted whenever a Web server attempts to send a cookie to your computer. Go to several of your favorite Web sites and watch for third-party cookies. When you receive a message from a third-party Web site, record the name of the third-party site and the contents of the cookie it is attempting to send. Finally, indicate whether you would accept such a cookie.

6

Interactive Summary

To review important concepts from this chapter, fill in the blanks to best complete each sentence. Where possible, use acronyms such as HTML rather than writing out the entire term. When using the NP9 BookOnCD or the NP9 Web site, click the Check Answers buttons to automatically score your answers.

The basic building blocks for today's Web were developed in 1990 by a British scientist named Tim Berners-Lee. The Web did not "take off," however, until 1993 when Marc Andreessen and his colleagues developed a Web [_____] called Mosaic. The Web is an abstract or imaginary space of information, whereas the [_____] is the communications network that carries Web data.

The Web is based on Ted Nelson's concept of a [_____]—a series of documents that are stored electronically and linked together according to logical relationships. On today's Web, these documents are stored in [_____] format and then displayed as Web [_____] by a browser. HTML is a set of specifications for creating documents that contain special instructions called HTML [_____], which specify how the document should appear when displayed on a computer screen.

In an HTML document, these tags are set apart from normal text by [_____] brackets. In addition to HTML documents, Web browsers are designed to deal with [_____] file formats, such as GIF, JPEG, and PNG. A browser can also work with other file formats if the necessary helper application, plug-in, or [_____] has been installed.

HTML documents are transmitted from a Web server to a browser using a protocol called [_____]. This protocol is [_____], which means that as soon as a request is fulfilled, the Web server "forgets" that your browser ever made a request. To keep track of an individual who clicks through several pages on a Web site, a Web server resorts to a [_____]—a small chunk of data that is generated by a Web server, sent to a browser, and then stored on the client computer's hard disk.

✦ CHECK ANSWERS

Many software tools are available today that make it easy to create Web pages. A Web page author can use a [_____] editor, such as Notepad, to create Web pages "from scratch" by manually embedding HTML tags within the text of a document. It is also possible to use the HTML conversion routines included with many standard software applications. Another route is to use specialized Web [_____] software, such as Microsoft FrontPage.

An HTML document is divided into two sections. The [_____] section contains information used to define global properties for the document. The [_____] section contains the text you want the browser to display, the HTML tags that format the text, and a variety of links. In addition to embedding HTML tags within the text, a Web page can be format-

ted with a [_____] style sheet, which allows Web page designers to change formats throughout an HTML document without modifying individual HTML tags. In addition to formatting specifications, HTML tags can be used to add graphics and links to Web pages. The <img src> tag can be used to specify a [_____]. The <a href> tag is used to specify a [_____] to another Web page or to a sound. Graphics and links can be combined to create an [_____] map that contains clickable hot spots. To control the position of text and graphics on a Web page, many authors place these elements in the cells of a Web page [_____]. In the context of Web pages, a [_____] is part of a Web page that scrolls independently of other parts of the Web page.

✦ CHECK ANSWERS

HTML was designed to create static Web pages. With basic HTML, once a Web page appears in a browser window, the only way to change the appearance of the page is to download an update to the entire page. [_____] is a method for updating Web pages "on the fly"—typically as the result of a mouseover or a mouse click. A technology called [_____] can be used to incorporate structured data, such as spreadsheet data or database records, into a text file by adding special-purpose tags. These tags explicitly identify a particular kind of information, much like a field heading in a [_____]. A technology called [_____] is similar to XML, but can be used to create customized HTML tags that control the appearance of an XML document.

Another way to add animation and interactivity to Web pages is to use [_____] languages, such as JavaScript and VBScript. Unfortunately, browsers offer slightly different support for these languages, which sometimes results in a [_____] error if the browser can't execute a particular instruction. In addition to JavaScript and VBScript, Java has become a popular programming tool for Web-based projects. Small Java programs are referred to as Java [_____]. ActiveX provides another Web development tool. An ActiveX [_____] is a compiled computer program that can be referenced from within an HTML document, downloaded, installed on your computer, and executed within the browser window. This technology has potential security loopholes, which can be avoided by the use of digital [_____].

✦ CHECK ANSWERS

6

The Internet was opened up to commercial use in 1991, and since then, e-commerce has become one of the fastest growing activities on the Web. E-commerce wares include physical products, [_____] products, and services. Most of the e-commerce activities that a typical Web surfer enjoys are classified as business-to-[_____], but with online auctions, consumer-to-[_____] e-commerce is also popular.

E-commerce merchants take advantage of automation and digitization to increase profit margins by cutting [_____]. Many online merchants attempt to gain income by providing space for banner ads and [_____] ads. Some Web pages—and not just those displayed by e-commerce sites—can contain [_____], such as ad-serving cookies and Web bugs, that surreptitiously gathers information and sends it to advertisers or other interested parties.

E-commerce customers typically collect the items they want to purchase in an online [_____] cart. These carts store a customer's selections in a [_____] on the client computer or in a server-side database.

When it is time to check out, a customer can use an electronic [_____] to automatically enter billing and shipping information. Many online customers are worried about their credit card numbers falling into the wrong hands. Most e-commerce sites establish a [_____] connection by using SSL or S-HTTP to avoid [_____] sniffer software that could intercept it. Savvy shoppers are also wary of [_____] storefronts that are designed to look like a legitimate store, but are operated by credit card thieves.

✦ CHECK ANSWERS

Key Terms

Make sure you understand all the boldfaced key terms presented in this chapter. If you're using the NP9 BookOnCD, you can use this list of terms as an interactive study activity. First, try to define a term in your own words, and then click the term to compare your definition with the definition presented in the chapter.

ActiveX control, 328
Ad-blocking software, 332
Ad-serving cookie, 335
AES, 343
Animated GIF, 317
ASP, 319
B2B, 331
B2C, 331
B2G, 331
Banner ad, 332
Body section, 314
Broken link, 319
Brute-force method, 341
Bytecode, 326
C2C, 331
Cascading style sheet, 315
Certificate authority, 329
CGI, 319
Ciphertext, 340
Clear GIF, 335
Click-through rate, 332
Client-side script, 325
Compact Privacy Policy, 310
Cookie, 309
Cryptographic algorithm, 340
Cryptographic key, 340
Decryption, 340
DES, 342
DHTML, 323
Digital certificate, 329
DTD files, 324
E-commerce, 331

Electronic wallet, 338
Encryption, 340
External link, 318
External style sheet, 315
Flash animation, 317
Formatting tags, 303
Head section, 314
Helper application, 305
Hot spot, 318
HTML document, 299
HTML form, 319
HTML frame, 320
HTTP status code, 307
Hypertext, 298
Hypertext link, 299
Image map, 318
Internal link, 318
Intrapage link, 318
Java applets, 326
JavaScript, 325
Java Virtual Machine, 326
Link tags, 303
Mailto link, 318
Markup language, 300
Media tags, 303
Mouseover, 323
Online shopping cart, 334
Operational tags, 303
P3P, 310
Packet sniffer, 336
Person-to-person payment, 339
PGP, 343

Plaintext, 340
Player, 305
Plug-in, 305
Pop-up ad, 332
Public key encryption, 342
RSA, 342
Script, 325
Scripting error, 326
Secure connection, 336
Self-closing tag, 301
Server farm, 308
Server-side script, 325
SET, 338
S-HTTP, 336
Socket, 306
Spyware, 335
SSL, 336
Stateless protocol, 307
Strong encryption, 341
Symmetric key encryption, 342
Text editor, 312
VBScript, 325
Weak encryption, 341
Web authoring software, 313
Web page header, 314
Web page table, 320
World Wide Web Consortium, 300
XHTML, 300
XML, 324
XML parser, 324
XSL, 324

Interactive Situation Questions

Apply what you've learned to some typical computing situations. When using the NP9 BookOnCD or the NP9 Web site, you can type your answers, and then use the Check Answers button to automatically score your responses.

1. Suppose that you are about to check out at an online store, but you don't see any indication that your transaction data will be protected by a secure connection. It would be best, under these circumstances, to use PGP software to encrypt your shipping and billing data. True or false? [＿＿＿＿]

2. Your friend, who is a little "computer phobic," is going to be creating his first Web page and asks you to recommend some software for the task. Which one requires the least knowledge of HTML tags: Notepad or Microsoft Word? [＿＿＿＿]

3. Suppose you visit a Web site that has eye-catching pages. You want to know how these pages were formatted, so you use one of the options on your browser's menu to view the [＿＿＿＿] HTML document.

4. Suppose you click a link at a Web site and get a message that the file cannot be displayed because it is in PDF format. To view the file, you need an updated version of your browser. True or false? [＿＿＿＿]

5. Suppose you're performing a local test of a Web page you created. All the page elements appear to be correctly positioned and formatted. You're also happy to discover that your large graphics files are displayed quite quickly by your browser. Can you expect similar performance after you post the page on a Web site? Yes or no? [＿＿＿＿]

6. You're poking around in an HTML document and you notice a tag that references a file with a .class file extension. You assume that this file contains the bytecode for a Java [＿＿＿＿].

7. Suppose your browser's security setting is Medium. You can expect your browser to display a security warning message any time that a(n) [＿＿＿＿] control tries to install itself on your computer.

8. One of your relatives wants to try online shopping, but is suspicious that her credit card number might get stolen from a merchant's server by a hacker using a packet sniffer. Is it correct to tell her that she can best avoid these potential rip-offs by a secure connection, such as SSL? Yes or no? [＿＿＿＿]

9. Suppose you're the high bidder in an online auction for a handmade quilt. The person who is selling the quilt does not accept credit cards and suggests that you use a(n) [＿＿＿＿] payment service to, in effect, wire your payment electronically.

10. You're looking through a list of cookies stored on your computer, but don't remember visiting sites such as bannerbank, hotlog, and ad.bb. You can assume that these cookies were created by [＿＿＿＿], such as ad-serving cookies.

✣ CHECK ANSWERS

6

Interactive Practice Tests

Practice tests that consist of 10 multiple-choice, true/false, and fill-in-the-blank questions are available on both the NP9 BookOnCD and the NP9 Web site. The questions are selected at random from a large test bank, so each time you take a test, you'll receive a different set of questions. Your tests are scored immediately, and you can print study guides that help you find the correct answers for any questions that you missed.

CLICK ✣ TO START

Projects

An NP9 Project is an open-ended activity that will help you apply the concepts you have learned. Many projects require resources in addition to your textbook, such as current magazines, library materials, or Web access. When you tackle a project, be prepared to use your critical thinking skills, logical analysis, and your creativity.

CRITICAL THINKING

In this chapter you read about some of the pitfalls of shopping online. Reflect on what you read within the context of your own online usage habits. What aspects of your online activities could you change to become more secure, more private, or more efficient? What do you have to give up to get these benefits? Is it worth it to you? Incorporate your thoughts in a one-page summary. Follow your instructor's guidelines for submission.

CYBERCLASSROOM

Work with your team to create a blog on any topic. You can use the tools provided at any free blogging site, such as *www.blogger.com*. Make sure that each person on the team posts at least one message to the blog. Send your instructor instructions for logging onto your blog. When all the blogs are up and running, your instructor might post the URLs so everyone in the class can judge whose blog is best.

GROUP PROJECT

Brainstorm with a group of three to five students to come up with an idea for an e-business. For this project, your group will complete several tasks. Look at the task list, assign tasks, and create a schedule for completing them. Compile your work into a single document for submission.
Tasks:
- Decide on a name for the business after finding an available URL.
- Design a Web site for the business. Mock up the Web site home page using Web authoring software or simply a graphics program, such as Paint.
- Locate at least five partner sites that might provide synergistic cross-marketing.
- Make a list of 10 keywords that can be used in your Web page header so customers can easily find your site when using a search engine.
- Find a site to host your online business and work up a spreadsheet showing your monthly and annual hosting costs.

MULTIMEDIA PROJECT

Surf the Web to select a home page that needs improvement. Use the Print Screen key on your keyboard to take a screenshot of the original page. Paste the page into graphics software such as Paint and store it as Home Page Original [Your Name]. Use your graphics software to create an improved home page by following some of the tips and recommendations offered in the chapter. Save your makeover as Home Page Makeover [Your Name]. Make a list of the changes you made. Submit the before, after, and list to your instructor.

RESUME BUILDER

Many companies have a Web site that provides information on their products and services. Use a search engine to locate a company in your career field. Suppose you are a recruiter for that company and you'll be attending a series of college career fairs. Create a one-page information flyer that you can hand out to prospective recruits. The flyer should include:

- The company name and URL
- A brief description of the company's mission, products, and services
- A description of typical working conditions
- Company location(s)
- Instructions on how to submit a resume electronically

ISSUE

The Issue section of this chapter addressed the controversy over censorship on the Web. Free speech is in constant struggle with individual rights and public safety. On the Web, some sites contain pornography, bigotry, and terrorist rhetoric that many people would rather not be public. One of the cornerstones of democracy, however, is freedom of speech. Where do you draw the line when it comes to censoring and filtering on the Internet? Explain your views, making sure you consider questions such as: Do parents have the right to monitor, screen, and filter their children's Web use? Are governments ever justified in regulating what their citizens can access? Should anyone be responsible for policing the Internet? Incorporate your ideas in a two-page summary and submit it to your instructor.

GLOBALIZATION

Technology has taken commerce into a new global dimension that provides access to products and services on an unprecedented scale. For this project, examine trends in global e-commerce, and submit your answers to the following questions.

- Which countries are the top players in the e-commerce market?
- How big is your country's share in the e-commerce pie?
- Is your country's share of the e-commerce pie increasing or decreasing?
- How does e-commerce affect developing countries?
- What are the advantages and disadvantages of a global market?

COMPUTERS IN CONTEXT

The Computers in Context section of this chapter focused on computers in the fashion industry. For this report, create a visual timeline that traces a garment from the time it is conceived by a designer to the time it is placed on a designer's rack or store shelf. Indicate technologies that are used at various stages of this process. Follow your instructor's guidelines for submitting your report as a printed document or by e-mail. Make sure that you provide citations for your text and graphical sources.

6

Study Tips

Study Tips help you to organize and consolidate the information in a unit by making lists, outlines, charts, and sketches. You can use paper and pencil or word processing software to complete most of the Study Tip activities.

1. Make sure you can use your own words to correctly answer each of the orange focus questions that appear throughout the chapter.

2. Draw a multi-panel "cartoon" that shows how a Web server and browser interact. Include the following terms: Web server, browser, HTTP, HTML, Port 80, socket, HTML document, graphic file, and URL.

3. Make sure you can explain the relationship between an HTML document and a Web page.

4. In your own words, explain what the term "stateless protocol" means, then describe how it relates to cookies.

5. List the port numbers that are traditionally used for HTTP traffic, SMTP e-mail, and FTP.

6. List the major security and privacy features of cookies.

7. Describe the advantages and disadvantages of each type of Web page development tool discussed in this chapter.

8. Explain how the term "header" is used in word processing, and how that differs from the way it is used in Web page authoring. Also explain how the term "frame" in desktop publishing differs from its use in Web page authoring.

9. Describe some of the ways that Web page designers use links. Describe external links, mailto links, intrapage links, and internal links.

10. In your own words, create definitions for HTML, DHTML, XML, XSL, and XHTML that clearly describe each technology.

11. Explain the differences between a server-side script and a client-side script.

12. In your own words, create definitions for Java applet, ActiveX control, JavaScript, VBScript, CGI, and ASP that clearly distinguish one technology from the others.

13. Make a list of security and privacy concerns discussed in this chapter. Describe each one and then describe procedures and technologies available to make your online experience more secure and private.

14. TechTalk: List the types of encryption mentioned in the TechTalk section, then arrange the list in order from strongest to weakest.

15. Fill in the blanks on the concept map below to show the hierarchy of HTML concepts presented in this chapter.

Review on the Web

TECHTV VIDEO PROJECT

The TechTV segment Find the Best Deals Online offers tips for using the e-pinions Web site. While watching the video, make a note of the features that make e-pinions such a helpful site. Go online and check out these features for yourself. Suppose you're looking for a digital music player and a hotel in Savannah, Georgia. Print a few sample pages showing choices, opinions, and detailed information. Indicate your personal selections using a highlighter. Did the e-pinions site live up to your expectations?

To work with the Video Projects for this chapter, connect to the New Perspectives NP9 Web site.

www.course.com/np/concepts9/ch06

ONLINE GAMES

Test your comprehension of the concepts introduced in Chapter 6 by playing the NP9 Online Games. At the end of each game, you have three options:

- Submit your results to your instructor using the Universal Gradebook through CoursePort
- Print your results to be submitted to your instructor
- Print a comprehensive study guide complete with page references

To work with the Online Games for this chapter, connect to the New Perspectives NP9 Web site.

www.course.com/np/concepts9/ch06

6

 LIGHTNING   DON'T TELL ME   FAKE OUT

ONLINE END-OF-CHAPTER ACTIVITIES

The following NP9 Review Activities are also available at the New Perspectives NP9 Web site:

- Interactive Summary
- Interactive Situation Questions
- Interactive Practice Tests
- Concept Map

If you are using the Web site to complete these activities, you can automatically score your answers and share the results with your instructor.

www.course.com/np/concepts9/ch06

7

Digital Media

FOCUS ON THESE LEARNING OBJECTIVES

Describe the advantages, disadvantages, and uses for digital media, such as bitmap graphics, vector graphics, 3-D graphics, 3-D animations, desktop video, waveform audio, and MIDI music

List the equipment and software that can be used to work with various types of digital media

Identify digital media files by their file extensions

Understand the advantages and disadvantages of using each type of digital media on the Web

Explain how resolution, image size, color depth, and color palettes can be manipulated to adjust the file size of a bitmap graphic

Describe procedures required to convert bitmap graphics into vector graphics and vector graphics into bitmaps

Explain how wireframes, rendering, and ray tracing apply to 3-D graphics

Define the differences between digital video and 3-D animation

Describe how to shoot, capture, edit, and process digital video

Explain how window size, frame rate, and compression affect file size for a desktop video

Summarize the process for creating DVD-video

Describe the formats used for digital music

Explain how to download music files and transfer them to portable audio players

A detailed list of learning objectives is provided at the New Perspectives NP9 Web site:

www.course.com/np/concepts9/ch07

UNDERSTAND THE CHAPTER CONTENTS

TIP

When using the BookOnCD, the ✳ icons are "clickable" to access resources on the CD. The ☩ icons are clickable to access resources on the Web. You can also access Web resources by using your browser to connect directly to the New Perspectives NP9 Web site at: www.course.com/np/concepts9/ch07

DIGITAL MEDIA, SUCH AS PHOTOS, MOVIES, 3-D GAMES, AND MUSIC ARE ALL part of today's lifestyle. Most of these technologies originated as computer applications but are increasingly migrating off the desktop. A new generation of photo printers requires no computer connection. Handheld arcade-style games offer a pocket-sized way to pass time while sitting in an airport or waiting in long lines. Portable audio players keep you rocking wherever you go. Chapter 7 looks at digital technologies on the desktop and on the go.

TAKE A PRE-ASSESSMENT QUIZ

to find out how much you know about bitmap graphics, vectors, 3-D animation, digital video and audio. Armed with your results, you can focus your study time on concepts that will round out your knowledge of digital media and improve your test scores.

www.course.com/np/concepts9/ch07

LISTEN TO A CHAPTER OVERVIEW

Get your book and highlighter ready, then connect to the New Perspectives NP9 Web site, where you can listen to an overview that points out the most important concepts for this chapter.

www.course.com/np/concepts9/ch07

BEFORE YOU READ ON, TRY IT

WHAT KINDS OF GRAPHICS, AUDIO, AND VIDEO FILES ARE ON MY COMPUTER?

You can use your computer to work with many types of media, such as photos, music, and videos. Your computer stores media that you've created and downloaded. It also stores images from Web sites you've recently visited. To discover what sort of media is stored on your computer, do the following steps:

1. Make sure your computer is turned on.

2. Click the Start button, then click Search. The Search Results dialog box appears. In the next two steps, you'll check some settings so that you have a visual display of your media files and so that you can see their file extensions.

3. Click the View menu and then select Thumbnails from the list.

4. Click the Tools menu and select Folder Options. Click the View tab and then make sure there is no check mark in the box for Hide extensions for known file types. Click the OK button to accept the settings you made in steps 3 and 4.

5. On the left side of the Search Results window, click the button for Pictures, Music, or Video.

6. Check the box for Pictures and Photos, then click the Search button. Your computer shows you a list of image files. Take note of the file extensions.

7. Repeat step 6 for the Music option and then for the Video option.

8. When you're finished looking at your media files, click the ⊠ button to close the Search Results dialog box.

Search for all files of a certain type, or search by type and name.

☑ **Pictures and Photos**
☐ Music
☐ Video

All or part of the file name:

You may also want to...

☑ Use advanced search options

[Back]   [Search]

A

SECTION

Bitmap Graphics

A digital camera seems easy to use. Point it, shoot the photo, and….what next? How do you transfer digital photos from camera to computer? How can you print them? How do you get them ready to become e-mail attachments? How do you prepare them for inclusion on Web pages? To understand the wide range of possibilities for digital photos, you'll need some background information about bitmap graphics—the topic for this section of the chapter.

BITMAP BASICS

What is a bitmap graphic? A **bitmap graphic**, also called a "raster graphic" or simply a "bitmap," is composed of a grid of dots, and the color of each dot is stored as a binary number. Think of a grid superimposed on a picture. The grid divides the picture into cells, called pixels. Each pixel is assigned a color, which is stored as a binary number. Figure 7-1 illustrates these basic characteristics of a bitmap graphic.

> **TERMINOLOGY NOTE**
>
> The term "pixel" is derived from "picture element." It is the smallest element that can be manipulated by a computer display device or printer.

FIGURE 7-1

A bitmap graphic is divided into a grid of individually colored pixels. The color number for each pixel is stored in binary format.

Where would I encounter bitmap graphics? Bitmap graphics are typically used to create realistic images, such as photographs. You might also encounter bitmaps in the form of cartoons, images that appear in computer games, and rendered images produced by 3-D graphics software. When you use a digital camera or camera-enabled cell phone, your photos are stored as bitmaps. A scanner produces bitmaps. The photos you send or receive as e-mail attachments are bitmaps, as are most Web page graphics.

How do I create bitmap images? You can create a bitmap graphic from scratch using the tools provided by graphics software—specifically a category of graphics software referred to as **paint software**. You might be familiar with paint software such as Adobe Photoshop, Jasc Paint Shop Pro, and Microsoft Paint (included with Windows). These programs have tools for freehand sketching, filling in shapes, adding realistic shading, and creating effects that look like oil paints, charcoal, or watercolors. If your freehand sketching talent maxes out with stick figures, you can also create bitmap graphics by using a scanner or digital camera.

SCANNERS AND CAMERAS

How do I convert a printed image into a bitmap? When you have a printed image, such as a photograph, a page from a magazine, or a picture from a book, you can use a **scanner** to convert the printed image into a bitmap graphic. A scanner essentially divides an image into a fine grid of cells and assigns a digital value for the color of each cell. As the scan progresses, these values are transferred to your computer's hard disk and stored as a bitmap graphics file. Scanners, such as the one pictured in Figure 7-2, are inexpensive and easy to use.

INFOWEBLINKS

For more information about scanning equipment, connect to the **Scanner Buyers Guide InfoWeb**.

www.course.com/np/concepts9/ch07

FIGURE 7-2

To scan an image, turn on the scanner and start your scanner software. Place the image face down on the scanner glass, and then use the scanner software to initiate the scan. The scanned image is saved in RAM and can then be saved on your computer's hard disk.

CLICK TO START

When should I use a digital camera rather than a scanner? Whereas a scanner digitizes printed images, a **digital camera** digitizes real objects. Instead of taking a photo with a conventional camera, developing the film, and then digitizing it with a scanner, a digital camera, such as the one in Figure 7-3, takes a photo in digital format, which you can then transfer directly to your computer.

INFOWEBLINKS

You'll learn more about digital cameras and accessories at the **Digital Camera Buyers Guide InfoWeb**.

www.course.com/np/concepts9/ch07

7

Shutter release button   Viewfinder   Built-in flash

Lens

FIGURE 7-3

The controls for a digital camera are very similar to those for an analog, or film, camera. To take a photo, you simply point and shoot.

CLICK TO START

How does a digital camera store images? Some digital cameras store images on floppy disks, CDs, mini-CDs, or miniature hard disk drives. Other digital cameras store images in removable solid-state storage modules, sometimes called "memory cards." Solid state storage is a popular technology for digital cameras. Like RAM, it can be erased and reused. Unlike RAM, solid state storage holds data without consuming power, so it doesn't lose data when the camera is turned off. Figure 7-4 illustrates several digital camera storage options.

FIGURE 7-4

Storage options for digital cameras vary in capacity from 8 MB to 1 GB. The number of photos that can be stored depends on their resolution. High-resolution photos require more storage space than low-resolution photos. As few as two high-res photos might fit on a 32 MB card, whereas the same card might hold hundreds of low-res images.

CompactFlash   Memory stick

SmartMedia card   xD-Picture card

Microdrive

How can I get images out of the camera? Digital cameras allow you to preview images while they are still in the camera and delete those you don't want. The photos you want to keep can be transferred directly to some printers, but typically you transfer the photo data to your computer's hard disk. Depending on your camera, this transfer can be achieved in several ways:

■ **Media transfer.** If your camera stores data on floppy disks or CDs, you can simply remove the media from your camera and insert it into the appropriate drive of your computer.

■ **Direct cable transfer.** If your computer and your camera have FireWire ports (also called IEEE-1394 ports), you can connect a cable between these two ports to transfer the photo data. You can use a similar transfer method if your computer and camera have USB ports or serial ports. A USB-2 or FireWire port provides good transfer speed. USB-1 ports are somewhat slower, and serial ports are quite slow.

■ **Infrared port.** Some cameras can "beam" the data from your camera to your computer's infrared port. This method eliminates the need for a cable but is much slower than using a FireWire, USB, or serial port.

■ **Card readers.** A card reader is a small device designed to read data contained in a solid state memory card. Card readers can be connected to your computer's USB port or built into the system unit. To transfer photo data from a memory card, you remove it from the camera and insert it into the card reader, as shown in Figure 7-5.

■ **Floppy disk adapters.** A **floppy disk adapter** is a floppy disk-shaped device that contains a slot for a memory card. You simply insert the memory card into the floppy disk adapter, and then insert the adapter into your computer's floppy disk drive.

■ **Docking station.** Some camera manufacturers offer a camera docking station that connects to a computer by cable. A camera can be placed in the docking station to transfer photos to the computer's hard disk.

FIGURE 7-5

A card reader transfers photo data from a memory card to your computer's hard disk.

■ **E-mail.** Cell phone photos can be transferred to a computer by e-mailing the photo to your e-mail account. The photo arrives as an attachment, which can be saved as a separate file.

Regardless of the technology you use, transferring photo data from your camera to your computer requires software, which might be supplied along with your camera, with your card reader, or by a standalone graphics software package, such as Adobe Photoshop. This software allows you to select a file format, specify a file name, and determine the location for each image file. You'll learn about your choices for file formats later in this section, but most cameras store photos in JPEG or TIFF formats.

After you store your digital photos on your computer's hard disk, you can modify them, send them as e-mail attachments, print them, post them on Web pages, or archive them onto a CD.

MODIFYING BITMAP GRAPHICS

What characteristics of a bitmap can I modify? Because bitmap graphics are coded as a series of bits that represent pixels, you can use graphics software to modify or edit this type of graphic by changing individual pixels. You can retouch old photographs to eliminate creases, spots, and discoloration (Figure 7-6). You can modify photos to wipe out red eye or erase the "rabbit ears" that ruined an otherwise good family portrait. You can even design eye-catching new pictures with images you cut and paste from several photos or scanned images.

Whether you acquire an image from a digital camera or a scanner, bitmap graphics tend to require quite a bit of storage space. Although a large graphics file might provide the necessary data for a high-quality printout, these files take up space on your hard disk and can require lengthy transmission times that clog up mailboxes and make Web pages seem sluggish. The size of the file that holds a bitmap depends on its resolution and color depth. Read on to see how these factors affect file size and how you can alter them to create smaller graphics files, suitable for e-mail attachments and Web pages.

IMAGE RESOLUTION

How does resolution pertain to bitmap graphics? The dimensions of the grid that forms a bitmap graphic are referred to as its resolution. The resolution of a graphic is usually expressed as the number of horizontal and vertical pixels it contains. For example, a small graphic for a Web page might have a resolution of 150 x 100 pixels—150 pixels across and 100 pixels high.

How does resolution relate to image quality? High-resolution graphics contain more data than low-resolution graphics. With more data, it is possible to display and print high-quality images that are sharper and clearer than images produced using less data. For example, a photograph of a cat taken with an inexpensive digital camera might produce a graphic with a resolution of 1600 x 1200, but a more expensive camera with 2272 x 1712 resolution contains more pixels and produces a higher-quality image.

Camera manufacturers sometimes express the resolution of digital cameras as megapixels. A **megapixel** is 1 million pixels. A camera with resolution of 1600 x 1200 has the capability of producing photos containing 1.9 megapixels (1600 multiplied by 1200). A camera with 2272 x 1712 resolution is technically 3.88 megapixels, but might be rounded off and called a 4.0 megapixel camera by its manufacturer.

FIGURE 7-6

Bitmap graphics can be easily modified. Many graphics software products include wizards that help you retouch photographs.

Before

After

7

How does resolution relate to the file size of a graphic?
Each pixel in a bitmap graphic is stored as one or more bits. The more pixels in a bitmap, the more bits needed to store the file.

How does resolution relate to the physical size of an image? A bitmap graphic is simply a collection of data. Unlike a printed photograph, a bitmap has no fixed physical size. The size at which a bitmap is displayed or printed depends on the density as well as the resolution (dimensions) of the image grid.

Imagine that each bitmap image and its grid come on a surface that you can stretch or shrink. As you stretch the surface, the grid maintains the same number of horizontal and vertical cells, but each cell becomes larger and the grid becomes less dense. As you shrink the surface, the grid becomes smaller and more dense. The graphic retains the same resolution no matter how much you stretch or shrink the graphic's physical size, as shown in Figure 7-7.

FIGURE 7-7

When this bitmap graphic is enlarged, it still retains its original resolution—24 x 24.

Original graphic at 24 x 24 resolution

Enlarged graphic still has 24 x 24 resolution

This concept of stretching and shrinking without changing resolution is important for understanding what happens when bitmaps are displayed and printed. The denser the grid, the smaller the image will appear. The density of an image grid can be expressed as dots per inch (dpi) for a printer or scanner or as pixels per inch (ppi) on a monitor.

How do I specify the size of a printed image? Most graphics software allows you to specify the size at which an image is printed without changing the resolution of the bitmap graphic. You'll get the highest print quality if the resolution of the graphic meets or exceeds the printer's dpi. An ink jet printer with a resolution of 1440 x 720 dpi produces a very dense image grid. If each pixel of a 1600 x 1200 graphic was printed as a single dot on this printer, the resulting image would be very high quality but just a bit wider than 1 inch. You can specify a larger size for the printout, in which case the printer must create additional data to fill the print grid. This process can produce a fuzzy and blocky image if the printed image gets very large.

As a general rule, when you incorporate an image in a desktop-published document, or when you print photographs, you should work with high-resolution bitmaps so that you can produce high-quality output. To capture high-resolution bitmaps, use the highest resolution provided by your digital camera. When scanning an image, choose a dpi setting on your scanner that is at least as high as the dpi for the printout.

How does a bitmap's resolution relate to what I see on the screen? In Chapter 2, you learned that you can set your computer monitor to a particular resolution, such as 1024 x 768. When you display a bitmap graphic on the screen, each pixel of the graphic typically corresponds to one pixel on the screen. If the resolution of your graphic is 1024 x 768 and your monitor is set at 1024 x 768 resolution, the image appears to fill the screen. If you view a 4.0 megapixel image on the same monitor, the image is larger than the screen, and you have to scroll or change the zoom level to view it (Figure 7-8).

Can I change a graphic's file size? The resolution and corresponding file size of a graphic might not be right for your needs. For example, if you take a photo with a 4.0 megapixel camera, it is unsuitable for a Web page. Not only would it take a long time to download, but it would be larger than most screens. A 4.0 megapixel graphic is also not suitable for an e-mail attachment. Uploading and downloading such a large file—especially over a dial-up connection—would take much too long. Reducing the resolution of a bitmap can reduce its file size and on-screen display size. Most experts recommend that Web graphics not exceed 100 KB and that e-mail attachments not exceed 500 KB.

You can reduce the size of a bitmap by cropping it. **Cropping** refers to the process of selecting part of an image—just like cutting out a section of a photograph. Cropping decreases resolution and file size by reducing the number of pixels in a graphic. You can also reduce file size by removing pixels from the entire graphic; however, this process changes the image quality.

Bitmap graphics are **resolution dependent**, which means that the quality of the image depends on its resolution. If you reduce the resolution, the computer eliminates pixels from the image, reducing the size of the image grid. For example, if you reduce the resolution from 2160 x 1440 (3.1 megapixels) to 1080 x 720 (.8 megapixels), the image grid becomes a quarter of its original size. The file size is reduced by a similar amount. However, the computer threw away data with the pixels, which can reduce image quality.

If you attempt to enlarge a bitmap by increasing its resolution, your computer must somehow add pixels because no additional picture data exists. But what colors should these additional pixels become? Most graphics software uses a process called **pixel interpolation** to create new pixels by averaging the colors of nearby pixels. For some graphics, pixel interpolation results in an image that appears very similar to the original. Other images—particularly those with strong curved or diagonal lines—develop an undesirable **pixelated**, or "bitmappy," jagged appearance (Figure 7-9).

FIGURE 7-8

When viewing an image larger than the screen, you must scroll to see all parts of the image or set the zoom level of your graphics software to less than 100%. You should understand, however, that changing the zoom level stretches or shrinks only the size of the image grid. It has no effect on the printed size of a graphic or the graphic's file size.

7

The figure above has a resolution of 130 x 130. The figure at right was enlarged to a resolution of 260 x 260, but it has a rough, pixelated appearance.

FIGURE 7-9

When you increase the resolution of an existing graphic, the file size increases, but the quality might deteriorate.

COLOR DEPTH AND PALETTES

What is color depth? **Color depth** is the number of colors available for use in an image. As the number of colors increases, image quality improves, but file size also increases. You can limit color depth to decrease the file size required for a graphic. To find out how this works, take a look at the storage requirements for various color depths. Then you can turn to the procedures for reducing color depth.

How does color depth relate to file size? To answer this question, go back to the old days of computing when monitors were simple monochrome devices. Each screen pixel could be either "on" or "off." A **monochrome bitmap** is displayed by manipulating the pattern of "off" and "on" pixels displayed on-screen. To store the data for a monochrome bitmap, an "on" pixel is represented by a 1 bit. An "off" pixel is represented by a 0 bit. Each row of the bitmap grid is stored as a series of 0s and 1s, as shown in Figure 7-10.

FIGURE 7-10

Each pixel in a monochrome bitmap graphic is stored as a bit.

1. This image originated as a black-and-white silhouette.

2. The computer divides the picture into a matrix.

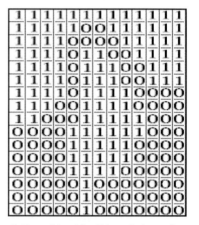

3. If a cell is white, it is coded as a 1. If the cell is black, it is coded as a 0.

Monochrome bitmaps require very little storage space. Suppose you create a full-screen monochrome bitmap with your monitor's resolution set to 640 x 480. Your screen displays 307,200 pixels (that's 640 multiplied by 480). Each pixel is set to display a black dot or a white dot. When you store the graphic, each dot requires only one bit. Therefore, the number of bits required to represent a full-screen picture is the same as the number of pixels on the screen. At a resolution of 640 x 480, a full-screen graphic requires 307,200 bits of storage space. The number of bytes required to store the image is 307,200 divided by 8 (remember that there are eight bits in a byte). Your full-screen monochrome bitmap would, therefore, require only 38,400 bytes of storage space.

But what about color? Today's color monitors require a more complex storage scheme. Each screen pixel displays a color based on the intensity of red, green, and blue signals it receives. A pixel appears white if the red, green, and blue signals are set to maximum intensity. If red, green, and blue signals are equal but at a lower intensity, the pixel displays a shade of gray. If the red signal is set to maximum intensity, but the blue and green signals are off, the pixel appears in brilliant red. A pixel appears purple if it receives red and blue signals, and so forth.

Each red, green, and blue signal is assigned a value ranging from zero to 255. Zero represents the absence of color, and 255 represents the highest intensity level for that color. These values produce a maximum of 16.7 million colors. A graphic that uses this full range of colors is referred to as a **True Color bitmap** or a **24-bit bitmap**. You might be able to guess where the "24-bit" term comes from. The data for each pixel requires three bytes of storage space—eight bits for blue, eight bits for green, and eight bits for red—for a total of 24 bits. Although True Color bitmaps produce photographic-quality images, they also produce very large files. Because each pixel requires three bytes, a 3.1 megapixel True Color bitmap would require a 9.3 MB file!

You might occasionally encounter a **32-bit bitmap**. Just like a 24-bit bitmap, it displays 16.7 million colors. The extra bits are used to define special effects, such as the amount of transparency, for a pixel. These files are even larger than those containing 24-bit bitmaps. A 3.1 megapixel 32-bit bitmap would be about 10 MB.

Files containing full-screen 24-bit and 32-bit bitmaps are typically too large for e-mail attachments and Web pages because they require excessively long upload and download times. Earlier in the chapter, you learned that you can reduce a bitmap's file size by removing pixels. Another way to shrink a bitmap file is to reduce its color depth.

How can I reduce color depth? To reduce the color depth of a bitmap, you can use your graphics software to work with color palettes. A **color palette** (also called a "color lookup table" or "color map") is the digital version of a kidney-shaped artist's palette that holds the selection of colors an artist uses for a particular painting. A digital color palette allows you to select a group of colors to use for a bitmap graphic.

The advantage of a palette is that if it contains only 256 colors, you can store the data for each pixel in 8 bits instead of 24 bits, which reduces the file to a third of the size required for a True Color bitmap.

How does a color palette work? A color palette is stored as a table within the header of a graphics file. Each palette contains a list of 256 color numbers. Each of these numbers is mapped to a 24-bit number that corresponds to the actual levels of red, green, and blue required to display the color. Figure 7-11 explains how this table works.

Pixels in the upper-left corner of an image

Color Palette	
Index #	**RGB Value**
0	000 000 000
1	060 000 255
2	020 167 167
3	120 060 060
4	180 060 060
5	255 000 000
.	
.	
.	
253	255 060 060
254	255 000 255
255	255 255 255

FIGURE 7-11

A color palette is a subset of all possible colors. Each color in the palette is numbered, and its number points to the full 24-bit RGB (red, green, blue) value stored in the graphics file header.

7

How do I select a color palette? Most graphics software offers a selection of ready-made palettes that you can choose by using the color palette or color picker tool. Ready-made palettes usually include a grayscale palette, a system palette, and a Web palette.

A **grayscale palette** uses shades of gray, or "gray scales," to display images that look similar to black-and-white photographs. Most grayscale palettes consist of 256 shades of gray. Figure 7-12 illustrates a grayscale palette and a grayscale bitmap graphic.

FIGURE 7-12

Grayscale bitmaps look like black-and-white photographs.

A **system palette** is the collection of colors the operating system uses for graphics that represent desktop icons and controls. Windows, for example, uses a system palette containing 20 permanent colors and 236 colors that can be changed, depending on the application.

FIGURE 7-13

The Windows system palette and Web palette are usually provided by graphics software.

A **Web palette** (also called a "Web-safe palette" or a "browser palette") contains a standard set of colors used by Internet Web browsers. Because most browsers support this palette, it is typically regarded as a safe choice when preparing graphics for Internet distribution. Figure 7-13 shows the collection of colors used by system and Web palettes.

Your graphics software might offer additional palettes. They are likely to include a "woodsy" palette that works well for outdoor photographs, a pastel palette that works well with images filled with predominantly light colors, and a flesh-tone palette that's designed to work nicely for portraits.

What if a palette doesn't contain the colors needed for an image? A particular 256-color palette sometimes does not contain the "right" selection of colors for an image. For example, the Windows system palette does not have a wide selection of orange tones for a Halloween or sunset photo. To make up for the lack of colors, your graphics software can dither the image. **Dithering** uses patterns composed of two or more colors to produce the illusion of additional colors and shading, relying on the human eye to blend colors and shapes.

Most graphics software provides options that let you control dithering. You can experiment with these options to find the best one for a particular image. Figure 7-14 illustrates different types of dithering.

True Color
No dithering
66 KB

256 Color
No dithering
23 KB

256 Color
Pattern dithering
23 KB

256 Color
Scattered dithering
23 KB

FIGURE 7-14

Dithering produces different results, depending on whether you use scattered or patterned dithering.

When should I reduce color depth? Generally, bitmap graphics that you want to print should remain in True Color format. Any graphics that will be sent as e-mail attachments, posted on a Web site, or viewed only on-screen can be reduced to a 256-color palette or compressed into a small file using a file format such as JPEG.

BITMAP GRAPHICS FORMATS

Are there different kinds of bitmap graphics? Many graphics file formats exist, and most graphics software offers a choice of popular formats, such as BMP, PCX, TIFF, JPEG, GIF, and PNG.

BMP, pronounced "bee-em-pee" or "bump," is the native bitmap graphics file format of the Microsoft Windows environment. Microsoft Paint, included as part of Microsoft Windows, creates BMP graphics files. The BMP format supports True Color and can be used for a wide variety of graphics applications, such as photographs, illustrations, and graphs. BMP files are not compressed in any way, so this format typically creates the largest graphics files of any file format. BMP graphics are not supported by most browsers, so they are not used on the Web.

PCX is one of the original personal computer bitmap graphics file formats. PCX graphics are usually 8-bit (256 colors) and are automatically compressed to reduce file size without any loss of image quality. Because it's not supported by browsers, PCX is not used on the Web.

TIFF (Tag Image File Format), or TIF, is a flexible and platform-independent graphics file format supported by most photo-editing software packages. Scanners and digital cameras commonly store bitmaps in TIFF format because it supports True Color and can be easily converted into other graphics file formats. TIFF is an excellent choice for DTP projects, but it is not supported by most browsers.

JPEG (pronounced JAY peg), which stands for Joint Photographic Experts Group, is a graphics format with built-in compression that stores True Color bitmap data very efficiently in a small file. The JPEG format is popular for Web graphics and for photos attached to e-mail messages. When creating or converting an image in JPEG format, you can control the level of compression and the resulting file size. The compression process eliminates

7

some image data, however, so highly compressed files suffer some quality deterioration. The TechTalk section of this chapter covers compression in more detail.

GIF (pronounced GIF or JIFF), or Graphics Interchange Format, was specifically designed to create images that can be displayed on multiple platforms, such as PCs and Macs. GIF graphics are a very popular format for Web graphics, but they are limited to 256 colors. In addition, the compression algorithm that's built into the GIF format is patented by UniSys Corporation. Currently, UniSys allows individuals to freely use GIF graphics on Web sites, as long as those graphics are created by using graphics software that contains GIF routines licensed by UniSys. Although the GIF format is popular, some Web developers express concern about further restrictions or fees that UniSys might require in the future.

PNG (Portable Network Graphic), pronounced "ping," is a graphics format designed to improve on the GIF format. A PNG graphic can display up to 48-bit True Color (trillions of colors). Unlike JPEG, PNG compresses bitmap data without losing any data, so compressed images retain the same high quality as the originals. Unlike GIF, PNG is a public domain format without any restrictions on its use.

How do I know which graphics format to use? Selecting the best graphics file format to use depends on what you intend to do with the image. Figure 7-15 summarizes popular uses for each format.

BMP	Graphical elements, such as buttons and other controls used in computer programs
PCX	Not used with much frequency today
TIFF	High-resolution scanned images and digital photos used in desktop publishing; high-quality digital photos reproduced on special photo printers
JPEG	Photographic or scanned images that might be used in a variety of applications, such as DTP or Web pages, where flexibility in file size is important
GIF	Popular format for Web graphics
PNG	An alternative to GIF for Web graphics

FIGURE 7-15

Choosing a bitmap graphics format depends on how the image is used.

QuickCheck

1. Images from a digital camera can be transferred to a computer by using a USB cable, serial cable, or [_____] cable.

2. A 3.5 megapixel digital camera captures images with a 2160 x 1440 [_____].

3. Bitmap graphics are resolution [_____], so that reducing the resolution also reduces the image quality.

4. A(n) [_____] palette produces images that resemble black and white photographs.

5. The [_____] format is a good choice for desktop publishing, but not for Web graphics. Hint: Use the acronym.

6. The most popular 256-color formats for Web graphics include [_____] and PNG. Hint: Use the acronym.

 CHECK ANSWERS

SECTION B

Vector and 3-D Graphics

If you've played any computer games recently or watched an animated movie, you've seen the product of computer-generated 3-D animated graphics. To the uninformed, these photorealistic action characters might seem little more than fancy cartoons. After you understand the way they are created, however, you'll appreciate the incredible amount of computing power they required.

This section of the chapter begins with two-dimensional vector graphics, one of the basic building blocks for 3-D animated graphics. You'll find out how they differ from bitmaps and why you might want to use them. After covering the basics for two-dimensional graphics, the section progresses to static 3-D graphics and then to animated 3-D graphics.

VECTOR GRAPHICS BASICS

What is a vector graphic? Unlike a bitmap graphic created by dividing an image into a grid of pixels, a **vector graphic** consists of a set of instructions for re-creating a picture. Instead of storing the color value for each pixel, a vector graphic file contains the instructions the computer needs to create the shape, size, position, and color for each object in an image. These instructions are similar to those a drafting teacher might give students: "Draw a 2-inch (or 112-pixel) circle. Locate this circle 1" down and 2" in from the right edge of the work area. Fill the circle with yellow." The Stonehenge image shown in Figure 7-16 was created as a vector graphic.

FIGURE 7-16

A vector graphic is formed from lines and shapes, which can be colored or shaded.

7

The parts of a vector graphic are created as separate objects. For example, the Stonehenge image was created with a series of roughly rectangular objects for the stones and a circular object for the sun. These objects are layered according to the artist's specifications. In the Stonehenge image, the sun object is layered behind the stones and clouds. This characteristic of vector graphics gives artists a great amount of flexibility in arranging and editing image elements.

How can I identify vector graphics? It can be difficult to accurately identify a vector graphic just by looking at an on-screen image. One clue that an image might be a vector graphic is a flat, cartoon-like quality. Think of clip art images—they are typically stored as vector graphics. For a more definitive identification, however, you should check the file extension. Vector graphics files have file extensions such as .wmf, .dxt, .mgx, .eps, .pict, and .cgm.

How do vector graphics compare with bitmap graphics? Vector graphics are suitable for most line art, logos, simple illustrations, and diagrams that might be displayed and printed at various sizes. When compared to bitmaps, vector graphics have several advantages and disadvantages. You should take the following distinctions into account when deciding which type of graphic to use for a specific project.

■ **Vector graphics resize better than bitmaps.** When you change the size of a vector graphic, the objects change proportionally and maintain their smooth edges. Whereas a circle in a bitmap graphic might appear to have jagged edges after it is enlarged, a circle in a vector graphic appears as a smooth curve at any size, as shown in Figure 7-17.

FIGURE 7-17

Unlike bitmaps, vector graphics can be resized without becoming pixelated and blurry.

Vector graphic at 200% (above) and 50% (left)

Bitmap graphic at 200% (above) and 50% (right)

■ **Vector graphics usually require less storage space than bitmaps.** The storage space required for a vector graphic reflects the complexity of the image. Each instruction requires storage space, so the more lines, shapes, and fill patterns in the graphic, the more storage space it requires. The Stonehenge vector graphic used as an example in this chapter requires less than 4 KB of storage space. A True Color photograph of the same image requires 1,109 KB.

■ **It is easier to edit an object in a vector graphic than an object in a bitmap graphic.** In some ways, a vector graphic is like a collage of objects. Each object can be layered over other objects, but moved and edited independently. You can individually stretch, shrink, distort, color, move, or delete any object in a vector graphic. For example, if you delete some of the stones from the Stonehenge vector image, the background layers remain. In contrast, most bitmap graphics are constructed as a single layer of pixels. If you erase the pixels for some of the stones in the Stonehenge photograph, you'll create a "hole" of white pixels (Figure 7-18).

FIGURE 7-18

Vector graphic objects are layered, so it is easy to move and delete objects without disrupting the rest of the image. In contrast, deleting a shape from a bitmap image leaves a "hole" because the image is only one layer of pixels.

■ **Vector graphics are not usually as realistic as bitmap images.** Most vector images tend to have a cartoon-like appearance instead of the realistic appearance you expect from a photograph. This cartoon-like characteristic of vector images results from the use of objects filled with blocks of color. Your options for shading and texturing objects are limited, which tends to give vector graphics a "flat" appearance.

What tools do I need to create vector graphics? Neither scanners nor cameras produce vector graphics. Architects and engineers sometimes use a digitizing tablet, such as the one in Figure 7-19, to turn a paper-based line drawing into a vector graphic. A **digitizing tablet** (sometimes called a "2-D digitizer") is a device that provides a flat surface for a paper-based drawing and a pen or "puck" that you can use to click the endpoints of each line on the drawing. The endpoints are converted into vectors and stored.

Usually, vector graphics are created "from scratch" with vector graphics software, referred to as **drawing software**. Popular drawing software includes Adobe Illustrator, Macromedia Freehand, and Corel Designer. Drawing software is sometimes packaged separately from the paint software used to produce bitmap graphics. In other cases, it is included with bitmap software as a graphics software suite.

FIGURE 7-19

A digitizing tablet allows you to trace line drawings for a vector graphic.

7

Vector graphics software provides an array of drawing tools that you can use to create objects, position them, and fill them with colors or patterns. For example, you can use the filled circle tool to draw a circle filled with a solid color. You can create an irregular shape by connecting points to outline the shape. Figure 7-20 illustrates how to use drawing tools to create a vector graphic.

FIGURE 7-20

To draw a circle, select the filled circle tool, and then drag the mouse pointer to indicate the circle's location and size. A color palette allows you to select the circle color. After you create the circle object, you can move it and change its size or color. You can also create irregular shapes for objects, such as clouds, by connecting short line segments.

CLICK TO START

The clouds are created as a series of short line segments and filled with color.

The stones are created as a series of short line segments and filled with black.

The background is a filled rectangle.

Vector graphics software helps you easily edit individual objects within a graphic by changing their sizes, shapes, positions, or colors. For example, the data for creating a circle for the sun is recorded as an instruction, such as CIRCLE 40 Y 200 150, which means create a circle with a 40-pixel radius, color it yellow, and place the center of the circle 200 pixels from the left of the screen and 150 pixels from the top of the screen. If you move the circle to the right side of the image, the instruction that the computer stores for the circle changes to something like CIRCLE 40 Y 500 150—500 pixels from the left instead of 200.

INFOWEBLINKS

To learn more about popular vector graphics software, you can connect to the **Vector Graphics Software InfoWeb**.

www.course.com/np/concepts9/ch07

When filling in a shape with color, your graphics software might provide tools for creating gradients. A **gradient** is a smooth blending of shades from one color to another or from light to dark. Gradients, as shown in Figure 7-21, can be used to create shading and three-dimensional effects.

FIGURE 7-21

Gradients can create the illusion of three dimensions, such as making this shape appear to be a tube.

Some vector graphics software provides tools that apply bitmapped textures to vector graphic objects, giving them a more realistic appearance. For example, you can create a vector drawing of a house, and then apply a brick-like texture derived from a bitmap photograph of real bricks. A graphic that contains both bitmap and vector data is called a **metafile**.

VECTOR-TO-BITMAP CONVERSION

Is it possible to convert a vector graphic into a bitmap? A vector graphic can be converted quite easily into a bitmap graphic through a process called rasterizing. **Rasterization** works by superimposing a grid over a vector image and determining the color for each pixel. This process is typically carried out by graphics software, which allows you to specify the output size for the final bitmap image. On a PC, you can also rasterize a vector graphic by using the Print Screen key to take a screenshot of a vector image. It is important to rasterize images at the size you ultimately need. If you rasterize a vector image at a small size and then try to enlarge the resulting bitmap image, you will likely get a poor-quality pixelated image, such as the one in Figure 7-22.

After a vector graphic is converted to a bitmap, the resulting graphic no longer has the qualities of a vector graphic. For example, if you convert the Stonehenge vector graphic into a bitmap, the sun is no longer an object that you can easily move or assign a different color.

How about converting a bitmap graphic into a vector graphic? Converting a bitmap graphic into a vector graphic is more difficult than converting from a vector to a bitmap. To change a bitmap graphic into a vector graphic, you must use tracing software. **Tracing software** locates the edges of objects in a bitmap image and converts the resulting shapes into vector graphic objects.

Tracing software products, such as Adobe Streamline and ImpressionX, work best on simple images and line drawings. They do not usually produce acceptable results when used on complex, detailed photos. Tracing capabilities are included in some general-purpose graphics software, but standalone tracing software offers more flexibility and usually produces better results.

INFOWEBLINKS

Looking for software to convert between vector images and bitmaps? You'll find helpful links at the **Vector-Bitmap Conversion InfoWeb**.

www.course.com/np/concepts9/ch07

FIGURE 7-22

When vector images are rasterized, they become bitmaps and can't be enlarged without becoming pixelated.

7

VECTOR GRAPHICS ON THE WEB

Do vector graphics work on the Web? Web browsers were originally designed to support a limited number of graphics formats—GIF and JPEG—and these formats were exclusively bitmaps. Built-in browser support for vector graphics has been slow, but plug-ins and players are currently available for several of the most popular Web-based vector graphics formats.

Which vector graphics formats can be used on the Web? A graphics format called **SVG** (Scalable Vector Graphics) is designed specifically for the Web (Figure 7-23). Graphics in SVG format are automatically resized when displayed on different screens or when printed. SVG supports gradients, drop shadows, multiple levels of transparency, and other effects, along with portability to other platforms, such as handheld computers and cellular phones. SVG graphic objects can include regular and irregular shapes, images, and text, and they can be animated. You can add SVG files to HTML and XML documents by using the <embed> tag.

Flash is another popular vector graphics format for the Web. As Chapter 6 explained, Macromedia's Flash software creates vector graphics that are stored in files with .swf extensions. Flash graphics can be static or animated. Flash players are shipped with most browsers, and player updates can be downloaded from the Macromedia site.

Flash animations have advantages over other formats, such as animated GIFs. Recall from Chapter 6 that an animated GIF is essentially a series of slightly different bitmap images displayed in sequence to achieve animation effects. As a bitmap-based format, GIF files are fairly large. Most Flash animations fit in compact files and, therefore, can be transferred from a Web server to a browser more rapidly than animated GIFs.

What are the advantages of using vector graphics on the Web? Vector graphics have several advantages:

■ **Consistent quality.** On Web pages, vector graphics appear with the same consistent quality on all computer screens. This capability makes it possible for browsers to adjust the size of an image "on the fly" to fit correctly on a screen, regardless of its size or resolution. These adjustments don't carry any penalty in terms of image quality—a "large" version of a vector graphic displayed on a monitor set at 1024 x 768 resolution has the same sharp detail and smooth curves as the original image sized to fit a smaller screen set at 640 x 480 resolution. This flexibility is important for Web pages that might be viewed at different resolutions on PCs, Macs, or other platforms.

■ **Searchable.** Another advantage is that any text contained in a vector image is stored as actual text, not just a series of colored dots. This text can be indexed by search engines so that it can be included in keyword searches. For example, suppose a vector drawing was used to produce a diagram describing the service box where your telephone line enters your house. One of the components in this diagram is labeled "telephone test jack." If you enter "telephone test jack" into a search engine, the service box diagram will likely turn up in the list of search results.

■ **Compact file size.** A third advantage of vector graphics on the Web is their compact file sizes. A fairly complex graphic can be stored in a file that is under 30 KB—that's kilobytes, not megabytes. These files require little storage space and can be transmitted swiftly from a Web server to your browser.

FIGURE 7-23

SVG graphics are typically used on the Web for maps, ads, organizational charts, and flowcharts.

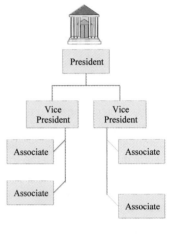

INFOWEBLINKS

Connect to the **Web-based Vector Graphics InfoWeb** for an update on the latest vector graphics formats for the Web.

www.course.com/np/concepts9/ch07

3-D GRAPHICS

How do vector graphics relate to 3-D graphics? Like vector graphics, **3-D graphics** are stored as a set of instructions. For a 3-D graphic, however, the instructions contain the locations and lengths of lines that form a wireframe for a three-dimensional object. The **wireframe** acts in much the same way as the framework of a pop-up tent. Just as you would construct the framework for the tent, and then cover it with a nylon tent cover, a 3-D wireframe can be covered with surface texture and color to create a graphic of a 3-D object. The process of covering a wireframe with surface color and texture is called **rendering**. The rendering process, shown in Figure 7-24, outputs a bitmap image.

FIGURE 7-24

3-D graphics are based on a wireframe, which can be rendered into a bitmap image that looks three-dimensional.

For added realism, the rendering process can take into account the way that light shines on surfaces and creates shadows. The technique for adding light and shadows to a 3-D image is called **ray tracing**. Before an image is rendered, the artist selects a location for one or more light sources. The computer applies a complex mathematical algorithm to determine how the light source affects the color of each pixel in the final rendered image. This process can take time—hours for a complex image, even using today's most powerful personal computers. Figure 7-25 shows the image from the previous figure rendered with an additional light source and ray tracing.

FIGURE 7-25

Ray tracing adds realism to 3-D graphics by adding highlights and shadows that are produced by a light source.

7

What tools do I need to create 3-D graphics? To create 3-D graphics, you need 3-D graphics software, such as AutoCad or Caligari trueSpace. This software has tools for drawing a wireframe and viewing it from any angle. It provides rendering and ray tracing tools, along with an assortment of surface textures that you can apply to individual objects. Figure 7-26 takes you on a tour of a popular 3-D graphics software package.

FIGURE 7-26

3-D graphics software provides tools for drawing a wireframe and then specifying colors and textures for rendering.

CLICK TO START

3-D graphics software runs on most personal computers, although some architects and engineers prefer to use high-end workstations. A fast processor, lots of RAM, and a fast graphics card with its own video RAM all speed up the rendering process. Experts recommend using at least a 1 GHz Pentium PC or a Macintosh G3 equipped with a high-resolution, 17" or larger monitor. A graphics card designed for 3-D work and loaded with at least 128 MB of memory is also useful.

Is it possible to animate 3-D graphics? 3-D graphics can be animated to produce special effects for movies or to create interactive, animated characters and environments for 3-D computer games. Animated special effects, such as massive battle scenes, are created by rendering a sequence of bitmaps, in which one or more objects are moved or otherwise changed between each rendering. In traditional hand-drawn animation, a chief artist draws the keyframes, and then a team of assistants creates each of the in-between images—24 of these images for each second of animation. For 3-D computer animation, the computer creates the in-between images by moving the object and rendering each necessary image. All the images are then combined into a single file, creating essentially a digital movie.

Graphics design companies such as Pixar Animation Studios and DreamWorks use 3-D animation techniques to produce animated feature films as well as special effects. The first full-length animated 3-D movie was *Toy Story*, released in 1995 by Walt Disney Studios and Pixar. Digitally animated films, such as *Ice Age II*, *Ratatouille*, and *Shrek 3*, illustrate the growing sophistication of 3-D animation.

INFOWEBLINKS

For additional resources about 3-D software (and shareware), rendering, ray tracing, and 3-D animated graphics, check out the **3-D Graphics InfoWeb**.

www.course.com/np/concepts9/ch07

Do game and movie animation require similar tools and techniques? An important characteristic of special effects and animated films is that rendering can be accomplished during the production phase of the movie and incorporated into the final footage. In contrast, 3-D computer game animation happens in "real time." Each frame that makes the image seem to move must be rendered while you are playing the game—a process that requires an incredible amount of computer power. To give you a handle on the immensity of the task, consider a game like Doom displayed on a computer monitor that's set at 1024 x 768 resolution (Figure 7-27). At this resolution, the screen contains 786,432 pixels (1024 multiplied by 768). If the game is presented in 32-bit color, each frame of the animation requires 25,165,824 bits (multiply 786,432 times 32).

Computer game designers believe that on-screen animation looks smoothest at 60 frames per second, which means your computer must handle 1,509,949,440—that's more than 1 billion—bits of information every second just to put the 3-D image onto the screen. In addition, the computer must process even more data to keep track of the movements of each player. To handle all this data, your computer's main processor gets help from a graphics processor located on your computer's graphics card. These graphics processors vary in their capabilities. For the fastest graphics capability, look for graphics cards billed as 3-D accelerators.

Can I create my own animated 3-D graphics? You can create 3-D animations on a standard PC or Mac with commercially available software, but professional 3-D software, such as Maya and Autodesk 3ds max, is expensive and has a steep learning curve. If you want to dabble with 3-D animations before making an expensive software investment, you might try Curious Labs Poser, Corel Bryce, or one of the shareware programs listed in the 3-D Graphics InfoWeb (page 378). Whether you use a commercial or shareware package, be prepared to spend lots of time with the manual before you are able to produce any original animations.

FIGURE 7-27

Classic computer games, such as Doom, established building blocks for animation technologies used to create today's fast-action, visually detailed computer games.

7

QuickCheck

SECTION B

1. Unlike bitmaps, vector graphics can be enlarged without becoming pixelated. True or false? [   ]

2. Whereas the software used to work with bitmap graphics is often referred to as paint software, vector graphics software is usually referred to as [   ] software.

3. 3-D graphics are based on a(n) [   ] that can be covered with surface texture and color.

4. The technique of adding light and shadows to a 3-D image is called ray [   ].

5. A vector graphic can be easily converted into a bitmap through a process called [   ].

6. Today, SVG and [   ] are the most popular vector graphics formats for the Web.

CHECK ANSWERS

Digital Video

In the previous sections, you learned about GIF and Flash animations—popular options for adding motion to Web pages. You also learned about using animated 3-D graphics for movie special effects and computer games. Digital animation is typically created from scratch by an artist with the help of a computer. In contrast, digital video is based on footage of real objects filmed and then stored as bits. Digital video encompasses several technologies, including those that produce theater-quality DVD movies, desktop videos, Web-based videos, and PDA videos. In this section, you'll take a look at what you can do with affordable, easy-to-use desktop video tools. You'll also explore how to transfer digital videos onto DVD and then add interactive menus to access selected scenes and special features.

DIGITAL VIDEO BASICS

What is digital video? A video is a series of still frames, like those in Figure 7-28, projected at a rate fast enough to fool the human eye into perceiving continuous motion. **Digital video** uses bits to store color and brightness data for each video frame. The process is similar to storing the data for a series of bitmap images in which the color for each pixel is represented by a binary number.

Unlike analog video, digital video retains image quality no matter how many times it is copied. Videos in digital format can be easily manipulated on a personal computer, putting the world of movie-making at your fingertips.

Footage for digital videos can be supplied by a video camera, videotape, television, DVD, or even a digital video recording device such as TiVo. You can shoot footage with a consumer-quality camcorder and use your personal computer to edit this footage into videos suitable for a variety of personal and professional uses, such as video wedding albums, product sales videos, training videos, video holiday greeting cards, documentaries for nonprofit organizations, and video scrapbooks. These videos can be stored on a hard disk or distributed on CDs, DVDs, videotapes, memory cards, or the Web.

Are there different kinds of digital videos? Digital video is sometimes classified by its platform. The term **desktop video** refers to videos that are constructed and displayed using a personal computer. **Web-based video** is incorporated in Web pages and accessed with a browser. **DVD-video** refers to a DVD format used for commercial DVDs that contain feature-length films. **PDA video** refers to small-format video designed to be viewed on a PDA or cell phone screen.

FIGURE 7-28

A video is composed of a series of bitmap graphics, each one called a frame.

How do I create digital video? To understand how you can create your own digital videos, you'll need information about four procedures summarized in Figure 7-29 and explained in the rest of this section.

FIGURE 7-29

Desktop video requires a few fairly simple steps.

1. Produce video footage. Select equipment for filming videos and use effective filming techniques.

2. Transfer video footage to a computer. Use cable-to-cable transfer or a video capture card to move video footage from cameras, videotapes, television, and DVDs to your computer's hard disk.

3. Edit video footage. Use software to select video segments, arrange them into a video, and add a soundtrack.

4. Store and play video. Select digital video file formats for playback on desktop, Web, PDA, and DVD platforms.

PRODUCING VIDEO FOOTAGE

Is it necessary to use a digital video camera for filming digital video? You can use a digital or an analog video camera to shoot video footage. As you might expect, a **digital video camera** stores footage as a series of bits. The video data can be stored on a tape in much the same way that computer data is stored on a backup tape. Video data can also be stored on 3" miniDVDs. Digital videotape formats include miniDV, DVCPro, and DVCam. MiniDV is the most popular and generally the format used by consumer digital video cameras.

You can also use an analog video camera to shoot footage that eventually becomes digital video. As with digital video cameras, the footage is stored on tape, but instead of storing bits, an **analog video camera** stores video signals as a continuous track of magnetic patterns. The three most popular analog video formats are Hi8, S-VHS, and VHS.

Another option for shooting video footage is a small, inexpensive **videoconferencing camera** (often called a "Web cam" or "Web camera") that attaches directly to a computer (see Figure 7-30). These cameras capture a series of still photos, which are stored in digital format directly on your computer's hard disk. Web cameras typically produce rather low-quality video. These cameras are not usually battery powered and must remain tethered to your computer, which tends to limit your videos to "talking heads."

FIGURE 7-30

A Web camera, such as this popular D-Link model, sits on top of a computer monitor. It is designed mainly for "talking head" applications, such as online video chats and video conferences.

7

What are the advantages of a digital video camera? A digital video camera captures video data in digital format, which can then be transferred directly to a computer for editing. In addition, digital cameras generally produce higher quality video than analog or videoconferencing cameras. Images tend to be sharper and more colorful. A common misconception is that because desktop, Web-based, and PDA videos are shown on a small computer screen at a fairly low resolution, a cheap camera won't make a difference. Just the opposite is true. The higher the quality of the original video, the better the final video will look.

Does desktop video require special filming techniques? When videos are processed and stored on a personal computer, some of the image data is eliminated to reduce the video file to a manageable size. Simpler videos tend to maintain better quality as they are edited, processed, and stored. Camera movements, fast actions, patterned clothing, and moving backgrounds all contribute to the complexity of a video and should be minimized. The techniques listed in Figure 7-31 can help you produce video footage that maintains good quality as it is edited and processed.

- Use a tripod to maintain a steady image.
- Move the camera slowly if it is necessary to pan from side to side.
- Zoom in and out slowly.
- Direct your subjects to move slowly, when possible.
- Position your shot to eliminate as much background detail and movement as possible.
- Ask the subjects of your video to wear solid-colored clothing, if possible.

FIGURE 7-31

Video Filming Tips

VIDEO TRANSFER

How do I transfer video footage to my computer? Video footage can originate from a variety of sources, including video cameras, videotape, DVRs (digital video recorders), and even your TV. To digitally edit and process digital video, you must transfer the video footage from its source to your computer. After the footage is transferred and stored on a random-access device, such as your computer's hard disk, you can easily cut out unwanted footage, rearrange clips, and add a soundtrack.

The basic method for transferring video footage to your computer is to send the data over a cable that connects your video source to your computer (Figure 7-32). Analog video footage from TV, videotape, and analog video cameras must be converted into digital format before it is stored on your computer's hard disk. Video that originates as a digital signal usually can be transferred directly to your computer without conversion.

How do I convert video from analog devices? The process of converting analog video signals into digital format is referred to as **video capture** and requires a video capture device that connects your computer to the video source with a cable. Your computer's graphics card might include video capture capabilities. If not, you can purchase a separate video capture device that connects to your computer's USB port or a video capture card that plugs into one of your computer's PCI slots.

FIGURE 7-32

You can transfer video footage to a hard disk by connecting a cable between a video camera and a computer. When the transfer is complete, the cable can be disconnected.

Most video capture devices support a variety of analog video sources, such as cameras and VCRs. The trick is to find a cable with a connector at one end that plugs into the video output port of your analog video source and a plug at the other end that's compatible with your video capture device. Figure 7-33 illustrates the equipment necessary for capturing video from an analog camera.

FIGURE 7-33

After it has been installed in your computer, a video capture card can be connected to an analog camera's video-out and audio-out ports.

How do I transfer data from a digital camera to my computer?
The data from a digital camera typically requires no conversion, so it can be transferred directly to your computer's hard disk. Most digital cameras provide a USB or FireWire port for this purpose. Your computer needs a corresponding port to accept the cable from the camera. Figure 7-34 explains where to find your computer's FireWire and USB ports.

Can I capture video from a digital video recorder?
A digital video recorder (DVR), like those used with TiVo service, is a device that records television signals received by an antenna, through a cable, or from a satellite. Signals that originate from antenna or cable are converted from analog into digital format and stored on a built-in hard disk. Satellite signals, already in digital format, are converted or unscrambled as necessary before being stored. DVRs are controlled by customized operating systems, usually based on Linux.

It seems like it would be easy to transfer video files from this computer-like device to your personal computer for editing, but some DVRs store data in proprietary formats designed to discourage copying and distribution. These proprietary formats can make it difficult to convert DVR videos into formats that can be manipulated on a computer. Consumers, however, are demanding more compatibility between DVRs and computers. Until DVR manufacturers provide standard video formats, you can capture analog video direct from the TV using a video capture device.

How do I control the transfer process?
Whether you transfer footage from an analog camera or a digital camera, you must use **video capture software** to control the transfer process. Video capture software allows you to start and stop the transfer, select a file format for storing your video footage, and specify the file name for each video clip. Video capture software is supplied with video editing software and with video capture devices.

FIGURE 7-34

FireWire ports (top) and USB ports (bottom) can be located on the front, sides, or back of the computer's system unit.

7

Videos are easier to edit if you divide them into several files, each containing a one- or two-minute video clip. Some video capture software automatically creates clips by detecting frame changes, such as when you turn your camera off, pause, or switch to a new scene (Figure 7-35).

FIGURE 7-35

Videos should be transferred as a series of short clips.

What format should I use for video files? For the best quality final product, experts recommend that you store video in a raw, non-compressed AVI format for editing. After you trim out unwanted footage, arrange your clips, and add a soundtrack, you might want to convert your completed video into other formats for distribution. You learn more about distribution formats later in this section.

Most digital video cameras store data in DV format. Despite the use of real-time compression to filter out unnecessary data as you record with your camera, DV format contains lots of data. When transferred to your computer, a DV clip requires roughly 1 GB of storage per 5 minutes of video. If you have the disk capacity, you'll get the best quality video if you transfer all this data. If disk space is tight, however, you can whittle digital video down to a more manageable size by using your video capture software to decrease the video display size, reduce the frame rate, and compress file data.

■ **Decrease video display size.** A smaller video window contains fewer pixels than a full-screen window and requires fewer bits to represent the data. Whereas a 720 x 480 video window contains 345,600 pixels, a 320 x 240 window contains only 76,800 pixels and fits in a file one-fourth the size. That's a big advantage. If you're creating Web-based videos designed to be displayed in a small window, or if you're designing video for handheld devices, consider decreasing the resolution at this stage of the process.

■ **Reduce the frame rate. Frame rate** refers to the number of frames shown per second. Digital video cameras record 30 frames per second (fps). Feature films are typically projected at a rate of 24 frames per second. If you intend to output your digital videos to DVDs, you should maintain a high frame rate. Most desktop video, however, has a frame rate of only 15 fps. Reducing the frame rate tends to increase the blurriness of a video, especially for fast-action sequences. If your videos are destined for desktop, Web, or PDA playback, you can reduce the frame rate at this stage of the process because the finished video will be displayed at a lower frame rate.

■ **Compress data.** Most video capture software offers AVI, MOV, or MPEG formats for storing video files. MPEG offers the most compression and produces the smallest files. MPEG compression works by eliminating data, however, and that can decrease image quality. MPEG format is an acceptable option if storage space is a concern or if your videos are destined for the Web or a PDA. It is, however, somewhat slow to work with. Most video experts prefer it as a distribution format rather than as a format for storing files during the editing process.

VIDEO EDITING

Do I need special equipment for video editing? Before camcorders went digital, editing a video consisted of recording segments from one videotape onto another tape. This process, called **linear editing**, required two VCRs at minimum. Professional video editors used expensive editing equipment, beyond the budget of most consumers.

Today's **nonlinear editing** simply requires a computer hard disk and video editing software. The advantage of nonlinear editing is that you can use a random-access device to easily edit and arrange video clips. Video editing requires lots of hard disk space, however, so before you begin an editing session, make sure your computer's hard disk has several gigabytes of available storage space. It is also a good idea to have at least 512 MB of RAM—professionals opt for at least 2 GB.

How do I edit a video? After your video footage is transferred to your computer and stored on the hard disk, you can begin to arrange your video clips by using video editing software, such as Adobe Premiere, Roxio VideoWave, Windows Movie Maker, or Ulead VideoStudio. Your completed video consists of video tracks containing video segments and transitions, plus audio tracks containing voices and music. Most video editing software allows you to overlay a video track with several audio tracks. Figure 7-36 illustrates how to lay out video and audio tracks.

INFOWEBLINKS

The **Video Editing InfoWeb** contains tips about editing digital videos, updates on the latest consumer-level software, and links to the most popular digital video sites.

www.course.com/np/concepts9/ch07

FIGURE 7-36

A timeline stretches across the top of the video editing window and provides the structure for each second of your video.

Place video tracks on the timeline to indicate the sequence for your video clips and transitions.

Timeline

Use the audio tracks to add sound clips.

The video and sound clips that you import for the project appear in a list.

Preview your video to see how the video segments, transitions, and soundtrack all work together.

Cruisin' the Caribbean

VIDEO OUTPUT

How does video footage become a digital video?

After you edit your video clips, arrange them on a timeline, and specify a soundtrack, your video editing software combines the data from all the video and audio files you selected into a single file, which is stored on your computer's hard disk as a digital video.

You can save your digital video in a variety of file formats and select compression techniques to achieve a file size that's best for videos played on computers, the Web, PDAs, or DVD players. Figure 7-37 describes some popular video file formats—**AVI**, **QuickTime**, **MPEG**, **RealMedia**, **WMV**, and **VOB**.

FIGURE 7-37

Popular Digital Video Formats

Format	Extension	Platform	Description and Use
AVI (Audio Video Interleave)	.avi	PC	Often the format for storing digital clips from video cameras; used for desktop video on the PC platform
QuickTime Movie	.mov	PC, Mac, UNIX, Linux	One of the most popular formats for desktop and streaming Web videos
MPEG (Moving Pictures Experts Group)	.mpg or .mpeg	PC, Mac, UNIX, Linux	Versions include MPEG1, MPEG2, and MPEG4; used for desktop video, PDA video, and streaming Web video
RealMedia	.rm	PC, Mac, UNIX, Linux	Produced by RealNetworks, a popular format for streaming Web videos
WMV (Windows Media Video)	.wmv	PC	Offers sophisticated compression options for high-quality images; used for desktop video, PDA video, and streaming video over the Web
VOB (Video Object)	.vob	Standalone DVD players, PCs, Macs, Linux	Industry-standard format for standalone DVD players

Which compression techniques should I use?

Suppose you decide to store your video as an AVI file for desktop viewing. You can compress that AVI file using various compression ratios and by reducing the frame rate or frame size. The videos in Figure 7-38 illustrate the differences in image quality and file size that result from using different compression ratios and frame rates.

FIGURE 7-38

Different compression ratios and frame rates can have a remarkable effect on video quality and file size.

Uncompressed video

Compression ratio: 35:1
Frame rate: 3
File size: 35 KB

CLICK TO START

Compression ratio: 14:1
Frame rate: 10
File size: 76 KB

CLICK TO START

Compression ratio: 3:1
Frame rate: 15
File size: 353 KB

CLICK TO START

A **codec** (compressor/ decompressor) is the software that compresses a file when a video is created and decompresses the file when the video is played. Popular codecs include MPEG, Indeo, Cinepak, DivX, and Windows Media Video 9. Each codec uses a unique compression algorithm and allows you to specify a level of compression. The TechTalk section of this chapter provides details about how video compression works.

It is important to understand that the codec used to compress a video also must be used to decompress the video when it is played. Videos intended for a widespread audience should use one of the codecs included in popular video players, such as QuickTime or Windows Media Player.

DESKTOP, PDA, AND WEB VIDEO

How are desktop videos used? Desktop videos are usually displayed on a computer screen with popular video player software, such as the RealMedia player, Windows Media Player, or Apple's QuickTime player. Desktop videos are typically stored on hard disk or CD, and they are sometimes sent as e-mail attachments.

Can I view movies on my PDA? Some PDAs and smartphones can be configured to play digital videos (Figure 7-39), including movie trailers, TV shows, and even feature-length movies. The device requires video or multimedia player software, such as Pocket TV or Windows Media Player, and storage capacity for the video file—usually on a solid-state memory card. Videos specially optimized for handheld devices can be downloaded from Web sites to your computer, then transferred to handheld storage and played. Popular formats for handheld video include MPEG and WMV.

How do Web-based videos work? A video for a Web page is stored on a Web server in a file. Usually, a link for the video file appears on the Web page. When you click the link, the Web server transmits a copy of the video file to your computer. If you have the correct video player installed on your computer, the video appears on your computer screen.

The transfer of a digital video file from the Web to your computer can happen in one of two ways, depending on the video format. In one case, your computer waits until it receives the entire video file before starting to play it. For large video files, you might wait several minutes or more before the video starts. An alternative method, called **streaming video**, sends a small segment of the video to your computer and begins to play it. While this first segment plays, the Web server sends the next part of the file to your computer, and so on, until the video ends. With streaming video technology, your computer essentially plays the video while it continues to receive it.

How do I add a video to a Web page? You can add two styles of video to your Web pages. The first style, called external video, simply displays a link to a video file. An HTML tag, such as <a href="ducks.avi"> 1.5 MB AVI Video </a>, indicates the file that contains the video (ducks.avi) and the text for the link (1.5 MB AVI Video). When the link is clicked, the video file is downloaded, and the video player is opened and displayed as a separate window in which the video appears.

A second style of Web video uses the <embed> tag to create an internal video, also referred to as an "in-place video." Instead of opening a separate window for the video player, an internal video plays within the Web page. Figure 7-40 on the next page illustrates external and internal Web page videos.

TERMINOLOGY NOTE

MPEG is potentially confusing because it is a file format and a codec. Files in MPEG format use the MPEG codec. Files in other formats, such as AVI and MOV, can also use the MPEG codec to compress file contents.

FIGURE 7-39

You can watch digital videos on some PDAs and cell phones.

7

INFOWEBLINKS

The **Video Players InfoWeb** provides lots of handy information about Microsoft Media Player, QuickTime, and other video player software.

www.course.com/np/concepts9/ch07

FIGURE 7-40

An external Web video (below) displays the player as a separate window. An internal, or in-place, video (left) displays the clip as though it were part of the Web page.

Internal Web video plays "in place."

External Web video displays video in a separate window.

How does Internet connection speed affect Web videos? Although it is possible to play streaming videos over a dial-up connection, it is truly an unsatisfying experience. New compression techniques are able to jam more video data into a smaller package, but with a dial-up connection images tend to be fuzzy and motion is often jerky.

High-speed Internet connections provide much more bandwidth for streaming video. Videos designed to be transmitted over high-speed connections can play in a larger video window, use less compression, and display better image quality. Until everyone has a high-speed connection, however, many Web sites provide one video file that's optimized for dial-up connections and a better quality video file that's optimized for DSL, cable, and ISDN connections.

What are the best formats for Web videos? Today's most popular Web video formats include MPEG4, MOV, WMV, and RM. All these formats offer streaming video and allow developers to adjust compression levels to produce file sizes optimized for dial-up or broadband connections.

DVD-VIDEO

Can I incorporate my digital videos onto DVDs with interactive menus like commercial movies? Suppose you've used video editing software to create a really spectacular video of your class reunion. You can package your completed video footage into a professional-style DVD that can be played on computer DVD drives (if your computer is equipped with DVD player software) or standalone DVD players. It can include interactive menus with options, such as Play Video, Select a Scene, and Special Features, that viewers can select using their DVD remote controls.

What equipment do I need? To create video DVDs, you need a writable DVD drive (sometimes called a "DVD burner") plus software that includes tools for DVD menu creation and DVD-video burning. These tools are offered by DVD authoring software, such as Adobe Encore, Sonic MyDVD, Nero, and Ulead DVD MovieFactory Disc Creator. Many video editing software packages and suites also include tools for creating DVD menus and burning projects onto DVDs.

What's the process for making a video DVD? To create a video DVD, you usually begin by selecting one or more completed videos that include soundtracks, transitions, titles, special effects, and so on. You then use DVD authoring software to design menus and buttons that viewers can use to navigate to specific parts of your video. To complete the project, you can test your project and then output it to DVD, a process often referred to as "burning."

What are my options for creating interactive DVD menus? A DVD menu is a screen that provides viewers with navigation tools to start a video, skip to specific scenes, play special features, and link to other menus. A typical DVD menu consists of a decorative background and option buttons that viewers can select using their DVD players' remote control. Static backgrounds are simply bitmap images, such as a frame from the video or an abstract design. Motion backgrounds display animations or video segments.

Option buttons can be a variety of shapes and sizes. They typically change appearance when selected. For example, when a viewer selects the Play button, it might light up or an icon might appear next to it.

Some DVD authoring software offers a selection of predesigned menu and button templates that you can easily incorporate with your videos. Your software might also provide the option to create your own backgrounds and buttons using graphics software, such as Adobe Photoshop or Microsoft Paint. Figure 7-41 illustrates a DVD menu being created using a simple DVD authoring software package.

7

FIGURE 7-41

Sonic's MyDVD software offers a selection of backgrounds and button styles for creating DVD menus.

Are menus easy to create? Yes, they just require a little advance planning. As you design the menu flow, remember that you want to provide viewers with a way to return to the main menu from each submenu. You might also want viewers to return to the main menu after viewing individual clips. If a submenu offers options for outtakes or other special features, you should provide a way for viewers to return to the submenu when the special feature ends. To help visualize the way your menus will work you can draw a diagram similar to the one in Figure 7-42.

FIGURE 7-42

Sketching a diagram of the menus for your DVD can help you envision how viewers will navigate to selected scenes and special features.

How do I output my video to DVD? To create a DVD that can be viewed on a standalone DVD player, you have to output your video in DVD-video format, which requires video encoded in MPEG2 format and stored in VOB (video object) files. Your DVD authoring software can generate MPEG2-encoded video clips and menus, store them in VOB files, and lay them out on a DVD according to industry standards.

Most DVD authoring software can accomplish the MPEG encoding "on the fly" as it burns the DVD. This process takes time, however, so if you are burning more than one copy, or if you want to test your menu structure before burning the video onto a DVD, you might want to consider creating a DVD image.

What's a DVD image? A **DVD image** (sometimes called a "DVD volume") is essentially a prototype of your DVD, but it is stored on your computer's hard disk. If you have space to store a DVD image, it is a good idea to make one before burning a DVD. You can use a DVD image for testing. You can also use the image to burn multiple DVDs without waiting for your software to prepare the files for each burn.

Can I simply copy a desktop video to a DVD using Windows Explorer or My Computer? Desktop videos are typically stored in AVI or MOV format and most standalone DVD players are not equipped to handle those formats. So, although you can use Windows Explorer to copy MOV and AVI files to a DVD and distribute them, these files can be viewed on most computers, but not on most DVD players.

Even copying files stored in MPEG format might not produce a DVD that works in a standalone player. The DVD-video format specification requires a specific layout for data on the DVD surface. The method you use to copy computer data files does not produce the required layout, so most DVD players will not be able to play the video.

How do I test my DVD image? Your DVD is ready for production and distribution if the video quality looks good and the menus work correctly. Use the tips listed below to test your DVD on your computer before you burn a DVD.

- Test each button to make sure it links to the correct clip.

- Play each clip to the end and make sure it returns to the correct menu when completed.

- Watch the video carefully and look for any poor quality segments with distracting artifacts. Artifacts can sometimes be removed by revisiting your MPEG coding options.

- Listen to the soundtrack to make sure the audio is clear, smooth, and synchronized with the video.

Does it make a difference if I use recordable or rewritable DVDs? Commercial DVD movies are stamped onto DVD-ROM disks during the manufacturing process—something you can't do with your computer's DVD drive. Your computer can burn data on DVD-R, DVD+R, or DVD-RW disks. Because the DVD industry has not achieved a single media standard, some standalone DVD players—particularly those manufactured before 2004—are not able to read one or more of these disk types. DVD+R and DVD-R seem to be compatible with the widest variety of DVD players, whereas DVD-RWs seem to be the least compatible. Before you distribute your DVDs make sure you test them in a standalone DVD player.

TERMINOLOGY NOTE

In the world of video production, an artifact is any visible degradation in the image quality, such as shimmering where contrasting colors meet or backgrounds that become wavy during fast pans or zooms.

QuickCheck SECTION C

1. Desktop video refers to digital videos constructed and displayed using a personal computer.

2. The process of converting analog video signals into digital format is referred to as video Capture.

3. The size of a video file can be reduced by three techniques: shrinking the size of the video window, reducing the frame rate, and compressing the video data.

4. When transferring video to your computer's hard disk, you get the best quality if you use MPEG compression. True or false? False

5. PDA videos are stored in MP3 files, similar to those used on portable audio players. True or false? False

6. Some Web pages feature Streaming video, which sends a small segment of the video to your computer and begins to play it. While this first segment plays, the Web server sends the next part of the file to your computer, and so on, until the video ends.

7. DVD-video requires files stored in VOB format.

 CHECK ANSWERS

SECTION

D

Digital Audio

Computers can record, store, and play back sounds, such as narrations, sound effects, and music. Swapping music files over the Internet is currently the most popular use of digital audio, but digital audio plays a key role in other very interesting applications. How would you like to quit messing with your computer keyboard and enter commands and documents simply by speaking into a microphone? Would you like to add music and sound effects to your Web pages? Maybe you'd like to pull tracks from your audio CDs and remaster them into your own collection of favorite songs. This section of the chapter covers a wide-ranging selection of digital audio concepts and technologies that you're likely to find handy for personal and professional use.

WAVEFORM AUDIO

What is waveform audio? **Waveform audio** is a digital representation of sound. Music, voice, and sound effects can all be recorded as waveforms. To digitally record sound, samples of the sound are collected at periodic intervals and stored as numeric data. Figure 7-43 shows how a computer digitally samples a sound wave.

FIGURE 7-43

Sampling a Sound Wave

Sample	Sample Height (Decimal)	Sample Height (Binary)
1	130	10000010
2	140	1000110
3	160	10100000
4	175	10101111
5	185	10111001

The height of each sample is converted into a binary number and stored. The height of sample 3 is 160 (decimal), so it is stored as its binary equivalent—10100000.

Does sampling rate affect sound quality? **Sampling rate** refers to the number of times per second that a sound is measured during the recording process. It is expressed in hertz (Hz). One thousand samples per second is expressed as 1,000 Hz or 1 KHz (kilohertz). Higher sampling rates increase the quality of the sound recording but require more storage space than lower sampling rates.

The height of each sample can be saved as an 8-bit number for radio-quality recordings or a 16-bit number for high-fidelity recordings. The audio CDs you buy at your favorite music store are recorded at a sampling rate of 44.1 KHz, which means a sample of the sound is taken 44,100 times per second. Sixteen bits are used for each sample. To achieve stereo effects, you must take two of these 16-bit samples. Therefore, each sample requires 32 bits of storage space. When you sample stereo CD-quality music at 44.1 KHz, you can store only eight seconds of music on a 1.44 MB floppy disk. Forty-five minutes of music—the length of a typical album—require about 475 MB.

To conserve space, applications that do not require such high-quality sound use much lower sampling rates. Voice is often recorded with a sampling rate of 11 KHz (11,000 samples per second). This rate results in lower quality sound, but the file is about one-fourth the size of a file for the same sound recorded at 44.1 KHz. Figure 7-44 illustrates how sampling rate affects sound quality.

FIGURE 7-44

A higher sampling rate produces more true-to-life sound quality. Use your BookOnCD to compare the quality of these audio clips, which were digitized at different sampling rates. You'll have to listen carefully to notice the differences.

Low sampling rate: File size = 66 KB

Medium sampling rate: File size = 124 KB

High sampling rate: File size = 235 KB

CLICK TO START

CLICK TO START

CLICK TO START

How does a computer produce waveform audio? Your computer's sound card is responsible for transforming the bits stored in an audio file into music, sound effects, and narrations. A **sound card** is a device that contains a variety of input and output jacks, plus audio-processing circuitry. A desktop computer's sound card (Figure 7-45) is usually plugged into a PCI expansion slot inside the system unit. Alternatively, sound card circuitry might be built into the system board. Notebook computers rarely feature a separate sound card because manufacturers save space by incorporating sound circuitry into the system board.

FIGURE 7-45

A sound card that plugs into a slot in a desktop computer's system unit is standard equipment on many PCs.

7

A sound card is typically equipped to accept input from a microphone and send output to speakers or headphones. For processing waveform files, a sound card contains a special type of circuitry called a **digital signal processor**, which performs three important tasks. It transforms digital bits into analog waves when you play back a waveform audio file. It transforms analog waves into digital bits when you make a sound recording. It also handles compression and decompression, if necessary.

To play a digitally recorded sound, the bits from an audio file are transferred from disk to the microprocessor, which routes them to your computer's sound card. The digital signal processor handles any necessary decompression, and then transforms the data into analog wave signals. These signals are routed to the speakers and voilà! You have sound (Figure 7-46).

FIGURE 7-46

Most sound cards use a digital signal processor to convert bits into an analog signal.

The sound card receives data from the microprocessor.

The sound card's digital signal processor decompresses data and converts it to analog signals.

The sound card sends analog signals to speakers.

How can I recognize a waveform audio file? You can recognize a waveform audio file by looking at its file extension. Waveform audio can be stored in a variety of file formats. The table in Figure 7-47 provides an overview of the most popular waveform audio formats, including **AAC**, **AIFF**, **MP3**, **RealAudio**, **Wave**, and **WMA**.

FIGURE 7-47

Popular Waveform Audio File Formats

Audio Format	File Extension	Advantages	Disadvantages
AAC (Advanced Audio Compression)	.aac	Very good sound quality; compressed format, used on iTunes music download site	Files are copy protected and use is limited to approved devices
AIFF (Audio Interchange Format)	.aif	Excellent sound quality; supported in browsers without a plug-in	Audio data is stored in raw, uncompressed format, so files are very large
MP3 (also called MPEG-1 Layer 3)	.mp3	Good sound quality even though the file is compressed; can be streamed over the Web	Requires a standalone player or browser plug-in
RealAudio	.ra, rx	High degree of compression produces small files; data can be streamed over the Web	Sound quality is not up to the standards of other formats; requires a player or plug-in
Wave	.wav	Good sound quality; supported in browsers without a plug-in	Audio data is stored in raw, uncompressed format, so files are very large
WMA (Windows Media Audio)	.wma	Compressed format, very good sound quality; used on music download sites	Files can be copy protected; requires Windows Media Player 9 or above

What type of software is required to record and play waveform audio files? To play an audio file on your computer, you must use audio or media player software. Player software tends to support several audio file formats. In the Windows environment, for example, you can use Windows Media Player to play Wave, AIF, and MP3 formats. Some players, however, do not allow you to record audio data. For example, you cannot use Windows Media Player to record sound. For recording, you must use Microsoft Sound Recorder.

Software that plays and records various audio file formats might be included with your computer's operating system, packaged with your sound card, or available on the Web.

Can I add waveform audio files to my Web pages? Yes. Waveform files can be embedded into a Web page using an HTML tag, such as <embed src="daisy.wav"> or <bgsound src="imagine.wav">. Wave format files are supported by most Web browsers, so it is a popular audio file format. RealAudio, AIFF, and MP3 can also be delivered over the Web.

Web-based waveform audio is often delivered in streaming format to avoid lengthy delays while the entire audio file is downloaded. As with videos, waveform audio files can be streamed over the Internet so that they play as they are downloaded. Streaming audio provides the technology for real-time Internet radio broadcasts and voice chat sessions.

PORTABLE AUDIO PLAYERS

How can I listen to my digital music collection when I'm away from my computer? A **portable audio player** like the one in Figure 7-48 is a pocket-sized, battery-powered device that stores digital music. You can transfer a series of digital music tracks, called a "playlist," from your computer's hard disk to your portable audio player and you'll have your personal collection of music wherever you go.

Where can I get digital music? Digital music is available from a wide variety of sources. At online music stores, such as iTunes Music Store, MusicMatch, Napster 3.0, MSN Music, and Walmart Music Downloads, individual songs can be downloaded for less than $1 each. The download price of an entire album is typically less than $10.

You can find free digital music, too. Famous performing artists and rock star wannabes post sample tracks from their CDs on Web sites. If fans like the music in these samples, they can purchase and download the entire song or CD.

You can also digitize music from your CD collection by using CD ripper software that converts CD-audio music into computer-friendly waveform audio format.

What are the most popular file formats for portable audio players? The first generation of online music was distributed in MP3 format. MP3 is a compressed waveform audio format that stores digitized music, vocals, and narrations in such a way that the sound quality is very good, but the file size remains relatively small—small enough to download from the Web. A CD track that requires 32 MB of storage space shrinks to approximately 3 MB in MP3 format.

Although MP3 remains a popular audio file format, newer standards offer better sound quality and compression. Apple is promoting the AAC format at its iTunes Music Store. Microsoft is promoting its WMA format at the Walmart Music Downloads site and at MSN Music.

TERMINOLOGY NOTE

Portable audio players are also called MP3 players and digital music players.

FIGURE 7-48

A Portable Audio Player

7

Can I play any digital music format on my portable audio player? Some portable audio players support a variety of digital music formats, whereas others support only one format. For example, Sony's first digital audio Walkman supported only a proprietary ATRAC3plus format and required conversion for music downloaded in AAC or MP3 format. In contrast, Apple's iPod supports several digital music formats, including AAC, MP3, WAV, and AIFF. When purchasing a portable audio player, you should consider which music formats you are likely to use.

What's all the buzz about the iPod? Consumers demand convenience and prefer not to purchase two devices when a single device meets their needs. Market demand and technological innovation produce convergence, such as when PDAs gain Wi-Fi compatibility or when cell phones feature digital cameras.

As an example of convergence, take a portable audio player, outfit it with a screen, add a high capacity mini-hard disk, include personal organizer software, throw in a few games, and provide connections for an external microphone and memory card reader. What you get is the Apple iPod (Figure 7-49). Not only can you use it to store a huge collection of digital music, you can use the hard disk drive as a portable mass storage device for document, photo, and video files. You can use it as a voice recorder and as a personal organizer for storing contacts and appointments. The iPod's versatility has led at least one college to experiment with issuing them to all incoming students.

MIDI MUSIC

What is MIDI music? Waveform audio is a digital version of a real analog sound signal. In contrast, **synthesized sound** is an artificially created, or synthetic, sound. Synthesized sound can be classified as MIDI music or synthesized speech.

MIDI (Musical Instrument Digital Interface) specifies a standard way to store music data for synthesizers, electronic MIDI instruments, and computers. Unlike waveform sound files, which contain digitized recordings of real sound passages, MIDI files contain instructions for creating the pitch, volume, and duration of notes that sound like various musical instruments.

MIDI is a music notation system that allows computers to communicate with music synthesizers. The computer encodes the music as a **MIDI sequence** and stores it as a file with a .mid, .cmf, or .rol file extension. A MIDI sequence is analogous to a player-piano roll that contains punched information indicating which musical notes to play. A MIDI sequence contains instructions specifying the pitch of a note, the point at which the note begins, the instrument that plays the note, the volume of the note, and the point at which the note ends.

Most computer sound cards are equipped to generate music from MIDI files, and many can capture music data from a MIDI instrument as well. A MIDI-capable sound card contains a **wavetable** (sometimes called a "patch set"), which is a set of prerecorded musical instrument sounds. The sound card accesses these sounds and plays them as instructed by the MIDI file. For example, if a sound card receives a MIDI instruction for a trumpet to play middle C, it accesses the trumpet's middle C patch and routes it to the speaker until it receives a MIDI instruction to stop the note.

What are the advantages and disadvantages of MIDI? MIDI files are much more compact than waveform audio files. Depending on the

INFOWEBLINKS

The **Portable Music InfoWeb** is chock full of information on where to download digital music, how to rip tracks from your CDs, and what you can expect from the newest portable audio players.

www.course.com/np/concepts9/ch07

FIGURE 7-49

Apple's iPod portable audio player is also a handy mass storage device.

exact piece of music, three minutes of MIDI music might require only 10 KB of storage space, whereas the same piece of music stored in a high-quality, uncompressed waveform file might require 15 MB of storage space.

One of the big disadvantages of MIDI is that it does not produce high-quality vocals. Another disadvantage is that it does not have the full resonance of "real" sound. Most musicians can easily identify MIDI recordings because they simply lack the tonal qualities of symphony-quality sound. You can compare the differences by using the Click to Start buttons in Figure 7-50.

FIGURE 7-50

MIDI music tends not to have the full resonance of waveform audio. Use your BookOnCD to listen to these two sound clips and see if you can hear a difference.

CLICK TO START

CLICK TO START

When would I use MIDI music? MIDI is a good choice for adding background music to multimedia projects and Web pages. Using a procedure similar to that for waveform audio files, you can add a link to a MIDI file by inserting a tag such as <embed src="sousa.mid"> within an HTML document. Most browsers include built-in support for MIDI music.

You can use music composition software, such as Finale, to create your own snappy tunes or get permission to use MIDI files you find on the Web. For composing your own MIDI music, you can input notes from a MIDI instrument directly to your computer. The input is typically handled by music composition software (Figure 7-51), which you can also use to edit notes and combine the parts for several instruments.

7

FIGURE 7-51

Music composition software provides tools for entering notes, specifying instruments, printing sheet music, and saving compositions in formats such as MIDI.

CLICK TO START

SPEECH RECOGNITION AND SYNTHESIS

What's the difference between speech synthesis and speech recognition? Speech synthesis is the process by which machines, such as computers, produce sound that resembles spoken words. **Speech recognition** (or "voice recognition") refers to the ability of a machine to "understand" spoken words.

If you've dialed Directory Assistance lately to obtain a telephone number, you've probably encountered speech recognition and speech synthesis. An automated operator asks you to speak the name of the person whose telephone number you seek. The name you speak is collected by a speech recognition unit, which attempts to spell out the name and then look for it in a database. If it locates the name and telephone number, a synthesized voice "speaks" the telephone number.

How does speech synthesis work? A basic sound unit, such as "reh" or "gay" is called a **phoneme**. Most speech synthesizers string together phonemes to form words. For example, the phonemes "reh" and "gay" produce the word "reggae." A basic speech synthesizer consists of **text-to-speech software**, which generates sounds that are played through your computer's standard sound card. As an alternative, some speech synthesizers are special-purpose hardware devices.

Speech synthesis is a key technology in wireless communication, such as accessing your e-mail using a cell phone—a speech synthesizer "reads" your e-mail messages to you. A speech synthesizer can also read a computer screen aloud, which unlocks access to computers and the Internet for individuals with visual disabilities.

How does speech recognition work? On a personal computer, a speech recognition system typically collects words spoken into a microphone that's attached to the sound card. The sound card's digital signal processor transforms the analog sound of your voice into digital data. This data is then processed by speech recognition software.

Speech recognition software analyzes the sounds of your voice and converts them to phonemes. Next, the software analyzes the content of your speech. It compares the groups of phonemes to the words in a digital dictionary that lists phoneme combinations along with their corresponding English (or French, Spanish, and so on) words. When a match is found, the software displays the correctly spelled word on the screen.

Speech recognition software can be integrated with word processing software so that you can enter text simply by speaking into a microphone. Going beyond word processing, speech recognition can be used to activate Windows controls instead of using a mouse. Most speech recognition software also works with your browser, allowing you to "voice surf" the Web.

Microsoft Office includes speech recognition software you can activate by using the Speech icon in Control Panel. The first step in using Microsoft speech recognition is training the computer to recognize your speaking style—your accent, pronunciation, and idiomatic expressions. Training consists of reading a series of short text passages into a microphone attached to your computer. Figure 7-52 lists tips for successful voice recognition training.

INFOWEBLINKS

You'll find lots of neat links at the **Speech Synthesis & Recognition InfoWeb**, including a speech synthesis Web site and information about adding voice recognition capabilities to your word processor.

www.course.com/np/concepts9/ch07

FIGURE 7-52

Tips for Voice Recognition Training

■ Speak at a consistent volume.

■ Speak at a steady pace, without speeding up and slowing down.

■ Speak naturally, without exaggerated pauses between words or syllables.

■ Work in a quiet environment so that the computer hears your voice instead of the sounds around you.

■ Use a good quality microphone and keep it in the same position.

You can train your computer by using the Voice Training Wizard, which displays paragraphs of text, waits for you to read them, and creates your personal speech profile (Figure 7-53).

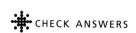

FIGURE 7-53

The Windows Voice Training Wizard displays short text passages. As you read each passage, the computer listens to the way you pronounce each word and stores it in your speech profile.

When training is complete, you can use Microsoft speech recognition to verbally issue commands in Windows and dictate text in Microsoft Word and Excel, plus any other Windows applications designed to support this feature.

QuickCheck

SECTION D

1. [waveform] audio can deal with vocals, music, and narrations, whereas [MIDI] music is primarily designed for instrumental sounds. Hint: Use the acronym.

2. The number of times per second that a sound wave is measured is referred to as the [＿＿＿＿＿] rate.

3. The most popular waveform audio formats for music downloads are MP3, WMA, and [＿＿＿＿＿]. Hint: Use the abbreviation.

4. You can transfer digital music tracks, called a [＿＿＿＿＿], from your computer's hard disk to your portable audio player, and you'll have a great collection of music wherever you go.

5. Speech [＿＿＿＿＿] software translates spoken words into text that appears on a computer screen or is stored in a file.

CHECK ANSWERS

TechTalk

Data Compression

As you learned throughout this chapter, digital media files can be quite large. For example, one second of video requires 56 MB of storage space; a 1024 x 768 True Color bitmap graphic requires 2.3 MB; and a 45-minute waveform audio file might be as large as 475 MB. Large files need lots of storage space, require lengthy transmission times, and easily become fragmented, thereby reducing the efficiency of your computer's hard disk drive. If you could reduce the size of a file without losing any of its data, you would be able to minimize these problems. This TechTalk is designed to help you understand the basic way that compression algorithms work and how to apply compression to the files you store on your computer, post on Web sites, and transmit as e-mail attachments.

What is data compression? **Data compression** is the general term used to describe the process of recoding data so that it requires fewer bytes of storage space. The process is similar in concept to condensing and reconstituting orange juice. To condense orange juice, water is removed. To compress a file, bytes are removed, which reduces the file size. Data compression is reversible. Just as water can be added to reconstitute orange juice, bytes previously removed from a file can be restored so that the data is returned to its original form (Figure 7-54). The process of reversing data compression is sometimes referred to as uncompressing, decompressing, unzipping, extracting, or expanding a file.

FIGURE 7-54

Compression reduces the number of bytes in a file.

The original file contains 20 MB of data.

The file is compressed.

The size of the compressed file depends on its data and the compression algorithm.

The file is uncompressed.

"Lossless" compression algorithms reconstitute the file to its original size.

When data is compressed, the size of the file that holds the data shrinks. The amount of shrinkage is referred to as the **compression ratio**. A compression ratio of 20:1, for example, means that a compressed file is 20 times smaller than the original file. The advantages of compressed files are that they can often fit on a single removable disk, and they take less time to upload or e-mail. The disadvantage of compressed files is that you might be required to manually uncompress them before using them.

Data compression is based on a **compression algorithm**—the steps that are required to shrink the data in a file and reconstitute the file to its original state. Many compression algorithms, such as Huffman, Lempel-Ziv Welch, and Shannon-Fano, are named after their inventors. As you learned earlier in this chapter, a compression algorithm is incorporated into a codec, which a computer uses to compress and decompress file data.

How do compression algorithms work? Some compression algorithms are designed to shrink text files; other algorithms are for graphics, sound, or video data. Some compression algorithms are generalized and work for any type of data. Although most of today's codecs contain sophisticated compression algorithms beyond the scope of this book, you can look at some examples of simple compression algorithms to get a general idea of how they work.

Dictionary-based compression replaces common sequences of characters with a single codeword, or symbol, which points to a dictionary of the original characters or to the original occurrence of the word. Figure 7-55 illustrates how this type of compression might work on a short text sample.

FIGURE 7-55

Dictionary-based Text Compression

The original sentence requires 107 bytes of storage space.

The compressed sentence requires only 73 bytes of storage space, but the dictionary adds 24 bytes of storage space, for a total of 97 bytes.

Dictionary
#1kids
#2trouble
#3whether

He didn't know whether the kids were looking for trouble or whether trouble always tracked down those kids.

He didn't know #3 the #1 were looking for #2 or #3 #2 always tracked down those #1.

Statistical compression, such as the well-known Huffman algorithm, takes advantage of the frequency of characters to reduce the file size. Characters that appear frequently are recoded as short bit patterns, and those that appear infrequently are assigned longer bit patterns.

For example, in the word "passages," the letter "s" appears with the most frequency. It is used for three of the eight characters—a probability of .375 (3 divided by 8). The letter "a" appears twice—a probability of .25. The letters "p," "g," and "e" each appear once, so each has a probability of .125. To compress this word, you can replace the ASCII codes for each letter with new shorter codes. The letters that appear most frequently have the shortest codes. After compression, the original word, which required 64 bits, requires only 18 bits. Figure 7-56 illustrates.

FIGURE 7-56

Statistical Text Compression

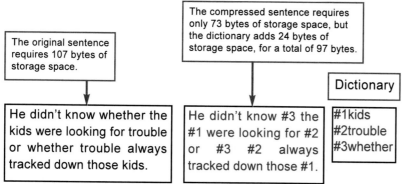

passages

To compress the word "passages," you can recode each letter according to its frequency.

Original Letter	p	a	s	g	e
Original ASCII Code	01110000	01100001	01110011	0110011	01100101
Frequency	1	2	3	1	1
Probability	.125	.25	.375	.125	.125
New Code	001	01	1	0000	0001

0111000001100001011100110111001101100001011001110110010101110011

The original ASCII code for "passages" was 64 bits.

001011101000000011

The compressed code is only 18 bits.

In the two examples of text compression described on the previous page, file size is reduced without any data loss. This **lossless compression** provides the means to compress a file and then reconstitute all the data into its original state. TIFF, PCX, and GIF graphics formats also use lossless compression. In contrast, **lossy compression** "throws away" some of the original data during the compression process. Lossy compression can be applied to graphics, videos, and sounds because, in theory, the human eye or ear won't miss the lost information. JPEG, MP3, and MPEG file formats use lossy compression. Most lossy compression techniques have adjustable compression levels so that you can decide how much data you can afford to lose.

Spatial compression takes advantage of redundant data in a file by looking for patterns of bytes and replacing them with a message that describes the pattern. **Run-length encoding** (RLE) is an example of a lossless spatial compression technique that replaces a series of similarly colored pixels with a code that indicates the number of pixels and their colors. As a simple example, suppose that a section of a picture has 167 consecutive white pixels, and each pixel is described by one byte of data, as in a 256-color bitmap image. An RLE codec compresses this series of 167 bytes into as few as two bytes, as shown in Figure 7-57.

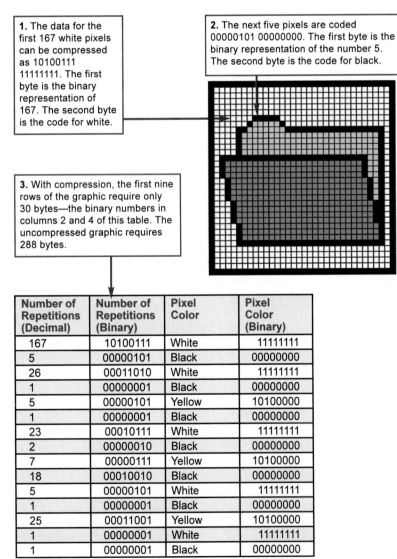

1. The data for the first 167 white pixels can be compressed as 10100111 11111111. The first byte is the binary representation of 167. The second byte is the code for white.

2. The next five pixels are coded 00000101 00000000. The first byte is the binary representation of the number 5. The second byte is the code for black.

3. With compression, the first nine rows of the graphic require only 30 bytes—the binary numbers in columns 2 and 4 of this table. The uncompressed graphic requires 288 bytes.

FIGURE 7-57

In an uncompressed file, each pixel of a 256-color bitmap requires one byte to indicate its color. For example, a white pixel might be coded 11111111. Run-length encoding compresses graphical data by recoding like-colored pixels when they appear in a series.

Number of Repetitions (Decimal)	Number of Repetitions (Binary)	Pixel Color	Pixel Color (Binary)
167	10100111	White	11111111
5	00000101	Black	00000000
26	00011010	White	11111111
1	00000001	Black	00000000
5	00000101	Yellow	10100000
1	00000001	Black	00000000
23	00010111	White	11111111
2	00000010	Black	00000000
7	00000111	Yellow	10100000
18	00010010	Black	00000000
5	00000101	White	11111111
1	00000001	Black	00000000
25	00011001	Yellow	10100000
1	00000001	White	11111111
1	00000001	Black	00000000

JPEG is a lossy version of run-length encoding that can be applied to images, such as photographs, that don't have large areas of solid color. A True Color photograph might not have any adjoining pixels of the same color. Applying RLE to such a photo would not result in any compression whatsoever. JPEG "preprocesses" an image by tweaking the colors in adjoining pixels so that they are the same color whenever possible. After this preprocessing is complete, run-length encoding techniques can be applied with more success. Figure 7-58 illustrates a section of a non-compressed image and a section of that same image after JPEG compression has been applied.

FIGURE 7-58

JPEG compression can slightly adjust the colors of adjacent pixels to make them the same. These like-colored pixels can then be compressed with RLE.

Non-compressed JPEG image

JPEG image with 35% compression

What about compressing sound and video files? **Temporal compression** is a technique that can be applied to video footage or sound clips to eliminate redundant or unnecessary data between video frames or audio samples. For example, if you are working with a video of a "talking head," the background image is likely to contain lots of redundant information that doesn't change from one frame to the next.

As the temporal compression algorithm begins to analyze frames, the first frame becomes a **key frame** that contains all the data. Key frames are stored at preset intervals or whenever a cut, wipe, or transition changes the scene. As the compression algorithm analyzes subsequent frames in the video, it stores only the data that is different from data in the key frame. If the image data from all frames is maintained, the compression is lossless. If slight changes between frames are eliminated, the compression is lossy. MPEG uses temporal and spatial compression algorithms, both of which are lossy. As a result, videos compressed with MPEG codecs have some image quality degradation.

Can I compress any kind of file? Some file formats automatically compress file data. Other formats allow you to select whether you want to compress the file and specify a level of compression. PCX, GIF, and MP3 files are always compressed. The software you use to save and open these files contains the codecs necessary to compress and decompress them. Codecs for JPEG, MPEG, AVI, DivX, and QuickTime files typically allow you to select compression levels before saving a graphics or video file. Some TIFF files are compressed, but others are not—it depends on the software used to store the file.

Most files that contain documents and databases are not stored in compressed format. BMP and Wave files are also stored as "raw," noncompressed bits. If you want to compress these files before sending them as e-mail attachments, for example, you can do so manually using compression software. BMP and DOC file sizes might shrink by as much as 70%. Other noncompressed file formats, such as Wave, might compress by about 20%. File formats such as GIF, MP3, MPEG, and JPEG hardly shrink at all when you zip them because they are already stored in a compressed format.

7

How do I manually compress files? To manually compress a file, such as a Word document or a Windows bitmap image, you can work with a **file compression utility**, which uses lossless compression to shrink one or more files into a single new file. PKZIP and WinZip are popular shareware programs that compress and decompress files. You can zip any kind of file, including program or data files. You cannot use a compressed file until it has been decompressed.

Compressing a file is sometimes called "zipping," and decompressing a file is sometimes called "unzipping." Technically, however, zipping not only compresses files, but can also combine several files into a single compressed file that can be unzipped into the original separate files.

For example, suppose you want to send three files to your boss. The original files are called Technology.xls, Award.doc, and Insurance.mdb. You can zip all three files into a single compressed file called Report.zip (Figure 7-59). Simply attach this one file to an e-mail and send it to your boss. When Report.zip is unzipped, it produces the three original files.

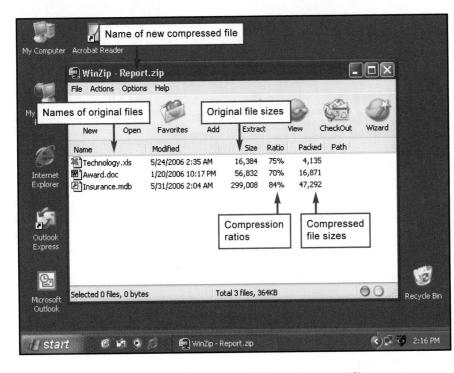

FIGURE 7-59

Popular file compression utilities, such as WinZip, zip one or more files into a new compressed file with a .zip extension.

CLICK TO START

Zipping can come in handy when you want to send several files as an e-mail attachment. It works particularly well for bitmap graphics and documents because they contain raw, uncompressed data. Remember, however, that JPEG graphics are already compressed and do not shrink significantly if you zip them.

Windows XP includes a built-in compression feature that allows you to create compressed folders. Any files that you drag into a compressed folder are automatically compressed. Compressed folders are fairly easy to use. You don't have to do anything special to open a file from a compressed folder. Simply double-click the file as usual, and Windows automatically decompresses the file before displaying its contents.

When you create a compressed folder, Windows automatically adds a .zip extension to the folder name. In this way, the folder is treated like a zipped file by other compression utilities, such as PKZIP and WinZip. So if you want to e-mail several bitmap graphics, for example, you can save them as usual in BMP format. Next, create a compressed folder called Photos (Figure 7-60). Windows automatically adds a .zip extension to the folder name. Drag the three bitmaps into the Photos folder. Attach the Photos folder to your e-mail message. The attachment will be named Photos.zip. The recipient of your e-mail can open the attachment by using Windows or a file compression utility.

FIGURE 7-60

The Compressed Folder menu option creates a folder into which you can drag files you want to compress.

Compressed folder icons feature a zipper. The folder name has a .zip extension, which is visible only if you have file extensions turned on in Windows.

QuickCheck   TECHTALK

1. A compression [   ] is a measurement of the amount of shrinkage—the original file size compared to the compressed file size.

2. A compression [   ] is the steps required to shrink the data in a file and reconstitute the file back to its original state.

3. Dictionary-based and statistical text compression are examples of [   ] compression, which loses no data during the compression process.

4. JPEG is an example of [   ] compression, in which data is eliminated during the compression process.

CHECK ANSWERS

Issue
Digital Rights Management

Suppose you purchase a music CD of your favorite recording group. Now you want to transfer the file to your computer, rip the best tracks, and transfer them to your portable audio player. But wait! That CD is copy protected and your computer CD drive won't read it. You purchased the disk. Can't you listen to the music on any device you choose? The answer is "yes" and "no." Yes, copyright law gives you the right to make copies for your personal use and transfer works into a format that works on your equipment. However, the growing pervasiveness of digital rights management may curtail your ability to exercise these rights.

It is easy to copy digital material. Before the dawn of the digital age, copies produced by analog equipment, such as photocopiers and audio tape dubbing machines, were of considerably poorer quality than the originals. Copies of digital materials, however, are indistinguishable from the originals, and that factor has encouraged an alarming increase in software, music, and movie piracy.

Piracy made world headlines in a dispute about sharing music on Napster. In 1999, an 18-year-old student named Shawn Fanning developed a Web-based technology for sharing MP3 music files. This technology, dubbed "Napster" after Shawn's nickname, quickly became one of the hottest applications on the Internet. In less than a year, its user base exceeded 25 million. Many of these music lovers downloaded hundreds of songs without paying for any of them.

Almost immediately, Napster ran afoul of the Recording Industry Association of America (RIAA), a watchdog organization that represents record companies, such as Columbia Records, Motown Records, and Epic Nashville. The RIAA compiled a list of 12,000 copyrighted songs that Napster technology made available as free downloads.

The RIAA filed suit, accusing Napster of contributing to copyright infringement, which considerably reduced the revenues of record companies and artists. The ensuing court battle stirred up a caldron of issues that relate to the use and abuse of digital media, including music, photos, and videos. After shutting down Napster's free download network, music piracy continued unabated. The RIAA then initiated a series of lawsuits targeting individuals who allegedly maintained large collections of pirated music.

The Napster experience hardened the resolve of digital stakeholders to stop illegal copying. The battle against piracy took shape as a concept called digital rights management (DRM), vigorously supported by Microsoft and backed by a host of industry leaders.

Today, digital rights management encompasses a variety of technologies implemented by copyright holders, such as record companies and software publishers, which restrict the usage of digital material. DRM systems address piracy by using a variety of technologies for manipulating data, media, devices, and transactions.

Software copy protection techniques include reading data written to places on a disk or CD-ROM that the drive cannot normally access, using hardware that must be plugged into the computer when the software is run, requiring a serial number during the installation process, and using Internet product activation that checks the validity of an installation. Most software copy protection schemes have proved to be costly for publishers or inconvenient for consumers.

Cable television has a long history of signal scrambling and encryption to prevent piracy. Consumers seem to tolerate this form of DRM because once the signal arrives, it is descrambled and can be archived to TiVo or videotape just as any broadcast television program.

Many consumers are not aware that they pay a surcharge for every blank audio tape or CD they purchase. Collected revenues from this surcharge go to music publishers to compensate recording artists for the fact that many people duplicate works without authorization.

Most of today's music download sites encrypt music files and embed codes that limit the number of times they can be copied and the devices on which they can be played. Apple's FairPlay DRM system is used on the iTunes Music Store. Microsoft's DRM-enabled Windows Media Player 9 is used on Walmart's Music Download site and Yahoo! Music Unlimited. RealNetworks secure RealAudio (.rax) format protects files downloaded from the RealPlayer Music Store. These formats are not compatible with each other and require different players. Music from several different download sites cannot be compiled into a single playlist.

It is becoming more common for music CDs to use play-protection technology designed to make the CD unusable in devices, such as computer CD-R drives, that can also be conveniently used for duplicating CDs. Consumers who purchase these protected CDs find that they cannot be copied to a computer hard disk, then ripped to produce an MP3 file for a portable audio player.

Commercial movie DVDs use CSS (Content-Scrambling System) encryption to make DVDs playable only on authorized DVD players equipped with decryption key circuitry. Movies purchased in the United States and Canada cannot be played on devices manufactured for the European or Asian markets, so continent-jumping travelers and expatriates have to take along their DVD players or abandon their DVD collections.

Despite DRM technologies and the inconveniences imposed on consumers, digital piracy remains rampant. According to an article about digital rights management posted on Wikipedia, "To date, all DRM systems have failed to meet the challenge of protecting the rights of the rights holder while also allowing the use of the rights of the purchaser. None have succeeded in preventing criminal copyright infringement by organized, unlicensed, commercial pirates."

Current DRM technologies do not seem able to distinguish between pirates and legitimate consumers. As a result, DRM technologies essentially pose restrictions on consumers that go beyond the intended limitations of copyright law.

Circumventing DRM is possible and it would seem okay to do so for legitimate reasons, such as making a backup copy. However, the Digital Millennium Copyright Act makes it illegal to circumvent any technological measure that controls access to a work.

The current status of DRM seems to conflict with the original intent of copyright law to allow consumers to manipulate and copy works for their own use. Can technology eventually offer a solution that prevents piracy, but allows individuals to exercise their rights to fair use of copyrighted materials?

7

INFOWEBLINKS

You'll find information related to this controversy at the **Digital Rights Management InfoWeb**.

www.course.com/np/concepts9/ch07

What Do You Think?

ISSUE

1. Have you had trouble using software, music CDs, or movie DVDs because of copy protection? ○ Yes ○ No ○ Not sure

2. In your opinion, do sites like the iTunes Music Store provide consumers with enough flexibility for copying files and creating playlists? ○ Yes ○ No ○ Not sure

3. Do you think digital rights management technologies are justified because of the high rate of piracy? ○ Yes ○ No ○ Not sure

SAVE RESPONSES

Computers in Context
Film

In 1895, eager Parisians crowded into a busy café to watch the first public presentation of an exciting new invention—the Cinematograph. The 10-minute film, mostly scenes of everyday life, was a smashing success and ushered in the motion picture era. Early films were short, grainy, grayscale, and silent, but technology quickly improved. In the New York debut of *The Jazz Singer* (1927), Al Jolson spoke the first words in a feature film, "Wait a minute, wait a minute. You ain't heard nothin' yet!" The audience rose to its feet, applauding wildly. In 1935, RKO studios released *Becky Sharp*, the first feature-length movie filmed from beginning to end in Technicolor—a real milestone for the film industry.

Even before "talkies" and Technicolor, filmmakers sought ways to escape the bounds of reality through special effects. As early as 1925, directors such as Willis O'Brien used stop-motion photography to animate dinosaurs, giant gorillas, and sword-wielding skeletons. Special-effects technologies—miniatures, blue screens, puppets, claymation, and composite shots—were used with varying degrees of skill over the next 50 years. Films such as Stanley Kubrick's masterpiece, *2001: A Space Odyssey* (1968), and George Lucas's original *Star Wars* (1977) stretched these technologies to their limits, but audiences demanded even more spectacular, yet "realistic," effects.

In 1982, Disney released *TRON*, a movie about a computer programmer who becomes trapped in the depths of a computer where programs are human-like creatures that serve every whim of an evil Master Control Program. The movie included the first primitive attempts at computer-generated footage—30 minutes of computer-generated imagery (CGI) created by two Cray XMP supercomputers.

CGI uses rendering techniques to create a 3-D scene from a 2-D image, a camera angle, and a light source. Sophisticated algorithms determine how textures, colors, and shadows appear in the rendered scene. Camera angles can be changed at will, and fantastic effects can be created by bending or stretching the image, manipulating light, creating textures, and adding movement to the scene.

Rendered scenes can be set in motion with computer animation techniques. Manual animation requires a painstaking process called "in-betweening," in which an artist draws a series of incrementally different images to produce the illusion of movement. Computers can easily generate in-between images and free up human animators for more challenging work.

A captivating animation special effect called morphing was first seen on the big screen in James Cameron's *Abyss* (1989) and later used in *Terminator 2* (1991) and other movies. Like in-betweening, morphing starts out with animators defining the morph's start and end points—for example, in *Terminator 2*, the liquid metal face of the T-1000 robot and actor Robert Patrick's face. The start and end points are rendered into digital images, and then the computer generates all the in-between images. Human animators tweak the images by inserting small discrepancies for a touch of less-than-perfect realism in the final image.

Although the process might sound simple, morphing complex objects realistically and believably takes a tremendous amount of time and computer power. The five-minute morphing sequence in *Terminator 2* took special-effects company Industrial Light and Magic a year to create.

Memorable computer-generated scenes from 2002 blockbusters include the breathtaking aerial scenes in *Spiderman*, a furry blue monster called Sully careening downhill in *Monsters, Inc.*, and the endless army of Uruk-hai marching down the valley toward Helm's Deep in *The Two Towers*. Spiderman's acrobatic swing through Manhattan was generated with three professional rendering products: Maya, Houdini, and RenderMan. The Uruk-hai were created with MASSIVE, a custom program that gave each computer-generated warrior a unique sequence of actions. To individually animate each of Sully's 2,320,413 blue hairs, animators developed software called Fizt, a dynamic simulator.

Rendering, morphing, and other special-effects processing require sophisticated computer systems. Pixar Inc., the company that provided the technology behind *Toy Story*, *Shrek*, *Monsters, Inc.*, and many other feature-length animated films, uses a cluster of computers dubbed the "RenderFarm." Consisting of more than 100 Sun SPARCstation computers, the network can process 16 billion instructions per second. A movie such as *Toy Story* took more than 800,000 computer hours to produce using the RenderFarm. That might seem like a long time, but if Pixar animators had attempted to use a single-processor computer, it would have taken 43 years to finish the job!

Other CGI variations are being used for increasingly sophisticated effects. Special-effects guru John Gaeta developed bullet time and image-based rendering for *The Matrix* (1999). They have been used for stunning visual effects in movies such as *The Matrix: Reloaded* (2003), *The Matrix: Revolutions* (2003), and *Hero* (2002/2004). Bullet time produces reality-defying action sequences that slow time to a tantalizing crawl and then crank it back up to normal speed as the camera pivots rapidly around the scene. The effect requires a computer to meticulously trigger a circular array of more than 100 still cameras in sequence. Image-based rendering generates a digital image based on photos of objects, scenes, or people. The 2-D photos can be digitally manipulated to create 3-D objects, eliminating the need for conventional CGI's computationally intensive 3-D wireframes and ray tracing.

Films, such as *Sky Captain And The World Of Tomorrow* (2004) and *Sin City* (2005), took green screen special effects to a new level. Filmed entirely indoors on a sound stage, these movies used a technique called compositing that layers two or more video clips over each other and merges them into one image. Actors were filmed against a green background screen. During post-production, video editing software removed the background and layered in scenery created with CGI or from real footage on location.

Sin City is also notable as one of the first fully digital live action motion pictures. It was filmed in full color with high-definition digital cameras. The footage was converted to black and white and then color was reintroduced digitally with the use of a DLP Cinema projector.

Sophisticated animation and rendering techniques now come close to producing realistic human figures. Animations were once clearly two-dimensional and far from lifelike, but CGI renderings are becoming more difficult to distinguish from real actors. What might happen in the future is the subject of *Simone* (2002), starring Al Pacino as a washed-up director who is given a hard disk containing code for a computer-generated movie star. Pacino uses her as the leading lady in a string of hits, all the while keeping her identity secret. According to reviewer Leigh Johnson, it becomes clear that Simone, a computer-generated image, is more authentic than the people watching her. It is one of the film's main themes, expressed by Pacino's character: "Our ability to manufacture fraud now exceeds our ability to detect it."

The implications of computer-generated actors are just emerging. Not only do they blur the line between reality and fiction, but they also raise puzzling questions for actors and their agents, directors, and programmers. Is it possible to create CGI doubles for long-dead actors, such as Marilyn Monroe and James Dean? If so, who controls their use and profits from their work? Can aging actors sign contracts for use of their "young" CGI counterparts? Would it be legal and ethical for programmers to create and market virtual characters based on real actors or a compilation of the best traits of popular stars? As is often the case, new technologies present issues along with their benefits—issues you might want to consider the next time you watch a movie.

INFOWEBLINKS

To find more information on this topic, visit the **Computers and Film InfoWeb**.

www.course.com/np/concepts9/ch07

7

Labs

Student Edition Labs

On the Web
Student Edition Labs

To access the Student Edition labs, connect to the New Perspectives NP9 Web site and click the link for Student Edition Labs. The link also provides access to lab assignments.

www.course.com/np/concepts9/ch07

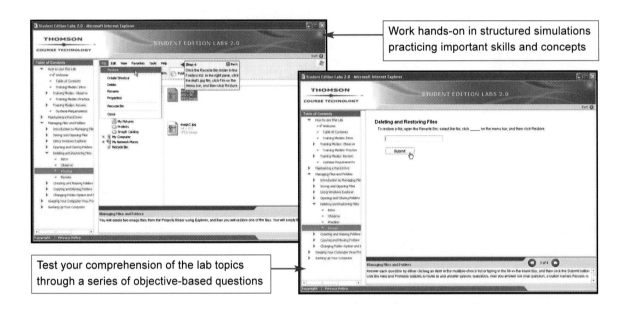

Work hands-on in structured simulations practicing important skills and concepts

Test your comprehension of the lab topics through a series of objective-based questions

WORKING WITH GRAPHICS

In the Working with Graphics Student Edition Lab, you will learn the following topics and skills:

- Downloading images from the Web
- Enhancing an image with filters and manipulating brightness, contrast, and sharpness
- Incorporating type in an image and working with layers
- Cropping vs. resizing and reducing file size
- Creating Web graphics

WORKING WITH VIDEO

In the Working with Video Student Edition Lab, you will learn the following topics and skills:

- Viewing digital video
- Importing and working with clips
- Using the storyboard
- Adding transitions and including audio
- Saving the video

WORKING WITH AUDIO

In the Working with Audio Student Edition Lab, you will learn the following topics and skills:

- Audio file formats and extensions
- Importing and downloading audio files
- Burning audio CDs
- Including audio files on a Web site

on the BookOnCD
New Perspectives Labs

To access the New Perspectives labs for Chapter 7, start the BookOnCD and then click the ✛ icon next to the lab title below.

✛ WORKING WITH BITMAP GRAPHICS

IN THIS LAB YOU'LL LEARN:

How to identify common bitmap graphics file extensions

How to capture an image from the Web

How to find the properties of a graphic

How to eliminate red eye and manipulate brightness, contrast, and sharpness of photos

How to make a photo look "old"

How to select a palette and apply a dithering technique

How to prepare graphics for the Web and e-mail attachments

The effects of lossy compression

LAB ASSIGNMENTS

1. Start the interactive part of the lab. Make sure you've enabled Tracking if you want to save your QuickCheck results. Perform each lab step as directed, and answer all the lab QuickCheck questions. When you exit the lab, your answers are automatically graded and your results are displayed.

2. Use the Start button to access the Programs menu for the computer you typically use. Make a list of the available bitmap graphics software.

3. Capture a photographic image from a digital camera, scanner, or Web page. Save it as "MyGraphic." Open the image using any available graphics software. Use this software to discover the properties of the graphic. Indicate the source of the graphic, and then describe its file format, file size, resolution, and color depth.

4. Prepare this graphics file to send to a friend as an e-mail attachment that is smaller than 200 KB. Describe the steps that were required.

5. Suppose you want to post this image on a Web page. Make the necessary adjustments to file size and color depth. Describe the resulting graphic in terms of its resolution, color depth, palette, and dithering.

✛ VIDEO EDITING

IN THIS LAB YOU'LL LEARN:

How to identify and use the basic tools provided by video editing software

How to select clips for a video and arrange them on the timeline

How to add transitions

What sound formats are acceptable for video sound clips

How to select sound clips for a video and arrange them on the timeline

How to preview a video

How to identify popular video formats and codecs

How characteristics such as frame rate, frame size, sound sampling, and codecs affect file size

How to specify a codec and other video attributes

How to find out which video players are installed on a computer

How to find the properties of a Web-based video

The differences between streaming and non-streaming video formats

LAB ASSIGNMENTS

1. Start the interactive part of the lab. Make sure you've enabled Tracking if you want to save your QuickCheck results. Perform each lab step as directed, and answer all the lab QuickCheck questions. When you exit the lab, your answers are automatically graded and your results are displayed.

2. Use the Control Panel's Add or Remove Programs icon to make a list of the video players available on your computer.

3. Locate a video clip on the Web and indicate the URL of the Web page on which it can be found. Describe the video's properties, including file size and format.

4. Play the video you located for Lab Assignment #3. Describe the video's visual and sound qualities, and discuss how they relate to your Internet connection speed. Also, describe the length and content of the video, the use of transitions or special effects (if any), and the use of sound tracks. If you could edit this video yourself, what changes would you make to produce a more effective video?

7

Interactive Summary

To review important concepts from this chapter, fill in the blanks to best complete each sentence. When using the NP9 BookOnCD or the NP9 Web site, click the Check Answers buttons to automatically score your answers.

A [_____] graphic is composed of a grid of dots, and the color of each dot is stored as a binary number. Both scanners and cameras produce images in bitmap format. The [_____] of the grid that forms a bitmap graphic is referred to as its resolution. High-resolution graphics typically produce better image quality than low-resolution graphics, but require more storage space. It is possible to change the resolution and/or the file size of a bitmap graphic, but because bitmaps are resolution [_____], these changes can reduce image quality. For example, enlarging a bitmap requires your computer to fill in missing pixels, which often results in a jagged or [_____] image. As a general rule, images that you intend to print should remain at full size and resolution. When sending bitmap files as e-mail attachments, they can be [_____]

in size or resolution to produce a file that is less than 500 KB.

Color [_____] refers to the number of colors available for use in an image. For example, a bitmap graphic composed of 256 colors requires only [_____] bits to store the data for each pixel, whereas 24 bits are required for each pixel in a [_____] Color graphic. Grayscale, system, and Web palettes use eight bits to represent each pixel. If a palette does not contain the right selection of colors, an image can be [_____] using scattered or patterned techniques. Popular bitmap graphics formats include BMP, PCX, TIFF, GIF, JPEG, and PNG. Of these formats, GIF, JPEG, and PNG are supported by most Web browsers.

CHECK ANSWERS

Unlike a bitmap graphic, created by superimposing a grid of pixels over an image, a [_____] graphic consists of a set of instructions for creating a picture. These graphics are created by using a type of graphics software called [_____] software. They are stored as a collection of [_____] and their corresponding sizes, colors, and positions. You can identify these graphics by their flat cartoon-like appearance and their file extensions: .wmf, .dxt, .mgx, .eps, .pict, and .cgm.

A vector graphic can be converted into a bitmap by a process called [_____]. Once converted, however, the resulting graphic loses the object-editing qualities it had in its vector state. In contrast, changing a bitmap image to a vector graphic is not easy. It requires the help of [_____] software, which works best on simple line drawings. Vector

graphics have not been popular on the Web because they have not been supported by browsers. Two vector graphics formats, [_____] and Flash, are gaining popularity, despite the fact that they might require browser plug-ins or players.

3-D graphics are stored as a set of instructions that contain the locations and lengths of lines that form a [_____] for a 3-D object. These lines form a framework that can be covered by colored, patterned, and textured surfaces. This process, called [_____], produces a bitmap image of the 3-D object. [_____] tracing adds highlights and shadows to the image. 3-D graphics can be animated to produce special effects for movies and animated characters for 3-D computer games.

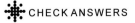 CHECK ANSWERS

Whereas animated 3-D graphics are created from scratch by an artist, digital video is usually based on footage of real objects, filmed and then stored as bits. Videos that are constructed and played on a personal computer are called [   ] videos. Video footage is typically stored on a computer's [   ] disk for editing, and then it can be transferred to CDs, DVDs, or videotape.

A video is composed of a series of bitmap graphics. Each one is called a [   ]. Popular desktop video file [   ] include AVI, QuickTime, MPEG, RealMedia, WMV, and VOB. When video footage is filmed using an analog camera, it can be converted into digital format by a video [   ] device. Footage from a digital video camera requires no conversion and can be streamed directly from camera to computer through a serial, [   ], or USB port. After video footage has been stored on a [   ]-access device, such as a hard disk, it can be easily edited.

Raw video footage contains a huge amount of data. The size of a video file can be reduced by three techniques: shrinking the size of the video window, reducing the [   ] rate, and [   ] the video data. A [   ] is the software or hardware that compresses and decompresses files, such as graphics and videos. Videos can be added to Web pages by using techniques such as [   ] video, which transmits the first segment of a video, begins to play it, and then continues to transfer additional segments. Digital videos can be transferred to DVDs, which use files in the [   ] format.

✦ CHECK ANSWERS

Music, voice, and sound effects can all be recorded and digitally stored as [   ] audio. To digitally record sound, [   ] of the sound are collected at periodic intervals and stored as numeric data. High-quality sound is usually sampled at 44.1 [   ], and each stereo sample requires 32 bits of storage space. To conserve space, radio-quality recordings of speaking voices are often recorded at lower sampling rates.

A computer's [   ] card is responsible for transforming the bits stored in an audio file into music, sound effects, and narrations. It contains digital [   ] processing circuitry that transforms bits into analog sound, records analog sounds as digital bits, and handles audio compression. Waveform audio file formats include Wave, Audio Interchange Format, RealAudio, AAC, WMA, and MP3. Most portable audio players work with waveform formats, such as [   ], used by the iTunes Music Store.

MIDI music is [   ] sound that is artificially created. Unlike waveform sound files, which contain digitized recordings of real sound passages, MIDI files contain [   ] for creating the pitch, volume, and duration of notes made by musical instruments. MIDI files are typically much smaller than waveform audio files for similar musical passages, so they are ideal for Web pages. However, MIDI music tends to lack the full resonance of symphony-quality sound that can be achieved with waveform audio.

Speech [   ] is the process by which machines, such as computers, produce sound that resembles spoken words. Speech [   ] refers to the ability of machines to "understand" spoken words.

✦ CHECK ANSWERS

7

Key Terms

Make sure you understand all the boldfaced key terms presented in this chapter. If you're using the NP9 BookOnCD, you can use this list of terms as an interactive study activity. First, try to define a term in your own words, and then click the term to compare your definition with the definition presented in the chapter.

24-bit bitmap, 367
32-bit bitmap, 367
3-D graphics, 377
AAC, 394
AIFF, 394
Analog video camera, 381
AVI, 386
Bitmap graphic, 360
BMP, 369
Codec, 387
Color depth, 366
Color palette, 367
Compression algorithm, 400
Compression ratio, 400
Cropping, 365
Data compression, 400
Desktop video, 380
Dictionary-based compression, 401
Digital camera, 361
Digital signal processor, 394
Digital video, 380
Digital video camera, 381
Digitizing tablet, 373
Dithering, 368
Drawing software, 373
DVD-video, 380
DVD image, 390
File compression utility, 404
Flash, 376
Floppy disk adapter, 362
Frame rate, 384
GIF, 370

Gradient, 375
Grayscale palette, 368
JPEG, 369
Key frame, 403
Linear editing, 385
Lossless compression, 402
Lossy compression, 402
Megapixel, 363
Metafile, 375
MIDI, 396
MIDI sequence, 396
Monochrome bitmap, 366
MP3, 394
MPEG, 386
Nonlinear editing, 385
Paint software, 360
PCX, 369
PDA video, 380
Phoneme, 398
Pixel interpolation, 365
Pixelated, 365
PNG, 370
Portable audio player, 395
QuickTime, 386
Rasterization, 375
Ray tracing, 377
RealAudio, 394
RealMedia, 386
Rendering, 377
Resolution dependent, 365
Run-length encoding, 402
Sampling rate, 393

Scanner, 361
Sound card, 393
Spatial compression, 402
Speech recognition, 398
Speech recognition software, 398
Speech synthesis, 398
Statistical compression, 401
Streaming video, 387
SVG, 376
Synthesized sound, 396
System palette, 368
Temporal compression, 403
Text-to-speech software, 398
TIFF, 369
Tracing software, 375
True Color bitmap, 367
Vector graphic, 371
Video capture, 382
Video capture software, 383
Videoconferencing camera, 381
VOB, 386
Wave, 394
Waveform audio, 392
Wavetable, 396
Web-based video, 380
Web palette, 368
Wireframe, 377
WMA, 394
WMV, 386

Interactive Situation Questions

Apply what you've learned to some typical computing situations. When using the NP9 BookOnCD or the NP9 Web site, you can type your answers, and then use the Check Answers button to automatically score your responses.

1. You have an old photograph that you want to incorporate in a brochure for your antiques business. To convert the photo into digital format, you use a(n) [_____].

2. Suppose you receive a bitmap image from one of your friends, but it seems curiously "blocky" or pixelated. Either this image was captured using a very low-resolution camera, or the size of the image was [_____].

3. Imagine that you are preparing a series of bitmap graphics for a Web site. To decrease the download time for each graphic, you can remove pixels or reduce the color [_____].

4. Suppose you are designing a logo for a client. You know the design will undergo several revisions, and you understand that the logo will be used at various sizes. You decide it would be best to use drawing software to create the logo as a(n) [_____] graphic.

5. What if you created a diagram as a vector graphic, but you want to post it on the Web as a bitmap so that it can be viewed without a plug-in or player. You can convert the vector into a bitmap using a process called [_____].

6. After you finish arranging video clips and adding a soundtrack, you can select a video file format and a compression technique. For example, you might store the video in AVI format and use the Cinepak [_____] to compress the file.

7. Suppose you click a Web page link to a video, but it is barely watchable because it is so jerky, and the sound doesn't coordinate with the images. You would expect this type of problem if you are using a slow, [_____] Internet connection.

8. Suppose you are creating an English-as-a-Second-Language Web page and you want to add links to sound files that pronounce English phrases. Would it be better to store the files in Wave or MIDI format? [_____]

9. Imagine that you're a musician and you are asked to synthesize some music for the opening screen of a Web site. For this project, you would most likely work with [_____] music.

10. Suppose you visit a Web site that allows you to enter sentences, and then it reads the sentences back to you. The site even gives you a choice of a female or male voice. You assume that this site uses speech [_____] technology.

✦ CHECK ANSWERS

7

Interactive Practice Tests

Practice tests that consist of 10 multiple-choice, true/false, and fill-in-the-blank questions are available on both the NP9 BookOnCD and the NP9 Web site. The questions are selected at random from a large test bank, so each time you take a test, you'll receive a different set of questions. Your tests are scored immediately, and you can print study guides that help you find the correct answers for any questions that you missed.

CLICK ✦ TO START   www.course.com/np/concepts9/ch07 ✦

Projects

An NP9 Project is an open-ended activity that will help you apply the concepts you have learned. Many projects require resources in addition to your textbook, such as current magazines, library materials, or Web access. When you tackle a project, be prepared to use your critical thinking skills, logical analysis, and your creativity.

CRITICAL THINKING

Copyright laws are changing as digital sound, image, and video technologies evolve and become easier to use. Although the courts seem to clearly hold that it is illegal to copy media for profit, they are not as clear about the acceptability of modifications. For example, video editing software makes it relatively simple for people to clip out parts of movies they find to be objectionable for themselves or their children. Should it be legal to do so for personal use? What if an organization wanted to rent out such edited copies? What if DVD players and movies were set up so that the devices would edit and display the revised version "on the fly?" After you consider your own opinion, you might check the Web to see the latest information about this issue. Explain your opinions on modifying copyrighted material and submit them to your instructor as a one- to two-page document.

CYBERCLASSROOM

Each person on your team should e-mail a photo in JPEG format to the other members of the group. The photo can be one you've taken or one you find on the Web. If you get your photo from the Web, keep track of the Web site so you have a record of your source. You should also check the site to make sure it doesn't contain any prohibitions for using its images for a personal project. Images at the NASA site are available for public use. You can use a search engine to look for "public domain photos" to find other sites with photos that are permissible to use. When you receive the photos from your team-mates, be creative and use Photoshop or similar photo editing software to create a composite image that contains elements from all the photos. Submit your original photo and your composite photo to your instructor.

GROUP PROJECT

Work with a group of four students to research Web-based music download sites. Create one PowerPoint slide for each site. The slide should give a basic overview of the site, including its name, URL, price, pros, and cons. For the final slide in the presentation, create a table comparing the features and prices of each site.

MULTIMEDIA PROJECT

Use Windows Sound Recorder or similar software to record your own 15-second radio ad for your favorite music download service, such as iTunes. Submit the text of your script along with the .wav file containing your ad.

RESUME BUILDER

Artists routinely create a portfolio containing examples of their best work. How can you apply the portfolio concept to your job search? Suppose you've decided to create a multimedia portfolio that showcases your talents. Describe what you'd like your portfolio to contain, indicating which of the items you currently have and which you'd like to create and add in the future. Also, describe the format for each item: photo, document, scan, audio, or video. Finally, describe whether you envision delivering your portfolio on CD or the Web, and then discuss the advantages and limitations of your choice.

GLOBALIZATION

The United States has been accused of exporting its culture and values through films and television. Sometimes referred to as "Coca Colonization" the mass exportation of American culture is expected to increase as more and more people have access to the Internet. But is digital distribution a two-way street? What can you find out about the *importation* of cultures to the United States (or your country)? Incorporate your findings into a two-page paper. Make sure you cite specific examples and offer your ideas on how technology aids or discourages cross cultural interchanges. Include a list of references on a third page.

ISSUE

The Issue section of this chapter focused on digital rights controversies, such as your rights to share music files, copy DVD movies, or use software to break copy protection. To begin the project, consult the Digital Rights Management InfoWeb and link to the recommended Web sites to get an in-depth overview of the issues. With this background, work with a partner and select a digital rights controversy that seems interesting. Use the Web to research the controversy. You should focus on the laws and arguments presented by one side of the controversy while your partner focuses on the other side of the controversy. Collaborate with your partner to write a dialog between two people who are arguing both sides of the issue. Follow your instructor's guidelines for submitting your work as a printed document or using e-mail.

COMPUTERS IN CONTEXT

The Computers in Context section of this chapter focused on digital special effects technology used in recent films. For this project, conduct your own exploration of the special effects that have appeared in your favorite movies. To begin the project, browse through the material presented in the Computers and Film InfoWeb on page 409. Look for information about specific movies using Web sites such as the Internet movie database (*www.imdb.com*). Many movies also have dedicated Web sites that you can find using a search engine. To complete the project, select one of your favorite movies and write a two- to four-page movie review that focuses on how its special effects contribute to the movie's overall quality. Try to incorporate information about how the special effects were developed—the company that provided the effects and the type of equipment used. You can also consider comparing the special effects in your chosen movies with the effects in other movies. You might also incorporate some frames from the film as illustrations in your paper. Before doing so, however, make sure you understand their copyright restrictions. Follow your professor's instructions for formatting and submitting your movie review.

Study Tips

Study Tips help you to organize and consolidate the information in a unit by making lists, outlines, charts, and sketches. You can use paper and pencil or word processing software to complete most of the Study Tip activities.

1. Make sure you can use your own words to correctly answer each of the orange focus questions that appear throughout the chapter.

2. Make a list of the file extensions that were mentioned in this chapter and group them according to digital media type: bitmap graphic, vector graphic, digital video, waveform audio, and MIDI. Circle any formats that are used on the Web.

3. Make a list of the software mentioned in this chapter, indicating the type of task that it helps you accomplish.

4. Describe the devices that transfer photos from a digital camera to a computer.

5. Describe how resolution and color depth contribute to the size of a graphics file.

6. Summarize how you would prepare bitmap graphics for the following uses: e-mail attachment, Web page, desktop publishing, and printed photo.

7. Explain how a computer monitor displays color, and how that relates to the way it stores a color palette.

8. Describe the effects of applying different types of dithering to a bitmap graphic.

9. Explain how the concept of layering relates to your ability to modify a vector graphic.

10. Make a list of the advantages and disadvantages of bitmaps and vector graphics.

11. Make a series of quick sketches that illustrates the evolution of a 3-D graphic from wireframe to rendered image, and to ray-traced image.

12. Explain the different procedures required to transfer analog or digital video from camera to computer.

13. Define the differences between linear and non-linear editing.

14. List three ways in which you can reduce the file size of a desktop video.

15. Explain how streaming audio and video work, and contrast them to non-streaming technology.

16. Use your own words to make a list of the steps required to burn video onto a DVD that can be viewed on standalone DVD players.

17. Make a list of 10 digital audio applications and indicate whether each one would use Wave or MIDI.

18. TechTalk: In your own words describe each type of compression mentioned in the TechTalk for Chapter 7.

19. Fill in the blanks on the concept map shown below to show the hierarchy of digital media described in this chapter.

Review on the Web

TECHTV VIDEO PROJECT

The TechTV segment *Online Music Stores and Services* highlights some of the most popular sites for downloading music. The host for this segment evaluates music sites based on five criteria. Watch the video and make a list of these criteria. Then go online and create your own comparison of two music download sites using these criteria.

To work with the Video Projects for this chapter, connect to the New Perspectives NP9 Web site.

www.course.com/np/concepts9/ch07

ONLINE GAMES

Test your comprehension of the concepts introduced in Chapter 7 by playing the NP9 Online Games. At the end of each game, you have three options:

- Submit your results to your instructor using the Universal Gradebook through CoursePort
- Print your results to be submitted to your instructor
- Print a comprehensive study guide complete with page references

To work with the Online Games for this chapter, connect to the New Perspectives NP9 Web site.

www.course.com/np/concepts9/ch07

TECHBUZZ

The TechBuzz article at the New Perspectives NP9 Web site includes new trends in networks, the Internet, and digital media. As you look at the directions technology is headed and as you consider your own lifestyle, which of these trends might be the most useful for you in the next year? What about in the next five years? Before you answer these questions, you might want to browse the Web to find additional information about the trends mentioned in TechBuzz. When you report about the trends that will be most useful to you, discuss them in the context of your own lifestyle, and then expand your discussion to the broader population of consumers in your country and others. Submit your summary, making sure you cite your sources.

www.course.com/np/concepts9/techbuzz

ONLINE END-OF-CHAPTER ACTIVITIES

The following NP9 Review Activities are also available at the New Perspectives NP9 Web site:

- Interactive Summary
- Interactive Situation Questions
- Interactive Practice Tests
- Concept Map

If you are using the Web site to complete these activities, you can automatically score your answers and share the results with your instructor.

www.course.com/np/concepts9/ch07

7

QUICK CHECK ANSWERS

ORIENTATION

QuickCheck A
1. unit
2. Start
3. False
4. Backspace
5. menu

QuickCheck B
1. save
2. browser
3. search
4. @
5. account

QuickCheck C
1. False
2. security
3. Spyware
4. spam

QuickCheck D
1. annotation
2. False
3. labs
4. Tracking

QuickCheck E
1. True
2. Home
3. Overview
4. Labs

CHAPTER 1

QuickCheck A
1. output
2. False
3. notebook
4. False
5. bits
6. compatible

QuickCheck B
1. backbone
2. IP
3. downloading
4. blog, Web log
5. voiceband
6. False
7. DSL
8. service
9. case
10. password

QuickCheck C
1. hypertext
2. URL
3. HTML
4. search
5. query, key words, search term
6. operators
7. language

QuickCheck D
1. @
2. MIME
3. spam
4. forward
5. SMTP;
   POP

QuickCheck TechTalk
1. operating
2. POST, power-on self-test
3. Safe
4. True

CHAPTER 2

QuickCheck A
1. digital
2. binary
3. ASCII
4. character;
   binary
5. gigabyte
6. integrated
7. system

QuickCheck B
1. registers
2. control
3. processor
4. instruction
5. clock
6. volatile
7. virtual
8. CMOS

QuickCheck C
1. head
2. lands
3. access
4. random;
   sequential
5. density
6. crashes
7. True
8. double layer

QuickCheck D
1. pointing
2. refresh, vertical scan
3. resolution
4. duplex
5. slots
6. USB
7. device

QuickCheck TechTalk
1. Machine
2. op, operation
3. pointer
4. accumulator, register

CHAPTER 3

QuickCheck A
1. executable
2. source
3. high
4. interpreter
5. application

QuickCheck B
1. resources
2. RAM, memory
3. user
4. kernel
5. True
6. False

QuickCheck C
1. document
2. False
3. spreadsheet
4. Database
5. ripper
6. DVD

QuickCheck D
1. requirements
2. installation
3. setup
4. True
5. patch
6. Control
7. open
8. public

QuickCheck TechTalk
1. True
2. Windows
3. HKEY
4. setup

CHAPTER 4

QuickCheck A
1. conventions
2. True
3. native
4. C
5. subdirectories
6. folders
7. size

QuickCheck B
1. Save
2. metaphor, model
3. Explorer
4. tracks;
   sectors
5. shredder

QuickCheck C
1. True
2. backdoor
3. spoofed
4. engineering
5. botnet
6. signature

QuickCheck D
1. Registry
2. folder
3. external
4. incremental
5. recovery

QuickCheck TechTalk
1. header
2. support
3. native
4. True

CHAPTER 5

QuickCheck A
1. resources
2. LANs
3. True
4. packet;
   circuit

QuickCheck B
1. Ethernet
2. Wi-Fi
3. Bluetooth
4. PNA;
   PLC

QuickCheck C
1. service
2. Ping, Packet Internet Groper
3. TCP;
   IP
4. static, permanent
5. domain

QuickCheck D
1. downstream;
   upstream
2. Always-on
3. DSL, digital subscriber line
4. False
5. hotspots

QuickCheck TechTalk
1. False
2. firewall
3. virtual

CHAPTER 6

QuickCheck A
1. link
2. HTTP
3. XHTML, extensible HTML
4. browser
5. True
6. stateless
7. cookie

QuickCheck B
1. ASCII
2. authoring
3. head
4. cascading
5. JPEG
6. Flash
7. mailto
8. hot spot
9. True
10. post

QuickCheck C
1. XML
2. scripts
3. Java
4. ActiveX
5. certificate

QuickCheck D
1. False
2. GIF
3. SSL
4. sniffer
5. wallets

QuickCheck TechTalk
1. plaintext, cleartext;
   ciphertext
2. Symmetric, Secret, Conventional
3. Asymmetric, Public
4. PGP

CHAPTER 7

QuickCheck A
1. FireWire
2. resolution
3. dependent
4. grayscale
5. TIFF
6. GIF

QuickCheck B
1. True
2. drawing
3. wireframe
4. tracing
5. rasterization, rasterizing
6. Flash

QuickCheck C
1. desktop
2. capture
3. frame
4. False
5. False
6. Streaming
7. VOB, video object

QuickCheck D
1. waveform;
   MIDI
2. sampling
3. AAC
4. playlist
5. recognition

QuickCheck TechTalk
1. ratio
2. algorithm
3. lossless
4. lossy

CREDITS

Orientation 2, Courtesy of Sony Electronics, Inc.
Orientation 6, Courtesy of Kensington Technology Group
Orientation 7, PhotoDisc/Getty Images
Orientation 15, Courtesy of ART + COM AG
Figure 1-02, Courtesy of Fujitsu Ltd. and Microsoft Corporation
Figure 1-03a, Courtesy of the Hewlett-Packard Company
Figure 1-03b, Courtesy of PalmOne
Figure 1-04, Courtesy of Sun Microsystems
Figure 1-05, Courtesy of Microsoft Corporation
Figure 1-06, Courtesy of the IBM Corporation
Figure 1-07c, MediaTechnics
Figure 1-07a, Courtesy of Alienware
Figure 1-07b, Courtesy of Apple Computer, Inc.
Figure 1-07d, Courtesy of Sony Electronics, Inc.
Figure 1-07e, Courtesy of Acer Inc. and Microsoft Corporation
Figure 1-07f, Courtesy of Apple Computer, Inc. Apple IMAC 17"
Figure 1-10a, Courtesy of Epson America, Inc.
Figure 1-10b, Courtesy of Olympus
Figure 1-10c, Courtesy of Epson America, Inc.
Figure 1-16, Courtesy of Linksys
Figure 1-27, Courtesy of Google, Inc.
Figure 1-29, Courtesy of Yahoo! Inc.
Figure 1-36, Courtesy of Yahoo! Inc.
CinC-1a, Courtesy of The Advertising Archives
CinC-1b, Courtesy of Napster
Issue-1a, Ron Chapple/Getty Images
Issue-1b, Dennis MacDonald/Photoedit
Figure 2-11, Courtesy of Intel Corporation
Figure 2-15, Courtesy of Intel Corporation
Figure 2-15, Courtesy of AMD
Figure 2-23, Courtesy of IBM Research
Figure 2-24, Courtesy of Intel Corporation
Figure 2-28, Courtesy of Sematech, Inc.
Figure 2-34a, Courtesy of Sony Electronics, Inc.
Figure 2-34b, Courtesy of Kingston Technology
Figure 2-34c, Courtesy of SanDisk Corp.
Figure 2-34d, Courtesy of SanDisk Corp.
Figure 2-34e, Courtesy of Kingston Technology
Figure 2-35, Courtesy of Research in Motion Limited
Figure 2-35a, Courtesy of Logitech Inc.
Figure 2-35b, Courtesy of Microsoft Corporation
Figure 2-35c, Courtesy of Think Outside Inc. and Palm Inc.
Figure 2-35d, Courtesy of Research in Motion
Figure 2-37a, Courtesy of IBM Corporation
Figure 2-37b, Courtesy of Kensington Technology Group
Figure 2-37c, Courtesy of X-Gaming Inc.
Figure 2-38a, Courtesy of Sony Electronics, Inc.
Figure 2-38b, Courtesy of Sony Electronics, Inc.
Figure 2-38c, Courtesy of ViewSonic
Figure 2-41, Courtesy of ATI Technologies, Inc.
Figure 2-42, Courtesy of Epson America, Inc.
Issue-2a, Gabe Palmer/CORBIS
Issue-2b, Courtesy of Lexmark International
CinC-2a, Computer History Museum
CinC-2b, Courtesy of Business Wire and Lages & Assoc.
Figure 3-20a, Courtesy of PalmOne, Inc.
Figure 3-20b, Courtesy of Microsoft
Figure 3-20c, Courtesy of Symbian
Figure 3-21, Courtesy of Microsoft
Figure 3-22a, b, c, Courtesy of Microsoft Corporation
Figure 3-23a, Courtesy of Microsoft Corporation
Figure 3-23b, Reprinted with permission of Quark Inc., and its affiliates
Figure 3-23c, Courtesy of Macromedia, Inc.

Figure 3-32a, Courtesy of Julie Cooke, www.lightdrawing.com
Figure 3-32b, Courtesy of Wolfram Research
Figure 3-42a, Courtesy of Microsoft Corporation
Figure 3-42b, Courtesy of Symantec Corp.
Figure 3-42c, Courtesy of Adobe Systems Inc.
Figure 3-42d, Courtesy of InterVideo, Inc.
Issue-3a, Courtesy of Software and Information Industry Association
Issue-3b, Courtesy of Software and Information Industry Association
CinC-3a, Eli Reed/ Magnum Photos
CinC-3b, Ashley Gilbertson/AURORA
Figure 4-18, © F-Secure Corporation
Figure 4-30, © 2005 Sonic Solutions
Figure 4-31, Courtesy of Maxtor Corporation
Issue-4a, Dennis O'Clair/ Getty Images
CinC-4a, A. Ramey/PhotoEdit
CinC-4b, Peter Macdiarmid/Reuters/Corbis
Figure 5-01, Courtesy of Bob Metcalfe
Figure 5-02, Steve Chenn/Corbis
Figure 5-10a, Courtesy of Linksys
Figure 5-10b, Courtesy of Linksys
Figure 5-21a, Courtesy of D-Link Systems
Figure 5-21b, Courtesy of D-Link Systems
Figure 5-22, Courtesy of Linksys
Figure 5-24a, Courtesy of Nokia
Figure 5-24c, Courtesy of NETGEAR, Inc
Figure 5-25, Courtesy of Dell
Figure 5-27, Courtesy of Motorola
Figure 5-33, Courtesy of the Computer History Museum
Figure 5-46, Courtesy of Zoom telephonics, Inc.
Figure 5-55, Royalty-Free/CORBIS
Figure 5-56, Courtesy of Hewlett-Packard, Inc.
Figure 5-56, Courtesy of Motorola Inc.
Figure 5-57, Courtesy of Hewlett-Packard
Issue-5a, Courtesy of Ken Pau and Stone Creek Coffee Company
Issue-5b, Courtesy of Rob Flickenger
CinC-5a, University of Illinois @Urbana-Champaign Archives
CinC-5b, John Henley/CORBIS
Figure 6-12, Courtesy of Fujitsu Siemens Computer
Figure 6-42, Nicholas DeVore/ Getty Images
Figure 6-52, A. Ramey/ PhotoEdit
CinC-6a, Courtesy of ArahWeave www.arahne.si and fabric courtesy of MTT Maribor
CinC-6b, Steve Allen/ Getty Images
Figure 7-01, Archivo Iconografico, S.A./CORBIS
Figure 7-04b, Courtesy of Sony Electronics, Inc.
Figure 7-04d, Courtesy of Lexar Media, Inc.
Figure 7-04e, Courtesy of IBM Corporation
Figure 7-19, Courtesy of Numonics Corporation
Figure 7-27, Courtesy of id Software
Figure 7-42a, Courtesy of Creative Labs, Inc
Figure 7-42b, Courtesy of Creative Labs, Inc
Figure 7-45a & b, Courtesy of Creative Technology, Ltd.
Figure 7-48, Courtesy of Apple Computer, Inc.
Figure 7-49, Courtesy of Rio Audio
Figure 7-52, Photodisc/Getty Images
Issue-7a, Victor Spinelli/www.photomillennium.com/
CinC-7a, DA SILVA PETER/CORBIS SYGMA
CinC-7b, CORBIS/SYGMA

GLOSSARY

24-bit bitmap A True Color graphic, which requires 24 bits for each pixel, used for photographic-quality images that can include any of 16.7 million colors. 367

32-bit bitmap A True Color graphic, which requires 32 bits for each pixel, used for photographic-quality images that can include any of 16.7 million colors. 367

3-D graphics A type of digital graphics format that displays a three dimensional image on a two dimensional space. 377

3-D graphics software The software used to create three-dimensional wireframe objects, then render them into images. 149

AAC (Advanced Audio Compression) A file format that provides highly compressed audio files with very little loss of sound quality and is promoted by Apple on its iTunes Web site. 394

Absolute reference In a worksheet formula, cell references (usually preceded by a $ symbol) that cannot change as a result of a move or copy operation. 144

Access time The estimated time for a storage device to locate data on a disk, usually measured in milliseconds. 81

Accounting software A category of software that includes accounting, money management, and tax preparation software. 155

ActiveX control A set of commands and components that can be used by programmers to add interactive features to Web pages. 328

Ad-blocking software A type of software that prevents ads from appearing on your computer screen. 332

Ad-serving cookie A cookie installed by a marketing firm to track user activities on Web sites containing their ads. 335

AES (Advanced Encryption Standard) An encryption standard that uses three separate key sizes and is based on the Rajndael encryption algorithm. 343

AGP Short for accelerated graphics port, an AGP is a type of interface, or slot, that provides a high-speed pathway for advanced graphics. 97

AIFF (Audio Interchange Format) An audio file format developed by Apple that is a popular cross-platform audio format. 394

ALU (arithmetic logic unit) The part of the CPU that performs arithmetic and logical operations on the numbers stored in its registers. 69

Always-on connection A permanent connection, as opposed to a connection that is established and dropped as needed. 18, 270

Analog device A device that operates on continuously varying data, such as a dimmer switch or a watch with a sweep second hand. 62

Analog video camera A device used to collect, store, and process video in an analog format on a magnetic tape. 381

Animated GIF A type of GIF image that displays a sequence of frames to create the appearance of continuous motion. 317

Antivirus software A computer program used to scan a computer's memory and disks to identify, isolate, and eliminate viruses. 205

Application software Computer programs that help you perform a specific task such as word processing. Also called application programs, applications, or programs. 12, 125

ARCnet (Attached Resource Computer network) One of the oldest, simplest, and least expensive LAN technologies. 249

ASCII (American Standard Code for Information Interchange) A code that represents characters as a series of 1s and 0s. Most computers use ASCII code to represent text, making it possible to transfer data between computers. 63

ASP (Active Server Page) An HTML document which includes scripts that are processed by a Microsoft Web server before sending a response back to the user. 319

Audio editing software A program that enables users to create and edit digital voice and music recordings. 151

Audio encoding software A computer program designed to convert sound files into a digital sound format, such as MP3 or AAC. 151

Automated system recovery A set of recovery disks that users are able to create using the Windows XP Backup utility. 216

Automatic recalculation A feature found in spreadsheet software that automatically recalculates every formula after a user makes a change to any cell. 144

AVI (Audio Video Interleave) A video file format, developed by Microsoft, that is the most common format for desktop video on the PC. 386

B2B (Business-To-Business) An e-commerce exchange of products, services, or information between businesses. 331

B2C (Business-To-Consumer) An e-commerce exchange of products, services, or information between businesses and consumers. 331

B2G (Business-To-Government) An e-commerce exchange of products, services, or information between businesses and governments. 331

Backdoor In the context of computer security, a backdoor is a method of bypassing normal procedures to gain access to a computer system. Some backdoors, such as a hidden password, are inadvertently or intentionally left open, whereas others are opened by viruses and worms. 200

Backup A backup is a duplicate copy of a file, disk, or tape. Also refers to a Windows utility that allows you to create and restore backups. 208

Backup software A set of utility programs that performs a variety of backup related tasks, such as helping users select files for backup. 213

Bandwidth The data transmission capacity of a communications channel. Digital signals are measured in bits per second, analog signals in Hertz. 246

Banner ad A type of advertisement typically embedded at the top of a Web page. 332

Baud rate The number of times per second that a signal in a communications channel varies. 268

Beep code A series of audible beeps used to announce diagnostic test results during the boot process. 41

Benchmarks A set of tests used to measure computer hardware or software performance. 72

Binary digits Series of 1s and 0s representing data. 62

Binary number system A method for representing numbers using only two digits, 0 and 1. Contrast to the decimal number system, which uses ten digits: 0, 1, 2, 3, 4, 5, 6, 7, 8, and 9. 62

Bit The smallest unit of information handled by a computer. A bit is one of two values, either a 0 or a 1. Eight bits comprise a byte, which can represent a letter or number. 11

Bitmap graphic An image, such as a digital photo, that is stored as a grid work of colored dots. 360

Blended threat A combination of more than one type of malicious program. 200

Blog (WeB LOG) A publicly-accessible personal journal posted on the Web. Blogs often reflect the personality of the author and are typically updated daily. 16

Bluetooth A wireless technology used in conjunction with standard Ethernet networks that allows data transfer rates between 200 and 700 Kbps up to a maximum range of 35 feet. 254

BMP The native bitmap graphic file format of the Microsoft Windows OS. 369

Body section A part of a Web page that begins with the <BODY> tag and contains the text, graphics, and links. 314

Boot disk A floppy disk or CD that contains the files needed for the boot process. 215

Boot process The sequence of events that occurs within a computer system between the time the user starts the computer and the time it is ready to process commands. 40

Boot sector virus A computer virus that infects the sectors on a disk that contain the data a computer uses during the boot process. The virus spreads every time the infected disk is in the computer when it boots. 198

Bootstrap program A program stored in ROM that loads and initializes the operating system on a computer. 129

Bot An intelligent agent that autonomously executes commands behind the scenes. Sometimes used to refer to a remote access Trojan horse that infects computers. 202

Botnet A group of bots under the remote control of a botmaster, used to distribute spam and Denial of Service attacks. 202

Bridge A device that connects two similar networks by simply transferring data without regard to the network format. 243

Broadband A term used to refer to communications channels that have high bandwidth. 246

Broken link A non-functioning Web link. 319

Browser A program that communicates with a Web server and displays Web pages. 26

Brute-force method A method of breaking encryption code by trying all possible encryption keys, usually employing supercomputers. 341

Bus topology A network arranged on a common backbone that connects all the network devices. If the backbone fails the network becomes unusable. 242

Byte An 8-bit unit of information that represents a single character. 11

Bytecode A compiled Java applet that is executed by Java Virtual Machine. 326

C2C (Consumer-To-Consumer) An e-commerce exchange of products, services, or information between consumers. 331

Cable Internet service A type of Internet connection offered to subscribers by cable television companies. 18

Cable modem A communications device that can be used to connect a computer to the Internet via the cable TV infrastructure. 18, 270

Cache Special high-speed memory that gives the CPU rapid access to data that would otherwise be accessed from disk. Also called RAM cache or cache memory. 71

CAD software (Computer-Aided Design software) A program designed to draw 3-D graphics for architecture and engineering tasks. 150

Capacitors Electronic circuit components that store an electrical charge; in RAM, a charged capacitor represents an "on" bit, and a discharged one represents an "off" bit. 74

Card reader A device that can be used to read and record data on a solid stage storage device. 80

Cascading style sheet (CSS) A template that can be set to control the layout and design of Web pages. 315

Case sensitive A condition in which uppercase letters are not equivalent to their lowercase counterparts. 21

CD (Compact disc) An optical storage medium used to store digital information. CD-ROMs are read only. CD-R and CD-RWs can be used to record data. 86

CD drive An optical drive that can work with one or more CD formats, such as CD-ROM, CD-R, or CD-RW. 10

CD ripper software Software that converts the music on an audio CD to a WAV file. 151

CD-DA An acronym for compact disc-digital audio. The format for commercial music CDs, typically recorded by the manufacturer. 87

CD-R An acronym for compact disc-recordable. CD-R is a type of optical disk technology that allows the user to create CD-ROMs and audio CDs. 87

CD-ROM An acronym for compact disc read-only memory. The read-only data format that is stamped onto a CD, usually by the manufacturer. 87

CD-RW An acronym for compact disc-rewritable. CD-RW is a type of optical disk technology that allows the user to write data onto a CD, then change that data much like on a floppy or hard disk. 87

Cell In spreadsheet terminology, the intersection of a column and a row. In cellular communications, a limited geographical area surrounding a cellular phone tower. 142

Cell references The column letter and row number that designate the location of a worksheet cell. For example, the cell reference C5 refers to a cell in column C, row 5. 143

Central processing unit (CPU) The main processing unit in a computer, consisting of circuitry that executes instructions to process data. 4

Certificate authority A company that issues digital certificates and verifies the correct identity of the recipient. 329

CGI (Common Gateway Interface) An interface that allows a user to access a Web-based database from a Web browser. 319

Character data Letters, symbols, or numerals that will not be used in arithmetic operations (name, social security number, etc.). 63

Chat group A discussion in which a group of people communicates online simultaneously. 16

Checksum A value, calculated by combining all the bytes in a file, that is used by virus detection programs to identify whether any bytes have been altered. 205

Ciphertext An encrypted message. 340

Circuit switching The method used by the telephone network to temporarily connect one telephone with another for the duration of a call. 247

CISC A general-purpose microprocessor chip designed to handle a wider array of instructions than a RISC chip. CISC stands for complex instruction set computer. 71

Clear GIF A small graphic on a Web page that installs cookies designed to track your online activities. Also known as a Web bug. 335

Click-through rate The number of times Web site visitors click an ad to connect to an advertiser's site. 332

Client A computer or software that requests information from another computer or server. 9

Client/server network A network where processing is split between workstations (clients) and the server. 241

Client-side script Scripting statements embedded in an HTML document that are executed by a client's browser. 325

Clip art Graphics designed to be inserted into documents, Web pages, and worksheets; available in CD-ROM or Web-based collections. 141

Cluster 1) A group of sectors on a storage medium that, when accessed as a group, speeds up data access. 2) A group of two or more devices connected together to share processing, storage, input, or output tasks. 195

CMOS memory A type of battery-powered integrated circuit that holds semi-permanent configuration data (acronym for complementary metal oxide semiconductor). 76

Coaxial cable A type of cable constructed of a center wire surrounded by a grounded shield of braided wire. Used for cable TV and to connect nodes on a network (also called coax cable). 244

Codec Derived from the terms COmpressor and DECompressor. A hardware or software routine that compresses and decompresses digital graphics, sound, and video files. 387

Color depth The number of bits that determines the range of possible colors that can be assigned to each pixel. For example, an 8-bit color depth can create 256 colors. 93, 366

Color palette The selection of colors used in graphics software. 367

Command-line interface A style of user interface which requires users to type commands, rather than use a mouse to manipulate graphics. 128

Commercial software Copyrighted computer applications sold to consumers for profit. 163

Communications channel Any pathway between the sender and receiver; channel may refer to a physical medium or a frequency. 243

Communications protocol A set of rules that ensures the orderly and accurate transmission and reception of data. 247

Communications satellites Satellites used to send and receive data to and from ground stations. 245

Compact Privacy Policy A header that defines a standard set of security tags that become part of the HTTP header for cookies. 310

CompactFlash (CF) A solid state storage card designed for digital cameras with a built in controller about the size of a matchbook that provides high storage capacity and access speed. 89

Compiler Software that translates a program written in a high-level language into low-level instructions before the program is executed. 123

Compression algorithm The steps that are required to shrink data in a file and reconstitute it to its original state. 400

Compression ratio A measurement of the amount of shrinkage that occurs when data is compressed. 400

Computer A device that accepts input, processes data, stores data, and produces output. 4

Computer network A collection of computers and related devices, connected in a way that allows them to share data, hardware, and software. 8

Computer program A detailed set of instructions that tells a computer how to solve a problem or carry out a task. 4

Computer programmers People who design, code, and test computer programs. 122

Computer virus A program designed to attach itself to a file, reproduce, and spread from one file to another, destroying data, displaying an irritating message, or otherwise disrupting computer operations. 198

Computer-aided music software Software used to generate unique musical compositions with a simplified set of tools, such as tempo, key, and style. 151

Concurrent-use license Legal permission for an organization to use a certain number of copies of a software program at the same time. 162

Control unit The part of the ALU that directs and coordinates processing. 69

Controller A circuit board in a hard drive that positions the disk and read-write heads to locate data. 84

Cookie A message sent from a Web server to a browser and stored on a user's hard disk, usually containing information about the user. 309

Copyright A form of legal protection that grants certain exclusive rights to the author of a program or the owner of the copyright. 162

Copyright notice A line such as "Copyright 2002 by ACME CO" that identifies a copyright holder. 162

Cropping The process of selecting and removing part of an image. 365

CRT (cathode ray tube) A display technology that uses a large vacuum tube, similar to that used in television sets. 92

Cryptographic algorithm A specific procedure for encrypting and decrypting data. 340

Cryptographic key A specific word, number, or phrase that must be used to encrypt or decrypt data. 340

CSMA/CD (Carrier Sense Multiple Access with Collision Detection) A method of responding to an attempt by two devices to use a data channel simultaneously. Used by Ethernet networks. 251

Data In the context of computing and data management, data refers to the symbols that a computer uses to represent facts and ideas. 4

Data bus An electronic pathway or circuit that connects the electronic components (such as the processor and RAM) on a computer's motherboard. 97

Data compression The process of condensing data so that it requires fewer bytes of storage space. 400

Data file A file containing words, numbers, and/or pictures that the user can view, edit, save, send, and/or print. 11

Data representation The use of electronic signals, marks, or binary digits to represent character, numeric, visual, or audio data. 62

Data transfer rate The amount of data that a storage device can move from a storage medium to computer memory in one second. 81

Database A collection of information that might be stored in more than one file or in more than one record type. 146

Database software The software designed for entering, finding, organizing, updating, and reporting information stored in a database. 146

Decryption The process of converting ciphertext into plaintext. 340

Defragmentation utility A software tool used to rearrange the files on a disk so that they are stored in contiguous clusters. 197

Demodulation The process of changing a received signal back to its original state (for example, when a modem changes an audio signal back to a digital pulse). 267

Denial of Service attacks An attack designed to overwhelm a network's processing capabilities, shutting it down. 204

DES (Data Encryption Standard) An encryption method based on an algorithm developed by IBM and the National Security Agency that uses 56-bit symmetric key encryption. 342

Desktop computers Computers small enough to fit on a desk and built around a single microprocessor chip. 6

Desktop operating system An operating system specifically designed for use on personal computers, such as Windows Me or Mac OSX. 130

Desktop publishing software The software used to create high-quality output suitable for commercial printing. DTP software provides precise control over layout. 137

Desktop video Videos stored in digital format on a PC's hard disk or CD. 380

Device driver The software that provides the computer with the means to control a peripheral device. 98

DHTML (dynamic HTML) A variation of the HTML format that allows elements of Web pages to be changed while they are being viewed. 323

Dial-up connection A connection that uses a phone line to establish a temporary Internet connection. 17

Dictionary-based compression A data compression scheme that uses a code word to represent common sequences of characters. 401

Differential backup A copy of all the files that changed since the last full backup of a disk. 214

Digital Any system that works with discrete data, such as 0s and 1s, in contrast to analog. 11

Digital camera A camera that takes and stores a digital image instead of recording onto film. 361

Digital certificate A security method that identifies the author of an ActiveX control. A computer programmer can "sign" a digital certificate after being approved. 329

Digital device A device that works with discrete (distinct or separate) numbers or digits. 62

Digital signal processor Circuitry that is used to process, record, and playback audio files. 394

Digital video A series of still frames stored sequentially in digital format by assigning values to each pixel in a frame. 380

Digital video camera A device used to collect, store, and process video in a digital format. 381

Digitize To convert non-digital information or media to a digital format through the use of a scanner, sampler, or other input device. 64

Digitizing tablet A device that provides a flat surface for a paper-based drawing, and a "pen" used to create hand-drawn vector drawings. 373

Directory A list of files contained on a computer storage device. 186

Disk density The closeness of the particles on a disk surface. As density increases, the particles are packed more tightly together and are usually smaller. 82

Distribution media One or more floppy disks or CDs that contain programs and data, which can be installed to a hard disk drive. 156

Dithering A means of reducing the size of a graphics file by reducing the number of colors. Dithering uses patterns composed of two or more colors to produce the illusion of additional colors and shading. 368

DOCSIS (Data Over Cable Services Interface Specification) A security technology used for filtering packets to certain ports. 271

Document production software Computer programs that assist the user in composing, editing, designing, and printing documents. 137

Domain name Short for "fully qualified domain name;" an identifying name by which host computers on the Internet are familiarly known (for example, "cocacola.com"). 263

Domain name servers Computers that host the domain name system database. 264

Domain Name System (DNS) A large database of unique IP addresses that correspond with domain names. 264

DOS (Disk Operating System) The operating system software shipped with the first IBM PCs, then used on millions of computers until the introduction of Microsoft Windows. 134

Dot matrix printer A printer that creates characters and graphics by striking an inked ribbon with small wires called "pins," generating a fine pattern of dots. 94

Dot pitch The diagonal distance between colored dots on a display screen. Measured in millimeters, dot pitch helps to determine the quality of an image displayed on a monitor. 92

Double layer DVD A DVD that essentially stacks data in two different layers on the disk surface to store 8.5 GB, twice the capacity of a standard DVD. 86

Downloading The process of transferring a copy of a file from a remote computer to local computer's disk drive. 15

Downstream Refers to transmitted data that flows from a host or server to a local computer (Contrast with upstream). 269

Drawing software Programs that are used to create images with lines, shapes, and colors, such as logos or diagrams. 149, 373

Drive bays Areas within a computer system unit that can accommodate additional storage devices. 80

Drive mapping A process of assigning a drive letter to a storage device located on a different network workstation. 256

DSL (Digital Subscriber Line) A high-speed Internet connection that uses existing telephone lines, requiring close proximity to a switching station. 19

DSL modem A device that sends and receives digital data to and from computers over telephone lines. 272

DSLAM (DSL Access Multiplexer) Special equipment used to interpret, separate, and route digital data in telephone lines for DSL providers. 272

DTD files (Document Type Definition files) A type of file that defines how markup tags are interpreted by a browser. 324

Dual core processor A single integrated circuit containing circuitry for two microprocessors. 72

Duty cycle A measurement of how many pages a printer is able to produce per day or month. 95

DVD (Digital Video Disc) An optical storage medium similar in appearance and technology to a CD-ROM but with higher storage capacity. The acronym stands for "digital video disc" or "digital versatile disc." 86

DVD authoring software Computer programs that offer tools for creating DVD menus and transferring digital video onto DVDs that can be played in a computer or standalone DVD player. 152

DVD drive An optical storage device that reads data from CD-ROM and DVD disks. 10

DVD image A series of files containing the data needed for a video DVD. The image is typically stored on a hard disk for testing before the image is transferred or "burned" to the DVD. 390

DVD+R, DVD-R Acronym for digital versatile disk recordable. A DVD data format that, similar to CD-R, allows for writing data in multiple sessions. 87

DVD+RW, DVD-RW A DVD technology that allows users to record and change data on DVD disks. 87

DVD-ROM A DVD disk that contains data that has been permanently stamped on the disk surface. 87

DVD-video A DVD format used for commercial movies shipped on DVDs. 87, 380

Dye sublimation printer An expensive, color precise printer that heats ribbons containing color to produce consistent, photograph-quality images. 95

Dynamic IP address A temporarily assigned IP address usually provided by an ISP. 262

Ear training software Software used by musicians to develop tuning skills, recognize keys, and develop musical skills. 151

EBCDIC (Extended Binary-Coded Decimal Interchange Code) A method by which digital computers, usually mainframes, represent character data. 63

E-commerce Short for electronic commerce, it is the business of buying and selling products online. 16, 331

Educational software Software used to develop and practice skills. 153

Electronic wallet Software that stores and processes customer information needed for an e-commerce transaction. 338

E-mail Messages that are transmitted between computers over a communications network. Short for electronic mail. 16

E-mail account A service that provides users with an e-mail address and a mailbox. 33

E-mail attachment A separate file that is transmitted along with an e-mail message. 34

E-mail client software Software that is installed on a client computer and has access to e-mail servers on a network. This software is used to compose, send, and read e-mail messages. 38

E-mail message A computer file containing a letter or memo that is transmitted electronically via a communications network. 33

E-mail servers A computer that uses special software to store and send e-mail messages over the Internet. 37

E-mail system The collection of computers and software that works together to provide e-mail services. 37

Encryption The process of scrambling or hiding information so that it cannot be understood without the key necessary to change it back into its original form. 340

Ethernet A type of network in which network nodes are connected by coaxial cable or twisted-pair wire; the most popular network architecture, it typically transmits data at 10 or 100 megabits per second. 250

Ethernet card A type of network interface card designed to support Ethernet protocols. 251

EULA A version of the license agreement that appears on the computer screen when software is being installed and prompts the user to accept or decline. 162

Executable file A file, usually with an .exe extension, containing instructions that tell a computer how to perform a specific task. 11

Expansion bus The segment of the data bus that transports data between RAM and peripheral devices. 97

Expansion card A circuit board that is plugged into a slot on a PC motherboard to add extra functions, devices, or ports. 97

Expansion port A socket into which the user plugs a cable from a peripheral device, allowing data to pass between the computer and the peripheral device. 98

Expansion slot A socket or "slot" on a PC motherboard designed to hold a circuit board called an expansion card. 97

Extended ASCII Similar to ASCII but with 8-bit character representation instead of 7-bit, allowing for an additional 128 characters. 63

External link A hyperlink that links to a location outside the Web site. 318

External style sheet A template that contains formatting specifications for a group of Web pages. 315

Extranet A network similar to a private internet that also allows outside users access as well. 261

FAT32 A file system used by Microsoft Windows 95, 98, and Me operating systems to keep track of the name and location of files on a hard disk. 195

FDDI (Fiber Distributed Data Interconnect) A high-speed network that uses fiber-optic cables to link workstations. 250

Fiber-optic cable A bundle of thin tubes of glass used to transmit data as pulses of light. 244

Field The smallest meaningful unit of information contained in a data file. 146

File A named collection of data (such as a computer program, document, or graphic) that exists on a storage medium, such as a hard disk, floppy disk, or CD-ROM. 11

File allocation table (FAT) A special file that is used by some operating systems to store the physical location of all the files on a storage medium, such as a hard disk or floppy disk. 195

File compression utility A type of data compression software that shrinks one or more files into a single file that occupies less storage space than the files did separately. 404

File date The date that a file was created or last modified. 187

File extension A set of letters and/or numbers added to the end of a filename that helps to identify the file contents or file type. 11

File format The method of organization used to encode and store data in a computer. Text formats include DOC and TXT. Graphics formats include BMP, TIFF, GIF, and PCX. 185

File header Hidden information inserted at the beginning of a file to identify its properties, such as the software that can open it. 65

File management utilities Software, such as Windows Explorer, that helps users locate, rename, move, copy, and delete files. 190

File name A series of letters and characters used to identify a file stored on a computer. 11

File-naming conventions A set of rules, established by the operating system, that must be followed to create a valid filename. 184

File shredder software Software designed to overwrite sectors of a disk with a random series of 1s and 0s to ensure deletion of data. 196

File size The physical size of a file on a storage medium, usually measured in kilobytes (KB). 187

File specification A combination of the drive letter, subdirectory, filename, and extension that identifies a file (such as, A:\word\filename.doc). Also called a "path." 186

File system A system that is used by an operating system to keep files organized. 195

File virus A computer virus that infects executable files, such as programs with .exe filename extensions. 198

Firewall software Software designed to analyze and control incoming and outgoing packets on a network, used to enhance security by filtering out potential intrusion attempts. 279

Fixed wireless Internet service High-speed, wide area Internet service alternative to cable and DSL that transmits data wirelessly using RF signals. 274

Flash A file format developed by Macromedia that has become popular for animations on Web pages. 376

Flash animation A popular proprietary animation format developed by Macromedia and frequently used on the Web. 317

Floppy disk A removable magnetic storage medium, typically 3.5" in size, with a capacity of 1.44 MB. 81

Floppy disk adapter A device that contains a slot for a flash memory module that, when inserted into a floppy disk drive, enables users to transfer data to their PCs. 362

Floppy disk drive A storage device that writes data on, and reads data from, floppy disks. 10

Folders The subdirectories, or subdivisions of a directory, that can contain files or other folders. 186

Font A typeface or style of lettering, such as Arial, Times New Roman, and Gothic. 139

Footer Text that appears in the bottom margin of each page of a document. 140

Format Specified properties for setting a document's appearance. 139

Formatting The process of dividing a disk into sectors so that it can be used to store information. 194

Formatting tags HTML code that is used to change the appearance of text. 303

Formatting utilities Software usually included in an operating system that assists with formatting disks. 195

Formula In spreadsheet terminology, a combination of numbers and symbols that tells the computer how to use the contents of cells in calculations. 143

Fragmented files Files stored in scattered, noncontiguous clusters on a disk. 197

Frame rate Refers to the number of frames displayed per second in a video or film. 384

Frames An outline or boundary, frequently defining a box. For document production software, a pre-defined area into which text or graphics may be placed. 141

Freeware Copyrighted software that is given away by the author or owner. 164

Full backup A copy of all the files for a specified backup job. 214

Full-system backup A backup, or copy, of all of the files stored on a computer. 209

Fully justified The horizontal alignment of text where the text terminates exactly at both margins of the document. 140

Function In worksheets, a built-in formula for making a calculation. In programming, a section of code that manipulates data, but is not included in the main sequential execution path of a program. 143

Gateway A device or software code used to join two dissimilar networks by converting data sent from one network into a format compatible to the receiving network. 243

GIF (Graphics Interchange Format) A bitmap graphics file format, popularized by CompuServe, for use on the Web. 370

Gigabit (Gb or Gbit) Approximately one billion bits, exactly 1,024 megabits. 65

Gigabyte (GB) Approximately one billion bytes; exactly 1,024 megabytes (1,073,741,824 bytes). 65

Gigahertz (GHz) A measure of frequency equivalent to one billion cycles per second. 70

Gradient A smooth blending of shades of different colors, from light to dark. 375

Grammar checker A feature of word processing software that coaches the user on correct sentence structure and word usage. 139

Graphical user interface (GUI) A type of user interface that features on-screen objects, such as menus and icons, manipulated by a mouse. Abbreviated GUI (pronounced "gooey"). 128

Graphics Any picture, photograph, or image that can be manipulated or viewed on a computer. 149

Graphics card A circuit board inserted into a computer to handle the display of text, graphics, animation, and videos. Also called a "video card." 93

Graphics software Computer programs for creating, editing, and manipulating images. 149

Grayscale palette Digital images that are displayed in shades of gray, black and white. 368

Groupware Software that enables multiple users to collaborate on a project, usually through a pool of data that can be shared by members of the workgroup. 155

Handheld computer A small, pocket-sized computer that is designed to run on its own power supply and provide users with basic applications. 7

Handshaking A process where a protocol helps two network devices communicate. 247

Hard disk drive A computer storage device that contains a large-capacity "hard disk" sealed inside the drive case. A hard disk is NOT the same as a 3.5" floppy disk that has a rigid plastic case. 10

Hard disk platter The component of the hard disk drive on which data is stored. It is a flat, rigid disk made of aluminum or glass and coated with a magnetic oxide. 83

Head crash A collision between the read-write head and the surface of the hard disk platter, resulting in damage to some of the data on the disk. 84

Head section A part of a Web page that begins with the <HEAD> tag and contains information about global properties of the document. 314

Head-end A satellite dish "farm" at which television broadcasts are received and retransmitted. 269

Header Text that is placed in the top margin of each page of a document. 140

Helper application A program that understands how to work with a specific file format. 305

High-level language A programming language that allows a programmer to write instructions using human-like language. 123

Home page (1) A document that is the starting, or entry, page at a Web site. (2) The Web page that a browser displays each time it is started. 27

HomePLC network A network that uses a building's existing power line cables to connect nodes. 254

HomePNA network A network that uses a building's existing phone lines to connect nodes. 254

Horizontal market software Any computer program that can be used by many different kinds of businesses (for example, an accounting program). 155

Hot spot An area on a Web page that is designated as a hyperlink. (See Wi-Fi hotspot) 318

HTML (Hypertext Markup Language) A standardized format used to specify the layout for Web page documents. 25

HTML document A plain text or ASCII document with embedded HTML tags that dictate formatting and are interpreted by a browser. 299

HTML form An HTML document containing blank boxes that prompt users to enter information that can be sent to a Web server. Commonly used for e-commerce transactions. 319

HTML frame Part of a Web page that scrolls independently of other parts of the Web page. 320

HTML tags A set of instructions, such as <b>, inserted into an HTML document to provide formatting and display information to a Web browser. 28

HTTP (Hypertext Transfer Protocol) The communications system used to transmit Web pages. HTTP:// is an identifier that appears at the beginning of each Web page URL (for example, http://www.fooyong.com). 24

HTTP status code A code used by Web servers to report the status of a browser's request. 307

Hub A network device that connects several nodes of a local area network. 242

Hypertext A way of organizing an information database by linking information through the use of text and multimedia. Helped the development of the Web. 298

Hypertext link Also called "link," an underlined word or phrase that when clicked, takes you to its designated URL. 299

ICANN (Internet Corporation for Assigned Names and Numbers) A global organization that coordinates the management of the Internet's domain name system, IP addresses, and protocol parameters. 264

Image map An area on a Web page consisting of a single graphic image containing multiple hot spots. 318

IMAP (Internet Messaging Access Protocol) A protocol similar to POP that is used to retrieve e-mail messages from an e-mail server, but offers additional features, such as choosing which e-mails to download from the server. 37

Incremental backup A copy of the files that changed since the last backup. 214

Information The words, numbers, and graphics used as the basis for human actions and decisions. 11

Infrared light A transmission technology that uses a frequency range just below the visible light spectrum to transport data. 245

Ink jet printer A non-impact printer that creates characters or graphics by spraying liquid ink onto paper or other media. 94

Input As a noun, "input" means the information that is conveyed to a computer. As a verb, "input" means to enter data into a computer. 4

Install The process by which programs and data are copied to the hard disk of a computer system and otherwise prepared for access and use. 157

Instant messaging A private chat in which users can communicate with each other in real time using electronically transmitted text messages. 16

Instruction cycle The steps followed by a computer to process a single instruction; fetch, interpret, execute, then increment the instruction pointer. 101

Instruction set The collection of instructions that a CPU is designed to process. 70

Integrated circuit (IC) A thin slice of silicon crystal containing microscopic circuit elements such as transistors, wires, capacitors, and resistors; also called chips and microchips. 66

Internal link A hyperlink that links to a location within the same Web site. 318

Internet The worldwide communication infrastructure that links computer networks using TCP/IP protocol. 14

Internet backbone The major communications links that form the core of the Internet. 14

Internet telephony A set of hardware and software that allows users to make phone-style calls over the Internet, usually without a long-distance charge. 16

Interpreter A program that converts high-level instructions in a computer program into machine language instructions, one instruction at a time. 123

Intranet A LAN that uses TCP/IP communications protocols, typically for communications services within a business or organization. 261

Intrapage link A hyperlink that links to a different location on the same Web page. 318

IP (Internet Protocol) One of the main protocols of TCP/IP that is responsible for addressing packets for routing to their destinations. 261

IP addresses Unique identifying numbers assigned to each computer connected to the Internet. 262

ISA (Industry Standard Architecture) A standard for moving data on the expansion bus. Can refer to a type of slot, a bus, or a peripheral device. An older technology, it is rapidly being replaced by PCI architecture. 97

ISDN (Integrated Services Digital Network) A telephone company service that transports data digitally over dial-up or dedicated lines. 18, 273

ISDN terminal adapter A device that connects a computer to a telephone jack and translates the data into a signal that can travel over an ISDN connection. 273

ISP A company that provides Internet access to businesses, organizations, and individuals. 19

Java applets Small programs that add processing and interactive capabilities to Web pages. 326

Java Virtual Machine (JVM) A component found in most browsers that executes Java applets. 326

JavaScript A scripting language, based on Java, that is used to design interactive Web sites. 325

Joystick An input device that looks like a small version of a car's stick shift. Popular with gamers, moving the stick moves objects on the screen. 91

JPEG (Joint Photographic Experts Group) A format that uses lossy compression to store bitmap images. JPEG files have a .jpg extension. 369

Kernel The core module of an operating system that typically manages memory, processes, tasks, and disks. 129

Key frame Frames at equal intervals in a digital video clip that contain all data for that frame. The rest of the frames in the video contain only the information that is different from the preceding key frame. 403

Keylogger A program, sometimes part of a Trojan Horse, that records a person's keystrokes, saves them, and then sends them to a system administrator or remote hacker. 199

Keyword 1) A word or term used as the basis for a Web page search. 2) A command word provided by a programming language. 30

Kilobit (Kbit or Kb) 1024 bits. 65

Kilobyte (KB) Approximately one thousand bytes; exactly 1,024 bytes. 65

Label In the context of spreadsheets, any text used to describe data. 142

LAN (Local Area Network) An interconnected group of computers and peripherals located within a relatively limited area, such as a building or campus. 8, 241

Lands Non-pitted surface areas on a CD that represent digital data. (See Pits) 79

Laser printer A printer that uses laser-based technology, similar to that used by photocopiers, to produce text and graphics. 94

Latency The elapsed time it takes for a packet of data to arrive at its destination. 259

LCD (liquid crystal display) A type of flat panel computer screen that is typically found on notebook computers. 92

LCD screen (liquid crystal display) A type of flat panel computer screen, typically found on notebook computers. (See LCD) 10

Leading Also called line spacing, the vertical spacing between lines of text. 140

Level 1 cache (L1 cache) Cache memory built into a microprocessor chip. L1 cache typically can be read in one clock cycle. 71

Level 2 cache (L2 cache) Cache memory that is located in a chip separate from the microprocessor chip. 71

Line spacing Also called leading, the vertical spacing between lines of text. (See Leading) 140

Linear editing A video editing technique involving recording segments of video from one tape to another. 385

Link tags HTML code that is used to designate text as a hyperlink in a document. 303

Links Underlined areas of text that allow users to jump between Web pages. 24

Linux A server operating system that is a derivative of UNIX and available as freeware. 133

Logical storage models Also referred to as metaphors, are any visual aid that helps a computer user visualize a file system. 191

Lossless compression A compression technique that provides the means to reconstitute all of the data in the original file, hence "lossless" means that this compression technique does not lose data. 402

Lossy compression Any data compression technique in which some of the data is sacrificed to obtain more compression. 402

Mac OS The operating system software designed for use on Apple Macintosh and iMac computers. 132

Machine code Program instructions written in binary code that the computer can execute directly. 100

Machine language A low-level language written in binary code that the computer can execute directly. 123

Macro virus A computer virus that infects the macros that are attached to documents and spreadsheets. (See Macro) 199

Macs (Macintosh computers) A personal computer designed and manufactured by Apple Computers. 13

Magnetic storage The recording of data onto disks or tape by magnetizing particles of an oxide-based surface coating. 79

Mail merge A feature of document production software that automates the process of producing customized documents, such as letters and advertising flyers. 141

Mailing list server Any computer and software that maintains a list of people who are interested in a topic, and facilitates message exchanges among all members of the list. 16

Mailto link A link in a Web page that automatically opens a pre-addressed e-mail form. 318

Mainframe computer A large, fast, and expensive computer generally used by businesses or government agencies to provide centralized storage processing and management for large amounts of data. 8

Malicious code Any program or set of program instructions, such as a virus, worm, or Trojan horse, designed to surreptitiously enter a computer and disrupt its normal operations. 198

MAN (Metropolitan Area Network) A public, high-speed network that can transmit voice and data within a range of 50 miles. 241

Markup language A language that provides text and graphics formatting through the use of tags. Examples of markup languages include HTML, XML, SGML. 300

Mass-mailing worm A worm that sends itself to every e-mail address in the address book of an infected computer. 200

Master File Table An index file used in NTFS systems used to maintain a list of clusters and keep track of their contents. 195

Mathematical modeling software Software for visualizing and solving a wide range of math, science, and engineering problems. 145

Mathematical operators Symbols such as + - / * that represent specific mathematical functions in a formula. 143

Media tags HTML code that specifies how to display media elements in a document. 303

Megabit (Mb or Mbit) 1,048,576 bits. 65

Megabyte (MB) Approximately one million bytes; exactly 1,048,576 bytes. 65

Megahertz (MHz) A measure of frequency equivalent to 1 million cycles per second. 70

Megapixel Millions of pixels, expresses the resolution and quality of an image. 363

Memory The computer circuitry that holds data waiting to be processed. 5

Mesh topology A network arranged in such a way that each device is connected to many other devices. Data traveling on a mesh network can take any of several possible paths. 242

Message header The section of an e-mail document that contains the address, subject, and file attachment information. 33

Metafiles Graphics files that contain both vector and bitmap data. 375

Microcomputer A category of computer that is built around a single microprocessor chip. The computers typically used in homes and small businesses (also called a personal computer). 6

Microprocessor An integrated circuit that contains the circuitry for processing data. It is a single-chip version of the central processing unit (CPU) found in all computers. 6, 69

Microprocessor clock A device on the motherboard of a computer responsible for setting the pace of executing instructions. 70

Microsoft Windows An operating system, developed by Microsoft Corporation, that provides a graphical interface. Versions include Windows 3.1, Windows 95, Windows 98, Windows Me, Windows NT, Windows 2000, and Windows XP. 130

Microwaves Electromagnetic waves with a frequency of at least 1 gigahertz. 245

MIDI (Musical Instrument Digital Interface) A standardized way in which sound and music are encoded and transmitted between devices that play music. 396

MIDI sequence Digitally encoded music stored on a computer. Usually is a file with a .mid, .cmf, or .rol file extension. 396

MIDI sequencing software Software that uses a standardized way of transmitting encoded music or sounds for controlling musical devices, such as a keyboard or sound card. 151

MIME (Multi-purpose Internet Mail Extensions) A conversion process used for formatting non-ASCII messages so that they can be sent over the Internet. 34

Modem A device that sends and receives data to and from computers. (See Voice band modem *and* Cable modem) 10

Modulation The process of changing the characteristics of a signal (for example, when a modem changes a digital pulse into an analog signal). 267

Money management software Software used to track monetary transactions and investments. 145

Monitor A display device that forms an image by converting electrical signals from the computer into points of colored light on the screen. 10

Monochrome bitmap A bitmap image that contains only the colors black and white. 366

Motherboard (See System board)

Mouse An input device that allows the user to manipulate objects on the screen by clicking, dragging, and dropping. 10

Mouseover The action of passing the pointer over a Web page element, typically a graphic, to trigger a change, such as making an image, link, or tooltip appear. 323

MP3 A file format that provides highly compressed audio files with very little loss of sound quality. 394

MPEG (Moving Pictures Expert Group) A highly compressed file format for digital videos. Files in this format have a .mpg extension. 386

MultiMedia cards (MMC) Solid state storage cards about the size of a stamp with a built in controller used in mobile phones, pagers, MP3 players and some digital cameras. 89

Multi-partite viruses A computer virus that is able to infect many types of targets by hiding itself in numerous locations on a computer. 206

Multiple-user license Legal permission for more than one person to use a particular software package. 162

Multiprocessing The ability of a computer or operating system to support dual core processors or multiple processors. 127

Multitasking The ability of a computer, processor, or operating system to run more than one program, job, or task at the same time. 127

Multithreading A technology that allows multiple parts or threads from a program to run simultaneously. 127

Multiuser operating system An operating system that allows a single computer to deal with simultaneous processing requests from multiple users. 130

NAN Neighborhood area network with a range of a few blocks, such as a Wi-Fi hotspot offered by a coffee shop or neighborhood Free Wi-Fi organization. 241

Nanoseconds Units of time representing 1 billionth of a second. 75

Narrowband A term that refers to communications channels that have low bandwidth. 246

Native file format A file format that is unique to a program or group of programs and has a unique file extension. 185

Natural language query A query using language spoken by human beings, as opposed to an artificially constructed language such as machine language. 148

Netiquette Internet etiquette or a set of guidelines for posting messages and e-mails in a civil, concise way. 36

Network access points (NAPs) Access points that link together different network service providers so that data can be transferred from one service provider to the other. 259

Network Address Translation (NAT) An Internet standard that allows a LAN to use one type of IP address for LAN data and another type of address for data to and from the Internet. 281

Network card An expansion board mounted inside a computer to allow access to a local area network. Also called a network interface card (NIC). 10

Network operating system Programs designed to control the flow of data, maintain security, and keep track of accounts on a network. 130

Network service providers (NSP) Companies that maintain a series of nationwide Internet links. 259

Newsgroups An online discussion group that focuses on a specific topic. 16

Node In a network, a connection point; in a hierarchical database, a segment or record type. 242

Non-executing zip file A type of file that has to be unzipped manually to extract the file or files contained within it. 160

Nonlinear editing A digital video editing technique that requires a PC and video editing software. 385

Notation software Software used to help musicians compose, edit, and print their compositions. 151

Notebook computers Small, lightweight, portable computers that usually run on batteries. Sometimes called laptops. 6

NTFS (New Technology File System) A file system used by Microsoft Windows NT, 2000, and XP operating systems to keep track of the name and location of files on a hard disk. 195

Numeric data Numbers that represent quantities and can be used in arithmetic operations. 62

Object code The low-level instructions that result from compiling source code. 123

Octet One of four sections of an IP address. 262

Online shopping cart An e-commerce cookie that stores information about items selected and collected for purchase. 334

Op code Short for operation code, an op code is an assembly language command word that designates an operation, such as add (ADD), compare (CMP), or jump (JMP). 100

Open source software Software that includes its source code, allowing programmers to modify and improve it. 164

Operands The part of an instruction that specifies the data, or the address of the data, on which the operation is to be performed. 100

Operating system The software that controls the computer's use of its hardware resources, such as memory and disk storage space. Also called OS. 12

Operational tags HTML code used to specify the basic setup and database integration for Web pages. 303

Optical storage A means of recording data as light and dark spots on a CD, DVD, or other optical media. 79

Output The results produced by a computer (for example, reports, graphs, and music). 5

P3P (Platform for Privacy Preferences Project) A specification that allows Web browsers to automatically detect a Web site's privacy policies. 310

Packet A small unit of data transmitted over a network or the Internet. 247

Packet sniffer A program that monitors data as it travels over networks. 336

Packet switching A technology used by data communications networks, such as the Internet, where a message is divided into smaller units called "packets" for transmission. 247

Page layout The physical positions of elements on a document page such as headers, footers, page numbering, and graphics positioning. 140

Paint software The software required to create and manipulate bitmap graphics. 149, 360

Palm OS A popular type of operating system produced by PalmSource specifically for handheld computers. 134

PAN (personal area network) An interconnected group of personal digital devices located within a range of about 30 feet. 241

Paragraph alignment The horizontal position (left, right, justified, centered, for example) of the text in a document. 140

Paragraph style A specification for the format of a paragraph, which includes the alignment of text within the margins and line spacing. 140

Parallel processing The simultaneous use of more than one processor to execute a program. 71

Password A special set of symbols used to restrict access to a user's computer or network. 21

Path A file's location in a file structure. (See File specification) 186

Payload The action taken by a virus, ranging from displaying an annoying message to corrupting the data on a computer's hard disk. 199

Payroll software A type of horizontal market software used to maintain payroll records. 155

PC card (PCMCIA card) A credit card-sized circuit board used to connect a modem, memory, network card, or storage device to a notebook computer. 98

PCI (Peripheral Component Interconnect) A method for transporting data on the expansion bus. Can refer to type of data bus, expansion slot, or transport method used by a peripheral device. 97

PCMCIA slot A PCMCIA (Personal Computer Memory Card International Association) slot is an external expansion slot typically found on notebook computers. 97

PCs (Derived from the term Personal Computers) Microcomputers that use Windows software and contain Intel-compatible microprocessors. 13

PCX The PC Paintbrush file format that incorporates a compression algorithm. 369

PDA (personal digital assistant) A computer that is smaller and more portable than a notebook computer (also called a palm-top or handheld computer). 7

PDA video Digital video formatted for viewing on a PDA or other handheld device. 380

Peer-to-peer The process by which one workstation/server shares resources with another. Refers to the capability of a network computer to act as both a file server and workstation. 15

Peer-to-peer network A network where workstations act as both file servers and clients. 241

Peripheral device A component or equipment that expands a computer's input, output, and storage capabilities, such as a printer or scanner. 11

Personal computer A microcomputer designed for use by an individual user for applications such as Internet browsing and word processing. 6

Personal finance software Software geared toward individual finances that helps track bank account balances, credit card payments, investments, and bills. 145

Person-to-person payment An e-commerce method of payment that bypasses credit cards and instead, uses an automatic electronic payment service. 339

PGP (Pretty Good Privacy) A popular program used to encrypt and decrypt e-mail messages. 343

Phoneme A unit of sound that is a basic component of words, and is produced by speech synthesizers. 398

Photo editing software The software used to edit, enhance, retouch, and manipulate digital photographs. 149

Physical storage model A representation of data as it is physically stored. 194

Physical topology The actual layout of network devices, wires, and cables. 242

Ping (Packet INternet Groper) A command on a TCP/IP network that sends a test packet to a specified IP address and waits for a reply. 259

Pipelining A technology that allows a processor to begin executing an instruction before completing the previous instruction. 71

Pits Spots on a CD that are "burned," representing digital data. 79

Pixel interpolation A process that is used by graphics software that averages the color of adjacent pixels in an image. 365

Pixelated Describes the effect of increasing the size and thus decreasing the quality of an image. 365

Pixels Short for picture element, a pixel is the smallest unit in a graphic image. Computer display devices use a matrix of pixels to display text and graphics. 92

Plaintext An original, un-encrypted message. 340

Plasma screen A compact, lightweight, flat panel computer screen that displays the pixels of an image using a technology similar to that of neon lights. 92

Platform A "family" or category of computers based on the same underlying software and hardware of a computer. 13

Player Standalone software, helper applications, and plug-ins, that work with one or more file formats, such as MP3, MIDI, or AAC. 305

Plug and Play The ability of a computer to automatically recognize and adjust the system configuration for a newly added device. 98

Plug-in A software module that adds a specific feature to a system. In the context of browsers, a plug-in adds the ability to play files referenced from the EMBED tag. 305

PNG (Portable Network Graphics) A type of graphics file format similar to but newer than GIF or JPEG. 370

Point size A unit of measure (1/72 of an inch) used to describe the height of characters. 139

Pointing device An input device such as a mouse, trackball, pointing stick, or trackpad, that allows users to manipulate an on-screen pointer and other screen-based graphical controls. 91

Pointing stick A mouse-substitute input device that looks like the tip of an eraser embedded in the keyboard of a notebook computer. 91

Polymorphic viruses Viruses that can escape detection from antivirus software by changing their signatures. 206

POP The Post Office Protocol (POP) is used to retrieve e-mail messages from an e-mail server. 37

POP server A computer that receives and stores e-mail data until retrieved by the e-mail account holder. 38

Pop-up ad A type of advertisement that usually appears in a separate window when you enter a Web site. 332

Portable audio player A small, lightweight, battery-powered device designed to store and play audio files stored in formats such as MP3 and AAC. 395

PostScript A printer language, developed by Adobe Systems, which uses a special set of commands to control page layout, fonts, and graphics. 96

POTS An acronym for "plain old telephone service." 266

Power-on self-test (POST) A diagnostic process that runs during startup to check components of the computer, such as the graphics card, RAM, keyboard, and disk drives. 40

Presentation software Software that provides tools to combine text, graphics, graphs, animation, and sound into a series of electronic "slides" that can be output on a projector, or as overhead transparencies, paper copies, or 35-millimeter slides. 150

Printer Control Language (PCL) PCL is the unofficial standard language used to send page formatting instructions from a PC to a laser or ink jet printer. 96

Private IP addresses IP addresses that cannot be routed over the Internet. 281

Processing The manipulation of data using a systematic series of actions. 4

Programming language A set of keywords and grammar (syntax) that allows a programmer to write instructions that a computer can execute. 123

Properties The characteristics of an object in a program. 122

Public domain software Software that is available for public use without restriction except that it cannot be copyrighted. 164

Public key encryption (PKE) An encryption method that uses a pair of keys, a public key (known to everyone) that encrypts the message, and a private key (known only to the recipient) that decrypts it. 342

Query A search specification that prompts the computer to look for particular records in a file. 30

Query by example (QBE) A type of database interface in which the user fills in a field with an example of the type of information that she is seeking. 148

Query language A set of command words that can be used to direct the computer to create databases, locate information, sort records, and change the data in those records. 148

QuickTime A video and animation file format developed by Apple Computer that can also be run on PCs. QuickTime files have a .mov extension. 386

RAM Random access memory is a type of computer memory circuit that holds data, program instructions, and the operating system while the computer is on. 73

Random access The ability of a storage device (such as a disk drive) to go directly to a specific storage location without having to search sequentially from a beginning location. 81

Ransomware Software, usually launched by hackers, that encrypts files without authorization, and then demands payment for the decryption key and software. 205

Rasterization The process of superimposing a grid over a vector image and determining the color depth for each pixel. 375

Ray tracing A technique by which light and shadow are added to a 3-D image. 377

Readability formula A feature found in some word processing software that can estimate the reading level of a written document. 139

Read-write head The mechanism in a disk drive that magnetizes particles on the storage disk surface to write data, or senses the bits that are present to read data. 79

RealAudio (.ra) An audio file format, developed by Real Networks, created especially for streaming audio data over the Web. 394

RealMedia A video file format, developed by Real Networks, that is popular for streaming Web videos. 386

Record In the context of database management, a record is the fields of data that pertain to a single entity in a database. 146

Recordable technology (R) A technique of writing data permanently on CD and DVD disks, the data cannot be changed once it has been recorded. 86

Recovery CD A CD that contains all the operating system files and application software files necessary to restore a computer to its original state. 216

Reference software Software that contains a large database of information with tools for sorting, viewing, and accessing specific topics. 153

Refresh rate The speed at which a computer monitor is rewritten, measured in Hertz. Faster refresh rates reduce flickering. 92

Registers A sort of "scratch pad" area of the ALU and control unit into which data or instructions are moved so that they can be processed. 69

Relative reference In a worksheet, cell references that can change if cells change position as a result of a move or copy operation. 144

Rendering In graphics software, the process of creating a 3-D solid image by covering a wireframe drawing and applying computer-generated highlights and shadows. 377

Repeater A network device that receives and retransmits amplified signals so that they can retain the necessary strength to reach their destination. 242

Reserved words Special words used as commands in some operating systems that may not be used in filenames. 185

Resolution The density of the grid used to display or print text and graphics. The greater the horizontal and vertical density, the higher the resolution. 93

Resolution dependent Graphics, such as bitmap, where the quality of the image is dependent on the number of pixels comprising the image. 365

Resource A component, either hardware or software, that is available for use by a computer's processor. 126

Restore The act of moving data from a backup storage medium to a hard disk in the event original data has been lost. 209

Retro viruses Viruses designed to corrupt antivirus software. 205

Rewritable technology (RW) A technique of writing data on CD and DVD disks that is rewritable. The data can be changed, or deleted after being recorded. 86

RF signals (Radio Frequency Signals) Used to transmit data on wireless networks. 245

Ring topology A network in which all devices are connected in a circle with each device having exactly two neighbors. 242

RISC (Reduced Instruction Set Computer) Refers to a microprocessor chip designed for rapid and efficient processing of a small set of simple instructions. 71

ROM (Read-Only Memory) Refers to one or more integrated circuits that contain permanent instructions that the computer uses during the boot process. 75

ROM BIOS A small set of basic input/output system instructions stored in ROM, which causes the computer system to load critical operating files when the user turns on the computer. 75

Root directory The main directory of a disk. 186

Router A network device that examines the IP address of incoming data, and forwards the data towards its destination. 243

RSA A commonly used public key encryption algorithm developed by Rivest, Shamir and Adelman. 342

Run-length encoding A graphics file compression technique that looks for patterns of bytes and replaces them with messages that describe the patterns. 402

Safe Mode A menu option that appears when Windows is unable to complete the boot sequence. By entering Safe Mode, a user can gracefully shut down the computer, then try to reboot it. 42

Sampling rate The number of times per second a sound is measured during the recording process. 393

Satellite Internet service A high-speed Internet service that uses a geosynchronous or lowearth orbit satellite to send data directly to satellite dishes owned by individuals.19

Scanner A device that converts a printed image into a bitmap graphic. 361

Script A program that contains a list of commands that are automatically executed as needed. 325

Scripting error An error that occurs when a browser or server cannot execute a statement in a script. 326

Search and Replace A feature of document production software that allows the user to automatically locate all instances of a particular word or phrase and substitute another word or phrase. 139

Search engine A program that uses keywords to find information on the Internet and returns a list of relevant documents. 29

Search operator A word or symbol that has a specific function within a search, such as "AND or +". 30

Sectors Subdivisions of the tracks on a storage medium that provide a storage area for data. 194

Secure connection An internet connection that encrypts data transmitted between your computer and a Web site. 336

SecureDigital (SD) A solid state storage card based on MultiMedia card technology, but features significantly faster data transfer rates and cryptographic security protection. Usually used for MP3 storage. 89

Self-closing tag An HTML tag that includes a closing symbol in the opening tag, and therefore does not require a separate closing tag. 301

Self-executing zip files A type of file that can be run to unzip the file or files contained within it. 160

Self-installing executable file A program that automatically unzips and then initiates and runs its setup program. 160

Semiconducting materials (semiconductors) Substances, such as silicon or germanium, that can act either as a conductor or insulator. Used in the manufacture of computer chips. 66

Sequential access A form of data storage, usually on computer tape, that requires a device to read or write data one record after another, starting at the beginning of the medium. 81

Serial processing Processing of data one instruction at a time, completing one instruction before beginning another. 71

Server A computer or software on a network that supplies the network with data and storage. 9

Server farm A group of multiple Web servers used to handle large volumes of requests. 308

Server-side script Scripting statements that are executed by a Web server in response to client data. 325

Service pack A collection of patches designed to correct bugs and/or add features to an existing software program. 160

SET (Secure Electronic Transaction) A system that ensures the security of financial transactions on the Web. 338

Setup program A program module supplied with a software package for the purpose of installing the software. 158

Shared resources On a network, resources such as hardware, software, and data, made available for authorized users to share. 238

Shareware Copyrighted software marketed under a license that allows users to use the software for a trial period and then send in a registration fee if they wish to continue to use it. 163

Shrink-wrap license A legal agreement printed on computer software packaging, which becomes binding when the package is opened. 162

S-HTTP (Secure HTTP) A method of encrypting data transmitted between a computer and a Web server by encrypting individual packets of data as they are transmitted. 336

Single-user license Legal permission for one person to use a particular software package. 162

Single-user operating system A type of operating system that is designed for one user at a time with one set of input devices. 130

Site license Legal permission for software to be used on any and all computers at a specific location (for example, within a corporate building or on a university campus). 162

SmartMedia The least durable portable solid state storage medium that does not include a built-in controller. 89

Smileys Text-based symbols used to express emotion. 36

SMTP server (Simple Mail Transfer Protocol Server) A computer used to send e-mail across a network or the Internet. 39

Socket A communication path over a network between two remote programs. 306

Software The instructions that direct a computer to perform a task, interact with a user, or process data. 4

Software license A legal contract that defines the ways in which a user may use a computer program. 162

Software patch A section of software code designed to modify an existing program to fix a specific error or add a feature. 160

Software publishers Companies that produce computer software. 122

Software suite A collection of individual applications sold as one package. 152

Solid ink printer A printer that melts a stick of solid ink and sprays it onto paper where it is fused to produce photograph-quality images without the use of special paper. 95

Solid state storage A technology that records data and stores it in a microscopic grid of cells on a non-volatile, erasable, low-power chip. 80

Sound card A circuit board that gives the computer the ability to accept audio input from a microphone, play sound files stored on disks and CD-ROMs, and produce audio output through speakers or headphones. 10, 393

Source code Computer instructions written in a high-level language. 123

Spam Unsolicited e-mail typically sent as a bulk or mass-mailing and used for fraudulent of deceptive marketing. 37

Spam filter Software that identifies unsolicited and unwanted e-mail messages and blocks them from the recipient's inbox. 37

Spatial compression A data compression scheme that replaces patterns of bytes with code that describes the patterns. 402

Speech recognition The process by which computers recognize voice patterns and words, then convert them to digital data. 398

Speech recognition software The software that analyzes voice sounds and converts them into phonemes. 398

Speech synthesis The process by which computers produce sound that resembles spoken words. 398

Spelling checker A feature of document production software that checks each word in a document against an electronic dictionary of correctly spelled words, then presents a list of alternatives for possible misspellings. 138

Spelling dictionary A data module that is used by a spelling checker as a list of correctly spelled words. 138

Spoofed address A fake return address on an e-mail message designed to hide the address of the real sender. 200

Spreadsheet A numerical model or representation of a real situation, presented in the form of a table. 142

Spreadsheet software Software for creating electronic worksheets that hold data in cells and perform calculations based on that data. 142

Spyware Any software that covertly gathers user information without the user's knowledge, usually for advertising purposes. 335

SSL (Secure Sockets Layer) A security protocol that uses encryption to establish a secure connection between a computer and a Web server. 336

Star topology A network configured with a central connection point or hub for all workstations and peripherals. 242

Stateless protocol A protocol, such as HTTP, that allows one request and response per session. 307

Static IP address A permanently assigned and unique IP address, used by hosts or servers. 262

Statistical compression A data compression scheme that uses an algorithm that recodes frequently used data as short bit patterns. 401

Statistical software Software for analyzing large sets of data to discover patterns and relationships within them. 145

Stealth viruses Viruses that can escape detection from antivirus software by removing their signatures and hiding in memory. 206

Storage The area in a computer where data is retained on a permanent basis. 5

Storage device A mechanical apparatus that records data to and retrieves data from a storage medium. 78

Storage medium The physical material used to store computer data, such as a floppy disk, a hard disk, or a CD-ROM. 78

Storage metaphor A likeness or analogy that helps people visualize the way that computers store files. 191

Store-and-forward technology A technology used by communications networks in which an e-mail message is temporarily held in storage on a server until it is requested by a client computer. 37

Stored program A set of instructions that resides on a storage device, such as a hard drive, and can be loaded into memory and executed. 5

Streaming video An Internet video technology that sends a small segment of a video file to a user's computer and begins to play it while the next segment is being sent. 387

Strong encryption Encryption that is difficult to decrypt without the encryption key. 341

Style A feature in many desktop publishing and word processing programs that allows the user to apply numerous format settings in a single command. 140

Subdirectory A directory found under the root directory. 186

Supercomputer The fastest and most expensive type of computer, capable of processing more than 1 trillion instructions per second. 8

SVG (Scalable Vector Graphics) A graphics format designed specifically for Web display that automatically re-sizes when displayed on different screens. 376

SVGA (Super Video Graphics Array) SVGA typically refers to 800 x 600 resolution. 93

SXGA (Super eXtended Graphics Array) A screen resolution of 1280 x 1024. 93

Symbian OS An operating system typically used on mobile phones and open to programming by third-party developers. 134

Symmetric key encryption An encryption key that is used for both encryption and decryption of messages. 342

Synthesized sound Artificially created sound, usually found in MIDI music or synthesized speech. 396

System board The main circuit board in a computer which houses chips and other electronic components. 67

System palette A selection of colors that are used by an operating system to display graphic elements. 368

System requirements 1) The specifications for the operating system and hardware configuration necessary for a software product to work correctly. 2) The criteria that must be met for a new computer system or software product to be a success. 156

System software Computer programs that help the computer carry out essential operating tasks. 12, 125

System unit The case or box that contains the computer's power supply, storage devices, main circuit board, processor, and memory. 10

Table An arrangement of data in a grid of rows and columns. In a relational database, a collection of record types with their data. 141

Tablet computer A small, portable computer with a touch-sensitive screen that can be used as a writing or drawing pad. 7

Tape backup A copy of data from a computer's hard disk, stored on magnetic tape and used to restore lost data. 85

Tax preparation software Personal finance software that is specifically designed to assist with tax preparation. 145

TCP (Transmission Control Protocol) One of the main protocols of TCP/IP that is responsible for establishing a data connection between two hosts and breaking data into packets. 261

TCP/IP Acronym for Transmission Control Protocol/Internet Protocol. A standard set of communication rules used by every computer that connects to the Internet. 14

Temporal compression A data compression scheme that, when applied to video or audio data, eliminates unnecessary data between video frames or audio samples. 403

Text editor Software, such as NotePad, that is similar to a word processor, but used to create plain, unformatted ASCII text. 312

Text-to-speech software Software that generates speech, based on written text, that is played back through a computer's sound card. 398

Thermal transfer printer An expensive, color-precise printer that uses wax containing color to produce numerous dots of color on plain paper. 95

Thesaurus A feature of documentation software that provides synonyms. 139

TIFF (Tag Image File Format) A file format (.tif extension) for bitmap images that automatically compresses the file data. 369

Token Ring network A type of network in which the nodes are sequentially connected in the form of a ring; the second most popular network architecture. 249

Topic directory A list of topics and subtopics arranged in a hierarchy from general to specific. 31

Top-level domain The major domain categories into which groups of computers on the Internet are divided: com, edu, gov, int, mil, net, and org. 263

Traceroute A network utility that records a packet's path, number of hops, and the time it takes for the packet to make each hop. 260

Tracing software Software that locates the edges of objects in a bitmap graphic and converts the resulting shape into a vector graphic. 375

Trackball An input device that looks like an upside down mouse. The user rolls the ball to move the on-screen pointer. 91

Trackpad A touch-sensitive surface on which you slide your fingers to move the on-screen pointer. 91

Tracks A series of concentric or spiral storage areas created on a storage medium during the formatting process. 194

Transceiver A combination of a transmitter and a receiver used to send and receive data in the form of radio frequencies. 245

Transponder A device on a telecommunications satellite that receives a signal on one frequency, amplifies the signal, and then retransmits the signal on a different frequency. 245

Tree topology Multiple star networks connected into a bus configuration by a backbone. 243

Trigger event An event that activates a task, often associated with a computer virus. 199

Trojan horse A computer program that appears to perform one function while actually doing something else, such as inserting a virus into a computer system or stealing a password. 199

True Color bitmap A color image with a color depth of 24 bits or 32 bits. Each pixel in a true color image can be displayed using any of 16.7 million different colors. 367

Twisted-pair cable A type of cable, with RJ-45 connectors on both ends, where two separate strands of wire are twisted together. Used to connect nodes on a network. 244

Unicode A 16-bit character-representation code that can represent more than 65,000 characters. 63

Uninstall routine A program that removes software files, references, and registry entries from a computer's hard disk. 161

UNIX A multi-user, multitasking server operating system developed by AT&T's Bell Laboratories in 1969. 133

Unzipped Refers to files that have been uncompressed. 159

Uplink port A connection port on a router to which additional hubs can be attached. 252

Uploading The process of sending a copy of a file from a local computer to a remote computer. 15

Upstream The process of transmitting data from your home computer to the Internet. 269

URL A Uniform Resource Locator is the address of a Web page. 25

USB flash drive A portable solid state storage device nicknamed "pen drive" or "keychain drive" that plugs directly into a computer's USB port. 88

Usenet A worldwide Internet bulletin board system of newsgroups that share common topics. 16

User ID A combination of letters and numbers that serves as a user's "call sign" or identification. Also referred to as a user name. 21

User interface The software and hardware that enable people to interact with computers. 128

Utility software A type of system software provided by the operating system or third-party vendors that specializes in tasks such as system maintenance, security, or file management. 135

UXGA (Ultra eXtended Graphics Array) A screen resolution of 1600 x 1200. 93

Validation code A series of letters and numbers usually shipped on disk media or delivered by e-mail. Used to verify that downloads and upgrades go to legitimate users. 161

Value A number used in a calculation. 142

VBScript A scripting language, based on Visual Basic, that is used to design interactive Web sites. 325

Vector graphic An image generated from descriptions that specify the position, length, and direction in which lines and shapes are drawn. 371

Vertical market software Computer programs designed to meet the needs of a specific market segment or industry, such as medical record-keeping software for use in hospitals. 155

VGA (Video Graphics Array) A screen resolution of 640 x 480. 93

Video capture The process of converting analog video signals into digital data stored on a hard drive. 382

Video capture software Software used to control the capture process of digital and analog video data. 383

Video editing software Software that provides tools for capturing and editing video from a camcorder. 152

Videoconferencing camera (Also called a Web camera.) An inexpensive digital camera that attaches directly to a computer and creates a video by capturing a series of still images. 381

Videogame console A computer specifically designed for playing games using a television screen and game controllers. 8

Viewable image size (vis) A measurement of the maximum image size that can be displayed on a monitor screen. 92

Viewing angle width The angle at which you can still clearly see the screen image from the side. 92

Virtual memory A computer's use of hard disk storage to simulate RAM. 74

Virtual private network (VPN) A network connection that typically carries encrypted data over the Internet to and from a remote access server. 281

Virus hoax A message, usually e-mail, that makes claims about a virus problem that doesn't actually exist. 206

Virus signature The unique computer code contained in a virus that helps with its identification. Antivirus software searches for known virus signatures to identify a virus. 206

VOB (Video OBject) An industry-standard video format for standalone DVD players. 386

Voiceband modem The type of modem that would typically be used to connect a computer to a telephone line. (See Modem) 17

Voice over IP (VOIP) A technology that allows computer users with Internet access to send and receive both data and voice simultaneously. 248

Volatile A term that describes data (usually in RAM), which can exist only with a constant supply of power. 74

WAN (Wide Area Network) An interconnected group of computers and peripherals that covers a large geographical area, such as multiple branches of a corporation. 241

WAP (Wireless Access Protocol) A communications protocol that provides Internet access for handheld devices. 275

Wave (.wav) An audio file format created as Windows "native" sound format. 394

Waveform audio A digital representation of sound, in which a sound wave is represented by a series of samples taken of the wave height. 392

Wavetable A set of pre-recorded musical instrument sounds in MIDI format. 396

Weak encryption Encryption that is relatively easy or simple to decrypt without the encryption key. 341

Web Short for World Wide Web. An Internet service that links documents and information from computers located worldwide, using the HTTP protocol. 24

Web authoring software Computer programs for designing and developing customized Web pages that can be published electronically on the Internet. 137, 313

Web-based e-mail An e-mail system that allows users to access e-mail messages using a browser. 37

Web-based video Digital video designed to be stored and played on a computer. 380

Web page header Also called "header," a subtitle that appears at the beginning of a Web page. 314

Web page table A grid of cells that are used as layout tools, for elements such as text and graphics placement in a Web page. 320

Web pages Documents on the World Wide Web that consist of a specially coded HTML file with associated text, audio, video, and graphics files. A Web page often contains links to other Web pages. 24

Web palette A standard selection of colors that all Internet browsers can display. 368

Web servers Computers that use special software to transmit Web pages over the Internet. 25

Web site Usually a group of Web pages identified by a common domain name, such as www.cnn.com. 25

WEP (Wired Equivalent Privacy) An encryption algorithm used to transmit data on Wi-Fi networks so that the data is useless to hackers. 253

What-if analysis The process of setting up a model in a spreadsheet and experimenting to see what happens when different values are entered. 142

Wi-Fi An Ethernet-compatible wireless network that uses 802.11 a, b, g, and n standards. 252

Wi-Fi card A type of network interface card that includes a transmitter to send data and plus a receiver and an antenna to transmit signals using Wi-Fi protocols. 253

Wi-Fi hotspot The geographical area in which you can connect to a Wi-Fi signal, such as a Wi-Fi equipped campus or coffeehouse. 275

WiMAX Fixed wireless Internet service based on Ethernet protocols with range of 30 miles and transmission speed of 70 Mbps. 274

Windows Explorer A file management utility included with most Windows operating systems that helps users manage their files. 192

Windows Mobile OS An operating system designed by Microsoft for hand-held computers. 134

Windows Registry A crucial set of data files maintained by the operating system that contains the settings needed by a computer to correctly use any hardware and software that has been installed. 165

Wired network A network that uses cables or wires to transmit data from one network device to another. 243

Wireframe A representation of a 3-D object using separate lines, which resemble wire, to create a model. 377

Wireless access point A network device that connects several devices of a local area network by broadcasting signals to any device with compatible Wi-Fi cards. 253

Wireless network Networks that use radio or infrared signals (instead of cables) to transmit data from one network device to another. 243

WISP (Wireless ISP) A wireless internet service provider that maintains a public Wi-Fi network. 275

WMA (Windows Media Audio) A file format that provides highly compressed audio files with very little loss of sound quality and is promoted by Microsoft. 394

WMV Windows Media or Windows Media Video is format for storing digital video. 386

Word processing software Computer programs that assist the user in producing documents, such as reports, letters, papers, and manuscripts. 137

Word size The number of bits that a CPU can manipulate at one time, which is dependent on the size of the registers in the CPU, and the number of data lines in the bus. 71

Worksheet A computerized, or electronic, spreadsheet. 142

Workstation (1) A computer connected to a local area network. (2) A powerful desktop computer designed for specific tasks. 8

World Wide Web Consortium (W3C) An international consortium of companies involved with the Internet and with the purpose of developing open standards. 300

Worm A software program designed to enter a computer system, usually a network, through security "holes" and then replicate itself. 200

Write-protect window A small hole and sliding cover on a floppy disk that restricts writing to the disk. 82

XGA Extended Graphics Array or XGA usually refers to 1024 x 768 resolution. 93

XHTML The follow-up version to HTML 4. 300

XML (eXtensible Markup Language) A document format similar to HTML, but that allows the Web page developer to define customized tags, generally for the purpose of creating more interactivity. 324

XML parser A tool in most browsers used for reading XML documents. 324

XSL (eXtensible Stylesheet Language) A technology that is similar to XML, and is used to create customized tags for displaying data in an XML document. 324

Zipped Refers to one or more files that have been compressed. 159

INDEX

EM C5977 37742 441 03/02/06--LM